WIPED!
DOCTOR WHO'S MISSING EPISODES

WIPED!
DOCTOR WHO'S MISSING EPISODES

RICHARD MOLESWORTH
INTRODUCTION BY TERRANCE DICKS

First published in England in 2010, and in this revised edition in 2013, by
Telos Publishing Ltd

www.telos.co.uk

Telos Publishing Ltd values feedback. Please e-mail us with any comments you may have about this book to: feedback@telos.co.uk

ISBN: 978-1-84583-080-9 (paperback) 978-1-84583-081-6 (hardback)

Wiped! Doctor Who's *Missing Episodes* © 2010, 2013 Richard Molesworth

Index prepared by Ian Pritchard

The moral right of the author has been asserted.

Internal design, typesetting and layout by Arnold T Blumberg
www.atbpublishing.com

British Library Cataloguing in Publication Data.
A catalogue record for this book is available from the British Library.

This book is sold subject to the condition that it shall not by way of trade or otherwise, be lent, resold, hired out or otherwise circulated without the publisher's prior written consent in any form of binding or cover other than that in which it is published and without a similar condition including this condition being imposed on the subsequent purchaser.

Printed in the UK by 4edge Limited

ACKNOWLEDGEMENTS

There are a number of people that I would like to thank for either their help in the research for this book, or for directly or indirectly helping me in years gone by.

This book comes out of a long obsession with the history of the *Doctor Who* archives that I've had since *Doctor Who Magazine* published an historic article in 1981's Winter Special. I'd like to thank Jeremy Bentham, the writer of that groundbreaking article, for being the original inspiration.

I've had occasion to write about the subject of missing episodes a number of times in the past. The first was for the excellent fanzine-turned-magazine *DWB* (*Doctor Who Bulletin*, later *DreamWatch Bulletin*, later still, just plain old *DreamWatch*), and my thanks go to editor Gary Leigh for giving me that opportunity. More recently, *Doctor Who Magazine* allowed me to explore the subject further in print, and my thanks go to then-editor Gary Gillatt for letting me do so. Thanks also to subsequent editors Alan Barnes, Clayton Hickman and Tom Spilsbury for the help they've given me in recent years. And lastly, the superb labour of love that is a fanzine called *Nothing at the End of the Lane*: an infrequent publication put together by Richard Bignell, Bruce Robinson, and Robert Franks, which covers the subject of lost and found *Doctor Who* in meticulous detail, and which first published the details of the two-inch videotape junkings. Go track copies down. Now!

The research into the overseas sales and broadcasting of *Doctor Who* has been another ongoing obsession of mine for the best part of 20 years. Over that time, a vast number of people have contributed nuggets of information that have added to the pool of knowledge. So my heartfelt thanks go to Ken Carriere, Dylan Crawfoot, Martin Dunne, Robert Franks, John Freeman, Graham Howard, David J Howe, Dominic Jackson, Dallas Jones, John Lavalie, Ian Levine, Ralph Montagu, Philip Morris, Andrew Pixley, Damian Shanahan, Dean Shewring, Stephen James Walker and Nigel Windsor, plus the following publications: Marvel Comics' and latterly Panini's *Doctor Who Magazine*, the New Zealand fanzine *Time/Space Visualizer* edited and published by Paul Scoones (especially for material about 'The Lion') and the Australian fanzine *Zerinza*, edited and published by Antony Howe. But by far the single biggest contributor to this area of research over the years has been the astonishing Jon Preddle, who has spent far more time visiting dusty old libraries in far-flung corners of the globe than any sane person should ever have to do.

I'd like to thank the numerous people who've helped, aided and abetted me in the writing of this book. In particular, my thanks go to Mark Ayres, Keith Barnfather, Glen Barnham, Ian Bayes and *Equity*, Jeremy Bentham, Steve Broster, Steve Bryant, Bruce Campbell, Stephen Cranford, Peter Crocker, John de Rivaz, Terrance Dicks,

WIPED!

Anne Hanford, David Holman, Richard Landen, Neil Lambess, Roger LeGree, Dennis Lensveld, Ian Levine, Simon M Lydiard, Ian McLachlan, Sue Malden, Andrew Martin, Enid Mawson, Ralph Montagu, Jon Preddle, Ian Pritchard, Steve Roberts, Gary Russell, James Russell, Paul Scoones, Damian Shanahan, Ian Sheward, Michael Smallman, David Stead, Roger Stevens, Ed Stradling, Graham Strong and Jan Vincent-Rudzki. Special thanks go to Richard Bignell, who came up with some excellent last-minute information, and Paul Vanezis, who has helped talk through some of my barmier ideas regarding missing episodes over many weeks, months and years. Also, my thanks to Telos Publishing, and to my editors David J Howe and Stephen James Walker, for giving me the opportunity to write this book. It's a project I've been itching to do for quite some time now, and thanks to them, it's happened.

Last, but by no means least, I'd like to thank my parents, Anthony and Gwyneth Molesworth, for putting up with my *Doctor Who* obsession for so long!

PUBLISHER'S NOTE

In this book the author has chosen to refer to the 1960s *Doctor Who* serials using the titles retrospectively allocated to them by various employees of the BBC and BBC Worldwide and used on the video and DVD releases of those stories. These titles differ in some cases from those used in other Telos books and by the official *Doctor Who Magazine*, which are the titles in use by the production team at the time of first transmission.

Note also that individual episodes of *Doctor Who* were referred to as 'Episode' for every story from 'The Savages' to 'The Green Death' (with the exception of 'The Ice Warriors', where each episode was titled with just the episode number). Thereafter, each episode was referred to as 'Part' with the exception of the four episodes that made up 'Destiny of the Daleks'. These naming conventions have been retained for this book. For 'The Ice Warriors', as well as the stories from 'An Unearthly Child' through to 'The Gunfighters', we have used the 'Episode' convention for convenience.

CONTENTS

Introduction by Terrance Dicks 8
Foreword 9
1 The BBC, Broadcasting, and Archiving 13
2 The Making of *Doctor Who* 27
3 Wiping the Transmission Videotapes 43
4 The BBC Film Library 77
5 BBC Enterprises: Villiers House 97
6 Reclaiming the Past – The Beginning of the End of the Junkings 141
7 The Big Breakthrough 159
8 *The Lively Arts*: 'Whose Doctor Who' 189
9 The Returned Episodes 203
10 Recovering the Third Doctor 251
11 Recolourisation, Reverse Standards, and Chroma Dots! 271
12 Recovered Fragments – Clips and Audios 287
13 Missing *Doctor Who* abroad in the 1960s and 1970s: The Hartnell and
    Troughton Years 333
14 The Overseas Sales of the Jon Pertwee Episodes 411
15 The Myth of the Missing Episodes 423
Appendix I The Missing Episodes: Overseas Sales and Transmissions 439
Appendix II The Archives Today: 1963-1989 475
Appendix III Glossary of Terms 543
Appendix IV *Doctor Who*: The Missing Episodes 548
Index 553
About the Author 576

INTRODUCTION

I must admit that during my time as script editor on *Doctor Who* – which was the end of Patrick Troughton's era, all of Jon Pertwee's, and the beginning of Tom Baker's – I was only vaguely aware of the problems and issues dealt with in this book. We – that is my producer, Barry Letts, and I – weren't so much concerned with shows that were over and done with, as with those currently going through the mill. There were ideas and storylines for new shows to be discussed, draft scripts to be edited, current scripts to be nursed through rehearsal and recording, tapes of finished shows to be edited … often all at the same time!

I was vaguely aware that occasionally Barry was consulted about shows to be saved: I remember he was very keen to preserve 'The Dæmons'. But it wasn't really a matter of great concern.

Today this attitude seems shocking, but at the time *Doctor Who* still hadn't quite attained its current legendary status. The BBC's justification was that tapes were expensive – if wiped, they could be re-used. And with its immense output there just wasn't room to save everything.

I became much more aware of the question of show survival when I became heavily involved with the Target novelisation programme. I worked from the PasB – the Programme as Broadcast – script, the final script for the show. In addition the BBC would arrange a private viewing of the serial in question for me – if it was still available. If the show was partly missing, I'd work from the script and whatever episodes had survived, plus production photographs.

Later, when VHS arrived, I'd be sent a VHS tape of the show – later still a DVD. I kept a television plus VHS/DVD player in my office, and could alternate between script and screen. Mostly things seemed to work out, though I occasionally had to use quite a bit of imagination to plug the gaps.

Today of course, the whole question of missing shows is taken far more seriously – hence this excellent book. It will tell you far more than I ever knew about vanished shows, and the sterling efforts made to recover them. I hope you enjoy it, and that still more missing *Who* continues to emerge from the mists of time!

Terrance Dicks
Script Editor, *Doctor Who*, 1968-1974

FOREWORD

Doctor Who was an immense part of the British television landscape back in the 1960s and 1970s, despite the modest protests of Terrance Dicks in his introduction to this book! That halcyon era of BBC television programming, which many self-respecting television enthusiasts hark back to with a deep-seated sense of nostalgia. The names of the classic BBC programmes of these two decades just trip off the tongue: *Steptoe and Son*, *The Goodies*, *Dad's Army*, *Grandstand*, *Basil Brush*, *Fawlty Towers*, *Parkinson*, *Top of the Pops*, *Jim'll Fix It*, *Multi-Coloured Swap Shop*, *Blue Peter*, *Monty Python's Flying Circus*, *Blake's 7* ... ah, those were the days! All worthy classics, and all hugely important in the cultural history of the nation.

Of course, *Doctor Who* continued on BBC1 until the end of the 1980s, but it was the early years of the programme, in that pre-video age, that interested many fans of the series in the 1980s and 1990s. And of course, the BBC's revival of the series, with Christopher Eccleston, David Tennant and Matt Smith, has ensured its immortality for generations to come.

There comes a point in any *Doctor Who* fan's life when they learn of the many, many, many adventures of the good Doctor that came *before* they began watching. Is David Tennant the earliest Doctor you can remember, or can you recall Christopher Eccleston? Or did you first tune in to Colin Baker? Or perhaps Jon Pertwee? No matter, because unless you started watching in 1963, then there are new (old) adventures to discover, new (old) Doctors to acquaint yourself with, and new (old) stories to watch.

That age-old fan pastime comes into play at around this point – the writing of the list. In this case, a list of all the good Doctor's television adventures from the very first story, 'An Unearthly Child', in 1963, through to ... well, who knows when it will stop, now? You might glean this list from a reference book, or download it from the internet. But the list tells you how many stories you've seen, how many stories the seventh Doctor has appeared in, how many Dalek stories there have been ... and how many stories took place before you started watching the series.

That last one is important. The totality of the Doctor's adventures on television is quantified. Now you know exactly what you have to see to catch up.

In 1981, *Doctor Who* fans had their lists. They had only four Doctors to contend with at that point, although the debut of the fifth was imminent. Video recorders had only just begun making their impact in mainstream society: most people knew at least someone who had one. For the first time, people could marvel at watching a television programme again. And again. And again.

WIPED!

It sounds really stupid and naive today, but the novelty of this concept was simply massive. Until the wider marketing of domestic video recorders in the late 1970s, television had been a disposable, transient medium. Old programmes lived on in the consciousness of the nation, but if you missed an episode of your favourite soap, or action series, or comedy, then chances were that it was gone, lost to you forever, unlikely ever to be repeated.

Doctor Who fans had enjoyed some repeats on television over the years. But not many. It took five years until the BBC first repeated a whole *Doctor Who* story, when 'The Evil of the Daleks' was shown for a second time in 1968. During Jon Pertwee's time as the Doctor, there were omnibus edition repeats every so often (where a story was edited down into a single long episode). And during Tom Baker's stint in the TARDIS, the chances were that the BBC would choose two stories from the season that had just aired to trot out again over the summer evenings a few months later.

But in late 1981, things changed. For the first time *ever*, the BBC decided to show some vintage *Doctor Who* repeats. 'An Unearthly Child', 'The Krotons', 'The Three Doctors' and 'Carnival of Monsters' were dusted down and shown on BBC2 to huge acclaim. How ironic that at roughly the same time that old *Doctor Who* episodes were being screened by the BBC for the first time, the full state of the BBC's archive of surviving *Doctor Who* episodes was made public.

In November 1981, Marvel's *Doctor Who Magazine* published a Winter Special that contained a groundbreaking interview by Jeremy Bentham with the BBC's then archive selector, Sue Malden. Accompanying the interview was a list.

Yet another list!

But this one was special. It was a list of which *Doctor Who* episodes still survived at the BBC. And which ones didn't.

It's hard to describe the shock that this list generated amongst *Doctor Who* fans at the time. Of course, there had been dark whispers for some years previously that some old episodes of *Doctor Who* had been junked, or wiped, or lost, or whatever. But no-one knew for sure which ones, or how many. The only story that ever got mentioned as definitely being missing was 'The Tomb of the Cybermen', but not many fans knew more than that.

But the *DWM* Winter Special had the full details, all presented in a neat list. Each *Doctor Who* story was listed: from 'An Unearthly Child' through to 'Logopolis'. Some stories had the magic word 'all' typed next to them. As in 'all episodes exist'. But a disappointing number of stories had the dreaded word 'none' next to them. As in 'none of the episodes exist'. Stories like 'The Daleks Masterplan', 'The Celestial Toymaker', 'The Power of the Daleks' and 'Fury from the Deep' were all gone.

FOREWORD

But more baffling still were those stories where some, but not all, of the episodes survived. Why keep 'The Tenth Planet' Episodes One, Two and Three, but not Episode Four? Why did only Episode One of 'The Web of Fear' survive, and not the rest?

And so began a multitude of questions, queries and conspiracy theories that would surround the subject of the missing episodes of *Doctor Who* for the next 30 years.

The *DWM* article also seemed to be the catalyst that triggered a seismic shift within *Doctor Who* fandom. From here on in, throughout the 1980s, fans seemed more focused on the programme's past glories of the 1960s and 1970s, rather than on the new material that was being offered up by the BBC.

In November 1981, I had just turned 13. I purchased *Doctor Who Magazine* and the Target *Doctor Who* books with vigour, and had not missed an episode of *Doctor Who* on television for, oooooh ... about seven years. I'd even begun making audio recordings of recent episodes, thinking of myself as something of a pioneer at the time. (How little did I know!) I could just about remember old *Doctor Who* stories as far back as 'Day of the Daleks', and desperately wished I could have seen some of the first two Doctors' adventures. Those stories that were so enchantingly detailed in my ragged copy of the 1973 *Radio Times Doctor Who* Special. The first Doctor's battles with the Daleks and the Celestial Toymaker, the second Doctor's fights with the Cybermen, Yeti and Ice Warriors ... even the third Doctor's early tussles with the Autons. Most shown before I was born, all shown before I started watching the series, and yet ... and yet ... perhaps one day, somehow, I could get to see them. Somehow ...

The harsh reality of the 1981 *DWM* Winter Special's list of lost *Doctor Who* episodes was a body-blow from which – if I'm brutally honest – I've never really fully recovered. The dawning realisation, as I scanned story after story on that list, that there was so much old *Doctor Who* I would never, ever get to see, was truly depressing.

And yet, in the years that followed, there were odd rays of hope. The news pages of *Doctor Who Magazine*, *DWB*, or the *Doctor Who* Appreciation Society (DWAS) newsletter *Celestial Toyroom* would occasionally report the recovery of another missing episode, and another one could get ticked off the list. Yes, another list. This was 'The List of Missing Episodes'. We all had one of those, didn't we?

And as the years went by, the realisation set in that perhaps the mystique of the missing episodes somehow *added* to the whole ethos of *Doctor Who*. If every single episode of the series still survived, to be repeated relentlessly on UK Gold, or to be sold in VHS or DVD box sets, then would *Doctor Who* have become as iconic and enthralling as it undoubtedly is?

The subject of missing episodes has burned at the heart of the *Doctor Who* community for nearly 30 years now. It has piqued many people's interest, not least mine. And as we have perhaps reached a point where the archive of *Doctor Who*'s past

WIPED!

programmes is as complete as it will ever be, then it seems appropriate to try to look back on why so many episodes are missing, and equally, why so many survived.

'As complete as it will ever be ...' That is, until the next episode turns up. And the lists have to be re-written.[1]

---

[1] Just a little note about this book. I'll be presenting as much of the information as possible as cold, hard facts. But occasionally, I'll feel the need to editorialise or pass comment on a subject. When I'm doing so, you'll find a footnote like this. And another thing – you'd better like lists ...

CHAPTER 1
THE BBC, BROADCASTING, AND ARCHIVING

Doctor Who was created by the BBC in 1963. As unlikely as it might now seem, it was the result of the toils and tribulations of an internal focus group of BBC creative types, who were trying to come up with an idea for a programme that could fit into an identified gap in the Saturday teatime television schedules. The initial group consisted of Donald Wilson, Head of the BBC's Script Department, writer C E Webber, and Script Department members Alice Frick and John Braybon. All sorts of viewer demographics were debated when formulating the concepts of the new programme's format, and the group's ideas were then fed back to and refined by Sydney Newman, the BBC's Head of Drama, who had set this work in train. Further revisions to what *Doctor Who* should be about were subsequently made by the programme's production team in the shape of producers Rex Tucker and Verity Lambert, story editor David Whitaker, and early writers such as Anthony Coburn, Terry Nation and John Lucarotti. Initially, *Doctor Who* was the product of a committee sat around a table, but as an idea, it soon became an organic, living thing, surviving weeks, months, years, decades … even into the next century. Not bad work, for a focus group.

More than anything else, however, *Doctor Who* was a child of the BBC. It was made in keeping with BBC budgets, by (mostly) BBC staff, and watched by people who knew exactly what to expect from the BBC. Its production methods followed the same patterns as most other contemporary BBC programmes, be it in the 1960s, the 1970s or the 1980s. In addition, the same factors that influenced what happened to episodes of *Doctor Who* after they'd been shown on BBC1 also affected each and every one of the BBC's other programmes at the same time – *Doctor Who* was far from unique.

To understand a little about the way *Doctor Who* was made and archived over the years, it is necessary to know a little about the BBC itself.

BBC EARLY HISTORY

The BBC was founded on 18 October 1922 as the British Broadcasting Company Ltd, a commercial organisation formed by a collection of both British and American electrical companies looking to expand into the field of wireless broadcasting, an area that had particularly taken off in America following the end of the First World War in 1918. The BBC received its first broadcasting licence in November 1922, and in the following month John C W Reith was appointed as its Managing Director. It soon began regular broadcasts of radio programmes, although initially only to a limited number of regional transmitters. On 28 September 1923, the first edition of the *Radio Times* magazine was printed, giving details of the forthcoming programmes on the BBC's radio service.

If you wanted to listen to the BBC in 1923, you first had to own a radio, and then you had to buy a licence for your radio from your local post office. By the end of 1924, over a million radio licences had been sold in the UK, and the BBC had over 20 transmitters relaying its programmes up and down the country.

On 20 December 1926, the BBC received a Royal Charter, signed by King George V. A Royal Charter changes a body from a collection of individuals into a single legal entity. Once incorporated by a Royal Charter, amendments to the Charter require government approval. This paved the way for the BBC to become a publicly funded corporation, and so the British Broadcasting Corporation was born. It was totally funded by the licence fee, and over the next few years, the BBC continued with its programme of radio broadcasts, expanding its transmitter network across the country, making it accessible to more and more of the population.

THE BBC TELEVISION SERVICE

The BBC began experimental television transmissions as early as 1929, initially with a system that broadcast a picture containing only 30 horizontal lines of resolution, developed by John Logie Baird. Baird, who had once been a student contemporary of BBC Managing Director John Reith in Glasgow, is now widely credited as having actually invented television, although prototypes for other systems were in circulation at the time. However, television was seen as a distraction to the BBC's main function as a radio service provider, and wasn't particularly embraced by the Corporation. Baird didn't work for the BBC, but the BBC Control Board allowed him access to their facilities in order for him to progress his experiments into television technology.

On 14 July 1930, the BBC transmitted the first ever play to be shown on British television, when a live performance of *The Man with a Flower in His Mouth* by Luigi Pirandello was screened. It was produced by the BBC's Programme Branch, but the screening was carried out under Baird's supervision. The BBC Control Board was not pleased with the results of this broadcast, and suspended its television involvement with Baird on 22 July 1930. However, the BBC still continued to give Baird some limited engineering support, on the orders of the Postmaster General, and test transmissions continued until 1932.

Baird persevered, overseeing the first ever television live outside broadcast in 1931, and the BBC began grudgingly to accept that television had a future. The BBC once again began undertaking experimental television transmissions from 22 August 1932, this time from the basement studio BB in Broadcasting House, London. For

CHAPTER 1

the first time, the BBC had control of both programme production and transmission. In February 1934, the BBC moved its television broadcasts away from Broadcasting House and into a specially converted studio at 16 Portland Place, London.

On 1 October 1936, the BBC moved its television service again, this time to Alexandra Palace in London, which housed two television studios. By now, the BBC Television Service, as it had been named, was broadcasting two hourly slots a day, 3.00 pm to 4.00 pm and 9.00 pm to 10.00 pm. It was also alternating between two different television systems: a 240-line system developed by Baird, and a 405-line system from Marconi-EMI. The transmission system was rotated on a weekly basis, and both were supported by the television sets of the day. After just under six months of dual standard broadcasts, the 240-line system was dropped altogether, and the BBC became totally a 405-line television network. Reception was limited to roughly a 25-mile radius of the Alexandra Palace transmitter, and so the BBC's audience was limited mostly to Londoners. Programming consisted mainly of short films and live studio broadcasts.

The outbreak of the Second World War in 1939 saw television transmissions by the BBC suspended on 1 September of that year. The nation's screens would remain dark for the duration of the War, until transmissions recommenced on 7 June 1946, beginning with the same Mickey Mouse cartoon, *Mickey's Gala Premiere*, that had been the BBC's last programme in 1939.

By 1947, television was still only available in the London area courtesy of the Alexandra Palace transmitter, but plans were being drawn up to establish transmitters in other areas of the country. The number of television licenses stood at around 15,000 in 1947, but increased to 125,000 in 1948.

The BBC's Sutton Coldfield transmitter was opened in 1949, allowing its signals to be received by the population of Birmingham and much of the West Midlands. By the early 1950s, more transmitters had been opened up and down the country, and so most of the UK's population at last had access to the BBC's television service.

Technically, not much had changed for the BBC in the years it was off-air during the War, and in the years following its return. Its programmes were captured by 405-line electronic cameras in the studios, and transmitted live to the nation's 405-line television sets. 35mm black and white film was used for the purposes of news and current affairs programmes, and was soon embraced as a means of pre-recording material for live comedy and drama programmes. These film inserts could then be 'played in' live during the broadcast.

But the BBC did not retain copies of its live programmes. They just disappeared into the ether …

FILM RECORDING/TELERECORDING

The BBC began experimenting with a process known as film recording, or

WIPED!

telerecording[2], which basically involved pointing a black and white film camera at a specially designed flat television screen. The television would show a live programme, while the film camera would record the image on film, along with the sound. One of the first experiments with this system captured the live BBC broadcast on 20 November 1947 of the marriage of Princess Elizabeth to the Duke of Edinburgh.

Princess Elizabeth had become Queen after the death of her father in 1952, and was crowned Queen Elizabeth II on 2 June 1953. The BBC announced that they were to broadcast the Coronation ceremony live on television. In the months that led up to the event, over two million television sets were sold in the UK, as public interest in the event reached fever pitch. The final viewing figure for the Coronation was later given at over 20 million, with people gathered around television sets belonging to friends, family and neighbours. For a lot of people, this would be their first ever experience of watching television.

The BBC's experiments with the telerecording system continued into the 1950s. The earliest surviving telerecording of a BBC drama, the play *It Is Midnight, Dr Schweizer*, hails from February 1953. In July 1953, the month after the Queen's Coronation, the BBC screened its groundbreaking science fiction serial *The Quatermass Experiment*, which was broadcast live on Saturday nights in six weekly instalments. The BBC began telerecording each episode as it went out live, but stopped after the first two. The final four instalments weren't recorded, as the quality of the telerecordings was felt to be too poor to justify the exercise. The process needed refinements.

Parliament passed the Television Act 1954, which gained Royal Assent on 30 July 1954. This law permitted the creation of the first commercial television network in Great Britain, which would be in competition with the BBC. The Independent Television Company (ITC, often known as ITV) was launched on 22 September 1955, and so the ratings war began.

The BBC turned to Professor Bernard Quatermass again, and presented a second adventure, *Quatermass II*, which began screening on the BBC on Saturday 22 October 1955. By this time, the telerecording process had been successfully refined enough to enable 35mm black and white film recordings of the live broadcasts to be made. Each episode was then repeated by the BBC on the Monday following its live Saturday debut. Prior to using telerecordings for repeats, if the BBC wanted to show a programme again, it had to re-engage the cast and crew to re-perform the programme live for a second time. But now it had a way of presenting exactly the same material again, and this also created a method of archiving its live television programmes.

---

2 Technically, the term 'telerecording' was used to cover a number of different recording techniques at the BBC, including the use of videotape. The BBC Television Recording Department used the term 'film recording' exclusively for the production of film sourced from a video screen. For the purposes of this book, the two terms are used interchangeably.

CHAPTER 1

The BBC's Film Library had begun in the 1930s, primarily as a repository for news films. BBC Television news had begun in earnest in 1948, and from then through to July 1954 took the form of BBC Television Newsreels made by the BBC Television Film Unit.[3] The BBC carried out its entire news gathering on film, and once the items had been transmitted, the films were retained for potential re-use, or for stock footage. Cataloguing and indexing of the film holdings was begun early on, and it became the BBC's main archive of its footage. With the advent of telerecording programmes onto film, the BBC Film Library also began archiving complete programmes.

The advantage that film had as a storage medium was that it was effectively permanent. But this was also a disadvantage. The BBC needed a format that would better suit the electronic environment of the television studio, and that was also re-usable.

Other independent television companies, such as ITC, began the practice of completely making some of their programmes on film, as a way of getting around the confines of broadcasting shows live from television studios. This gave programme-makers a great deal of flexibility, in rehearsing shots, editing out mistakes, and shooting in locations far and wide. However, mainly down to the extremely high cost of this practice, the BBC steadfastly continued making programmes live, although the use of pre-filmed inserts became more and more common.

The BBC relocated its television service from Alexandra Palace to Lime Grove studios in 1950. Lime Grove had opened as a film studio in 1915, but was sold to the BBC in 1949 by the Rank Organisation. The BBC saw Lime Grove as a temporary stop-gap, as plans to build the new BBC Television Centre at nearby White City in London were nearing fruition. In actual fact, Lime Grove studios would service the BBC for over 40 years: the final programme transmitted from there was an edition of *The Late Show* in August 1991.

TWO-INCH VIDEOTAPE

The BBC began experimenting with the idea of using video tape to record a programme in 1958, based on the already established principles of magnetic audio tape. The BBC's first videotape recorder was a machine called VERA (Visual Electronic Recording Apparatus), which was designed and built in-house by the BBC's own research and development team. VERA used fixed video heads, with the videotape travelling over them at an extremely fast speed of 200 inches-per-second – which not only caused technical problems, in that the tape was prone to snap, but was also expensive, because

---

3 News was an entirely separate production from the rest of the Film Unit. The man in charge was a New Zealander called Tahu Hole who didn't trust television not to slant the news. Before then, sound news bulletins had been repeated on BBC Television without pictures since the 1930s.

WIPED!

it used up a large amount of tape. This system was first used in April 1958 to transmit some pre-recorded material into an edition of *Panorama*, but its BBC career was to be short-lived. Over in America, engineers for a company called Ampex (<u>A</u>lexander <u>M</u> <u>P</u>oniatoff <u>Ex</u>cellence, named after the founder of the company) were working on a videotape machine called the Ampex VR1000. Ampex had started developing their videotape system in 1952, and had first marketed it in the United States in 1956.

The Ampex VR1000 machine essentially was composed of two parts: the tape transport unit, and the electrical racks unit. It was capable of recording and playing back only in black and white, and it contained no time-base corrector (a later refinement that was necessary to counteract any errors introduced into the recording and/or replay processes by the mechanics of the machine, by buffering the video signal and releasing it at a steady rate).

The early Ampex models also didn't have any tape timers, or any erase facilities. The two-inch wide videotape that they used ran at a speed of 15 inches per second, and the picture was recorded across the tape from top to bottom using four heads on a rotating drum – a technique known as Quadruplex recording, or Quad for short. Being an American system, it was devised to record and play 525-line television pictures (the American standard at the time), but machines could be easily modified to work with the BBC's 405-line standard output.

The BBC purchased two Ampex VR1000 machines in 1958. The first was installed at the Lime Grove studios on 16 August of that year, and was first used on 1 October 1958 to transmit a three-minute trailer for *A Tale of Two Cities*. The second was installed soon after. It was quickly followed by a newly-purchased third machine, and by early 1959, an operator shift system was begun. Complete schools programmes and various sporting items were now being shown from videotape by the BBC.

However, this new format of two-inch videotape was still treated with a degree of mistrust by the BBC. Frequently, transmissions would be backed-up onto 35mm film, and kept on standby just in case the new videotape equipment broke down while playing out programmes to the nation. The BBC initially kept a stock of only about half-a-dozen two-inch videotapes, which were re-used over and over again. No thought at all was given to the storage and preservation of videotaped material for future use. Once a tape had been screened, it was quickly erased (using a magnetic bulk-erasure machine) and then made ready for another programme.

In addition, the system wasn't exactly cheap. The VR1000 machine cost something in the region of $70,000 in 1958, which in today's money would be equivalent to £500,000. A 60-minute blank two-inch tape cost over £100, which in the late 1950s would be several months' income for the average worker.

BBC Television Centre opened for production in June 1960. This was a prestigious

CHAPTER 1

building based in West London, and was the world's first purpose-built television production facility. Two more Ampex VR1000 machines were purchased and installed in the new building, and three more were soon added, bringing the BBC's total number of two-inch videotape machines up to eight. These were joined by four new two-inch machines that had been developed by the RCA company, with help from Ampex themselves, the RCA TR-22. These were specifically designed to record and play 625-line signals onto two-inch tapes, and were purchased in readiness for the launch of BBC2 in April 1964, which was designed as a 625-line channel from the outset. The BBC was determined to improve the picture quality of its service, and increasing the number of picture 'lines' made a significant difference.

The rapid introduction of two-inch videotape saw a big change in the way the BBC made programmes. In the short space of two or three years, it moved away from broadcasting material live, and began pre-recording programmes on two-inch tape. However, the disciplines of programme-making remained the same, with directors, actors and studios still working to the principles of live television. This became known as 'as live' recording, with the efforts of the cast and crew being directed towards ensuring that a programme was recorded in as few takes as possible, in as near to real-time as was practicable. Thus, by the time *Doctor Who* began production in 1963, the BBC was routinely pre-recording its programmes on two-inch videotape 'as live'.

In 1964, the BBC launched BBC2, the UK's third television channel. This made use of the superior 625-line television system from the outset, which in turn meant that the BBC had to install line-converters in all their transmitters, allowing programmes to be broadcast in both 405-line and 625-line formats. This enabled viewers with either 405-line or 625-line television sets to watch both channels. Colour transmissions came to BBC2 in 1967, and then to BBC1 in November 1969.

By the early 1970s, the BBC had over 35 two-inch machines at Television Centre, with almost the same number again located throughout the rest of the Corporation's regional production centres across the UK.

SO WHY WERE BBC PROGRAMMES NOT KEPT?

The BBC had a number of historical issues surrounding the preservation of its programmes. One of the biggest was the way internal policies and procedures had evolved over the 1950s, 1960s and 1970s.

The BBC Film Library had initially been set up to be reactive to the demands of a live broadcaster. It would decide whether or not to keep a programme in its archive only after that programme had been shown by the BBC. Even with the advent of telerecording in the mid-1950s, the process was used only as a way of preserving programmes as they went out live on air. Once something was committed to film, the

WIPED!

film couldn't be re-used, and so it became a permanent record. But the retention and storage of the film material after broadcast was still a secondary consideration. The BBC was geared up to maintaining a public television service, and ensuring that its live programmes were made and transmitted was its priority. This reflected the fact that its Royal Charter made no specific provision for it to archive its programmes.

The introduction of videotape, and the move to pre-recording programmes, was essentially a way of building safeguards into the live transmission system. It allowed for a degree of editing, and took away many of the variables that had to be considered and addressed for a live broadcast. It gave the BBC more control over what was screened. But videotape was viewed as just the medium used to get programmes onto air, and not as a means to retain them after transmission.

The purchase of new videotapes was the responsibility of the BBC's Engineering Department, as was managing the pool of already used ones. The onus was on them to recycle as many as possible, thus cutting down on the number of new ones that had to be purchased each year. Although the initial purchase of the tapes was funded out of the Engineering Department's budget, they would then charge all internal BBC production departments for using the tapes to make their programmes, via the BBC's internal market accounting system. So a programme like *Doctor Who* would have to pay a sum out of its production budget for each use of a two-inch tape to record or transmit an episode.

This meant that BBC production departments were encouraged to issue Wipe/Junk Authorisation forms for as many two-inch tapes as possible, in order to release funds back to the programme-making budget. The more tapes that could be wiped, the more money that could then be released back for the production of new material. Lists of material held on two-inch tapes were regularly circulated by the Engineering Department to the various production departments, inviting them to release the tapes for erasure and re-use.

Thus, in practice, it remained the case that the only programme material seriously considered for retention after broadcast was that telerecorded onto 35mm film – as recalled by Anne Hanford, the senior librarian in the BBC Film Library from 1968 to 1996.

> **Anne Hanford:** In the pre-videotape days of the BBC, the only way of retaining programmes was to make black and white film recordings of live transmissions. The BBC had a policy back then of retaining some of its material this way, but there was only a very limited budget for this. So the BBC only made film copies of selected episodes from its output. They did not necessarily keep whole series.

CHAPTER 1

The selection of material to be recorded and retained was an almost arbitrary process. Some consideration was given to material that could be repeated, or considered for sale overseas. But again, this was mainly a reactive process, probably completed by someone with no more than a marker pen and a copy of that week's *Radio Times*. There was no consolidated policy about the retention of material, and there was not much thought beyond what the practicalities of the archive were, above and beyond its servicing of the programme-making function. The BBC was looking forward to the following day's or week's programmes, not back at what was shown the day or week before.

While telerecording was a viable system for the retention of black and white programmes, the results of colour telerecording from two-inch colour videotape were very poor indeed. Thus by 1970, when a full colour service was introduced on BBC1 as well as BBC2, the use of film as a method of retaining programmes was essentially obsolete. Only limited black and white telerecording continued, for the purposes of overseas sales to countries that hadn't introduced a colour service as yet.

The BBC had made provisions, funds and resources available for its Film Library since its inception in 1948, but no similar arrangement had been put in place for videotaped material in the 1950s and 1960s. Videotaped programmes appear to have fallen through a gap in policy. Programme-makers and their departments (in *Doctor Who*'s case, the Drama Department) had the power to ensure that specified material was retained – for repeat, overseas sale, or some other use – by issuing a Retention Authorisation sheet. But the problem with this system was that it relied on the personnel concerned making decisions based on an arbitrary and inconsistent set of criteria. Put simply, it was a system based on keeping nothing unless someone instructed otherwise, rather than keeping everything unless someone decided to junk material. The question was always 'What should we keep?', not 'What should we throw away?'

To add to the complexity, Retention Authorisation sheets could also be raised by BBC Enterprises, a separate arm of the BBC, which sold its programmes overseas. At best, this led to a duplication of paperwork. At worst, it meant that there were two different systems running in parallel, with different sets of criteria being applied in each case towards the retention of the material. And it relied on someone, somewhere, issuing the correct paperwork. Should a programme, for whatever reason, not have a Retention Authorisation sheet issued for it, either by the production department or by Enterprises, then the two-inch tape was fair game for wiping and re-use.

The Retention Authorisation sheets could be overturned by the issuing of Wipe/Junk Authorisation forms, which again could be raised by either the relevant BBC production department or by Enterprises. This led to the inevitable situation where a hierarchy evolved as to which bits of paper had precedence over which other bits of

WIPED!

paper, and the whole system became an administrative nightmare.

Another factor was the complex agreement for repeats that the BBC had struck with the actors' union Equity in the mid-1950s. The need for this agreement – which remained in force pretty much unchanged until the mid-1980s – arose due to the BBC having acquired the ability to repeat programmes from telerecordings or two-inch videotapes. Actors no longer had to be re-hired to give literal repeat performances, and so received less money than before. This was of great concern to Equity, who saw it as a threat to the livelihoods of their members. They also reasoned that if the BBC were to build up an archive of old television programmes and then begin repeating them, this would surely cut down on the number of new programmes it needed to make to fill its schedules, adversely affecting actors still further.

The agreement essentially limited any repeats to a two-year period after a programme's first transmission. After this, the programme became known as 'out-of-time'. Initially, if the BBC wanted to screen an out-of-time programme, it had to get Equity's specific permission for this and pay all of the actors a proportion of their original fee again. In December 1974, the agreement was refined so that 52 out-of-time repeats could be shown each calendar year without securing specific permission – 26 on BBC1, 26 on BBC2. This was still the situation in 1981, when BBC2 ran its season of old *Doctor Who* repeats under the umbrella title 'The Five Faces of *Doctor Who*'. Of the five four-part stories selected for this season, four were classed as out-of-time, which used up 16 of BBC2's 26 slots for that whole year.

Glen Barnham was the BBC Radio and Television Organiser for Equity between 1975 and 2005. As such, he was responsible for liaising and negotiating with the BBC on the issue of archive repeats, amongst other things. I asked him to explain the relationship between Equity and the BBC at the time:

Glen Barnham: People imagine that Equity was somehow opposed to the BBC repeating material, but that really wasn't the case at all. As long as the repeats were done with the agreement of our members, and were fully paid for, then we were quite happy. Our repeats agreement with the BBC had been in effect for a long time before I got involved in 1975, and so I don't know how it originated, or who suggested the framework. But one of the basic details was that the BBC could repeat any programme within two years of its first broadcast without having to renegotiate with our members. There was also a limitation on the number of programmes that were older than two years that could be shown on the BBC. But as far as I can recall it was purely arbitrary, and if the BBC had asked us to review it, then we'd have been happy to talk to them.

CHAPTER 1

My principal contact at the BBC was the Head of Programme Contracts in the Commercial Rights Department, and we had a number of conversations over the years about ways that the rules could be changed that would benefit both our membership and the BBC itself. There was obviously a communications issue within the BBC, because the rest of the departments couldn't have known that we were not advocating that older material needed to be destroyed.

The main change in the agreement came in the mid-1980s, when we suggested to the BBC that we'd consider allowing more archive material to be screened in the afternoon, and negotiated a reduction of the fee they'd have to pay the actors down from 80% of the original fee, to 50%. We thought it was better for the BBC to repeat old British programmes than for them to buy in foreign programmes to fill the afternoon schedules.

We were committed to ensuring that our members got a fair deal from the BBC, and we did want to always guarantee that there would be a certain level of output of new production. This wasn't really an issue when I started in the mid-1970s, as the BBC was producing so much new material every week – their studios were always in constant use. But the agreement on out-of-time repeats was more of a gentlemen's agreement between us and the BBC. Equity never ever monitored the BBC's output to check that they kept to their annual out-of-time allocation, and if the BBC had approached us about increasing the amount of old material they could screen, then I'm sure something could have been sorted out.

But it's sad that this agreement might be even partly responsible for the destruction of all those wonderful old programmes. That was something that was never Equity's intention at all when the arrangement was made. We expected all of the BBC's programmes to be available for overseas sales, and it was BBC Enterprises who perhaps did not appreciate that this was a potential goldmine for them. Equity did press for less restrictive overseas sales arrangements, which eventually did come about under a more enlightened BBC, who realised that the archive was there to be exploited both for the BBC and the performers. It was Equity that suggested to the BBC that old radio programmes be made available for sale on tape, many years before that become a reality. At the time we were told there simply was no market. In the 1980s, everybody woke up to the potential of the archive, and it is a crime that old material was destroyed to make shelf space. And sadly, after I left Equity in 2005, someone decided to junk all my paperwork, which included all the details of these old agreements, and so the mentality which led to the loss of all these programmes still exists today.

WIPED!

Other programme rights were also an issue for the BBC. Unlike ITV productions, which usually had total buy-out clauses in their contracts (in exchange for one big fee, a contributor would sign over all his or her rights in the material in perpetuity), most BBC programmes had contracts providing for just a single screening. This applied not only to the actors, but also to writers, musicians and any other freelance contributors to the programme in question. For the BBC to repeat a programme, even within the two-year window, could lead to quite substantial costs.

The final factor was the arrival of colour television at the BBC in the late 1960s and early 1970s. A standard television licence cost £5 in 1968, but this was just for owning a black and white television set. 1968 saw the introduction of a 'colour supplement' charge to the standard television licence, which was an additional cost of £5, effectively doubling the licence fee for those with colour sets. These additional licence fee funds were made directly available to the BBC to help pay for the introduction of the new colour technology, but this created both a political and an editorial need for colour programmes.

Although senior executives such as BBC2 Controller David Attenborough initially stated that black and white programmes might still be made from time to time for artistic reasons, in practice this did not happen. From November 1969, the BBC's television service was in colour on both channels; all new programmes were made in colour, and there was a conscious move away from repeating older black and white material. After all, the BBC now had to justify the cost of the colour licence, and black and white repeats would hardly help their position with either the viewers or the government. Andrew Martin of the BBC Film and Videotape Library explains how black and white was used in the late 1960s and early 1970s at the BBC:

> **Andrew Martin:** Occasional programmes were made in black and white for artistic reasons e.g. Alan Bennett's *A Day Out* and Brecht's *The Gangster Show: The Resistible Rise of Arturo Ui*. Many more programmes were made in black and white until the mid-1970s for economic or logistical reasons – for example, not all studios at Television Centre were colour equipped until 1975, and some regions also took time to convert. Certainly not all new programmes were made in colour immediately, e.g. *Z Cars* took until early 1970 to convert, and *Blue Peter* was in black and white until after the 1970 summer break. Many schools and further education programmes took years to change.

And so, several disparate factors were coming into play at the BBC in the 1960s and 1970s, all contributing to the way that old programme material was dealt with. These factors resulted in the majority of programmes being junked semi-methodically either straight after being screened, or just after the second anniversary of their broadcast.

CHAPTER 1

Somewhere along the line, BBC Enterprises might step in and decide that a particular programme ought to remain available for overseas sales purposes. Once this was decided, then a whole raft of other commercial, economic and practical forces would exert themselves; but that's for another chapter ...

It wasn't all one-way traffic for old BBC programmes. There was a growing understanding within the BBC during the early-to-mid 1970s of the historical and cultural significance of its output, coupled with the first stirrings of the realisation that the full possibilities of the commercial exploitation of its archive had yet to emerge. The general consensus amongst BBC management was that something needed to be done to change things at the Corporation. But what, exactly?

Before we explore these questions further, let's pause to look at how *Doctor Who* fitted into the BBC's production strategy over the years. To understand better how the BBC treated *Doctor Who* as a programme, it's perhaps useful to understand how it was made.

WIPED!

CHAPTER 2
THE MAKING OF DOCTOR WHO

*D*octor Who was made in more or less the same way throughout the entire 26 years of its original run on air. That's a slight simplification – there were actually two different ways the programme was made, but both were similar. *Doctor Who* began in 1963 with a production schedule that saw an episode a week being rehearsed and then recorded. This method remained relatively unchanged for the remainder of the decade. The 1970s saw this production process evolve, initially to the point where two episodes were made per fortnight. This may sound more or less the same, but it allowed for a longer uninterrupted rehearsal period, which was then followed by two studio days in which to record two episodes' worth of material. This technique was further refined in the 1970s and 1980s to allow for location filming and outside broadcast recording to be integrated into the production when and if required.

This method of programme making remained in effect until the BBC ended the series in 1989, and it helps throw some light on the short-term and long-term archival foibles that the programme has been affected by since 1963.

CASE STUDY – 'THE RESCUE': EPISODE ONE

The production of *Doctor Who* from 1963 to 1969, when William Hartnell and then Patrick Troughton played the Doctor, followed an almost identical pattern for each and every story. As an example of 1960s production methods, we'll look at the making of one early William Hartnell story, 'The Rescue'.

The first production block (i.e. the first continuous block of rehearsing and recording episodes on a weekly, uninterrupted, basis) of *Doctor Who* ended on Friday 23 October 1964, with the studio recording of the last episode of the story 'The Dalek Invasion of Earth'.

The standard weekly schedule for *Doctor Who* at this time would begin on a Monday morning, with the first day's rehearsal for that week's episode, which would usually take place in a Territorial Army drill hall on Uxbridge Road in the Shepherd's Bush area of London, not far from the show's production office. Four days of rehearsal would take place for an episode, from Monday through to Thursday, with the episode then recorded in the studio on the Friday of that same week. Once an episode had been completed, the cast then had the weekend to themselves, only to return to the Drill Hall again on Monday morning to begin rehearsing the next episode, and so on. One episode of *Doctor Who* was made a week.

The production and recording of a given episode was usually about three weeks in

WIPED!

advance of its BBC transmission. So, for example, the day after the final episode of 'The Aztecs' was recorded at Lime Grove (Friday 22 May 1964), the opening episode of that same story was screened on BBC1 (Saturday 23 May 1964). This short period between recording and transmission was the only opportunity for any post-production work to be done, in order to get the episode ready for transmission from (in most cases) its two-inch black and white master videotape.

'The Rescue' was slightly atypical, in that it was essentially the first two episodes of a six-episode mini-production block, which also included the four-part story 'The Romans'. All six episodes were directed by Christopher Barry and shared many of the same production crew.

The story's in-studio production was being planned as early as Wednesday 7 October 1964, when producer Verity Lambert wrote to all the directors lined up to oversee *Doctor Who* in the coming months, informing them that only five planned breaks were allowed in each studio recording. This was a critical piece of technical planning, as each break in recording would result in the two-inch videotape of the studio session undergoing a physical edit to remove the extraneous material, and allow the resultant completed scenes to be spliced together, to become the transmission tape of the episode in question.

A small amount of pre-filming was done for this story at the BBC's Ealing Film Studios on Monday 16 November 1964. This was of the model shot of the TARDIS materialising in the cave at the start of the first episode, and also various model shots of the crashed rocket ship. These film sequences would then be played into the studio during the recording of this episode, along with the film of the opening titles for the series. Playing in film inserts was a regular part of studio recording sessions.

The first rehearsal day on Monday 30 November began at 11.00 am, which was an agreed late start each week to allow William Hartnell time to travel up to London from his home near Mayfield in Sussex. It finished at around 6.00 pm, which was later than usual due to the late start. The cast and director would return the following day at 10.00 am to resume proceedings, finishing this time at 5.00 pm. Wednesday and Thursday would follow the same pattern, with a final rehearsal probably performed in front of producer Verity Lambert on the Thursday afternoon – this was known as the 'producer's run'. For 'The Rescue', rehearsals took place at the London Transport Assembly Rooms opposite Television Centre.

After four days of solidly rehearsing the episode, the cast and director would then have a single day in the studio – in the case of this episode, at Riverside Studios in Hammersmith – to record the episode. Beginning at 10.30 am, the whole of the morning and afternoon of Friday 4 December 1964 was spent on camera and costume rehearsals, which were as much for the studio crew's benefit as the cast's.

CHAPTER 2

Studio rehearsals allowed for all the camera moves to be practiced. The director would generally have pre-planned which of the five cameras would capture any given shot, which would prepare for the next shot, and so on, allowing the studio vision mixer to know which camera to cut to next, but this would be the first opportunity to see how the director's plan would pan out on the studio floor. It was necessary to work out the sequence of shots in such a way that the cables of any two cameras never crossed each other, otherwise there was a risk they would snag and restrict the ability of the cameramen to get the shots they needed.

The morning rehearsals would finish at 1.00 pm, and the cast and crew would then have an hour's lunch break. They would then resume at 2.00 pm, and would go on to 7.00 pm, which would then be followed by an hour's supper break. Then it was back to the studio again, and the serious business of actually recording the episode would begin. There would be a technical run-through and line up of all the studio equipment at 8.00 pm, which took about 30 minutes, in readiness for the recording to finally start at 8.30 pm

The scripts for 'The Rescue' had been written by the programme's outgoing story editor, David Whitaker, and had been structured so that nearly all of the action could be recorded in a single studio utilising just six new sets plus the established TARDIS interior set.

The script for the first episode was structured as follows:

Telecine insert: Opening titles
Telecine insert: TARDIS arrives
Telecine insert: Crashed rocket ship
Scene 1: Int. Rocket Ship – Compartment One
Scene 2: Int. Rocket Ship – Compartment Two
Scene 3: Int. Rocket Ship – Compartment One
Scene 4: Int. TARDIS

RECORDING BREAK 1

Scene 5: Int. Cave with TARDIS
Scene 6: Ext. Rocky Ledge
Telecine Insert: Crashed Rocket
Scene 7: Ext. Rocky Ledge
Telecine Insert: Crashed Rocket
Scene 8: Ext. Rocky Ledge
Scene 9: Int. TARDIS

WIPED!

RECORDING BREAK 2

Scene 10: Ext. Rocky Ledge
Scene 11: Int. Cave with TARDIS
Scene 12: Ext: Rocky Ground with Scrub Bushes
Scene 13: Int. Cave with TARDIS

RECORDING BREAK 3

Scene 14: Int. Rocket Ship – Compartment One
Scene 15: Int. Rocket Ship – Compartment Two
Scene 16: Int. Rocket Ship – Compartment One
Scene 17: Int. Rock Tunnel with Ledge
Scene 18: Int. Rocket Ship – Compartment One
Scene 19: Int. Rock Tunnel with Ledge
Scene 20: Int. Cave with Rock Backing
Scene 21: Int. Rock Tunnel with Ledge
Scene 22: Int. Cave with Rock Backing
Scene 23: Int. Rock Tunnel with Ledge
End Titles: Caption roller

The episode was to be recorded in scene order, with the cast and crew moving from set to set as required. The actual recording would begin at 8.30 pm, and was due to conclude at 9.45 pm, giving the cast and crew just 75 minutes to record everything needed for the one 25-minute episode.

Three recording breaks were scheduled, which meant that four chunks of continuous action were planned to be recorded. If you consider that these four together were to account for the 25-minute running time of the episode, then the schedule allowed for no more than 15 minutes on average for each recording break. And that was if everything went smoothly in the studio …

The action was to be recorded onto a black and white two-inch 405-line videotape, given the recording number VT/4T/25136. Most two-inch tapes could record a maximum of 61 minutes' worth of material, and so this tape wouldn't be kept running during the recording breaks.

Recording for this episode began as scheduled at 8.30 pm, and the first chuck of action was all recorded without a hitch. The recording began with a shot of a VT timeclock, onto which one of the studio cameras was trained, as it counted down 30 seconds to the start of the programme. This then cued the first telecine insert, a 35mm

CHAPTER 2

film of the *Doctor Who* opening titles, which ran for 27 seconds. This was followed by another telecine film insert of the stills montage filmed at Ealing of the model TARDIS materialising. Over this, two caption slides were superimposed, giving the title of the episode ('The Powerful Enemy'), and then the writer's credit ('Written by David Whitaker').

This was then faded to black by the studio vision mixer for a few seconds, and then another telecine film insert was faded up, this time of the crashed rocket ship model. Throughout these telecine inserts, the studio grams operator would be responsible for playing in the title music, the sound effects of the TARDIS materialisation, and the 'ping' of the rocket ship's radar scanner. Once the model shot had established the rocket ship as the location for the action, it was straight into the first studio scene, Scene 1. This was the first action to be recorded in the studio for this episode, and featured Maureen O'Brien playing Vicki, looking at the radar screen of the ship. Only three of the studio's five cameras were required to record this scene.

All of the action required for this episode from the studio's five cameras, plus the output of the telecine machine, was selected live, shot-by-shot, by the vision mixer in the studio gallery, with the selection being sent to be recorded on the two-inch black and white videotape. Music and sound effects were played in 'live' into the studio by the grams operator, and these were recorded as part of the soundtrack to the television pictures on the two-inch videotape.

Recording for this episode stopped at the planned recording break, after the first TARDIS interior scene. The first 6 minutes and 28 seconds of the episode had now been captured on the two-inch tape as a continuous sequence. The videotape was then stopped, as the cameras, the crew and the cast all repositioned themselves to begin work on the second chunk of action. During this break, actor Ray Barrett changed out of Bennett's costume and into Koquillion's robes and mask. Recording breaks were not always a technical requirement – often practical necessities such as costume changes dictated them.

The Ampex two-inch videotape machine was restarted, and once it was up to speed (two-inch machines needed up to 30 seconds to get the video heads fully working at speed, which would slowly allow the on-tape recording to stabilise), the second chunk of action from this episode was successfully enacted for the studio cameras. This section of action again concluded with a TARDIS interior scene, and ran for 5 minutes and 12 seconds. The time in the studio would by now have been approaching 9.00 pm.

After the studio was reset, the third chunk of action was ready to be recorded. The two-inch machine was restarted, and the cast and crew went onwards with scene 10 of the script. All went well, until the final scene in this section came to be recorded, in

WIPED!

which the Doctor walks out of the TARDIS to find that the cave has been sealed and Ian is unconscious in the rubble. Something went awry with this scene in the studio, and so a second take had to be recorded, immediately after the initial take of the action. Recording then eventually came to a halt at the planned third recording break of the night. The TARDIS set was quickly removed ('struck') from the studio, and in its place was erected the backdrop that was to be used for all the scenes featuring the Sand Beast.

After resetting, the studio prepared to record the fourth – and final – planned chunk of action. Recording began with Scene 14, only for an unplanned stop to occur, as action was suspended after the completion of Scene 16, set in the interior of the crashed rocket.

The final scenes of the episode (from Scene 17 onwards) called for a technique known as inlay to be used in the studio. Inlay allowed the output of one camera to be inserted into the shot from another. In this instance, a shot of the Sand Beast was meant to be inlaid into a shot of the Doctor and Ian standing on a ledge above the creature. Three inlay shots in total were planned for this sequence, but there were technical difficulties with the technique on the day, which caused delays in the studio.

The studio was reset, and recording resumed on the final scenes of the episode, which mainly concentrated on the attempt by the Doctor and Ian to escape from the sealed cave by clambering along a ledge in a rocky tunnel, intercut with a single scene set back on board the crashed rocket. The rest of the episode's action was recorded in sequence, but there were continuing problems with the inlay equipment in the studio, rendering the recorded material unusable.

Director Christopher Barry was forced to go back and re-record everything from Scene 17 onwards. But time was marching on in the studio, and the 9.45 pm finish time was fast approaching. If the recording overran this time, then additional payments would need to be made to the studio crew, and to the cast, which ate into *Doctor Who*'s already meagre budget. Barry knew that an overrun was now inevitable, but opted to at least minimise the overrun payments by quickly arranging a re-take of Scene 18, the one remaining scene set inside the crashed rocket ship. Once this single scene was recorded, he was able to release Jacqueline Hill, Maureen O'Brien and Ray Barrett for the evening, and they were able to leave the studio at the agreed time of 9.45 pm. William Hartnell, William Russell and Tom Sheridan (the actor playing the Sand Beast) had to remain behind to conclude the recording, which triggered overtime payments for the trio.

Christopher Barry now decided to record the remaining scenes out of order, almost certainly because there were still issues with the studio's inlay equipment. He began with retakes of all the action from the beginning of Scene 19, and continued

CHAPTER 2

right through to the end of the episode. He then went back and did a re-take of Scene 17, which ran to one minute exactly. Still not happy with the final scenes of the episode, he ordered a third take of the action leading up to the end of the episode, starting with Scene 21. This third take ran for 1 minute and 55 seconds. Eventually, all the material required for this episode was successfully recorded, but not before the studio session overran by 15 minutes.

The two-inch black and white videotape of the studio recording session, spool VT/4T/25136, now had to be edited, to put the episode together in scene order, cutting out all the recording breaks. In total, Christopher Barry had the following chunks of action that needed to be strung together to make the episode:

Material	Duration	Total Duration
Titles & Scenes 1-4	06.28	06.28
Scenes 5-9	05.12	11.40
Scenes 10-12	00.43	12.23
Scene 13: Take 2	02.28	14.41
Scenes 14-16	04.45	19.36
Scene 17: Take 2	01.00	20.36
Scene 18: Take 2	01.23	21.59
Scenes 19-20: Take 2	02.21	24.20
Scenes 21-23: Take 3	01.55	26.15

EDITING 'THE RESCUE': EPISODE ONE

Director Christopher Barry reviewed the studio recording tape of the first episode shortly after the studio day, in early December 1964, and made editing notes about which parts of the recording he wanted to use to make the finished episode. These notes, and the original two-inch studio recording spool, were then handed over to a BBC videotape editor. The nine sections of tape that were required to make up the final transmitted episode were carefully cut out from the parent spool, and spliced together in order to make the final transmission videotape spool for this episode.

When the process was over, spool VT/4T/25136 now ran to just over 25 minutes, and contained the first episode of 'The Rescue' in full. It was now ready to be screened on BBC1 on Saturday 2 January 1965. The BBC kept tape VT/4T/25136 until August 1967, when it was junked from the Engineering Department's tape store – see Chapter 3 for the full story.

The cast and director would return to the London Transport Assembly Rooms at 11 am on Monday 7 December for four more days of rehearsal, this time for the second and final episode of the serial. Then it was back to Riverside Studios on Friday 11 December to record the episode. The structure of the studio day was identical to that of the previous week, and most of the same sets were re-erected for the recording.

This was the basic template *Doctor Who* followed from 1963 through to early 1969. Retakes such as those that occurred on the first episode of 'The Rescue' were not uncommon, and out-of-scene-order recording took place more often than is sometimes supposed. This meant that Verity Lambert's entreaty to directors to have no more than five recording breaks per episode was frequently not adhered to in practice.

TWO-INCH VIDEOTAPE EDITING AND THE BBC

The BBC had experimented with two types of two-inch videotape machines in 1958, the Ampex VR1000 from America, and the BBC's own VERA system. The Ampex machine proved to be more practical, and this two-inch format won the day. Amazingly, it would continue to be the transmission format for the Corporation throughout the 1960s and 1970s. It was phased out for new programme making only in 1983, when it was replaced by the more lightweight one-inch tape format.

Ampex two-inch machines had four video heads located on the drum of the machine, which broke the television picture down into 16 separate stripes. Each stripe, containing one-sixteenth of an entire television field, was then recorded onto the two-inch tape.

The concept of physically editing film, or even quarter-inch audio tape, had been around for a long time by the late 1950s. With film, the editor had physical pictures to refer to when cutting the desired footage away from unwanted material. However, every splice made between two sections of film had the unwanted side-effect of making the film 'bounce' around the join when passed through a projector's gate. A system of working with film was introduced in the industry to minimise these side effects, by having graded prints made from cut negatives, which eliminated this problem. Cutting magnetic audio tape was slightly trickier, as there were no visual cues to work to. But it was still a common discipline, and edited audio tape was widely used in the film, television and music industries. Two sections of disparate sound, music or dialogue could be quite seamlessly spliced together, and if done in the correct manner, the edited audio tape would be playable on most types of reel-to-reel machines without any technical problems or concerns.

Two-inch videotape was a different proposition. As with audio tape, there were no visual guides on the magnetic tape to show an editor exactly where to cut, and so precise notes of stop and start times needed to be logged before editing. Each frame of video was recorded on a number of successive tracks spread transversely across the tape. Each track was one ten-thousandth of an inch wide, and was separated from the next by a guard band one five-thousandth of an inch wide. If a cut was to be successfully made to the videotape, it needed to be made directly in the middle of the guard band.

CHAPTER 2

Ampex developed a simple worktop splicing block for two-inch videotape, which was used in conjunction with a liquid treatment that was applied to the physical tape itself. This treatment was a highly volatile solution of Edivue (a developing fluid marketed by Ampex) mixed with iron filings. As the Edivue evaporated, it left the iron filings on the surface of the tape, visibly aligned along the paths of the magnetic tracks beneath. Identifying track one on the tape could be done by locating the edit pulse recorded on the control track at the bottom edge of the tape, and then counting eight tracks to one side. The tape was cut at an angle in the correct position using a razor blade, and then the process was repeated with the next section of tape. Once this too had been cut, the two sections of tape could be spliced together, making sure that the alternation of odd/even fields of the picture wasn't disturbed. The iron filings needed to be completely cleaned off the tape afterwards, and the two ends would be joined together with sticky tape. If the edit was technically successful (meaning that all the tracks were still in the right order, and the cuts had been made on the guard bands), the edited two-inch tape would play back correctly. If not, white flashes and/or picture break-ups would occur on replay, and the editor usually had to have another attempt to get the splice done correctly.

This method of two-inch tape editing was later superseded by a piece of equipment called a Smiths Splicer. This incorporated a precision thumbwheel that controlled the tape position, and a built-in microscope that allowed joins to be more precisely aligned. But in the days before videotape timecode, accurate cuts could be determined only by running the tape until the appropriate point was reached, hitting the stop button, and marking the videotape with a wax pencil. The bottom line remained that for most of the 1960s, the only way to edit videotape was to physically cut the tape, and then splice the required sections together.

As evidenced by Verity Lambert's 7 October 1964 memo to her directors, the BBC were concerned about the integrity of tapes that had numerous splices in them. The drum of a two-inch videotape machine would spin at 15,000 revolutions per minute, putting the tape under severe pressure. Any weaknesses would be severely tested under these conditions, and the weakest areas on any tape would naturally be the splice points. So the BBC powers-that-be decreed that no more than five splices should be made in a 30 minute tape. Any tape that had more than five splices in it couldn't be re-used, and re-using videotape was something the BBC was keen on, considering the costs of new tape[4].

Apart from the risk of tapes breaking on transmission, there were other problems

---

4 By the time the BBC switched to broadcasting 625-line colour pictures from their two-inch tapes in the 1970s, the number of splices allowed before a tape became unsuitable for reuse was reduced to just three per 90-minute spool.

caused by splices. Due to the head positioning on the videotape recorder, the sound recorded on the tape was at a position about half a second ahead of the corresponding picture. Thus any physical edit made to the two-inch tape would result in having sound spliced at a point half a second away from the required picture. To get around this problem, sometimes the soundtrack from a studio recording was copied onto quarter-inch audio tape, and then dubbed back onto the edited videotape so that it remained in sync with the action.

Any physical cuts or splices made to a two-inch videotape were charged to the programme's production budget under the BBC's internal rules. (In the 1970s, the cost of each splice was £60.00, and the programme's producer had to agree to accept the charge before the cut was made.)

Despite the somewhat crude nature of the editing and splicing methods described above, the end results were usually excellent. The downside was the limitation on the number of edits that could be made.

With the introduction of colour for BBC2 in 1967, the practice of physically splicing videotapes in order to edit them was quickly phased out[5]. Instead, the process of electronically duplicating sections of tape (or tapes) onto another tape was introduced. Editing by copying material was the next step in the evolution of programme making.

ONE-INCH VIDEOTAPE AND OTHER TRANSMISSION FORMATS

One-inch format videotape had been around since the 1960s. The first one-inch system was known as the A Format, and was developed by Ampex, but didn't particularly interest the BBC as it didn't meet with broadcast specifications. The C Format one-inch videotape system was co-developed by Ampex and Sony in 1976 as a replacement for Ampex two-inch tape format, and was designed to be fully broadcastable.

As its name suggests, the tape was only half the width of two-inch videotape, and was again an open reel format. It used the same helical scan method of recording onto tape that later domestic machines, such as VHS video recorders, utilised. The video head was on a rotating drum, but because of the tape path and the drum angle, the head swept across the tape in a diagonal strip, rather than a vertical one. The video heads of one-inch machines spun at the exact same field rate as the BBC's PAL television system, 3,000 rpm (revolutions per minute).

Unlike the quadruplex recording system employed on two-inch machines, the helical scan method enabled an entire television field to be recorded onto a section

---

5 Physical splices were still used in the 1970s to remove generic titles from shows like *I, Claudius* (originally in the strand 'The BBC2 Serial') and the *Porridge* pilot 'Prisoner and Escort' (from the *Seven of One* Ronnie Barker series).

CHAPTER 2

of tape in a single pass. This enabled one-inch machines to play back a single still frame if required, or to show a viewable image when shuttling backwards or forwards through a tape at speed – something that two-inch technology couldn't do. This greatly facilitated the editing process, enabling portions of recordings to be quickly located and reviewed.

The one-inch machines were much smaller than their two-inch counterparts, used less power than two-inch machines, and generally required less maintenance.

Of course, the switch from two-inch to one-inch didn't happen overnight at the BBC. Programmes were still being edited on two-inch tape as late as 1984, and the format was still being used in 1987 as way of recording live programmes such as *Breakfast Time* for posterity (presumably to use up the remaining tape stock).

The first C Format one-inch machines were purchased by the BBC in 1978, but at the time, the quality of the recordings wasn't considered quite good enough for broadcast. The format was mainly used for making Programme-as-Broadcast recordings of live shows in the late 1970s. Around about 1982, the BBC changed its attitude towards the one-inch tape format. To begin with, some programmes that were recorded in the studio on two-inch tape were then edited on one-inch tape for broadcast. (Examples include the first series of *The Young Ones* and *The Black Adder*.)

Doctor Who switched directly from two-inch to one-inch production after the making of the twentieth anniversary special 'The Five Doctors'. 'Warriors of the Deep' was thus recorded and edited completely on one-inch tape, as were all subsequent *Doctor Who* stories through to 1989's 'Survival' (although the flashback scenes in 'Resurrection of the Daleks' were all edited on two-inch tape).

One-inch tape continued to be the BBC's broadcast format until the early 1990s, when it was replaced with the D3 format, the first digital videotape system used by the BBC. Unlike two-inch and one-inch tapes, D3 tapes came in a single cassette unit, roughly twice the size of a domestic VHS tape. The system was developed by Panasonic in 1991, and the BBC began converting its edit suites to the format in 1992. Although D3 was a digital format, it recorded material as uncompressed composite signals on a tape that was now just half an inch wide.

D3 was not to be around at the BBC for too long though. A tape format called Betacam SP had been launched in 1986 by Sony. This had been used by the BBC for newsgathering and in post-production, and was seen as a replacement for Sony's U-MATIC video cassette system, which had been used for these purposes since 1971. In 1993, Sony launched Digital Betacam (commonly referred to as DigiBeta), which recorded television pictures as compressed component video signals. Unlike Betacam SP, Digital Betacam was an immediate rival to the D3 format.

In the late 1990s, the BBC began to look ahead towards making programmes in

WIPED!

a different aspect ratio to the standard 4x3 picture, which had been the screen size of televisions since they were first invented. The BBC decided that 16x9 programmes would be the way forward, and slowly began moving production over to this new aspect ratio. D3 remained the format for 4x3 programme making, but anything made 16x9 was to be produced on Digital Betacam. Initially 16x9 programmes were made only for the BBC's digital channels, such as BBC Choice, which launched in 1998 alongside digital versions of BBC1 and BBC2.

71 EDITS

All recorded material (from either studio or location sessions) for any given programme would be edited together during post-production to produce the actual programme itself. Although atypical for the BBC, the method widely used on *Doctor Who* in the 1980s was to start by compiling a first edit that basically contained all the footage recorded for an episode, edited into scene order. No real attention was paid to the actual running time of the episode on this edit. Under the BBC internal system, this was known as a 71 edit. In some cases, a 71 edit might end up being the final, transmitted version of a programme. More often, however, there was further editing required, and the next version of the programme was referred to as a 72 edit. In the case of *Doctor Who*, most episodes from the 1980s were transmitted as 72 edits, i.e. had been edited twice before transmission.

Once a programme had been edited to the correct length, and the producer was happy with the content, only then would it be approved for further post-production, such as the addition of music and sound effects, in readiness for transmission.

Occasionally, further edits were required, and so the programme would become a 73 edit, or even in some extreme cases a 74 edit. For example, 'Revelation of the Daleks' Part Two was initially edited together as a 71 edit, then edited to its correct length for transmission as a 72 edit, which was then fully syphered (i.e. had music and sound effects added). Shortly before transmission, the final scene of the story was altered to remove the last word of dialogue (the Doctor saying 'Blackpool'), thus making the transmitted version a 73 edit.

Another example is 'Resurrection of the Daleks', which was initially produced and edited as four episodes of approximately 25 minutes' duration. Initial 71 edits were prepared, which were then cut to length and syphered, ready for transmission as 72 edits. When the late decision was taken to broadcast the story as two approximately 50-minute episodes (to accommodate the BBC's Winter Olympics television coverage), the versions that came out of the editing suite for transmission were then 73 edits.

For Part Fourteen of 'The Trial of a Time Lord', the production team were struggling to bring the episode in at the normally-required duration of 24 minutes

CHAPTER 2

and 30 seconds. A 71 edit (running to 30 minutes and 33 seconds), a 72 edit (running to 30 minutes and 21 seconds) and a 73 edit (running to 29 minutes and 30 seconds) were prepared. The production team were very happy with the latter, but obviously it was still too long for the standard slot. A shorter 74 edit (duration 27 minutes and 6 seconds) was then produced, but the production team felt that it compromised the story too much. Producer John Nathan-Turner appealed to his superiors for a longer timeslot, and was given the go-ahead for a 30-minute one. Consequently the production team elected to return to the 73 edit, which became the transmission master for this episode.

The 71/72/73 edit definition system was introduced to the BBC in the late 1970s, as a way of accurately logging programme versions. Prior to this, the BBC had a system of just putting the letters 'ED'[6] after a recording number, to denote how many electronic edits it had undergone. 'Carnival of Monsters' Episode Two is one of only a few examples from the 1970s where an earlier-than-transmitted edit of a *Doctor Who* episode still survives to this day. This version of Episode Two has a different arrangement of the *Doctor Who* theme on its opening and closing titles (the 'Delaware' theme, created by Delia Derbyshire using a Delaware synthesiser for the programme's tenth anniversary with the intention that it would replace the existing version, arranged by Derbyshire back in 1963 – at the last minute, producer Barry Letts changed his mind, and retained that existing version), had extra scenes not in the transmitted episode, and had scenes arranged in a different order. This version of the episode was given the programme number VTC/6HT/79344/ED, to show that it was the first edited version of the programme. When the 'old' theme was added back to the episode, and the episode's scenes were re-arranged or edited out to make the episode as transmitted, the programme number for this tape was VTC/6HT/79344/ED/ED, which showed that it was a further edit on from the former version.

EPISODES TRANSMITTED FROM FILM

Jon Pertwee's debut four-part story, 'Spearhead from Space', was the only *Doctor Who* story between 1963 and 1989 to be both made and transmitted from film, and this was due to circumstances (a strike by BBC studio technicians) rather than a deliberate alteration in production policy.

However, in the 1960s, a handful of episodes were transmitted from film. But unlike the episodes of 'Spearhead from Space', these weren't shot using film cameras (except for any film insert sequences). Instead, production followed the usual pattern,

---

6 'ED' stood for 'Electronic Dub'. Another suffix used by the BBC was 'D' for 'Dub', which was used to indicate a straight dub of a recording, with no editing involved.

WIPED!

with most of the studio scenes being performed in front of a television studio's electronic cameras. The difference was that the cameras' output was captured not on videotape, but on film. The transmission masters were, to all intents and purposes, telerecordings.

The first episode to be aired in this manner was the fourth episode of 'The Daleks', which was recorded out-of-sequence (unlike most episodes of *Doctor Who* at this time, which – as previously discussed – were made largely in scene order). It was transmitted from a 35mm black and white film recording of the material shot electronically in Lime Grove Studio D. Instead of the output of the vision mixing desk being recorded on a two-inch 405-line videotape, it was sent directly to a telerecording suite, where the footage was captured on 35mm film. This was probably done with the foreknowledge that the episode would require a larger than usual number of edits to be made in order to get it into shape for transmission, editing being much easier to accomplish on film than on video. This was not an uncommon technique for the BBC to employ in its programme making. For instance, the first season of the 1966 series *Adam Adamant Lives!* (which was also produced by Verity Lambert, *Doctor Who*'s first producer) was handled in this way too, with the output of the electronic television cameras being captured on 35mm black and white film. The 35mm film was then edited to create the film transmission masters of the finished episodes.

The next episode of *Doctor Who* to be screened from film was mastered in this way for entirely different reasons. The story 'Planet of Giants' was written and recorded as a four-part adventure towards the end of *Doctor Who*'s first recording block. When it was decided that *Doctor Who* would come back for a second year, it was also decided to hold back the final two stories from the first production block and use them to start the second season on screen. 'Planet of Giants' would therefore become the story to launch the programme's second season. However, Head of Serials Donald Wilson felt that it was not ideal for this purpose, and particularly that the narrative of the third and fourth episodes was too slow-moving. Given that there was some breathing time between seasons, producer Verity Lambert consequently had those two episodes cut down and edited together into a single, pacier final episode. Both episodes had already been recorded and edited on 405-line two-inch videotape, so 35mm black and white telerecordings were made of them in order to facilitate this further editing work.

The BBC internal programme number for each episode of *Doctor Who* records exactly how it was screened. The standard programme number format for the series in 1963 was VT/T/XXXXX, where 'XXXXX' was a unique five digit number given to each episode. The 'VT' prefix indicated that the programme was to be broadcast from videotape, and the 'T' showed that it was originally made on (video) tape as well.

In 1964, with the advent of BBC2 (which was a 625-line channel, as opposed to

CHAPTER 2

BBC1's 405-line service), the mid-section of the programme number was altered from just 'T' to either '4T' or '6T'. '4T' indicated that the programme was made on 405-line videotape, '6T' showed that 625-line videotape was used. This was then refined still further when colour television was introduced, with the codes '6LT' used for low band (i.e. black and white) recordings and '6HT' used for 625-line high-band (i.e. colour) recordings . Videotaped episodes of *Doctor Who* would be coded '4T' up until 'The Enemy of the World' Episode Three, when the code would change to '6LT', indicating a switch to 625-line videotape. At about the same time, the 'VT' prefix would change to 'VTM' (for Video Tape – Monochrome). From 'Doctor Who and the Silurians' in 1970, this would alter to 'VTC' (Video Tape – Colour) followed by '6HT'.

The programme numbers of episodes shown from film would have a different prefix. Instead of 'VT', this could be either '16' or '35', indicating that the master consisted of either 16mm or 35mm film – although in *Doctor Who*'s case, all episodes transmitted from film in the 1960s used 35mm stock.

The programme number for the fourth episode of 'The Daleks' is 35/T/20398, which tells us that it was a 35mm film print taken from a video source. However, the programme number for the transmitted version of the third episode of 'Planet of Giants' is 35/6T/23675. Taken at face value, this seemingly tells us that it was a 35mm film print taken from a 625-line video source. This must be an error, however, because the videotape-recorded third and fourth episodes of the original version of 'Planet of Giants' both had programme numbers VT/4T/XXXXX, showing that they were recorded on 405-line videotape – as usual for *Doctor Who* at that time. This meant it was impossible for the 35mm film to have come from a 625-line source.

That this error occurred casts a question mark over the origins of the next episode to be transmitted from film – Episode Five of 'The Dalek Invasion of Earth'. This would appear to have been a film recording made directly from the studio feed (like the fourth episode of 'The Daleks'), and yet its programme number is 35/6T/24329, indicating that it was shot using 625-line cameras in the studio. Although this is not impossible, the fact that the 'Planet of Giants' code is patently wrong suggests that this one could be too. If it were correct, then technically 'The Dalek Invasion of Earth' Episode Five would be the first episode of *Doctor Who* to have been made in 625-lines. Examination of the surviving 35mm film print does not disprove this, as the picture quality is exceptionally good.

The remaining episodes of William Hartnell's era of *Doctor Who* were all transmitted from 405-line videotape. Well, probably ... There is a very small amount of contradictory evidence to suggest that episodes of 'The Celestial Toymaker' and 'The Gunfighters' just might have been screened from 35mm film, although the programme numbers for these episodes are all in the VT/4T/XXXXX format. (This is discussed further in later chapters.)

The final episode of Patrick Troughton's debut adventure, 'The Power of the Daleks' was screened from 35mm film, as were the final two episodes of 'The Wheel in Space', the third episode of 'The Dominators', the final episode of 'The Mind Robber', the first episode of 'The Krotons', the fifth episode of 'The Seeds of Death' and the second episode of 'The Space Pirates'. All of these episodes have programme numbers that begin '35/6T', showing that 625-line cameras were used in the studio. This was almost certainly the case for all of the episodes from 'The Wheel in Space' onwards. It's plausible that it is correct for the final episode of 'The Power of the Daleks' as well. Certainly, the BBC's Film Recording Viewing Report for that episode indicates it came from a 625-line source. (It also notes that there was some visible microphony – i.e. sound disturbance on the picture – during some of the gunshots in the action sequences, and grades the film recording as 'S-', which stands for 'Generally substandard or with objectionable but brief faults'.)

In some of these cases, the episodes could have been recorded and screened in this manner due to the complexity of editing they required, coupled with the comparative ease of editing film compared with videotape. Having said that, however, there's no evidence of particularly numerous editing splices in the surviving 35mm film prints of these episodes. In other cases, the reason might have been as mundane as the BBC not having a free two-inch videotape suite available to record a given episode's studio session, hence 35mm film was used instead.

Unlike the majority of 1960s episodes of *Doctor Who* screened on videotape, the small number of episodes that were transmitted from 35mm film had their transmission master film prints sent to the BBC Film Library afterwards.

Although the information in this chapter may seem very detailed, it helps to explain the wide variety of different physical forms that *Doctor Who* material took over the years. From VT spools to telerecordings, from filmed inserts to different edits, different takes of the same scenes, and a variety of black and white filmed versions of sequences, episodes and whole stories ... any and all of which are fair game in the hunt for elements of the show that are now considered missing.

All two-inch videotape at the BBC in the 1960s and early 1970s was totally under the jurisdiction of the BBC's Engineering Department. They were responsible for the physical tape spools. But they weren't responsible for what might actually be recorded on them ...

CHAPTER 3
WIPING THE TRANSMISSION VIDEOTAPES

Once an episode of *Doctor Who* was made and screened by the BBC, what then physically happened to it?

As we have seen, the vast majority of '60s *Doctor Who* episodes were transmitted on BBC1 from two-inch black and white videotapes. Throughout the 1960s and the early part of the 1970s, the storage and management of all of the BBC's videotapes was controlled by the Engineering Department. However, the Engineering Department had no mandate to keep or preserve the actual programmes recorded on the videotapes. Their primary function was to ensure that the studio sessions for each programme were recorded, that the master transmission tape was ready for broadcast, and that the broadcast went ahead successfully. After any given programme had been screened, there was usually no perceived need for it to be retained on tape – unless BBC Enterprises wanted it for overseas sale. Thus the tape became a resource that could be re-used. It's important to realise here that the BBC as a whole had no mandate to retain any of its output. There was no BBC Film and Videotape Library as exists today. There was just the BBC Film Library, which catered exclusively for material originated or stored on film.

When *Doctor Who* began in 1963, the BBC had just a single channel of programmes. But with the launch of BBC2 in April 1964, there were now two channels to manage. And, therefore, double the amount of videotape to keep track of. Storage of this ever-increasing stock of videotape became a growing problem. Early in 1962, part of the basement of the BBC's Television Centre, next to the main transmission area, had been given over to become a tape storage facility. An even bigger tape storage area was then built under Studio TC1. Later, this was adapted to incorporate a moveable racking system to hold even more tapes. When these areas became full, then further temporary storage facilities in Television Centre were sought. Basement dressing rooms located around the VT area were requisitioned to store the ever-growing mountain of videotapes. This situation only increased the pressure on the Engineering Department to re-use as many of the tapes as it could. By 1968, the BBC had over 12,000 two-inch videotapes tucked away in its various storage areas. Around 120 of these tapes were *Doctor Who* episodes, but even at this point in time, 80 episodes had already been junked.[7]

As outlined in Chapter 1, two separate types of internal BBC paperwork were

---

[7] Trying to establish a full and clear picture of when and how the BBC's *Doctor Who* master videotapes were wiped is nigh-on impossible, as the surviving paperwork is incomplete, comes from a variety of disparate BBC departments, and is sometimes contradictory. But nevertheless, I will try!

issued in relation to the master two-inch videotapes of *Doctor Who* episodes held by the BBC Engineering Department. Retention Authorisation forms were issued for tapes that needed to be kept for any reason, but these could be overruled at any time by the issuing of Wipe/Junk Authorisation forms against the same tapes. The general rule of thumb, at least in regard to the black and white *Doctor Who* videotapes, seems to have been that once a Retention Authorisation form was submitted for a particular videotape by a particular department, then this could be overruled only by a Wipe/Junk Authorisation form raised by the same department.

The two BBC departments that would issue these forms were the Drama Department and BBC Enterprises. The Drama Department was the parent department for the *Doctor Who* production office, and was ultimately responsible for all the tapes that the *Doctor Who* team used. The *Doctor Who* production office was most likely consulted on which tapes of old programmes were to be singled out for either retention or destruction, but the details of how this took place in practice are sketchy. Enterprises' sole interest in relation to these tapes was in ensuring that *Doctor Who* episodes didn't get junked until they had managed to make 16mm film copies for overseas sales. Once Enterprises had their 16mm film prints, then their interest in retaining the parent videotape material would quickly dissipate.

1963-1966

The earliest surviving examples of paperwork relating to the two-inch master videotapes of the *Doctor Who* episodes are a batch of Retention Authorisation sheets issued to the Engineering Department as a formal instruction by either the *Doctor Who* production office, or possibly by the Drama Department centrally, dating from sometime in early 1964. These early forms theoretically required that the person who was requesting the retention be identified, and that a reason be given, but in many cases these details were left blank on the paperwork.

The paperwork covers all the episodes of *Doctor Who* from the first episode of 'An Unearthly Child' through to the third episode of 'The Sensorites'. From it, we learn that all four episodes of 'An Unearthly Child' were requested to be kept, with director Waris Hussein named as the originator of the request for the first three episodes. (He is identified with just the word 'Hussein' entered onto the paperwork.) This section is left blank on the paperwork for the fourth episode. 'Possible Repeat' is the stated reason for the retention of the opening episode – no reason is given for the other three.[8]

---

8 The opening episode was repeated on 30 November 1963, but this document apparently post-dates that event. Not that this suggests that more repeats of this episode were planned – it's more likely that a bogus reason was given on the Retention Authorisation paperwork, perhaps by a director who really didn't want his work to be destroyed if he could help it. 'Possible Repeat' was the reason stated on the forms for virtually every episode where one was given.

CHAPTER 3

Director Christopher Barry (or just 'Barry' as the paperwork states) was the person responsible for the request to keep five of the seven episodes of 'The Daleks'. This section of the paperwork is left blank on the request to keep the first episode, while the name 'Russell' is cited as the person asking for the final episode to be kept. What is slightly puzzling with this paperwork is that the tape number and recording date given on the form for the first episode of this story, entitled 'The Dead Planet', is for the initial untransmitted recording of the episode, and not for the completely remounted version that was eventually shown. This could just be down to the wrong information being inadvertently transcribed onto the form. The fourth episode of 'The Daleks' was transmitted from 35mm film, and on the retention paperwork, the film print is likewise cited for retention. Again, 'Possible Repeat' is given as the reason on the paperwork for one of the episodes, this time the fourth.

'Russell' was again the named saviour of both episodes of 'The Edge of Destruction'. And again 'Possible Repeat' was the reason cited on the form for keeping the first episode. The next story, 'Marco Polo', was also requested to be kept, with director Waris Hussein again named as the person behind the paperwork being issued.[9]

All six episodes of 'The Keys of Marinus' were listed for retention, with director John Gorrie cited as the person behind the request for Episodes Two to Six – this section of the form for the first episode was left blank. The cited reason for four of the episodes (Episodes Two, Three, Four and Six) was 'Possible Repeat', while that for the other two (Episodes One and Five) was 'Transfer'.[10]

All four episodes of 'The Aztecs' were listed for retention, with director John Crockett named as the person behind the request. 'Possible Repeat' was again the reason given in each case.

The surviving paperwork only goes up to the third episode of 'The Sensorites', but these three episodes were again retained for 'Possible Repeat', and two more mystery names were attributed to the request – a 'Scott' for the second episode, and a 'T Cook' (almost certainly Terence Cook, Acting Drama Organiser for Television at the time)

---

9 What is slightly unusual about this 'Marco Polo' request is that the reason given for the retention of the first episode (only) – is 'Possible Transfer'. Transfer to what? It could mean transfer to 16mm film, for purposes of overseas sales, although as this was standard practice for all episodes of *Doctor Who* (as we'll see later), why mention it just for this episode? Or it could mean that the programme on the master 405-line videotape needed transferring to another 405-line tape for retention, possibly due to a problem with the tape itself (such as too many physical edits in the tape causing playback problems).

10 Again, transfer to what?

WIPED!

for the third.

For the remainder of 1964, all of 1965 and most of 1966, records are sketchy or completely missing, but it seems likely that all episodes of *Doctor Who* transmitted from 1963 through to 1966 were kept on their original 405-line two-inch videotapes throughout this period, at least until the end of 1966.

NOVEMBER-DECEMBER 1966

By the time William Hartnell's Doctor transformed into Patrick Troughton's at the end of 'The Tenth Planet' in October 1966, the BBC had screened 134 episodes of *Doctor Who*. And at this point in time, it would appear that the Engineering Department still held a full set of all of these episodes on their original transmission tapes.

The next piece of available paperwork dates from Wednesday 9 November 1966, the week after Patrick Troughton's full debut in the first episode of 'The Power of the Daleks'. Again, this is in the form of a Retention Authorisation sheet. But by 1966, the format of these sheets had altered slightly, and they now recorded which BBC department was asking for the programme(s) to be retained. In most cases, 'Television Enterprises' (or BBC Enterprises as it is better known) was the department cited. But occasionally, the Drama Department would also issue its own forms.

It seems that sheets were now being compiled and submitted on a weekly basis (possibly with reference to a copy of that week's *Radio Times*) by Enterprises, and covered the programmes due to be shown by the BBC over the coming week (e.g. w/c 12 November 1966 in this first instance). Each sheet detailed all the week's programmes that Enterprises wanted to have transferred onto 16mm film, in order that they could then try to sell them to overseas television stations. So the Retention Authorisation form dated Wednesday 9 November 1966 covered seven days' worth of programmes on the BBC commencing Saturday 12 November 1966, and included 'The Power of the Daleks' Episode Two. As noted before, this system was designed to ensure that the tapes were not wiped or junked *before* Enterprises could get around to accessing them for telerecording.

Further Retention Authorisation forms were then raised on an ongoing weekly basis by Enterprises for the rest of 'The Power of the Daleks', with the final episode being detailed on the one dated Monday 5 December 1966.

Then, on Friday 16 December 1966, Enterprises decided that they needed to issue Retention Authorisation forms for a whole batch of William Hartnell episodes – basically the complete run of stories from 'An Unearthly Child' through to 'The Gunfighters'. The videotapes of these episodes had already been copied to black and white 16mm film for overseas sales purposes by this point (as the series was first sold overseas in 1964), so the reason why Enterprises needed to ask for this huge batch of

CHAPTER 3

material to be kept at this point in time is unclear. Certainly, no reason is put forward on the paperwork.[11] Whatever the reason, though, this does seem to confirm that, at the end of 1966, all the William Hartnell episodes of *Doctor Who* still survived on their original transmission videotapes. And now, thanks to Enterprises, these videotapes would remain at the BBC for some time further.

---

11 One explanation may be that all of the *Doctor Who* film prints made by BBC Enterprises up to this point in time used the Suppressed Field method of telerecording, which essentially captured images made up of 188 scan lines. With the introduction of the more advanced Stored Field telerecording system, which was brought in at about the time that BBC2 launched in 1964, it was now possible to make film copies of old programmes at the full 377-line resolution. (See Chapter Five for more details of the different telerecording processes.) Perhaps BBC Enterprises decided that they wanted better resolution copies of early *Doctor Who* stories to sell? The important New Zealand market was showing interest in purchasing more stories from the first two seasons in late 1966/early 1967, so this could have been the catalyst for such a move. Certainly, we know from the film prints that survived that Suppressed Field recordings of most William Hartnell stories were made close to their original transmission dates, and that Stored Field prints were also made a few years later. A date of around late 1966/early 1967 would nicely fit the production of the later Stored Field prints, tying in with this paperwork. Most of the Patrick Troughton-era Stored Field prints were made on the day and time of the episode's BBC1 transmission.

In the first edition of this book, I put forward the theory that the change between Stored Field and Supressed Field prints might have taken place around the time that 'The Gunfighters' was initially telerecorded for overseas sales, which would have neatly accounted for the stories that were selected for retention in late 1966. Since then, the ABC print of 'Galaxy 4' Episode Three has turned up, and this is a Stored Field print. No Suppressed Field print of any Season Three episode has ever been located, and so it would appear that only Seasons One and Two stories had Suppressed Field prints distributed by BBC Enterprises.

It could be that Season Three episodes telerecorded on different days in different telerecording suites *might* have been a random mix of Stored and Suppressed field prints, depending on which suites had been converted to the new process. Could BBC Enterprises have been in a position where they knew that they needed to replace their sales prints of all of the first two seasons, and were also unsure what they had (in term of Stored / Suppressed Field prints) of the Season Three stories prior to 'The Savages'?

Another possible answer may be that Enterprises at this point weren't actually keeping a master negative of each William Hartnell episode. They may have initially had a certain set number of film prints made of each story, which by 1966 were all in circulation in various countries and overseas markets. Occasionally, Enterprises may have needed quick access to copies of certain stories, only to find they had no film copies available themselves. 'The War Machines', for example, was certainly film recorded twice, initially just after its original BBC1 transmission, and then again in 1967 to furnish the Australian Broadcasting Corporation (ABC) with a new set of film prints for the story. (Did ABC somehow lose one or all of their film prints of this story's episodes? Later events would suggest so …)

Alternatively, perhaps the mass retention request was triggered by a desire by BBC Engineering to re-use a number of these early *Doctor Who* videotapes, which to their way of thinking, had been hanging around, unused, for the best part of three years now?

WIPED!

Also lodged on the same date, for reasons unknown, was retention paperwork for the two-inch videotape of the unbroadcast pilot version of the first episode of 'An Unearthly Child'. Perhaps it was at this point that the 16mm film recording of that tape (which still survives to this day) was actually made?

Some inconsistencies begin to crop up in the paperwork at this point. A few episodes from this huge Hartnell run were specifically mentioned on the Retention Authorisation forms as having 35mm films as their transmission masters. These were 'The Daleks' Episode Four, 'The Dalek Invasion of Earth' Episode Five, 'The Celestial Toymaker' Episodes One, Two and Three, and 'The Gunfighters' Episodes Two, Three and Four. Now, as far as can be ascertained, only the first two of these episodes were actually transmitted from 35mm film. The programme numbers for all four episodes of 'The Celestial Toymaker' and 'The Gunfighters' show they were originally transmitted from 405-line videotape. As noted in Chapter Two, this discrepancy remains a mystery.

For some reason, the two-inch videotape of Episode Six of 'The Dalek Invasion of Earth' was not included in this mass retention order. Neither was the final episode of 'The Celestial Toymaker'. The third episode of 'Planet of Giants' was listed as being on two-inch videotape, when – as we know – it was actually transmitted from 35mm film.[12]

Friday 16 December 1966 was also the date on which Enterprises lodged its regular weekly retention order for the following week's BBC programmes, which included Episode One of 'The Highlanders', due to be screened on Saturday 17 December 1966. Further retention orders were then submitted by Enterprises on a weekly basis for the rest of this four-part story.

1967

The surviving paperwork indicates that 1967 began as the previous year ended, with Enterprises issuing their weekly Retention Authorisation forms for the next week's BBC television output. Thus forms were lodged on a weekly basis for all episodes of 'The Underwater Menace' and 'The Moonbase', which takes us up to March 1967.

However, the other type of previously-mentioned BBC paperwork now surfaces for the first time. These are the Wipe/Junk Authorisation forms; and in this instance

---

12 Theorising again, could this possibly suggest that the episode was originally edited on videotape and then transferred to film for transmission? Probably not ... The BBC's production file for 'Planet of Giants' indicates that the original Episodes Three and Four were both telerecorded twice; once onto 16mm film, and then again onto 35mm film. The 16mm prints were probably used to view the episodes, to allow the director to make editing notes, and perhaps prepare a rough cut of the new Episode Three. The 35mm prints were then used to make the transmission copy.

CHAPTER 3

they were also instigated by Enterprises. These forms effectively told the Engineering Department that Enterprises no longer had any interest in retaining the transmission videotapes of the specific episodes of *Doctor Who* detailed on the forms. Unless there were any other outstanding reasons to keep the tapes, then the Engineering Department would now be free to re-use or dispose of them. Indeed, the reason for the forms being issued by Enterprises is simply given in the three-word statement written upon them: 'No Further Interest.'

On Thursday 9 March 1967, Enterprises issued Wipe/Junk Authorisation forms stating they had 'No Further Interest' in all four episodes of 'The Highlanders' and the first two episodes of 'The Underwater Menace'. As both these stories were subsequently sold overseas, it is safe to assume that the six episodes concerned had already had 16mm black and white film copies made from the two-inch tapes prior to the forms being issued. These 16mm copies would almost certainly have been made at the time of transmission on BBC1 – a practice that would, more often than not, continue well into the 1970s.

Although the two-inch videotapes of the first two episodes of 'The Underwater Menace' survived for quite some time after this point, it seems that those of all four episodes of 'The Highlanders' were either junked or erased for re-use very soon after, possibly within days of the forms being issued. Given that retention orders had been issued by Enterprises for the great majority of the William Hartnell episodes only a few months previously, it seems highly likely that 'The Highlanders' was the first *Doctor Who* story to have its transmission master videotapes junked by the BBC.[13]

On 29 March 1967, Enterprises issued Wipe/Junk Authorisation forms for Episodes One, Two and Three of 'The Moonbase'. Again, this was probably due to them having by now made their 16mm black and white film sales prints of these

---

13 Why did the first two episodes of 'The Underwater Menace' survive (as evidenced by the fact that, as we shall see, they crop up again on later junking forms) when all those of 'The Highlanders' apparently didn't? There is no corroborating paperwork to suggest what actually occurred, but one workable theory is that the Drama Department had issued its own Retention Authorisation forms for these two episodes, which would then have taken priority over the junking forms raised by BBC Enterprises. But this would also suggest that the Drama Department had by this point either issued its own junking forms for 'The Highlanders' or somehow hadn't issued any retention forms at all for the story. BBC Enterprises' junking request was therefore the last bureaucratic hurdle needed to be overcome by the Engineering Department in order to be able to junk the two-inch transmission tapes of 'The Highlanders'. Was this at all tied to the fact that 'The Highlanders' was the last historical story to be made, as this type of story had been deemed unpopular with viewers at the time? Or was the reason more mundane than that – such as the recent change in *Doctor Who*'s production team, with Innes Lloyd and Gerry Davis replacing John Wiles and Donald Tosh as producer and script editor the previous year, causing some sort of hiccup in standard procedures?

particular episodes. However, these three episodes weren't junked at this point in time, presumably because Drama Department retention orders were still in place for all three of them.

Weekly retention orders were issued by Enterprises for all four episodes of 'The Macra Terror' throughout late March and early April 1967. For 'The Faceless Ones', Enterprises for some reason decided to change its method of informing the Engineering Department of its desire for material to be kept. For this story, all six episodes had a single 'block' retention order raised, dating from early May 1967. But no retention form was apparently filed at all by Enterprises for the seven episodes of 'The Evil of the Daleks', the next and final story shown as part of the programme's fourth season.[14]

Just a few short months after the transmission tapes of 'The Faceless Ones' were marked for retention, the first large batch of *Doctor Who* episode wipings was to take place at the BBC. Prior to this, only the four episodes of 'The Highlanders' had been junked.

On 17 August 1967, Enterprises elected to issue Wipe/Junk Authorisation forms for the majority of the William Hartnell episodes of *Doctor Who*. Whatever reason had motivated them to ask for most of these episodes to be retained in the November of the previous year must have by now been superseded.[15] These junking forms effectively cancelled the retention forms raised late in 1966. At least some of the early episodes listed on them had also been subject to the retention orders issued by the Drama Department in early 1964. What isn't known is whether, by August 1967, the Drama Department had issued its own Wipe/Junk forms for those episodes, or if the Wipe/Junk forms that Enterprises now raised were enough to overrule those earlier

---

14 It's tempting to surmise that this omission of retention paperwork may have led to 'The Evil of the Daleks' not being telerecorded for overseas sale by BBC Enterprises at this time. Every single one of the countries that eventually purchased this story did so some considerable time after they purchased the rest of the fourth series, almost as if it was not part of the package originally on offer. The first overseas sale of the story was to Australia in late 1968, which fits the theory nicely. Additionally, there is later evidence – as we shall see – that BBC Enterprises issued retention paperwork for this story only after it was repeated on BBC1 in the summer of 1968. If this was indeed the first time they asked for the story to be kept, perhaps it was also the first time that 16mm film telerecordings were made of it?

15 As mentioned above, this reason was almost certainly the desire to create new Stored Field film recordings. Looking at the BBC's surviving 16mm telerecordings of 'The Daleks', only Suppressed Field recordings of Episodes Five and Seven now survive. Theorising again, perhaps the two-inch tapes of these episodes had been damaged in some way, or were just unplayable, when they came to be used for making new Stored Field prints? If so, Suppressed Field prints would be all the BBC ever had for those episodes. Looking at the surviving 16mm print of Episode Two of 'The Edge of Destruction', the last five minutes has been patched in from a Suppressed Field print, while the rest of the episode is a Stored Field recording. Could this have been done as a way of working around more two-inch tape damage, which was found only in 1967?

CHAPTER 3

Drama Department retentions.

Regardless, Wipe/Junk Authorisation forms were raised by Enterprises for the two-inch transmission tapes of the following episodes:

Story	Episodes
The Pilot Episode	
An Unearthly Child	1-4
The Daleks	1, 2, 3, 6, 7
The Edge of Destruction	1
Marco Polo	1-7
The Keys of Marinus	1-6
The Aztecs	1-4
The Sensorites	3, 4, 5
The Reign of Terror	1, 2, 3, 4, 6
The Dalek Invasion of Earth	1, 2, 4, 6
The Rescue	1
The Romans	1-4
The Web Planet	2, 3, 5
The Space Museum	1, 3, 4
The Chase	2, 4, 6
The Time Meddler	1, 3, 4
Galaxy 4	1, 2, 4
The Myth Makers	2, 3, 4
The Daleks Masterplan	1, 2, 4, 5, 7, 8, 9
The Massacre	1-4
The Ark	1-4
The Gunfighters	1

As a result of this junking order, the BBC destroyed the transmission tapes of practically all of the listed episodes. Due either to oversight or to a stroke of good fortune, the tapes of the unscreened pilot episode, the first episode of 'An Unearthly Child' and Episode Four of 'The Keys of Marinus' managed to survive this purge. But each and every one of the other episodes listed had its two-inch transmission tape either wiped or junked very soon after these forms were issued, possibly within a few days.

There was and is no ready explanation for the seemingly arbitrary selection of episodes singled out for destruction. Some of the stories had every episode marked down for junking, but others – like 'The Sensorites' and 'The Web Planet' – had only selected episodes put forward. If there was any sort of selection for preservation methodology being applied to the BBC's archive of *Doctor Who*'s two-inch tapes, then

WIPED!

it's unlikely that Enterprises would have been dictating it. A more likely reason is that the tapes were stored in specific sections of the Engineering Department's facilities, and wipe forms were issued for just certain sections of tapes.

By the time the fifth season of *Doctor Who* began screening, with 'The Tomb of the Cybermen', in September 1967, the transmission videotapes of 79 episodes of William Hartnell's *Doctor Who* had been disposed of by the BBC. This was in addition to the four episodes of 'The Highlanders' junked earlier in 1967.

This August 1967 junking of most of the Hartnell episodes was almost certainly responsible for the complete and irretrievable loss of one *Doctor Who* episode. While Enterprises held 16mm film prints of every other episode that was junked at this point, Episode Seven of 'The Daleks Masterplan' was never telerecorded for overseas sale, as far as can be established. The erasure of the two-inch transmission master tape of this episode meant that, from this point on, the BBC no longer held a full set of episodes of *Doctor Who*.

Enterprises continued issuing Retention Authorisation paperwork for the fifth season episodes of *Doctor Who* on a weekly basis again, although this time the forms were raised during the actual week of an episode's broadcast on BBC1, and not a week in advance as before. The last retention form issued by Enterprises in this year was for the first episode of 'The Enemy of the World', which was shown on Saturday 23 December 1967. This retention form was raised during week 52 in the BBC's calendar, which was w/c 24 December 1967.

1968

This year began with a change in production for *Doctor Who*, away from the old video format of 405-lines, to the new 625-line standard (albeit still all on two-inch videotape). This change occurred between the studio recordings of Episode Six of 'The Web of Fear' and Episode One of 'The Enemy of the World'.

There is a gap in the surviving BBC paperwork at this point, which means that there are no details of any further retention orders being lodged by Enterprises for the last five episodes of 'The Enemy of the World', or for the first episode of the subsequent story, 'The Web of Fear'. However, the retention paperwork does survive for the other five episodes of 'The Web of Fear', and for the opening episode of 'Fury from the Deep', although none of these is dated at all. But no other retention orders survive for the remainder of the fifth season of *Doctor Who*.

On Monday 4 March 1968, a Wipe/Junk Authorisation form was raised by Enterprises for a single episode – Episode Four of 'The Abominable Snowmen'. However, this didn't lead to the episode being junked at this point. The form was annotated to the effect that the BBC Drama Department/*Doctor Who* production office had asked for this tape – and others not specified – to be retained for possible repeats.[16]

Then, on Monday 17 June 1968, Enterprises issued a Retention Authorisation form for another single episode of *Doctor Who* – Episode Four of 'The Tenth Planet'. The reason given on the paperwork was 'Held for Enterprises Possible Future Sales', although 16mm film copies of this episode had already been made by Enterprises and the story sold to a number of countries prior to this date.

On Tuesday 1 August 1968, Enterprises finally issued forms for the retention of all seven episodes of 'The Evil of the Daleks', which at the time was being repeated on BBC1 on Saturday evenings (the first repeats of *Doctor Who* since the opening episode of 'An Unearthly Child' was reshown on 30 November 1963). It's difficult to know for sure, because of the gaps in the existing BBC paperwork, but it could be that this was the first time that Enterprises had expressed an interest in this particular story.[17]

It seems that Enterprises' retention instructions on 'The Evil of the Daleks' were either overlooked or completely ignored, as the videotapes of the first six episodes of the story were apparently erased (as we shall later discover) in August 1968, barely a month after the repeat run on BBC1 had finished (but not before 16mm film copies had finally been made for Enterprises). For some reason, the final episode of the story was spared the fate of the other six, and the transmission master videotape survived in BBC Engineering Department storage – for the time being, at least.

The 1968 repeat of 'The Evil of the Daleks' on BBC1 was transmitted from the original 405-line two-inch videotapes, at least in the case of Episodes Two to Seven. A few lines of new voiceover dialogue, spoken by Patrick Troughton's Doctor, were added to the start of the first episode, to emphasise that he was showing an old story to new companion Zoe, as explained at the end of 'The Wheel in Space'. The Programme-as-Broadcast (PasB) information for the repeat of Episode One quotes the recording number as VT/4T/39237, which is exactly the same as for the original transmission. While this doesn't prove that the new overdubbed dialogue by Patrick Troughton was edited onto the original transmission videotape of this episode, the BBC Film and

---

16 Again, this probably isn't an indication that large-scale repeats of *Doctor Who* stories were actively considered at this time. It's more likely that someone, somewhere, was reluctant to let material be destroyed if they could possibly help it.

17 Interestingly, the retention forms for the repeat of 'The Evil of the Daleks' bear the instruction 'Hold all Programmes in this series for possible future sales'. This could be interpreted as BBC Enterprises deciding to sell this story for the first time, if 'this series' refers simply to the seven episodes of 'The Evil of the Daleks', hence the comments and the retention order. However, if 'this series' means *Doctor Who* as a whole, then it could be seen as an indication of a reversal of BBC Enterprises policy of issuing junking forms.

WIPED!

Videotape Library has only one tape number logged on the wiping record[18] they have for this story, which would seem to support that conclusion.

1969

On Friday 31 January 1969, the day before BBC1 screened the second episode of 'The Seeds of Death', Enterprises issued a batch of Wipe/Junk Authorisation forms for another large selection of Hartnell-era *Doctor Who* transmission tapes. As a result of this, the two-inch videotapes containing all of the following episodes were disposed of by the BBC:

The Edge of Destruction	2
The Keys of Marinus	4
The Sensorites	1, 2, 6
The Reign of Terror	4
Planet of Giants	1-3 [19]
The Dalek Invasion of Earth	3
The Rescue	2
The Web Planet	1, 4, 6
The Crusade	1, 4
The Space Museum	2
The Chase	3, 5
The Time Meddler	2
Galaxy 4	3
The Myth Makers	1
The Daleks Masterplan	3, 6

This tidying-up exercise meant that most of the Hartnell-era *Doctor Who* stories had now had their master tapes wiped.

On the same day, Enterprises also issued Wipe/Junk Authorisation forms for:

---

18 In the words of Andrew Martin of the BBC Film and Videotape Library, these current records are ' ...fairly useless generally as they just list spool numbers, recording numbers, and have a rubber-stamped "Wiped" on them, without any details of when this happened'.

19 The paperwork again details the third episode of 'Planet of Giants' as a videotape holding, rather than as a 35mm film print, which is at least consistent with the earlier retention paperwork. Is this just a clerical error? Whatever the reason, the issuing of this junking authorisation seems to have been responsible for the destruction of the 35mm transmission film print of the episode at this time.

CHAPTER 3

The Tenth Planet	4
The Moonbase	2-4
The Macra Terror	4
The Faceless Ones	1-4
The Ice Warriors	4

However, none of these ten episodes actually appears to have been junked at this time. The paperwork for most of the Patrick Troughton episodes in this batch had 'No longer required by Enterprises but held by Drama Serials' noted on it. So even though Enterprises no longer needed these episodes, the Drama Department was – for now – blocking the Engineering Department from disposing of the videotapes. If the William Hartnell serials were now considered fair game for junking, it seems that at least the Patrick Troughton episodes were still being intentionally kept.

Six months later, on Thursday 17 July 1969, roughly a month after BBC1 viewers saw Troughton bow out of *Doctor Who* in the final episode of 'The War Games', a further batch of Wipe/Junk Authorisation forms were issued by Enterprises. These were for the following episodes:

The Daleks	5
The Chase	1
Mission to the Unknown	1
The Daleks Masterplan	10, 11, 12
The Evil of the Daleks[20]	1, 2, 3, 4, 5, 6

Despite the existence of this order, it is highly likely that the first six episodes of 'The Evil of the Daleks' had already been wiped by this point (as later paperwork would indicate). But if these episodes had somehow escaped junking in August 1968, they certainly didn't now. The transmission tapes of all of the other episodes listed above were also wiped at this point, apart from that of 'Mission to the Unknown', which seemingly managed to survive this purge either by luck or by design.

With the wiping of these episodes in July 1969, we have come to the point where the vast majority of the Hartnell episodes of *Doctor Who* transmitted from videotape had seen their original two-inch tapes wiped or junked by the BBC. The tapes of the pilot episode and 'An Unearthly Child' Episode One were still held, as were those

---

20 It does seem that someone had it in for the Dalek episodes at this point, doesn't it? Perhaps this was some hang-over from the legal to-ing and fro-ing that had dogged Terry Nation's proposed Dalek television series, as is discussed more fully in Chapter 5.

WIPED!

of 'Mission to the Unknown', all four episodes of 'The War Machines' and the final episode of 'The Tenth Planet'. But by August 1969, this was probably all that remained on videotape at the BBC of Hartnell's era as the Doctor.

The two-inch tape of the third episode of 'The Crusade' might possibly still have been in existence too, as no documentation survives at all regarding when this episode was wiped, although in all probability it went in one of the earlier purges with the other episodes of the story. Similarly, the fates of the two-inch transmission tapes of 'The Celestial Toymaker', 'The Gunfighters' Episodes Two, Three and Four, 'The Savages', 'The Smugglers' and 'The Tenth Planet' Episodes One, Two and Three are not documented at all. But they were almost certainly all junked prior to August 1969.

A few days after the purge of this batch of Hartnell episodes, more Wipe/Junk Authorisation forms were issued on Monday 21 July 1969, this time for episodes featuring Patrick Troughton's Doctor. But rather than originating from Enterprises, these forms were generated by the BBC Drama Department, who had, up until now, requested the retention of a number of Troughton episodes that had been authorised for junking by Enterprises.

The timing of these forms is curious. Troughton had just left the series, and Jon Pertwee had recently been announced as his successor. When *Doctor Who* returned to BBC1 the following year, his adventures would be made and screened in colour. Behind the scenes, Peter Bryant had recently vacated the producer's role, leaving Derrick Sherwin in charge. Sherwin's stay as producer would last only a few months, before he too left to be replaced by Barry Letts. While Troughton was still the current Doctor, perhaps it was felt that his old stories were an asset worth keeping. But now it would seem that someone within the Drama Department had decided that the BBC had no great desire to screen his old black-and-white adventures again, when stories with a new Doctor, in full colour, were just around the corner.

The full list of *Doctor Who* episodes earmarked for destruction at this point in time by the Drama Department were:

The Underwater Menace	1-4
The Moonbase	1-4
The Macra Terror	1-4
The Faceless Ones	1-6
The Evil of the Daleks	1-7
The Tomb of the Cybermen	1-4
The Abominable Snowmen	1-6
The Ice Warriors	1-6
The Enemy of the World	1-6

CHAPTER 3

The Web of Fear	1-6
The Wheel in Space	1-6
The Dominators	1-5
The Mind Robber	1-5
The Krotons	1-4
The Seeds of Death	1-6
The Space Pirates	1-6

Although all of this material was now cleared by the BBC Drama Department for junking, some of the episodes were still covered by old retention orders made by Enterprises – a reversal of the usual scheme of things – which resulted in a number of them being spared from destruction at this time.

Episodes Three and Four of 'The Underwater Menace' were amongst these episodes that survived, due to the Enterprises retention orders issued in early 1967 (see above), although the first two episodes had already been wiped in March 1967.

All four episodes of 'The Moonbase' were junked at this time, as Enterprises had released Episodes One, Two and Three for junking in March 1967, and had cleared Episodes Two, Three (both for a second time) and Four for junking in January 1969.

All four episodes of 'The Macra Terror' managed to escape destruction at this time, despite this junking order; the first three episodes escaped apparently because it wasn't possible to cross-reference the spool numbers of the transmission videotapes with those quoted on the Wipe/Junk paperwork, while the fourth episode was still the subject of an Enterprises retention order dating from April 1967.

The first four episodes of 'The Faceless Ones' had already been cleared for junking by Enterprises in January 1969, so they were now wiped as a result of these new Drama Department authorisations. However the two-inch tape of Episode Five survived this purge, as Enterprises still had a retention order on it. According to the existing BBC paperwork, Enterprises should have had an outstanding retention order on Episode Six as well, but this had either been revoked, or was ignored, as this episode was wiped along with the first four.

For 'The Evil of the Daleks', the paperwork notes that the two-inch tapes for Episodes One through to Six had already been wiped in August 1968 (as has been referred to previously). However, Episode Seven managed to survive this new purge, as it was noted on the paperwork that Enterprises still had a retention order for it – presumably the one raised in August 1968. All four episodes of 'The Tomb of the Cybermen' were saved for the same reason; the relevant retention orders for this story had been raised by Enterprises in September/October 1967.

Nearly every episode of 'The Abominable Snowmen' also survived being junked

WIPED!

at this time due to existing Enterprises retention orders issued between November 1967 and January 1968. The sole exception was Episode Four, which Enterprises later issued a lone Junk/Wipe form for in March 1968.

Enterprises had issued retention orders for all six episodes of 'The Ice Warriors' in February 1968, although in January 1969 it had issued a junking authorisation for Episode Four only. The two-inch tape of this episode was therefore disposed of as a result of the Drama Department's new junking authorisation, but the other five episodes were spared for now.

The Enterprises retention order from December 1967 for the opening episode of 'The Enemy of the World' still seemed to be in effect, and spared this particular videotape from destruction. As previously mentioned, no records exist of any Enterprises retention orders for the other five episodes, and presumably back in 1969, no-one could find any reason to keep these five episodes. It is possible that Episode Six managed to avoid destruction at this point, but Episodes Two, Three, Four and Five were all wiped.

All six episodes of 'The Web of Fear' manage to survive being junked at this point in time, even though there was no Enterprises retention order for the first instalment.

With 'The Wheel in Space', things get more complicated. The Wipe/Junk form correctly noted that the final two episodes of this story were held as 35mm films, but decreed that they were to be junked as well as the videotapes of the first four episodes. The tapes of Episodes One to Four were indeed wiped, and it would appear that the 35mm film of Episode Five was also destroyed as a result of this paperwork. The 35mm film of Episode Six, however, managed to survive.

For 'The Dominators', initially the paperwork was filled in incorrectly, with all five episodes noted as being made on two-inch videotape. The form was then amended by hand to note that the transmission format for Episode Three was actually a 35mm film print. This 35mm film print managed to survive, but the videotaped Episodes One, Two, Four and Five were all wiped

The paperwork for 'The Mind Robber' had Episode Five correctly identified as being broadcast from a 35mm film print. This print also managed to avoid destruction, but the two-inch videotapes of the first four episodes were all wiped. Similarly with 'The Krotons', Episode One was noted as being a 35mm film print on the junking paperwork and this managed to survive, but the remaining three videotaped episodes were all wiped.

For 'The Seeds of Death', the paperwork noted that there was a retention order from Enterprises on Episode Four alone. A copy of this retention order has never surfaced, so it's not known from when it dates, but it meant that Episode Four was not junked. The 35mm transmission print of Episode Five, although scheduled for

CHAPTER 3

junking, also survived. But Episodes One, Two, Three and Six were all wiped.

And finally, the junking paperwork for 'The Space Pirates' had Episode Two correctly noted as being transmitted from a 35mm film print, and although this was scheduled to be junked, it managed to escape. But the other five episodes, which were held on two-inch videotape, were all wiped.

The BBC paperwork for all these junkings was then annotated by hand, confirming that the destruction was actioned on the same day that the paperwork was raised, Monday 21 July 1969.

So, to summarise all the above, the episodes that were junked on this day were:

The Underwater Menace	1, 2
The Moonbase	1-4
The Faceless Ones	1, 2, 3, 4, 6
The Abominable Snowmen	4
The Ice Warriors	4
The Enemy of the World	2, 3, 4, 5
The Wheel in Space	1, 2, 3, 4, 5
The Dominators	1, 2, 4, 5
The Mind Robber	1, 2, 3, 4
The Krotons	2, 3, 4
The Seeds of Death	1, 2, 3, 6
The Space Pirates	1, 3, 4, 5, 6

'The Power of the Daleks' isn't logged on any BBC Wipe/Junk forms at all, so details of when this story's tapes were wiped are not known. However, it seems certain that they had already gone by this point in time, despite the retention forms raised by Enterprises in late 1966. Similarly, 'The Highlanders' was one of the first – if not *the* first – *Doctor Who* story to have its videotapes junked by the BBC, in 1967. But by targeting nearly all the stories from 'The Underwater Menace' through to 'The Space Pirates', the BBC was getting rid of virtually the whole Troughton era of the show. The only second Doctor stories that were now still being kept on their original transmission videotapes were 'Fury from the Deep', 'The Invasion' and 'The War Games'.

As we have seen, selected episodes from the initial big list of unwanted Troughton stories had been spared, mainly due to there being outstanding Enterprises retention orders on them. It's highly likely that this Drama Department-originated purge of episodes then triggered Enterprises into reviewing the episodes that had been spared on their say-so. Just under two months after this batch of junkings, on Monday 22 September 1969, Enterprises issued Wipe/Junk forms for the following episodes:

WIPED!

The Underwater Menace	3, 4
The Faceless Ones	5
The Evil of the Daleks	7
The Tomb of the Cybermen	1-4
The Abominable Snowmen	1, 2, 3, 5, 6
The Ice Warriors	1, 2, 3, 5
The Enemy of the World	1
The Web of Fear	1, 2, 3, 4, 5, 6

For some reason, not all of the two-inch tapes of these episodes were wiped as a result of this. 'The Abominable Snowmen' Episodes Three, Five and Six, 'The Ice Warriors' Episodes One, Two, Three and Five, 'The Enemy of the World' Episode One and 'The Web of Fear' Episodes One, Three, Five and Six all managed to survive for a very short while longer, although all the other episodes detailed had their master videotapes wiped at this point.

On the very same day, for reasons unknown, Enterprises raised Retention Authorisation paperwork for 'The Seeds of Death' Episode Four (on videotape) and Episode Five (on 35mm film), and 'The Space Pirates' Episode Two (on 35mm film).

Perhaps realising that not all the junkings that they'd authorised on 22 September had been carried out, Enterprises issued another Wipe/Junk Authorisation form just four days later, on Thursday 25 September. This time it was for:

The Abominable Snowmen	3, 5, 6
The Ice Warriors	1, 2, 3

And this time, all the episodes detailed on the paperwork were disposed of.

A month or so later, on Monday 20 October 1969, Enterprises decided to issue yet more junking forms for another batch of *Doctor Who* episodes:

The Tenth Planet	4
The Ice Warriors	5, 6
The Enemy of the World	3
The Web of Fear	1, 3, 5, 6
Fury from the Deep	1, 2

The two 'Fury from the Deep' episodes were spared from destruction – presumably as the BBC Drama Department hadn't yet also issued Wipe/Junk forms for this story. But the two-inch tapes of all the other episodes were destroyed. Not all of these two-inch tapes were thrown away, however – the tape that held 'The Enemy of the World'

CHAPTER 3

Episode Three was erased, and later re-used to record an episode of *Blue Peter*, which survives on this spool to this day.[21]

1970

Colour came to BBC1, and Jon Pertwee's Doctor sprang into action on the nation's screens. His debut story, 'Spearhead from Space', was made entirely on location on 16mm colour film. But from Pertwee's second story, 'Doctor Who and the Silurians', normal production practice was resumed, and the series returned to being made on 625-line two-inch videotape, only this time in colour.

The sum total of Hartnell and Troughton *Doctor Who* episodes that still survived on their two-inch transmission videotapes at the beginning of 1970 was as follows:

The Pilot Episode	
An Unearthly Child	1
Mission to the Unknown	1
The War Machines	1, 2, 3, 4
The Macra Terror	1, 2, 3, 4
Fury from the Deep	1, 2, 3, 4, 5, 6
The Invasion	1, 2, 3, 4, 5, 6, 7, 8
The War Games	1, 2, 3, 4, 5, 6, 7, 8, 9, 10

It's possible too that the final episode of 'The Enemy of the World' might still have survived at this point, as there was no record if it being wiped or junked – although in all probability it was destroyed alongside Episodes Two to Five the previous year. Similarly, there is no wiping record for Episode Four of 'The Seeds of Death', but it doesn't appear on any subsequent paperwork, so it's very doubtful that it survived into the 1970s.

Paperwork relating to the two-inch colour videotapes of the Pertwee episodes from the early 1970s is scarcer than that relating to the episodes of the previous decade, so definitive conclusions about when tapes were wiped are harder to arrive at. However, a single undated Retention Authorisation form, originated at Enterprises and presumably issued sometime in early 1970, noted that the two-inch videotapes of Episodes One, Two, Three and Five of 'Doctor Who and the Silurians' were all to be kept.

---

21 Andrew Martin of the BBC Film and Videotape Library explained that two-inch spools had been checked to see if any previously recorded programme material was still lurking at the end of a tape. 'No-one has ever found any *Doctor Who* that way (so far) but there are a few examples of the end of a programme being found after the programme that was next recorded on a spool – the earliest of these is the end of episode one of *Vanity Fair* from 1967 on the end of another *Blue Peter*. I assume this sort of thing happened only when someone either forgot to wipe the old recording off or didn't do it properly'.

WIPED!

1971-1973

Another year would pass by before the BBC would again pay close scrutiny to its stock of two-inch videotapes of black and white *Doctor Who* episodes. On Thursday 20 May 1971, the Drama Department issued Wipe/Junk Authorisation forms for:

The Pilot Episode	
An Unearthly Child	1
Fury from the Deep	1, 2, 3, 4, 5, 6
The Invasion	1, 2, 3, 4, 5, 6, 7, 8
The War Games	1, 2, 3, 4, 5, 6, 7, 8, 9, 10

These junking forms are signed by 'R Marsh', who presumably was Ronnie Marsh, the then head of the Drama Department. As such, he was effectively *Doctor Who* producer Barry Letts' boss at the time. Somehow, the two-inch tapes of all six episodes of 'Fury from the Deep' managed to evade destruction this time around, but all the other episodes detailed on the forms were junked.

Pamela Nash at Enterprises (of whom we'll be hearing more later) issued a retention order for the 16mm film prints of all four episode of 'Spearhead from Space' in September 1971. The story had been repeated on BBC1 in July of that year, and Nash quoted the repeat broadcast dates on the retention paperwork. It's possible that she thought this was a new story at the time.

A package of 13 Jon Pertwee stories was prepared for sale to the American market by Enterprises in late 1972, which saw NTSC two-inch colour videotape copies made of all the third Doctor's adventures from 1970's 'Doctor Who and the Silurians' to 1972's 'The Time Monster' inclusive. This demonstrates that the first three seasons of Pertwee's adventures were probably still intact on their 625-line broadcast tapes at this point in time – meaning that no colour episodes of *Doctor Who* had been junked by the end of 1972.[22]

In September 1973, Enterprises issued Wipe/Junk forms for all seven episodes

---

[22] One iconic BBC series that almost suffered from having its two-inch master tapes wiped was *Monty Python's Flying Circus*. *Python* member Terry Jones, speaking in a BBC Radio 4 documentary *Long Live the Dead Parrot*, noted: 'We were tipped off by a friend in the video department that they were about to wipe all the television shows – the first series of *Python* – and we sort of clandestinely smuggled the tapes out of the BBC and put them onto Philips VCR cassettes, which was the only domestic video available at the time. I had them in my cellar for a period of about six months, and we felt that that was going to be the only record of our television series left. And then what happened was that suddenly the BBC sold the shows in America, and so they didn't wipe them. So we were saved by the bell, but it was a very close-run thing.'

Fellow *Python* Michael Palin notes in his autobiography that on 13 September 1973, he visited Terry Jones's house and spent the evening watching videotapes of the early *Monty Python* shows, along with Graham Chapman and John Cleese.

CHAPTER 3

of 'The Evil of the Daleks'. This was a bit of a waste of time, as all seven episodes had already been wiped some years previously.

1974

There was a long gap before the next batch of Wipe/Junk Authorisation forms were instigated by Enterprises, in March 1974[23]. These junking orders were for the two-inch videotapes of 'The War Machines' Episodes One to Four, and 'The Macra Terror' Episodes One to Four. These eight episodes were all duly destroyed as a result.

A rogue Wipe/Junk Authorisation form was raised by Enterprises for the fourth episode of 'Day of the Daleks' sometime in the summer of this year, but this was apparently ignored.

In July 1974, Enterprises issued a Wipe/Junk form for the last surviving episode from William Hartnell's time in the programme that was still held by the BBC on two-inch videotape – 'Mission to the Unknown' (an episode that Hartnell himself didn't actually feature in). This was destroyed as a result.

The following month, August 1974, saw Enterprises quickly moving to issue Wipe/Junk forms for all six parts of the Pertwee story 'Invasion of the Dinosaurs', which had only been shown on BBC1 earlier in the year.[24]

As 1974 drew to a close, the final piece of *Doctor Who* paperwork we have from Enterprises declared that they had 'No further interest' in all six episodes of 'Fury from the Deep', and the last black and white videotaped episodes of *Doctor Who* that the BBC held were erased.

1975-1976

It was around this time that the control of the BBC's two-inch videotapes was taken

---

Jones's illicit video copies were presumably therefore made at some point prior to this, which suggests the NTSC masters of *Monty Python's Flying Circus* were probably prepared at around the same time as those of the Pertwee *Doctor Who*s.

23 This gap is, of course, only apparent in the *extant* BBC paperwork found years later. In reality, the earlier Jon Pertwee episodes would have almost certainly begun being junked soon after the second anniversary of their initial screening, starting in early 1972.

24 It's highly probable that the first episode of this story was wiped at around this time as a result of this paperwork. It's possible that the other five episodes had their transmission tapes earmarked for wiping at this point in time as well, as the production team of the 'Whose Doctor Who' edition of *The Lively Arts* documentary series found that there were no colour two-inch tapes of *any* of the episodes of this story at the BBC in late 1976 ... However, the tapes of Episodes Two to Six *weren't* actually wiped, even if they were taken out of the system in 1974; they somehow survived, and were ultimately sent to the NFTVA – the National Film and Television Archive – in the late 1990s. But to all intents and purposes, the BBC considered the story to have been junked.

WIPED!

out of the hands of the Engineering Department and given over to the BBC Film Library, which was consequently renamed the BBC Film and Videotape Library. With this move, the routine wiping of episodes of *Doctor Who* came to a halt. Anne Hanford was the Head of the Film and Videotape Library at this time.

> **Anne Hanford:** I think it was sometime in 1975 when the control of the BBC's two-inch tapes was taken out of the hands of the Engineering Department, and instead passed to the BBC Film Library, which then duly changed its name to the BBC Film and Videotape Library. There was something of a battle between ourselves and BBC Engineering in the period building up to this – the '100 Year War' as I always think of it! But it was a war that the Archive won, and at last we could stop the wiping of the two-inch tapes. But most of the BBC's output pre-1973 had already suffered badly.

By this point in time, a large number of colour Jon Pertwee episodes of *Doctor Who* had met the same fate as the black and white episodes from the 1960s, and had been wiped. From the spread of the episodes junked, it would seem that Jon Pertwee's first three seasons had all been cleared for wiping at some point, with random episodes spared along the way, in much the same way that random William Hartnell and Patrick Troughton episodes had dodged the initial junkings of the late 1960s. If the destruction hadn't been halted, then the remainder of the episodes from seasons seven, eight and nine would probably have gone the same way in a very short space of time.[25]

Exactly when these episodes were destroyed isn't known, although the standard practice at the time in the BBC was to junk material on the second anniversary of its television broadcast. There's no reason to doubt that the majority of the Pertwee era master tapes went in this way. But surviving paperwork from the production of the 'Whose Doctor Who' episode of the BBC2 programme *The Lively Arts*, which dates from late 1976, gives a good indication of which of the Pertwee episodes had survived up to this point. During preparatory research by the documentary's production team, an inventory of the BBC's remaining stock of old *Doctor Who* episodes was undertaken by them, and a rough catalogue of available two-inch tapes was put together, in a listing dated 24 November 1976.

This showed that by this point in time, the following Pertwee episodes had had their two-inch videotapes wiped, and so no longer existed in the Film and Videotape Library:

---

[25] The retention of the two-inch tapes of all four episodes of 'Day of the Daleks' smacks of a deliberate act of preservation on someone's part. However, there isn't any evidence to back up this theory.

CHAPTER 3

Doctor Who and the Silurians	1, 2, 3, 4, 5, 6, 7
The Ambassadors of Death	2, 3, 4, 5, 6, 7
Inferno	1, 2, 3, 4, 5, 6, 7
Terror of the Autons	1, 2, 3, 4
The Mind of Evil	1, 2, 3, 4, 5, 6
The Claws of Axos	2, 3
Colony in Space	1, 2, 3, 4, 5, 6
The Dæmons	1, 2, 3, 5
The Curse of Peladon	1, 2, 3, 4
The Sea Devils	1, 2, 3
The Mutants	1, 2
The Time Monster	1, 2, 3, 4, 5, 6
Frontier in Space	1, 2, 3, 6
Planet of the Daleks	3
Invasion of the Dinosaurs	1, 2, 3, 4, 5, 6

Prior to the two-inch tapes being wiped, Enterprises had made 16mm black and white telerecordings of all of the third Doctor's adventures from seasons seven to ten. Clips used in the transmitted 'Whose Doctor Who' programme (shown on BBC2 in early 1977) from the stories 'Doctor Who and the Silurians' (Episodes Three and Four), 'Terror of the Autons' (Episode Two), 'The Claws of Axos' (Episode Three) and 'The Time Monster' (Episode Four) were all sourced from these prints. The colour transmission tapes may have been wiped, but at least black and white copies still survived at Enterprises.

1977-1978

There are no details of any further retention or junk authorisations for *Doctor Who* episodes from 1977 onwards. But by now, all the black and white two-inch videotapes of the William Hartnell and Patrick Troughton episodes were long gone, and over half of the Jon Pertwee episodes had been junked or erased as well.

Although practically all of the Pertwee episode junkings happened prior to November 1976, one episode that was apparently lost by the BBC after this period is the first episode of 'Death to the Daleks'. The transmission tape of this episode was listed as still surviving by the 'Whose Doctor Who' production team on 24 November 1976, but it was not among the episodes found to be held by the BBC in 1978, when Sue Malden was appointed as the BBC's first Archive Selector.

One other piece of *Doctor Who*'s televisual history was marginally affected during this period. For the repeat of Part Three of the Tom Baker story 'The Deadly Assassin' in August 1977, the original transmission tape of the episode (which was the only broadcast

WIPED!

copy held by the BBC) was edited to remove the original cliff-hanger freeze-frame of the Doctor's head being held underwater, due to complaints from 'clean up television' campaigner Mary Whitehouse following the initial screening of the programme.

By the summer of 1978, the BBC's collection of *Doctor Who* episodes held on their original two-inch videotapes was small. Although they had a full set of Tom Baker episodes (from 'Robot' in 1974 through to 'The Invasion of Time', which had been screened earlier in 1978), they had an extremely depleted collection of Pertwee episodes. These consisted of:

Episode	Parts
The Ambassadors of Death	1
The Claws of Axos	1, 4
The Dæmons	4
Day of the Daleks	1, 2, 3, 4
The Sea Devils	4, 5, 6
The Mutants	3, 4, 5, 6
The Three Doctors	1, 2, 3, 4
Carnival of Monsters	1, 2, 3, 4
Frontier in Space	4, 5
Planet of the Daleks	1, 2, 4, 5, 6
The Green Death	1, 2, 3, 4, 5, 6
The Time Warrior	1, 2, 3, 4
Death to the Daleks	2, 3, 4
The Monster of Peladon	1, 2, 3, 4, 5, 6
Planet of the Spiders	1, 2, 3, 4, 5, 6

There were no two-inch videotapes of episodes from the '60s at all. However, not all the episodes from *Doctor Who*'s past had been transmitted from videotape – there were still those odd few that had been transmitted from film. The Film Library's holdings of *Doctor Who* are discussed in more detail in the next chapter.

THOSE VIDEOTAPE WIPING DETAILS IN FULL ...

SEASON ONE

Episode	Wipe Date	Recording No.
Pilot Episode	20/05/71	VT/P/19491

CHAPTER 3

An Unearthly Child: 1	20/05/71	VT/T/19789
An Unearthly Child: 2	17/08/67	VT/T/19781
An Unearthly Child: 3	17/08/67	VT/T/19788
An Unearthly Child: 4	17/08/67	VT/T/19873
The Daleks: 1 (Original – Not TX'd)	Pre-1970	VT/T/19964
The Daleks: 1 (Remount – TX version)	17/08/67	VT/T/20192
The Daleks: 2	17/08/67	VT/T/20023
The Daleks: 3	17/08/67	VT/T/20171
The Daleks: 4	n/a 35mm film	35/T/20398 A & B
The Daleks: 5	17/07/69	VT/T/20439
The Daleks: 6	17/08/67	VT/T/20675
The Daleks: 7	17/08/67	VT/T/20685
The Edge of Destruction: 1	17/08/67	VT/T/20679
The Edge of Destruction: 2	31/01/69	VT/T/20810
Marco Polo: 1	17/08/67	VT/T/20820
Marco Polo: 2	17/08/67	VT/T/21019
Marco Polo: 3	17/08/67	VT/T/21017
Marco Polo: 4	17/08/67	VT/T/21248
Marco Polo: 5	17/08/67	VT/T/21260
Marco Polo: 6	17/08/67	VT/T/21275
Marco Polo: 7	17/08/67	VT/T/21332
The Keys of Marinus: 1	17/08/67	VT/T/21636
The Keys of Marinus: 2	17/08/67	VT/T/21516
The Keys of Marinus: 3	17/08/67	VT/T/21645
The Keys of Marinus: 4	31/01/69	VT/T/22069
The Keys of Marinus: 5	17/08/67	VT/T/22078
The Keys of Marinus: 6	17/08/67	VT/T/21826
The Aztecs: 1	17/08/67	VT/T/21840
The Aztecs: 2	17/08/67	VT/T/21990
The Aztecs: 3	17/08/67	VT/T/22203
The Aztecs: 4	17/08/67	VT/T/22159
The Sensorites: 1	31/01/69	VT/T/22283
The Sensorites: 2	31/01/69	VT/T/22377
The Sensorites: 3	17/08/67	VT/T/22445
The Sensorites: 4	17/08/67	VT/T/22636
The Sensorites: 5	17/08/67	VT/T/23150
The Sensorites: 6	31/01/69	VT/T/23191
The Reign of Terror: 1	17/08/67	VT/4T/23217
The Reign of Terror: 2	17/08/67	VT/4T/23350
The Reign of Terror: 3	17/08/67	VT/4T/23095
The Reign of Terror: 4	31/01/69	VT/4T/23097
The Reign of Terror: 5	17/08/67	VT/4T/23400
The Reign of Terror: 6	17/08/67	VT/4T/23405

WIPED!

SEASON TWO

Episode	Wipe Date	Recording No.
Planet of Giants: 1	31/01/69	VT/4T/23309
Planet of Giants: 2	31/01/69	VT/4T/23421
Planet of Giants: 3 (Original)	Pre-1970	VT/4T/23675
Planet of Giants: 4 (Original)	Pre-1970	VT/4T/23891
Planet of Giants: 3 (TX version)	n/a 35mm film	35/6T/23675
The Dalek Invasion of Earth: 1	17/08/67	VT/4T/23897
The Dalek Invasion of Earth: 2	17/08/67	VT/4T/24194
The Dalek Invasion of Earth: 3	31/01/69	VT/4T/24198
The Dalek Invasion of Earth: 4	17/08/67	VT/4T/24189
The Dalek Invasion of Earth: 5	n/a 35mm film	35/6T/24329
The Dalek Invasion of Earth: 6	17/08/67	VT/4T/24590
The Rescue: 1	17/08/67	VT/4T/25136
The Rescue: 2	31/01/69	VT/4T/25137
The Romans: 1	17/08/67	VT/4T/25260
The Romans: 2	17/08/67	VT/4T/25423
The Romans: 3	17/08/67	VT/4T/25428
The Romans: 4	17/08/67	VT/4T/25749
The Web Planet: 1	31/01/69	VT/4T/25751
The Web Planet: 2	17/08/67	VT/4T/26040
The Web Planet: 3	17/08/67	VT/4T/26052
The Web Planet: 4	17/08/67	VT/4T/26056
The Web Planet: 5	31/01/69	VT/4T/26129
The Web Planet: 6	31/01/69	VT/4T/26302
The Crusade: 1	31/01/69	VT/4T/26305
The Crusade: 2	17/08/67	VT/4T/26482
The Crusade: 3	Pre-1970	VT/4T/26485
The Crusade: 4	31/01/69	VT/4T/26733
The Space Museum: 1	17/08/67	VT/4T/26730
The Space Museum: 2	31/01/69	VT/4T/26894
The Space Museum: 3	17/08/67	VT/4T/26898
The Space Museum: 4	17/08/67	VT/4T/27154
The Chase: 1	17/07/69	VT/4T/27163
The Chase: 2	17/08/67	VT/4T/27547
The Chase: 3	31/01/69	VT/4T/27551
The Chase: 4	17/08/67	VT/4T/27555
The Chase: 5	31/01/69	VT/4T/27559/B
The Chase: 6	17/08/67	VT/4T/27876
The Time Meddler: 1	17/08/67	VT/4T/27879
The Time Meddler: 2	31/01/69	VT/4T/27953
The Time Meddler: 3	17/08/67	VT/4T/27959
The Time Meddler: 4	17/08/67	VT/4T/28195

CHAPTER 3

SEASON THREE

Episode	Wipe Date	Recording No.
Galaxy 4: 1	17/08/67	VT/4T/28205
Galaxy 4: 2	17/08/67	VT/4T/28426
Galaxy 4: 3	31/01/69	VT/4T/28436
Galaxy 4: 4	17/08/67	VT/4T/28443
Mission to the Unknown	July 1974	VT/4T/28457
The Myth Makers: 1	31/01/69	VT/4T/29157
The Myth Makers: 2	17/08/67	VT/4T/29160
The Myth Makers: 3	17/08/67	VT/4T/29165
The Myth Makers: 4	17/08/67	VT/4T/29419
The Daleks Masterplan: 1	17/08/67	VT/4T/29715
The Daleks Masterplan: 2	17/08/67	VT/4T/29718
The Daleks Masterplan: 3	31/01/69	VT/4T/29723
The Daleks Masterplan: 4	17/08/67	VT/4T/29727
The Daleks Masterplan: 5	17/08/67	VT/4T/29899
The Daleks Masterplan: 6	31/01/69	VT/4T/29904
The Daleks Masterplan: 7	17/08/67	VT/4T/30363
The Daleks Masterplan: 8	17/08/67	VT/4T/30369
The Daleks Masterplan: 9	17/08/67	VT/4T/30379
The Daleks Masterplan: 10	17/07/69	VT/4T/30617
The Daleks Masterplan: 11	17/07/69	VT/4T/30614
The Daleks Masterplan: 12	17/07/69	VT/4T/30939
The Massacre: 1	17/08/67	VT/4T/30935
The Massacre: 2	17/08/67	VT/4T/30930
The Massacre: 3	17/08/67	VT/4T/30925
The Massacre: 4	17/08/67	VT/4T/31107
The Ark: 1	17/08/67	VT/4T/31154
The Ark: 2	17/08/67	VT/4T/31264
The Ark: 3	17/08/67	VT/4T/31269
The Ark: 4	17/08/67	VT/4T/31463
The Celestial Toymaker: 1	Pre-1970	VT/4T/31529
The Celestial Toymaker: 2	Pre-1970	VT/4T/31653
The Celestial Toymaker: 3	Pre-1970	VT/4T/31657
The Celestial Toymaker: 4	Pre-1970	VT/4T/32137
The Gunfighters: 1	17/08/67	VT/4T/32032
The Gunfighters: 2	Pre-1970	VT/4T/32205
The Gunfighters: 3	Pre-1970	VT/4T/32152
The Gunfighters: 4	Pre-1970	VT/4T/32535
The Savages: 1	Pre-1970	VT/4T/32548
The Savages: 2	Pre-1970	VT/4T/32718
The Savages: 3	Pre-1970	VT/4T/32723
The Savages: 4	Pre-1970	VT/4T/32909
The War Machines: 1	March 1974	VT/4T/32897

WIPED!

The War Machines: 2	March 1974	VT/4T/33163
The War Machines: 3	March 1974	VT/4T/33168
The War Machines: 4	March 1974	VT/4T/33408

SEASON FOUR

Episode	Wipe Date	Recording No.
The Smugglers: 1	Pre-1970	VT/4T/33489
The Smugglers: 2	Pre-1970	VT/4T/33893
The Smugglers: 3	Pre-1970	VT/4T/33892
The Smugglers: 4	Pre-1970	VT/4T/34127
The Tenth Planet: 1	Pre-1970	VT/4T/34830
The Tenth Planet: 2	Pre-1970	VT/4T/34827
The Tenth Planet: 3	Pre-1970	VT/4T/34974
The Tenth Planet: 4	20/10/69	VT/4T/35067
The Power of the Daleks: 1	Pre-1970	VT/4T/35809
The Power of the Daleks: 2	Pre-1970	VT/4T/35685
The Power of the Daleks: 3	Pre-1970	VT/4T/35583
The Power of the Daleks: 4	Pre-1970	VT/4T/35575
The Power of the Daleks: 5	Pre-1970	VT/4T/35242
The Power of the Daleks: 6	n/a 35mm film	35/6T/36252
The Highlanders: 1	09/03/67	VT/4T/36028
The Highlanders: 2	09/03/67	VT/4T/36299
The Highlanders: 3	09/03/67	VT/4T/36500
The Highlanders: 4	09/03/67	VT/4T/36559
The Underwater Menace: 1	21/07/69	VT/4T/36845
The Underwater Menace: 2	21/07/69	VT/4T/36700
The Underwater Menace: 3	22/09/69	VT/4T/37123
The Underwater Menace: 4	22/09/69	VT/4T/37124
The Moonbase: 1	21/07/69	VT/4T/37215
The Moonbase: 2	21/07/69	VT/4T/37185
The Moonbase: 3	21/07/69	VT/4T/37337
The Moonbase: 4	21/07/69	VT/4T/37352
The Macra Terror: 1	March 1974	VT/4T/37894
The Macra Terror: 2	March 1974	VT/4T/38315
The Macra Terror: 3	March 1974	VT/4T/37965
The Macra Terror: 4	March 1974	VT/4T/37961
The Faceless Ones: 1	21/07/69	VT/4T/38259
The Faceless Ones: 2	21/07/69	VT/4T/38245
The Faceless Ones: 3	21/07/69	VT/4T/38571
The Faceless Ones: 4	21/07/69	VT/4T/38574
The Faceless Ones: 5	22/09/69	VT/4T/38855
The Faceless Ones: 6	21/07/69	VT/4T/38857
The Evil of the Daleks: 1	August 1968	VT/4T/39237

CHAPTER 3

The Evil of the Daleks: 2	August 1968	VT/4T/39242
The Evil of the Daleks: 3	August 1968	VT/4T/39361
The Evil of the Daleks: 4	August 1968	VT/4T/39382
The Evil of the Daleks: 5	August 1968	VT/4T/39603
The Evil of the Daleks: 6	August 1968	VT/4T/39604
The Evil of the Daleks: 7	22/09/69	VT/4T/39826

SEASON FIVE

Episode	Wipe Date	Recording No.
The Tomb of the Cybermen: 1	22/09/69	VT/4T/39819
The Tomb of the Cybermen: 2	22/09/69	VTM/4T/40034
The Tomb of the Cybermen: 3	22/09/69	VTM/4T/40031
The Tomb of the Cybermen: 4	22/09/69	VT/4T/40262
The Abominable Snowmen: 1	22/09/69	VTM/4T/40837
The Abominable Snowmen: 2	22/09/69	VTM/4T/40981
The Abominable Snowmen: 3	25/09/69	VTM/4T/41084
The Abominable Snowmen: 4	21/07/69	VTM/4T/41216
The Abominable Snowmen: 5	25/09/69	VTM/4T/41319
The Abominable Snowmen: 6	25/09/69	VTM/4T/41440
The Ice Warriors: 1	25/09/69	VTM/4T/41472
The Ice Warriors: 2	25/09/69	VTM/4T/41632
The Ice Warriors: 3	25/09/69	VTM/4T/41656
The Ice Warriors: 4	21/07/69	VTM/4T/41821
The Ice Warriors: 5	20/10/69	VTM/4T/41840
The Ice Warriors: 6	20/10/69	VTM/4T/42232
The Enemy of the World: 1	20/10/69	VTM/6LT/42231
The Enemy of the World: 2	21/07/69	VTM/6LT/42378
The Enemy of the World: 3	21/07/69	VTM/6LT/42351
The Enemy of the World: 4	21/07/69	VTM/6LT/42764
The Enemy of the World: 5	21/07/69	VTM/6LT/42924
The Enemy of the World: 6	Pre-1970	VTM/6LT/42774
The Web of Fear: 1	20/10/69	VTM/6LT/42888
The Web of Fear: 2	22/09/69	VTM/6LT/43370
The Web of Fear: 3	20/10/69	VTM/6LT/43230
The Web of Fear: 4	22/09/69	VTM/6LT/43430
The Web of Fear: 5	20/10/69	VTM/6LT/43401
The Web of Fear: 6	20/10/69	VTM/6LT/43474
Fury from the Deep: 1	late 1974	VTM/6LT/43513
Fury from the Deep: 2	late 1974	VTM/6LT/43559
Fury from the Deep: 3	late 1974	VTM/6LT/43621
Fury from the Deep: 4	late 1974	VTM/6LT/43980
Fury from the Deep: 5	late 1974	VTM/6LT/44214
Fury from the Deep: 6	late 1974	VTM/6LT/44248
The Wheel in Space: 1	21/07/69	VTM/6LT/44312

WIPED!

The Wheel in Space: 2	21/07/69	VTM/6LT/44427
The Wheel in Space: 3	21/07/69	VTM/6LT/44520
The Wheel in Space: 4	21/07/69	VTM/6LT/44628
The Wheel in Space: 5	n/a 35mm film	35M/6T/44753
The Wheel in Space: 6	n/a 35mm film	35/6T/44894

SEASON SIX

Episode	Wipe Date	Recording No.
The Dominators: 1	21/07/69	VTM/6LT/44992
The Dominators: 2	21/07/69	VTM/6LT/45000
The Dominators: 3	n/a 35mm film	35M/6T/45251
The Dominators: 4	21/07/69	VTM/6LT/45321
The Dominators: 5	21/07/69	VTM/6LT/45505
The Mind Robber: 1	21/07/69	VTM/6LT/45610
The Mind Robber: 2	21/07/69	VTM/6LT/45700
The Mind Robber: 3	21/07/69	VTM/6LT/45777
The Mind Robber: 4	21/07/69	VTM/6LT/45897
The Mind Robber: 5	n/a 35mm film	35M/6T/45916
The Invasion: 1	20/05/71	VTM/6LT/47017
The Invasion: 2	20/05/71	VTM/6LT/47058
The Invasion: 3	20/05/71	VTM/6LT/47461
The Invasion: 4	20/05/71	VTM/6LT/47463
The Invasion: 5	20/05/71	VTM/6LT/47044
The Invasion: 6	20/05/71	VTM/6LT/47792
The Invasion: 7	20/05/71	VTM/6LT/48315
The Invasion: 8	20/05/71	VTM/6LT/48091
The Krotons: 1	n/a 35mm film	35M/6T/48284
The Krotons: 2	21/07/69	VTM/6LT/48518
The Krotons: 3	21/07/69	VTM/6LT/48540
The Krotons: 4	21/07/69	VTM/6LT/48847
The Seeds of Death: 1	21/07/69	VTM/6LT/49252
The Seeds of Death: 2	21/07/69	VTM/6LT/49339
The Seeds of Death: 3	21/07/69	VTM/6LT/49533
The Seeds of Death: 4	Pre-1972	VTM/6LT/49550
The Seeds of Death: 5	n/a 35mm film	35M/6T/49686
The Seeds of Death: 6	21/07/69	VTM/6LT/49789
The Space Pirates: 1	21/07/69	VTM/6LT/49991
The Space Pirates: 2	n/a 35mm film	35M/6T/50189
The Space Pirates: 3	21/07/69	VTM/6LT/50185
The Space Pirates: 4	21/07/69	VTM/6LT/50342
The Space Pirates: 5	21/07/69	VTM/6LT/50400
The Space Pirates: 6	21/07/69	VTM/6LT/50626
The War Games: 1	20/05/71	VTM/6LT/50811
The War Games: 2	20/05/71	VTM/6LT/50902

CHAPTER 3

The War Games: 3	20/05/71	VTM/6LT/51149
The War Games: 4	20/05/71	VTM/6LT/51084
The War Games: 5	20/05/71	VTM/6LT/51295
The War Games: 6	20/05/71	VTM/6LT/51483
The War Games: 7	20/05/71	VTM/6LT/51584
The War Games: 8	20/05/71	VTM/6LT/51744
The War Games: 9	20/05/71	VTM/6LT/51922
The War Games: 10	20/05/71	VTM/6LT/52067

SEASON SEVEN

Episode	Wipe Date	Recording No.
Spearhead from Space: 1	n/a 16mm film	23/4/8/3060[26]
Spearhead from Space: 2	n/a 16mm film	23/4/8/3061
Spearhead from Space: 3	n/a 16mm film	23/4/8/3062
Spearhead from Space: 4	n/a 16mm film	23/4/8/3063
Doctor Who and the Silurians: 1	Between 12/72 – 11/76	VTC/6HT/55280
Doctor Who and the Silurians: 2	Between 12/72 – 11/76	VTC/6HT/55685
Doctor Who and the Silurians: 3	Between 12/72 – 11/76	VTC/6HT/55686
Doctor Who and the Silurians: 4	Between 12/72 – 11/76	VTC/6HT/56771
Doctor Who and the Silurians: 5	Between 12/72 – 11/76	VTC/6HT/56842/ED
Doctor Who and the Silurians: 6	Between 12/72 – 11/76	VTC/6HT/57113
Doctor Who and the Silurians: 7	Between 12/72 – 11/76	VTC/6HT/57083/ED
The Ambassadors of Death: 1	NOT WIPED	VTC/6HT/57251/ED
The Ambassadors of Death: 2	Between 12/72 – 11/76	VTC/6HT/57463/ED
The Ambassadors of Death: 3	Between 12/72 – 11/76	VTC/6HT/57478/ED
The Ambassadors of Death: 4	Between 12/72 – 11/76	VTC/6HT/57615/ED
The Ambassadors of Death: 5	Between 12/72 – 11/76	VTC/6HT/57674/ED
The Ambassadors of Death: 6	Between 12/72 – 11/76	VTC/6HT/57881/ED
The Ambassadors of Death: 7	Between 12/72 – 11/76	VTC/6HT/57945/ED
Inferno: 1	Between 12/72 – 11/76	VTC/6HT/58651/ED
Inferno: 2	Between 12/72 – 11/76	VTC/6HT/58652/ED
Inferno: 3	Between 12/72 – 11/76	VTC/6HT/58975/ED
Inferno: 4	Between 12/72 – 11/76	VTC/6HT/58976/ED
Inferno: 5	Between 12/72 – 11/76	VTC/6HT/59131/ED
Inferno: 6	Between 12/72 – 11/76	VTC/6HT/59183/ED
Inferno: 7	Between 12/72 – 11/76	VTC/6HT/59325/ED

---

26 The recording numbers quoted here for "Spearhead from Space" are actually the project numbers – these were allocated to almost all programmes (one main exception being the News) and indicate producing department, commissioning year, channel and whether black and white or colour, with the second half of the number just being a sequential number. Filmed programmes, not having recording numbers, had only project numbers, but these would change when a programme was repeated, unlike the later programme number.

WIPED!

SEASON EIGHT

Episode	Wipe Date	Recording No.
Terror of the Autons: 1	Between 02/73 – 11/76	VTC/6HT/62564/ED
Terror of the Autons: 2	Between 02/73 – 11/76	VTC/6HT/62565/ED
Terror of the Autons: 3	Between 02/73 – 11/76	VTC/6HT/62787/ED
Terror of the Autons: 4	Between 02/73 – 11/76	VTC/6HT/62788/ED
The Mind of Evil: 1	Between 03/73 – 11/76	VTC/6HT/63220/ED
The Mind of Evil: 2	Between 03/73 – 11/76	VTC/6HT/63221/ED
The Mind of Evil: 3	Between 03/73 – 11/76	VTC/6HT/63222/ED
The Mind of Evil: 4	Between 03/73 – 11/76	VTC/6HT/63223/ED
The Mind of Evil: 5	Between 03/73 – 11/76	VTC/6HT/63224/ED
The Mind of Evil: 6	Between 03/73 – 11/76	VTC/6HT/63225/ED
The Claws of Axos: 1	NOT WIPED	VTC/6HT/63227/ED
The Claws of Axos: 2	Between 04/73 – 11/76	VTC/6HT/63228/ED
The Claws of Axos: 3	Between 04/73 – 11/76	VTC/6HT/63229/ED
The Claws of Axos: 4	NOT WIPED	VTC/6HT/63230/ED
Colony in Space: 1	Between 05/73 – 11/76	VTC/6HT/63231/ED
Colony in Space: 2	Between 05/73 – 11/76	VTC/6HT/63232/ED
Colony in Space: 3	Between 05/73 – 11/76	VTC/6HT/63233/ED
Colony in Space: 4	Between 05/73 – 11/76	VTC/6HT/63234/ED
Colony in Space: 5	Between 05/73 – 11/76	VTC/6HT/63235/ED
Colony in Space: 6	Between 05/73 – 11/76	VTC/6HT/63236/ED/ED
The Dæmons: 1	Between 05/73 – 11/76	VTC/6HT/63237/ED
The Dæmons: 2	Between 05/73 – 11/76	VTC/6HT/63238/ED
The Dæmons: 3	Between 05/73 – 11/76	VTC/6HT/63239/ED
The Dæmons: 4	NOT WIPED	VTC/6HT/63240/ED
The Dæmons: 5	Between 05/73 – 11/76	VTC/6HT/63241/ED

SEASON NINE

Episode	Wipe Date	Recording No.
Day of the Daleks: 1	NOT WIPED	VTC/6HT/68909/ED
Day of the Daleks: 2	NOT WIPED	VTC/6HT/68910/ED
Day of the Daleks: 3	NOT WIPED	VTC/6HT/68911/ED
Day of the Daleks: 4	NOT WIPED	VTC/6HT/68912/ED
The Curse of Peladon: 1	Between 02/74 – 11/76	VTC/6HT/76488/ED
The Curse of Peladon: 2	Between 02/74 – 11/76	VTC/6HT/76521/ED
The Curse of Peladon: 3	Between 02/74 – 11/76	VTC/6HT/76722/ED
The Curse of Peladon: 4	Between 02/74 – 11/76	VTC/6HT/76723/ED
The Sea Devils: 1	Between 04/74 – 11/76	VTC/6HT/89568/ED
The Sea Devils: 2	Between 04/74 – 11/76	VTC/6HT/69569/ED/ED
The Sea Devils: 3	Between 04/74 – 11/76	VTC/6HT/69570/ED
The Sea Devils: 4	NOT WIPED	VTC/6HT/69571/ED
The Sea Devils: 5	NOT WIPED	VTC/6HT/69572/ED

CHAPTER 3

The Sea Devils: 6	NOT WIPED	VTC/6HT/69573/ED
The Mutants: 1	Between 05/74 – 11/76	VTC/6HT/77399/ED
The Mutants: 2	Between 05/74 – 11/76	VTC/6HT/77400/ED
The Mutants: 3	NOT WIPED	VTC/6HT/77714/ED
The Mutants: 4	NOT WIPED	VTC/6HT/77720/ED
The Mutants: 5	NOT WIPED	VTC/6HT/77945/ED
The Mutants: 6	NOT WIPED	VTC/6HT/77955/ED
The Time Monster: 1	Between 06/74 – 11/76	VTC/6HT/78493/ED
The Time Monster: 2	Between 06/74 – 11/76	VTC/6HT/78498/ED
The Time Monster: 3	Between 06/74 – 11/76	VTC/6HT/78720/ED
The Time Monster: 4	Between 06/74 – 11/76	VTC/6HT/78729/ED
The Time Monster: 5	Between 06/74 – 11/76	VTC/6HT/78942/ED
The Time Monster: 6	Between 06/74 – 11/76	VTC/6HT/78960/ED

SEASON TEN

Episode	Wipe Date	Recording No.
The Three Doctors: 1	NOT WIPED	VTC/6HT/82370/ED
The Three Doctors: 2	NOT WIPED	VTC/6HT/82371/ED
The Three Doctors: 3	NOT WIPED	VTC/6HT/82569/ED
The Three Doctors: 4	NOT WIPED	VTC/6HT/82579/ED
Carnival of Monsters: 1	NOT WIPED	VTC/6HT/79332/ED/ED
Carnival of Monsters: 2	NOT WIPED	VTC/6HT/79344/ED/ED
Carnival of Monsters: 3	NOT WIPED	VTC/6HT/79608/ED/ED
Carnival of Monsters: 4	NOT WIPED	VTC/6HT/79612/ED/ED
Frontier in Space: 1	Between 03/75 – 11/76	VTC/6HT/81462/ED
Frontier in Space: 2	Between 03/75 – 11/76	VTC/6HT/81504/ED
Frontier in Space: 3	Between 03/75 – 11/76	VTC/6HT/81725/ED
Frontier in Space: 4	NOT WIPED	VTC/6HT/81733/ED
Frontier in Space: 5	NOT WIPED	VTC/6HT/81918/ED/ED
Frontier in Space: 6	Between 03/75 – 11/76	VTC/6HT/81919/ED
Planet of the Daleks: 1	NOT WIPED	VTC/6HT/83751/ED/ED
Planet of the Daleks: 2	NOT WIPED	VTC/6HT/83760/ED/ED
Planet of the Daleks: 3	Between 04/75 – 11/76	VTC/6HT/83951/ED
Planet of the Daleks: 4	NOT WIPED	VTC/6HT/83952/ED/ED
Planet of the Daleks: 5	NOT WIPED	VTC/6HT/84122/ED/ED
Planet of the Daleks: 6	NOT WIPED	VTC/6HT/84130/ED
The Green Death: 1	NOT WIPED	VTC/6HT/84962/ED
The Green Death: 2	NOT WIPED	VTC/6HT/84963/ED
The Green Death: 3	NOT WIPED	VTC/6HT/85251/ED/ED
The Green Death: 4	NOT WIPED	VTC/6HT/85252/ED
The Green Death: 5	NOT WIPED	VTC/6HT/85471/ED/ED
The Green Death: 6	NOT WIPED	VTC/6HT/85481/ED

WIPED!

SEASON ELEVEN

Episode	Wipe Date	Recording No.
The Time Warrior: 1	NOT WIPED	VTC/6HT/85882/ED
The Time Warrior: 2	NOT WIPED	VTC/6HT/85885/ED
The Time Warrior: 3	NOT WIPED	VTC/6HT/86084/ED
The Time Warrior: 4	NOT WIPED	VTC/6HT/86085/ED
Invasion of the Dinosaurs: 1	August 1974	VTC/6HT/88448/ED
Invasion of the Dinosaurs: 2	August 1974 *	VTC/6HT/88372/ED
Invasion of the Dinosaurs: 3	August 1974 *	VTC/6HT/88613/ED/ED
Invasion of the Dinosaurs: 4	August 1974 *	VTC/6HT/88642/ED/ED
Invasion of the Dinosaurs: 5	August 1974 *	VTC/6HT/88911/ED/ED
Invasion of the Dinosaurs: 6	August 1974 *	VTC/6HT/88915/ED
Death to the Daleks: 1	Between 11/76 – 12/78	VTC/6HT/89269/ED
Death to the Daleks: 2	NOT WIPED	VTC/6HT/89270/ED
Death to the Daleks: 3	NOT WIPED	VTC/6HT/99486/ED
Death to the Daleks: 4	NOT WIPED	VTC/6HT/89487/ED
The Monster of Peladon: 1	NOT WIPED	VTC/6HT/90340/ED
The Monster of Peladon: 2	NOT WIPED	VTC/6HT/90342/ED
The Monster of Peladon: 3	NOT WIPED	VTC/6HT/90433/ED
The Monster of Peladon: 4	NOT WIPED	VTC/6HT/90461/ED
The Monster of Peladon: 5	NOT WIPED	VTC/6HT/90712/ED
The Monster of Peladon: 6	NOT WIPED	VTC/6HT/90718/ED
Planet of the Spiders: 1	NOT WIPED	VTC/6HT/91637/ED
Planet of the Spiders: 2	NOT WIPED	VTC/6HT/91646/ED/ED
Planet of the Spiders: 3	NOT WIPED	VTC/6HT/91962/ED
Planet of the Spiders: 4	NOT WIPED	VTC/6HT/91973/ED
Planet of the Spiders: 5	NOT WIPED	VTC/6HT/92372/ED
Planet of the Spiders: 6	NOT WIPED	VTC/6HT/93065/ED

* The transmission tapes of these episodes were later found and archived some time prior to 1981.

From the programme's twelfth season, which debuted on BBC1 in December 1974, no more transmission tapes were junked by the BBC.

CHAPTER 4
THE BBC FILM LIBRARY

The BBC Film Library was created in the 1930s, a development that went hand in hand with the formation of the BBC News Unit. This Unit began generating lots of newsreel footage, especially after the BBC re-opened for business after the second World War. This was all shot on film. Not only was there a need to retain and store this film, but there was also a requirement to catalogue it, so that it could be quickly located again if needed. These were the Film Library's tasks. Its operations were spread over three different BBC premises in London – the Lime Grove studios, the Film Studios in Ealing and a warehouse storage unit at Windmill Road in Brentford.

At about the same time as the Film Library was founded, the BBC began experimenting with the process of telerecording its live programmes – the technique of creating film recordings of images from an electronic television screen. It was decided quite early on by the BBC policy-makers that any programme telerecorded onto film for eventual rebroadcast would utilise 35mm black and white film stock, as 16mm film, with its lower resolution, produced results that were thought to be too poor to be acceptable to television viewers. Over the course of its first ten years, the Film Library became the home of an increasing number of these 35mm telerecordings, in addition to its news holdings. These ranged from comedies and dramas, to children's programmes and documentaries. Anything that the BBC transmitted was fair game for telerecording.

Of course, not everything that was shown by the BBC was kept, and there was no real long-term archival strategy behind the Film Library's existence. The BBC had lots of films, it needed somewhere to store them, and it needed a catalogue of what it had so that footage could be quickly located again. That was the Film Library's purpose.

In November 1968, the Film Library moved to a single location, a new set of purpose-equipped premises in Windmill Road, Brentford, closing down its operations at Lime Grove and Ealing. At around about the same time, the News Unit separated its film archive away, into a separate, independent entity, locating itself at Television Centre. Thus it was all of the BBC's non-news films that were now housed at the new facility in Brentford.[27]

The move to this new facility was covered in some depth by the BBC's in-house

---

[27] Andrew Martin from the BBC Film and Videotape Library explains just how haphazard film storage at the BBC was: 'Windmill Road was used as an overflow store for the Ealing Film Library since c.1963. In 1968 the library migrated there wholesale though there was still film storage at Ealing until TFS closed c.1992, but apart from some *Z Cars* film inserts someone saved, anything there was probably junked at that time. Could have been *Doctor Who* stuff in theory …'

WIPED!

magazine *Ariel* in February 1969, in an article written by Anne Hanford, the senior Film Librarian. The article gave some details about how the Film Library was used at the time:

> The main function of the Film Library is to provide film material for re-use, and make available information which happens to be on film. Approximately 450 enquiries per week are received by the Enquiry Section, resulting in the issue of 1,250 cans. An average of two hours 30 minutes of reused material is transmitted each week, and six hours of repeated programmes on film. The Film Library also holds material for the production departments' current programme needs and master material for programmes in which Television Enterprises have a sales interest.
>
> The Film Library takes in the majority of BBC produced material on film, including complete programmes, film sequences, and items related to complete programmes and news stories. It is also responsible for building up a useful stock-shot collection. These different categories of material now mean an annual intake of 17,000 cans, or approximately 9,000,000 ft of 16mm material and 7,000,000 ft of 35mm material. An increasing proportion of this is in colour, which requires different storage conditions and modified handling methods.

Hanford went on to describe the various facilities that the new Windmill Road unit had incorporated into it. First, there were two separate film vaults. The larger general archive covered 27,000 square feet and stored film at a temperature that never exceeded 70° F. The second, smaller area held films specifically for archival storage, and was a mere 7,500 square feet in size. The temperature in this vault was kept at a strict 55° F. There was an Accessions area in the building, where new film items were identified, numbered and catalogued, and a viewing area, which contained ten cubicles for watching material ordered up from the archive.

The article also mentioned that a new computer system was being introduced – '… an Ultronic machine for preparing the necessary punched paper tape has been installed' – which, it was hoped, would in time be able to provide information on all the BBC's various libraries, including limited information about programmes that had been recorded on videotape.

FILM DURATIONS

The film used in the making of *Doctor Who* in the early 1960s was almost always black and white 35mm stock. When it came to quantifying material held in the Film Library, it was the actual physical length of the film that was usually recorded, not the

CHAPTER 4

running time.

35mm film contains 16 frames per foot of film, and the film would always be shot at 25 frames per second. So, for example, a 35mm film insert for *Doctor Who* might be logged as consisting of 380 feet of material. The calculation 380 x 16 would tell us that this equates to 6,080 frames of footage. Played at 25 frames per second, this would run for 243.2 seconds. Or, in other words, for just over four minutes.

When it came to making telerecordings for overseas sales, 16mm black and white film was always used. Because this film is less than half the width of 35mm film, the number of frames per foot is more than double – 40, to be exact. A typical 16mm film print of an episode of *Doctor Who* would run to about 900 feet. 900 x 40 would give us 36,000 frames of footage. Running this at the standard speed of 25 frames per second would give us 1,440 seconds – exactly 24 minutes – of on-screen time.

EPISODES TRANSMITTED FROM FILM

When *Doctor Who* began, it adopted the standard BBC model of programme making at the time, and so episodes were pre-recorded on two-inch videotape some weeks in advance of transmission. However, as discussed in earlier chapters, there were a few exceptions, where episodes were transmitted from 35mm film.

During the Hartnell era, these exceptions were the fourth episode of 'The Daleks', the final episode of 'Planet of Giants' and the fifth episode of 'The Dalek Invasion of Earth'. Thus, by the end of 1964, the BBC Film Library held the master prints of these three episodes in its archive. According to practically all of the available evidence, no further Hartnell episodes of *Doctor Who* were transmitted from 35mm film.

But then we come to 'The Celestial Toymaker' and 'The Gunfighters'. In Chapter 3, it was noted that a Retention Authorisation form for most of the Hartnell era stories was raised in late 1966 by BBC Enterprises, presumably to enable new Stored Field telerecordings of these stories to be made. Listed in this paperwork were a number of 35mm film telerecordings of *Doctor Who* episodes. Both 'The Daleks' Episode Four and 'The Dalek Invasion of Earth' Episode Five were noted as being held on 35mm film (but oddly enough, not 'Planet of Giants' Episode Three, as has been commented upon). But also listed for retention in this paperwork were 35mm film telerecordings of 'The Celestial Toymaker' Episodes One, Two and Three, and 'The Gunfighters' Episodes Two, Three and Four.

A quick examination of the BBC's PasB ('Programme-as-Broadcast') records for these episodes seemingly indicates that they were originally transmitted on BBC1 from 405-line two-inch videotape. Programmes shown from 35mm film would have the transmission reference 35/6T/XXXXX, whereas those shown from two-inch videotape would have the reference VT/4T/XXXXX. All of the episodes of both these stories were logged as being shown from videotape.

BBC PasB Details—'The Celestial Toymaker' and 'The Gunfighters'

Story Title	Episode Title	Transmission Tape
The Celestial Toymaker: 1	The Celestial Toyroom	VT/4T/31529
The Celestial Toymaker: 2	The Hall of Dolls	VT/4T/31653
The Celestial Toymaker: 3	The Dancing Floor	VT/4T/31657
The Celestial Toymaker: 4	The Final Test	VT/4T/32137
The Gunfighters: 1	A Holiday for the Doctor	VT/4T/32032
The Gunfighters: 2	Don't Shoot the Pianist	VT/4T/32205
The Gunfighters: 3	Johnny Ringo	VT/4T/32152
The Gunfighters: 4	The OK Corral	VT/4T/32535

Could the PasB information be wrong? It's possible, but unlikely, as errors on PasB forms were very rare. Film review paperwork for 'The Gunfighters' Episodes One, Two and Three mentions only 35mm comopt inserts, not complete programmes. There is a record of a 35mm telerecording under 'The Gunfighters' Episode Four, but it is a 200 foot insert of the recap.

Could the information on the Retention Authorisation form be wrong? Perhaps whoever filled it in made a mistake, and wrote codes for film down against these episodes, when they actually meant to write videotape codes? Again, it's possible.

Perhaps whoever was making up the retention order was working from the catalogue of Film Library holdings at the time, and all these episodes were listed as being held on 35mm film. But why would that be? One possibility is that all that was actually held for them was a few minutes of telerecorded material from the cliffhanger, to be used as the opening reprise of the following episode. That might explain why only the first three episodes of 'The Celestial Toymaker' are listed, as their closing scenes would have been used for the reprises in Episodes Two, Three and Four. As later evidence will show, at least one episode of 'The Celestial Toymaker' did have such cliffhanger footage held by the Film Library at about this time. But 'The Gunfighters' had Episodes Two, Three and Four listed, which undermines this theory. (The notion that Episode Four could have been film recorded so that its final scenes could be re-used as the opening scenes of 'The Savages' Episode One would appear to be disproved by the fact that the latter episode did not actually feature such a reprise.) Perhaps these were inserts from Episodes One, Two and Three, but as they were used in Episodes Two, Three, and Four, they were now listed under these episodes ...? Admittedly, this is now clutching at straws.

It would be very easy to dismiss this one piece of evidence of these six episodes of 'The Celestial Toymaker' and 'The Gunfighters' existing as 35mm film recordings. However,

CHAPTER 4

there is another piece of corroborating evidence. In November 1976, a list of the BBC Film Library's holdings of *Doctor Who* episodes was drawn up for the makers of the 'Whose Doctor Who' documentary, and a single episode of 'The Gunfighters' was detailed as still existing on film. This was Episode Four of the story, and the listing crucially noted that it was a 35mm ComOpt negative (i.e. a negative with an optical soundtrack) ...

So can we assume that both pieces of information are correct? Is it conceivable that all the episodes of 'The Celestial Toymaker' and 'The Gunfighters' were transmitted from videotape in April and May 1966, and yet by December 1966, when Enterprises issued their retention order including these stories, only 'The Gunfighters' Episode One still existed in that format, with the rest of both stories now surviving as 35mm telerecordings instead (and remember, no mention was made of the fourth episode of 'The Celestial Toymaker' on this retention order)? Well, yes!

Perhaps, sometime between the transmission of these stories in April and May 1966 and December 1966, when the Retention Authorisation forms were issued, something had already happened to the master videotapes of these episodes. Or had something been *scheduled* to happen to them? Perhaps the videotapes of these episodes needed to be wiped, or junked or re-used, or were found to be damaged or faulty in some way. As a stop-gap safeguard, they might have been telerecorded onto 35mm film, until such time as either the Drama Department or Enterprises could give a final ruling on the retention or junking of the material? Admittedly, as theories go, it's a bit of a long shot, but it's one that fits all the facts as they stand.[28]

'The Power of the Daleks' was Patrick Troughton's first outing as the Doctor, and the final episode of this adventure was the next to be made as a 35mm telerecording rather than a two-inch videotape. Afterwards, the 35mm print was sent to the Film Library. The remainder of the episodes of the fourth season were all made and transmitted from videotape.

The final story of the fifth season, 'The Wheel in Space', was shunted between studios during production. The first episode was recorded at Lime Grove Studio D,

---

28 One other theory, which only really accounts for the existence of Episode Four of 'The Gunfighters' on 35mm film, revolves around a well-documented dispute between the story's director, Rex Tucker, and the producer Innes Lloyd. Lloyd requested that a sequence from the final shootout in the episode be removed prior to transmission, but Tucker refused. Lloyd pulled rank, and insisted on the cut, leading Tucker to ask that his name be taken off the final episode. The surviving 16mm print of this episode does indeed have Tucker's name absent from the end credits, although when the print is examined frame by frame, it can be seen that it does appear for just two frames. If a last-minute edit was required on the episode, it would have made sense to have the original version dubbed onto 35mm film from its two-inch tape master in order to undertake the cut. Lloyd's requested edit could then have been easily made, and Tucker's director's credit would have been snipped at the same time too.

WIPED!

Episodes Two to Four were made at Television Centre, while the final two episodes were recorded at Riverside Studios. This may have had some bearing on the fact that, while the first four episodes were made and transmitted on two-inch videotape, the final two were made as 35mm telerecordings (although, having said that, many other episodes allocated to Riverside were recorded on videotape in the usual way).

During the remainder of Patrick Troughton's time in the series, quite a few odd episodes were made and broadcast as 35mm telerecordings, rather than as two-inch videotapes. These were: 'The Dominators' Episode Three, 'The Mind Robber' Episode Five, 'The Krotons' Episode One, 'The Seeds of Death' Episode Five and 'The Space Pirates' Episode Two. All of these episodes were sent to the Film Library after transmission.

Once the production of *Doctor Who* moved into colour with Jon Pertwee's debut season, there was no longer the option of making 35mm film telerecordings of episodes for broadcast, as the process didn't work at all well with colour (although some colour telerecordings of other shows do exist). Additionally, the changeover to colour production saw location filming permanently switch to colour 16mm film stock, as colour 35mm film was prohibitively expensive.

As previously noted, due to a strike at the BBC in late 1969, Jon Pertwee's first story, 'Spearhead from Space', ended up being made totally on location on 16mm colour film. These were the last episodes of *Doctor Who* to be made on film by the BBC.

FILM SEQUENCES

One aspect of production that featured increasingly on *Doctor Who* over the years was the pre-filming of material for inclusion in an episode made on videotape in the television studio. This was usually to allow for extensive location work (as for example on 'The Dalek Invasion of Earth'), or for model and effects shots. Occasionally, studio-based material would be pre-filmed at places like the BBC's Ealing studios, either for ease of editing or because of technical complexity of the required sequence (e.g. a fight scene). 35mm black and white stock was used extensively for these pre-filmed inserts, although 16mm film gradually took over towards the end of the 1960s.

These film sequences (also known as film inserts) would invariably find their way to the Film Library after they had been used in the making of the episodes for which they had been shot. The Library would mostly decide that this material wasn't worth keeping, and the films would be routinely junked just a short time after the parent programme had been completed and screened. But some examples from the 1960s did survive.

The film sequences for the first two episodes of 'The Daleks Masterplan' are examples of this, although those for the first episode were mis-filed for many years. Those for the third episode of 'The War Machines' were junked by the library not

CHAPTER 4

long after the story's BBC1 transmission, but managed to find their way into private collections. The BBC was later able to borrow back some of them to make a copy.

As previously noted, another use of film in the production of *Doctor Who* was the telerecording onto 35mm film of the action from the end of one episode for use as the reprise at the beginning of the next. The reprises were not always done this way, though. Sometimes the cast just re-performed the action from the previous week's cliffhanger.

Some of these 35mm film recordings of cliffhanger scenes also ended up at the Film Library. One such example was the final four minutes of the second episode of 'The Celestial Toymaker' ('The Hall of Dolls'), material from which would have been played into the studio recording of Episode Three as the opening reprise.

At some point during 1967, the 16mm film sequences for the second episode of 'The Abominable Snowmen' found their way to the Film Library for retention. In 1969, some of the 35mm film sequences for the first episode of 'The Space Pirates' were also sent to the Film Library, but were misfiled for a number of years as sequences from *Dad's Army*.

Additionally, the Film Library retained two trailers (one 'short' and one 'long') for 'The Dalek Invasion of Earth' on 16mm black and white film.[29]

JUNKINGS AND LOSSES

As noted in the chapter on the videotape wipings, Wipe/Junk Authorisation forms were sporadically issued by either BBC Enterprises or the BBC Drama Department. These forms signalled that material was no longer required and could be disposed of. The vast majority of the forms related to episodes held on videotape, and videotape had one property that film didn't – the ability to be erased and re-used.

Undoubtedly, some of the impetus behind the wiping of many episodes of *Doctor Who* was the necessity to re-use the videotapes on which they were held. But this didn't apply to film. Any Wipe/Junk Authorisation issued for a programme that existed only

---

29 In the mid-1980s, a 1981 print-out of information from the BBC's Film and Videotape Library was circulated amongst a few *Doctor Who* fans, including this writer. This showed details of film inserts from 'The Power of the Daleks', 'The Moonbase' and 'The Faceless Ones', which seemingly still survived in 1981 but had since been lost. However, the truth was rather different. The details of the BBC's film holdings were being transferred from the old card index system (used up until the late 1970s) into the BBC's first computer index system, and an over-diligent employee had processed some cards for material that had already been junked. The film inserts for these three stories had been destroyed by the BBC many years prior to 1981, but the print-out made it *look* as if this material was still at the Library at that time. This led to some unfounded rumours circulating about the material's survival, and about the BBC apparently continuing to get rid of old footage.

WIPED!

on film would achieve no freeing up of a resource (apart from shelf space). So it's more difficult to rationalise what happened as result of these orders in relation to the episodes transmitted from 35mm film telerecordings.

Aside from the confusing indications as to whether some episodes of 'The Celestial Toymaker' and 'The Gunfighters' were held on film or on videotape, the first mention in the surviving paperwork of the fate of any of the black and white episodes transmitted from 35mm film came when a batch of William Hartnell episodes were earmarked for junking on Friday 31 January 1969. The print of the third episode of 'Planet of Giants' was included in this batch (along with the videotapes of the other episodes of the story). It is almost certain that this 35mm film print was destroyed by the Film Library at this point in time. It's also pretty likely that the 35mm film of Episode Six of 'The Power of the Daleks' had been junked at some point prior to this (again, along with the videotapes of the story's other episodes).

On Monday 21 July 1969, further *Doctor Who* junkings were authorised by Enterprises, and this batch included the 35mm film prints of Episode Five and Episode Six of 'The Wheel in Space', Episode Three of 'The Dominators', Episode Five of 'The Mind Robber', Episode One of 'The Krotons' and Episode Two of 'The Space Pirates'. However, it seems that only Episode Five of 'The Wheel in Space' was actually destroyed as a result of this, with all the others on the list surviving. Later paperwork notes that the 35mm film prints of 'The Seeds of Death' Episode Five and 'The Space Pirates' Episode Two were to be retained specifically for Enterprises' use. This was confirmed by a Retention Authorisation form for these two episodes, raised by Enterprises on Monday 22 September 1969 despite the earlier junking order.

So the summary details of the Film Library's destruction of film-originated *Doctor Who* episodes from the 1960s are as follows:

Episode	Junk Date	Programme No.
The Daleks: 4	Pre-1970	35/T/20398 A & B
Planet of Giants: 3	31/01/69	35/6T/23675
The Dalek Invasion of Earth: 5	NOT JUNKED	35/6T/24329
The Power of the Daleks: 6	Pre-1970	35/6T/35252
The Wheel In Space: 5	21/07/69	35M/6T/44753
The Wheel In Space: 6	NOT JUNKED	35/6T/44894
The Dominators: 3	NOT JUNKED	35M/6T/45251
The Mind Robber: 1	NOT JUNKED	35M/6T/45916
The Krotons: 1	NOT JUNKED	35M/6T/48284
The Seeds of Death: 5	NOT JUNKED	35M/6T/49686
The Space Pirates: 2	NOT JUNKED	35M/6T/50189

CHAPTER 4

If there were ever any 35mm telerecordings of any of the episodes of 'The Celestial Toymaker' or 'The Gunfighters' held at the Film Library, then they aren't mentioned again in any further retention or junking paperwork. Whatever was held must have been junked by 1970, with the possible exception of a 35mm print of Episode Four of 'The Gunfighters' (see the section on *The Lively Arts*: 'Whose Doctor Who').

The upshot of all this is that by 1970, the Film Library would have contained 35mm black and white telerecordings of the following episodes of *Doctor Who*:

The Dalek Invasion of Earth	5
(The Gunfighters	4 – possibly?)
The Wheel in Space	6
The Dominators	3
The Mind Robber	5
The Krotons	1
The Seeds of Death	5
The Space Pirates	2

Plus, the Library would have held the transmission 16mm colour films prints and negatives of all four episodes of Jon Pertwee's debut story, 'Spearhead from Space'.

During the late 1960s and early 1970s, the Film Library would occasionally find itself in possession of 16mm film telerecordings of complete episodes of *Doctor Who* – films that would have originated at Enterprises. How these came to be sent to the Film Library is something that's not completely understood, although several plausible reasons have been suggested.

One theory is that film copies ordered up from Enterprises by various BBC departments over the years would then sometimes be sent to the Film Library in error, rather than be returned to Enterprises. Another possible scenario is that some of these films were returned to the BBC from overseas, and were sent to the Film Library rather than to Enterprises. Sometimes these films were kept, sometimes they were destroyed. Also, 16mm prints were routinely ordered up as viewing copies of programmes by various BBC departments. This was in the pre-portable-video days, when film was the only alternative to replaying material on two-inch tape. Given the high hourly cost of booking a two-inch machine, any way of avoiding this expense was embraced.

A few specific records of *Doctor Who* material that was junked over the years were kept by the Film Library. None of these junkings were dated, but all must have taken place prior to 1976 at the latest (and the junking of the 35mm transmission print of 'The Wheel in Space' Episode Five can certainly be dated to July 1969). These details are:

WIPED!

Episode	Film Library Card Details	What this means…
'The Crusade' Episode One ('The Lion')	F/R 16/4ENT/26305 16 comopt neg: EN10409 – <u>Spare neg (943 ft)</u> JUNKED	The programme number for this episode was VT/4T/26305. The film code here is F/R (for film recording) 16 (16mm) / 4 (from 405 line material) ENT (BBC Enterprises print) / 26305 (the same five-figure code as the VT transmission spool it was made from). The print is further described as 16 (16mm again) comopt (with an optical soundtrack) neg (negative), with the BBC Enterprises library number EN10409. It's identified as a spare neg, and runs to 943 ft (just over 25 minutes). JUNKED speaks for itself…
'The Celestial Toymaker' Episode Two ('The Hall of Dolls'):	T/R 35/4R/31653 35 comopt neg CL13930 (3801 feet) – Junked <u>Film Sequences</u> <u>35 sepmag (150 ft)</u> 35 mute pos: JUNKED 35 mag trk; JUNKED 35 reh pos: JUNKED 35 mute neg: JUNKED <u>Also for programme 1 (628 ft)</u> <u>Film sequences and Trailer</u> <u>35 sepmag – Reel 1 of 2 (400 ft)</u> 35 mute pos: JUNKED 35 mag track: JUNKED	The programme number for this episode was VT/4T/31653. The film code here is T/R (for telerecording) 35 (35mm) / 4 (from 405-line material) R (a code given to a recording not made for direct transmission) 31653 (the five-figure part of the programme number). The print is further described as a 35mm negative with optical soundtrack, and given the library number CL13930. However, the length of the film – 3801 feet – would give a duration of just over 40 minutes to this footage, which is very suspect, given that the episode had a standard

		25-minute transmission slot. Bearing in mind that the longest 35mm film used by the BBC Film Library was 3000 feet, then it's fair to say that this is a misprint on the card. If the duration was actually 380 feet, or 381 feet, then this would be about four minutes, which would be about right for a film of a telerecorded cliffhanger, which of course, wouldn't have been made for direct transmission. The rest of the information on the card is for the various film sequence components for this episode, which were also junked.
'The Power of the Daleks' Episode Six.	T/R 6T/36252 35 sepmag (2236 ft) 35 comopt pos : CL 52091 (OS) Junked 35 mag trk : CL52092 (OS) Junked Film sequences 35 sepmag (350 ft) 35 mute pos: CL 29259 Junked 35 mag trk: CL 29260 Junked 35 mute neg: CL 51881 (273 ft) Junked 35 mute neg: CL 30593 (2293 ft) Junked 35 mute neg: CL 30594 Junked	The programme number of this episode was 35/6T/36252, and so this record is for the 35mm transmission print of this episode. The length – 2236 feet – gives a running time of just under 24 minutes. This 35mm print had both an optical soundtrack (which would have been unsyphered due to the way the film was edited) and a 35mm separate magnetic track, which was probably the fully edited soundtrack. The rest of the information on the card is for the various film sequence components for this episode, which were also junked.

WIPED!

'The Ice Warriors' Episode Three	F/R 16/4ENT/41656 16 mute neg : EN11383 (901ft) junked	As with 'The Lion' above, this is a spare BBC Enterprises film negative, running to just over 24 minutes (901 feet). The Film Library record shows that this was a mute (i.e. silent) negative, although this has to be questionable.
'The Wheel in Space' Episode Five	F/R 35/6T/47753 PL87960 JNK 35 COMPOPT POS 2135 ft PL87961 JNK 35 MAG TRK 2135 ft PL89016 JNK 35 COMOPT NEG 2135 ft RL. 1 OF 2 PL89017 JNK 35 COMPOT NEG RL. 2 OF 2 EN12204 JNK 35 FGDP 2135 ft RL. 1 OF 2 EN12205 JNK 35 FGDP RL. 2 OF 2	The programme number of this episode was 35M/6T/44753, and so this record is for the 35mm transmission print of this episode. This film record is in a different format from the others above. It lists the library number of each element first, followed by the code JNK for Junked. Then is detailed exactly what that element was. So PL87960 was a 35mm positive film print with an unsyphered optical soundtrack that ran to 2135 feet, or just under 23 minutes. There was also the corresponding magnetic soundtrack of mixed programme sound, a 35mm negative split into two reels, and a BBC Enterprises 35mm positive print, split into two reels.

Additionally, a 16mm film copy of Episode Four of 'The Daleks Masterplan' was held by the Film Library until November 1973. It was then borrowed by the *Blue Peter* production team so that a clip from it could be used in their show's celebration of *Doctor Who*'s tenth anniversary, and was never returned, despite numerous requests and memos sent between the Film Library and the *Blue Peter* office. What exactly

CHAPTER 4

happened to this print remains a mystery.

But despite these occasional junkings and losses, more 16mm episodes of *Doctor Who*, probably all originating at Enterprises, began finding their way to the Film Library, whose staff then added them to the permanent archive, as Anne Hanford recalls:

> **Anne Hanford:** The BBC Film Library rarely intentionally made any 16mm black and white film recordings of *Doctor Who* episodes in the 1960s and early 1970s. These were mainly done by BBC Enterprises. However, I know that some episodes of *Doctor Who* came our way on film from other sources during this time. Our policy towards them was quite simple, if never expressly authorised by the management! We knew that the BBC hadn't kept the original two-inch tapes, so if a BBC department sent us an episode it had finished with on 16mm film, we made a deliberate point of archiving it. Sometimes these were duplicates from BBC Enterprises, but we still kept them.

1976 AND 1977

In 1976, work began on production of 'Whose Doctor Who', a documentary about *Doctor Who*, which was to feature in the BBC2 series *The Lively Arts*. In November 1976, the documentary's production team prepared a list of which old *Doctor Who* episodes survived at the BBC at the time, and in which particular archive they were kept (either the BBC Film Library at Windmill Road, or the BBC Enterprises vault at Villiers House). This list gives an indication of what the Film Library's holdings were at that point in time, plus some comments about the subjective quality of the material:

Story	*Film Library*	*What this probably means…*
An Unearthly Child	Episodes 1-4: '*16mm CO*'	All four episodes were held as 16mm black and white film prints with optical soundtracks.
The Dalek Invasion of Earth	Episode 5: '*35 CO*'	Episode Five held as a 35mm black and white film print with optical soundtrack.
The Crusade	Episode 3: '*Very Bad*'	Episode Three held, but the format is unrecorded. The comment 'Very Bad' may refer either to the quality of the print, or to the episode's adjudged suitability as a source for clips for the documentary.

WIPED!

The Chase	Episode 1: 'No Neg'	Probably an overspill of information from the BBC Enterprises column on the list – the episode wasn't actually at the Film Library.
Galaxy 4	Episode 2: 'No Neg'	Again, almost certainly an overspill of information from the BBC Enterprises column on the list – the episode wasn't actually at the Film Library.
The Daleks Masterplan	Episode 2: 'Film Seqs Only' Episode 4: 'Lost'	The film sequences for Episode Two were held, but the format is not recorded. A complete print of Episode Four was supposed to be held, but was missing.
The Gunfighters	Episode 4: '35 CO neg'	Episode Four held as a 35mm black and white film negative with optical soundtrack. Yes, 35mm!
The Faceless Ones	Episode 1: '16 CO neg'	Episode One held as a 16mm black and white film negative with optical soundtrack.
The Enemy of the World	Episode 3: '16 CO'	This episode is seemingly listed as being held by *both* BBC Enterprises *and* the Film Library. However, the notes in the BBC Enterprises column are probably just an overspill from the Film Library information. This episode was probably held at the Film Library only.
The Wheel in Space	Episode 6: '35 comopt'	Episode Six held as a 35mm black and white film print with optical soundtrack.

CHAPTER 4

The Dominators	Episode 3: '35 CO'	Episode Three held as a 35mm black and white film print with optical soundtrack.
The Mind Robber	Episode 5: '35 CO'	Episode Five held as a 35mm black and white film print with optical soundtrack.
The Krotons	Episode 1: '35 CO pos'	Episode One held as a 35mm black and white film print with optical soundtrack. Defined as a positive print (rather than a negative), but it can't be assumed that the omission of the word 'pos' in the other listings automatically means they were held as negatives.
The Seeds of Death	Episode 5: '35 CO pos'	Episode Five held as a 35mm black and white film print (positive) with optical soundtrack.
The Space Pirates	Episode 2: '35 mute pos'	Episode Two held as a 35mm black and white film print (positive), but with no soundtrack.
Spearhead from Space	Episode 1: '35 mag + pos col' Episodes 2-4: '16 col pos + mag'	The listing states that Episode One was held as a 35mm colour film print positive with a separate magnetic soundtrack, which is totally inaccurate (although the new title sequence material *was* held on 35mm, and logged under this story for many years, which may be where the confusion stemmed from). Episodes Two, Three and Four were held as 16mm colour positive film prints with separate magnetic soundtracks.

WIPED!

Doctor Who and the Silurians	Episodes 6-7: '16 col pos + mag (sequences)'	The film sequences for Episodes Six and Seven were held as 16mm colour positive film prints, with separate magnetic soundtracks.
Inferno	Episode 1: 'film sequences?'	The film sequences for Episode One may have been held. The question mark written next to this listing casts doubt as to the certainty of this material existing at the time. Although unrecorded on the paperwork, these would have been on 16mm colour film.
The Three Doctors	Episodes 2-4: 'film sequences'	The film sequences for Episodes Two, Three and Four were held. Although unrecorded, these would have been on 16mm colour film.
Frontier in Space	Episodes 1-2: 'sequences 16 cl mt neg'	The film sequences for Episodes One and Two were held as 16mm colour negatives, which had no soundtrack on them (hence mute).
Planet of the Daleks	Episodes 1, 3-6: 'film seqs'	The film sequences for Episodes One, Three, Four, Five and Six were held. Although unrecorded, these would have been on 16mm colour film. It seems from this point in the listing, the compiler made no reference to the film being colour or being 16mm, probably because these were taken for granted for the later material.
The Time Warrior	Part 4: 'film seqs'	The film sequences for Part Four were held on 16mm colour film.

CHAPTER 4

Invasion of the Dinosaurs	Parts 1-3: *'film seqs + print'* Parts 4-6: *'film seqs'*	The film sequences for all six episodes were held on 16mm colour film. Although open to interpretation, the listing seems to imply that 16mm black and white film telerecordings for Parts One, Two and Three were held by the Film Library as well.
Death to the Daleks	Parts 1-4: *'film seqs'*	The film sequences for all four episodes were held on 16mm colour film.
The Monster of Peladon	Parts 1-6: *'film seqs'*	The film sequences for all six episodes were held on 16mm colour film.
Planet of the Spiders	Parts 1-2: *'film seqs'*	The film sequences for Parts One and Two were held on 16mm colour film.
The Ark in Space	Part 1: *'film seqs'*	The film sequences for Part One were held on 16mm colour film.
Genesis of the Daleks	Parts 1-4: *'film seqs'*	The film sequences for Parts One, Two, Three and Four were held on 16mm colour film.
Revenge of the Cybermen	Parts 1-4: *'film seqs'*	The film sequences for all four episodes were held on 16mm colour film.
Planet of Evil	Parts 1-4: *'film seqs'*	The film sequences for all four episodes were held on 16mm colour film.
Pyramids of Mars	Parts 1-4: *'film seqs'*	The film sequences for all four episodes were held on 16mm colour film.
The Android Invasion	Parts 2+4: *'film seqs'*	The film sequences for Parts Two and Four were held on 16mm colour film.

WIPED!

Although there is no reason to doubt the details relating to the various film sequences held at this point in time by the Film Library, the rest of the details on this listing are open to some debate. This will be examined in full in the chapter on 'Whose Doctor Who' later in the book. But for now, the listing is notable for giving a rough approximation of the relatively small amount of *Doctor Who* material held by the Film Library at this point in time. Most of the film sequences would end up being junked within a few years – as was the standard BBC practice for programme components when the whole transmitted programme also survived in the archives.

Barely 12 months after the 'Whose Doctor Who' team had drawn up their list, there was another audit of the Library's holdings. This came about because the BBC began making private sales of episodes of *Doctor Who*, and initially offered copies of the ones held at Windmill Road. The story of these sales will be told in a later chapter. But for now, suffice to say that the details of the full holdings of William Hartnell and Patrick Troughton episodes at the BBC Film Library at Windmill Road as listed in 1977 were as follows (with a blank entry against a title indicating no holdings for that story):

Story	Film Library
An Unearthly Child	Episodes 1-4 (all 16mm)
The Daleks	
The Edge of Destruction	
Marco Polo	
The Keys of Marinus	Episode 5 (16mm)
The Aztecs	
The Sensorites	
The Reign of Terror	
Planet of Giants	
The Dalek Invasion of Earth	Episode 5 (35mm)
The Rescue	
The Romans	Episodes 1 & 3 (both 16mm)
The Web Planet	Episode 2 (16mm)
The Crusade	Episode 3 (16mm)
The Space Museum	Episode 3 (16mm)
The Chase	
The Time Meddler	Episode 2 (16mm)
Galaxy 4	
Mission to the Unknown	
The Myth Makers	
The Daleks Masterplan	
The Massacre	
The Ark	Episode 3 (16mm)
The Celestial Toymaker	
The Gunfighters	Episode 4 (16mm)

CHAPTER 4

The Savages	
The War Machines	
The Smugglers	
The Tenth Planet	Episodes 1-3 (all 16mm)
The Power of the Daleks	
The Highlanders	
The Underwater Menace	Episode 3 (16mm)
The Moonbase	Episodes 2 & 4 (both 16mm)
The Macra Terror	
The Faceless Ones	Episode 1 (16mm)
The Evil of the Daleks	
The Tomb of the Cybermen	
The Abominable Snowmen	
The Ice Warriors	
The Enemy of the World	Episode 3 (16mm)
The Web of Fear	
Fury from the Deep	
The Wheel in Space	Episode 6 (35mm)
The Dominators	Episodes 1, 2, 4, 5 (all 16mm)
The Mind Robber	Episode 5 (35mm)
The Invasion	Episodes 2, 3, 5-8 (All 16mm)
The Krotons	Episode 1 (35mm), Episodes 2 & 3 (16mm)
The Seeds of Death	Episodes 1, 2, 4, 6 (all 16mm, Episode 2 'fine grain'), Episode 5 (35mm)
The Space Pirates	Episode 2 (35mm)
The War Games	Episodes 2, 5, 8, 9 (all 16mm)

A lot had seemingly changed at the Film Library since the previous list was compiled. From the programme's first season, a 16mm print of 'The Keys of Marinus' Episode Five had turned up. From the second, Episodes One and Three of 'The Romans' had also appeared, where only Enterprises had Episode One before. Episode Two of 'The Web Planet' and Episode Two of 'The Time Meddler' had made their way to the Film Library at this point as well. From the third season, 'The Ark' Episode Three had arrived, while the 35mm print of 'The Gunfighters' Episode Four had now become a 16mm print[30]. From Season Four, the first three episodes of 'The Tenth Planet' had seemingly been sent from Enterprises, who were listed as having them in 1976, although perhaps the details were simply entered into the wrong column in the 'Whose Doctor Who' report.

For Patrick Troughton's Doctor, 'The Underwater Menace' Episode Three had

---

30 I can't offer any explanation for this, other than that the film might not have been 35mm in the first place, and is only now correctly identified as 16mm.

WIPED!

appeared from nowhere, as had 'The Moonbase' Episode Two – Episode Four was apparently held by Enterprises in 1976, but had passed to the Film Library in the intervening time. The details listed for Season Five were unchanged, but there had been lots of additions of episodes from Season Six. Perhaps these had also come from Enterprises in the previous year?

Now, let us examine what was going on at Enterprises, who had begun making 16mm film copies of *Doctor Who* episodes in 1963 …

CHAPTER 5
BBC ENTERPRISES: VILLIERS HOUSE

BBC Enterprises was set up by the BBC in 1960 to act as the BBC's commercial division, handling the small number of requests that came in from outside companies seeking to obtain merchandise licences for such programmes as *Andy Pandy* and *Muffin the Mule*. It superseded a department called BBC Exploitation, run almost single-handedly by a man named Roy Williams. Enterprises would also occasionally publish books based on BBC programmes, or issue LP records of some of its best-loved radio shows. It was also, from its inception, the division responsible for selling copies of the BBC's programmes to overseas broadcasters, thereby generating revenue that could be ploughed back into programme-making. The BBC had made occasional forays into the overseas sales arena in the 1950s, but the refinement of its telerecording technology and the introduction of two-inch videotape in the later years of that decade meant that, by 1960, it could begin to offer its television programmes to more and more foreign stations, many of which were significantly behind the UK, technology-wise, when it came to broadcasting.

SALES FORMATS

The biggest problem for the BBC in terms of overseas sales was that of the differing television formats and standards in its potential foreign markets. In the early 1960s, the BBC was broadcasting 405-line black and white pictures, at 25 fps (frames per second). But it was also gearing up for the launch of BBC2 in 1964, initially as a 625-line black and white service, again with pictures broadcast at 25 fps. Inevitably, it would be looking to sell programmes made in both of these formats.

Some of the countries that Enterprises looked to sell programmes to also used one of these two systems. But not many used both. And countries such as Canada, America and Japan used a third system altogether, with a 525-line black and white picture running at 29.97 fps. And as if all that that wasn't confusing enough, colour television was just around the corner ...

The easiest way that Enterprises found to get around these format and compatibility issues was to sell their programmes not on videotape at all, but as 16mm black and white film prints. Unlike videotape, film could be screened by every television station in every country around the world, regardless of line structure and frame rate of their own systems.

The way that the BBC made these telerecordings of its programmes was really quite ingenious. Film had a standard running speed throughout the world, which was 24 fps. To overcome the difference between this and the 25 fps speed of the BBC's television pictures was extremely problematical. Had they simply recorded the 25 fps television picture onto film running at 24 fps, this would have resulted in flickery, strobing film recordings that would have been virtually unwatchable. What they instead did was to increase the speed of their film recorders, so that they now ran at 25 fps. When programmes were now recorded to film, every pair of video fields was captured onto a single frame of film at 25 fps.

This worked perfectly for overseas sales purposes. If the film copy of the programme was sold to a country that used the same 25 fps video system, then they would simply play it back on their telecine equipment at 25 frames per second, exactly as the BBC would. Countries using 29.97 fps (59.94 fields per second) video systems, on the other hand, would play it with their telecine running at 23.98 fps. Using a system of repeating every fifth field coming off the film (known as 3:2 pulldown), the telecine produced a 29.97 fps video signal, even though the film itself was running at 23.98 fps. The programme would play back approximately 4% slower than the BBC transmission and the sound would be pitched down by a corresponding amount, around a semitone. Generally only viewers with perfect pitch might notice this slight shift; for the majority it would be unnoticeable.[31]

TELERECORDING

The telerecording process works by using a film camera that records at 25 fps (frames per second) linked to a specially adapted flat television screen, onto which the programme plays out from its videotape master recording or from a live broadcast. The film camera records the output of the flat screen at the same 25 fps rate, synchronised to the video frame of the television signal.

---

31 A quick note to try to explain the whole 60 versus 59.94, 30 versus 29.97 thing. Basically, the video standard was based around the prevailing mains frequency at the time television was developed – so 50 Hz in the UK and 60 Hz in the US. The original US television transmissions were at 60 Hz, but when colour capability was bolted on in the mid '50s, it was discovered that the chosen colour subcarrier frequency of 3.58 MHz could, under certain conditions, beat with the FM audio carrier to produce stationary dot patterns on the screen. Two options were available – change the field frequency or change the FM audio carrier frequency. The latter was discounted, because it risked introducing an incompatibility with existing monochrome receivers, which would cause loss of audio. However, there was much more latitude in the television scanning systems. With the field rate slightly reduced to 59.94 fps, the dot patterns were no longer fixed and were lost in the random movement of on-screen action, and compatibility with monochrome receivers was maintained. Given the problems this field rate reduction would cause in the following years (particularly in the area of conversion between various worldwide video standards), many would argue that the wrong choice was made!

CHAPTER 5

The BBC had been recording live transmissions onto film since the late 1940s, as a way of preserving copies of their programmes. But with the advent of videotape, the process could be adapted, with the film recorders linked to a two-inch machine.

The equipment required for such an operation was detailed in the very first BBC Engineering Monograph, entitled *The Suppressed Frame System of Telerecording*. Written by C B B Wood, A V Lord, E R Rout and R F Vigurs, it was published by the BBC Engineering Division in June 1955.

Bearing in mind that this was written some *three years* before the BBC's first experimentation with either the VERA video system or the introduction of two-inch videotape in 1958, the paper demonstrated an impressively full working knowledge of the detailed equipment needed to make a telerecording suite. This was:

a) Two film recording machines. One machine was to be reloaded with film, whilst the other was kept in operation. Film recording could then be switched between each machine without having to stop or pause the videotape playback.
b) Videotape playback equipment.
c) A picture control desk to allow for the monitoring and adjustment of the videotape replay levels during the recording
d) A video control bay containing equipment for the correction of the frequency and amplitude of the video signal
e) A sound control bay allowing for the monitoring and adjustment of the programme's audio levels
f) Two sound amplifiers

When these telerecording machines were eventually constructed, all of this equipment was incorporated (with some refinement) into a huge self-contained unit – apart from the videotape playback equipment, which was always separate[32]. At one end was the video input, which could be linked to either a studio feed or a videotape machine. This in turn was connected to a flat television monitor pointed towards the middle of the unit. This television picture display area was fed by a 12 inch cathode ray tube, and used a piece of equipment known as a time base corrector to stabilise the picture's signal, ensuring a smooth playback.

Also located towards the middle of the unit was a fixed position 16mm film

---

32 The film recorders were always standalone units. The input was a video signal – originally a live feed from studio, then in later years a feed from the VT area if they were recording from tape. The VT and FR areas were not in the same place, indeed at Television Centre they weren't even on the same floor.

camera, with its lens aimed squarely at the flat television monitor. On top of this camera was a magazine for holding the raw 16mm film stock, with reels for two film spools – one to feed the film through the gate of the camera, and one to take it up after it had been exposed. At the other end of the unit were all the main controls, switches, dials and monitoring equipment.

The sound of the videotaped programme was recorded at the same time onto the 16mm film, fed into the film recorder directly from the VT machine. The 16mm film stock used to make telerecordings had perforations running down only one edge. Where you'd normally expect the corresponding set of perforations to be on the other edge of the film was instead the area where the sound was captured. This was known as an optical soundtrack. This area of the film was 'read' by a beam of light when replayed, and reproduced the programme's mono soundtrack (which was the only television sound system in use at the time). All *Doctor Who* 16mm film prints made by Enterprises had the programme's soundtrack recorded onto the film in this manner.

The sound was always recorded 16 frames behind the picture it accompanied. This was because the sound head had to be slightly offset from the picture gate in film projectors and players – they both couldn't be in exactly the same place. So the sound was physically recorded slightly behind the accompanying picture, but when played back, it would be in perfect sync.

FRAME RATES AND FIELDS

In the early 1960s, the BBC's television standard was the 405-line system. Of these 405 lines, only 377 horizontal lines made up the actual picture; the other 28 contained pulses used by the television receiver to synchronise the system – ensuring that the start of the picture appeared at the top of the screen, rather than halfway down it etc. Somewhat confusingly to the layperson, although the picture is made up of 377 horizontal lines, this is known as the vertical resolution – i.e. the number of lines that you would cross travelling vertically down the picture.

Ideally, a television receiver would draw line 1, then line 2, and so on all the way down to line 377, then fly back to the top of the picture and draw the next frame in the same way. However, with a frame rate of 25 fps, this would have produced an unacceptable level of flicker on the cathode ray tube displays of the time. Rather than increase the frame rate, engineers decided to use an interlaced system, in which the frame would be broken down into two 'fields' of 188.5 lines each and written out to the screen in two passes. The first pass writes all the odd numbered horizontal lines onto the screen, then the second pass, 1/50th of a second later, writes all the even numbered lines into the gaps between the odd-numbered lines. The half-lines mean that field one starts halfway along the top of the picture and field two ends halfway along the bottom.

CHAPTER 5

If the image is from a frame-based source such as a film print, then both fields of the television picture originate from the same point in time (because the image was captured onto a single frame of film), although they are displayed 1/50th of a second apart. A moving object, for example a football, would be in the same position in both fields. However, if the image is from a field-based source such as a live video camera, then the fields originate 1/50 of a second apart *and* are displayed 1/50th of a second apart. The aforementioned football would be in a different position in field two than in field one. This distinction is known as temporal resolution and is fundamental to the difference in look between film- and video-sourced material on television. The temporal resolution of pictures originating from film is 1/25th of a second, whereas that of pictures from a video camera is 1/50th of a second. This explains the visible motion differences observed between a transmission of, say, a movie and the more fluid 'live video' look of a studio chat show.

Telerecording video signals in a way that allowed the film to clearly capture the full television image was not easy. Half the battle was won by having the film run at 25 fps, when the television picture also ran at this frame rate. But the time taken physically to move the film on by one frame and stop it so the gate (the part of the camera that exposes a frame of film to the image it's capturing) could be opened was much longer than the vertical blanking interval between the two fields – i.e. the time difference between the last line of one field being displayed, and the first of the next. If this problem wasn't corrected, then the film would still be moving through the gate when the next field to be displayed was starting to appear on the television screen. The film couldn't be speeded up to get it into position in time (as this would throw out the 25 fps speed, which was critical to the process working), and so other solutions were needed.

SUPPRESSED FIELD RECORDINGS

The first solution the BBC adopted to get around this problem was to make Suppressed Field telerecordings (also known as Skip Field recordings) – the method used for the first batch of *Doctor Who* episodes to be done in 1963 and 1964. The television monitor in the telerecording equipment was set so that it displayed either only field one or only field two of a normal 377-line picture. This was achieved by the use of a special control unit that emitted a pulse to blank out the tube display for one of the fields during the pulldown time of each frame of film in the camera. One side-effect of this was that no shutter mechanism was required in the camera. The blanking pulse for the blackout unit was physically generated by the film camera itself, whenever it was running, which meant that the television picture being captured was now truly updated just 25 times a second, not 50. But as only one field was ever displayed on the television monitor, then the film camera could see only lines 1, 3, 5, 7, 9, 11, 13 … etc, of the television picture, or only lines 2, 4, 6, 8, 10, 12, 14 … etc, depending on whether the odd or the even fields were being blanked.

So, in effect, the resultant recording made onto the 16mm film wasn't of a 377-line television image, but of a 188.5-line television image. The images captured using this Suppressed Field system were therefore of a comparatively low resolution. The line structure of the picture was quite apparent to the naked eye, objects with smooth edges now looked slightly jagged on screen, and any on-screen movement could appear quite jerky.

STORED FIELD RECORDINGS

Within a few years of *Doctor Who* being first telerecorded by Enterprises, the BBC had switched to another system of telerecording altogether, that of Stored Field recordings.

This was a considerable improvement on the Suppressed Field system, in that it did not involve the blanking out of fields. Instead, the image sent to the television monitor within the telerecording equipment was altered slightly. The first field of each video frame was displayed at a much higher intensity than the second. This meant that when a frame of film in the gate of the film camera was exposed to the screen, the luminosity of the phosphor of the first field's image had decayed to match exactly that of the second field's image. So now the two fields appeared to be displayed simultaneously and at the same luminance level to the film camera.

This process was aided by another innovation called 'spot wobble'. The lines making up each field of video were 'written' onto the television screen by an electron beam – effectively, a moving spot – starting at the top of the screen and finishing at the bottom, and all done in $1/50^{th}$ of a second. The addition of a high frequency – but low voltage – sine wave to the vertical deflection plate of the television screen gave the moving spot a more elongated oval shape. While this 'wobble' made the image on the screen slightly more blurred than normal, it helped remove the visible line structure, and prevented moiré patterns appearing on screen when the film was subsequently rebroadcast.

Most importantly, the Stored Field telerecording system allowed television images to be captured at their full 377-line resolution, removing all the inherent resolution problems of the Suppressed Field recordings.

When it came to the later Patrick Troughton *Doctor Who* stories, which were made using the BBC's new 625-line equipment – which had 576 lines of active picture area – the resolution of the telerecordings would improve still further.

CHAPTER 5

OUT-OF-PHASE FILM INSERTS

One new problem inherent in the Stored Field telerecording method was to do with how it captured any images from the videotape master of a programme that had originally been shot on film.

When location work was done for 1960s *Doctor Who*, either 16mm or 35mm film was used to capture the sequences required, shot at the television standard rate of 25 fps. When these sequences came to be edited into the finished programme, the film was telecined onto two-inch videotape (either 405-line up to 1967, or 625-line from 1968 onwards), which was running at 50 fields a second. Ideally, field one and field two of any given frame of the video image should both capture information from the same frame of film. However, this was not always the case.

For many years, the telecines used by the BBC used a simple field servo. This meant that as they were starting up, they would slightly slip the speed of the film until the top of a film frame sychronised with the top of a video field – achieving what was known as a 'lock'. 50% of the time it provided the ideal situation where a frame of film was recorded in fields one and two of the same video frame – in which case the insert was said to be in-phase. But it also meant that 50% of the time a frame of film was captured in field two of one video frame and field one of the next – producing an out-of-phase insert. To a viewer watching the output of the telecine or the videotape made from it on transmission, the results would appear identical. The eye has no sensitivity to temporal phase. However, it was a very bad situation for any subsequent telerecording.

Ideally, one frame of a film insert in the programme would be transferred to one frame of the film recording, which would be the case with an in-phase insert. Unfortunately, an out-of-phase insert would result in each frame of the insert appearing on two frames of the film recording. Or, to put it another way, each frame of the film recording would contain a blend of images from two consecutive frames of the film insert. This would result in noticeable double-imaging of moving objects.

Out-of-phase inserts plague a good number of the surviving *Doctor Who* 16mm telerecordings. It's one of the technical problems that has, to date, proved almost impossible to correct when remastering the telerecordings for DVD release.

But enough of all this technical gubbins. Let's get back to BBC Enterprises …

VILLIERS HOUSE

Thanks to the system of telerecording to film, the BBC had the equipment it needed to make film copies of its programmes, which could then be sold to overseas broadcasters. From 1960, these sales were handled by the Television Sales and Production Operations Department of Enterprises, based in a building called Villiers House in Ealing, located

WIPED!

directly above Ealing Broadway Station.

It was this department that was responsible for deciding that *Doctor Who* was a suitable programme for potential overseas sales in the first place, back in 1963. As such, it made the initial arrangements to have the videotape masters of each episode from 'An Unearthly Child' Episode One onwards telerecorded onto 16mm black and white film.

The first batch of 16mm Suppressed Field telerecordings of William Hartnell's *Doctor Who* episodes were generally made within a few weeks of each episode's BBC1 transmission, if not actually at the time of broadcast. The actual instruction to make each telerecording was issued by a film recording clerk at Enterprises, and the scant paperwork that survives shows that in most instances this was Pamela Nash.

Once the 16mm film prints of any given *Doctor Who* episode had been made for overseas sales, they were then sent to Villiers House. The building wasn't designed for large-scale film storage, but a small number of rooms and offices had been fitted out with Dexion racking, and the 16mm films were stored on these racks, from floor to ceiling.

ORDERING THE TELERECORDINGS

As already discussed, Enterprises issued Retention Authorisation forms on a regular basis for any programmes of which they wanted to order 16mm film recordings. These were sent to the BBC's Engineering Department, who looked after all the two-inch transmission tapes in the 1960s. Occasionally, the forms would also be sent to the Film Library, which housed the odd *Doctor Who* episode that had been transmitted from 35mm film. The purpose of the forms was to ensure that Enterprises had the opportunity to arrange the production of 16mm telerecordings of the material they required for overseas sales – in this case every episode of *Doctor Who* (except, probably, the seventh episode of 'The Daleks Masterplan' ('The Feast of Steven')) – before the transmission tapes were junked or re-used.

The dates on which these Retention Authorisation forms were issued give a good indication of when Enterprises made some of their 16mm film prints. Sadly, the surviving records are not complete. But this may be because a lot of *Doctor Who* telerecordings were made at the time of the episode's broadcast on BBC1. In such cases, there would be no need to ask for the videotape of the episode to be kept in order to make a telerecording at a later date. Listed below are details of the surviving authorisation requests, which begin with Episode Two of 'The Power of the Daleks':

CHAPTER 5

Date	Story / Episode	Notes
09/11/66	The Power of the Daleks: Episode Two	Issued three days before BBC1 tx
18/11/66	The Power of the Daleks: Episode Three	Issued one day before BBC1 tx
25/11/66	The Power of the Daleks: Episode Four	Issued one day before BBC1 tx
05/12/66	The Power of the Daleks: Episode Five	Issued one day before BBC1 tx
05/12/66	The Power of the Daleks: Episode Six	Issued eight days before BBC1 tx (for 35mm)
16/12/66	Pilot Episode – An Unearthly Child An Unearthly Child: All The Daleks: All The Edge of Destruction: All Marco Polo: All The Keys of Marinus: All The Aztecs: All The Sensorites: All The Reign of Terror: All Planet of the Giants: All The Dalek Invasion of Earth: Episodes One – Five The Rescue: All The Romans: All The Web Planet: All The Crusade: All The Space Museum: All The Chase: All The Time Meddler: All Galaxy 4: All Mission to the Unknown The Myth Makers: All The Daleks Masterplan: All The Massacre: All The Ark: All The Celestial Toymaker: Episodes One – Three The Gunfighters: All	All these retention forms were issued for two-inch videotapes, apart from 'The Daleks' Episode Four, 'The Dalek Invasion of Earth' Episode Five, 'The Celestial Toymaker' Episodes One to Three and 'The Gunfighters' Episodes Two to Four, which were all issued for 35mm films. (The episodes of 'The Gunfighters' and 'The Celestial Toymaker' mentioned were all made on two-inch tape according to all other BBC paperwork. Conversely, 'Planet of Giants' Episode Three was shown from 35mm film, and not two-inch tape.) Seemingly no retention sheets were issued for 'The Dalek Invasion of Earth' Episode Six or 'The Celestial Toymaker' Episode Four. These retention forms were almost certainly issued so that new, Stored

WIPED!

		Field 16mm telerecordings could be made of all these episodes, to replace the 16mm Suppressed Field copies made originally for BBC Enterprises.
16/12/66	The Highlanders: Episode One	Issued one day prior to BBC1 tx
19/12/66	The Highlanders: Episode Two	Issued five days prior to BBC1 tx
09/01/67	The Highlanders: Episode Three	Issued nine days after BBC1 tx

It would appear that from 1967 onwards, Enterprises' system altered slightly. Instead of the Retention Authorisation forms being given a specific date, they were now issued by week. They were then in most cases annotated by hand with a date, which presumably is the date when the 16mm telerecording was actually made of that particular episode.

Week	Story / Episode	Handwritten Date	Notes
2/67	The Highlanders: Episode Four	-	
3/67	The Underwater Menace: Episode One	-	
4/67	The Underwater Menace: Episode Two	02/02/67	Telerecording made 19 days after BBC1 tx
5/67	The Underwater Menace: Episode Three	01/03/67	Telerecording made 31 days after BBC1 tx
6/67	The Underwater Menace: Episode Four	01/03/67	Telerecording made 24 days after BBC1 tx
7/67	The Moonbase: Episode One	01/03/67	Telerecording made 17 days after BBC1 tx
8/67	The Moonbase: Episode Two	01/03/67	Telerecording made ten days after BBC1 tx
9/67	The Moonbase: Episode Three	01/03/67	Telerecording made three days after BBC1 tx
10/67	The Moonbase: Episode Four	01/03/67	Telerecording made three days before BBC1 tx
11/67	The Macra Terror: Episode One	13/03/67	Telerecording made two days after BBC1 tx

CHAPTER 5

12/67	The Macra Terror: Episode Two	23/03/67	Telerecording made five days after BBC1 tx
13/67	The Macra Terror: Episode Three	23/03/67	Telerecording made two days before BBC1 tx
14/67	The Macra Terror: Episode Four	14/04/67	Telerecording made 13 days after BBC1 tx
19/67	The Faceless Ones: Episode One The Faceless Ones: Episode Two The Faceless Ones: Episode Three The Faceless Ones: Episode Four The Faceless Ones: Episode Five The Faceless Ones: Episode Six	-	Week 19 was w/c 08/05/67, which was the week after Episode Five of this story was screened, leading up to the Saturday of Episode Six's tx. The story was therefore retained as a 'job lot'.
	The Evil of the Daleks: Episodes One - Seven		No forms were apparently raised for this story at this time.
36/67	The Tomb of the Cybermen: Episode One	18/09/67	Telerecording made 16 days after BBC1 tx
37/67	The Tomb of the Cybermen: Episode Two	09/10/67	Telerecording made 30 days after BBC1 tx
38/67	The Tomb of the Cybermen: Episode Three	09/10/67	Telerecording made 23 days after BBC1 tx
39/67	The Tomb of the Cybermen: Episode Four	11/10/67	Telerecording made 18 days after BBC1 tx
40/67	The Abominable Snowmen: Episode One	03/11/67	Telerecording made 34 days after BBC1 tx
41/67	The Abominable Snowmen: Episode Two	08/01/68	Telerecording made 93 days after BBC1 tx

WIPED!

42/67	The Abominable Snowmen: Episode Three	08/01/68	Telerecording made 86 days after BBC1 tx
43/67	The Abominable Snowmen: Episode Four	08/01/68	Telerecording made 79 days after BBC1 tx
44/67	The Abominable Snowmen: Episode Five	08/01/68	Telerecording made 72 days after BBC1 tx
45/67	The Abominable Snowmen: Episode Six	08/01/68	Telerecording made 65 days after BBC1 tx
46/67	The Ice Warriors: Episode One	07/02/68	Telerecording made 88 days after BBC1 tx
47/67	The Ice Warriors: Episode Two	07/02/68	Telerecording made 81 days after BBC1 tx
48/67	The Ice Warriors: Episode Three	29/02/68	Telerecording made 95 days after BBC1 tx
49/67	The Ice Warriors: Episode Four	29/02/68	Telerecording made 88 days after BBC1 tx
50/67	The Ice Warriors: Episode Five	29/02/68	Telerecording made 81 days after BBC1 tx
51/67	The Ice Warriors: Episode Six	29/02/68	Telerecording made 74 days after BBC1 tx
52/67	The Enemy of the World: Episode One	01/03/68	Telerecording made 68 days after BBC1 tx
	The Enemy of the World: Episodes Two - Six		No forms were apparently raised for these episodes at this time.
	The Web of Fear: Episode One		No form was apparently raised for this episode at this time.
-	The Web of Fear: Episode Two	04/04/68	Telerecording made 54 days after BBC1 tx

CHAPTER 5

-	The Web of Fear: Episode Three	04/04/68	Telerecording made 47 days after BBC1 tx
-	The Web of Fear: Episode Four	04/04/68	Telerecording made 40 days after BBC1 tx
-	The Web of Fear: Episode Five	04/04/68	Telerecording made 33 days after BBC1 tx
-	The Web of Fear: Episode Six	04/04/68	Telerecording made 26 days after BBC1 tx
-	Fury From the Deep: Episode One	04/04/68	Telerecording made 19 days after BBC1 tx

During this time, no retention orders were apparently issued for any of the seven episodes of 'The Evil of the Daleks', 'The Enemy of the World' Episodes Two to Six or the first episode of 'The Web of Fear'. Or, if there were, the paperwork no longer survives. 'Fury from the Deep' Episode One is the last episode to appear on this run of paperwork – there is no mention of any retention order being made for the rest of the episodes of that story, or for those of the final story of the season, 'The Wheel in Space'.

The next batch of retention orders that Enterprises issued for *Doctor Who* went back to the system of having specific dates on them, and referred to episodes from a couple of years earlier:

Date	*Story / Episode*	*Notes on the paperwork*
17/06/68	The Tenth Planet: Episode Four	Hold for Enterprises possible Future Sales
01/08/68	The Evil of the Daleks: Episode One The Evil of the Daleks: Episode Two The Evil of the Daleks: Episode Three The Evil of the Daleks: Episode Four The Evil of the Daleks: Episode Five The Evil of the Daleks: Episode Six The Evil of the Daleks: Episode Seven	Hold all programmes in this series for possible future sales

The last piece of surviving Retention Authorisation paperwork from Enterprises in the 1960s was seemingly issued as a response to a Wipe/Junk Authorisation form that the BBC Drama department issued on 21 July 1969, which saw most of the Patrick

WIPED!

Troughton stories from 'The Underwater Menace' to 'The Space Pirates' cleared for destruction. For some reason, Enterprises decided to spare just three of these episodes on 22 September 1969:

Date	Story / Episode	Notes
22/09/69	The Seeds of Death: Episode Four The Seeds of Death: Episode Five The Space Pirates: Episode Two	The first episode was held on two-inch tape, the other two were on 35mm film

These are the last retention forms for the black and white episodes of *Doctor Who*. Apart from the three episodes mentioned above, nothing more has come to light for the stories from 'The Wheel in Space' to 'The War Games'.

SALES CONTRACTS

When it came to overseas sales of *Doctor Who*, just what could BBC Enterprises sell, and to whom, and for how long? The answers to these questions are to be found in most of the BBC contracts that the writers for the series had to sign. As well as covering terms of payment, repeat fees and so on, these set out the BBC's terms and conditions for any overseas sales of the writer's programmes. Here are the relevant passages (sections (3) and (4)) from a typical 1960s BBC writer's contact. (All spelling and punctuation are as on the original.):

> 3) During a period of 6 months from the date of the initial BBC performance of the last of the scripts the EXCLUSIVE RIGHT TO ACQUIRE AN EXCLUSIVE OPTION (which may be taken up during a period of one year from the date of the initial BBC performance) to PURCHASE THE RIGHT TO TELEVISE OR TO LICENCE THE WORK TO BE TELEVISED IN ANY OVERSEAS COUNTRY subject to payment of a fee (which shall not be returnable in any event and which shall be set off against any subsequent payments due in respect of overseas sales under (4) below) to be calculated at the discretion of the BBC in either the following ways:-
>
> For an option for world rights   4% of the initial BBC fee
> For an option on particular countries only   25% of the fee which would be payable under (4) below if the option for those particular countries is taken up by the BBC
>
> 4) In respect of those countries for which the BBC has taken up an exclusive

option acquired in accordance with (3) above the EXCLUSIVE RIGHT TO TELEVISE OR TO LICENCE A RECORDING OF THE WORK TO BE TELEVISED during a period of five years from the date of the initial BBC performance of the last of the scripts without restriction as to the number of transmissions, subject to payment to the Writer of the amounts specified below on such right being taken up by the BBC within one year from the date of the initial BBC performance of the last of the scripts:-

i) USA and its dependant territories	100% of initial fee
ii) Canada	35% of initial fee
iii) Australia and New Zealand	25% of initial fee
iv) Each British Commonwealth or English speaking territory other than those in (i) to (iii) above	½% of initial fee
v) Other countries	Percentage to be agreed

What this all meant in (reasonably) plain English is as follows.

Enterprises had six months from the date of transmission to decide if the programme that the writer had written was going to be offered for sale abroad. Where *Doctor Who* was concerned, this was a given, but not so for every other show. Once a decision had been taken, Enterprises then had one year from the date of transmission to actually take that option up. Once taken up, the exclusive overseas sales rights would then belong to Enterprises for a period of five years, again beginning from the date of first transmission of the final episode on the BBC. So, for example, Enterprises' initial option to sell all four episodes of 'An Unearthly Child' overseas would expire on 13 December 1968, the day before the fifth anniversary of the BBC1 debut transmission of the final episode.

There was also an option whereby some of the money due to the writer could be paid up-front, depending on whether the BBC decided to buy the world rights for the story or whether it was done on a country-by-country basis.

This contract also helps illuminate Enterprises' sales policy in terms of target markets in the 1960s. Sales to the American television networks appear to have been the number one target, presumably because the revenue to be gained was very healthy (as evidenced by the fact that a writer's fee was effectively doubled if one of his/her programmes was sold to America). The rewards for a writer for sales to Canada, Australia and New Zealand were all quite reasonable as well.

But for sales to the whole of the rest of the Commonwealth, the poor writer could expect to only get ½% of his original fee. So if, for example, a writer had been paid £200.00 per episode to write a four-part story (which wasn't an unheard of figure in

WIPED!

the 1960s), earning him £800.00 in total, he would have received only £4.00 for each sale of that story to television stations in Hong Kong, or Barbados, or Malta.

Of course, once the initial five-year sales options had expired, they could always be renewed, provided the writer – or his/her agent – agreed. Enterprises' usual procedure was to seek a renewal for a further five year period each time. For example, in the case of 'Marco Polo', for which the original contract expired in April 1969, Enterprises was able to renew the sales rights for a second five-year period, up to April 1974. Sometime during the 1970s, the length of sales rights specified in new BBC contracts was changed from five years to seven years, but this had no impact on the 1960s episodes of *Doctor Who*.

By examining the sales records for the William Hartnell and Patrick Troughton *Doctor Who* adventures (see the chapter on Overseas Sales for more details), it's possible to determine which stories seemingly had their sales contracts renewed for a second term.

Story	Initial Sales Expiry Date[33]	Renewed Expiry Date	Date of Last Sale[34]	Country of Last Sale
An Unearthly Child	13/12/68	13/12/73	24/07/73	Algeria
The Daleks	31/01/69	31/01/74	24/07/73	Algeria
The Edge of Destruction	14/02/69	14/02/74	24/07/73	Algeria
Marco Polo [35]	03/04/69	03/04/74	26/10/70	Ethiopia
The Keys of Marinus	15/05/69	15/05/74	24/07/73	Algeria
The Aztecs	12/06/69	12/06/74	24/07/73	Algeria
The Sensorites	31/07/69	31/07/74	24/07/73	Algeria
The Reign of Terror	11/09/69	11/09/74	26/10/70	Ethiopia
Planet of Giants	13/11/69	13/11/74	24/07/73	Algeria
The Dalek Invasion of Earth	25/12/69	25/12/74	24/07/73	Algeria
The Rescue	08/01/70	08/01/75	24/07/73	Algeria
The Romans	05/02/70	05/02/75	22/10/71	Ethiopia
The Web Planet	19/03/70	19/03/75	25/07/73	Nigeria
The Crusade	16/04/70	16/04/75	22/10/71	Ethiopia
The Space Museum	14/05/70	14/05/75	22/10/71	Ethiopia
The Chase	25/06/70	25/06/75	22/10/71	Ethiopia

---

[33] In law, a contract period running for five years from an episode's original transmission date would expire on the day before the fifth anniversary of that date, rather than on the anniversary itself.

[34] This covers only sales of telerecordings up to the mid-1970s, not sales of surviving episodes on videotape in later decades.

[35] A memo dated 11 March 1969 exists relating to 'Marco Polo', recording BBC Enterprises' wish to extend the sales rights for another five years. This confirms that the initial rights period would end on 3 April 1969, and seeks agreement from writer John Lucarotti's representatives to renew the sales rights up to 3 April 1974.

CHAPTER 5

Title	Date 1	Date 2	Date 3	Country
The Time Meddler	23/07/70	23/07/75	25/07/73	Nigeria
Galaxy 4	01/10/70	01/10/75	18/12/72	Singapore
Mission to the Unknown	08/10/70	08/10/75	--/10/66	Australia
The Myth Makers	05/11/70	05/11/75	18/12/72	Singapore
The Daleks Masterplan (11 episodes)	28/01/71	-	--/10/66	Australia
The Massacre	25/02/71	25/02/76	18/12/72	Singapore
The Ark	25/03/71	25/03/76	18/12/72	Singapore
The Celestial Toymaker	22/04/71	22/04/76	18/12/72	Singapore
The Gunfighters	20/05/71	20/05/76	18/12/72	Singapore
The Savages	17/06/71	17/06/76	24/02/72	Singapore
The War Machines	15/07/71	15/07/76	25/07/73	Nigeria
The Smugglers	30/09/71	30/09/76	24/02/72	Singapore
The Tenth Planet	28/10/71	28/10/76	24/02/72	Singapore
The Power of the Daleks	09/12/71	09/12/76	24/02/72	Singapore
The Highlanders	06/01/72	-	06/03/70	Zambia
The Underwater Menace	03/02/72	-	06/03/70	Zambia
The Moonbase	03/03/72	-	06/03/70	Zambia
The Macra Terror	31/03/72	-	06/03/70	Zambia
The Faceless Ones	12/05/72	-	06/03/70	Zambia
The Evil of the Daleks	30/06/72	-	24/07/70	New Zealand
The Tomb of the Cybermen	22/09/72	-	25/09/70	New Zealand
The Abominable Snowmen	03/11/72	03/11/77	24/10/74	Nigeria
The Ice Warriors	15/12/72	15/12/77	04/10/73	Zambia
The Enemy of the World	26/01/73	26/01/78	24/10/74	Nigeria
The Web of Fear	08/03/73	08/03/78	24/10/74	Nigeria
Fury from the Deep	19/04/73	-	19/04/73	Gibraltar
The Wheel in Space	31/05/73	31/05/78	? 1974	Nigeria
The Dominators	06/09/73	06/09/78	20/11/75	Nigeria
The Mind Robber	11/10/73	-	16/05/72	Gibraltar
The Invasion	20/12/73	-	09/08/72	Gibraltar
The Krotons	17/01/74	17/01/79	06/02/76	Nigeria
The Seeds of Death	28/02/74	28/02/79	14/02/76	Zambia
The Space Pirates	11/04/74	11/04/79	01/04/76	Zambia
The War Games	20/06/74	20/06/79	17/05/76	Zambia

WIPED!

It would thus seem that all of the William Hartnell stories, with the possible exceptions of 'Mission to the Unknown' and 'The Daleks Masterplan', had their contracts extended for a second five-year term, as they were all still being sold abroad after the initial contract expiry dates. And even 'Mission to the Unknown' was still listed as being available for purchase in 1974, in Enterprises' *A Quick Guide to Dr Who* brochure (which we'll come to shortly), so this single-episode story possibly also had its overseas sales rights renewed for a second period, even if 'The Daleks Masterplan' (the story to which it acted as a precursor) didn't.

It would appear that while 'The Power of the Daleks' had its sales contract renewed for a second stretch by Enterprises, the batch of stories that followed it, from 'The Highlanders' through to 'The Tomb of the Cybermen', did not. Of the other fifth season stories, however, it would seem that only 'Fury from the Deep' did not have its contract renewed. The fact that the last sale of 'Fury from the Deep', to Gibraltar, came on the *very date* the rights lapsed seems almost *too* convenient – perhaps there was some sort of 'last-chance-to-buy' offer by Enterprises?

Turning to the sixth season, it appears that the rights for 'The Mind Robber' and 'The Invasion' were both allowed to expire without renewal, but that the rest of the stories from Patrick Troughton's final year had their rights extended for a second term.

'THE DALEKS' – A TERRY NATION TELEVISION SHOW ...

It is possible that the unusually low number of overseas sales of – and apparent non-renewal of overseas sales rights to – the early Patrick Troughton stories might have had something to do with the plans that writer Terry Nation had at that time for producing a spin-off series featuring his creations the Daleks.

Nation had spent a great deal of time and effort in 1966 trying to negotiate for the production of a pilot episode for this proposed spin-off, to be made on film and shot in colour. He had scripted the pilot, which he had called *The Daleks*, and set up a production company to handle the actual filming. He was also negotiating with the BBC – who held 50% of the rights to the Daleks – about them providing co-funding, and possibly screening the series on BBC2.

Towards the end of November 1966, as the proposed production inched nearer to becoming a reality, Nation's solicitors drew up a draft contract for the BBC. This included a clause that would have prevented Enterprises from selling any episodes of *Doctor Who* that featured the Daleks (regardless of who had written them) to *any* overseas markets, with immediate effect. This embargo would have continued for up to a year after the last episode of *The Daleks* was screened on television, whenever that might be. However, there is no indication that this contract was ever formally agreed upon or signed.

A few months further down the road, and the BBC had pulled out of the deal to

CHAPTER 5

co-finance production of *The Daleks*, and decided not to screen the series. Nation tried to press on regardless, and a new contract was presented to the BBC in January 1967, which offered them a percentage of the merchandising and script rights to a potential series of *The Daleks*. As part of this deal, the BBC again had to agree that no new overseas sales of any episodes of *Doctor Who* that featured the Daleks could be made – although any prior sales would be honoured. Additionally, under the terms of the agreement, no *Doctor Who* episodes featuring the Daleks could be repeated in the UK at all. It seems that the BBC agreed to these terms, and this time the contract was signed.

'The Daleks', 'The Dalek Invasion of Earth' and 'The Chase' had all been widely sold around the world by Enterprises over the previous few years, and these existing sales weren't affected. Additional overseas sales of these three stories continued to be healthy in 1967 and 1968, so the BBC clearly didn't think that these were covered by the terms of the new Nation agreement. 'Mission to the Unknown' and 'The Daleks Masterplan' had initially been sold to ABC in Australia in 1966, but issues with the country's censors had prevented their transmission, and the stories weren't offered to any other foreign broadcasters. The agreement with Nation might have had a bearing on this.

'The Power of the Daleks', made in late 1966, was only ever sold abroad to three countries by Enterprises. The first sale was to ABC in Australia in October 1967, and the details of this are logged on the BBC's sales sheet for the story. However, this typed sheet has been crossed through, and the word 'Withdrawn' written on it in pen. This is the only *Doctor Who* sales sheet for a 1960s story to indicate such a withdrawal. Next to the Australian sales details on the sheet is the handwritten note: 'Although programme withdrawn, pay when invoiced. No other sales permitted. 18/8/67.'

However, at some later point, the handwritten 'Withdrawn' has been crossed out, and the word 'Re-raised' written in pen next to it. The story was then sold to New Zealand in 1969 and Singapore in 1972. Presumably the initial withdrawal was rescinded sometime between August 1967 and May 1969. The sale to Singapore in 1972 would indicate that the rights to this story were indeed re-negotiated for a second five-year period.

The BBC's sales sheet for 'The Evil of the Daleks' has no notations on it whatsoever to indicate that it was ever withdrawn from being offered for overseas sale, although it ultimately was sold to only four countries – the three that had purchased 'The Power of the Daleks' plus Hong Kong. But by 1974, it was the only Patrick Troughton story that Enterprises was no longer offering for sale, according to *A Quick Guide to Dr Who*.

'The Evil of the Daleks' was repeated by the BBC in the summer of 1968, perhaps indicating that the eventual collapse of Nation's *The Daleks* project in 1967 somehow rendered the agreement with the BBC void. But the situation with that project seems to have created some degree of confusion within the BBC over their rights to sell Dalek stories overseas. And as one of the affected stories was the one that introduced the second Doctor, then the commercial viability of the whole initial run of Patrick Troughton episodes was seemingly adversely affected.

With this in mind, it's perhaps no wonder that the series underwent some degree of a re-boot with 'The Tomb of the Cybermen', the opening episode of which seems designed as a perfect starting point for new viewers.

SALES PRINTS

As discussed earlier, Enterprises would issue Retention Authorisation forms for all programmes that it wished to sell abroad, in order for them to be telerecorded before the tapes were wiped for re-use. Beginning with 'An Unearthly Child' in 1963, a 16mm Suppressed Field telerecording of each episode was made around the time of its BBC1 transmission. Enterprises would then keep a master negative of the episode, from which any number of prints could be made, depending on how many countries wanted to purchase it. However, not every overseas sale saw a new film print being made. Sometimes a country that had already screened the series would be asked to send its film copies of the episodes on to another country that had just purchased it.

It would appear to have been in late 1966, around the time 'The Savages' was transmitted, that the BBC changed from the Suppressed Field system of telerecording to the superior Stored Field system. It seems that Enterprises used this switch as an opportunity to have new Stored Field film recordings made of all of the earlier *Doctor Who* stories, from 'An Unearthly Child' through to 'The Gunfighters' (with the probable exception of 'The Daleks Masterplan' Episode Seven). The master transmission tapes (and films) for all of these episodes were all still in existence at this point.[36]

From 'The Savages' onwards, it seems likely that all further 16mm film recordings of *Doctor Who* were made using the Stored Field system. The surviving BBC records

---

36 This in itself raises some interesting questions. Did this new batch of Stored Field telerecordings really include 'Mission to the Unknown' and 'The Daleks Masterplan', despite the lack of any overseas sales whatsoever for the earlier Suppressed Field telerecordings of those stories, and despite the rights complications surrounding Dalek episodes? The fact that the surviving prints of episode two, five and ten of 'The Daleks Masterplan' are all of the Stored Field variety, along with the fact that both stories were included in the 1966 retention order issued by BBC Enterprises (which we must assume was for the creation of the Stored Field telerecordings), would seem to confirm that they were. So presumably BBC Enterprises hadn't given up trying to sell these stories abroad at this point.

What did BBC Enterprises do with its old collection of Suppressed Field telerecordings of the stories from 'An Unearthly Child' to 'The Gunfighters'? A few Suppressed Field telerecordings do survive to this day, but mainly because the films were returned from an overseas market that had originally purchased Suppressed Field prints. Most probably the collection was simply junked by BBC Enterprises very soon after it had taken delivery of the new, superior Stored Field prints, in late 1966 or early 1967.

CHAPTER 5

show that, more often than not, these later telerecordings would be made direct from the actual BBC1 transmissions of the episodes. This makes a great deal of sense, as it would have cost substantially less than booking both a telerecording suite *and* a two-inch videotape machine in order to make the telerecordings at a later date.

Even after *Doctor Who* started to be produced on colour videotape at the beginning of the 1970s, Enterprises continued making 16mm back and white telerecordings of the episodes for overseas sale, again usually direct from their BBC1 transmissions. Most of the rest of the world still had only black and white television in the early years of this decade.

One significant issue with the making of 16mm black and white telerecordings directly from colour videotape was that the colour signal would manifest itself as a detailed pattern of grey 'chroma dots' embedded in the black and white picture. This was regarded as an unwelcome intrusion. To get around the problem, BBC Engineers developed a filter system that could be used in telerecording suites; but the fact that the system relied on the operator to remember to apply it each time, coupled with the fact that the BBC had up to 20 film recording channels but just two of these filters, meant that more often than not it just wasn't used. The overwhelming majority of the 16mm black and white telerecordings of the colour Jon Pertwee episodes contain this chroma dot information – which would prove to be a blessing in disguise in years to come …

By 1974, Enterprises began to wind down its sales of black and white material, as colour was at last beginning to take off in most of the overseas markets it sold material to. The last Jon Pertwee story to have 16mm black and white telerecordings made for overseas sale was 'The Time Warrior', although there is evidence that 'Invasion of the Dinosaurs' was also telerecorded[37]. Colour sales on videotape quickly became the order of the day for Enterprises.

JUST HOW MANY 16MM SALES PRINTS WERE THERE?

For each programme that it decided to have telerecorded, Enterprises would be supplied with both a 16mm film negative and one or more 16mm film positive prints struck from that negative. What isn't clear is just how many positive prints would have been supplied of a typical *Doctor Who* episode.

---

37 Part One of 'Invasion of the Dinosaurs' was certainly telerecorded, as the film still exists as the only surviving record of this episode. The BBC has the recording cards for the rest of the story, which tells us that all the other episodes (with the exception of Part Four) had film recordings made of them. And although there is no mention of a film recording being made of Part Four, it probably was recorded and just not noted on the card. Two dates are noted for Part Five's recording, so one of these could be for Part Four, noted in error against the wrong episode.

WIPED!

One noted commentator, Ian Levine (of whom we will be hearing more later), has in the past claimed that Enterprises made as many as 28 film print copies of each episode. While this seems inconceivable for the later black and white stories, bearing in mind their relatively modest sales prospects, that figure may not be too far wide of the mark for some of the early Hartnell ones. 'An Unearthly Child', 'The Daleks' and 'The Edge of Destruction', for instance, were all sold to four countries in 1964, 11 in 1965 and a further 20 by 1970, which comes to 35 in total. Over the same period, 'Marco Polo' was sold to 25 countries and 'The Keys of Marinus' sold to 32.

The best-guess scenario is that Enterprises would order up to perhaps half a dozen film prints to begin with, along with the single negative for each episode. It would certainly have made good financial sense to run off multiple film copies in one batch. If further prints were needed later on, the negative could be pressed into service again at that stage. Somewhere around the programme's third season, the number of positive prints of each episode that Enterprises would have ordered would probably have been drastically reduced, perhaps down to just one or two, based on the decreasing number of overseas sales.[38]

It's also possible that *two* 16mm film negatives could have been made for some, if not all, '60s *Doctor Who* stories (not including the new set of negatives made when the stories originally telerecorded using the Suppressed Field process were later redone using the Stored Field system). BBC Sydney in Australia was certainly supplied with negatives of some, if not most, William Hartnell and Patrick Troughton stories. What is unclear is if these really were second negatives, or if they were Enterprises' originals, which would have left only a stockpile of positive prints in England. If the latter was the case, possibly the negatives were returned from Australia at some later date. Alternatively, the negatives could have been sent to BBC Sydney only after Enterprises had finished with them.

In the surviving paperwork in the production file for 'The War Machines' (currently held at the BBC's Written Archive Centre in Caversham), there is a memo dating from 1968 from Pamela Nash, the Film Recording Clerk at Enterprises, asking for another set of negatives (not prints, note) of this story to be made. This was seemingly done at the behest of ABC in Australia. A comparison between the two surviving prints of Episode Two of this story – one recovered from Australia, the other from Nigeria – shows that they are indeed from separate transfers. (Presumably the Nigerian returned print is from the 1968 transfer, while the Australian one is from the 1966 original, which then went missing.)

This sort of thing was probably happening all the time. Factor into the equation

---

[38] But this is pure speculation, based on conversations I've had with several people in the BBC, both past and present.

CHAPTER 5

the new set of Stored Field telerecordings made in late 1966/early 1967, and it clearly becomes impossible to say just how many prints, or even negatives, Enterprises really had made of each episode.

As previously noted, however, not every new overseas sale would have required a new 16mm print of the episode to be supplied. Enterprises employed a system known as 'bicycling', whereby prints were regularly sent from one country to another, once the first country had finished with them. Some information about this system has come to light via programme traffic records for countries such as New Zealand, Australia and Cyprus, but the full details remain sketchy at best.

Geographical proximity would seem to be the obvious requirement for an efficient bicycling chain, but that's not necessarily how it was organised. For example, we know that Cyprus sent prints to Hong Kong and Uganda, while New Zealand sent prints to Denmark, Nigeria and Singapore. So expediency was more likely the key to how the bicycling system worked.

To suggest anything further would be no more than an educated guess. But nevertheless, here goes…

The stories from the first two seasons of *Doctor Who* were sold to over 30 countries, and trying to plot the possible movements of the various prints of these stories is like trying to plot the paths of snowflakes in a blizzard. Okay, perhaps not quite that complicated, but you get the idea!

Seasons One and Two initially were supplied as Suppressed Field prints. ABC in Australia had its own set of Suppressed Field prints of Seasons One and Two, and apart from the four Hartnell stories it sent to New Zealand in 1967[39], those prints stayed at ABC.

The distributor Television International Enterprises Ltd handled the initial sales of Doctor Who to Gibraltar, Aden, Trinidad and Tobago and Bermuda. It's possible that only one set of prints was supplied to TIE Ltd for all these markets to share in turn. We know that Rhodesia and Zambia certainly shared the same set of Suppressed Field prints of early Hartnell stories, and possibly also Nigeria and Kenya too.

It seems likely that Singapore and Hong Kong shared their prints of the early Hartnell stories, and as Hong Kong's sales were linked to Aden's, then they could have been part of the TIE distribution system.

So far that's three sets of Suppressed Field prints of Seasons One and Two, servicing 11 countries.

One set of Supressed Field prints was sent to Cyprus; perhaps these had originated with Canada and/or Malta? Some of these prints ended up in Uganda and Hong Kong.

---

39 'The Reign of Terror', 'Planet of Giants', 'The Dalek Invasion of Earth' and 'The Rescue'.

WIPED!

In all, there could have been as few as six sets of Suppressed Field prints of Seasons One and Two criss-crossing the globe in the 1960s.

Then we have the Spanish and Arabic dubbed Stored Field prints made in 1967. One simple assumption that can be made is that the countries that aired the series dubbed into another language shared a common set of prints for that language. So a single set of Arabic-dubbed prints could have been shared by Tunisia, Morocco, Saudi Arabia, Iran, Jordan, Libya and Algeria, while a single set of Spanish dubbed prints could have been shared by Venezuela, Chile and Mexico.

By the time Stored Field prints of Seasons One and Two were made in 1967, only two countries purchased the stories in English (rather than the dubbed versions): Sierra Leone and Ethiopia. It's probable that this was just a single set of prints, shared between the two countries.

For Seasons Three, Four, Five and Six (which were all Stored Field prints only), the number of overseas sales dramatically decreased, and it would appear that there were no more than four prints of each story made in most instances. The best 'guesstimate' (and there is a lot of guesswork here, which is why some of this information doesn't appear in Appendix i later in this book) for how these prints moved around the world is as follows:

Story	*Print A*	*Print B*	*Print C*	*Print D*
Galaxy 4	Australia	New Zealand Singapore	Barbados	Zambia Sierra Leone
Mission to the Unknown	Australia			
The Myth Makers	Australia	New Zealand Singapore	Barbados	Zambia Sierra Leone
The Daleks Masterplan (11 eps)	Australia			
The Massacre	Australia	New Zealand Singapore	Barbados	Zambia Sierra Leone
The Ark	Australia	New Zealand Singapore	Barbados	Zambia Sierra Leone
The Celestial Toymaker	Australia	New Zealand Singapore	Barbados	Zambia Sierra Leone

CHAPTER 5

Story				
The Gunfighters	Australia	Singapore	Barbados	Zambia Sierra Leone
The Savages	Australia	New Zealand Singapore	Barbados	Zambia Sierra Leone
The War Machines	Australia	New Zealand Singapore Nigeria	Barbados	Zambia Sierra Leone
The Smugglers	Australia	New Zealand Singapore	Barbados	Zambia Sierra Leone
The Tenth Planet	Australia	New Zealand Singapore		
The Power of the Daleks	Australia	New Zealand Singapore		
The Highlanders	Australia	Singapore New Zealand	Hong Kong	Uganda Zambia
The Underwater Menace	Australia	Singapore New Zealand	Hong Kong	Uganda Zambia
The Moonbase	Australia	Singapore New Zealand	Hong Kong	Uganda Zambia
The Macra Terror	Australia	Singapore New Zealand	Hong Kong	Uganda Zambia
The Faceless Ones	Australia	Singapore New Zealand	Hong Kong	Uganda Zambia
The Evil of the Daleks	Australia	Singapore New Zealand	Hong Kong	

WIPED!

The Tomb of the Cybermen	Australia	Singapore New Zealand	Hong Kong	
The Abominable Snowmen	Australia	Singapore New Zealand	Hong Kong	Gibraltar Zambia Nigeria
The Ice Warriors	Australia	Singapore New Zealand	Hong Kong	Gibraltar Zambia
The Enemy of the World	Australia	Singapore New Zealand	Hong Kong	Gibraltar Zambia Nigeria
The Web of Fear	Australia	Singapore New Zealand	Hong Kong	Gibraltar Zambia Nigeria
Fury from the Deep	Australia	Singapore New Zealand	Hong Kong	Gibraltar
The Wheel in Space	Australia	Singapore New Zealand	Hong Kong	Gibraltar Nigeria
The Dominators	Australia	Singapore	Hong Kong	Gibraltar Nigeria
The Mind Robber	Australia	Singapore Gibraltar	Hong Kong	
The Invasion	Australia	Singapore Gibraltar	Hong Kong	
The Krotons	Australia	Singapore Gibraltar	Hong Kong Nigeria	
The Seeds of Death	Australia	Singapore Gibraltar	Hong Kong Zambia	
The Space Pirates	Australia	Singapore Gibraltar	Hong Kong Zambia	
The War Games	Australia	Singapore Gibraltar	Hong Kong Zambia	

CHAPTER 5

Things get initially simpler for the sales of the Jon Pertwee stories in the 1970s. ABC in Australia purchased Seasons Seven through to Ten on 16mm black and white film (bar 'Inferno', 'The Mind of Evil', 'The Dæmons' and 'The Green Death'), and again probably retained their own set of prints. Singapore and Hong Kong also purchased these stories on 16mm black and white film, and probably shared prints. Gibraltar had the same stories too, so it would seem that the same set of prints was used for them in the main.

All of the sales of the 13 NTSC stories from Seasons Seven, Eight and Nine to the US between 1972 and 1978 would have been handled by Time-Life, who had their own set of videotape masters, while the Canadian NTSC sales were all handled by BBC Toronto, who also had their own set of tapes.

Things get more complicated from 1975, when PAL one-inch tapes of mainly Season Ten and Eleven stories started being sold overseas, There is documentation that shows that New Zealand sent its PAL tapes of 'Death to the Daleks' to Brunei at the BBC's request in February 1976, and other stories might also have made the same journey.

It's important to stress once again – most of the above is mainly conjecture!

FOREIGN LANGUAGE VERSIONS

When it came to selling *Doctor Who* to non-English speaking countries, Enterprises looked to give the purchasing broadcasters all the components they would need to produce their own 16mm film prints with soundtracks in their own language. This meant supplying a 16mm film print of each episode, complete with the optical soundtrack of the original broadcast sound, a 16mm film negative of the same episode, and a separate magnetic music and effects (M&E) soundtrack. The M&E track would contain suitable incidental music and sound effects – although these might not be the same as on the original UK broadcast – but none of the actors' dialogue. A copy of the script of the episode would probably be supplied as well, which would then need to be translated into the broadcaster's own language.

This would enable the overseas broadcaster to hire in voice actors to dub all the speaking parts of the story, working from the translated script. This could be mixed with the M&E soundtrack and combined with the picture elements from the negative to produce a new 16mm film print incorporating the foreign language soundtrack. Alternatively, the M&E track could be simply mixed with the newly-recorded dialogue to produce a new magnetic audio soundtrack in the foreign language, which could then be played in tandem with the original English language 16mm film print, with the optical soundtrack muted for transmission.

It was written into all the BBC Enterprises sales contracts with foreign broadcasters that any newly created foreign language soundtracks would automatically become

WIPED!

the property of Enterprises, and would therefore need to be returned to them (or destroyed, if that was what they stipulated instead) alongside the other elements of the programme once the broadcaster's contract had expired.

The surviving sales paperwork for the William Hartnell and Patrick Troughton episodes lists which stories had M&E soundtracks available for these purposes. The paperwork also records which stories had specific foreign language versions available for purchase:

Story	M&E Track	Foreign Language Version Available
An Unearthly Child	M&E track available	Spanish version available
The Daleks	M&E track available	Spanish version available
The Edge of Destruction	M&E track available	Spanish version available
Marco Polo	None listed	None listed
The Keys of Marinus	M&E track available	Spanish version available
The Aztecs	M&E track available	Spanish version available
The Sensorites	M&E track available	Spanish version available
The Reign of Terror	None listed	None listed
Planet of Giants	M&E track available	Spanish version available
The Dalek Invasion of Earth	M&E track available	Spanish version available
The Rescue	M&E track available	Spanish version available
The Romans	None listed	None listed
The Web Planet	M&E track available	Spanish version available
The Crusade	None listed	None listed
The Space Museum	M&E track available	Spanish version available
The Chase	No records for this story	
The Time Meddler	None listed	Spanish version available
Galaxy 4	None listed	Spanish version available
Mission to the Unknown	No records for this story	
The Myth Makers	None listed	Spanish version available
The Daleks Masterplan	No records for this story	
The Massacre	None listed	Spanish version available
The Ark	None listed	Spanish version available
The Celestial Toymaker	None listed	Spanish version available
The Gunfighters	None listed	Spanish version available
The Savages	None listed	Spanish version available
The War Machines	No records for this story	
The Smugglers	None listed	Spanish version available
The Tenth Planet	None listed	Spanish version available
The Power of the Daleks	None listed	None listed
The Highlanders	None listed	Spanish version available
The Underwater Menace	None listed	Spanish version available

CHAPTER 5

The Moonbase	None listed	Spanish version available
The Macra Terror	None listed	Spanish version available
The Faceless Ones	None listed	Spanish version available
The Evil of the Daleks	None listed	None listed
The Tomb of the Cybermen	None listed	Spanish version available
The Abominable Snowmen	None listed	Spanish version available
The Ice Warriors	None listed	Spanish version available
The Enemy of the World	None listed	Spanish version available
The Web of Fear	None listed	Spanish version available
Fury from the Deep	None listed	None listed
The Wheel in Space	No records for this story	
The Dominators	No records for this story	
The Mind Robber	None listed	None listed
The Invasion	No records for this story	
The Krotons	None listed	None listed
The Seeds of Death	None listed	None listed
The Space Pirates	No records for this story	
The War Games	None listed	None listed

On the face of it, that's an awful lot of Spanish versions of *Doctor Who*! Nearly every story from the programme's first five seasons has a sales code listed on the BBC Clearance History Sheet for a Spanish language version. But did all these actually exist? And if so, who produced them?

It would seem on the balance of probability that most of the stories listed as having a Spanish soundtrack available in fact never did. The main BBC markets for such episodes would have been Venezuela, Mexico and Chile (Spain itself never purchased the series in the 1960s), and these three countries purchased only a fraction of the stories listed as having Spanish soundtracks. So the paperwork is wrong, basically. But why?

If the handful of early episodes bought by Venezuela, Mexico and/or Chile did have Spanish language versions made, then perhaps at some later date, these were returned to the BBC along with the original negatives, prints and M&E tracks? The apparent existence at Enterprises of Spanish dubbed episodes in 1976, listed in the 'Whose Doctor Who' research, indicates that this might well have happened. Perhaps the BBC then had to come up with a sales code for these Spanish language versions? And once that was done, then perhaps some bureaucratic requirement saw a Spanish language sales code applied to nearly all the other stories as well? Hence all the Spanish language codes on the sales sheets.

Of course, for a Spanish language version to have been made, there would have had to have been an M&E track already available to use in the first place. The stories that are listed above as having M&E tracks available are probably the only ones that

WIPED!

actually had Spanish language versions made for them at the time. And the list of stories with available M&E soundtracks corresponds neatly to the list of stories purchased by Mexico in 1967, which we know were all definitely dubbed into Spanish.

The M&E tracks would also have been used for the production of any Arabic soundtracks of the series. One of the few countries that would have screened *Doctor Who* in Arabic was Algeria, and significantly, when they purchased the series in 1973, the only stories they took were those listed as having available M&E tracks. It is just a theory, but perhaps some of these early Hartnell stories exist today only because Algeria purchased them and then returned them? And perhaps Algeria purchased them only because of the random availability of M&E tracks? Such big consequences hang on such tiny twists of fate ...

There is no mention on any of the sales paperwork of the existence of any Arabic dubbed stories, as there is for the Spanish dubbed ones. Yet we know there were Arabic dubbed episodes made. The 1976 'Whose Doctor Who' listing shows Arabic versions of 'An Unearthly Child', 'The Daleks', 'The Edge of Destruction', 'The Keys of Marinus', 'The Aztecs', 'The Sensorites', 'Planet of Giants', 'The Dalek Invasion of Earth', and 'The Rescue' at Enterprises.

Episodes that survive today at the BBC in either Arabic or Spanish

Episode	Format Retained
An Unearthly Child: 1	Spanish Print
The Daleks: 7	Spanish Sound Negative
The Edge of Destruction: 2	Arabic Print
The Keys of Marinus: 1	Arabic Print
Planet of Giants: 1	Arabic Print
Planet of Giants: 2	Arabic Print
Planet of Giants: 3	Arabic Print
The Dalek Invasion of Earth: 1	Arabic Print
The Dalek Invasion of Earth: 2	Arabic Print
The Dalek Invasion of Earth: 4	Arabic Print
The Dalek Invasion of Earth: 6	Arabic Print
The Rescue: 1	Arabic Print
The Rescue: 2	Arabic Print

CHAPTER 5

A Spanish dubbed version of 'Planet of Giants' Episode Three and an Arabic dubbed copy of 'The Aztecs' Episode Four also both exist in private hands A copy of the latter was loaned to the BBC in 2002 to enable its Arabic soundtrack to be included on the DVD release of 'The Aztecs' as an optional extra.[40] When this print was examined, the film recording was found to date from 1967, some six months after the initial Stored Field telerecordings were made for this story.

One final note on the subject of foreign language soundtracks. When *Blue Peter* did a retrospective feature on *Doctor Who*'s tenth anniversary in November 1973, they used an excerpt from Episode Four of 'An Unearthly Child' dubbed into Arabic. An Arabic-dubbed copy of this episode no longer exists at the BBC.

AUDITION PRINTS

While it has taken many years to discover and analyse what scant BBC paperwork remains about its overseas sales of *Doctor Who* in the 1960s and 1970s, there is virtually no surviving documentation about the use of audition prints in such sales. There certainly isn't any paperwork that has surfaced at the BBC over the years that throws any light on the subject. And yet audition prints were an important tool in BBC Enterprises' sales and promotion of the series.

In an age where there was no domestic videotape system like Betamax or VHS – let alone DVD or Blu-ray – it stands to reason that that the only way BBC Enterprises could let potential customers actually see the programmes they were trying to sell to them was to send them 16mm film copies. This seems to be exactly what they did.

What we do know about the use of audition prints by the BBC all comes from paperwork and programme traffic records of other television stations and countries.

The best example is that of ABC in Australia. It was sent 16mm copies of all the William Hartnell and Patrick Troughton episodes to view in advance of officially purchasing the episodes from BBC Sydney. For example, the ABC was sent 16mm prints of 'The Wheel in Space' and 'The Dominators' to view in August 1968. Once they had agreed to purchase the stories, these then became the 'official' prints of the stories purchased, and ABC then in turn had to submit these prints to the country's censors, in March and April 1969 respectively. Similarly, the ABC was sent audition prints of 'The Invasion' on 24 December 1968, but the story wasn't actually submitted to the Australian censors until 24 February 1970.

In New Zealand, the BBC asked for some of their 16mm films of *Doctor Who* to be sent to other overseas foreign broadcasters once NZBC had finished with them. The first two episodes of 'Marco Polo' were sent to Iran in October 1967, while

---

40 The M&E track for this was one of those with incidental music and sound effects that differed from the UK version.

WIPED!

'An Unearthly Child', 'The Daleks' and 'The Edge of Destruction' were all sent to a broadcaster in Denmark in March 1968. None of these stories was eventually sold to these countries, so the supply of prints is not recorded in the BBC sales paperwork.

We also know that the German broadcaster ZDF was sent audition prints of 'The Ice Warriors' in 1968, but that this didn't lead to them purchasing the series (and they no longer hold the prints they were sent).

There might be dozens of other examples of audition prints of *Doctor Who* episodes or whole stories being sent out either directly by the BBC or by others at their request, which we simply don't know about. And probably never will ...

BBC ENTERPRISES IN THE 1970S

As the 1960s turned into the 1970s, BBC Enterprises' stockpile of *Doctor Who* episodes held on black and white 16mm film grew ever larger, as each new Jon Pertwee adventure was added to their sales catalogue. But sales of the William Hartnell and Patrick Troughton stories were beginning to dry up.

This was due to a number of factors. Markets wanted new material, not old. And more and more television stations were taking their first steps into colour broadcasting. In the early 1970s, ABC in Australia were still taking all the new Jon Pertwee *Doctor Who* stories that Enterprises could offer them in black and white, as were RTV in Hong Kong, RTS in Singapore and GBC in Gibraltar. But as far as *Doctor Who*'s back-catalogue was concerned, there were few further sales. RTS in Singapore, Midwest TV in Nigeria, and TVA in Algeria purchased small batches of Hartnell episodes in 1972 and 1973 respectively. Nigeria and Zambia purchased a handful of Troughton stories between 1973 and 1976. But such instances were increasingly few and far between – black and white sales were waning.

In 1972, Enterprises sold *Doctor Who* into the American market for the first time, making a batch of the 13 Jon Pertwee stories from 'Doctor Who and the Silurians' through to 'The Time Monster' available as 525-line two-inch colour videotapes. This was the first attempt to sell the series abroad in colour, and met with only limited success.

To illustrate *Doctor Who*'s place in Enterprises' scheme of things, we can examine an existing document detailing all the programmes sold in the three months from July to September 1972. Popular shows such as *Dad's Army*, *Doomwatch*, *The Basil Brush Show*, *The Benny Hill Show*, *Elizabeth R*, *Horizon*, *Ivanhoe*, *The Onedin Line*, *Panorama*, *The Six Wives of Henry VIII*, *Steptoe and Son* and *Trumpton* were all doing good business, alongside *Doctor Who*. But *Doctor Who* was just one of 360 different titles that Enterprises was selling at that point in time. A quick count reveals that 3,534 individual episodes or programmes were sold in this three-month period. Only 248 of

CHAPTER 5

these episodes were *Doctor Who* episodes. These are listed as the sales of the 13 NTSC colour Pertwee stories to the US channels KHOL, WFTV and KPHO (72 episodes x 3 = 216 episodes); the black and white stories 'The Krotons', 'The Seeds of Death', 'The Space Pirates and 'The War Games' to Gibraltar (26 episodes); and 'Colony in Space', also in black and white, to Australia (6 episodes).

Another BBC Enterprises sales document exists covering the period from July to September 1975. The *Doctor Who* sales in this three month period consisted of the stories 'Planet of the Spiders' to ABC in Australia; 'Robot', 'The Ark in Space', 'The Sontaran Experiment', 'Genesis of the Daleks' and 'Revenge of the Cybermen' to Dubai; and 'Genesis of the Daleks' to the Netherlands, plus a sale of the 13 NTSC Pertwee stories to the American channel WVIA. There were very few black and white sales of *Doctor Who* episodes after this point in time.

Doctor Who was a very small part of Enterprises' portfolio, and in the early 1970s, colour episodes were demonstrably more in demand than black and white ones. By 1975, both New Zealand and Australia had started buying the Pertwee stories in colour; both countries used the PAL television format, and so were supplied with two-inch tapes copied directly from the BBC's broadcast masters.

Coupled to this, the rights to sell the Hartnell and Troughton stories were beginning to expire in the early 1970s. The lack of demand saw to it that, this time, the rights weren't renewed. So what was Enterprises going to do with its old 16mm black and white *Doctor Who* film prints?

A QUICK GUIDE TO DR WHO

In the mid-1970s, Enterprises produced an A4 photocopied sales brochure for *Doctor Who*, presumably for the benefit of prospective overseas buyers, entitled *A Quick Guide to Dr Who*. Although the brochure is undated, it lists every story from 'An Unearthly Child' to 'Planet of the Spiders'. There is no mention of Tom Baker's debut story, 'Robot', so this would probably date it to sometime in the last six months of 1974.

The information presented in *A Quick Guide to Dr Who* is surprisingly sparse for a sales brochure. The front cover has a basic sketch of the TARDIS emblazoned inside a crude star or explosion, alongside the name of the document, printed in a lovely 1970s Letraset font!

The second page of the brochure tells the reader that for each story, five key bits of information are listed. First up is the *identifying letter* (or production code, as we've since become accustomed to calling these alphanumeric notations). Second is the *title of adventure*. This is followed by point three, the number of episodes each story runs to. Points four and five are, respectively, the *Setting* of each story, and the *Monsters or Characters involved*.

WIPED!

Further notes then inform us:

* Serials A – ZZ available in monochrome only (i.e. black and white 16mm film prints).
* Serials AAA onwards available in colour or monochrome (i.e. colour two-inch videotape or black and white 16mm film prints).
* Not all materials are available for copyright reasons. These are indicated after the identifying letter of the serial.

Finally, details of who played the Doctor in each story are presented. William Hartnell's, Patrick Troughton's and Jon Pertwee's eras in the series are all correctly identified by the production codes of their first and last adventures, whilst Tom Baker is listed as being the Doctor from story 4A onwards. As story 4A isn't listed in *A Quick Guide to Dr Who* then one can only assume that the plan was to type up new pages for the guide each year, as new stories became available for sale, while at the same time presumably more *Not Available* comments would be added to older Hartnell and Troughton tales as they were either junked or their rights periods expired.

The list of all the stories then follows. Here is – word for word – what the guide has to say about them:

Code / Availability	*Title*	*No Eps*	*Setting*	*Monsters or Characters*
A – Not Available	(No title given)	4 eps	100,000BC	Palaeolithic tribesmen
B – Not Available	The Mutants	7 eps	The planet Skaro	Daleks
C	(No title given)	2 eps	Inside spaceship, snowy plateau	A Giant
D – Not Available	Marco Polo	7 eps	Encampment of Kublai Khan	Assassins
E – Not Available	The Keys of Marinus	6 eps	From 15th century Earth to distant space and far future	
F – Not Available	Dr. Who & the Aztecs	4 eps	Aztec Mexico	Aztecs
G – Not Available	Dr. Who & the Sensorites	6 eps	Planet of the Sensorites	The telepathic Sensorites
H – Not Available	The Reign of Terror	6 eps	French Revolution	

CHAPTER 5

J – Not Available	Dr. Who & Planet of Giants	3 eps	England, 1964	Dr. Who and companions reduced to one-inch
K – Not Available	Dalek Invasion of Earth	6 eps	London, 2164	Daleks
L – Not Available	Dr. Who & the Rescue	2 eps	Planet Dido	Koquillion
M – Not Available	Dr. Who & the Romans	4 eps	AD64 – the court of Nero	Great Fire of Rome
N	The Web Planet	6 eps	Lunar Planet Vortis	Menoptra and Zarbis
P – Not Available	Dr. Who & the Crusades	4 eps	Palestine, with Richard the Lionheart at the Crusades	Saracens
Q	The Space Museum	4 eps	Planet Xeros – far distant future	Moroks and Xerons – people of the future
R – Not Available	The Chase	6 eps	The Arid Planet. Planet Mechanus	The Mirebeast, The Mechanoids. The Daleks
S	The Time Meddler	4 eps	England, the Norman Conquest	Dr. Who meets a time-travelling monk
T	Galaxy 4	4 eps	A doomed planet	Chumblies (robots), Drahvins and Rills
U – Not Available	The Myth Makers	4 eps	The besieged city of Troy	(A high comedy adventure)
	Dalek Cutaway (Mission to the Unknown)		Jungle in solar system	Daleks
V – Not Available	The Daleks Master Plan	11 eps	Galaxy wide struggle	Daleks
W – Not Available	The Massacre of St Bartholomew	4 eps	16th Century Paris	
X – Not Available	Dr. Who & the Ark	4 eps	Space ship version of the Ark	The reptilian Monoids
Y – Not Available	The Celestial Toymaker	4 eps		Dolls of human size

WIPED!

Z – Not Available	Dr. Who & the Gunfighters	4 eps	American Wild West (Tombstone)	Doc Holliday, Wyatt Earp and other famous cowboy figures.
AA – Not Available	Dr. Who & the Savages	4 eps	Prehistoric Age	Savage Cavemen
BB	The War Machines	4 eps	Present day London	The War Machine (mobile computer)
CC	Dr. Who & the Smugglers	4 eps	17th century Cornwall	Pirates
DD	The Tenth Planet	4 eps	The year 2000	The Cybermen
EE	The Power of the Daleks	6 eps	2020AD Planet Vulcan	The Daleks In this episode, Patrick Troughton appears for the first time as Dr. Who
FF	Dr. Who & the Highlanders	4 eps	Culloden 1746	
GG	The Underwater Menace	4 eps	Atlantis	The Atlanteans
HH	Dr. Who & the Moonbase	4 eps	Moon 2070	The Cybermen
JJ	Dr. Who & the Macra Terror	4 eps	Strange Planet. Distant future	
KK	The Faceless Ones	6 eps	1966 Gatwick Airport and a space satellite	The Chameleons
LL – Not Available	The Evil of the Daleks	4 eps	Victorian London	Daleks
MM	The Tomb of the Cybermen	4 eps	The Planet Telos	Cybermen
NN	The Abominable Snowmen	6 eps	Tibet	The Yeti
OO	Dr. Who & the Ice Warriors	6 eps	The Second Ice Age	The Martian Ice Warriors
PP	The Enemy of the World	6 eps	Australia	

CHAPTER 5

QQ	The Web of Fear	6 eps	The London Underground	The Yeti and menacing cobwebs
RR	The Fury from the Deep	6 eps	Present Day. North Sea Gas Refinery	Seaweed creatures
SS	The Wheel in Space	6 eps	Space Station	The Cybermen and Cybermats
TT	The Dominators	5 eps	Present Day	The Quarks
UU	The Mind Robbers	5 eps	Distant Future	Legendary Monsters, a controlling computer and the White Robots
VV	The Invasion	8 eps	Present Day	The Cybermen
WW	The Krotons	4 eps	Distant Future	Crystalline monsters
XX	The Seeds of Death	6 eps	Distant Future	The Ice Warriors
YY	The Space Pirates	6 eps	Distant Future	Featuring inter-stellar ships
ZZ	The War Games	10 eps	Distant Future	Soldiers bought from many periods of time by an alien enemy
AAA	The Spearhead from Space	4 eps	Present Day	The Autons – plastic men The series goes into colour and Jon Pertwee takes over as the Doctor
BBB	The Silurians	7 eps	Present Day	Lizard-like men
CCC	The Ambassadors of Death	7 eps	Present Day	Martians, masquerading as returned astronauts
DDD	The Inferno	7 eps	Present Day	Primords – men degenerated into primeval apes

WIPED!

EEE	The Terror of the Autons	4 eps	Present Day	The Autons again, and the first appearance of the Master (Roger Delgado)
FFF	The Mind of Evil	6 eps	Present Day	An alien mind-eating parasite, brought to Earth by the Master
GGG	The Claws of Axos	4 eps	Present Day	The golden Axons, the Master's latest tools
HHH	Colony in Space	6 eps	25th Century	The Primitives, the Doomsday Machine and the Master
JJJ	The Dæmons	5 eps	Present Day	An immensely powerful Lucifer-like Alien, and two other gothic monsters
KKK	The Day of the Daleks	4 eps	25th Century	Ogrons and the Daleks
LLL	The Sea Devils	6 eps	Present Day	Undersea relations of the Silurians – and the Master
MMM	The Curse of Peladon	4 eps	Far distant future	Ice Warriors, Arcturus, Alpha Centuri and Aggedor
NNN	The Mutants	6 eps	Far Distant Future	Humanoids who degenerate into monstrous form
OOO	The Time Monster	6 eps	Back to Legendary Atlantis	Kronos – from outside time – and the Master
PPP	Carnival of Monsters	4 eps	Distant future	The dragon-like Drashigs

CHAPTER 5

RRR	The Three Doctors	4 eps	Present Day	All three manifestations of the Doctor, played by Jon Pertwee, Patrick Troughton and William Hartnell, battle with former Time Lord Omega
QQQ	Frontier in Space	6 eps	25th Century	The Draconians. The Ogrons, the Master and the Daleks
SSS	Planet of the Daleks	6 eps	25th Century	The Spiridons, the Daleks and the Doctor's old allies, the humanoid Thals. Note: in spite of the lettering, SSS follows directly on from QQQ
TTT	The Green Death	6 eps	Present Day	Pollution, two-foot maggots and a green sickness
UUU	The Time Warrior	4 eps	England, Middle Ages	Commander Linx, Sontaran Warrior, and Irongron and UNIT
WWW	The Invasion of the Dinosaurs	6 eps	Present Day	Dinosaurs, pterodactyls, a stegosaurus, a brontosaurus, and a tyrannosaurus rex
XXX	Death to the Daleks	4 eps	Planet Exxilons	Daleks

WIPED!

| YYY | The Monster of Peladon | 6 eps | Far Distant Future | Aggedor |
| ZZZ | Planet of the Spiders | 6 eps | Present Day | UNIT and the spiders of Metebelis |

That the compiler of the list seemed to think that 'The Evil of the Daleks' was a four-part story can be put down to simple human error, whilst the episode count for 'The Daleks Masterplan' being given as 11 confirms that this story was only ever offered for sale minus its seventh episode, rather than this being a similar oversight. The placing of 'Carnival of Monsters' before 'The Three Doctors' mirrors the production order, and the order in which many overseas stations would show these two stories.

What *A Quick Guide to Dr Who* illustrates is that the earlier stories were, by 1974, starting to come out of their window of sales rights exploitation. But can we assume that every story listed as *Not Available* had been junked by this point? And can we assume that ever other Hartnell and Troughton story, listed by default as available, was still in existence at Enterprises?

The stories that appear to have been still available from the first three seasons – 'The Edge of Destruction', 'The Web Planet', 'The Space Museum', 'The Time Meddler', 'Galaxy 4', 'Mission to the Unknown' and 'The War Machines' – seem a somewhat random selection. As we have seen, the rights for the first season stories would have expired initially in 1968/69, and again in 1973/74, so the fact that 'The Edge of Destruction' still crops up as for sale is just about plausible. But why just this one story, especially as most of the others from that season were definitely still sitting on Enterprises' shelves (where they were found in 1978)? Is it perhaps because the cast comprised only the four regular members, thus making it potentially easier for the rights to be renegotiated should a new sale arise?

The sales rights to the programme's second season would have expired from November 1974 through to July 1975, and it is perhaps telling that the three stories still listed as available from this season come from its tail end. 'The Web Planet' and 'The Time Meddler' had both been sold to Nigeria as recently as July 1973, along with 'The War Machines' from the third season.

The fact that most of the third season stories are listed as unavailable is somewhat mystifying, as the overseas sales rights to these adventures (the Dalek episodes aside) would not have been due to expire until between November 1975 ('The Myth Makers') and June 1976 ('The Savages'). That 'Mission to the Unknown' is still listed as available would seem to suggest that the sales rights for this single episode had been extended for another five years after their initial expiry in October 1970.

The availability of nearly all of the stories from the programme's fourth season

CHAPTER 5

(apart from 'The Evil of the Daleks') is in some ways reassuring, demonstrating that the pool of available stories was being reduced in some sort of date order, with the oldest generally being the first to be withdrawn. But it also seems to contradict the evidence that most of the early Troughton stories didn't have their sales rights renewed once the initial five year period had expired, which would have been in 1971/2.

Why 'The Evil of the Daleks' is the only Troughton story to be listed as *Not Available* is also something of a mystery. Later evidence shows that it was junked by Enterprises in 1974, but so were many other stories. Perhaps it simply went into the skip outside Villiers House significantly earlier in the year than the others?

One possibility – and it is only a theory – is that the brochure was produced to see if there was still a market for the old *Doctor Who* stories. Perhaps the lack of sales that it generated – only a few odd Troughton stories were sold after this point – sealed the fate of the large number of *Doctor Who* prints that Enterprises junked in 1974?

The brochure was revised and re-issued by Enterprises the following year. It now included the first five Tom Baker stories from Season 12 (with 'Revenge of the Cybermen' and 'Genesis of the Daleks' being listed in production order rather than transmission order), which suggests a date sometime around the spring of 1975.

Code/ Availability	Title	No Eps	Setting	Monsters or Characters
4A	Robot	4 eps	Present Day	UNIT
4C	The Ark in Space	4 eps	Far distant future (on the spaceship 'Nerva')	The Wirrn
4B	The Sontaran Experiment	2 eps	Far distant future – Earth	Styre and The Sontarans
4D	The Revenge of the Cybermen	4 eps	Distant future	Nerva (the space-station) & Cybermen
4E	The Genesis of the Daleks	6 eps	Distant future – planet Skaro	Daleks, Thals & Kaleds

Some of the Hartnell stories listed as available in the previous catalogue were now marked as *Not Available* some 12 months later. These were 'The Edge of Destruction', 'Mission to the Unknown', 'The War Machines', 'The Smugglers' and 'The Tenth Planet'. This left 'The Web Planet', 'The Space Museum', 'The Time Meddler' and 'Galaxy 4' as the only Hartnell stories still seemingly being sold by Enterprises.

For Troughton's Doctor, now every story from 'The Power of the Daleks' through to 'The Enemy of the World' had *Not Available* typed next to it, as did 'The Mind Robber' and 'The Krotons'. Does this indicate that a whole batch of *Doctor Who* 16mm telerecordings had been junked by Enterprises in the 12 months or so between the two versions of the catalogue?

BLUE PETER AND 'THE TENTH PLANET' EPISODE FOUR

One of the greatest fan myths surrounding the subject of missing *Doctor Who* episodes is that Episode Four of the final Hartnell adventure, 'The Tenth Planet', was lost by the *Blue Peter* production team after they borrowed the telerecording so that they could show a brief clip of the Doctor's first regeneration. The facts of the situation are rather different.

The edition of *Blue Peter* broadcast on 5 November 1973 ran a retrospective feature celebrating *Doctor Who*'s tenth anniversary on air. A number of clips from old episodes were featured, and these did indeed include a 30-second sequence from Episode Four of 'The Tenth Planet'. But is there any truth to the story that *Blue Peter* then lost the episode? Well, the original 405-line broadcast tape for this episode was wiped by the BBC in October 1969, and *Blue Peter* could hardly be blamed for that. Telerecordings of the first three episodes were found to be held by the Film Library in 1977, and it's possible that people assumed the absence of the fourth episode was somehow proof that *Blue Peter* had lost the print in 1973. But the Film Library never held a print of 'The Tenth Planet' Episode Four; there was never any index card for it in their card system.

In fact, the film print that the *Blue Peter* production team used was borrowed from Enterprises, and there is nothing to suggest that they failed to return it afterwards. Even if the print had been mislaid, Enterprises would almost certainly still have had a negative of the episode at that point. And the story was still being offered for sale in 1974, according to the first *A Quick Guide to Dr Who* brochure. If Enterprises were still selling the story in 1974, then Episode Four can't have been lost in 1973!

THE DWAS AND 'GALAXY 4'

The Lively Arts documentary 'Whose Doctor Who', broadcast in 1977, looked at the history of the series in a manner that had never been done before, and utilised a large number of archive clips. Producer Tony Cash had been assisted in his background research for this by members of the newly-formed Doctor Who Appreciation Society, including in particular Society President Jan Vincent-Rudzki.

The DWAS held the first ever *Doctor Who* convention in 1977, and organiser Keith Barnfather then began planning for a follow-up to be held in August 1978. In January 1978, on the recommendation of *Doctor Who* producer Graham Williams, Barnfather

CHAPTER 5

contacted BBC Enterprises to see if it would be possible for the DWAS to screen an old story at the event. As they anticipated that they would have to pay clearance fees to any actors featured in the episodes they screened, the DWAS decided to ask for a story with a relatively small cast. 'Galaxy 4' fitted the bill well, in that apart from the three main cast members, there were only four other artistes featured. Also, the story was thought to still exist, as this had been seemingly established in the research for 'Whose Doctor Who' in late 1976, to which Vincent-Rudzki had been privy.

The Film and Video Sales department of Enterprises was contacted by Barnfather in early March 1978 with a formal approach to buy film prints of all four episodes of 'Galaxy 4', on the understanding that the DWAS could show the story at their convention only if they were able to clear this with the principal cast members, or their representatives, and any other rights holders. Barnfather then received a letter dated 9 March 1978 from Enterprises, telling him:

Re: *Doctor Who* and the Chumblies.

I regret to inform you that, after considerable research, we have discovered that all master material relating to the above series has been destroyed. I am sorry to give you this disappointing news.

This was one of the first instances of the BBC making details of the destruction of specific old episodes of *Doctor Who* known outside of the Corporation. Obviously, this letter put paid to the notion of the DWAS buying 16mm film copies of this story, and the matter was not pursued further (although the DWAS would later buy 16mm film copies of 'An Unearthly Child', 'The Edge of Destruction' and 'The Rescue'). However, it has somehow led to the latter-day myth that 'Galaxy 4' was junked mere days or weeks prior to the DWAS approaching the BBC, or that the DWAS had come close to preventing its destruction. In fact, the story could have been junked at any point between November 1976, when the researchers for 'Whose Doctor Who' had compiled their listings of the BBC's *Doctor Who* holdings, and Barnfather's enquiry to Enterprises in March 1978.

THE BFI

Occasionally the British Film Institute would be offered material that BBC Enterprises was disposing of. The BFI would regularly contact various BBC departments in the 1970s, and ask if they were throwing any films away. If so, they would say, could those films perhaps be given to the BFI instead? After all, one of the aims of the BFI was to try to preserve selected examples of the nation's television heritage. It was sometimes down to sheer luck and good timing that would see them being offered material, and

WIPED!

one such instance occurred in 1977.

At that time, Enterprises were disposing of their 16mm film negatives of three Troughton stories: 'The Dominators', 'The Krotons' and 'The War Games'. All three had been selected to be 'Withdrawn, De-accessioned and Junked', but instead of them being sent to the skip, and then on to the incinerator, they were handed over to the BFI, who transferred them to their own archive.

The details of why and how this happened weren't fully uncovered for another couple of years, and the ramifications were potentially massive, as we shall later discover …

AFTER TRANSMISSION …

Under BBC Enterprises' standard overseas sales contracts, which applied to *Doctor Who* as well as to other shows, foreign broadcasters would have the rights to transmit a given programme a set number of times within a set period. If they had used up the allowed number of screenings, or the time period had expired, then they had to do one of three things:

i. Send the films back to BBC Enterprises in London.
ii. Send the films on to another foreign broadcaster if BBC Enterprises requested them to do so.
iii. Destroy the films, and issue a certificate of destruction back to BBC Enterprises.

Although we know from third-hand sources which of these three actions was taken in relation to some copies of some episodes from some countries (see Appendix (i) for details), *no* surviving BBC documentation has yet been uncovered that records exactly what happened to any of the *Doctor Who* films that Enterprises sold around the world in the 1960s and 1970s.

CHAPTER 6
RECLAIMING THE PAST —
THE BEGINNING OF THE END OF THE JUNKINGS ...

The BBC in the early 1970s were not blind to the problems that had been inherited from the previous decade, or to the circumstances, procedures and policies that had led to the position whereby old programmes were being routinely destroyed. Not only were there internal pressures to improve matters, but there was also public scrutiny by outside bodies such as the BFI, who by this point were openly questioning the BBC's lack of clarity regarding its archives and archiving procedures.

THE ANNAN COMMITTEE REPORT

The Annan Committee on the Future of Broadcasting was established in April 1974, to look specifically at new television technologies and their funding, within the framework of the existing two BBC channels and the ITV network. The Committee reported its findings in February 1977, the two significant actioned recommendations of which were an increase in the BBC's licence fee, and the setting up of Channel 4, which eventually began broadcasting in November 1982.

The report also touched briefly on the topic of programme archiving, and drew the conclusion that videotape technology was sufficiently advanced in 1977 to be able to record every programme that was broadcast on the three UK channels, and therefore that the only obstacle to preserving the totality of Britain's television programme output was financial, not technical. However, when the cost of keeping just all of ITV's programmes from a single year was estimated at £1.2 million plus a further £400,000 in operating costs, it accepted that such a financial burden was not one that the television companies could be expected to shoulder.

The report made well-intentioned recommendations about a three-tiered approach to television archiving, whereby the television companies would keep what programmes they could; the rest would be offered to the National Film Archive (NFA); and any that the NFA rejected would then be offered to the people involved with the original production, to see if any of them wanted to keep the tapes. However, this proposal was roundly condemned as unworkable by all parties, including the BBC.

MEDIA INTEREST IN THE BBC'S WIPING OF OLD PROGRAMMES

An article by Nicholas Wapshott in the *Scotsman* on 21 August 1975, entitled *Why TV Wipes out its Masterpieces*, was one of the first public examinations of the BBC's policy

WIPED!

of junking old shows. This was sparked by the BBC's recent *Festival 40* series of archive programmes celebrating 40 years of its television broadcasts. Wapshott reported on the elaborate arrangements that had to be made to allow the broadcast of so much archive material, and noted:

> The contract [between the BBC and the artists' unions] allows a first showing and a repeat showing within two years, and there is a stipulated repeat fee for the artists involved. Any repeat showing after that date must be negotiated individually with every artist involved in the production.
>
> This has led to very little repeating after two years, because of the administrative cost of renegotiating, the reluctance of some artists to [have] their earlier work reshown and the repeat fees demanded …
>
> In this impossible situation the BBC have, with their limited resources, tried to keep tapes – ostensibly for their own use and not for rebroadcasting – which are of historical or artistic value. By strict letter of the two-year contracts, the programme would, after that period, have been automatically junked.
>
> With rising costs, the BBC have been forced – reluctantly by those with an informed and intelligent approach to archive material – to keep only the most obviously valuable or useful material
>
> The future, however, is optimistic. The latest annual contract between the television companies and the artists' unions has considerably relaxed the position of repeating after a two-year period. Equity have agreed to allow the BBC 52 'out of time' repeats a year, as long as repeat fees are paid according to an agreed code and that the number of such repeats is deducted from the 'bought film' quota – the category of cinema-based feature films and bought, mainly American, film series – so that their members' livelihoods are not put in jeopardy by their own past work.
>
> This contract, signed last December, has allowed the *Festival 40* season to go ahead with little friction and allow similarly ambitious retrospectives to be organised on a regular basis.

A few months later, in its November 1975 issue, the trade magazine *Video & Audiovisual Review* ran a three-page feature on the state of the BBC's television archive. Written by Adrian Hope, the article revolved around an interview between Hope and Anne Hanford, the then head of the Film Library. It carefully explained the difference between the public perception of what the BBC's archive policy should be and the financial reality of the situation. The most telling statement was: '…the BBC neither

CHAPTER 6

needs nor can afford to preserve a copy of every videotape or film it transmits.'

At the time, Hanford was in the process of unifying the BBC's two major visual archives, the Film Library and the videotape storage library. As the article noted:

> The idea of videotape shelves being cleared by the metre length, or wiped at the whim of a clerk for economical re-use, is strongly contested at the BBC, on the grounds that all decisions are made after careful consideration, and anyway old black and white video recordings cannot be shown in colour, and so on and so on. There is nevertheless still plenty of routine erasure.
>
> Videotape has done much for broadcasting but its prime blessing is also sometimes a terrible disadvantage: it is awfully easy to erase. There is of course nothing to prevent a clerk from ordering film into a dustbin, but a dustbin full of film is much more difficult to explain away than a reel of blank tape.

Some of the costs associated with keeping and viewing old programmes were disclosed in the article. At the Film Library, the cost for a private viewing of a film was £20 an hour. For a two-inch videotape, it was £60 an hour. To cut down its in-house costs, the Film Library had begun making off-air recordings on domestic Philips videotape recorders of all the BBC's output, and was using these tapes to determine the cataloguing requirements of each and every programme. If a two-inch videotape was to be copied onto film, the transfer cost was £10 a minute. To copy an hour-long colour two-inch tape onto another two-inch tape also incurred huge costs. Two two-inch machines would be required, plus an engineer to run them. A blank 60-minute tape would set the BBC back £100. The total rate for the job would be around £200 an hour.

THE BBC STARTS TO ACT

With Equity relaxing its rules on repeats late in 1974, it was down to the BBC itself to take the next step over its old programmes. That *something* needed to be done was no longer an issue. Exactly *what* needed to be done, and by *whom*, was less obvious. In 1978, the BBC's senior management decided that it needed to create a new position, that of an Archive Selector, whose responsibility it would be to ensure that things changed – that programmes were retained, and that the junking of old material was halted. The person chosen to fill this position was Sue Malden, who had previously been working in the intake area of the Film Library for some years.

Malden had seen first-hand for some time how the workings of the BBC had led to the archiving policy – or, more accurately, the lack of archiving policy – that the Corporation had arrived at in the mid-'70s, albeit more by default than by any kind of strategic planning decision.

When preparing this book, I was able to speak to Malden at length about what exactly was going on at the BBC in the 1970s:

Sue Malden: The key person for putting the question of the BBC's archiving policy on the map was Anne Hanford, who worked at the BBC Film Library when it moved to Brentford in 1968. Before her, there was someone called Brian Enright who ran the Film Library, and I think he was more of a professional librarian. But I think he began the practice of running it in a professional way, rather than it just being a film store.

But how stuff got there in the Film Library in the first place? I don't think there was a coherent selection policy in that sense, and so people just sort of passed stuff to the Library. I would think that once they moved the Library from the Film Studios down to Windmill Road in 1968, they would have introduced a more coherent way of getting stuff sent down there. I don't know that a selection policy as such existed, but Anne was obviously building up to all that.

And the other thing was, there were originally people called 'Selectors' in the Sound Archive. The Sound Archive structure was that there was the Current Library, which was the equivalent of Current Ops in television, and then there was the Archive. The ... 'Selectors' ... selected stuff from the Current Library and moved it into the Archive, and they catalogued the material at the same time. And in the Sound Library, they also created programme compilations. They might have decided that a whole edition of *World at One* – or whatever the equivalent was in those days – wasn't worth keeping, but all the bits about what the Prime Minister said about this or that were worth retaining, and so they compiled that section onto disc.

And so that was very much a radio practice, but I think that there was a similar set-up in television. Some film cans had a 'CL' code which stood for Current Library, and most of them were 'PL' which stood for Permanent Library, and then there were also some 'EN' codes, which stood for BBC Enterprises. And so there were these three different code sequences, all of which indicated the status of the given programme. Then colour television came along, and all colour material was given a 'K' code.

So when I was working in the intake area at Accessions, before my work as Selector, you had people generally wondering about why there were all these different code sequences for programmes. 'EN' was a 'dead' sequence,

CHAPTER 6

and 'CL' was also effectively 'dead' – they just weren't added to at all. And so what I did was to transfer all the 'EN's and 'CL's into the 'PL' range, so at least you had just one sequence. And what that indicated was that there was a similar process to the radio going on; when stuff came into the Current Library, it was held for a period of time, reviewed by the Selector and then moved into the Permanent Library – or if not, then junked at that point. And then BBC Enterprises indicated that they were also holding stuff – I don't know of any review process that happened on that.

So, although I was the first Television Selector, there had been people doing this job of selection before, but at a different kind of level. But it looked like they had just been going through the Current Library and saying 'Yes' or 'No'. They must have had some sort of archival criteria back then, but I don't recollect seeing anything about what system or rules they were working to, or whether it was just their own personal views about what needed to be retained. There'd clearly been some selection going on – or de-selection, perhaps – but I couldn't work out on what basis they'd made these selections. I don't think they had any criteria.

Later on, for example, when I became Television Selector, and was overseeing the whole review process, we'd find things that had been put into the Category As (the alphabetical system later devised to categorise the entire contents of the BBC Film and Television Library), and for the life of us we just couldn't work out why. So that is why I introduced this process and procedure of saying *why* something had been selected, and introduced a set of criteria. So you'd say, 'This was kept for … criterion A, B or C …', or whatever, so that at least people in the future could know what was on your mind when you decided what should be kept. And we occasionally added a few notes if we could, although the computer system wasn't very good at allowing that. So that was again learning from what had happened in the past.

Anne Hanford worked with a guy called Alan Shawcross, who I think came from more of a production side, and their role was to introduce a set of selection criteria or policy. I don't know if they were pre the Briggs report, or as a response to it. But certainly, they did a lot of early work on the mapping out of the criteria for selecting and retaining programmes.

THE BRIGGS REPORT

The Briggs report to which Sue Malden refers was the *Report on the Advisory Committee on Archives*, which was published in full by the BBC in 1979. The Committee had by that point been exploring for some time the background to the state of affairs at the

WIPED!

BBC in relation to *all* of its archives.

The need for the BBC to get to grips with its archival commitments and policies was first officially recognised in February 1975, when a draft paper on the subject was prepared for the BBC's General Advisory Council, which reported to the BBC's Board of Governors. This was to address the scope of the BBC's archival responsibilities, in terms of audio material, paperwork and television programmes. This draft paper noted:

> There are identifiable and important gaps, due not so much to custodial deficiencies as to the fact that, particularly in the earlier years, there was a less general recognition of the historical importance of written and sound archives than there is now and, even more important, a limit to the amount of money that it was considered appropriate to devote to these purposes.

The paper detailed the BBC's current (as of February 1975) destruction and retention practices as applied to all of its television material:

> Ideally, the BBC would keep all the material it accumulates, and house it in a vast integrated library open both to its own staff and to all bona-fide outside researchers. In practice this is impossible because of the costs of storage and of staff. A full list of the libraries in which archive material is kept, in the form of a 'Directory of BBC Libraries and Information Services' which has been prepared for use within the BBC, is attached to this paper as an Appendix. This shows not only the richness of the collections held, but the accommodation and staffing involved. The 'Directory' does not, however, describe the retention and destruction practices, and a summary of these, as currently pursued by the 14 libraries which deal with archive material, is as follows:-
>
> (i) Visual Material
>
> Film Library: all BBC-produced film material is initially taken in. Films are retained if the Head of the production department concerned, in consultation with the Film and Videotape Librarian, considers this should be done or if BBC Enterprises intends to make use of them for outside sales. Some stock shots are extracted by Library staff. The rest are destroyed. Some material, which would otherwise be destroyed, is donated to the National Film Archive.
>
> Videotape Library (now amalgamated with Film Library): as above except that video tapes not retained may be wiped and re-used …

CHAPTER 6

The report also noted:

> The Independent Television Companies Association make a grant to the NFA of £20,000 a year to enable it to buy ITV programmes. Although the BBC is in complete sympathy with the aims of the NFA, its system of financing does not allow it to make a grant of any kind – and indeed, were the NFA to apply similar criteria to the acquisition of BBC output, a substantially larger sum would be required.
>
> The NFA's committee grades some BBC films as 'A' and these may be acquired from the BBC at copying cost. It grades others as 'B', and these are handed over free of charge by the BBC if the time comes that the BBC no longer wishes to retain them itself.

The members of the Advisory Committee on Archives were chosen and appointed by the BBC's Board of Governors. The Chairman was respected academic Lord Asa Briggs, who was joined by other academics from various universities and libraries, plus the writer and broadcaster Benny Green. The actor Marius Goring[41] also sat on the Committee, in his then role as Vice-President of Equity, the actors' union.

The BBC formally announced the setting up of the Committee in a press release on 27 January 1976. The Committee actually held its first meeting on 22 January 1976, in which the various members set out an initial framework document that detailed the terms of reference for the study.

The Committee noted that, as the BBC's main source of income was the licence fee, this should be used primarily for broadcasting purposes, and that any archiving policies should reflect this. Thus any items retained and preserved should be either for re-use or for reference purposes.

The areas the Committee focused on were the BBC's archival policies in relation to its visual, audio and written archives, including storage and selection. Its aim was to advise the BBC as to how these resources could be best exploited in the BBC's and the national interest. The Committee met six times between January 1976 and December 1977, and during that time prepared an interim report, which was then presented to the BBC Board of Governors in January 1978.

The BBC's archival inventory was broken down into four areas: the Sound Archives; the Registry and Reference Services at the Written Archive Centre in Caversham; the Music Library; and the Television Film and Videotape Library. One of

---

41 Goring had played Theodore Maxtible in the Patrick Troughton story 'The Evil of the Daleks', the transmission tapes of which had ironically been junked by the BBC some years earlier.

WIPED!

the first observations the Committee made was about the speed at which the Film and Videotape Library was growing, as more and more new programmes were produced. Another issue the Committee struggled to get to grips with was that of external access to the BBC's archives. While the internal market of the BBC itself was well served, the needs of potential external users were flagged up for serious consideration when the Committee set out its final recommendations.

From the very start, the Committee was under no illusions as to the problems the BBC faced in terms of programme preservation:

> Some of those who contacted us seemed to feel that virtually everything ever broadcast should be preserved on the mere off-chance that it might one day prove valuable, but we unanimously rejected this view as unrealistic. We examined in some detail the criteria applied by the various selectors appointed by the BBC, and the extent to which it could be further standardised.

Another early passage from the interim report noted:

> We realised early on that to some extent preservation and use are mutually incompatible; the greater the access given to any document, film or tape, the shorter its life is likely to be. We considered, however, ways in which this basic difficulty could be overcome, for example, by preparing a non-accessible master copy from which access copies are made as necessary. The primary problem, however, is one of selection, and we agreed that as far as possible the same criteria should be applied throughout the BBC to determine whether a particular document or recording should be kept.

The area of rights and contracts was then considered. The interim report stated:

> We studied in some detail the contracts currently in use and we may be making recommendations as to whether or not it might be desirable, or indeed necessary, for the BBC to take wider rights than at present, to ensure that material it wishes to make available is not denied to would-be users on contractual grounds.

The interim report then concluded with a statement that seemed to be curiously out of step with the rest of the document:

> We believe the BBC is fortunate in having so many 'archive-minded' people

CHAPTER 6

among its staff, that the criticisms of the BBC which have been made over such matters as the alleged 'wiping' of irreplaceable tapes have largely been unfounded, and that the obstacles which exist to developing a more comprehensive and consistent archive policy are not insuperable, and by no means all financial.

The Committee's final report was prepared by Lord Asa Briggs and his team throughout the rest of 1978, and was presented to the BBC's Board of Governors in April 1979. An early recommendation was that the BBC's archival responsibilities should perhaps be included in the wording of the Corporation's Royal Charter upon its next renewal, which would establish beyond doubt that it had a right to spend some of its licence fee revenue on this purpose. Below are reproduced some of the other key conclusions and recommendations from the report:

The BBC Film and Videotape Library is the largest in the world. Altogether the Corporation holds approximately 350,000 cans of film and 60,000 spools of videotape. About 12,000 cans of film and 6,000 spools of videotape are added to its holdings each year.

The BBC's policy is to retain material for long-term re-use on the advice of Heads of Groups and Departments, with the final decision being taken by BBC's Film and Videotape Librarian, using the following agreed criteria:

a) Material on the history and development of television (this includes artistic and technical achievements, new television techniques and outstanding examples of existing techniques).
b) Material in which people of historic interest appear (sport, entertainment, drama, politics, science, etc).
c) Events (actuality) of historic interest (in all fields) including those moments when a live television programme itself makes history (and for which recording facilities have been found in time).
d) Material of sociological interest (i.e. examples of aspects of contemporary life, plays, documentaries, and light entertainment).
e) Material showing objects such as works of art, buildings, machinery and equipment, etc.
f) Material showing geographical places, especially related to stages in development.
g) Individual programmes or series of programmes (not less than six) which would be of use to future compilers of transmission schedules in

reflecting retrospectively the work of an outstanding artist or artists and for showing again significant programmes from all types of output.

The Film and Videotape Library is primarily for use within the BBC. It handles about 400 internal enquiries a week seeking information or material for re-use. Three hours of film extracts from the Library, ten hours of programmes previously broadcast on film and over 20 hours of programmes previously broadcast on tape, are transmitted each week.

Some concern was expressed to us that all the copies of a programme might be destroyed without the people involved in making it – writers, actors and production staff – being aware of what was happening or being given an opportunity to buy a copy for personal retention. While we recognise that the BBC cannot be expected to keep a copy of every programme it transmits, and that copyright difficulties might arise if all those concerned in making a programme were to be given an automatic right to obtain a copy of it, nevertheless the point seems to us to have substance. We also recognise that if such a right did exist it would serve one of the aims we feel to be desirable, namely to ensure that as many programmes as possible are kept in some form, and to facilitate access to them, if only for private reference.

BBC Enterprises and the Film Hire Library also hold material which could be stored at the Film and Videotape Library and recorded in its catalogue. Although Enterprises must retain viewing cassettes and sometimes viewing prints, and the Film Hire Library must control the actual film copies it distributes, material from which other copies are made should be controlled by the Library and surplus prints returned there. This will maximise a more efficient preservation and access policy.

We were concerned that most untransmitted material was not being considered by the selectors in the Film and Videotape Library. Selection can only take place if production staff prepare adequate shot lists and if editors sort and label material not used in the programme. This can only be done if programme budgets allow for the appropriate personnel time and facilities. Some system should be devised to ensure that this material is made available for selection with the appropriate information and in the appropriate form.

We found that the selection procedures and preservation techniques applied to programmes transmitted on videotape were not as thorough as those applied to film programmes. We recognised the historical and technical reasons for this, but could see no justifiable reasons for treating them differently in future.

CHAPTER 6

> We support the current policy of transferring all remaining 405 line material to 625 line videotape before the equipment which handles the former format is obsolete.

So the Committee looked at the historical reasons for the mish-mash of internal BBC procedures and practices, and recommended a new way of working. The aims of this were to introduce some clarity for those outside bodies looking inwards on the BBC; to help the BBC gain a better understanding of its own heritage; and to ensure that the BBC preserved what it could of the material surviving from its past, and worked responsibly to preserve programmes in the future. Although the report wasn't officially published until 1979, many of its findings and recommendations were discussed and anticipated by the BBC management for a considerable time prior to this.

Sue Malden: Lord Asa Briggs was asked to do a report on the BBC archives. My understanding was that it was against a background of BBC awareness that it ought to be more open about what it was doing, possibly in the light of some criticism thrown at it by the BFI and other organisations that cared about archives. By then, the BFI was beginning to get its teeth into the BBC. The BFI previously had only the national *film* archive, but they took on responsibility for television as well possibly at around about this time. Clearly, the people at the BFI had a concern about the retention of television, and so they had quite a lot of input into the Briggs report, coupled with, as I say, the BBC realising that they needed to be more open about what it was doing. And so the Briggs report came out with all sorts of interesting recommendations – not all of which I can remember – but one that was very good, and that is only now just beginning to happen in a way, was that there ought to be someone with an archive interest at the end of every production, to help the production team clear up, tidy up, and ensure that everything that was relevant found its way into the archives, and I think that approach applied to paperwork, tapes, rushes ... everything. That wasn't acted upon at the time. But I'd say that in the last two years or so, the BBC's Information and Archives have been very active in getting media asset managers positions with productions to do exactly that. And media asset management sounds a lot grander than tidying up after the end of a production! There's more to it than that, but obviously they're helping the production teams document and preserve stuff all through the production process, so that it's all there and identified, ready to go into the archive. So at long last – 30 years later – that's happened! There were all sorts of recommendations I can't remember ... But a key one was that the BBC should appoint an Archive Selector, who would be responsible for the selection and retention of BBC television output, because radio already had that process with these nine or ten Selectors that worked in their own different subject areas.

Prior to the creation of the post of Archive Selector in 1978, the Film Library had slowly begun implementing a whole range of new working practices, which had to be fought through with other BBC departments nearly every step of the way. One of the key policy changes that the Library had secured in the early 1970s was for it to take charge of all of the BBC's two-inch videotapes, which until then had been the prerogative of the Engineering Department. This was gradually phased in around 1974/1975, and was primarily the work of the then head of the Film Library, Anne Hanford.

Anne Hanford: All the BBC's two-inch tape was under the control of the Engineering Department to begin with. The Engineering Department were very anxious that they should be able to release for re-use as many tapes as possible as quickly as possible, mainly due to the high cost of the tape itself. The more tape that was re-used, the less money that needed to be spent on new tape. But this was coupled with the agreement we had with the unions, specifically Equity. When I first joined the BBC, it was written into the Equity agreement that all the programmes would be destroyed after two years of being transmitted. So there was a huge amount of pressure from the senior management to ensure that as many two-inch tapes as possible were erased for re-use; certainly anything that was over two years old was fair game. Production departments were also reluctant to authorise retention.

At the time, I continually made the point that we should be keeping this material, despite what the current agreements said. After all, agreements can always be re-negotiated and altered. In a way, BBC Enterprises offered a solution to this problem for *Doctor Who* and other popular programmes, in that they made 16mm black and white film copies for sale overseas.

Sue Malden: From the work that Anne Hanford had done with Alan Shawcross, clearly she was very aware, increasingly, that the Film Library was responsible for only a small – if significant – part of the BBC's output. So she began campaigning to get control of the videotape recordings as well. So that pre-dated my position, or my appointment. And there was some involvement from a woman called Kay Salway, who was in charge of what was

CHAPTER 6

called Cataloguing back then (which was looking after all the documentation of the archive material). So initially the three of us worked in pushing at these barriers regarding videotape to some extent. But really those two did more than I did, in terms of campaigning and actually achieving the transfer and documentation of videotape from Engineering to the Library. And it was a very bitter fight. It wasn't just with the troops, kind of thing, it was at management level as well, who were sticking their noses in, whatever. It didn't help much that the Film Library was in a different managerial structure at the BBC. It was part of the Film Department.

The Film Department was still a very strong BBC department, in that at that time in the 1970s, it was the height of the BBC's film productions really. All the big documentaries and dramas were done on film. It was a big department in itself, but didn't have that much to do with VT recording or studio recording. And clearly the VT department saw themselves as providing a service for production and transmission. Later, when I took over running the Sound Library, I found exactly the same process there, that the Current Library sound archive was servicing the production needs and the transmission needs, and certainly didn't see archiving as one of its priorities. The process of archiving was certainly ranked below servicing what production people wanted and what transmission people wanted, and that's what you also found happening in VT in the early 1970s. The way they saw it, the tapes were owned by production, they were required for transmission, or sometimes repeats, and so they would service them for that. Meanwhile they were operating the VT store for production, and if production said they didn't want to keep the tapes, well then they thought they must know what they were doing, so they didn't keep them.

But of course, the VT area would have also had, as part of their responsibility, the purchasing of all the new tape stock. And clearly, they had the responsibility for managing that as efficiently and as cheaply as possible, so that if they could recycle the tapes and re-use them quickly, they would. That was one of their *raisons d'être*, so that's what they did. So Anne was the main one rather than me that fought that battle with VT. I would have thought that would have been ongoing from 1974 through to about the time of the Briggs report. But a lot of that is really a 'chicken and egg' situation. Whether the Briggs report raised people's awareness, or people were already aware of this anyway …? Because sometimes an outsider coming in and telling you what to do is a very useful way for telling people what you think needs to be done and getting it publicised. The Library already had responsibility for videotape

WIPED!

by the time I was made Selector.

Before the Archive Selector post was even thought of, there was a guy called Gareth Morris, who was Senior Assistant in Enquiries. When Anne Hanford had succeeded in getting some kind of involvement in VT, the main thrust of that was taking over responsibility for the staff that documented the tapes, and took the information off the Engineer's Report Form and put it into the system. From that, the Library managed to get hold of print-outs of stuff that had been proposed for wiping. And Gareth Morris, the guy in charge of Enquiries, was given the job of checking these print-outs, and saying whether these things should be wiped or not. So that was the very beginning of the Library exercising any sort of responsibility over that.

He used to discuss with me the things that were on these lists, and we'd say: 'That's ridiculous – that shouldn't be on there. We'd put a big cross through them, and send the lists back off to somebody in VT. But we'd check up on one or two, and they didn't seem to have taken any notice of what we'd put on there. So we went back to Anne and said: 'There's something wrong here, even this system isn't working well enough, it needs to be better.' What she was then doing behind the scenes, I don't know, but the next thing that happened was that it was announced that there was a new post of Television Archive Selector being created at the BBC, and that people could apply for it.

I later found out, behind the scenes, that the new position couldn't be called a Television Archivist because they didn't require a qualified archivist for the job. What they required was someone who knew something about television, and probably also had librarianship skills, but those specialist skills of an archivist weren't necessarily what they saw as valuable. The BBC already had an Archivist at their Written Archive Centre in Caversham, who was a trained archivist, and you think of those professional archive qualifications and skills applied to paper documents and things like that. Through the BBC grading system, someone had objected to the post that I got being called an Archivist, so it was called Television Archive Selector. But I didn't know that until afterwards!

So I applied for the job. Several other people in the Library did. I don't know if it was advertised outside the BBC, it might well have been … Anyway, I was successful, and I started the job in 1978.

Sue Malden's appointment as the BBC's first Television Archive Selector in 1978 was a turning point for the Corporation. For the first time, there was somebody whose role it was to look at the retention of programmes as a priority, rather than as an afterthought.

CHAPTER 6

But having been given the role of Television Archive Selector, Malden then needed to define it, not only for herself, but for the various production departments at the BBC. Her early days in the post were mainly spent ensuring that the new systems and procedures were put into place with the BBC's programme-makers, so that new programmes could be effectively and efficiently preserved for the future.

Sue Malden: Anne Hanford was very good, and along with Alan Shawcross, had by then got the BBC's archive selection policy written up as a kind of formal document. So what she then did was arrange for me to be taken to visit all the heads of production, and we would talk them through my new role; what I was going to do, why I was needed, why it was important, and what the criteria were that we would now be using for selecting material for the archives. And, obviously, to clearly start telling them how the process was going to be changing, and that we would be overriding decisions that they had made for purely understandable short-term production needs; that, longer-term, we had a view, and that we would and could override their decisions. And they all accepted it, they accepted the intellectual argument.

Not one person argued about the value of the tape, despite the fact that, behind the scenes, this could have had a big impact on the budgets. But of course, this was all pre- the internal market (which the BBC under John Birt introduced in the 1990s), so quite how the BBC budgeted for all that, I don't quite know. Perhaps VT took over the entire budget for all the tape stock that was ordered by the BBC, and did not then attribute it to the production team, as they had done before. Or maybe they did. That bit I don't know. But you can see, if you were to suddenly say that you would be likely to be retaining, say 10%-20% more than before, then it does have cost implications in terms of recycling the tapes.

One of the things that helped in that was Kay Salway's input on the documentation side. She introduced ... something called an 'autowipe' system ... In the Intake area of the Film and Videotape Library, they would log the transmission tapes, the edited tapes, the original recordings, all under the programme number for a *Doctor Who* or whatever. Because the normal process was that what the BBC and its archive were interested in retaining would be the edited, transmitted programme. That's the one they can repeat, that's the one they can sell, that's the one they've cleared the rights for. And therefore, unless the production had a real need, all those other ancillary tapes could be released straight away for wiping and reuse. So what the Library offered VT was a more efficient way of releasing – in effect – the junk.

So you could focus on that which you knew you really needed to keep, and that was quite a good trade-off; it meant a lot more tape was released to be re-used …, but productions still had the right to say, 'No, we need that.' And from the archive, you could say, 'That was a particularly interesting bit of production …', and still keep something. It was I who put the hold on all the 'Shada' film and studio tapes from *Doctor Who*, for example. Or if a documentary had done a really good, really long interview with someone, you could keep the interview as well as the edited programme, and things like that. And that was for *all* tapes that were recorded in studio or as OB production.

So having been give the job of Archive Selector, and having had this great introduction to every head of production, and had the opportunity to tell them how important the archive was and that this was what we were going to do, I then had to toddle off and think about how I was actually going to do it! So what I decided to do, was that I took that set of archive selection criteria of Anne's, and enhanced it a bit, so you could look at it and not think, 'What does that mean?', and make it a bit more understandable.

The introduction of an alphabetical grading system to the contents of the BBC Film and Videotape Library was one of Sue Malden's early innovations. Everything that came into Windmill Road was assessed, and was then given a grade from 'A' to 'K'. 'A' signified the most important material, and 'K' was considered the least important. But the classifying of material was slightly more complex than just applying a simple sliding scale. For example, 'A' material was classified as 'Works of Artistic Importance', while 'B' was for 'Material Important in the History of Television'. The most commonly used grade was 'F', which was for 'Programmes that Represent the Output of BBC TV'. Most *Doctor Who* stories between 1963 and 1989 were awarded 'F' grades. A few, such as 'The Five Doctors' and 'The Caves of Androzani', were given 'B' grades. But there was an ulterior motive behind Malden's grading system …

Sue Malden: To each one of the reasons why you think you might want to keep something, I gave a letter. As I said before, I had found stuff that people had previously kept, but I just didn't know why. And also, it was a good sort of discipline. But if somebody said to me, 'Why have we kept all this stuff in the archive?', I could say, well 50% we've kept for its historical value, 10% because it contains personalities, or whatever … So, you know, you could then argue the case for the whole of the archive.

One thing I did have to do was get access to the transmission schedules.

CHAPTER 6

Everything that had happened with selection in the past had always been retrospective. So I decided that to be proactive, rather than reactive, was better, because otherwise you could miss things … So I then began going through the transmission schedules every week, identifying what I thought should be archived.

Actually, a little before that, when I was working in Intake, I'd introduced a system whereby you could go through the week's television schedules, and you'd see that there were certain key programmes. You'd think, 'We need to make sure we get that in,' and 'We need to make sure we get the negative of that,' and so on. And so I'd make a list of those, and check everything as it came in, and if something didn't come in, we'd introduced a chasing process, so that we could chase up with the labs, or the editor, or the producer, saying. 'Where is this?' This was, almost, an early start of the actual archive selection work. So I transferred that kind of process – going through the schedules, looking at film and VT original programmes, and marking up everything that I thought was of archive significance, and the reason why. We eventually transferred that into the BBC's Infax system[42]. And then, similarly, if something didn't come in, I'd get my team to chase and find out where it was and get it in, plus any relevant information we'd found out, and we'd pass all this on to the Intake team, so they could update the catalogue with the information we'd found out. Infax was actually relatively limited then; it was only the VT Department, VT engineers, and the Intake staff who could access it.

Another one of the things I did was have a couple of staff transferred to me, who were called Selectors …. What they'd been doing previously was viewing loads of stuff with a view to recommending whether it should be kept or not. And in order to justify that decision, they were writing down notes on the back of an index card about what the programme was about. Now that, to me, seemed to be a complete waste of time, because we were now saying we were going to keep everything. There wasn't much we were going to be getting rid of. And all this information they'd been compiling about programmes was not accessible by anybody else at the BBC, it was just written on the backs of index cards. So I changed the Selectors' role into that of retrospective cataloguing. Their main role was now to start cataloguing

---

42 Infax (which is sort-of short for Information Access) is the BBC's current in-house computer database for the contents of the Film and Videotape Library, which most BBC staff can access. It was introduced in 1993 and replaced a number of linked systems that included the two archive holdings systems VTOL (Video Tape On Line) and FLOL (Film Library On Line). Infax is due to be switched off in late 2012, to be replaced by a new system, Fabric.

programmes that *weren't* already catalogued, to review the holdings, and see if there was anything that wasn't necessary to keep, and recommend those for junking. It was more a case of tidying up the holdings rather than junking any complete programmes.

Malden at this point began turning her attention away from making sure that archival policies and practices were in place for newly-generated programme material, and looking back to the gaps in the archive that had been identified by her re-assigned Selectors. She found herself pondering on why so much material was missing, and what – if anything – could be done to try to fill the gaps …

CHAPTER 7
THE BIG BREAKTHROUGH

When Sue Malden began her new position as the BBC's Archive Selector in 1978, she started looking into the reasons why so many old programmes had been lost by the BBC over the years, and considering how the Corporation might plug the gaps in its archive. Fortunately, she decided to focus on one series – *Doctor Who* – as her pet project. She used this as a template in helping her understand the circumstances behind why certain programmes survived, and others didn't.

Sue Malden: The challenge of being given the Archive Selector role was having to set up the new job, and new processes and stuff like that. I went at it with great enthusiasm. And so I very quickly kept up these contacts with the production people, and had regular meetings with them, put in place the criteria for selection, informing the Intake areas, changing the review procedure, and so on. I would say that after about a year, maybe a bit less, I just thought, 'It would be interesting to find out why some stuff hadn't been kept.' So I just decided I'd pick on what was, to me, a seminal, classic, television series, that clearly had run for a long time, and was still running, and had influenced a lot of people, and find out what its history had been, in terms of retention, and *Doctor Who* came to mind. I liked watching *Doctor Who*, but I looked at it objectively as a classic television series. It would be really good to analyse what had happened to that series, from which I could learn, and do things. I just really did it because I wanted to learn what had happened. But when I made my first list of what had been transmitted, and then compared that to what existed, then I got these big gaps. And then I wondered *why* there were gaps.

It was then that I learned about the rights. That the BBC's deals with Equity allowed one showing and one repeat within two years, for nearly all its programmes. And after that, you'd junk it. And I could look back and see the old records, such as those for the first television Just William series with Dennis Waterman (*William*, 1962). You could see the records; see that it was junked two years to the day, almost, after it was screened. You could see the pattern a lot. So I learned that that was one reason why stuff had gone. Clearly, through doing the job, I had also picked up all this business about the cost of videotape, and the frailty of it, and the lack of confidence in it as a format. So for me it was all about learning *why* all this stuff hadn't survived, and I just happened to use, quite by chance, *Doctor Who* as an example.

WIPED!

In 1978, when Malden looked over what the Library still retained from *Doctor Who*'s 14 year history, she found that there were just 47 episodes out of the 253 broadcast between 1963 and 1969. Mainly, these were odd episodes from various stories over this six year period. Only one complete story had survived: the very first.

The full list of the 47 episodes was as follows:

WILLIAM HARTNELL

Story	16mm B&W film	35mm B&W film
An Unearthly Child	1, 2, 3, 4	
The Daleks		
The Edge of Destruction		
Marco Polo		
The Keys of Marinus	5	
The Aztecs		
The Sensorites		
The Reign of Terror		
Planet of Giants		
The Dalek Invasion of Earth		5
The Rescue		
The Romans	1, 3	
The Web Planet	2	
The Crusade	3	
The Space Museum	3	
The Chase		
The Time Meddler	2	
Galaxy 4		
Mission to the Unknown		
The Myth Makers		
The Daleks Masterplan		
The Massacre		
The Ark	3	
The Celestial Toymaker		
The Gunfighters	4	
The Savages		
The War Machines		
The Smugglers		
The Tenth Planet	1, 2, 3	

PATRICK TROUGHTON

Story	16mm B&W film	35mm B&W film
The Power of the Daleks		
The Highlanders		
The Underwater Menace	3	

CHAPTER 7

The Moonbase	2, 4	
The Macra Terror		
The Faceless Ones	1	
The Evil of the Daleks		
The Tomb of the Cybermen		
The Abominable Snowmen		
The Ice Warriors		
The Enemy of the World	3	
The Web of Fear		
Fury from the Deep		
The Wheel in Space		6
The Dominators	1, 2, 4, 5	
The Mind Robber		5
The Invasion	2, 3, 5, 6, 7, 8	
The Krotons	2, 3	1
The Seeds of Death	1, 4, 6 2 (Fine Grain)	5
The Space Pirates		2
The War Games	2, 5, 8, 9	

It's possible that the 35mm transmission print of 'The Dominators' Episode Three was also in existence at the Library at the time. I was recently able to raise this point with the Library's Andrew Martin:

> **Andrew Martin**: I'm very sceptical about the idea that the 35mm material for Episode Three of 'The Dominators' was ever anywhere but at the BBC Film Library – there is no evidence in the files that this was the case. Not that our files are exhaustive, but there would be a different provenance for this material than for the 16mm copies – the former is the original transmission material so would have been lodged with the Film Library after transmission, the latter are BBC Enterprises copies which would not have been. As far as I remember, we have the master film recording negatives, not dupes, as with the other existing 35mm *Doctor Who* episodes. We also had the master 35mm magnetic soundtracks, though these have since been transferred to CD and polyester track, as with all our original acetate master sound film.

From Jon Pertwee's time as the Doctor, Malden discovered that about half of the transmission two-inch videotapes had survived, but mainly from his last two seasons. These were screened in 1972/3 and 1973/4, so the tapes would have been just on the cusp of being prepared for wiping (using the two-years-from-transmission rule) when

WIPED!

the practice was effectively halted in 1975 or thereabouts. Also, Pertwee's debut story, 'Spearhead from Space', still survived, mainly because it was made on film, and there was no real incentive for junking films at the BBC – film couldn't be wiped and re-used like videotape. The surviving Pertwee episodes were:

JON PERTWEE

Story	625-line two-inch colour VT	16mm colour film
Spearhead from Space		1, 2, 3, 4
Doctor Who and the Silurians		
The Ambassadors of Death	1	
Inferno		
Terror of the Autons		
The Mind of Evil		
The Claws of Axos	1, 4	
Colony in Space		
The Dæmons	4	
Day of the Daleks	1, 2, 3, 4	
The Curse of Peladon		
The Sea Devils	4, 5, 6	
The Mutants	3, 4, 5, 6	
The Time Monster		
The Three Doctors	1, 2, 3, 4	
Carnival of Monsters	1, 2, 3, 4	
Frontier in Space	4, 5	
Planet of the Daleks	1, 2, 4, 5, 6	
The Green Death	1, 2, 3, 4, 5, 6	
The Time Warrior	1, 2, 3, 4	
Invasion of the Dinosaurs		
Death to the Daleks	2, 3, 4	
The Monster of Peladon	1, 2, 3, 4, 5, 6	
Planet of the Spiders	1, 2, 3, 4, 5, 6	

Out of the 128 episodes that comprised Pertwee's era, only 59 survived – just under half. But there were only eight complete third Doctor stories, out of the 24 that were made and screened.

From Tom Baker's debut adventure, 'Robot', Malden discovered that all the episodes of all the stories still survived in full on their original two-inch broadcast tapes (although that of Part Three of 'The Deadly Assassin' had been slightly edited for its 1977 repeat).

CHAPTER 7
IAN LEVINE AND THE BBC

Ian Levine was 10 years old when *Doctor Who* began in 1963, and was instantly captivated by the programme. He began making audio recordings of the episodes as he watched them go out on BBC1 every week, and made copious notes on them in various exercise books. By the early to mid-1970s, he was working as the main disc jockey at the legendary Blackpool Mecca nightclub in his home town of Blackpool, and had begun collecting soul and R&B records. This led to him becoming one of the central figures in the burgeoning Northern Soul dance movement of the early '70s, and from this he moved into the arena of record production, developing the distinctive hi-energy sound, which would prove to be an extremely popular musical niche in the late '70s and early '80s. This success meant that Levine was better placed than most people to indulge his passion for *Doctor Who*.

Levine had been involved with other fans in assisting the makers of the 'Whose Doctor Who' documentary in late 1976 and early 1977, and was shocked at how few episodes of the programme's early days had survived at the BBC. He was also aware that material was still being junked, having discovered that 'Galaxy 4', 'The Time Meddler' and some episodes of 'The War Games' had been disposed of by BBC Enterprises since the making of the documentary.

Levine had purchased his first video recorder in 1976, a Philips 1500, and had begun recording the series off-air from the start of the programme's fourteenth season (i.e. from 'The Masque of Mandragora' onwards). He had also managed to track down off-air videos of a few earlier Tom Baker episodes from other fans, and had made his own video copies of them. But he really wanted to get hold of episodes featuring the earlier three Doctors that he could enjoy again.

In January 1977, Levine was attending the annual MIDEM music conference in Cannes in France, and met up with Terry Sampson from Enterprises, who was representing BBC Records at the event. Levine and Sampson got chatting about *Doctor Who*, and Levine expressed an interest in purchasing copies of old programmes from the BBC. On returning to London, Sampson introduced Levine to Arthur Jearum, who worked in a division of Enterprises called Non-Theatrical Sales, set up mainly to enable schools and universities to buy copies of BBC programmes that had an educational value. As they were used to selling to organisations rather than individuals, there was some initial resistance to dealing with Levine, but he was eventually told that he could purchase selected old episodes of *Doctor Who,* with the proviso that he could choose only episodes that were less than seven years old at the time – the department didn't have the rights to sell any material that was older than that. So, in the summer of 1977, Levine elected to buy video copies of all six episodes of the Jon Pertwee story 'Frontier in Space':

WIPED!

Ian Levine: 'Frontier in Space' was the first private sale[43] in history to anyone of a *Doctor Who* story. I had to pay £3,000 for it. Which was highway robbery! It was supplied over three U-MATIC tapes; two episodes per tape. Only Episodes Four and Five were in colour. They had to make up prints off the negatives of the other episodes, as there were no film prints of them. So they had to make prints up first, get the prints themselves, and then transfer them onto U-MATIC tape. That's how I got them.

At least as far as the black and white episodes were concerned, Levine was being supplied with copies of materials held only at Villiers House, and not at the Film and Videotape Library (although this distinction wasn't particularly clear to him at the time). It would appear that at this point – the summer of 1977 – the Film and Videotape Library were actually still oblivious to the fact that Enterprises had their own archive of material that was missing from the main archive – including episodes One, Two, Three and Six of 'Frontier in Space'.

As far as Levine was concerned, spending £3,000 on six episodes of *Doctor Who* in 1977 was a very, very expensive exercise. (The equivalent sum in 2010 would be nearer to £16,000!) And besides, he really wanted to get his hands on William Hartnell and Patrick Troughton material, which was excluded by the less-than-seven-years-old rule.

Through other contacts at the BBC, Levine was soon introduced to another department of Enterprises. This was called Film Sales, and was actually based at the Film and Videotape Library. Film Sales had been set up to supply material from the Library to other British broadcasters – mainly for news reports and current affairs programmes.

Levine eventually started dealing with John Bridger at Film Sales, and was told that there were certain copyright rules that prevented the BBC selling him any copies of the Hartnell and Troughton episodes. These restrictions were mainly due to agreements with the Writers' Guild and Equity. Levine therefore contacted both of these organisations, and negotiated his own special dispensations that allowed him to buy old episodes of *Doctor Who* for his own private use. Bridger was eventually satisfied with Levine's diligence, and agreed that he could at last begin buying copies of the 47 Hartnell and Troughton episodes of *Doctor Who* that the Film and Videotape Library held at that point. And because Levine had got his own clearances from Equity and the Writers' Guild, the cost of buying an episode was significantly less than Non-Theatrical Sales were charging him – it now came to about £200 an episode.

---

43 Dalek creator Terry Nation's agent did purchase 16mm film prints of the first four episodes of 'The Dalek Invasion of Earth' from BBC Enterprises in 1965, although Levine wasn't aware of this.

CHAPTER 7

Ian Levine: I went through every single *Doctor Who* episode in the Film Library in 1977. I went in on six different days and watched them all on a Steenbeck[44]. As a prospective client, I was allowed to view material.

One day John Bridger said to me, 'I don't understand why there's this different version of 'An Unearthly Child' here with a different running time. What's this all about?'... He was going through it for me to buy it, because I bought that first story quite early on, as the Film Library had all four episodes. I wasn't going to buy Episode One, as I already had a copy from Keith Barnfather, who had got a copy from BBC Pebble Mill. In the week the BBC showed 'Whose Doctor Who' in 1977, *Pebble Mill at One* did a feature on the series, and one of the researchers ordered Episode One of 'An Unearthly Child' up on a Philips videocassette. She then gave the tape to Keith Barnfather for a couple of days, and I copied it, and then he gave it back! So I only bought U-MATICs of the other three episodes from the BBC. John Bridger said to me, 'There's something that doesn't add up here ...' So we went and got it out and watched it, and I realised that it was the unscreened pilot. It wasn't marked as the pilot, it was just marked 'An Unearthly Child', but it was a completely different running length.

Until Levine identified it as the pilot episode, the BBC were almost certainly unaware that they still held a copy of this material.

A NOTE ON THE PILOT EPISODE

The first episode of *Doctor Who*, entitled 'An Unearthly Child', was initially recorded on Friday 27 September 1963 at the BBC's Lime Grove Studios. It was always understood, however, that this was to some extent a trial run. If the BBC's Head of Drama, Sydney Newman, deemed the recording acceptable, then it would become the transmission master, and the weekly production of the subsequent episodes would begin some three weeks later. If not, there was a two-week gap in which further work could be done on the script and other aspects, and the episode would then be re-recorded in the week before the second episode was due in the studio.

Within days of the recording of the pilot, Newman had reviewed it and decided that there were several things that he wasn't happy with. Changes were made to the script in line with his instructions, and 'An Unearthly Child' was re-recorded on Friday 18 October 1963. This second version became the episode that launched the series on BBC1 on Saturday 23 November 1963.

---

44 A Steenbeck is a tabletop machine designed to enable film to be easily viewed, rather than having to project it.

WIPED!

It's entirely possible that the 16mm black and white film print that Levine and Bridger discovered in the BBC Film Library in 1977 was the very same one that had been made from the original two-inch videotape of the Friday 27 September 1963 studio recording specifically for Sydney Newman to review in late September 1963. However, the videotape of the studio recording did also appear on the Retention Authorisation paperwork raised by Enterprises in December 1966, when most of the Hartnell stories had Stored Field telerecordings made of them for the first time. And as the surviving print of the pilot episode is indeed a Stored Field telerecording, then there is also a chance that it was made in late 1966/early 1967 as a result of this order.

The film contains what we would now consider to be the full studio recording of the session in Lime Grove on Friday 27 September 1963. It begins with the VT countdown clock, before the familiar *Doctor Who* title sequence begins (but with a thunderclap sound effect that was dropped for the series proper). The episode is enacted in scene order with no breaks, including the occasional fluffed line, right up to the point where Ian and Barbara barge their way into the mysterious police box they have discovered in a junk yard, which is where the first recording break occurs, and the action stops. Recording then picks up on the TARDIS interior set (complete with main doors that flap about rather than closing on cue), and runs right through to the end of the episode. A retake of the whole of this second section of the episode is then attempted, but doesn't get very far at all before things grind to a halt. A third attempt at all the TARDIS scenes is then recorded, which continues all the way through to the end.

When the episode came to be released on VHS in the early 1990s (on *Doctor Who – The Hartnell Years*), it was edited down to just the first opening scenes up to the junkyard sequence, coupled with the *final* take of the complete TARDIS scenes. The episode then got its only ever screening on television as part of BBC2's *The Lime Grove Story* on Monday 26 August 1991. This time it was edited together from the opening scenes coupled with the *first* take of the TARDIS scenes. The full, unedited pilot episode footage was released on DVD in 2006, in the DVD box set entitled *Doctor Who – The Beginning*, along with a third edited-together version, utilising the best bits of both full takes of the TARDIS scenes.

IAN LEVINE AND THE BBC—CONTINUED

During his visits to Windmill Road in 1977, Levine went through all the Film and Videotape Library's index cards regarding their *Doctor Who* holdings, and discovered that there was one episode that should have been on their shelves but was absent – Episode Four of 'The Daleks Masterplan'. The relevant card indicated that (as previously discussed) the film had been loaned by the Library to *Blue Peter* in 1973, and had never been returned.

CHAPTER 7

Through Jan Vincent-Rudzki, Levine had known about the production of the BBC2 'Whose Doctor Who' documentary in late 1976, and had seen the list of archive holdings prepared by Tony Cash's team. From this, he knew that there was a BBC Enterprises film store at Villiers House, and that this too held episodes of *Doctor Who*, or at least had done so in 1976. And, if the 'Whose Doctor Who' research was correct, this could certainly include episodes that didn't exist at the Film and Videotape Library at all in 1977. Levine therefore started pressing to be given access to whatever *Doctor Who* material was held by Enterprises at Villiers House. He also quickly purchased copies of all 47 Hartnell and Troughton episodes that were held at Windmill Road (apart from Episode One of 'An Unearthly Child, as noted above). He discovered along the way that some of the Library's film prints weren't in that good a condition – Episode Three of 'The Ark' was badly scratched, for instance, and Episode Five of 'The Keys of Marinus' was quite poor too. But once Levine had completed all these purchases, Bridger at last arranged to take him to visit Villiers House. This was sometime in early 1978. The experience was an eye-opener for Levine.

> **Ian Levine:** I saw the film vault. It was just a little room with stuff on the shelves, and it was in a mess. I found ten *Out of the Unknown*s from Series One, which was supposed to have been junked years earlier … 'Andover and the Android' and 'The Fox and the Forest' weren't there, but the other ten of the 12 episodes from Series One were. It didn't make any sense …
>
> I and a chap named Perry from Villiers House just went through all the stuff on the shelves; it only took about an hour to look through every single can of film in the whole room. It wasn't like Windmill Road, where there were hundreds of thousands of film cans; there were probably only something like 500 film cans in the whole room. I can't remember what else was in there, it wasn't that much, but there were lots of *Doctor Who*s in there.
>
> Some of the *Doctor Who* films I found at Villiers House, like 'The Sensorites', and 'The Keys of Marinus', were only negatives, they had never been made into print form. 'Planet of Giants', we couldn't find the mag soundtrack for Episode Three, whereas the rest of the episodes were comopt prints, with an audio stripe. Some of the stories had no prints at all, some were just negatives, and some were both. And none of them was incomplete.
>
> I remember distinctly looking at all six cans of 'The Seeds Of Death', and thinking what a waste, when I had already seen five episodes of it also at Windmill Road. I thought, why couldn't we have found a different Troughton six-parter here that was all missing, not just missing only one episode of the six, like the set at Windmill Road?

WIPED!

At that time, the purge was continuing, and the first Dalek story had been requested for junking. The episodes hadn't *actually* quite been taken off the shelf yet, though. This guy, Perry, said, 'I could have just gone and thrown them in the skip.' Perry told us that when he threw films away, he'd first of all take them out of the can – the cans were re-used for something else; they didn't throw the cans away. The films weren't on reels, they were just on a yellow spool, which was in the centre of the film, and you just pushed the spool out, and the film would all tumble into the skip, and no-one could ever touch it again. It could never be reconstituted out of the skip, as they didn't want people stealing BBC copyright material. So it was put into a skip like that, and taken away to … wherever. As soon as films have been rained on and stuff, then they're finished. They were waiting to be thrown away, and that was his job. But because I said that I was going to buy them, Perry actually physically ripped off all the gaffer tape that had been wrapped around the tins, and I put the cans back on the shelf myself. Another guy from Enterprises who was there said, 'You can't do that,' but John Bridger said, 'I work for BBC Enterprises, this is my customer, please can we try and sort it out – who do we need to speak to?' He said, 'Pamela Nash'. So we went to her office. Well we didn't get anywhere with her, so John Bridger said, 'We'd better get back to Windmill Road.' Because she was being so unhelpful, we feared that she was going to go and throw all these *Doctor Who* prints in the skip out of spite.

What Levine had discovered in early 1978 was that BBC Enterprises still held a number of complete *Doctor Who* stories on 16mm black and white film. Those stories were:

William Hartnell	Episodes
An Unearthly Child	1, 2, 3, 4
The Daleks	1, 2, 3, 4, 5, 6, 7
The Edge of Destruction	1, 2
The Keys of Marinus	1, 2, 3, 4, 5, 6
The Aztecs	1, 2, 3, 4
The Sensorites	1, 2, 3, 4, 5, 6
Planet of Giants	1, 2, 3
The Dalek Invasion of Earth	1, 2, 3, 4, 5, 6
The Rescue	1, 2
The Romans	1, 2, 3, 4
The Web Planet	1, 2, 3, 4, 5, 6

CHAPTER 7

The Space Museum	1, 2, 3, 4
The Chase	1, 2, 3, 4, 5, 6
The Ark	1, 2, 3, 4
The Gunfighters	1, 2, 3, 4

Patrick Troughton

The Mind Robber	1, 2, 3, 4, 5
The Seeds of Death	1, 2, 3, 4, 5, 6

Jon Pertwee

Spearhead from Space	1, 2, 3, 4
Doctor Who and the Silurians	1, 2, 3, 4, 5, 6, 7
The Ambassadors of Death	1, 2, 3, 4, 5, 6, 7
Inferno	1, 2, 3, 4, 5, 6, 7
Terror of the Autons	1, 2, 3, 4
The Mind of Evil	1, 2, 3, 4, 5, 6
The Claws of Axos	1, 2, 3, 4
Colony in Space	1, 2, 3, 4, 5, 6
The Dæmons	1, 2, 3, 4, 5
Day of the Daleks	1, 2, 3, 4
The Curse of Peladon	1, 2, 3, 4
The Sea Devils	1, 2, 3, 4, 5, 6
The Mutants	1, 2, 3, 4, 5, 6
The Time Monster	1, 2, 3, 4, 5, 6
The Three Doctors	1, 2, 3, 4
Carnival of Monsters	1, 2, 3, 4
Frontier in Space	1, 2, 3, 4, 5, 6
Planet of the Daleks	1, 2, 3, 4, 5, 6
The Green Death	1, 2, 3, 4, 5, 6

This discovery meant that a further 56 Hartnell episodes and five Patrick Troughton episodes could be added to the total number of surviving *Doctor Who* episodes. And the discovery of a complete run of Pertwee episodes from 'Spearhead from Space' through to 'The Green Death' meant that his era was now missing only seven episodes; all six parts of 'Invasion of the Dinosaurs', and Part One of 'Death to the Daleks'.

Levine's arrival at Villiers House almost certainly came just in time to prevent the destruction of the 16mm film prints of all seven episodes of 'The Daleks'. The story had already been classified as Withdrawn, De-Accessioned and Junked, and the relevant tins of film were gaffer-taped together, sitting on a separate shelf, just awaiting final disposal. Levine recalls that there were 28 tins of film in total: one set of positive prints for all seven episodes, one set of negatives, one set of Arabic-dubbed positives, and one set of Arabic-dubbed negatives. If that truly was the case, then both sets of the Arabic films were discarded not long after the episodes were rescued, as only the original English-language positives and negatives were retained by the Film and Videotape Library (and years later it was discovered that the can supposedly holding the negative for Episode Seven actually contained a misfiled magnetic soundtrack of the episode instead).

Following his initial visit to Villiers House in 1978, Levine was able to spend some time going through Enterprises' records in relation to their complete archive of *Doctor Who* 16mm film prints over the years. He was also able to illuminate some of the working practices in place at the time.

ACCESSIONS RECORDS

BBC Enterprises, like the Film and Videotape Library, kept index record cards for all of its 16mm films, which detailed all the sales and other relevant information for them. These were known as Accessions Records. The cards for *Doctor Who* were examined thoroughly by Levine, who discovered that there was one for every single Hartnell, Troughton and Pertwee episode from 'An Unearthly Child' through to 'The Green Death' – with just one exception.

That exception was Episode Seven of 'The Daleks Masterplan' (entitled 'The Feast of Steven'), which had been shown on BBC1 on Christmas Day 1965. As this episode was something of a fun Christmas romp, largely divorced from the main action of the rest of the story, Enterprises had elected not to order a 16mm telerecording of it. The other episodes had then been offered for sale overseas as an 11-part adventure. Only ABC in Australia had ever been offered this story (and the single episode Doctor-less teaser 'Mission to the Unknown'), but had elected not to screen either. (See the section on overseas sales to Australia for more details of why this happened.) Perhaps because of the problems that the Australians had with them, Enterprises didn't subsequently offer 'Mission to the Unknown' or 'The Daleks Masterplan' to any other overseas broadcasters. However, they still kept films of them, and even loaned a 16mm print of Episode Three to *Blue Peter* in October 1971, so that a clip from it could be included in an edition of the programme.

From the index cards, Levine learned what exactly had happened to each and every episode once held by Enterprises, and when:

Ian Levine: There were no computers then. The index cards were these

CHAPTER 7

little pink cards that you could buy at any stationery shop. They had all the information for when each episode had been Withdrawn, De-Accessioned and Junked. I checked every card for every *Doctor Who,* and found out when they were junked. The only one they didn't have a card for was 'The Feast of Steven'.

Levine was able to establish that up until January 1972, Enterprises still had 16mm film copies of every episode of *Doctor Who* bar that one exception, from the first episode of 'An Unearthly Child' through to the last episode of 'The Dæmons', shown on BBC1 the previous year. But what had happened after that?

WITHDRAWN, DE-ACCESSIONED AND JUNKED

In 1972, for the first time, BBC Enterprises began disposing of its stock of 16mm *Doctor Who* stories, in a three-stage process.

Stage one was for a story to be Withdrawn from the back-catalogue of *Doctor Who* available to foreign television stations to purchase. After this point, no further overseas sales of that story could be made. As discussed in Chapter 5, one of the main reasons why stories could no longer be sold abroad was that the rights had expired. Rights could, of course, be re-negotiated, but the overseas sales of black and white episodes of *Doctor Who* had tailed-off considerably in the early part of the '70s.[45]

Stage two was for the Withdrawn story to be De-Accessioned, which meant that the Accessions Record card for each episode was taken out of its usual home in the index tray. The card was then placed in another file marked as Junked. This was stage three.

The films and negatives for each Withdrawn, De-Accessioned and Junked story were collected up from their homes in the film racks at Villiers House, and destroyed. As described above by Levine, the usual method was to take the can of film to a skip outside, open up the can and knock out the centre of the spool, so that the film would unspool into the skip. Once full, these skips were then usually sent for the contents

---

[45] But why did this happen in 1972 specifically? As we have seen, the rights to most Hartnell stories were extended for a second five-year period, which took them well beyond this date. As far as the Troughton stories were concerned, however, the BBC's sales records show that the batch from 'The Highlanders' to 'The Tomb of the Cybermen' weren't sold abroad at all after their initial five-year rights period had elapsed, which would have occurred between January and September 1972. It would appear that the rights for these adventures were not renewed. So this was *possibly* the first time since 1963 that BBC Enterprises found itself in possession of film prints of *Doctor Who* that it could no longer financially exploit. It therefore no longer had any legal or commercial reason to hold on to the material. (I say '*possibly*', as it appears that the rights to 'The Daleks Masterplan' may not have been renewed after their initial sales period expired in 1971.)

to be incinerated. Occasionally, however, Withdrawn, De-Accessioned and Junked material was passed to the British Film Institute (BFI) for them to keep, rather than being sent for destruction.

Levine's inspection of the Accessions Records index cards revealed that when a given story was junked, all the episodes of that story were disposed of together (unlike the transmission videotape wipings overseen by the BBC's Engineering Department, which saw seemingly random collections of episodes destroyed in batches).

By the time of Levine's visit to Villiers House in 1978, a significant number of Hartnell and Troughton stories had already had their 16mm films junked. None of the Pertwee stories had had their 16mm black and white films junked at all.

Levine's recollection[46] of the dates of the Hartnell and Troughton junkings by BBC Enterprises is as follows:

Story	Withdrawn, De-Accessioned & Junked Date
An Unearthly Child	Not Junked
The Daleks	Identified for junking in 1978, but not carried out
The Edge of Destruction	Not Junked
Marco Polo	Junked in 1972
The Keys of Marinus	Not Junked
The Aztecs	Not Junked
The Sensorites	Not Junked
The Reign of Terror	Junked in 1972
Planet of Giants	Not Junked
The Dalek Invasion of Earth	Not Junked
The Rescue	Not Junked
The Romans	Not Junked
The Web Planet	Not Junked
The Crusade	Junked in 1972
The Space Museum	Not Junked
The Chase	Not Junked
The Time Meddler	Junked in 1976
Galaxy 4	Junked in 1976
Mission to the Unknown	Junked in 1974

---

46 Although Levine recalls that 'The Dominators', 'The Krotons' and 'The War Games' were all junked prior to his first visit to Villiers House in early 1978, and the three stories were subsequently recovered from the BFI, there is a conflict of dates in the BFI's own records. These indicate that 'The Dominators' and 'The War Games' were acquired in July 1978, while 'The Krotons' didn't turn up until October 1980. These dates don't easily tie in with either Levine's or Malden's recollections of events, and so can't be easily explained.

CHAPTER 7

The Myth Makers	Junked in 1972
The Daleks Masterplan (11 eps)	Junked in 1974
The Massacre	Junked in 1974
The Ark	Not Junked
The Celestial Toymaker	Junked in 1973
The Gunfighters	Not Junked
The Savages	Junked in 1973
The War Machines	Junked in 1974
The Smugglers	Junked in 1974
The Tenth Planet	Junked in 1974
The Power of the Daleks	Junked in 1974
The Highlanders	Junked in 1974
The Underwater Menace	Junked in 1974
The Moonbase	Junked in 1974
The Macra Terror	Junked in 1974
The Faceless Ones	Junked in 1974
The Evil of the Daleks	Junked in 1974
The Tomb of the Cybermen	Junked in 1974
The Abominable Snowmen	Junked in 1974
The Ice Warriors	Junked in 1974
The Enemy of the World	Junked in 1974
The Web of Fear	Junked in 1974
Fury from the Deep	Junked in 1974
The Wheel in Space	Junked in 1974
The Dominators	Junked in 1977 (sent to the BFI)
The Mind Robber	Not Junked
The Invasion	Junked in 1974
The Krotons	Junked in 1977 (sent to the BFI)
The Seeds of Death	Not Junked
The Space Pirates	Junked in 1974
The War Games	Junked in 1977 (sent to the BFI)

What is somewhat surprising is that there appears to be no correlation between the dates of the rights to sell a particular story expiring, and the year in which BBC Enterprises decided to Withdraw, De-Accession and Junk that story. 'Marco Polo', 'The Reign of Terror', 'The Crusade', 'The Myth Makers', 'Mission to the Unknown', 'The Massacre', 'The Celestial Toymaker', 'The Savages', 'The War Machines', 'The Smugglers', 'The Tenth Planet', 'The Power of the Daleks', 'The Abominable Snowmen', 'The Ice Warriors', 'The Enemy of the World', 'The Web of Fear', 'The Wheel in Space', 'The Dominators', 'The Krotons', 'The Space Pirates' and 'The War Games' were all junked while Enterprises still had the rights to sell them. Only 'The Daleks Masterplan', 'The Highlanders', 'The Underwater Menace', 'The Moonbase', 'The Macra Terror', 'The Faceless Ones', 'The Evil of the Daleks', 'The Tomb of the

WIPED!

Cybermen', 'Fury from the Deep' and 'The Invasion' were junked *after* Enterprises' rights to sell them had expired. Yet all the Hartnell stories that were retained by BBC Enterprises up to 1978 had seen their sales rights expire in 1973, 1974, 1975 … The only story that seemingly survived because Enterprises still had the rights to sell it in 1978 was 'The Seeds of Death'. ('The Mind Robber' also survived through to 1978, yet seemingly the rights to sell this story had lapsed without renewal in 1973.)

The last Hartnell and Troughton *Doctor Who* stories to have their transmission videotapes wiped, in 1974, were 'Mission to the Unknown', 'The War Machines', 'The Macra Terror' and 'Fury from the Deep'. This was the same year that Enterprises junked their 16mm prints of the same stories. Without knowing the exact dates of the film junkings, it's impossible to say whether they occurred before or after the videotape wipings. But it's possible that – for these four stories at least – their destruction on film could have occurred while their two-inch transmission tapes were still being held by the BBC's Engineering Department, if only for a few more months. But for all the other stories junked by Enterprises between 1972 and 1977, the 16mm film prints were the last surviving copies that the BBC held of the material.

It's possible that some of the junked films found their way to the Film Library. This would explain the survival of odd episodes such as 'The Time Meddler' Episode Two and 'The Faceless Ones' Episode One at Windmill Road. And it's almost certain that the various missing episodes that have been returned over the years from UK-based private collectors (such as 'The Evil of the Daleks' Episode Two and 'The Faceless Ones' Episode Three) all originated from Enterprises, suggesting that the disposal process was not always 100% successful in destroying the material.

However, while Enterprises were diligently destroying their own stock of *Doctor Who* negatives and film prints between 1972 and 1978, they couldn't legislate for the actions of the various overseas broadcasters to which the programmes had already been sold. As previously noted, one of the options that such broadcasters had once their rights to screen the programmes had expired was to ship the films back to the BBC. Although some of the films returned in this way may have ended up at the Film Library over the years, most of them would have gone straight back to Enterprises. Enterprises, however, would have already decided that some of these programmes were Withdrawn, De-Accessioned and Junked, and had probably destroyed their own film holdings of them some months or years previously. These returned films probably sat about in limbo for some time, until someone got round to checking if they were still part of the current sales catalogue.

This is one possible explanation for the situation that arose early in 1978, when Levine visited Villiers House for the first time, and found 28 *Doctor Who* film cans marked up to be destroyed. It's possible that these films, along with those of a number of other early Hartnell stories, had recently been sent back to Enterprises from overseas (and almost certainly from the Arabic-speaking Algeria, given that some of the films were Arabic-dubbed), even though Enterprises may have destroyed its own copies some time previously.

IAN LEVINE AND PAMELA NASH

Pamela Nash began working at the Television Sales and Production Operations Department of BBC Enterprises in Villiers House in the mid-1960s. In her role as a Film Recording Clerk, she was the person who arranged for 16mm film telerecordings of episodes of *Doctor Who* (amongst other programmes) to be made for Enterprises for the purposes of overseas sales. Once the prints were sent to Villiers House, it was Nash who was responsible for them on a day-to-day basis.

Once the rights for Enterprises to sell a particular programme had expired, it was Nash who authorised the material to be Withdrawn, De-Accessioned and Junked from the Enterprises system. This would involve her stamping those words onto the Accessions Record card for each programme, and then overseeing the physical destruction of the material.⁴⁷

By his own admission, Levine 'freaked' when it was explained to him that the film prints of all seven episodes of 'The Daleks' were due to be destroyed by Enterprises. He urged John Bridger to find out who was responsible for this decision, in the hope that the story could be spared – at least until he had been able to get copies made. Bridger was introduced to Pamela Nash, who explained to him and Levine that the films were old programmes that no-one wanted to buy from Enterprises any more, and that she was just making room for newer material.

Levine in particular was convinced that their protests to Nash would somehow

---

47 Pamela Nash has over the years been pilloried by some *Doctor Who* fans for her actions, so it's important to understand her role in the whole sorry affair of the destruction of so many episodes of *Doctor Who*. All the Hartnell and Troughton episodes had their transmission videotapes erased or junked by the BBC in the late 1960s and early 1970s. It was Pamela Nash who, by dint of her job at BBC Enterprises, ensured that 16mm film copies were made of all but one of those episodes. She was not aware that so much of this material had subsequently had its original videotapes destroyed, or that the BBC Enterprises films were, in some instances, the last surviving copies of some of the programmes. At the time, the various internal departments of the BBC were fragmented, and were usually working to different procedures and systems. As soon as the situation was fully understood by the Film and Videotape Library, then corrective action was applied.

Although not all of the current 147 surviving episodes of 1960s *Doctor Who* were returned directly from BBC Enterprises, the fact is that they *nearly all* survive as 16mm black and white film prints. And the fact that they were copied onto 16mm film in the first place is solely down to BBC Enterprises, and Pamela Nash. There would be almost no Hartnell and Troughton episodes surviving to this day without Nash and Enterprises – just the handful that survived as 35mm transmission prints.

WIPED!

encourage her to junk the story quickly, and perhaps even to authorise the junking of still more material.

> **Ian Levine**: She didn't like anyone telling her how to do her job. Because, let's face it, she'd had all these episodes sitting on her shelves for all those years. She'd actually had to order up the print of Episode One of 'Galaxy 4' to copy it for Tony Cash [for 'Whose Doctor Who'], and then put it back, and then within months of it actually being copied and used, she still went and destroyed the negatives. So she can't claim, with any conscience, that nobody wanted them, that they had no use for them, when she'd already ordered clips from them for a documentary! It just makes no sense to me. She claimed, years later, that she only had BBC Enterprises copies, and she thought that all the originals were still at the BBC Film and Videotape Library. But they weren't at the Library; they didn't exist.
>
> So John Bridger drove me straight back that morning from Villiers House to Windmill Road, and we went to find Sue Malden. Sue had only been in the job a month or so, and we needed to tell her what was going on, and get these films protected. And so John brought me in, and introduced me, and said, 'This is Ian, who has been trying to buy all these *Doctor Who*s, and they're being destroyed.' Sue did not know that there were *Doctor Who* prints at Villiers House; I was the one who told her. She drew a letter up straight away, and had it sent to Pamela Nash's office, saying, 'Please do not destroy any more *Doctor Who*s, we need them.' She put in a holding order.

SUE MALDEN AND BBC ENTERPRISES

Sue Malden's recollection of how she came to be aware of the large archive of *Doctor Who* 16mm film prints at Villiers House differs quite dramatically from Levine's:

> **Sue Malden**: One of the objectives of my job was to improve the reputation of the BBC archive with the outside professional world. And that meant building up good relationships with the BFI, who were clearly the sort of organisation to be working with in partnership, but also they were very much the public face of television archives. A guy called Paul Madden was there then, who may well have been the first Television Officer in the BFI. So Paul and I worked together to produce a catalogue called *Keeping Television Alive*, which was a list of everything that was held at the BFI – it was for material from *all* broadcasters, it wasn't just for BBC stuff.
>
> It was when we were making this catalogue with Paul that he supplied me

CHAPTER 7

with a list of what was in the National Film Archive that was BBC material. There were some old records at the BBC, and sometimes in the BBC catalogue, if something had been sent to the BFI, it actually indicated it. I went through checking all their records, and all our records, and if I found records in the BBC that something had actually gone there, but it didn't appear on his lists, then we'd double check for it, and so on. So I got the BBC catalogue, and ensured it was up to date. As part of that process, I noticed they'd got various things at the BFI, but in particular I noticed these *Doctor Who*s.

What Malden had discovered was that the BFI held film prints of three complete Patrick Troughton stories – 'The Dominators', 'The Krotons' and 'The War Games'.

Sue Malden: So I said to Paul, 'How on Earth did you get hold of those?' Because for a lot of the other stuff, I was finding records saying 'Released to go to the National Archive', but not for these films. A whole lot of films that had been on nitrate[48] – a lot of the BBC's early news footage – had been sent to the BFI, who could store it safely. So for most things, there was a logic. But I didn't understand how he'd got hold of these *Doctor Who*s. So he explained that there was this really nice lady called Enid Mawson, who worked for BBC Enterprises, and who'd sent them to him. And I thought, 'Wow!'

So I rang up Enid and introduced myself, and said, 'Do you mind if I come and look at what you're offering to the National Archive, because you obviously don't realise it, but there are some gaps in the BBC archive, and this'd be a great way of filling those gaps'. And she said, 'Of course, I'd got no idea. I'd assumed the masters were still at the BBC, and these were just our spare copies. It never occurred to me.' Now I never found out how Paul Madden got to find Enid in the first place – I never thought to ask him that. I was more interested in getting to talk to her myself.

So I went to see Enid at Villiers House, and she showed me their vaults, and their stock, and their returns, and I asked her then if I could start going through what she had got. At one time I used to go up there to look at it, but eventually I got her to send it to me.

I recall at one meeting I went through all Enid's cards, and marked up

---

[48] Nitrate was the first type of plastic film base that was commercially available in the late 1800s. Unfortunately, it was extremely flammable, and also had a tendency to decompose in storage, producing a flammable gas that was prone to auto-ignite, which caused spontaneous fires. Acetate would later replace nitrate as the main film base medium in the 1950s, and was a whole lot safer!

everything I wanted her to send to the Library when they'd finished with it. It is possible that I didn't know about the returns from abroad then, but I thought I would have, because that's how Paul got hold of the three Patrick Troughton stories. They were all returns from overseas that she offered to him. But I honestly can't remember if I was as aware of the returns as I was of their holdings. I can remember very much, early on, going through all her stuff, and marking up what we wanted. But it was certainly not Pamela Nash I was dealing with at that time, it was only Enid.[49]

My first meeting with Ian Levine came in the middle of that. He was buying stuff through the Film Sales people, through a guy called John Bridger. I don't know how much earlier he'd been doing that, but I was in the post by 1978, and John Bridger brought Ian along to meet me ... I don't know exactly when, but it must have been a good few months into my starting the job, because I didn't start doing any of this until then. John bought him along because he knew I was interested particularly in *Doctor Who* stuff.

Windmill Road was quite a gossipy place, and so everybody quite quickly got to know what I was doing – it was a new job, people were interested, and so word had got round about my interest in *Doctor Who*. John Bridger, working for BBC Enterprises in the same building, was asked to deal with Ian Levine. And I think Keith Owen, who was the boss of Library Sales at the time, he'd sort of done the original deal, he'd been the one Ian had approached

---

49 Since I wrote the first edition of 'Wiped!', I have been able to correspond with Enid Mawson. This is what she was able to tell me of her time at the BBC, and her contribution to the saving of these three Patrick Troughton stories:

Enid Mawson: I joined the BBC Film Unit in January 1961 and started work as an assistant editor/neg cutter working mainly at Ealing TFS (and Television Centre for a short time). Sometime in the early 1970s, it was requested that I should go on a short-term loan to BBC Enterprises to replace Wally Morgan (who was in charge of their negative department) while he went into hospital. I ended up staying with them until I retired from the BBC in 1986. I'm at a loss as to why Sue Malden associated me with the *Doctor Who* films you speak about. The truth is that I don't think I can add any useful information about how decisions were made as to what film would be withdrawn. Decisions of this kind were made higher up and information was sent to me from Pamela Nash via one of her famous interoffice memos, in order that I could alter the records of what we held in the vaults. I have no memory of me personally having anything to do with sending material to Paul Madden. The film vault at Villiers House was looked after by a man called Reg, who also had a boy called Perry working with him (their surnames escape me), and as far as I'm aware, contained mostly telerecordings, which we mostly worked on. Villiers House was built on the bridge over the railway, so there was nowhere to put a skip – our film rubbish had to be wheeled down a narrow alleyway at the side of the building to the pavement.

CHAPTER 7

directly. And Keith, once he'd done the deal, delegated it to John to look after Ian. John must have said to Ian, 'You must meet Sue, she's interested in *Doctor Who*', and it went from there. So I would have told Ian everything I had found out so far, which would have included the Villiers House connection. But certainly Ian was the one that triggered me off in thinking of looking at what had been sold overseas, and in trying to find material that way.

It would appear, then, that Enid Mawson from BBC Enterprises took the initiative in 1977 to donate their unwanted 16mm film prints of 'The Dominators', 'The Krotons', and 'The War Games' to the BFI. Prints that, as far as Malden can recall, were returned to Enterprises by an unknown overseas broadcaster (although if we assume that they all came back from a single country, then the candidates are Australia, Gibraltar, Singapore or Hong Kong, these being the only countries that screened all three stories).

Anne Hanford recalls a similar set of circumstances:

Anne Hanford: There was some limited cross-department communication between the BBC Film Library and BBC Enterprises in the 1960s and 1970s, but not a great deal. We sometimes received recordings that BBC Enterprises no longer wanted, but it didn't happen systematically. Once Sue Malden became the BBC Archive Selector in 1978, then the search for material that had been lost by the BBC became something we could explore in earnest. The problem was that any individuals who had copies of BBC programmes were actually breaking copyright law, and so it was quite a thorny problem. The BBC Film and Videotape Library were best placed to handle these problems, though, and in conjunction with the National Film and Television Archive, could act with a certain amount of discretion to ensure material was returned.

By the end of 1978 the Film Library was in possession of significantly more *Doctor Who* material than it had been at the start of the year. All the 16mm black and white film prints from Enterprises had been transferred from Villiers House to Windmill Road (apart from those for a couple of Pertwee stories that already existed in full on colour videotape anyway). In addition, 16mm film print copies of the BFI's negatives of 'The Dominators', 'The Krotons' and 'The War Games' had been made by the BBC, and added to their archive (a haul that may or may not have also included the 35mm print of 'The Dominators' Episode Three – see Andrew Martin's comments earlier).

WIPED!

THE 'INVASION OF THE DINOSAURS' MYSTERY

I've made little mention of the Pertwee story 'Invasion of the Dinosaurs' until now, but it's a subject that needs to be addressed. The whole six-part story seems to have, at one point, been officially missing *in its entirety* from the BBC. This can be deduced from four disparate but relevant pieces of evidence:

1. The junking order raised by BBC Enterprises for all six episodes of this story in August 1974, which may well have been carried out. This is related to …
2. The fact that this story was never once sold abroad by BBC Enterprises at all in the 1970s. Coupled with …
3. The 625-line transmission tape of Part One was certainly junked by the BBC, presumably as a result of the August 1974 junking order. (Contrary to one long-standing fan myth, this had nothing to do with the on-screen story title of this episode being simply 'Invasion', and so being confused somehow with the opening episode of the Troughton story 'The Invasion' when that came to be junked. The two-inch tapes of 'The Invasion' were junked in 1971, three years before 'Invasion of the Dinosaurs' was even made and screened.) This episode survives only in black and white to this day. Which ties in to …
4. The list of available/surviving *Doctor Who* episodes drawn up by the 'Whose Doctor Who' production team in November 1976 didn't include a single episode of 'Invasion of the Dinosaurs' on two-inch tape. No spool numbers were logged for any episode of this story.

The only conclusion that can be reasonably drawn from this evidence is that, by 1976, the story was missing in its entirety from the BBC. But by 1981, the BBC had found two-inch 625-line colour tapes of Parts Two, Three, Four, Five and Six, plus an untransmitted 'ED' edit of Part Three. And these weren't just two-inch dubs of the episodes, these were the original transmission tapes (the 'ED' edit aside). Where had they come from?

When the story came to be released on VHS by BBC Video in 2003, the job of preparing the videotape master for this was done at BBC Pebble Mill, and was overseen by Paul Vanezis. He was given access to the original two-inch videotapes of Parts Two to Six, and noted that the tape cases had British Rail stickers plastered all over them. These dated back to 1974, when it appeared that the tapes had been sent to BBC Cardiff – the reason being that *Doctor Who*'s eleventh season had a different transmission slot in Wales than in the rest of the country[50]. BBC Cymru had decided

CHAPTER 7

to screen a regional opt-out programme at Saturday teatimes, a Welsh folk music programme called *Gwerin 74*. *Doctor Who* was instead screened first on a Monday night ('The Time Warrior' Part One only), then on Tuesday nights (from 'The Time Warrior' Part Two through to 'Invasion of the Dinosaurs' Part One) and then finally on Sunday afternoons (from 'Invasion of the Dinosaurs' Part Two onwards). Was this a clue as to where the tapes had perhaps re-appeared from?

The BBC Film and Videotape Library retains recording cards for the network transmission tapes of Parts Two to Six of 'Invasion of the Dinosaurs'. This is what is recorded on those cards:

> Part Two: Master tape was dubbed to film recording on 27/06 (1974?); a VT dub was made for BBC Wales on 08/01/74, spool number F4066
> Part Three: Film recording made on 27/06 (1974?). No mention of a BBC Wales dub.
> Part Four: No mention of film recording being made, or of a BBC Wales dub.
> Part Five: Film recordings made on 28/06 and on 10/07 (1974?); VT dub to F4010 for BBC Wales made on 06/02/74.
> Part Six: Film recording made on 28/06 (1974?); dub to F4153 for BBC Wales on 10/02/74

So were the BBC two-inch masters in 2003 actually the copies made by BBC Wales in 1974, and not the original network transmission masters, which might have all been junked by 1976? Andrew Martin of the BBC Film and Videotape Library is doubtful:

> **Andrew Martin:** Possibly Parts Three and Four were shipped overnight to Wales for transmission the next day, or dubs were made and not noted. The point though (regarding the mystery of why the masters were apparently missing in 1976) is that it does not appear to be because they were in Wales, as they had their own copies made. There is a different recording number on the Welsh PasBs suggesting the master tapes were not just played out later from London.
>
> On checking in the file of VT wiping slips we have, it does note that the transmission spool for 'Invasion of the Dinosaurs' Part One was wiped

---

50 It's probably worth mentioning at this point that, in 1967, 'The Abominable Snowmen' was also shown in a later time slot on BBC Wales, but on the same evening that the rest of the BBC network saw the episodes of this story. BBC Wales would have made their own two-inch transmission tapes of the episodes, either at the time of network transmission, or prior to transmission, using the BBCs own 'direct line' relay. These tapes would have been wiped/re-used within days of use.

(spool number 65170), but there is also a wiping slip for Part Three, listing the spools 62589, 94550, 94613, 43443 and 30490. Somebody has later noted 'exists' in pen against all but 94550. On Infax, 62589 is the first edit version, and 43443 was a protection dub made on 22 January 1974. 30490 was the re-edited original transmission version. 94613 is listed as 'incomplete parts' and was junked in 1991. 62589, 43443 and 30490 were all transferred to D3 in the 1990s. When BBC Choice repeated the story in 1999, they used the first edit by mistake, transmitting from a D3 copy of 62589. Both episodes are listed in the wiping file as 'Invasion' by the way. There are no slips for the other episodes.

So it's possible the network transmission tapes were sent by rail to Wales, though as I say there also seem to have been dubs made prior to transmission for some of the episodes at least – I wonder if Paul definitely remembers British Rail stickers on all the episodes, or just on Parts Three and Four, which do not list dubs being made? Perhaps the masters were sent as well, since they had been technically reviewed and were therefore to be preferred to the dubs made especially for Wales, which might not have been checked to the same standard. (This costs money to do these days; not sure if it would then.) The recording cards do not list the tapes as having been used for the Welsh transmissions – normally any transmission is noted on them. It is of course possible that someone neglected to note this, but would they have neglected to do it for all five episodes?

So the masters we had by 2003 must have been the originals since their numbers match the recording cards, whereas the Welsh dubs had different spool numbers (the ones starting with F on the recording cards). They would not (or should not at any rate) have renumbered the Welsh master tapes, certainly not to give them the same numbers as the originals. I think the original two-inch spools (including the longer Part Three) may just have been misfiled in 1976. The fact that the telerecordings are listed as having been made from the original two-inch tapes after transmission proves that the spools must have come back to London after the Welsh transmission, unless BBC Wales made them for BBC Enterprises, which seems unlikely – if the spools were needed and had been traced to Wales, there would have been no reason for Wales not to have sent them back to London.

So it would appear that the tapes the BBC retain for Parts Two to Six are the original network transmission tapes of these episodes, and not dubs for BBC Wales. And the tapes weren't kept for any significant length of time by BBC Wales in 1974. So

CHAPTER 7

perhaps the tapes were never missing in the first place. Perhaps the 'Whose Doctor Who' researchers just didn't look at the right files or shelves when researching their programme in late 1976/early 1977.

As we'll later learn, the list prepared for 'Whose Doctor Who' has quite a few other question marks hanging over it, and the inability of the researchers to find the two-inch tapes of any of the episodes of 'Invasion of the Dinosaurs' in November 1976 does not mean that they were not actually there at the BBC at the time. The 1974 junking order may have been responsible for the loss of only the first episode, and this in turn may have led to the story just not being offered for sale by Enterprises, as it was pointless without the opening instalment.

One person who can offer some insight on this is Jan Vincent-Rudzki. In 1976, he had assisted the production team of 'Whose Doctor Who' in his capacity as President of the DWAS. By 1978, however, he was working for the BBC ...

Jan Vincent-Rudzki: I joined the BBC in 1978 and started in the basement, in VT Current Ops, a department that dealt with the handling of videotape at Television Centre and sending the tapes around the country, and beyond. One of the first things I discovered there were the card index files holding the technical information about each videotape, whether the tapes were held at Television Centre or Windmill Road. At that time the tapes were split between the two locations, with no particular rhyme or reason. So of course I investigated what still existed. Windmill Road knew practically nothing about what was around, just a very rough idea.

One of the problems at the time was that there was a clash between the head of VT and Anne Hanford, the Head of the Film Library. Both wanted to increase the power of their departments, so there was little co-operation between the two departments. VT felt the tapes belonged to them, and didn't like Windmill Road trying to claim ownership.

After 'Whose Doctor Who', I had been given a list by Tony Cash of what the production team had discovered still existed, but it soon became clear to me that whoever had put together the list had no understanding of VT's filing system. For instance, the VT index cards were stored in the recording number order, not programme transmission order, and all it took was a misfiling for something to become 'lost' for a while.

As it happened, I hadn't seen Part One of 'Invasion of the Dinosaurs' in colour when it was shown on the BBC in 1974 because one of the guns of my TV tube had gone, so I was surprised to discover that it didn't exist when I first checked, but I am 99% sure the rest of the story was there on the shelves

WIPED!

in 1978.

At that time, the filing system of the VT holdings was being computerised onto a database called VTOL (Video Tape On Line), but it was a mess. Basically it was a list of VTC/XXX/XXXXX numbers and their corresponding computer 'dummy programme numbers' (which would be in the sequence LDL9XXXXX.). The information was sparse, and often inaccurate, but gave Windmill Road some idea of what was around.

Then six months later I got a job in the VT Cataloguing Unit, which by now was part of the Film Library, but I was still based in Television Centre, across the corridor from Current Ops (this was something of an attempt to forge a link between the two departments). Part of my work (and that of others) was maintaining VTOL, and I was given (i.e. I took) the task of tidying up the Drama listings, with particular attention paid to *Doctor Who*. This involved shelf checks to cross-check the data on the cards and computer.

It was at this point that VTOL started to show story titles and details of which edits were held (ED or ED/ED etc) and any other information. Again, I have no recollection of Parts Two to Six of 'Invasion of the Dinosaurs' being 'lost'! I also made sure that the series title was *Doctor Who* for every record, rather than all its variations (*Dr Who*, *Dr. Who*, *Who*, *D Who*, etc), which might not appear in a search...

One reason that the 'Whose Doctor Who' researchers thought all of 'Invasion of the Dinosaurs' no longer survived might be this: because so much videotape had been wiped, any old programmes were often assumed by Current Ops to no longer exist, and from my knowledge of some of my then-colleagues I can well believe that an enquiry about the story could be met with the answer 'It doesn't exist', because quite frankly, they couldn't be bothered to look it up, or the cards were mis-filed.

The arrival of the computer system VTOL didn't always help. In those early days of computers people didn't understand them at all, particularly the librarians at Windmill Road. I had to give them lessons on how to use the system after they started telling everyone that *I, Claudius* had been wiped. That was because I had entered it on the computer as an 'I' followed by a comma and a space, so if any other variation of this spelling was entered, the poor computer would not find the details! Hence the mis-information being sent out ...

So I disagree that all six parts of 'Invasion of the Dinosaurs' were ever lost by the BBC. I'm sure I knew Parts Two to Six were there, and I had seen the tapes on the shelves.

CHAPTER 7

What we know for certain is that the two-inch colour tapes of all but the first episode of this story were all stored safely in the BBC's Film and Videotape Library by November 1981. For argument's sake, let's assume that they were located (if missing at all) in late 1978, at around the time the BFI episodes and the Villiers House haul were also transferred to Windmill Road. If so, the Library's collection of *Doctor Who* at that time would have looked like this:

WILLIAM HARTNELL

Story	16mm b&w film	35mm b&w film	Missing
Pilot Episode	1		
An Unearthly Child	1, 2, 3, 4		
The Daleks	1, 2, 3, 4, 5, 6, 7		
The Edge of Destruction	1, 2		
Marco Polo			1, 2, 3, 4, 5, 6, 7
The Keys of Marinus	1, 2, 3, 4, 5, 6		
The Aztecs	1, 2, 3, 4		
The Sensorites	1, 2, 3, 4, 5, 6		
The Reign of Terror			1, 2, 3, 4, 5, 6
Planet of Giants	1, 2, 3		
The Dalek Invasion of Earth	1, 2, 3, 4, 6	5	
The Rescue	1, 2		
The Romans	1, 2, 3, 4		
The Web Planet	1, 2, 3, 4, 5, 6		
The Crusade	3		1, 2, 4
The Space Museum	1, 2, 3, 4		
The Chase	1, 2, 3, 4, 5, 6		
The Time Meddler	2		1, 3, 4
Galaxy 4			1, 2, 3, 4
Mission to the Unknown			1
The Myth Makers			1, 2, 3, 4
The Daleks Masterplan			1, 2, 3, 4, 5, 6, 7, 8, 9, 10, 11, 12
The Massacre			1, 2, 3, 4
The Ark	1, 2, 3, 4		
The Celestial Toymaker			1, 2, 3, 4
The Gunfighters	1, 2, 3, 4		
The Savages			1, 2, 3, 4
The War Machines			1, 2, 3, 4
The Smugglers			1, 2, 3, 4
The Tenth Planet	1, 2, 3		4

WIPED!

PATRICK TROUGHTON

Story	16mm b&w film	35mm b&w film	Missing
The Power of the Daleks			1, 2, 3, 4, 5, 6
The Highlanders			1, 2, 3, 4
The Underwater Menace	3		1, 2, 4
The Moonbase	2, 4		1, 3
The Macra Terror			1, 2, 3, 4
The Faceless Ones	1		2, 3, 4, 5, 6
The Evil of the Daleks			1, 2, 3, 4, 5, 6, 7
The Tomb of the Cybermen			1, 2, 3, 4
The Abominable Snowmen			1, 2, 3, 4, 5, 6
The Ice Warriors			1, 2, 3, 4, 5, 6
The Enemy of the World	3		1, 2, 4, 5, 6
The Web of Fear			1, 2, 3, 4, 5, 6
Fury from the Deep			1, 2, 3, 4, 5, 6
The Wheel in Space		6	1, 2, 3, 4, 5
The Dominators	1, 2, 4, 5	3	
The Mind Robber	1, 2, 3, 4	5	
The Invasion	2, 3, 5, 6, 7, 8		1, 4
The Krotons	2, 3, 4	1	
The Seeds of Death	1, 2, 3, 4, 6	5	
The Space Pirates		2	1, 3, 4, 5, 6
The War Games	1, 2, 3, 4, 5, 6, 7, 8, 9, 10		

JON PERTWEE

Story	625-line 2-inch colour VT	16mm colour film	16mm b&w film	Missing
Spearhead from Space		1, 2, 3, 4	1, 2, 3, 4	
Doctor Who & the Silurians			1, 2, 3, 4, 5, 6, 7	
The Ambassadors of Death	1		1, 2, 3, 4, 5, 6, 7	
Inferno			1, 2, 3, 4, 5, 6, 7	
Terror of the Autons			1, 2, 3, 4	
The Mind of Evil			1, 2, 3, 4, 5, 6	
The Claws of Axos	1, 4		1, 2, 3, 4	
Colony in Space			1, 2, 3, 4, 5, 6	

CHAPTER 7

Story				
The Dæmons	4		1, 2, 3, 4, 5	
Day of the Daleks	1, 2, 3, 4			
The Curse of Peladon			1, 2, 3, 4	
The Sea Devils	4, 5, 6		1, 2, 3, 4, 5, 6	
The Mutants	3, 4, 5, 6		1, 2, 3, 4, 5, 6	
The Time Monster			1, 2, 3, 4, 5, 6	
The Three Doctors	1, 2, 3, 4			
Carnival of Monsters	1, 2, 3, 4			
Frontier in Space	4, 5		1, 2, 3, 4, 5, 6	
Planet of the Daleks	1, 2, 4, 5, 6		1, 2, 3, 4, 5, 6	
The Green Death	1, 2, 3, 4, 5, 6			
The Time Warrior	1, 2, 3, 4			
Invasion of the Dinosaurs	2, 3, 4, 5, 6			1
Death to the Daleks	2, 3, 4			1
The Monster of Peladon	1, 2, 3, 4, 5, 6			
Planet of the Spiders	1, 2, 3, 4, 5, 6			

The tally of missing episodes now stood as follows: 61 William Hartnell episodes, 76 Patrick Troughton episodes, and two Jon Pertwee episodes. This meant that at the end of 1978 there were a total of 139 episodes of *Doctor Who* missing from the BBC archives.

WIPED!

CHAPTER 8
THE LIVELY ARTS—WHOSE DOCTOR WHO

Some light is potentially shed on the state of the BBC's *Doctor Who* holdings in the 1970s by the research done for the April 1977 BBC2 documentary 'Whose Doctor Who', an edition of *The Lively Arts* programme strand. In November 1976, a member of the documentary's production team spent some time trying to work out what exactly still survived from the show, and the results were typed up into a list, and then annotated by hand. The typed list is dated 24 November 1976.[51]

This list was compiled on a per-episode basis, giving the original transmission date of each episode, along with its on-screen title. Each episode was allocated three columns, into which information could be recorded by hand. The typed headers for those columns were *Ent*, *Film Lib* and *Foreign Version*.

As far as the Hartnell and Troughton stories are concerned, films marked in the *Ent* column of the list are almost certainly those that the researcher thought still existed as 16mm copies at BBC Enterprises' offices in Villiers House. Those listed in the *Foreign Version* column are also presumably ones that the researcher thought were held at Villiers House. Those listed in the *Film Lib* column were presumably the ones held in the Film and Videotape Library at Windmill Road.

However, whoever made the list was quite inconsistent in how they recorded the information on it. Sometimes, the existence of an episode is marked simply by having the relevant box in the particular column drawn round in pen on all four sides. Other boxes are not drawn round, but simply have odd bits of information jotted into them, or initials such as 'TR', which presumably stands for 'telerecording' (an almost universally recognised shorthand denotation within the BBC at the time). Other boxes have been drawn around, but have data recorded in the next column – is this meant to relate to the print marked in the first column, or to a second one held elsewhere?

How this information was collected is also unclear. It's probable that the researcher collated the information from card files, rather than inspecting rows of shelves. This might also explain why information is sometimes entered into the wrong column on the listing.

Bearing all that in mind, here's what the list *apparently* tells us existed from *Doctor Who*'s black and white era at Villiers House and the BBC Film Library in November

---

51 This list has been referenced a few times in the previous chapters of this book, but I've decided to hold back on any major discussion of it until now, as it contradicts quite a lot of the known facts – facts borne out, for example, by the discovery of exactly what *Doctor Who* material was still held at Villiers House in 1978, as discussed in the previous chapter.

1976 (along with the – sometimes pithy – comments from the original anonymous compiler of the list in brackets):

Story	Enterprises	Film Library	Foreign Version
An Unearthly Child	Episode 1 ('*Telerecording Poor Quality*')	Episodes 1-4 ('*16mm CO*')	Episodes 1-4 ('*Arabic*')
The Daleks	Episode 7 ('*Arabic*')		Episodes 1-7 ('*Arabic*')
The Edge of Destruction			Episodes 1-2 ('*Arabic*')
Marco Polo			
The Keys of Marinus			Episodes 1-6 ('*Arabic*')
The Aztecs			Episodes 1-4 ('*Arabic*')
The Sensorites			Episodes 1-6 ('*Arabic*')
The Reign of Terror			
Planet of Giants			Episodes 1-3 ('*Arabic*')
The Dalek Invasion of Earth		Episode 5 ('*35mm CO*')	Episodes 1-4, 6 ('*Arabic*') Episode 5 ('*Sp + Arabic 16mm FL*')
The Rescue			Episodes 1-2 ('*Arabic*')
The Romans	Episode 1 ('*Bad – <u>No</u>*')		
The Web Planet	Episodes 1-5 ('*TR*') Episode 6 ('*Very Bad – Panto*')		Episodes 1-6 ('*Spanish*')
The Crusade		Episode 3 ('*Very bad*')	
The Space Museum	Episode 1 ('*Boring, cheap*') Episode 2 ('*TR B&W TR NEG*') Episodes 3-4 ('*TR*')		Episode 3 ('*16mm mag Spanish*')

CHAPTER 8

The Chase	Episode 1 ('No print') Episodes 2-6 ('TR')	Episode 1 only ('No Neg')	
The Time Meddler	Episodes 1-4 ('TR'), Episode 4 ('TR, shrinking TARDIS')		
Galaxy 4	Episode 1 ('TR No negative') Episode 2 ('TR No print') Episodes 3-4 ('TR')	Episode 2 ('No Neg')	
Mission to the Unknown			
The Myth Makers			
The Daleks Masterplan		Episode 2 ('Film Seqs only') Episode 4 ('Lost')	
The Massacre			
The Ark	Episodes 3-4		
The Celestial Toymaker			
The Gunfighters		Episode 4 ('35 CO neg')	
The Savages			
The War Machines			
The Smugglers			
The Tenth Planet	Episodes 1-3		
The Power of the Daleks			
The Highlanders			
The Underwater Menace			
The Moonbase	Episode 4 ('OK')		
The Macra Terror			
The Faceless Ones		Episode 1 ('16mm CO neg')	
The Evil of the Daleks			
The Tomb of the Cybermen			

WIPED!

The Abominable Snowmen			
The Ice Warriors			
The Enemy of the World	Episode 3 ('*No*')	Episode 3 ('*16 CO*')	
The Web of Fear	Episode 1 ('*No Yeti*')		
Fury from the Deep			
The Wheel in Space		Episode 6 ('*35 comopt*')	
The Dominators	Episodes 2-5 ('*TR*')	Episode 3 ('*35 CO*')	
The Mind Robber		Episode 5 ('*35 CO*')	
The Invasion	Episodes 1-4, 7 & 8 only Episode 3 ('*A + B*')		
The Krotons	Episode 1 ('*Yes*') Episodes 2-4 ('*TR*')	Episode 1 ('*35 CO pos*')	
The Seeds of Death	Episodes 1-6 ('*TR*')	Episode 5 ('*35 CO pos*')	
The Space Pirates	Episode 2	Episode 2 ('*35 mute pos*')	
The War Games	Episodes 4, 7 & 9 Episode 10 ('*Neg – Time Lords*')		

What conclusions can be drawn from this document? Well, for starters, there's quite a lot of information that doesn't make sense, as noted before. But there is also a lot that *does*. When it comes to BBC internal documents in general, I tend to apply an Occam's Razor type of logic to the information contained therein. Is it consistent with what we already know? Can it be corroborated with other documents? Are there any reasons to doubt what we are being presented with?

Let's look at the episodes from the first two seasons. According to the list, most of these survived at Enterprises *only* as Arabic film prints. Come 1978, and these had *all* seemingly become English versions, and not Arabic ones at all. One *possible* explanation for this is that these episodes could have been returned to Enterprises from an overseas broadcaster (and being Arabic, this almost certainly means Algeria – it can't be co-incidence, surely, that Algeria purchased in July 1973 each and every episode listed above as being in Arabic?). These films could have been back at Villiers

CHAPTER 8

House for a relatively short time (or perhaps not – the use of an Arabic-dubbed clip of 'An Unearthly Child' Episode Four on *Blue Peter* back in 1973 might suggest otherwise), and an assumption was made that there were *only* Arabic-dubbed copies of the episodes in this batch. However, on closer examination, it might have been found to comprise:

- a 16mm B&W film print, English soundtrack
- a 16mm B&W film negative, English soundtrack
- a magnetic soundtrack
- a 16mm B&W film print, Arabic soundtrack

This would almost accord with what Ian Levine recalls finding for 'The Daleks' – i.e. four tins for each episode, containing an English print, an English negative, an Arabic print and an Arabic negative respectively. He might have mistakenly identified the magnetic soundtrack tins as Arabic negatives.

If this were the case, it would mean that, having purchased 'An Unearthly Child', 'The Daleks', 'The Edge of Destruction', 'The Keys of Marinus', 'The Aztecs', 'The Sensorites', 'Planet of Giants', 'The Daleks Invasion of Earth' and 'The Rescue' in 1973, Algeria returned Arabic prints, along with the original English prints, negatives and magnetic soundtracks, at some later date. These were then all lumped together as 'Arabic prints' by Enterprises, the truth being discovered only when the film cans were finally inspected by the Film Library in 1978. Could it be that *Blue Peter* had used that Arabic clip in November 1973 simply because they had been told by Enterprises that that was the only version of Episode Four of 'An Unearthly Child' that they held? It's only a theory – but it's a compelling one!

The 'Whose Doctor Who' list supports some of the information found in both versions of Enterprises' *A Quick Guide to Dr Who* sales brochure from 1974/75. That indicated that 'The Web Planet', 'The Space Museum', 'The Time Meddler' and 'Galaxy 4' were all still available for purchase. The overseas sales rights for those stories had certainly expired by 1976, and yet Enterprises still demonstrably had 16mm film copies of them at this point.

That there were Spanish soundtracks listed for all six episodes of 'The Web Planet' and a single episode of 'The Space Museum' suggests that a batch of material had also been returned to Enterprises from one of the Spanish-language territories at some point, of which these were the remnants. Of the two main Spanish-speaking countries that purchased these stories, the best bet for the one that returned them would be Chile, as it would seem that Mexico retained their films for some time, well into the 1980s. Or the supposed Spanish episodes, like the supposed Arabic ones, could perhaps have been English versions all the time.

WIPED!

The list could be taken to indicate that the second episode of 'Galaxy 4' had already been junked by this point, due to the '*No neg*' and '*No print*' comments added by hand to the paperwork. That seems, on the face of it, unlikely. Another possible reading is that the Film Library held a negative of the episode but no print, while Enterprises held a print but no negative. Again, though, this seems implausible.

The odd episodes of Seasons Four and Five that are listed as being held at Enterprises tally closely with those that were found at the Film Library in 1977; namely, 'The Tenth Planet' Episodes One, Two and Three, 'The Moonbase' Episode Four, and 'The Enemy of the World' Episode Three. Perhaps the details of these episodes had been listed in the wrong column of the document, and were at the Film Library all along? Alternatively, maybe these episodes were sent to the Film Library from Enterprises not long after the list was compiled? Or perhaps they were borrowed from Enterprises by *The Lively Arts* production team, and then sent to the Film Library after the programme was made – either in error, or because Enterprises just didn't want them back, as they weren't complete stories? (The information for 'The Enemy of the World' episode is confusingly entered in both columns, but did the BBC *really* hold two copies of this one episode at the time? It seems improbable.)

The apparent existence of Episode One of 'The Web of Fear' at BBC Enterprises in 1976 seems, on first glance, something of an anomaly. The 1981 *Doctor Who Monthly* Winter Special article on the Film and Videotape Library tells how Sue Malden rescued this episode from Enterprises. The way that the article is written has led many people to assume that this must have happened sometime *after* 1978, when all of the other Hartnell, Troughton and Pertwee 16mm film episodes held at Enterprises had already been transferred to the Library.

There are three possible explanations for this episode appearing on the 1976 list:

1. The film might have been returned to Enterprises as early as 1976 but stored somewhere separate from the main stock of episodes in Villiers House, by dint of it being a returned print and only one episode of an otherwise missing story (and thus unsuitable for overseas sale). It was then found by Malden some time after the initial 1978 discoveries.
2. There were two separate prints of 'The Web of Fear' Episode One over the years: one that existed at Enterprises in 1976, but had been junked by 1978, and another that was returned to Enterprises some time after 1978, and subsequently discovered by Malden.
3. *The Lively Arts* list, for this episode, is just wrong!

When it comes to the episodes listed from the sixth season, then a real hotchpotch of

CHAPTER 8

material is revealed. 'The Invasion', for example, has six of its eight episodes listed as still remaining, but not the *same* six episodes as were found at the BBC Film Library in 1977. The 1976 list has Episodes Five and Six down as missing, but it was Episodes One and Four that would be missing come 1977 (and to this day). Could it be that not only were the episodes logged against the wrong archive by the *Lively Arts* researcher, but that the *wrong* six episodes were identified as existing? Again, is the listing just plain *wrong*?

Similarly, for both 'The Dominators' and 'The War Games', the correct number of extant episodes was listed (correct in that, come 1977, four episodes of each story were found at the Film Library), but the actual episodes listed are different from those that were later discovered. At least the fact that they were listed as being at Enterprises is consistent with other evidence, as the complete stories were later sent to the BFI. But where were the other episodes of those stories in 1976? The list seemingly confirms that the 35mm transmission print of 'The Dominators' Episode Three was still at the Film and Videotape Library after all. Again, did the researcher mis-identify the exact episodes and the archive in which they were held?

Some of the extant material was definitely viewed by members of the *Lively Arts* production team. Researcher Ben Shepherd viewed 16mm black and white prints of 'The Crusade' Episode Three, 'The Space Museum' Episode One, 'The Enemy of the World' Episode Three and 'The Claws of Axos' Episode Three on 24 November 1976. Two days later, he and another researcher viewed film prints of 'The Web Planet' Episode Six, 'The Krotons' Episode One, 'The Seeds of Death' Episode Five, 'The War Games' Episode Ten, and 'Doctor Who and the Silurians' Episodes Four, Five and Seven. Shepherd was probably the person who made the 'pithy' comments on the existing paperwork that was mentioned earlier.

It is also worth looking at the listing put together by Tony Cash's production team for the BBC's various holdings of the Jon Pertwee and Tom Baker episodes. We've briefly examined the details presented in just the *Film Lib* column in Chapter 4, but the full entries were as follows:

Story	VT Spool Quoted	Enterprises	Film Library
Spearhead from Space		Episodes 1-4 '*TR*'	Episode 1: '35 *mag + pos col*' Episodes 2-4: '16 *col pos + mag*'

WIPED!

Doctor Who and the Silurians		Episodes 1-7 'TR' (Episodes 4, 5 and 7 described as 'Quite Good' Episode 7 also bizarrely listed as 'missing')	Episodes 6-7: '16 col pos + mag (sequences)'
The Ambassadors of Death	Episode 1	Episodes 1-7 'TR'	
Inferno		Episodes 1-7 'TR'	Episode 1: 'film sequences?'
Terror of the Autons		Episodes 1-4 'TR'	
The Mind of Evil		Episodes 1-6 'TR'	
The Claws of Axos	Episodes 1 & 4	Episodes 1-4 'TR' (Episode 3 described as 'Good')	
Colony in Space		Episodes 1-6 'TR'	
The Dæmons	Episode 4	Episodes 1-5 'TR'	
Day of the Daleks	Episodes 1-4	Episodes 1-4 'TR'	
The Curse of Peladon		Episodes 1-4 'TR'	
The Sea Devils	Episodes 4-6	Episode 1 'No print, No neg' Episodes 1-6 'TR'	
The Mutants	Episodes 3-6	Episodes 1-6 'TR'	
The Time Monster		Episodes 1-6 'TR'	
The Three Doctors	Episodes 1-4	Episodes 1-4 'Original Tape'	Episodes 2-4: 'film sequences'
Carnival of Monsters	Episodes 1-4	Episodes 1-4 'TR'	
Frontier in Space	Episodes 4 & 5	Episodes 1-6 'TR'	Episodes 1-2: 'sequences 16 cl mt neg'
Planet of the Daleks	Episodes 1, 2, 4-6	Episodes 1-6 'Original Tape'	Episodes 1, 3-6: 'film seqs'
The Green Death	Episodes 1-6	Episodes 1-5 'Original Tape'	
The Time Warrior	Parts 1-4	Parts 1-4 'Original Tape'	Part 4: 'film seqs'
Invasion of the Dinosaurs		'NO'	Parts 1-3: 'film seqs + print' Parts 4-6: 'film seqs'
Death to the Daleks	Parts 1-4	Parts 1-4 'Original Tape'	Parts 1-4: 'film seqs'

CHAPTER 8

The Monster of Peladon	Parts 1-6	Parts 1-6 *'Original Tape'*	Parts 1-6: *'film seqs'*
Planet of the Spiders	Parts 1-6 Repeat Compilation ('105' 14')	Parts 1-6 *'VTC'*	Parts 1-2: *'film seqs'*
Robot	Parts 1-4	Parts 1-4 *'VTC'*	
The Ark in Space	Parts 1-4	Parts 1-4 *'VTC'*	Part 1: *'film seqs'*
The Sontaran Experiment	Parts 1-2 Repeat Compilation	Parts 1-2 *'VTC'*	
Genesis of the Daleks	Parts 1-6	Parts 1-6 *'VTC'*	Parts 1-4: *'film seqs'*
Revenge of the Cybermen	Parts 1-4	Parts 1-4 *'VTC'*	Parts 1-4: *'film seqs'*
Terror of the Zygons	Parts 1-4	Parts 1-4 *'VTC'*	
Planet of Evil	Parts 1-4	Parts 1-4 *'VTC'*	Parts 1-4: *'film seqs'*
Pyramids of Mars	Parts 1-4	Parts 1-4 *'VTC'*	Parts 1-4: *'film seqs'*
The Android Invasion	Parts 1-4	Parts 1-4 *'VTC'*	Parts 2 & 4: *'film seqs'*
The Brain of Morbius	Parts 1-4		
The Seeds of Doom	Parts 1-6		
The Masque of Mandragora	Parts 1-4		
The Hand of Fear	Parts 1-4		
The Deadly Assassin	Parts 1-4		

Just a few words about how these details were presented on the page. Whereas the archival nature of the Hartnell and Troughton episodes fitted the format of the typewritten sheets quite well, the Pertwee and Baker episodes were less suited to the various columns and headings given. The *Foreign Version* column was still on all the sheets for these episodes, but wasn't used at all for any entry – it was just a blank column all the way through the listing, so has been omitted here.

The story title and episode number of each story were listed in transmission order, and where a two-inch tape was noted as existing, the tape/programme number was written on by hand. For example, the notation for 'The Three Doctors' Episode One was given as 'VTC/6HT/82370/ED'. But next to each handwritten tape number was another five-digit number in brackets, followed by the annotation 'ENT'. In the

WIPED!

case of the 'The Three Doctors' Episode One, this was '(65765) ENT'. This would appear to be the BBC Enterprises spool number for each videotaped episode, and could mean one of two things – either that BBC Enterprises had a duplicate two-inch copy of every episode, or – as seems more likely – that each tape was logged in both the Windmill Road system and the Enterprises system, under a different code in each case. The typewritten list only went up to the story 'The Android Invasion' (and erroneously detailed that it ran to five episodes; this has been corrected above), with the details for all the subsequent stories added and amended by hand on later pages.

As with the Hartnell/Troughton section, there is much to be deeply suspicious about in the Pertwee/Baker details collated by the 'Whose Doctor Who' team.

The mention of 35mm colour film next to 'Spearhead from Space' Episode One is almost certainly a reference to the 35mm film of the opening and closing titles, which was logged against this story for many years at the Film and Videotape Library. The notation 'TR' again seems to have been used as shorthand for 16mm black and white film prints, but whoever compiled the list stopped logging these after 'Frontier in Space'. But does this really mean that there were no such prints held for 'Planet of the Daleks' or 'The Green Death' in 1976? There certainly were in 1978.

The number of film sequences from Pertwee and Baker stories that were still seemingly around is quite a revelation, considering how few survived just a few short years later. However, given that the Film and Videotape Library was prioritising the preservation of complete transmitted programmes, then it is understandable why such programme elements might be junked in due course, especially as they were all from episodes that existed in full (if not in full colour). Of course, some of this information may not have been correct at the time, but there is no way of verifying this now.

The listing appears to indicate that Enterprises had two-inch colour tapes of all six episodes of 'Planet of the Daleks' at this point, but that the Film and Videotape Library was missing Episode Three. There is no reason to doubt the latter fact, but the former is highly unlikely, and smacks of an error. A two-inch colour tape of Part One of 'Death to the Daleks' seemingly existed at both Enterprises and Windmill Road, but Enterprises seemed to be missing the final episode of 'The Green Death'. The tape of 'Death to the Daleks' Part One would be missing by 1978.

THE LIVELY ARTS: WHOSE DOCTOR WHO—TAKE 2!

Having drawn up their list of which episodes they thought existed at either BBC Enterprises or the BBC Film Library in late 1976, the next step the 'Whose Doctor Who' production team took was to order up from Enterprises the films or negatives

CHAPTER 8

from which they wanted to take clips for their programme. So on Thursday 13 January 1977, producer Tony Cash sent a memo to Pamela Nash at Enterprises, asking for some specified 16mm negatives to be sent to the programme's film editor, David Martin.

Most of the episodes asked for were ones identified as existing in November 1976 – however, not all the requested material could be supplied by BBC Enterprises ... The typed memo of 13 January has been annotated by hand, and these details are reproduced below:

Story / Episode Requested	*Notes (All hand written)*
An Unearthly Child: Episode One	Print and Neg ordered. Want
The Daleks: Episode One	Scrapped. Don't Want
The Daleks: Episode Two	Scrapped. Don't Want
The Dalek Invasion of Earth: Episode Two	Neg ordered. Want – indicated
The Dalek Invasion of Earth: Episode Five	Neg ordered. Want – indicated
The Dalek Invasion of Earth: Episode Six	Scrapped. Don't Want
The Rescue: Episode Two	Scrapped. Want. Checking Neg
The Web Planet: Episode Two	Print and Neg ordered. Want
The Space Museum: Episode Two	No print. Want. Neg ordered
The Chase: Episode One	Scrapped. Does not exist
The Chase: Episode Two	Neg exists! Want. Don't paper up
The Chase: Episode Five	No print. Want. Neg ordered
Galaxy 4: Episode One	Neg exists. Don't Want. Print only – neg does not exist
Galaxy 4: Episode Two	Scrapped. Don't Want
The Tenth Planet: Episode Two	Telerecording. Print Only – Paper
The Tenth Planet: Episode Four	Scrapped. No neg – Print?
The Invasion: Episode Eight	Telerecording. Want. No Neg – Print?
The Krotons: Episode Two	Ordered. Want
The Krotons: Episode Three	Ordered. Want
The Seeds of Death: Episode One	Ordered. Want
The Seeds of Death: Episode Five	Ordered. Want
The Seeds of Death: Episode Six	Ordered. Want
The Space Pirates: Episode Two	Ordered. Want
The War Games: Episode Ten	Ordered. Want
The Silurians: Episode Four	No neg. Telerecording. Want
The Silurians: Episode Seven	No neg. Telerecording. Want
The Claws of Axos: Episode Three	Ordered. Want
The Dæmons: Episode Five	Neg ordered. Want
The Sea Devils: Episode Two	Scrapped – no neg & no print. Want
The Curse of Peladon: Episode One	Does not exist
The Curse of Peladon: Episode Two	Does not exist
The Curse of Peladon: Episode Three	Checking for neg. Want

WIPED!

The Time Monster: Episode Two	Neg, but awaiting. Want
The Time Monster: Episode Three	Scrapped. Don't Want
The Time Monster: Episode Four	Ordered. Want
The Time Monster: Episode Six	Ordered. Want

If this listing is to be believed, then copies of at least some of the episodes that apparently existed at Enterprises in November 1976 had been scrapped by January 1977. The first two (Arabic?) episodes of 'The Daleks' were requested, but both had seemingly been junked – had the rest of the story also followed at the same time? From what we can deduce from later events, then it's possible that all seven episodes were Withdrawn, De-Accessioned and Junked by this point in time, but the films were still awaiting their final trip to the skip.

This list would also seem to confirm that Episode Two of 'Galaxy 4' had indeed been junked, which ties in with the notes written on the November 1976 document. Episode One of 'Galaxy 4' certainly *was* still in existence, however, and this was ordered up. A six-minute section was duplicated on 16mm film, although the clip that appeared in the finished documentary ran for no more than 30 seconds, taken from the middle of this six-minute section. The unused sections of 16mm film, trimmed from either side of the 30-second clip, were presented to DWAS President Jan Vincent-Rudzki, as a thank you for the help that he had given the production team.

However, later evidence would indicate that some of the other episodes listed as having been scrapped by BBC Enterprises actually weren't. 'The Dalek Invasion of Earth' Episode Six, 'The Rescue' Episode Two, and 'The Chase' Episode One were all later found at Villiers House. And you have to wonder why Episode Four of 'The Tenth Planet' was ordered, when this episode wasn't even on the list of those available in November 1976.

As for the Pertwee era, the number of episodes listed as having been scrapped or lost in the intervening months is astonishing. And yet a full set of prints from 'Doctor Who and the Silurians' through to 'The Green Death' was found at BBC Enterprises in 1978.[52]

When looked at with hindsight, then, the paperwork prepared for the 'Whose Doctor Who' production team is a bit of a hotch-potch. In some respects, it makes perfect sense, and helps to explain certain events and anomalies in the other evidence. But in other instances, it appears contradictory with what we know happened just a year or so later, when material was found to exist either at the Film Library or at

---

[52] It's tempting to believe that someone, somewhere, didn't check too hard at Villiers House when asked to find these episodes in 1977.

CHAPTER 8

Enterprises.

If nothing else, it demonstrates that things are never entirely straightforward, and that past events can't be explained in shades of mere black and white ...

ONE FINAL MYSTERY ...

When the BBC hit upon the notion of doing a documentary about *Doctor Who* in 1976, it was originally to be made under the auspices of the series *2nd House*, which was edited by Tony Cash. *2nd House* was cancelled before the *Doctor Who* feature could be fully planned, and was replaced by *The Lively Arts*.

In the autumn of 1976, the makers of *2nd House* approached former *Doctor Who* script editor and writer Terrance Dicks about being a consultant on the documentary, and Dicks agreed. At the time, he was pitching the story 'The Vampire Mutation' to the *Doctor Who* production office, as well as writing novelisations of previous *Doctor Who* adventures and re-working his non-fiction book *The Making of Doctor Who* (which he had originally co-written with Malcolm Hulke in 1972).

Dicks spent a week at the BBC, going through old episodes of *Doctor Who* and preparing a 'Summary of recommended available material', which listed a number of clips he thought might be suitable for the documentary team to use in their programme. These included sequences from 'An Unearthly Child', 'The Dalek Invasion of Earth', 'The Romans', 'The Web Planet', 'The Crusade', 'The Space Museum', and 'The Time Meddler' to represent Hartnell's Doctor, all of which came from material we know existed at the time. For Troughton's Doctor, he recommended clips from 'The Moonbase', 'The Web of Fear', 'The Wheel in Space', 'The Dominators', 'The Seeds of Death' and 'The War Games', again all from material we know to have existed. But also included in the list was a clip of the Doctor meeting the Daleks in Victorian England from 'The Evil of the Daleks'.

Was Dicks able to view a copy of at least one episode of 'The Evil of the Daleks' at the BBC in 1976? If so, which archive was it in – the Film and Videotape Library at Windmill Road, or the BBC Enterprises library at Villiers House? Or was Dicks just suggesting the clip from his memory of the story, without knowing whether or not the material survived? I contacted Dicks in an attempt to clarify this issue:

> **Terrance Dicks**: Sorry, I can't remember! I vaguely remember the programme, but I don't remember if I viewed any *Who* episodes in connection with it or not. I might well have done!

This, then, must remain a mystery ...

WIPED!

CHAPTER 9
THE RETURNED EPISODES

By 1978, all of the BBC's two-inch videotapes were under the control of the Film and Videotape Library, and no more *Doctor Who* transmission tapes were being junked. All of the Tom Baker episodes and about half of the Jon Pertwee episodes existed on this format in colour, while the other half of the Pertwee episodes existed as black and white 16mm telerecordings (apart from 'Spearhead from Space', which was on 16mm colour film). Two Pertwee episodes were however missing altogether – Part One of 'Invasion of the Dinosaurs', and Part One of 'Death to the Daleks'. Out of the 253 episodes from the 1960s, 61 of William Hartnell's and 76 of Patrick Troughton's were still missing. All the surviving Hartnell and Troughton episodes were held as black and white film telerecordings; mainly as 16mm films, but with a smattering of 35mm films as well.

The total number of missing episodes: 139.

But this was set to reduce ...

THE WAR MACHINES: EPISODE TWO
RETURNED TO THE BBC – C1978

ABC TV in Australia had purchased nearly all of the Hartnell and Troughton *Doctor Who* stories for screening from 1964 onwards, and had shown most of them at least twice between 1965 and 1972. Like all other overseas broadcasters that purchased the series, they had been supplied with 16mm black and white film prints of the episodes.

Not long after a 1968 run of repeats, comprising all the stories from 'The Space Museum' through to 'The Faceless Ones' (bar 'Mission to the Unknown' and 'The Daleks Masterplan', the only black and white stories never shown in Australia), three 16mm *Doctor Who* film prints that had originated at ABC found their way into the hands of an Australian film collector. These were 'The Chase' Episode One, 'The War Machines' Episode Two and 'The Faceless Ones' Episode One.

It has been claimed in the past that these three episodes were somehow 'stolen' from the ABC, but there is no direct evidence to substantiate that. It's equally likely that the films were disposed of by the ABC as per their agreements with the BBC, and then 'rescued' at some point in the disposal chain – *en route* to a landfill site, for instance.

These three 16mm *Doctor Who* films have stayed in Australia ever since. The first private film collector soon passed them on to another, who sometime in 1970 gave them to his son, David Gee, who was something of a *Doctor Who* fan.

In 1977, Gee was put into contact with UK-based *Doctor Who* fan Jeremy Bentham, who at the time was running the Doctor Who Appreciation Society's Reference Department. Due to the advent of domestic video recorders in the mid- to late 1970s, many UK *Doctor Who* fans were contacting their Australian counterparts, seeking copies of the early Jon Pertwee and Tom Baker stories that were being repeated fairly regularly then by the ABC. Programmes taped off-air in Australia could be easily replayed in the UK, as fortunately the video standards of the two countries were identical. In return, Australian fans were sent copies of more recent episodes, which might not show up on the ABC for another year or two.

Bentham arranged with Gee to have all three of his '60s episodes copied onto U-MATIC videotape and sent to him in England. Bentham then showed the episodes to Ian Levine in 1978. Levine was in a position to find out if any of the three were missing from the BBC's archive. He quickly ascertained that one of them – 'The War Machines' Episode Two – most definitely was.

After discovering this, Levine contacted Gee himself, and asked if he could have a 16mm film copy of the episode. Gee took his print of 'The War Machines' Episode Two to a film laboratory in Sydney, and paid AU $280.00 to have a duplicate film print made, which he then air-mailed to Levine in London.

When the print arrived, Levine took it to the BBC, who then struck their own negative from it for the Film and Videotape Library. This effectively became the BBC's master copy of the episode. It was now two film generations down from Gee's original print, but was nevertheless the first ever 'missing' episode of *Doctor Who* to be located outside of the BBC and returned to the Corporation.

In late 1996, when the story was being prepared for VHS release by BBC Video, Gee was informally approached about the possibility of the BBC borrowing his original 16mm film of 'The War Machines' Episode Two, in order to make a first generation copy of it, but this never happened.

At the time of writing, Gee retains the 16mm film copies of all three of the episodes he acquired in 1970. (The film copy of 'The Faceless Ones' Episode One that he owns is incomplete, as it has censor cuts to remove both Inspector Gascoigne's death and the panning shot of the Chameleon at the episode's climax.) He has gone to great pains in recent years to try to set the record straight with regards to how the episodes came to be in his possession. As far as he is aware, the standard practice at ABC for dealing with BBC programmes after their rights had expired was to shred the films, incinerate the shredded remains, and send a Certificate of Destruction back to the BBC. As far as he's aware, Certificates of Destruction were issued in 1968 for all three of the 16mm films that he now owns.

CHAPTER 9

THE WEB OF FEAR: EPISODE ONE
RETURNED TO THE BBC—C1978

Not everything in the history of the lost and found episodes of *Doctor Who* makes perfect sense, and the story behind the recovery of 'The Web of Fear' Episode One is a case in point.

As the story goes, not long after becoming Archive Selector for the BBC Film and Videotape Library in 1978, Sue Malden made a chance return visit to Villiers House, the home of BBC Enterprises. On the day she visited, a batch of 16mm films had just arrived back at Enterprises from overseas, and amongst them was a lone episode of *Doctor Who*, which turned out to be the first part of 'The Web of Fear'. This was the only *Doctor Who* episode in the whole consignment.

Because the film was only a single episode of a six-part story, it hadn't been put back on the shelf for re-sale by the Enterprises staff, but had instead been left to one side, and was actually scheduled to be destroyed. Malden saw to it that the episode was immediately archived, and this also led to her issuing a new instruction to all Enterprises staff that from that point on, *all* returned material had to be forwarded to the Film and Videotape Library. Nothing further was to be destroyed.

As discussed above, none of this explains why Episode One of 'The Web of Fear' was on the list of surviving episodes drawn up in 1976 – two years earlier – by the researcher for the 'Whose Doctor Who' documentary!

DEATH TO THE DALEKS: PART ONE
RETURNED TO THE BBC—APRIL 1981

A 525-line two-inch colour videotape of this episode was returned to the BBC from BBC Canada in April 1981. The full details about this return will be covered in the following chapter, looking specifically at the Jon Pertwee era.

THE ABOMINABLE SNOWMEN: EPISODE TWO
RETURNED TO THE BBC—FEBRUARY 1982

In the early 1980s, Roger Stevens was working for the BBC as a film editor. Stevens was a *Doctor Who* fan, and was in contact with Ian Levine, who he knew at the time was purchasing 16mm film print copies of old *Doctor Who* episodes from the BBC. Stevens was interested in seeing old *Doctor Who* episodes himself, and so Levine would occasionally invite him to his house to view some of the material he had purchased so far.

At the time, Stevens was living in Maidenhead, and was regularly travelling into work via train. One morning, he found himself bumping into a BBC work colleague on the station platform, who explained that he usually travelled in by car, but was having some repairs done, hence the need to use public transport. Stevens has asked that this person not be identified in this book, so we'll call him 'Mr Agnew'[53] for the purposes of the story. Stevens found himself chatting to Agnew that morning, and once Agnew's car had been repaired, was regularly given lifts into work by him. The two of them would chat during the journeys, and one day, the subject of old *Doctor Who* episodes came up.

Agnew worked as a projectionist at the BBC, and had over the years acquired a number of 16mm film prints of various television programmes. These included a number of old variety shows and other mundane material, but his haul of films also included seven episodes of *Doctor Who*, all on 16mm black and white film. At the time, Stevens was unsure which episodes the BBC still had, but knew that Levine would be interested in the material regardless. Stevens asked Agnew if he was interested in selling the films to him, and a fee of £25.00 was arranged for all seven prints.

Stevens recalls that the seven 16mm black and white films he purchased were 'The Space Museum' Episode One, 'The Abominable Snowmen' Episode Two, 'The Moonbase' Episode Four, 'Invasion of the Dinosaurs' Part One, and three episodes of 'Carnival of Monsters'. Stevens purchased these seven prints in the summer of 1981, and then passed them all over to Levine, after Levine persuaded him that he had the necessary contacts to check the episodes against the BBC's holdings – this was before the publication in late 1981 of *Doctor Who Monthly*'s Winter Special, which detailed publicly for the first time which episodes the BBC retained.

Within months of the Winter Special article, a news report in issue 62 of *Doctor Who Monthly*, dated March 1982, briefly announced that Episode Two of 'The Abominable Snowmen' had been returned to the BBC:

> … the donator of the episode, who has been allowed to retain a copy of the episode, was unaware of the value of the item he held until he read the list in the Winter Special. Describing himself as an earnest fan of the *Doctor Who* series, he agreed to return the episode in the hope it would benefit other keen followers of the series.

This doesn't really cover the reality of the situation. Not long after receiving all seven of Stevens' 16mm prints in the summer of 1981, Levine had ascertained that the episodes of 'The Abominable Snowmen' and 'Invasion of the Dinosaurs' were both missing from the BBC. He arranged for the 16mm film print of 'The Abominable Snowmen' Episode Two to be loaned to the BBC in February 1982, and – as was the BBC's standard practice at the time – a 16mm film copy was made for the Film and

---

53 Not an original pseudonym in *Doctor Who* terms, I admit!

CHAPTER 9

Videotape Library, with the original then given back to the provider to retain. But Levine held back on letting the BBC know about the film print of 'Invasion of the Dinosaurs' Part One, at least for the time being.

THE REIGN OF TERROR: EPISODE SIX—PRISONERS OF CONCIERGE
RETURNED TO THE BBC—MAY 1982

The 1981 *Doctor Who Monthly* Winter Special feature on the BBC archives was apparently the catalyst for the next episode to be returned to the BBC as well. A film collector who held a 16mm print of the 'The Reign of Terror' Episode Six came forward soon after the return of 'The Abominable Snowmen' Episode Two. Details were reported in issue 68 of *Doctor Who Monthly*, dated September 1982:

> … the trail which led to the finding of this episode was one of the many to have been followed up since the plea to find the lost episodes was launched in last year's Winter Special. Up until last May all of the trails had proved fruitless with the exception of 'The Abominable Snowmen' find. Early that month, however, a source came to light which looked more concrete. Part-time contributor to the *Monthly*, Bruce Campbell, followed up the lead and received invaluable help in his endeavours from WTVA (Wider Television Access), the organisation dedicated to the preservation of old television. Contact with the collector and holder of the film episode was established with the major obstacle being, for a time, fear of prosecution for holding what is still, technically, BBC property. Once that fear was allayed, the physical recovery of the episode took place and, in a scene reminiscent of spy films, the can was picked up from a railway station in a fast car and whisked away to the BBC Film Library for Sue Malden to arrange a copy to be made for the BBC's retention. The film collector himself, who again has preferred to remain anonymous, was reportedly surprised to find what was, in his eyes, a very inconsequential part of his library of 16mm films was so sought after.

The full story behind this was as follows. Bruce Campbell often used to attend the various regular London sci-fi collectors' fairs in the late 1970s and early 1980s (also known at the time as 'movie jumbles'). He was a close friend of Jeremy Bentham, who was then the main feature writer for *Doctor Who Monthly*, and so was always on the lookout for *Doctor Who* films. At one fair in the early 1980s, he got talking to a stallholder who tipped him off that one of his regular customers, who collected 16mm films, had a missing *Doctor Who* episode in his collection.

WIPED!

> **Bruce Campbell:** It was so long ago that this episode was recovered, my memory is not too clear on the precise events, or the timescale. The bare bones of the matter are that a friend of mine who had a number of contacts with various 16mm film collectors got in touch with me to advise me that a 16mm film print of 'The Reign of Terror' Episode Six was available, and for sale for £50.00. The collector who was selling the print went round to my friend's house with the film. My friend had a 16mm projector, and so was able to view the print and verify that the film was indeed what the collector claimed it was. The film was then purchased on my behalf, and I donated it to the BBC in return for a copy for my collection. This was carried out by another friend of mine on my behalf, who knew the relevant authorities at the BBC. I was proud to be one of the people who at the time were returning missing episodes of *Doctor Who* to the BBC.

Once he had the episode, Campbell contacted Bentham, who in turn introduced him to Ian Levine. After something like six months of negotiations between Levine and the private collector – all conducted via Campbell – a deal was done that saw the 16mm film print of 'The Reign of Terror' Episode Six handed over to Levine. Levine, in turn, was then able to pass it to the BBC, who took a 16mm duplicate negative for their archive. The print was found to be a Stored Field telerecording of the episode.

INVASION (OF THE DINOSAURS): PART ONE
RETURNED TO THE BBC—JUNE 1983

This was the last Jon Pertwee episode to be missing from the BBC archive. Its recovery thus allowed the BBC once more to hold a complete run of the third Doctor's adventures.

The debut transmission of 'Invasion of the Dinosaurs' in 1974 (the opening episode was only called 'Invasion' on-screen, while all subsequent episodes of the story were called 'Invasion of the Dinosaurs') came at a time when BBC Enterprises were discovering that more and more of their overseas customers were requesting that programmes be supplied to them in colour. Australia had been one of the last countries still to buy Pertwee stories in black and white. From Season 11 onward, however, it too switched to colour.

Ironically, by the time the ABC came to purchase Season 11 in the latter half of 1974, Enterprises were unable to supply them with 'Invasion of the Dinosaurs' – presumably because the 625-line two-inch colour master copy of the opening episode (if not the whole story) had already been wiped.

'The Time Warrior' was the last *complete* story to have 16mm black and white film recordings made of its episodes, but it seems that at least the first three episodes of 'Invasion of the Dinosaurs' also went through this process.

As previously mentioned, in 1981 Ian Levine had Roger Stevens' 16mm black and white print of the episode, but initially he wanted to hold onto it, so that it could be used as a potential bargaining counter should any other missing episodes turn up. Eventually, Levine decided to return the episode to the BBC, and so loaned the Film and Videotape Library the print in June 1983. A 16mm film copy was made and retained by the BBC, and the original print was returned to Levine.

THE DALEKS MASTERPLAN: EPISODE FIVE—COUNTER PLOT
THE DALEKS MASTERPLAN: EPISODE TEN—ESCAPE SWITCH
RETURNED TO THE BBC—JULY 1983

The next episodes to be returned to the BBC have a long-standing reputation of a slightly mysterious background to their discovery. There is, people suspect, something fishy in the tale …

The news that Episodes Five and Ten of 'The Daleks Masterplan' had been found was first broken in Issue 82 of *Doctor Who Monthly*, dated November 1983:

> … the story of their recovery began when an assistant for the Church of Jesus Christ of Latter-Day Saints in Wandsworth was clearing out the basement cellar, and found six cans of film. The assistant phoned the BBC and asked if they would like them back even if they only wanted the cans. The phone message was transferred to Brentford Film Library where Sue Malden's successor Steve Bryant took the call. He naturally said that he was interested and [asked if] the cans [had] any titles on. The reply was [that the cans contained] one episode of *Warship*, one episode of *Adventure World*, a couple of schools programmes and two episodes of something called *Doctor Who*! Not long after, the films were taken to Brentford … How the films came to be under the church in the first place will probably remain one of life's mysteries.

The Doctor Who Appreciation Society's newsletter, *Celestial Toyroom*, reported a slightly different version of this story in its September 1983 edition:

> … in what can only be described as a sensational find, two episodes of the longest *Doctor Who* story ever, 'The Daleks Masterplan', have been found in the basement of a Mormon Unification Church in London … News of the find broke at the end of July, when BBC Film Archivist Steve Bryant, recently taken over from Sue Malden, accepted a phone call from one of the leaders of the Mormon Unification Church in England. Apparently, during a massive clear out of the church cellar, a

WIPED!

whole pile of 16mm film cans – all BBC marked – had been found buried beneath all the other rubbish ... Steve Bryant went down to the church to discover that two of the cans contained missing *Doctor Who* episodes.

To add to the confusion, a few years later, in a chapter on returned episodes in his book *Doctor Who: 25 Glorious Years* (WH Allen/Planet, 1988), author Peter Haining essentially reiterated the *Celestial Toyroom* report but added that the films were found in the 'newest temple' of the Mormon Unification Church of Great Britain in Clapham, South London. The number of film cans was now given as 'a dozen or so', and they were all said to be found in the corner of the church basement in a crate marked 'BBC Property'.

The true name and location of the church in question seem unclear at best. The Church of Jesus Christ of Latter-Day Saints does have a church in Wandsworth but not one in Clapham (although the two places are within about a mile of each other). However, there appears to be no such thing as the Mormon Unification Church. The Unification Church, a cult founded by the Reverend Moon, is a different organisation altogether, and has no sites in either Clapham or Wandsworth.

Although this did not feature in any of the initial reports, it has since been frequently suggested that the church may have been a converted property previously occupied and used as a storage facility by BBC Enterprises. In this version of the tale, Enterprises simply didn't clear out the basement thoroughly when they vacated the premises, and left a number of film cans behind – and this is not too far-fetched, as the later story of the discovery of the four surviving episodes of 'The Ice Warriors' will demonstrate. This would also tie in with the idea of the building being the 'newest temple' of whichever Church it was, as recounted by Haining.

The lack of clarity over the details of the discovery of these two episodes has led some to suspect that the whole account involving the church was merely a smokescreen, concocted to conceal a different set of circumstances altogether. Dark whispers have even suggested that the comedian and film collector Bob Monkhouse was somehow behind the recovery, although there is no evidence at all to support this.

In an attempt to try to get to the bottom of the matter, I contacted Steve Bryant, who is now the Senior Curator at the British Film Institute. This is what he had to say on the matter:

Steve Bryant: Nailing down the precise facts (or the background, anyway) of this matter is not too easy, but everybody enjoys the mystery and speculation anyway. It was not actually I who took the call from the Church – it was the then Deputy Head of the BBC Film and Videotape Library, Gareth Morris.

CHAPTER 9

He arranged the delivery of the cans to Windmill Road and then passed the job of identifying what may be worth keeping to me. He didn't really take much notice of the details – as far as he was concerned it was just a case of getting what was most likely to be a pile of junk delivered to the right address so that we could check it out. It is only his vague recollection, passed on to me in a jokey sort of way, that it was a Mormon Church, which is the basis of the story. It could be wrong.

Having identified that there were two important missing *Doctor Who* episodes amongst what was otherwise, indeed, a pile of junk, I was more interested in the ramifications of the recovery than in the details of where the cans had been and why. This was not out of a lack of interest, more out of a general approach to the recovery of missing material. This was in the days before the BBC took a more relaxed approach to recovering its lost treasures and, because it was a tricky area to deal with, I tended not to ask too many questions in order to ensure the continuing recovery of material. As a result, I'm afraid this story will need to remain largely a mystery ...

And so a mystery it must remain.

THE CELESTIAL TOYMAKER: EPISODE FOUR – THE FINAL TEST
RETURNED TO THE BBC – 15 FEBRUARY 1984

As previously noted, ABC Television in Australia had purchased and screened *Doctor Who* from 1964 onwards, omitting only 'Mission to the Unknown' and 'The Daleks Masterplan' from its run of Hartnell and Troughton episodes. Prior to 1984, the station had been responsible for returning a few colour 625-line two-inch videotapes of Jon Pertwee episodes to the BBC, in instances where only 16mm black and white film prints had previously been known to exist. Now, however, during a routine examination of its film archive, a lone 16mm black and white film print of the fourth and final episode of 'The Celestial Toymaker' ('The Final Test') was discovered. This was sent to the BBC's Sydney office, where it was passed to Basil Sands, who immediately sent it back to Steve Bryant at the Film and Videotape Library in London. It arrived on Monday 15 February 1984, where it was examined and found to be in excellent condition, apart from having the 'Next Episode' caption edited from the end.

The print apparently wasn't a direct survivor of Australia's 1960s screenings of the series, as the ABC destroyed their original copy of 'The Final Test' in 1974. Instead, it arrived there from TVS in Singapore, after it had aired in that country in the early 1970s. Once they had finished with the episode, TVS were supposed to send it back to the BBC's office in Sydney, but mistakenly sent it instead to ABC's Frenchs Forest studio, which was also in Sydney. Rather than forward it on to the BBC at the time, ABC put it into storage, where it sat for a number of years.[54]

Doctor Who producer John Nathan-Turner was already due to fly to Australia for a promotional visit in April 1984, and the discovery of this episode prompted him to arrange to visit the ABC during his trip, to ascertain if there was any possibility of other missing episodes still residing in their archives. He suspected that the title of the returned episode – 'The Final Test' – might be a coded indication that the ABC were waiting to see how the BBC would react to the long-overdue return of this copyright material before they sent back a whole lot more. Sadly, though, that wasn't the case, and Nathan-Turner's visit yielded no further finds.

Steve Bryant of the Film and Videotape Library also investigated the possibility that the survival of 'The Celestial Toymaker' Episode Four at the ABC might indicate the existence of other missing *Doctor Who* episodes in Australia. Within days of the print's return, he wrote to Basil Sands at BBC Sydney, asking if he could be put in contact with the person at the ABC who had sent the episode on to BBC Sydney in the first place.

Sands made a few enquiries with the ABC, and reported back to Bryant at the end of February:

> I very much fear that there is no chance of finding further old episodes of *Doctor Who* in Australia (or New Zealand). The episode of "The Celestial Toymaker" somehow survived the ABC Film Library purges of the early 1970s, having been misfiled and left at the back of a bin where it shouldn't have been! They have been clearing out their vaults very thoroughly in recent years and it is something of a miracle that this single episode survived. Having said that, ABC are very conscious of our interest in some of the old BBC programmes and if by chance something else of interest turns up I know they would pass it over to us.

THE WHEEL IN SPACE: EPISODE THREE
RETURNED TO THE BBC—APRIL 1984

It was at the September 1983 Doctor Who Appreciation Society convention at the Grand Hotel, Birmingham, that I was told by one of the organisers, Gary O'Hare, that a fan named David Stead had a copy of the missing third episode of the Patrick

---

54 One thing that backs up this odd turn of events is the missing 'Next Episode' caption. Singapore was sent the prints of all four episodes of 'The Celestial Toymaker' from New Zealand in 1972. New Zealand didn't screen 'The Gunfighters', making the removal of the 'Next Episode' caption a logical edit.

CHAPTER 9

Troughton story 'The Wheel in Space'. It was only when I returned home after the event that I noticed that one of the fanzines I had purchased that weekend – *Time Watcher* Volume 2 number 1 – was edited by Stead, and the editorial address of the 'zine was in Portsmouth. Towards the back of the 'zine was an off-screen photograph of a Cybermat from 'The Wheel in Space' …

Some months later, in April 1984, Issue 87 of *The Official Doctor Who Magazine* (as *Doctor Who Monthly* had now been renamed) featured an anonymous letter printed in the *Gallifrey Guardian* news section. It stated:

> I have written to you because I am unsure where at the BBC to write. You may be interested to know that an episode of *Doctor Who* which going by your listings, is missing from the archives, is alive and kicking in the Portsmouth area.

The news item went on to say that the episode in question had been identified as a Patrick Troughton/Cyberman episode, which also contained Cybermats … Could it be an episode of 'The Wheel in Space'? Or could it be an episode of 'The Tomb of the Cybermen'?

Following this exposure in print, Stead returned his 16mm film print of Episode Three of 'The Wheel in Space' to the BBC. And although it might seem that he was effectively 'outed' by the *Doctor Who Magazine* article as the owner of a missing episode, Stead was happy to explain subsequently just what had happened at the time:

> **David Stead**: In early February 1983, I put an advert in my local paper, *The Portsmouth News*, under the Wanted section. I said I was looking for privately owned 16mm film prints of old television programmes such as *Doctor Who*, *Muffin the Mule*, and so on, and asked for people to contact me if they could help. Only one person responded to the advert, and phoned me saying he couldn't help me himself, but that a man he was once in contact with back in 1979 had some episodes on film at the time. He recalled *Doctor Who* being amongst them. He gave me the details of the collector in question, and wished me well, and good luck!
>
> Well, luck was on my side. The collector was a chap called Mr Smith, of Pinedene Films in Southampton. I phoned him up, and told him what I was interested in. He was sure that he had some *Doctor Who* film prints in his collection, so I arranged to pop over to him that same evening. This would have been in the week before the BBC's Longleat *Doctor Who* convention in early April 1983. When I arrived, he had 'The Wheel in Space' Episode Three lined up in his projector, and so we were the first people to see the episode

in 15 years.

It turned out he also had a complete copy of Episode Five of 'The Dominators' (the BBC's prints at the time were all edited, although it was later discovered that the BFI held unedited copies of the episode), and a Spanish-dubbed copy of 'Planet of Giants' Episode Three. I bought his 16mm print of 'The Wheel in Space' Episode Three for £15.00 there and then, and he said he would call me when he had unearthed the others. I picked the other two episodes up at a later meeting, where he informed me he had owned all three since about 1973, when he took over the vast collection of films from his father, but couldn't say how they ended up with his father in the first place!

I contacted the BBC Film and Videotape Library in the summer of 1983, and spoke to a gentleman called Steve Bryant. We discussed the film print, and decided that it would be a lovely gesture if I were to officially hand over the film to the BBC on the date of the programme's twentieth anniversary – in November of that year. All the preparations were made, only for me to go down with 'flu. November quickly turned to Christmas and then to the New Year. Before I knew it, nearly six months had gone by before I could arrange to finally let the BBC have the episode in April 1984.

As was the norm by now, the BBC borrowed Stead's 16mm film, and struck a 16mm negative for the archive, which became their master copy, allowing Stead to keep his original print.

When the episode was chosen to be released on BBC Video in 1992 (on the VHS *Cybermen – The Early Years*), the copy used was a further film generation down from the BBC's negative, which resulted in a very poor quality presentation. The original 16mm film was borrowed a second time by the BBC on 27 March 1994. This time it was wetgate telecined[55] onto D3 videotape, which meant that now the BBC's copy was virtually as good as Stead's original film.

As for the 'outing' of Stead's ownership of the episode in *Doctor Who Magazine* in April 1984 … Prior to his actually returning the print to the BBC, Stead had been put in contact with Ian Levine. Levine was convinced that Stead was not going to return the print, but persuaded him to part with a video copy of it. And he wasn't the only person to get a copy. Very soon, pirate video copies were circulating amongst fans, and knowledge of the episode's existence and the owner of the print became

---

55 This is a method of making an excellent quality video copy of a film print. The film is run through a telecine machine that has the viewing gate submerged in a liquid with the same refractive index as the film stock. This reduces the effect of any dust, dirt or hairs, and helps cover up scratches and marks on the film's surface.

CHAPTER 9

commonplace. One person who had seen a copy of the episode prior to its return was Gary Russell, who at the time was a regular feature writer for *Doctor Who Magazine*. It was Russell who penned the 'anonymous letter'. Looking back on the event now, Russell is of the rueful opinion that the letter was '... not one of my finest moments'. Although Stead was quite peeved at the letter's publication at the time, the passing of years has mellowed his attitude somewhat:

> **David Stead**: My personal feeling on why Gary Russell did that was that it was probably to force me to return the episode. Even though, as Steve Bryant would confirm, I had already spoken to the BBC archives some months before, but hadn't been able to return the print due to illness.

THE TIME MEDDLER: EPISODE ONE — THE WATCHER
THE TIME MEDDLER: EPISODE THREE — A BATTLE OF WITS
THE TIME MEDDLER: EPISODE FOUR — CHECKMATE
THE WAR MACHINES: EPISODE ONE
THE WAR MACHINES: EPISODE THREE
THE WAR MACHINES: EPISODE FOUR
RETURNED TO THE BBC — JANUARY 1985

During 1984, Ian Levine was following up several clues about missing episodes of *Doctor Who* in his own time, and at his own expense. One of them revolved around the possibility of African countries retaining prints, triggered by a chance remark apparently made on a Radio 2 magazine programme earlier that year. An engineer being interviewed about a scheme to set up a satellite education and community television system in Nigeria joked that Nigerian television was so behind the times that Patrick Troughton was still the Doctor over there. This was reported back to Levine, and it got him thinking. Levine started making telephone calls to the various television stations in Nigeria (which numbered 32 at the time), until he finally got a positive response, as he explains:

> **Ian Levine:** A wonderful woman called Victoria Ezeokoli at Nigerian Television told me she knew that there were some old *Doctor Who* episodes over in Nigeria. It took her about a month to find them – 14 episodes. It was the first time complete stories had turned up rather than odd episodes.

What Levine had discovered were three complete Hartnell stories (and not Troughton ones, which he initially had been hoping to find) – 'The Web Planet' (six episodes), 'The Time Meddler' (four episodes) and 'The War Machines' (four episodes). These

WIPED!

three stories had indeed been sold as a package to Nigeria in July 1973 (which is the date recorded in the BBC paperwork). Only these 14 episodes had been sold in this package, and they were screened on the station Midwest TV between April and July 1973. Levine had thus found this whole sales batch in its entirety.

The BBC already had 16mm film copies of all six episodes of 'The Web Planet', although their copies of Episodes One and Six were slightly edited. Episode One was missing the reprise from the preceding story 'The Romans', whilst the final episode had had the caption 'Next Episode: The Space Museum' added to the end in place of the original 'Next Episode: The Lion' (a change presumably made for the benefit of an overseas broadcaster that did not buy 'The Crusade', of which 'The Lion' was the first episode). The Nigerian prints were complete, and contained the correct caption for 'The Lion' at the end of Episode Six.

The BBC also already held the respective second episodes of 'The Time Meddler' and 'The War Machines', but the discovery potentially enabled them to complete both those stories in their collection. However, although the existence of this batch of *Doctor Who* films was confirmed in October 1984, real-world events had implications for their recovery ...

On 5 July 1984, an ex-minister of the Nigerian Government living in London, Umaru Dikko, was abducted from outside his house. Acting on a tip-off, the Metropolitan Police swooped on Stanstead airport a few hours later, to find two large crates about to be loaded onto a flight bound for Nigeria. Inside one of the crates was the unconscious Mr Dikko, along with another man who was in possession of drugs and syringes. The resultant diplomatic row between the UK and Nigeria was huge – two members of the Nigerian High Commission were expelled from their London embassy, and diplomatic relations with Nigeria were completely broken off for two years.

These complications meant that it took quite a few months before the BBC actually received the *Doctor Who* films from Nigeria. It was only in early 1985 that they arrived back in the UK (by which time three missing episodes of 'The Reign of Terror' had been found and returned from Cyprus – see next section). On examination, it was discovered that Episodes One, Three and Four of 'The Time Meddler' and Episodes Two, Three and Four of 'The War Machines' had unfortunately been edited.

CHAPTER 9

Cuts to the Nigerian Prints of 'The Time Meddler' and 'The War Machines'

Episode	Missing Material
The Time Meddler: Episode One	Beginning at 00:25, the initial TARDIS scenes where the Doctor and Vicki discover Steven were all cut. This was a significant chunk of action, lasting about two-and-a-half minutes.
The Time Meddler: Episode Three	During the argument between the Vikings approximately half-way through the episode, 10 seconds of dialogue was cut, as one Viking dared the other to try to kill him.
The Time Meddler: Episode Four	Beginning at 16:18, about 13 seconds of action was cut at the end of the scene. This was of the Saxons stabbing the two Vikings.
The War Machines: Episode Two	At 04:00 into the episode, about four seconds of action was missing. This was a shot of a rag being soaked with chloroform to subdue the Doctor.
	At 09:33, about 17 seconds was cut, featuring the murder of the tramp by the War Machine.
	At 18:45, about 38 seconds of footage had been removed – the testing of the War Machine's weapons on one of the slave workers.
	At 22:59, the final cut from this episode was the loss of approximately four seconds from the sequence of the War Machine moving about the warehouse.
The War Machines: Episode Three	At 00:35, on the cut from an overhead shot to a frontal shot of the War Machine, approximately 21 seconds was cut from reprise from the previous episode.
	At 06:56, four seconds of material was missing in the middle of the close-up of Professor Krimpton's speech: 'Machines have been programmed TO DESTROY ANY FORM OF HUMAN LIFE THAT OPPOSES THEM. The order to attack must come from Wotan alone.' (The cut section is the material in capitals).
	At 07:32, almost 18 seconds was missing of Major Green giving orders.
	At 19:00 was the first of two sections missing from the army's attack on the warehouse, lasting for almost 56 seconds.
	At 19:47 is the second missing section from the attack on the warehouse, duration 37 seconds.

WIPED!

The War Machines: Episode Four	At 07:19, approximately nine seconds was missing from the telephone kiosk sequence.
	At 08:11, there were two small breaks in the film (of nine frames and six frames respectively) during the scene of the Doctor and Ben talking.
	At 09:32, there was a cut of seven-and-a-half seconds from the exchange between Polly, Brett and Krimpton, when Polly reports back to the Post Office Tower.

Further investigation showed that these cuts matched exactly those made to the episodes when they were screened by NZBC in New Zealand in 1968 and 1969. NZBC's programme traffic records showed that they had indeed sent their 16mm films of all four episodes of 'The Time Meddler' to Nigeria on 2 March 1973. However, the NZBC records also showed that all four episodes of 'The War Machines' were sent to Singapore on 20 September 1972, and that all six episodes of 'The Web Planet' – although never actually screened in New Zealand in the 1960s – were still in the NZBC storage facility in Harriett Street, Wellington when they did a stocktake on 1 April 1970. Given that 'The War Machines' was despatched to Singapore some six months before 'The Time Meddler' was sent to Nigeria, it is highly likely that Singapore was asked to send its films of that story on to Nigeria after it had finished with them. However, it's unlikely that the 16mm films of 'The Web Planet' that came back from Nigeria originated in New Zealand at all.

The edits to 'The Time Meddler' episodes, when they were discovered some time after the prints were returned to the BBC, caused something of a problem for Levine. Unknown to all but a few select friends of his, he was already in possession of 16mm film prints of the first and third episodes of 'The Time Meddler', which he had kept from the BBC. The irony of his finding in Nigeria what he thought were duplicate copies of the only two 'missing' episodes that he knew actually existed at this time wasn't lost on Levine. As the news of the Nigeria find spread, the fact that he already had copies of the first and third episodes also became common knowledge in *Doctor Who* fandom. But whereas the Nigerian prints were edited, Levine's were complete.

When and how did Levine acquire these two missing *Doctor Who* films?

THE TIME MEDDLER: EPISODE ONE—THE WATCHER
THE TIME MEDDLER: EPISODE THREE—A BATTLE OF WITS
FOUND 1981—RETURNED TO THE BBC 1992

Ian Sheward joined the BBC in Bristol in the summer 1978 as a Film Assistant (a position also sometimes referred to as a Film Projectionist), before moving to the Film Department at BBC Ealing Studios in late 1979. Later in his BBC career he would work in both the Light Entertainment Department and the Drama Department as an

CHAPTER 9

Assistant Floor Manager and then Floor Manager.

Sheward's interest in *Doctor Who* brought him into contact in early 1980 with Roger Stevens, who also worked as a Film Assistant at the BBC at the time. Sheward also got to know Ian Levine at around this time, and learned that Levine was buying copies of old *Doctor Who* episodes from the BBC Film Library. Sheward knew that Levine was also enthusiastically trying to track down copies of episodes that he knew the BBC no longer officially retained. Occasionally, Levine would invite both Sheward and Stevens to his house to watch some of his old *Doctor Who* episodes.

Sometime in late 1981 or early 1982, Sheward was on a year's secondment at BBC Enterprises at Villiers House, where he worked as a Film Print Examiner for the Overseas Sales division. While at Villiers House, Sheward witnessed first-hand the destruction of a batch of *Doctor Who* 16mm film prints that had recently been returned from an overseas broadcaster. Despite the clear instructions about returned material given to Enterprises by Sue Malden and the Film and Videotape Library some years previously, he could see that some individuals at Enterprises were still junking material without first checking if it was missing or not. Sheward related this incident back to a third party, and within days, the individuals responsible were reprimanded for their actions. But this still left Sheward feeling uneasy about the BBC's ability to retain material, as some personnel were clearly flouting procedures.

Sheward's job at the BBC brought him into contact with staff from many external BBC sites, and he would occasionally bring up the subject of *Doctor Who* with them. In the summer of 1980 or 1981 (Sheward can't recall precisely when), he had got to know a person who worked at the BBC's Alexandra Palace studios, who claimed to know the whereabouts in private hands of some *Doctor Who* 16mm prints. One of the episodes mentioned by this person was Episode Two of 'The Abominable Snowmen'. At the time, Sheward didn't know which episodes were and weren't missing from the BBC, but thought it would be a good idea to track the material down.

Sheward expressed an interest in obtaining these *Doctor Who* prints, only to be told that someone else had been promised the films. He found out later that this person was Roger Stevens, who had indeed obtained (from 'Mr Agnew') a haul of seven episodes, which included 'The Abominable Snowmen' Episode Two and 'Invasion of the Dinosaurs' Part One. Nevertheless, Sheward's contact at Alexandra Palace knew of some other *Doctor Who* film prints in private hands, and within weeks presented him with 16mm film prints of 'The Time Meddler' Episodes One, Two and Three. Sheward was still unsure about precisely which *Doctor Who* episodes were missing from the BBC at the time.

Like Stevens before him, Sheward was persuaded by Ian Levine to hand the three 16mm prints over to him, so that he could use his contacts to check if the episodes were missing from the BBC archive. It was quickly established that the BBC had only the second episode of the story, and that the first and third were indeed missing. But Levine decided to hold on to the films of these two missing episodes for the time being.

Levine's commitment to seeing missing *Doctor Who* material returned to the BBC is beyond question. But the fact remains that he held material back in a few instances. He did not return 'The Abominable Snowmen' Episode Two until a good nine months after it came into his possession, and he held on to 'Invasion of the Dinosaurs' Part One for nearly two years. Had all four episodes of 'The Time Meddler' not been found in Nigeria in 1984, how long would he have waited before returning his prints of Episodes One and Three?

> **Ian Levine:** I had 'Invasion of the Dinosaurs' Part One at the same time as I had 'The Abominable Snowmen' Episode Two, about 1981. I hadn't actually remembered holding on to 'Invasion of the Dinosaurs' Part One for that long! But I held on to them for the same reason as 'The Time Meddler' Episodes One and Three. Which was that people I knew had contacts, and rumours abounded. There were lots of film collectors around, saying they had missing episodes of *Doctor Who*, but that they wouldn't sell them for money, they'd only swap them for other missing episodes. In other words, you had to have a missing *Doctor Who* to get a missing *Doctor Who*. I purposely didn't give those few episodes back to the Film Library, because I had to have an ace up my sleeve if someone said, 'Here's "The Evil of the Daleks" Episode One, I want another missing *Doctor Who* for it'. That's the reason. I had to.
>
> It was because it looked at that time, from the rumours, as if there were lots of things out there, and that these film collectors wanted to trade. A guy who had a film shop in Huddersfield, I think it was, or Halifax, said he had all six prints of 'The Power of the Daleks'. He came out with every excuse in the book when we tried to corroborate it. I don't understand why people waste people's time like that. The Nigerian thing was just total perseverance. Victoria Ezeokoli worked for Nigerian Television, and she said she'd look in their archive, and she found all those *Doctor Who* prints. She found three complete stories, and I got all excited because she'd found 14 episodes for me. Sadly, only four of them were actually missing. Six were officially missing, but I already had those two episodes of 'The Time Meddler'. Getting four missing episodes back out of the 14 … It's a pity all of the 14 couldn't have been missing ones.

Levine was in a quandary over the 'Time Meddler' prints he had obtained from Sheward. Within months of the Nigerian prints being returned to the BBC, he knew that Episodes One and Three were edited, unlike his copies. But he wasn't sure how best to deal with the situation. A number of years passed ...

All four episodes of 'The Time Meddler' were then selected to be repeated on BBC2 in the January of 1992 (in a short run of old *Doctor Who* stories, which also included 'The Mind Robber' and 'The Sea Devils'). A member of BBC staff, Steve Roberts, got to know some weeks in advance that the repeats were to take place. He also knew that there were edits to the BBC's copies of the first and third episodes, and that Levine had complete prints. He contacted Levine, who agreed to loan the complete prints to the BBC so that D3 videotape copies could be made. Originally, only the first episode of 'The Time Meddler' was to be shown uncut on BBC2, but at the last minute, it was decided to screen the third episode complete as well.

THE REIGN OF TERROR: EPISODE ONE—A LAND OF FEAR
THE REIGN OF TERROR: EPISODE TWO—GUESTS OF MADAME GUILLOTINE
THE REIGN OF TERROR: EPISODE THREE—A CHANGE OF IDENTITY
RETURNED TO THE BBC—DECEMBER 1984

It is something of a rare occurrence when a batch of missing episodes is discovered. It's an even rarer – nay unique – occurrence when the same batch is discovered *twice* within a fortnight! But this is exactly what happened in the case of the next recovered haul of missing material.

In 1984, Paul Vanezis lived in Birmingham and was a member of the Doctor Who Appreciation Society. A keen television and video enthusiast, he was fascinated by the subject of the missing *Doctor Who* episodes. He started attending various local meetings in and around the Birmingham area, which brought him into contact with people such as Neville Watkins and Richard Down, fans who had taken it upon themselves to contact overseas television stations in the hope of finding long-forgotten archives of *Doctor Who* episodes. Vanezis decided it was time that he tried the same approach.

> **Paul Vanezis:** The reason I went looking for missing *Doctor Who* episodes was that I had read the Sue Malden article in *Doctor Who Monthly*'s Winter Special in 1981, and been horrified at the discovery that all these things had just been thrown away. In 1981, I was 14, 15, whatever, and I didn't think I could do anything about it, and I forgot about the missing episodes for a while. Then in 1984, I got more interested in the subject again, and got more involved in the fan side of things. I had joined the Doctor Who Appreciation Society a couple of years earlier, and saw that episodes were starting to come back to the BBC .... At that stage it was almost too much to hope for that everything might be back in the archives, and you would be able to watch it.

WIPED!

Because at the end of the day, if you were a *Doctor Who* fan in the 1980s, what you wanted to see was old *Doctor Who!* ... The new series ... was on, but you almost weren't that bothered about it, because you knew it was on, and could never foresee a time when *Doctor Who* wouldn't be on. You wanted to find old episodes, and *The Five Faces of Doctor Who* repeat season in 1981 had helped get people interested.

Because there was a lot of talk about finding episodes, I got more interested in that, and started thinking about where things might be. Of course, at that time, things were coming from private collectors, but there was talk of the possibility of episodes being found abroad. There were lots of rumours, all sorts of people would wind you up about all sorts of stuff. My renewed interest just happened to coincide with a visit in 1984 of my aunt and my uncle over from Cyprus, and so I asked them about an old programme called *Doctor Who* from the '60s, and if they remembered watching it. They said they didn't remember it at all. I was a bit disappointed. They said, 'Have you got anything you can show us, that might jog our memories?', and so I put on a Tom Baker story, and they had no recollections of it at all. They didn't even recognise the music. But I had a really ropy copy of 'An Unearthly Child' from *The Five Faces of Doctor Who* repeat, and so I put that on, and straight away, as soon as the opening titles began, they recognised them. They didn't remember the music, but they remembered the look, the swirly cloud sequence, and they both sort of said in unison, 'Oh, we used to watch this every week, in Cyprus'. I asked if they could remember what they saw, but they said they just recalled the 'atmosphere', they said it was for children, but that it was a good adventure series. So I knew then that *Doctor Who* had been shown in Cyprus. It's not something I could have asked my Dad, because he wasn't in Cyprus in the '60s, he was over here – he was watching *Doctor Who* in Britain!

So I think I then started to draw up a list of countries I could contact, and Cyprus was first on the list. So I wrote a letter to the Cyprus Broadcasting Corporation, and I think at the same time I wrote one other letter, to Mexican television. I think I may have written to a few others, which I didn't get any response from. The first letter I got back was from the Cyprus Broadcasting Corporation. I think it was probably about two or three weeks after I sent my letter, but it could have been longer than that. My letter probably went round the houses a bit in Cyprus! My way in was my surname, a Greek surname, and I explained that my father was a Greek Cypriot businessman, who was now living in the UK. I simplified it for them, and said I was interested in finding these old episodes of a television programme called *Doctor Who*, and that a member

CHAPTER 9

of my family remembered seeing it in Cyprus. I wondered when they showed them, and if they happened to have any of them still in their archive? I think I worded it something like that; that's the sort of wording I would have used.

The letter Vanezis received back from the Cyprus Broadcasting Corporation, dated 25 October 1984, read as follows:

Dear Mr Vanezis,

Thank you for your letter dated 4 October 1984. Indeed we have broadcast the BBC series *Doctor Who* back in 1966. We still have in our possession the following 13 episodes in black and white:

1. (F) Ep 1
2. (F) Ep 3
3. (F) Ep 4
1. (G) Ep 1
2. (G) Ep 2
3. (G) Ep 3
4. (G) Ep 4
5. (G) Ep 5
6. (G) Ep 6
1. (H) Ep 1
2. (H) Ep 2
3. (H) Ep 3
4. (H) Ep 6

Sincerely yours,

P Ioannides (Head of Programmes)

Paul Vanezis: I wasn't expecting the reply to be positive at all; I was expecting it to be negative. I was expecting them to say, "We did show this, but it was a long time ago. We don't have any records, and we certainly don't have the programmes any more." You would expect that. Some years ago, my father asked to borrow from me the original letter from the Cyprus Broadcasting Corporation for some reason, and I've never seen it again since! The only copy of it that's left is the one that was reprinted in the DWAS newsletter, *Celestial*

Toyroom. But anyway ... there was no list of titles, it just said '... we've got serial F, serial G and serial H', and only a certain number of episodes of each of them. I didn't have a bloody clue what F, G and H were! It was gobbledegook to me! I had to get the Jean Marc Lofficier *Doctor Who Programme Guide* out, and check the serial codes against what was in the letter, to make sure that what I thought was in the letter was what I suspected. Which was that there could be some missing episodes there. And, of course, there were three – the first three episodes of 'The Reign of Terror'.

I wasn't that interested in how quickly they could get back to the BBC archives, I was just interested in how fast I could see them! That was my overriding interest. Purely by coincidence, my Dad was in Cyprus on business at the time, and so I rang him up, and said, 'Can you have a word with this guy, because I would really like these films'. So he made an appointment on the phone with the guy who had sent me the letter, and went round to see him at Cyprus television. He was told, 'Look, if you can get a letter from the BBC saying you can have the films, then you can have them'. So, that was basically a 'No!'

Anyway, I was trying to work out if there was another way I could get hold of these films. I thought, maybe I should give the BBC a call, and see what they say. And that's how I heard, on the grapevine, purely by coincidence, that the episodes had actually been found by them in Cyprus, and that they were being returned. And I thought perhaps it was something to do with me, but it wasn't!

In an incredible twist of fate, Vanezis' efforts had collided with Ian Levine's own episode hunt. Encouraged by his recent discovery of the 14 William Hartnell episodes in Nigeria (even though they had yet to be returned to the BBC at this stage), Levine had been put in touch with Peter Lydiard-White and Roger Brunskill of BBC Enterprises by *Doctor Who* producer John Nathan-Turner, whom Levine had got to know personally over recent years. Brunskill and Levine had come up with a list of overseas broadcasters that could conceivably still hold old episodes of *Doctor Who*. They had then composed a written request for any information on potential holdings, which was sent via Brunskill's telex to the various broadcasters in early November 1984.

Ian Levine: There was a guy called Peter Lydiard-White (who they called Snowy Lydiard-White) who worked for BBC Enterprises at Villiers House, and who had once done some work on *Doctor Who*, and I had befriended him. I did all those telexes with Roger Brunskill. Peter Lydiard-White started it, and Roger finished it. And I sat there and physically did them country by country. We spent two days on the telex machine, which he operated, and

CHAPTER 9

I had a copy of the 1972 edition of *The Making of Doctor Who* by Malcolm Hulke and Terrance Dicks – there was no list at this time like you had years later. I'd also been through the BBC Enterprises cards, and worked out that there had been what they called the 'bicycle prints', which had been sent from country to country. That's where I got the information. I married it up with *The Making of Doctor Who*, and we sent telexes to all these countries. We wrote that we were desperate to get back any *Doctor Who*. We had to say, 'Even though you were asked to junk them years ago, please have a look. If you still have any in your libraries, we would desperately love them back'. Cyprus replied straight away with a list of their episodes.

CBC in Cyprus was one of only three television stations that replied to Brunskill's telex. The swiftness of its reply, which came on 19 November 1984, may perhaps have been due to the subject matter having been recently investigated in response to Vanezis' enquiries. But now that there had been a direct approach from the BBC, CBC could no longer deal with Vanezis. Within weeks, the episodes were returned directly to the BBC Film and Videotape Library.

The only other replies to Brunskill's telex came from a television station on the Ascension Islands, which owned up to having 16mm black and white films prints of all six episodes of the Jon Pertwee story 'The Sea Devils', and from a rather bemused television station in Iran, who asked 'In the name of Allah, what are you talking about?'[56]

Vanezis wrote to a number of other television stations around the world in 1984, and also discovered a large batch of Hartnell episodes at a station called Televisa SA in Mexico. Unfortunately, this batch contained no missing episodes whatsoever.

This wasn't quite the end to Vanezis' enquiries with the CBC though. A number of questions still intrigued him. What, for instance had happened to Cyprus's prints of the fourth and fifth episodes of 'The Reign of Terror', and the second of 'The Aztecs'? And what other BBC material might they still hold?

Paul Vanezis: I actually went over to Cyprus in 1989. It really bugged me that, when the BBC sent the telex about *Doctor Who* in 1984, they didn't ask them about anything else. And by that stage, I'd gotten interested in archive television in general, not just *Doctor Who*, and if you're going to get in contact

---

56 This response has been much derided by sections of *Doctor Who* fandom in recent years, but in Arab countries such wording is common etiquette in letter writing, in much the same way as 'Dear Sir' or 'Yours sincerely' are in Western culture.

WIPED!

with a television station, and they come back to you and say 'Yes, we've got these old *Doctor Who*s', you should perhaps say, 'I wonder what else you've got?' But Roger Brunskill and Steve Bryant certainly never did, and that really annoyed me. It seemed like common sense to ask that question.

So in 1989 I happened to get a job at the BBC, but before I started, I decided to have a holiday, and so I went to Cyprus with my Dad. While I was over there, I learned that one of the guys who was a friend of his was like the Monty Don of gardening programmes in Cyprus. He was a bit of a star, and so he had access to the television station. I told him I'd got this job at the BBC, and he said, 'You should visit our television station', and I said I'd love to. So he took me round there, and I saw a bit of editing and whatnot. I said, 'Do you know anyone in the television archive, or the film archive?' He said, 'Yes, I know a guy, he's been here for years, he knows everything. What do you want know?' So I explained I was looking for old BBC films, and he said 'Well, he's your man!'

And so he took me to see this guy, and I said I was looking for these old BBC films. I talked to him about the *Doctor Who* films returned to the BBC in 1984, but that there were some missing. He said, 'I remember the *Doctor Who*s – let me get my books out, and I'll see what happened'. So he got his books out, and he showed me the various pages in the book that were to do with *Doctor Who*. Basically, there was a record for each episode … A1, A2, A3, A4, B1 to B7, C1, C2 and so on. There was a record of all the episodes that had come in. He even knew which flight number they had come in from England on, and the date! It's a shame I didn't write any of this down, it would have been interesting information. And, also, they knew where the prints had been sent to, and the dates they were sent out. They were all in this book.

Cyprus had received the complete first season of *Doctor Who*, from 'An Unearthly Child' through to 'The Reign of Terror', between 1965 and 1966. (Why 'The Reign of Terror' had been included is something of a mystery, as the CBC never screened that story, and the surviving BBC records show that they never actually purchased it in the first place.) Vanezis discovered that the CBC had – on the BBC's instruction – sent their prints of 'An Unearthly Child', 'The Daleks' and 'The Edge of Destruction' to a television station in Uganda shortly after they had been screened. Similarly, their prints of 'Marco Polo' and 'The Keys of Marinus' had been sent to Hong Kong Rediffusion after they too had been screened in Cyprus. But the prints of *all* the episodes of 'The Aztecs', 'The Sensorites' and 'The Reign of Terror' had remained in Cyprus. The details were fastidiously recorded in the books.

CHAPTER 9

Paul Vanezis: I said, 'There's a star marked in red next to Episode Two of 'The Aztecs', and Episodes Four and Five of 'The Reign of Terror'. What happened to F2, and H4 and H5?' He said, 'Destroyed.' I said 'What do you mean, "Destroyed"? Did you destroy them?' He said, 'No, no they were in a vault where the whole Cypriot film archive was stored, and during the shelling in the civil war, when there was a coup in 1974, the television station was hit, and that building was destroyed.' It was blown up. A lot of people have said over the years that it was destroyed in the Turkish invasion of Cyprus, but the Turkish invasion came a little bit later, and was triggered by this unsuccessful coup on the island. So we knew what happened to 'The Reign of Terror' Episodes Four and Five, and 'The Aztecs' Episode Two: they were destroyed. He wouldn't have made that up, not when they lost the entire national film archive of Cyprus!

I then said, 'Is there anything else you've got, or you might have? Where were the returned *Doctor Who* films found?' He said, 'In the basement; we call it "the Grave", because no-one ever goes there.' I said 'Can you show me?' He took me straight down into 'the Grave'. And it was basically a room just rammed full of film. You've got to bear in mind it was in the middle of summer in Cyprus, and this basement room wasn't quite underground, the walls were very hot, very warm. It wasn't a cold place, and it just stank of vinegar. All the racks on the left hand side of the room contained about 60 episodes of the ABC series *Armchair Theatre*. At the time, I was only interested in the BBC programmes – I'm kicking myself now. On the floor, in small piles, were all the films from all the other countries, including all their BBC films. There were a few hundred BBC films. I tried putting things into order as I was writing things down.

The things that were interesting were … The first series of *Z Cars*, there were the first seven episodes there. And there were another five from the second series. They may well have bought others, but if so, they weren't there. Or they had been sent on to somewhere else. I should have really checked his book, and cross-referenced that, but I didn't, unfortunately. It's only now, when you look back on it in hindsight, that you think, I should have done this, I should have done that. There were some plays there. There was a 1970 episode of *No Trams to Lime Street*, which the BBC had. There was *The Desperate People*, which was a Francis Durbridge thriller from 1963 – the BBC didn't have that, although the BFI, I discovered later, did have the original 35mm copies. Most episodes, although not all, of a series called *Katy*, which I think Susan Hampshire was in. The entire 1959 series of *Bleak House*, which featured William Russell, which was missing from the BBC. There was a sports reel, I remember the date very clearly, it was 23 November 1963, so I'd remember that![57] All the 1950s episodes of *Captain Pugwash*. A real mixed bag of oddities. *Andy Pandy* was also in there.

I wrote them all down, and all the information was later given to Adam Lee at the BBC Film and Videotape Library. It was difficult for me to know what was missing at the time, as I didn't have access to the BBC computer or anything like that. I had no idea that the *Z Cars* episodes I'd found were missing, until Adam Lee told me. Two of the episodes of *Z Cars*, you couldn't close the lids on the tins because of the amount of mould on the film. Although, as I understand it, they managed to clean the film, scrape it off, and managed to save them. But there were some other things in there ... Something called *Zoo Quest for a Dragon* – all the *Zoo Quest*s were in there, which was the original 1950s David Attenborough series. There were about 200 missing episodes in total, I think. Quite a lot of material, anyway, which all went back to the BBC. It just goes to show you, if only they'd bothered to ask in 1984, when they got the *Doctor Who*s back, 'Have you got any other BBC film?', they would have got all that back then.

THE REIGN OF TERROR: EPISODE THREE—A CHANGE OF IDENTITY
RETURNED TO THE BBC (AGAIN!)—EARLY 1985

The discovery of a duplicate print of the third episode of 'The Reign of Terror' just a few months after the first three episodes of the story had been returned from Cyprus, was not particularly newsworthy at the time. By chance, the very same collector who came up with the 16mm copy of Episode Six in 1982 now came forward with a 16mm print of the third episode. Once again, he contacted Bruce Campbell, who purchased the print from him. Regardless of the Cyprus find, Campbell loaned the BBC his print of Episode Three, where it was found to be better quality than the Cyprus one – it was again a Stored Field print, whereas the Cyprus prints were all Suppressed Field recordings. There are some details that make the discovery of this print of some interest:

> **David Stead:** The print originated from the same collector who supplied Episode Six back in 1982, and it was located by Bruce Campbell again. It was, however, unearthed at the same time the Cypriot episodes of 'The Reign of Terror' were discovered and returned to the BBC archive. There wasn't much of a thing made about it, as the Cyprus episodes seemed to be more

---

57 23 November 1963 was the date on which the first episode of *Doctor Who* was transmitted on the BBC.

CHAPTER 9

interesting as news. I was at that time working for Steve Bryant as his assistant at Windmill Road, so I was the chap who returned the 16mm film to Bruce Campbell after the archive had taken a copy of it. Bruce told me that he wasn't keen on holding on to it, as he had no means of keeping it in good condition, and so gave me the print of Episode Three. He later also gave me his print of Episode Six. Both of these UK-originated prints are of a better quality film transfer than the Cyprus ones. However the copy of Episode Three has some pronounced sprocket damage, mainly during the scene on film of Ian breaking out of the cell, and Episode Six has the very start of the opening titles missing. I think that was why they released the Cyprus versions on VHS.

In the mid-1990s the BBC made arrangements to borrow again these 16mm films of Episode Three and Episode Six of 'The Reign of Terror', and on Sunday 27 March 1994, they were both wetgate telecined and transferred onto digital D3 tape. These D3 copies were of a better quality than the original transfers.

THE FACELESS ONES: EPISODE THREE
RETURNED TO THE BBC—APRIL 1987
THE EVIL OF THE DALEKS: EPISODE TWO
RETURNED TO THE BBC—MAY 1987

Just prior to the Doctor Who Appreciation Society's 1985 Panopticon convention, held on 27 and 28 July at the Grand Hotel in Brighton, representatives from the Society were approached out of the blue by a gentleman named Saied Marham, who had an unusual proposition. Marham arrived at the Hotel on the Friday before the event was due to begin on the Saturday, and met with deputy convention organiser Steve Pugsley and DWAS Co-ordinator David Saunders. He informed them that he was representing an unnamed individual who had film copies of two missing *Doctor Who* episodes, 'The Faceless Ones' Episode Three and 'The Evil of the Daleks' Episode Two. This person wanted to show them both at a special screening he had organised at a local Brighton cinema (the Duke of York) that Sunday evening, just as the Panopticon event would be finishing. Tickets for the screening would be priced at £2.00 each, and would be made available to purchase to any interested Panopticon attendees. Doubtful of these claims, Pugsley and Saunders arranged a further meeting with Marham the following day.

Marham duly arrived back at the convention on the Saturday morning, and met again with Steve Pugsley. This time, they were joined by Ian Levine and Gary Leigh, editor of the fan magazine *Doctor Who Bulletin* (*DWB*), who were both also attending the event. Marham could offer no actual proof of the existence of the two episodes,

WIPED!

and so all concerned were deeply sceptical of his claims, wary that some kind of hoax was being perpetrated. Marham was told that the Panopticon event would not be able to publicise the cinema screening without there first being some proof of the two episodes' actual existence. Furthermore, Marham was told that a guarantee would need to be given that both the episodes would be returned to the BBC following the screening. Marham left that evening, but returned to the convention on the Sunday morning, saying that the planned screening due later that evening had been cancelled.

This didn't stop a couple of Panopticon attendees – namely Dave Palfreyman and Paul Vanezis, who had been tipped-off by DWAS Co-ordinator David Saunders – from going to the Duke of York cinema on the Sunday evening, just to see if Marham or the mysterious person he claimed to represent would be willing to talk to them about the two episodes they claimed to have in their possession. Palfreyman and Vanezis found the cinema closed and seemingly deserted.

Marham did indeed represent an individual who planned to screen the two episodes at the Duke of York cinema, and the two 16mm films were at the time physically in the hands of this person. But this person didn't *own* the two films. They were owned by a collector named Gordon Hendry, who had loaned the films to an acquaintance of his, not knowing that they were missing episodes. This person found out that that was the case, and realised that perhaps he could exploit the situation, while at the same time keeping Hendry ignorant of the rarity of his two episodes. Marham, however, realised that Hendry was being excluded from something he felt he should know about, and pondered about how to resolve the situation.

The following month, Marham wrote directly to Steve Bryant at the BBC Film and Videotape Library, telling him that he knew of the existence of these two missing Patrick Troughton episodes. Marham explained that although he wasn't the owner of the episodes, he was hoping to be able to negotiate for the BBC to borrow the films in order for them to make their own copies. However, he was vague in terms of actual detail, and although Bryant sent Marham a cautious reply welcoming the initiative, there was nothing more the BBC could officially do in the matter.

Unofficially, however, something was done. One of Bryant's assistants at Windmill Road at the time was David Stead. Stead discussed Marham's letter with a friend of his, another *Doctor Who* fan named Michael Smallman. Smallman in turn was close friends with Paul Vanezis, who had gone to the Duke of York cinema in Brighton during the Panopticon convention to try and talk to Marham about the episodes. Smallman passed Marham's details onto Vanezis, reasoning that Vanezis' experience in finding the Cyprus material and dealing with the BBC at the time made him best placed to try to move matters forward.

Vanezis at last contacted Marham in late 1985, claiming he had been given his

CHAPTER 9

details by a film collector he'd met at a film fair. Vanezis explained that he was interested in obtaining rare episodes of *Doctor Who* on 16mm film, and he had been told that Marham might have access to some. Marham was initially quite wary, understandably, and although he didn't deny that this was the case, he didn't initially confirm anything either. Nevertheless, Vanezis did offer to try to furnish Marham with videotape copies of a number of old television programmes that Marham was interested in obtaining in exchange for anything interesting he might unearth on the *Doctor Who* front. Marham and Vanezis would keep in touch, albeit infrequently, over the next 18 months.

The story then moves forward to 1987. Vanezis and Smallman (along with this author, and a number of other individuals) were co-organisers of another convention, TellyCon, which was to be held in Birmingham. A one-day event, scheduled for Saturday 18 April 1987, the convention was planned as an appreciation of the whole genre of British fantasy television shows, including *UFO*, *The Tomorrow People*, *Adam Adamant Lives!*, *Doctor Who* and *Randall & Hopkirk (Deceased)*, with a number of guests from these programmes due to appear at the event. In the weeks leading up to the convention, the organisers were also talking to an individual who claimed to have a copy of the missing William Hartnell episode 'The Tenth Planet' Episode Four, and at one time were hopeful of securing the episode for screening at the convention. This claim was eventually exposed as a hoax with no grounding whatsoever in reality, but not before advertising flyers had been distributed confidently stating that 'a previously missing episode of *Doctor Who*' would be screened at TellyCon.

Then, just a matter of weeks away from the date of the event, Vanezis was contacted by Marham, who was interested in attending TellyCon. Vanezis carefully suggested to Marham that TellyCon would be interested in running some sort of a tribute to Patrick Troughton at the event – the second Doctor actor had died in late March 1987, only a few weeks previously.

Paul Vanezis: We were planning the first TellyCon convention in 1987, and we were desperate to screen a missing episode at the event. Out of the blue, I received a telephone call from the chap who had claimed to have 'The Evil of the Daleks' Episode Two and 'The Faceless Ones' Episode Three. He was interested in the event, and we were discussing the sad news of Patrick Troughton's recent death. The conversation turned to what a nice idea it would be to show something special at the convention as a tribute to Pat Troughton, and he readily agreed to send 'something special'. Two days before the event, a VHS tape arrived in the post, which contained Episode Three of 'The Faceless Ones'.

The convention organisers had already made all the necessary arrangements with the

WIPED!

BBC to screen old episodes of programmes such as *Doomwatch*, *Adam Adamant Lives!* and *Doctor Who*, and permission was quickly granted by the BBC for the missing episode to also be screened. The BBC were hopeful that this would lead to its eventual return to the Film and Videotape Library. To a packed hall of attendees, 'The Faceless Ones' Episode Three was screened – with no prior introduction or announcement, other than that what was to follow on the main screen was a tribute to Patrick Troughton – at TellyCon on the afternoon of Saturday 18 April 1987.

The episode was slightly damaged, with small portions of material missing, of no more than a few frames' duration at a time, leading the film to 'jump' on occasion. And because a film's optical soundtrack is 16 frames out of synch with the pictures, the soundtrack also jumped too during the damaged portions. (Contrary to fan myth, however, the BBC has never classified the episode as 'untransmittable', and clean-up work was subsequently done for its VHS and DVD appearances.) The rush for the telephone kiosks by scores of attendees after the episode's end-credits had rolled is now a thing of legend.

The episode was supplied as a VHS camera copy (i.e. a copy made by pointing a domestic video camera at a projector screen while the 16mm film was projected upon it). In the two years since the Brighton cinema incident, Gordon Hendry had been made aware of the rarity of his two film prints, and had spent a lot of the intervening time trying to get them back in his possession.

Hendry was a film collector, and he had acquired the two episodes in the summer of 1983, buying them at a car boot sale held at the Buckingham Movie Museum. They were amongst a number of films of other old television material that were being sold that day by an elderly dealer. It was the word 'Dalek' written on the film tin of 'The Evil of the Daleks' Episode Two that had drawn Hendry to the two cans, as he had fond recollections of *Doctor Who* from his younger days. Hendry had managed to haggle the price of the films down from the £12.00 originally asked to just £8.00 for the pair. At the time, he was unaware that both the episodes were missing from the BBC, so he was happy to play the films a number of times on his own home 16mm projection equipment. It was this that had caused the damage to the episode of 'The Faceless Ones', which had been in near pristine condition when he had first purchased it.

Following the TellyCon event, a short series of telephone calls and negotiations between Paul Vanezis, Saied Marham, Gordon Hendry and Steve Bryant from the BBC Film and Videotape Library, plus the involvement of Ian Levine, resulted in Hendry's 16mm film print of 'The Faceless Ones' Episode Three being loaned to the BBC late in April 1987. The 16mm film print of 'The Evil of the Daleks' Episode Two was then loaned to the BBC a month later, in May 1987.

The BBC made their own 16mm film copies of the two episodes, but the process used at that time resulted in the usual image clarity loss. The two films were consequently borrowed a second time on 27 March 1994, where they were wetgate telecined and transferred onto digital D3 tape, giving the archive much better quality copies.

THE ICE WARRIORS: EPISODE ONE
THE ICE WARRIORS: EPISODE FOUR
THE ICE WARRIORS: EPISODE FIVE
THE ICE WARRIORS: EPISODE SIX
'RETURNED' TO THE BBC — AUGUST 1988

During the late 1980s, the BBC began streamlining some of its sites, and Villiers House, the old home of BBC Enterprises in Ealing, was one of the properties scheduled to be cleared out and allocated to another BBC department. The building comprised nine floors and a basement, and had stood empty for some time, as BBC Enterprises had moved to its new home in Woodlands, down the road from Television Centre.

Before the property was fully emptied and refurbished in readiness for the new department, it was thoroughly searched for any items that BBC Enterprises might have left behind. It was only during this final search by a member of BBC Enterprises film storage staff that a long-forgotten batch of 16mm black and white films were found. As it was known that they would probably be of interest to the Film and Videotape Library, the films were despatched to Windmill Road immediately. Alongside a missing episode of the series *Adam Adamant Lives!* (the final episode of the second series, 'A Sinister Sort of Service'), were five cans of film marked as *Doctor Who* – Episodes Two, Four, Five and Six of 'The Ice Warriors' and Episode Six of 'Fury from the Deep'. However, a quick examination of the contents of the cans showed that two of them were incorrectly labelled. The one marked as Episode Two of 'The Ice Warriors' actually contained a print of Episode One of that story, and sadly the one for Episode Six of 'Fury from the Deep' contained a different programme altogether, which wasn't actually classed as missing by the BBC.

A representative from the BBC Film and Videotape Library visited Villiers House days after the films were sent to Windmill Road, to ensure that there was nothing else tucked away in the building, and found nothing further.

THE TOMB OF THE CYBERMEN: EPISODE ONE
THE TOMB OF THE CYBERMEN: EPISODE TWO
THE TOMB OF THE CYBERMEN: EPISODE THREE
THE TOMB OF THE CYBERMEN: EPISODE FOUR
RETURNED TO THE BBC — 5 JANUARY 1992

'The Tomb of the Cybermen' was considered to be the holy grail of *Doctor Who*'s lost stories by many fans throughout the 1970s and 1980s. This was *the* story to get back

WIPED!

into the archives.

At the BBC Film and Videotape Library, Archive Selector Adam Lee (who had replaced Steve Bryant in the role) had been contacted in December 1991 by a representative from Asia Television in Hong Kong, asking what they should do with a batch of BBC films they found they still had in their archive. Lee was sent a vague list of the films, which included episodes of *Softly, Softly*, plus four episodes of *Doctor Who*, but with no story titles or serial codes detailed. Lee asked for the films to be sent back to the BBC, knowing that he wouldn't find out what the episodes actually were until they arrived. But the films never arrived …

David Stead at this point in time was on temporary attachment to BBC Enterprises in Woodlands. He was at work one morning in early January 1992 when he received a phone call from Bruce Campbell.

David Stead: Bruce called and informed me that some *Doctor Who* episodes were returning to the BBC from overseas. He had been in contact with Adam Lee at the BBC Film and Videotape Library on another matter, and Adam had mentioned to him that some episodes of *Doctor Who* were on their way back, but it was not known what they were and they apparently hadn't arrived at Windmill Road yet. I told him I would look into it.

I immediately went down to the despatch area in Woodlands, where there are usually 16mm and 35mm films and various videotapes awaiting either despatch or booking in and removal. I searched through a large number of brown packages of film material, some of which had labels indicating Rediffusion television in Hong Kong. Strangely, some of the packages had been opened, and knowing the tendency for things to go astray in the past, I checked through them all. I found several unopened packages, one of which contained four prints of *Doctor Who*, though all the label said was 'MM'. I then took the prints from despatch to my office (more or less right above despatch, as it happens) and very carefully looked at the leader of each film, and had that heart-stopping moment when I saw the words 'The Tomb of the Cybermen'.

All in all, about 20 tins of film had been sent back from Hong Kong's Asia Television, which was the new name of the old Rediffusion Television station. The films had sat unclaimed in the loading bay for a few days, perhaps a few weeks even, until Stead found them. Why had no-one located them before? Possibly it was because BBC staff were looking for films coming back from Asia Television, when the returned parcels were marked up as Rediffusion Television. Or possibly it was because Asia Television

CHAPTER 9

had unknowingly sent them back to BBC Enterprises (who had, after all supplied them in the first place) rather than to the Film and Videotape Library. Regardless, 'The Tomb of the Cybermen' was back, and David Stead had the films under lock and key.

But now Stead was in a quandary. He knew that the films were valuable additions to the Film and Videotape Library's stock of '60s *Doctor Who* episodes. And their return had been arranged by the Film and Videotape Library in the first place. But they had actually been sent to BBC Enterprises – arguably quite rightly, as that had been the department that had sold them to Hong Kong in the 1960s – and so the films were technically theirs, and not the archive's. And in 1992, BBC Enterprises were making a very reasonable profit for the Corporation by releasing old episodes of *Doctor Who* on VHS. The release of a previously-missing story such as 'The Tomb of the Cybermen' would surely become a best-seller for the range ... but the potential sales could be damaged if pirate copies managed to leak out of the BBC to the thriving underground fan video circuit.

David Stead: The films were locked in the bottom drawer of my desk until the next morning, when I was able to take them straight over to David Jackson, who was head of BBC Enterprises' home video department. He was obviously delighted to have the story, and set the wheels in motion for the film to be transferred to video for the eventual VHS release, as they would then have the best quality transfer from the master prints to release, rather than a copy from a duplicate print (in effect two copies down), which is what the Film and Videotape Library would have supplied once they had archived the Hong Kong prints.

David Jackson phoned Adam Lee that day to let him know the prints had arrived, and much to Adam Lee's annoyance said he would return the prints after BBC Enterprises had finished with them, as after all, they were BBC Enterprises' property, and not the Film and Videotape Library's. At least not yet!

A viewing of the film prints was arranged by David Jackson for later that same day. Stead and Jackson became the first people in the UK for nearly 25 years to watch 'The Tomb of the Cybermen'.

In order for the story to be quickly released on video, the films had to be cleaned up, and then transferred onto videotape, in this instance onto Betacam SP. The film clean-up was done at the Film Clinic, a division of a company called Soho Images in London, where the prints were treated with an ultrasonic cleaner. The video transfer was also done outside the BBC, at a facilities company called JCA, where, by coincidence, David Stead's then wife, Alys, worked. She was able to oversee the transfer, and ensure that no rogue copies were made.

Another consideration for BBC Enterprises was that in the January of 1992, BBC2 had begun a repeat run of old *Doctor Who* stories, beginning with the William Hartnell story 'The Time Meddler', which were being transmitted weekly on Friday evenings. This was due to be followed in February by a Patrick Troughton adventure, with 'The Mind Robber' favourite for selection. But if the recovery of 'The Tomb of the Cybermen' was made public in early January, there was a good chance that 'The Mind Robber' could be dropped from the repeats and 'The Tomb of the Cybermen' quickly ushered into the schedules in its place. A great coup for BBC2, but a potential loss of sales revenue for Enterprises. But if the Film and Videotape Library didn't actually have the returned prints, then the programme couldn't be scheduled. For this reason, the news of the return of 'The Tomb of the Cybermen' was held back by all at the Film and Videotape Library and Enterprises until the *Radio Times* issue that listed 'The Mind Robber' Episode One as the Patrick Troughton repeat was published. By that point, it was too late to switch stories for transmission.

But in the weeks between the return of 'The Tomb of the Cybermen' in early January and the official announcement of its return at the end of the month, rumours of the find started creeping around both *Doctor Who* fandom and various BBC departments. Somewhere along the line, a cover story was put about to the effect that four episodes of *Doctor Who* had indeed been recently returned on 16mm black and white film, but that they were nothing more than a duplicate copy of 'An Unearthly Child'.

'The Tomb of the Cybermen' was released by BBC Video on VHS in the UK on 4 May 1992. Prior to this, the fanzine *DWB* announced in its April 1992 edition that BBC Enterprises would set up a 'missing episodes office' in the wake of the story's recovery, but only if the VHS went on to sell more than 30,000 units. As it transpired, the video actually sold 23,000 units within just four days of release, earning it the number one slot in the week's Gallup video sales chart, and also the top slot in the high-street retailer HMV's sales chart, beating the likes of *Aliens: Special Edition*, *The Silence of the Lambs* and *Robin Hood – Prince of Thieves*. However, BBC Enterprises never set up a 'missing episodes office', and as far as I have been able to establish, the idea was never seriously mooted by anyone within the BBC, no matter how many units 'The Tomb of the Cybermen' sold on VHS. By 1999, its sales had actually reached the 30,000 mark, making it the eleventh highest selling *Doctor Who* video so far.

THE CRUSADE: EPISODE ONE — THE LION
RETURNED TO THE BBC — 11 JANUARY 1999

New Zealand holds the honour of being the first country outside of the UK to have

CHAPTER 9

screened *Doctor Who*, although during the '60s its scheduling was rather erratic, with a number of stories going unbroadcast altogether – including all of Patrick Troughton's final season.

All programmes purchased by the New Zealand Broadcasting Corporation – NZBC – were assessed and assigned a rating prior to transmission. This rating was designed to give some guidance as to the content of the material. *Doctor Who* stories were usually either assigned a 'G' rating for General Viewing, or a 'Y' rating, meaning that they couldn't be screened before 7.30 pm.

'The Crusade' was amongst a batch of seven stories purchased in September 1967 for screening by NZBC[58]. From this batch, both 'The Dalek Invasion of Earth' and 'The Web Planet' were assigned a 'Y' rating by the New Zealand censors, and as *Doctor Who* had a transmission slot earlier in the evening than 7.30 pm, they were not screened. Four of the others – 'The Reign of Terror', 'Planet of Giants', 'The Rescue' and 'The Romans' – were given 'G' ratings, and were screened.

There is conflicting paperwork evidence as to what rating the seventh story, 'The Crusade', received at this point, but that story too was never screened by NZBC.

NZBC had a film storage unit in Harriett Street, Wellington, and all four episodes of 'The Crusade' were sent there some time before April 1970. The first episode, 'The Lion', was still held at the Harriett Street facility up until the spring of 1974, although it is possible that the other three episodes might have been destroyed prior to that date. But early in 1974, 'The Lion' was amongst a batch of several hundred films scheduled for destruction. Surviving paperwork seems to confirm that it was the only episode of *Doctor Who* in this batch.

The films were loaded into a truck and it was despatched to a local landfill site, where it was intercepted by a local film collector, who had been tipped off that a consignment of films was due to be thrown out. After talking to workmen at the dump, he was allowed to remove 321 of the junked films and take them away to safety. The balance of the consignment was thrown into the dump as evidence that the disposal took place.

By chance, the 16mm film of 'The Lion' was one of those that was rescued. It found its first home outside the NZBC with the film collector in Johnsonville, Wellington who had rescued it from the tip. It changed ownership a number of times over the next

---

58 It was thought for a long time that these seven stories were all prints sent from ABC in Australia. Newly found paperwork shows that it was only 'The Reign of Terror', 'Planet of Giants', 'The Dalek Invasion of Earth' and 'The Rescue' that were sent from ABC. Where NZBC got the prints of 'The Romans', 'The Web Planet' and 'The Crusade' from isn't known – they may have been sent from the BBC, but as the print of 'The Lion' is a Suppressed Field print, it's more likely they came from a broadcaster that had already screened these stories prior to 1967.

WIPED!

15 years, at one point passing through the hands of a collector named David Lascelles. It then rested for at least 10 years in the possession of an 'eccentric painter', who stored a huge collection of films at the property of Dean Fletcher in Wahine Gorge, New Zealand. Fletcher had agreed to hold the material for a small fee for six months, but after two years had passed with no contact with the owner, and more importantly no fee, he decided to cut his losses and dispose of the material. In January 1998, collector Larry Duggan took about 40 tins of film, including 'The Lion', off Fletcher's hands for $150.00. Duggan was not that impressed with the episode, and decided to sell it on, which he did at a members-only convention of the Film Buffs' Association in Napier in May 1998. The film was purchased at the event for $5.00 by Bruce Grenville – the low price being set by Duggan due to the episode being just one part of a longer story.

Grenville was also something of a film buff, and a science fiction fan to boot, but was completely unaware of the film's rarity. He advertised the contents of his collection on his own website, complete with details of his print of 'The Lion' – which went completely unnoticed until after it was eventually returned to the BBC!

Grenville lived in Auckland, New Zealand, and owned his own 16mm film projector. He was able to play his collection of films, and regularly did so for friends and colleagues. Cornelius Stone was one such friend, and was also something of a *Doctor Who* fan. Stone visited Grenville in the latter half of 1998 and was shown the episode along with other non-*Doctor Who* films in Grenville's collection. He too failed to realise that it was a missing episode, until a conversation some weeks later with fellow *Doctor Who* fan Neil Lambess.

It was Lambess who first realised that Grenville's print could be of a missing episode. He and another *Doctor Who* fan, Paul Scoones, made arrangements to visit Grenville at his Auckland flat. The visit took place on Sunday 3 January 1999, and the film print of the episode was projected for them, with Scoones making a crude copy of the episode with his video camera. Its existence having thus been verified, Lambess and Scoones explained to Grenville that he had a missing episode on his hands.

Grenville took some convincing of the film's rarity, and it took even further persuasion for him to make it available for return to the BBC. He was sceptical at first of the assertions of Lambess and Scoones that his print was the only known copy of the episode, and that the BBC would be very interested in borrowing it. He felt sure that the BBC must hold a complete set of *Doctor Who* episodes. It was only after he was shown evidence – in the form of a VHS copy of 'The Missing Years' documentary (from the VHS box set release of 'The Ice Warriors') – that he became quite excited.

An initial e-mail was sent by both Lambess and Scoones on Monday 4 January 1999 to the BBC's Steve Roberts. This explained the circumstances of the episode's discovery, and this led to Scoones and Roberts laying down the initial groundwork to

CHAPTER 9

get the 16mm film sent back to England.

> **Neil Lambess:** We were both in e-mail contact with Steve Roberts. On 4 January I emailed Steve explaining the poor condition of the print and letting him know that Bruce had used a chemical cleaner on it recently. As a fully qualified projectionist, I felt it important to give Steve a quick heads-up on the extent of the damage. Then, as I had to return to my home city of Whangarei, we mutually decided that Paul Scoones was the best person to negotiate between the BBC and Bruce. I realise that's probably superfluous information, but people tend to assume I just walked away and left Paul to it, when in fact we were both involved in the initial stages of the return.

Initially, Scoones made a VHS copy of his camera-copy of the projected episode to send to Roberts to verify the find, and then on Thursday 7 January, he met with Grenville to borrow the 16mm film print

Grenville initially agreed in principle to loan Scoones the print so that he could send it to the BBC, but then became concerned that if he did so, he might not get it back. It was only after Scoones made a number of phone calls to Grenville, and a couple of return visits to his flat to supply him with written assurances from both himself and Roberts, that he allowed Scoones to take the film print away with him on the evening of Thursday 7 January. It was sent to Roberts at the BBC in London by Federal Express the very next day.

In the next few days, the VHS camera-copy of the episode arrived with Roberts, followed by the 16mm film, which was delivered on Monday 11 January. The print was examined and cleaned by the BBC, and was found to be a standard 16mm positive viewing print with optical soundtrack. It was copied to Digital Betacam after being extensively cleaned up. The print was quite badly damaged in places, with visible tramline scratches during sections of the action, and one hole that had seemingly been caused by a mis-aligned projector sprocket at some point in the past.

However, in the meantime, Grenville had become quite excited about the discovery of his episode, and wrote his own press release, which he sent out to local newspapers, television and radio stations in New Zealand. The story was forwarded to other news agencies, and before long, newspaper, television and radio reports in both New Zealand and England featured the story of the return of the missing episode.

Part of Grenville's statement to the press concerned his idea to auction the film print over the internet once it was returned to him. This caused something of a problem for the BBC, as Steve Roberts pointed out in a letter to Grenville: 'Because the print should have been either returned or destroyed after the contract period had expired,

WIPED!

it is technically still the property of the BBC and therefore can be classed as stolen property ... If you proceed down this path, you may open yourself up to legal action.'

The situation was unique, as never before had a private collector made such a public declaration about the potential financial rewards that could be exploited from their found footage. Nevertheless, Grenville then sought to gain yet more publicity over the fact that the BBC was 'threatening' him (as he perceived it), which led to a second letter being sent out by Roberts. This time the tone was more conciliatory: 'I'm pleased to be able to confirm that the BBC's official position is now that the film is your property and that you may sell it on or otherwise dispose of it as you please. You bought the print in good faith and therefore you are entitled to be considered as the legal owner ... I have been asked to point out, however, that the ownership of the print is limited to the physical acetate film, not to the copyright of the programme contained on it. This must also be made clear to anyone who wishes to buy the film from you.'

The 16mm film print was sent back to Grenville on 5 February 1999. Grenville went ahead with his plan to auction it. The first auction was due to take place on 17 September 1999, but was postponed shortly before that because of the low number of pre-registered bidders. Eventually, in October 1999, the film was sold at auction for US $850, although Grenville didn't actually receive any of the money, due to the amount the auction house had spent on advertising the sale. The film was sold on again in January 2000, when the winning bid was US $1275.

Paul Scoones: As a fan of *Doctor Who*, I was of course very excited and proud to help reinstate a lost segment of its early history. I was, however, dismayed and frustrated over what occurred after the film was returned to the BBC. I had given Bruce Grenville repeated reassurances that the BBC would be very pleased to get the film back, so I felt let down by the Corporation's rather undiplomatic and frankly ungrateful response to Bruce's stated intention to auction his film print.

Then there was the matter of my expenses. I paid the not inconsiderable expense of sending the film via Federal Express delivery to London out of my own pocket, with the assurance that I would be promptly reimbursed. In fact I wasn't paid back until more than six months later, after I had sent numerous e-mails and faxes to various individuals at the BBC chasing this reimbursement.

To add insult to injury, when the BBC released the commercial VHS box set containing the episode in the UK, Neil and I were dismayed that although Bruce Grenville's name appeared several times, neither of us were acknowledged anywhere in the extensive sleeve notes.

CHAPTER 9

THE DALEKS MASTERPLAN: EPISODE TWO—DAY OF ARMAGEDDON
RETURNED TO THE BBC—15 JANUARY 2004

Francis Watson began work as an engineer at the BBC in the summer of 1972. One day, not long after this, he was given the task of clearing out a room full of junk at the Corporation's Film and Television Studios at Ealing, with instructions to dispose of everything therein. Amongst all the various items that Watson found in the room were two 16mm black and white films containing *Doctor Who* episodes. Watson was also a member of a local film club, Filmsoc (an associated society of the University College London Union), located in Gordon Street, just off Euston Road in central London. Consequently, rather than destroy the two *Doctor Who* films, he kept them so that they could be projected and watched by his fellow film enthusiasts. The two films Watson saved were 'The Daleks' Episode Five ('The Expedition') and 'The Daleks Masterplan' Episode Two ('Day of Armageddon').

The old Ealing Studios, known within the Corporation as Television Film Studios or TFS, was one of a number of BBC premises in London outside of Television Centre. At this time, it was used solely for work on either 16mm or 35mm film. It was home to two large sound stages, numerous film cutting rooms and nearly all of the BBC's film crews. Ealing was also home to BBC Enterprises, based at Villiers House – a 1960s office block that straddled Ealing Broadway station. This was where all the overseas sales of *Doctor Who* episodes were originated. BBC Enterprises had a 16mm viewing theatre at Villiers House, but would sometimes use the more extensive facilities at TFS, where would-be buyers of BBC programmes could be shown examples of the material they were interested in. These viewing studios were maintained by the BBC's Film Department, for whom Watson worked.

Watson took the films away from Ealing sometime in late 1972 or early to mid-1973, and they resided in the archive of Filmsoc for some years. At some point, they were taken out of their separate BBC films cans and both put into a single 35mm can. Watson left London in 1977 to work for Yorkshire Television in Leeds, and took his two *Doctor Who* films with him. The films spent much of the next 20 years in several of Watson's cupboards, until he eventually took them into his office at Yorkshire Television in the early 1990s. There they hung inside a carrier bag, slung on a coat hook for the next ten years!

At some point in the late 1980s, the 16mm film can that had once been home to 'Day of Armageddon' was spotted in the Filmsoc archives by a latter-day member who was also a *Doctor Who* fan, although he was disappointed when the contents were checked and found to be unrelated to the label.

Watson had the *Doctor Who* films transferred to Digital Betacam in late 2003, mainly as a training exercise for YTV's newly-installed Snell & Wilcox Archangel film stabilising equipment. The tapes, films and DVD viewing copies of the episodes were returned to Watson in January 2004, which prompted him to Google various *Doctor Who* sites on the internet. One site that drew his eye was the *Doctor Who* Restoration Team website, run by BBC engineer Steve Roberts. Reading this, Watson learned for the first time that his 'Day of Armageddon' episode was one that was missing from the BBC, and realised that he held the only known copy.

Watson sent an e-mail to Roberts on Monday 12 January 2004, informing him of the circumstances that led to him being in possession of the 'Day of Armageddon' film. Roberts rang him back within the hour to follow up his e-mail. Watson agreed to send both the 16mm films and his Digital Betacam copies (in separate parcels, in case one went astray) to Roberts, and they arrived at the BBC on Thursday 15 January 2004. By 2.00 pm that day, the news of the episode's return was announced on the BBC's *Doctor Who* website, and on the Restoration Team forum.

GALAXY 4: EPISODE THREE — AIR LOCK
FOUND — 19 JULY 2011
RETURNED TO THE BBC — DECEMBER 2011

Ralph Montagu, in his time away from his job at the BBC, helps supervise many aspects of the Montagu family home of Beaulieu. Beaulieu is a picturesque stately home located in Hampshire, and has been the home of the Montagu family since 1538. It is also home to the National Motor Museum, and as part of the visitor experience, has a small theatre that screens films of interest to the many motor fans who frequent the museum.

In order to ensure that the film projection equipment runs smoothly, Beaulieu employs a small number of staff to operate and maintain the film equipment, many of whom are retired ex-BBC engineers. On Monday 18 July 2011, Ralph Montagu met up with some Beaulieu staff at a local cafe for a chat and some coffees, along with some other ex-TV engineers that they knew. He was introduced to a friend of one of his workers, Terry Burnett, who used to work at Television South (TVS) in Southampton. Burnett, Montagu was informed, was a keen collector of old films.

Montagu went and spoke to Burnett, who mentioned that amongst the many films he had in his collection was an old episode of *Doctor Who*. He couldn't recall any specific details about the episode, but offered to lend Montagu the film the next time the two of them met. Burnett then left the gathering, but managed to leave his jacket behind. Montagu contacted Burnett, and offered to return his jacket to him the next day, and when the two of them met again, Burnett had dug out the 16mm film of his *Doctor Who* episode and handed it to Montagu.

The film can handed to Montagu offered only small clues as to the contents; it was

CHAPTER 9

not an original BBC/BBC Enterprises film tin, and there were no BBC labels on either the can or the film spool. There was a small label on the spool itself, with the title of a film, which was crossed out in biro. Underneath this, also written in biro, were the words 'Dr Who' and 'Air Lock'. Montagu quickly checked up on 1960s *Doctor Who* episode titles, and realised that this was the title for the third episode of the wholly-missing William Hartnell story 'Galaxy 4'. Would the contents match ...?

Intrigued as to what the film could be, Montagu took the reel to Beaulieu's AV theatre, which was equipped with a Rank Cintel Mk III telecine, and loaded the 16mm reel into the equipment.

The film was missing the standard BBC film leader countdown; instead a generic countdown had been spliced onto the start of the print. This was then followed by the original *Doctor Who* title sequence, which was followed by a small section of action featuring the first Doctor and Vicki. As the features of a Rill were exposed for the first time, a caption with the title 'Air Lock' appeared on the screen. What Montagu had discovered was indeed the missing third episode of 'Galaxy 4'.

The 16mm Stored Field print itself was in reasonably good condition, albeit in slightly truncated form. The print suffers from some moderate tramline scratches, most noticeable in a section that features the character of Maaga in close-up. However, at the episode's cliffhanger conclusion, featuring Steven trapped in Drahvin ship's airlock, the film abruptly ends. The final 27 seconds or so of action, plus the end credits, were all missing. (Chopping the end credits from films was a common practice amongst film collectors, as it was thought the easiest was of removing any tell-tale copyright notices from the print.)

Footage missing from the end of 'Air Lock' (Missing material is in capitals)

MAAGA: Why do you not give up, Earthman?

(Steven climbs to his feet and faces Maaga through the interior viewing panel of the airlock).

STEVEN: I'd rather face the CHUMBLIES THAN YOU ANY DAY.

(HE TRIES TO OPEN THE OUTER AIRLOCK DOOR).

MAAGA: (LAUGHS.) THAT WILL NOT WORK NOW. THE PRESSURE HAS LOCKED THE DOOR. YOU MUST SURRENDER! OR DIE!

WIPED!

(AS THE NEEDLE ON THE PRESSURE GUAGE INSIDE THE AIRLOCK MOVES ANTICLOCKWISE BACK TO ZERO, STEVEN'S BREATHING BECOMES LABOURED, AND HE SLUMPS TO THE FLOOR, UNCONSCIOUS).

(END CREDITS ROLL OVER STEVEN'S INERT BODY BEFORE FADING TO BLACK).

Montagu contacted Burnett and told him that his *Doctor Who* film print was one that was missing from the BBC, and asked him if he had any objection to a copy being made for eventual return to the BBC. Burnett was more than happy to comply. Montagu asked Burnett how he came to have the film in the first place. Burnett recalled that a friend of his was involved in organising a school fête in the Marchwood district of Southampton, sometime around 1982 or 1983. Burnett later told the *Radio Times* website:

> I've been interested in film since about 1947. I've built up a modest collection. I buy and sell, and keep the films I like. In the mid-80s, an electrician at TVS was organising a school fête over Marchwood way. Everybody down there knew I was a film buff, and he just mentioned to me, 'I've got a box of films if you're interested.' So I said, 'Bring 'em in.' We did a suitable deal, I took them home ...

Burnett told Montagu that when he looked through the films he had purchased, he discovered a lone episode of *Doctor Who* that was amongst the films – 'Air Lock'. The print had then sat in his collection for the next 30 years, where Burnett occasionally viewed it on his own 16mm film projector.

Montagu contacted Steve Roberts the next morning, Wednesday 20 July 2011, and told him that he had a 16mm film print on loan that he might be interested in seeing, but didn't tell him any further details. Later that day, Montagu met up with Roberts at BBC Television Centre, and they decided to transfer the film that same day. They both rang Paul Vanezis, who quickly motored down to London from Birmingham. The three of them had some initial discussions about the missing end section of the episode. Constructing new end credits was something of a standard practice for the Restoration Team when remastering black and white *Doctor Who* episodes for DVD release, and the audio from the missing end portion of the episode survived, courtesy of the off-air recordings of David Holman, John de Rivaz and Allen Wilson. A repair of some description would seem entirely possible.

Roberts prepared the film for transfer on one of the BBC's Spirit telecine machines. He spliced new white film leader onto the beginning and end of the 16mm reel, cleaned the film on an ultrasonic film cleaner, and prepared to transfer the film onto Digital Betacam. The transfer was completed, but on reviewing the tape later in the day, Roberts found that the sound was awful - the Spirit had developed a sound fault. The fault on the Spirit was eventually repaired, but in the meantime the 'sound' part of the film was re-transferred using a Rank Cintel Mark III telecine, and re-laid onto the Digital Betacam Spirit transfer of the film. A 2K scan[59] of the 16mm film was made a few days later by Roberts, as he knew the film was going back to Terry Burnett once they had finished with it. This was done mainly for preservation purposes, but on comparing the result of the 2K scan with the Spirit transfer, it was found that the Spirit transfer had in fact resolved all the image detail held on the 16mm film at standard definition.

When Steve Roberts solvent-cleaned the film, there were a number of markings written on the leader in chinagraph that were cleaned off. No-one took a note of these markings at the time, but Ralph Montagu recalls that the title 'Air Lock' was one of the things marked on the film. Roberts also started the transfer of the film after the countdown clock on the leader (which, as mentioned, was a generic leader known as an SMPTE (Society of Motion Picture and Television Engineers) film leader, and not the original BBC film leader) had begun, omitting a caption card that said 'Australian Broadcasting Corporation'. Thus it took some time to substantiate that this film was once the ABC transmission print of this episode from Australia. This episode, along with many more episodes of *Doctor Who*, were returned to BBC Enterprises in June 1975 from ABC. The film must have been appropriated by someone from the BBC at some point between 1975 and the time Burnett purchased the prints in 1982/3.

Once the film had been transferred by Steve Roberts, Montagu then took the original film back to Beaulieu, to be re-united with Burnett.

The recovery of this episode of 'Galaxy 4' was announced alongside a surprise screening of five minutes of material of the episode itself at the December 2011 *Missing Believed Wiped* annual event at the BFI, along with a second recovery ...

THE UNDERWATER MENACE: EPISODE TWO
FOUND — 19 SEPTEMBER 2011
RETURNED TO THE BBC — DECEMBER 2011

Ralph Montagu contacted Terry Burnett to return his 16mm film print of the 'Galaxy 4' episode in early September 2011. When he finally met up with Burnett to hand over the film, Burnett revealed that he had located a second episode of *Doctor Who* on

---

59 A 2K scan is a transfer of every frame of a film, at a resolution higher than the current HD specification.

WIPED!

16mm film in his collection.

What's more, this second film was obtained by Burnett at the same time as the 'Galaxy 4' episode, in the early 1980s, and Burnett said that he had simply forgotten about it when sorting out the 'Galaxy 4' film for Montagu. It was only some days after he had handed over the 'Galaxy 4' episode that he remembered the second print.

Once again, Montagu arranged to borrow the film of this episode, and took it to Beaulieu to view on the Rank Cintel Mk III telecine. He watched as the title 'The Underwater Menace' appeared on screen, followed by the words 'Episode Two'.

This time the episode was a complete print, in that it had both opening and closing credits intact. However, there were four small edits to the film. These were:

A syringe being filled from a bottle (0 min 02 sec)
More shots of the syringe (0 min 03 sec)
Polly cries as she is held down on the operating table (0 min 07 sec)
Damon is interrupted as he is about to inject Polly (0 min 08 sec)

These edits matched completely with the censored material from this episode that was discovered in Australia by Damian Shanahan in 1996 (see Chapter 12), which along with chinagraph markings on the film leader, indicated that this print was also one that had originated at ABC[60]. Shanahan's records showed that this print was returned to BBC Enterprises in June 1975.

Aside from this, the film suffered a noticeable central phosphor dot, which had been burned into the original film recorder screen, a couple of quite noticeable

---

[60] When the print of the 'The Underwater Menace' episode was located, it too had chinagraph markings on the film leader. This time, Roberts made a note of the marks before the film was cleaned. They said:

Dr Who No. 145 The Underwater Menace pt2   Ft926 – Dur 24.41

That this was noted as the 145th episode indicates that the ABC episode numbering system for *Doctor Who* must have included 'Mission to the Unknown' and the 11-episode version of 'The Daleks Masterplan'. Did the chinagraph markings on the 'Galaxy 4' episode indicate that it was 'No. 84'? Sadly, no-one can remember if this was the case. Both films had the same type of SMPTE film leaders spliced onto them, replacing their original BBC film leaders.

However, the 'Galaxy 4' print is a Stored Field print. In the first edition of this book, I theorised that the copies of this story originally supplied to ABC by the BBC in the summer of 1966 would almost certainly have been Suppressed Field prints. The existence of this Stored Field Print conclusively proves otherwise. In the light of this discovery, it would now therefore appear that only the first two seasons of *Doctor Who* were sold as Suppressed Field prints by BBC Enterprises, and for Season Three onwards, Stored Field prints would seem to have been used from day one.

CHAPTER 9

scratches, and a couple of splices where the film had snapped at some point over the years, leaving gaps of a few frames either side of the join. One bad splice covered a tear in the film, and around 40 to 50 frames of action were missing during a scene of Ben and Jamie in the Atlantean mines.

Once again, the film print was taken by Montagu to Steve Roberts at BBC Television Centre so that a Digital Betacam copy could be made of it (a 2K scan wasn't done this time, for the reasons stated earlier), before it was eventually returned to Terry Burnett.

In the meantime, Paul Vanezis contacted the Australian Archives to request that the BBC be allowed to have access to the 16mm film of all the *Doctor Who* censor cuts that they held from this story, so that the material from Episode Two of 'The Underwater Menace' in particular could be transferred in a similar manner to the episode itself, and so help better to restore the episode. The cut material was transferred on a 2K scanner and was sent to Steve Roberts in early 2012 on a USB pen drive. However, the transfer had dirt in the gate, and wasn't as clean as was needed, so a second one was done. When this arrived, the restoration work on the episode could begin at last. The unrestored episode itself was shown to a packed audience at the December 2011 *Missing Believed Wiped* annual event at the BFI.

2011 ONWARDS

In late 2011, the number of missing episodes of *Doctor Who* stood at 106. Exactly 30 episodes had been located in the 30 years since the 1981 article in the *Doctor Who Magazine* Winter Special had first made public the exact status of the BBC's archive holdings of the series.

The full details of how the various colour Jon Pertwee episodes have been recovered will be examined in the next chapter, but for now, here's how the first two Doctors are currently represented in the BBC archives:

WILLIAM HARTNELL

Story	16mm b&w film	35mm b&w film	Missing
(Pilot Episode)	1		
An Unearthly Child	1, 2, 3, 4		
The Daleks	1, 2, 3, 4, 5, 6, 7		
The Edge of Destruction	1, 2		
Marco Polo			1, 2, 3, 4, 5, 6, 7
The Keys of Marinus	1, 2, 3, 4, 5, 6		
The Aztecs	1, 2, 3, 4		
The Sensorites	1, 2, 3, 4, 5, 6		
The Reign of Terror	1, 2, 3, 6		4, 5

WIPED!

Story	16mm b&w film	35mm b&w film	Missing
Planet of Giants	1, 2, 3		
The Dalek Invasion of Earth	1, 2, 3, 4, 6	5	
The Rescue	1, 2		
The Romans	1, 2, 3, 4		
The Web Planet	1, 2, 3, 4, 5, 6		
The Crusade	1, 3		2, 4
The Space Museum	1, 2, 3, 4		
The Chase	1, 2, 3, 4, 5, 6		
The Time Meddler	1, 2, 3, 4		
Galaxy 4	3		1, 2, 4
Mission to the Unknown			1
The Myth Makers			1, 2, 3, 4
The Daleks Masterplan	2, 5, 10		1, 3, 4, 6, 7, 8, 9, 11, 12
The Massacre			1, 2, 3, 4
The Ark	1, 2, 3, 4		
The Celestial Toymaker	4		1, 2, 3
The Gunfighters	1, 2, 3, 4		
The Savages			1, 2, 3, 4
The War Machines	1, 2, 3, 4		
The Smugglers			1, 2, 3, 4
The Tenth Planet	1, 2, 3		4

PATRICK TROUGHTON

Story	16mm b&w film	35mm b&w film	Missing
The Power of the Daleks			1, 2, 3, 4, 5, 6
The Highlanders			1, 2, 3, 4
The Underwater Menace	2, 3		1, 4
The Moonbase	2, 4		1, 3
The Macra Terror			1, 2, 3, 4
The Faceless Ones	1, 3		2, 4, 5, 6
The Evil of the Daleks	2		1, 3, 4, 5, 6, 7
The Tomb of the Cybermen	1, 2, 3, 4		
The Abominable Snowmen	2		1, 3, 4, 5, 6
The Ice Warriors	1, 4, 5, 6		2, 3

CHAPTER 9

The Enemy of the World	3		1, 2, 4, 5, 6
The Web of Fear	1		2, 3, 4, 5, 6
Fury from the Deep			1, 2, 3, 4, 5, 6
The Wheel in Space	3	6	1, 2, 4, 5
The Dominators	1, 2, 4, 5	3	
The Mind Robber	1, 2, 3, 4	5	
The Invasion	2, 3, 5, 6, 7, 8		1, 4
The Krotons	2, 3, 4	1	
The Seeds of Death	1, 2, 3, 4, 6	5	
The Space Pirates		2	1, 3, 4, 5, 6
The War Games	1, 2, 3, 4, 5, 6, 7, 8, 9, 10		

WIPED!

CHAPTER 10
RECOVERING THE THIRD DOCTOR

As we have seen, unlike those of the William Hartnell and Patrick Troughton eras, not all of the master videotapes of Jon Pertwee's episodes of *Doctor Who* were wiped by the BBC. However, by the time the practise of wiping was stopped by the BBC, in 1975 or thereabouts, around half of the episodes that made up Pertwee's era as the Doctor had been destroyed.

625-LINE COLOR TWO-INCH TRANSMISSION TAPES

Sue Malden, newly appointed as Archive Selector for the BBC Film and Videotape Library in 1978, had the task of trying to piece back together the third Doctor's era. First, she looked to the remaining two-inch 625-line transmission tapes that the BBC still held.

Pertwee's last season as the Doctor (the programme's eleventh) was missing just two episodes – the first episodes of both 'Invasion of the Dinosaurs' and 'Death to the Daleks'. As we have seen, the two-inch tapes of all six episodes of 'Invasion of the Dinosaurs' were listed as missing in November 1976, in the audit of surviving *Doctor Who* episodes carried out for 'Whose Doctor Who'. But at some point prior to 1981, the tapes of all bar the first episode of this tale had turned up. Conversely, Part One of 'Death to the Daleks' was listed as still surviving on two-inch tape in the November 1976 list, but this had been lost by the time Malden started trying to preserve the series.

The tenth season was missing five of its 26 episodes on two-inch colour tape – 'Frontier in Space' Episodes One, Two, Three and Six, and 'Planet of the Daleks' Episode Three. Season Nine had suffered much worse, with only 11 of its 26 episodes remaining on their transmission tapes. 'The Sea Devils' Episodes One, Two and Three, all four episodes of 'The Curse of Peladon', 'The Mutants' Episodes One and Two, and all six episodes of 'The Time Monster' were missing from the BBC archive.

Just four episodes remained from the entirety of the seventh and eighth seasons – 'The Ambassadors of Death' Episode One, 'The Claws of Axos' Episodes One and Four and 'The Dæmons' Episode Four.

From a total of 124 Pertwee episodes originally broadcast from two-inch videotape, only 60 now survived, just less than half.

The colour 16mm transmission film prints of all four episodes of Pertwee's debut adventure, 'Spearhead from Space', were also located and archived, taking the tally of surviving episodes to 64. However, there were only eight complete stories amongst

WIPED!

this batch.

In summary, the Pertwee episodes held in the BBC archive at this point on their colour transmission masters were as follows:

Story	Colour 625-line Two-inch Tape	16mm colour film
Spearhead from Space		1, 2, 3, 4
Doctor Who and the Silurians		
The Ambassadors of Death	1	
Inferno		
Terror of the Autons		
The Mind of Evil		
The Claws of Axos	1, 4	
Colony in Space		
The Dæmons	4	
Day of the Daleks	1, 2, 3, 4	
The Curse of Peladon		
The Sea Devils	4, 5, 6	
The Mutants	3, 4, 5, 6	
The Time Monster		
The Three Doctors	1, 2, 3, 4	
Carnival of Monsters	1, 2, 3, 4	
Frontier in Space	4, 5	
Planet of the Daleks	1, 2, 4, 5, 6	
The Green Death	1, 2, 3, 4, 5, 6	
The Time Warrior	1, 2, 3, 4	
Invasion of the Dinosaurs	2, 3, 4, 5, 6	
Death to the Daleks	2, 3, 4	
The Monster of Peladon	1, 2, 3, 4, 5, 6	
Planet of the Spiders	1, 2, 3, 4, 5, 6	

BBC ENTERPRISES

BBC Enterprises had initially sold the Pertwee stories overseas in the same manner as they had the earlier Hartnell and Troughton ones – as 16mm black and white film recordings. Although the series had begun airing in colour on BBC1 in 1970, most of the countries purchasing these episodes were still transmitting only a black and white service, and so had no need of colour copies.

The process of film recording from a colour videotape was basically the same as from a black and white videotape, although some specific artefacts generated by the colour (or chroma) part of the picture could sometimes be seen in the black and white film recordings as very small dots in the picture. As noted in Chapter 5, a way of

CHAPTER 10

filtering out these chroma dots during the telerecording process was developed by the BBC, although more often than not, it wasn't applied in practice.

Between 1970 and 1974, Enterprises had made 16mm black and white film recordings (usually at the time of transmission, to save on costs) of all of Pertwee's first four seasons as the Doctor, from 'Spearhead from Space' through to 'The Green Death'. The practice had continued for the eleventh season's first two stories – 'The Time Warrior', and 'Invasion of the Dinosaurs' – before it was permanently stopped. By this time – early 1974 – the demand from overseas stations for colour material was steadily growing, and the days of Enterprises selling black and white prints abroad were numbered. Perhaps because the whole story wasn't telerecorded, Enterprises didn't keep the 16mm black and white films of the first three episodes of 'Invasion of the Dinosaurs'. These were sent to the Film Library instead, which kept them until at least the end of 1976, before junking them (if the 'Whose Doctor Who' listing is to be believed).

In 1978, the Film and Videotape Library were able to take from Enterprises a full set of 16mm black and white film negatives for all the third Doctor stories that were missing from the archive, either in part or in their entirety, from seasons seven through to ten. This ensured that nearly every Pertwee episode now at least had some representation in the archive.

So, by the end of 1978, the archive of the third Doctor's episodes comprised the following:

Story	Colour 625-line Two-inch Tape	16mm Colour Film	16mm Black and White Film Recordings
Spearhead from Space		1, 2, 3, 4	
Doctor Who and the Silurians			1, 2, 3, 4, 5, 6, 7
The Ambassadors of Death	1		1, 2, 3, 4, 5, 6, 7
Inferno			1, 2, 3, 4, 5, 6, 7
Terror of the Autons			1, 2, 3, 4
The Mind of Evil			1, 2, 3, 4, 5, 6
The Claws of Axos	1, 4		1, 2, 3, 4
Colony in Space			1, 2, 3, 4, 5, 6
The Dæmons	4		1, 2, 3, 4, 5
Day of the Daleks	1, 2, 3, 4		
The Curse of Peladon			1, 2, 3, 4
The Sea Devils	4, 5, 6		1, 2, 3, 4, 5, 6
The Mutants	3, 4, 5, 6		1, 2, 3, 4, 5, 6
The Time Monster			1, 2, 3, 4, 5, 6
The Three Doctors	1, 2, 3, 4		

WIPED!

Carnival of Monsters	1, 2, 3, 4		
Frontier in Space	4, 5		1, 2, 3, 4, 5, 6
Planet of the Daleks	1, 2, 4, 5, 6		1, 2, 3, 4, 5, 6
The Green Death	1, 2, 3, 4, 5, 6		
The Time Warrior	1, 2, 3, 4		
Invasion of the Dinosaurs	2, 3, 4, 5, 6		
Death to the Daleks	2, 3, 4		
The Monster of Peladon	1, 2, 3, 4, 5, 6		
Planet of the Spiders	1, 2, 3, 4, 5, 6		

As can be seen from the table, two Pertwee stories remained incomplete at this point, with 'Invasion of the Dinosaurs' and 'Death to the Daleks' both still missing their respective opening instalments. But the other 22 stories were now complete, even if only eight of them were in full colour.

CANADA—PART ONE

In late 1980, Ian Levine began investigating the possibility of US and Canadian television stations retaining colour transmission copies of Pertwee stories. He had obtained colour off-air domestic recordings of a number of these stories from American *Doctor Who* fans over the previous few years, including some that he knew the BBC now kept only in black and white. While his investigations into American broadcasters had yet to offer up any substantial leads, he had rather more luck with his Canadian enquiries. Levine explains how this came about:

> **Ian Levine:** There was a guy called Andrew Trentacosta at KCET in Los Angeles. He'd shown 'The Dæmons' and then wiped the tapes, which had been re-used for their own news programmes and stuff, only weeks before I met him. Otherwise he would have given me the actual two-inch tapes of 'The Dæmons'. All they had left at KCET were colour U-MATICs. They didn't have any two-inch tapes at all; they had all gone, they had all been wiped. But they did have U-MATICs of 'The Curse of Peladon', which he gave me, and I've actually still got them with his television station ident on them. They certainly transmitted one 90-minute tape of 'The Curse of Peladon' originally; a 90-minute omnibus kind of thing.[61] And 'The Dæmons' would have been

---

61 If KCET were transmitting *Doctor Who* from NTSC U-MATIC tapes (which makes sense, as advert breaks and station idents would have to be edited onto the local transmission tapes), then perhaps the other US PBS markets did the same thing. Which might very well mean that Time-Life kept hold of a single set of NTSC two-inch tapes, which were then bicycled round all the PBS stations as required, so that they could all make their own U-MATIC master transmission tapes. Only one set of NTSC Jon Pertwee episodes could have accounted for all the US screenings of the series in the 1970s.

CHAPTER 10

about two hours, wouldn't it? After topping and tailing the episodes.

Andrew said – because he was a bit of a *Doctor Who* fan – he'd heard on the grapevine that there were still colour two-inch tapes at BBC Canada. So I phoned them, on behalf of the Library – Sue Malden gave me permission to use her name. They said, 'No, they've all been junked long ago.' But Andrew Trentacosta said they were still there, he said he knew someone who knew the tapes were there, so I insisted. They said, 'Look according to the computer, they've been wiped.' I said 'Don't believe that, you go and look.' So they went into the basement, and there were all these tapes.

Levine had discovered that BBC Toronto still held two-inch 525-line colour copies of, amongst other stories, 'The Claws of Axos', 'The Curse of Peladon' and 'The Mutants', which they had supplied to either TV Ontario and/or CKVU for screenings in recent years. Once he knew that the two-inch tapes were in existence, Levine informed Malden at the Film and Videotape Library of his discoveries.

In January 1981, Malden wrote to Hilary Read at BBC Toronto, asking if the BBC in London could be supplied with two-inch colour copies of the 525-line tapes of 'The Claws of Axos' Episodes Two and Three, all four episodes of 'The Curse of Peladon', and Episodes One and Two of 'The Mutants'. Read replied in March 1981, saying that dubs could be made of all these episodes, if Malden was happy to authorise that the costs of making the copies would be met by the Windmill Road archive. Malden wrote back in late March to confirm that the costs would be met for these eight episodes, and also hastily added a handwritten PS to her letter, enquiring if BBC Toronto also had access to 525-line colour copies of 'Death to the Daleks'. If they did, she asked, could she also arrange to have Part One added to the list of episodes to be copied, making nine in total.

Read replied to Malden's letter in late April 1981, confirming that two-inch 525-line colour dubs of the eight episodes she requested were in the process of being made. She also confirmed the existence of two-inch colour copies of all four episodes of 'Death to the Daleks' in Canada, although the tapes weren't currently held by BBC Toronto. Her letter stated that the tapes were at that point in time with the OECA (Ontario Education Communications Authority), but that she had made arrangements for a 525-line two-inch copy of Part One to be made, which would be sent back to London along with the other eight episodes that had been requested. (A handwritten note on this letter states 'Received 5.6.81', which might be just the date the letter was received by Malden, but is more likely the date the actual two-inch tapes were received at Windmill Road. The archive data for the episodes of 'The Claws of Axos' held by Windmill Road gives 23/04/81 as the recording dates, which sounds about correct.)

WIPED!

The result of this first foray into the *Doctor Who* holdings of BBC Toronto was that by the end of 1981, another third Doctor story – 'Death to the Daleks' – had been completed (and in colour too), leaving just 'Invasion of the Dinosaurs' Part One as the sole missing episode from the Pertwee era. It also meant that three more third Doctor stories were now in full colour in the archive, whereas previously they had been held wholly or partly in black and white. Although the Canadian tapes were in the NTSC video format, PAL standards conversions could be easily made if required.

At some point prior to November 1981, the Film and Videotape Library also acquired 525-line NTSC two-inch colour tapes of all six episodes of 'The Time Monster'. It's uncertain where these tapes originated from, but all the evidence points to BBC Toronto in Canada again being the source. Anecdotal evidence indicates that the tapes returned were the original 525-line conversions, and not dubs thereof (unlike the previous nine episodes retrieved from Canada). These tapes had been less than a week away from being erased when the BBC found out about them.

It was in November 1981 that Marvel's *Doctor Who Monthly* Winter Special was published containing Jeremy Bentham's groundbreaking interview with Malden, as discussed in previous chapters. This was accompanied by a checklist of the episodes the BBC still retained (which did contain a few errors: 'The Wheel in Space' Episode Six was omitted from the list, whilst Episode Four of 'The Invasion' was wrongly included, and there were no black and white prints of 'The Time Monster' listed as existing, which was incorrect).

The part of the checklist devoted to Jon Pertwee's episodes detailed only which still survived in colour or black and white, but if it had been slightly more detailed, it would have read as follows:

Story	*Colour 625-line Two-inch Tape*	*Colour 525-line Two-inch Tape*	*16mm Colour Film*	*16mm Black and White Film Recordings*
Spearhead from Space			1, 2, 3, 4	
Doctor Who and the Silurians				1, 2, 3, 4, 5, 6, 7
The Ambassadors of Death	1			1, 2, 3, 4, 5, 6, 7
Inferno				1, 2, 3, 4, 5, 6, 7
Terror of the Autons				1, 2, 3, 4
The Mind of Evil				1, 2, 3, 4, 5, 6
The Claws of Axos	1, 4	2, 3		1, 2, 3, 4

CHAPTER 10

Colony in Space					1, 2, 3, 4, 5, 6
The Dæmons	4				1, 2, 3, 4, 5
Day of the Daleks	1, 2, 3, 4				
The Curse of Peladon		1, 2, 3, 4			1, 2, 3, 4
The Sea Devils	4, 5, 6				1, 2, 3, 4, 5, 6
The Mutants	3, 4, 5, 6	1, 2			1, 2, 3, 4, 5, 6
The Time Monster		1, 2, 3, 4, 5, 6			1, 2, 3, 4, 5, 6
The Three Doctors	1, 2, 3, 4				
Carnival of Monsters	1, 2, 3, 4				
Frontier in Space	4, 5				1, 2, 3, 4, 5, 6
Planet of the Daleks	1, 2, 4, 5, 6				1, 2, 3, 4, 5, 6
The Green Death	1, 2, 3, 4, 5, 6				
The Time Warrior	1, 2, 3, 4				
Invasion of the Dinosaurs	2, 3, 4, 5, 6				
Death to the Daleks	2, 3, 4	1			
The Monster of Peladon	1, 2, 3, 4, 5, 6				
Planet of the Spiders	1, 2, 3, 4, 5, 6				

The returned 525-line two-inch tapes of 'The Curse of Peladon' were soon to be pressed into service by the BBC. In the summer of 1982, a brief run of repeats of classic *Doctor Who* stories was sanctioned by BBC1 at very short notice. This had been prompted by the success of the repeat season *The Five Faces of Doctor Who* on BBC2 in November 1981, when 'An Unearthly Child', 'The Krotons', 'Carnival of Monsters', 'The Three Doctors' and 'Logopolis' were dusted down and shown again – the first ever 'out of time' *Doctor Who* repeats screened by the Corporation.

This time, *Doctor Who* had been granted six 50-minute midweek early-evening slots on BBC1, so only colour stories were deemed suitable for inclusion. The repeat season was given the umbrella title *Doctor Who and the Monsters*, and one story featuring each of the third, fourth and fifth Doctors would be selected, and edited into two 50-minute episodes. 'The Curse of Peladon' was chosen to represent the third Doctor and the Ice Warriors. ('Genesis of the Daleks' – edited down by a third of its running time – was chosen for the fourth Doctor and the Daleks, while 'Earthshock' showcased the fifth Doctor and the Cybermen.)

Episodes One, Two and Four of 'The Curse of Peladon' presented few problems for the BBC engineers who had to standards-convert the two-inch 525-line Canadian

WIPED!

tapes to create the 625-line PAL tapes needed for transmission. But the 525-line tape of the third episode kept sticking and jamming every few seconds each time a playback was attempted, and at one stage it was almost declared unplayable and junked. But with a lot of perseverance on the engineer's part, short sections of playback were able to be recorded – still in NTSC – from the tape, until every frame of material from the episode had been copied. All the small portions of playback were then copied back together in scene order to make a new NTSC version of the episode, which could then be converted back to 625-line PAL. The original 525-line two-inch tape of Episode Three was then disposed of by the BBC, but retained by Ian Levine:

> **Ian Levine:** When they threw the tape out, I hit the roof. I went to Sue Malden, and said 'I got them back, it was my bloody hard work, you can't just throw them away.' She said 'It's not good enough to keep.' So I said, 'Fine, give it to me then, rather than throw it out.' 'OK then, here you are.' Now they've had to borrow it back, to re-bake it, to re-use it again to get a better quality copy for the DVD. Imagine if I'd let them throw it away!

CANADA—PART TWO

In September 1982, a Chicago-based American *Doctor Who* fan, Nick Telizya, wrote a letter to *Doctor Who* producer John Nathan-Turner, telling him that he'd heard that BBC Canada were in possession of colour transmission tapes of the Pertwee stories 'Colony in Space' and 'The Sea Devils'. What inspired Telizya to send this letter isn't known, but presumably he'd done some research of his own, perhaps after reading the article in the 1981 Marvel Winter Special. Or perhaps the stories had recently screened on a PBS station in his area? Either way, Nathan-Turner forwarded Telizya's letter onto Sue Malden, asking her to look into this claim.

Malden duly followed up the lead in early October 1982, sending a letter to Giles Neal at BBC Canada in Toronto, asking if they did indeed hold two-inch 525-line copies of these two *Doctor Who* stories, or any others that might be useful to the main BBC archive. At the time, BBC Toronto didn't hold their two-inch tapes on-site, but had them stored with an outside shipping company, Thunder-North Broadcast Services Ltd in Ontario. Thunder-North quickly audited their *Doctor Who* two-inch NTSC tape holdings for BBC Toronto, and in early November reported that they held the following third Doctor stories in colour: 'The Claws of Axos', 'Colony in Space', 'Day of the Daleks', 'The Sea Devils', 'The Three Doctors', 'The Green Death', 'The Time Warrior', 'Death to the Daleks', 'The Monster of Peladon' and 'Planet of the Spiders'. Telizya had been correct.

This was reported back to Malden in London, and in early December 1982, she

CHAPTER 10

formally requested that the BBC in London be sent copies of 'The Sea Devils' Episodes One, Two and Three, and all six episodes of 'Colony in Space'. At the same time, she enquired when the rights to these two stories would expire with BBC Canada. If it was anytime soon, could the original tapes perhaps be sent to her in London, rather than just copies of them? In early February 1983, Evelyn Pagkalinawan from BBC Canada wrote to Malden to confirm that they would indeed send the original tapes back to England, and followed this up a few days later with a telex letting her know that the tapes had been despatched on Friday 18 February 1983 to Windmill Road.[62] This recovery was eventually reported in issue 77 of *Doctor Who Monthly*, dated June 1983.

Once the episodes had been received by the BBC, and 625-line PAL conversions of these NTSC colour episodes had been made, the tally of complete colour Pertwee stories now held by the BBC stood at 15. Just four stories now existed only in black and white, a further four in a mixture of black and white and colour. Only one – 'Invasion of the Dinosaurs' – was still missing an episode altogether.

1983 – A BUMPER YEAR FOR PERTWEE RECOVERIES

The recovery of the colour episodes of 'The Sea Devils' and 'Colony in Space' from Canada in early 1983 was just the beginning of a whole deluge of finds and returns of Pertwee material during this year.

First, and most significantly, Ian Levine returned his 16mm black and white film print of 'Invasion of the Dinosaurs' Part One in June (see the previous chapter for more details). This finally completed this story for the BBC.

Sue Malden vacated her position as Archive Selector at the Film and Videotape Library during this year, and was replaced by Steve Bryant. Bryant began making overseas enquiries of his own, and one of his first was with Basil Sands at the BBC's Sydney office in Australia. In mid-June 1983, Sands sent a telex to Bryant, informing him that ABC held 625-line two-inch colour videotapes of 'Frontier in Space', and were also in the process of obtaining 525-line copies of 'The Claws of Axos', 'The Mutants' and 'The Time Monster' from the BBC's US distributor Lionheart, to screen on the channel ABC1 that summer. ('Frontier in Space' was actually shown in colour on ABC1 between 2 and 9 June 1983.) Where ABC had got the two-inch tapes of 'Frontier in Space' from is a mystery, as the story had only been screened in black and white by the station prior to this time.

Bryant replied to Sands the next day, asking if he could arrange for ABC to make colour 625-line two-inch copies of Episodes One, Two, Three and Six of 'Frontier in

---

62 To put this into some kind of context, this was a couple of days after BBC1 had screened the second episode of the Peter Davison story 'Terminus'.

WIPED!

Space', and have them sent to him in London. He also asked if Sands could find out if Lionheart were in possession of 525-line colour copies of any other Pertwee stories, such as 'Terror of the Autons' and 'Planet of the Daleks'.

In early July, Sands confirmed that the new 625-line two-inch colour copies of the four episodes of 'Frontier in Space' were being made by ABC, and were due to be despatched to Windmill Road within the next four weeks. He also confirmed that ABC had got only NTSC copies of 'The Claws of Axos', 'Colony in Space', 'The Sea Devils', 'The Mutants' and 'The Time Monster' from Lionheart, and that no colour tapes of 'Terror of the Autons' or 'Planet of the Daleks' were available from the US distributor.

It was probably at around this point in time that it was realised that one of the BBC's long-held copies of Episode Five of 'Frontier in Space' was in fact not the transmitted version but an earlier edit (although it didn't contain any additional scenes – the cliffhanger reprise was longer, and the 'Delaware' theme had been dubbed onto the opening and closing titles).

Presumably after hearing about the initial stages of this dialogue between Sands and Bryant, the usually-reliable *Doctor Who Monthly* ran a story in the *Gallifrey Guardian* news page of its Issue 80, dated September 1983:

> Good news for archivists everywhere. More colour Pertwee episodes have turned up, this time in Australia. It seems that despite numerous checks and requests to ABC Television as to whether they still retained copies of *Doctor Who*, which returned negative results, they do still have the following mint two-inch video tape copies: 'Terror of the Autons', 'Claws of Axos', 'Colony in Space', The Curse of Peladon', 'The Sea Devils', 'The Mutants', 'The Time Monster', 'Frontier in Space' and 'Planet of the Daleks'. As you read this, perfect copies should be winging their way around the world to take their rightful place in the BBC Archive Library.

Unfortunately, only 'Frontier in Space' was returned from this list, and the rest of the news story was incorrect.

Bryant continued the search for more colour Pertwee episodes abroad. His enquiries took him back in the direction of Canada. In September 1983, Mary Paskewicz from Lionheart distributors in the US wrote to Bryant concerning the seven-part story 'Inferno'. Lionheart had recently been sent 525-line colour two-inch videotapes of all seven episodes of this story from BBC Toronto, which now allowed them to distribute the story in colour in the US.

Following this up, Bryant asked Paskewicz about obtaining copies of these tapes,

CHAPTER 10

but she suggested that he first contact BBC Toronto directly and seek to get either copies or the original tapes sent from them. Failing that, she'd be happy to help supply copies of the tapes that Lionheart had received. In October 1983, Bryant wrote to Paul Hodgson at BBC Toronto, and requested that the 525-line two-inch colour copies of all seven episodes of 'Inferno' that they were holding be sent back to the BBC in England. Within weeks of this, the Film and Videotape Library received the NTSC broadcast tapes, and made 625-line two-inch conversions. It was found that the NTSC copy of Episode Five was from an earlier edit than the one originally transmitted in the UK. It contained a scene – of the survivors of Project Inferno grouped around a radio listening to a newsreader, voiced a little too obviously by Jon Pertwee – that had been cut from the final version, and so was also missing from the 16mm black and white film print of the episode.

Doctor Who producer John Nathan-Turner was able to announce the return of 'Inferno' during an interview for the US science fiction magazine *Fantasy Empire* – however, he was misquoted! The magazine wrongly reported the return of colour copies of a seven-part *Patrick Troughton* story, leading to all sorts of false rumours of a colour copy of 'The Evil of the Daleks' being found!

1983 was the year of *Doctor Who*'s twentieth anniversary, and one of the ways the BBC marked the occasion was with a two-day convention at Longleat House, Wiltshire, over the Easter Bank Holiday weekend of Sunday 3 and Monday 4 April. Several old stories were scheduled to be shown in a 'theatre tent' at the event and, in order to save the BBC the cost of having to make new tapes for this purpose from their own archive, producer John Nathan-Turner asked Ian Levine if he would provide copies from his collection. The stories selected for screening were 'The Dalek Invasion of Earth', 'The Dominators', 'Terror of the Autons', 'Terror of the Zygons' and 'The Visitation'. Levine was able to supply the organisers with tapes of all these stories, but in the case of 'Terror of the Autons', he had colour copies of the episodes available, whereas the BBC held only black and white prints at the time.

In 1977, Levine had been in contact with an American fan, Tom Lundie, who had recorded a number of Pertwee stories off-air from his local Chicago television station, WTTW Channel 11. Lundie had colour copies of 'Doctor Who and the Silurians', 'Terror of the Autons', 'The Claws of Axos', 'Day of the Daleks' and 'The Sea Devils'. These recordings were made on domestic 525-line Betamax tapes, from which Levine had made his own colour 525-line Betamax copies. Lundie had also recorded about six minutes of material from the final episode of 'The Mind of Evil', which he passed onto Levine in the same manner. (Lundie would later make his footage from 'The Mind of Evil' available to another friend of his, Larry Charet, who would copy it to NTSC Betacam in 1996.)

WIPED!

On Levine's behalf, Lundie was able to contact a fellow US fan who had colour off-air domestic recordings of 'The Ambassadors of Death' and 'Inferno', made from broadcasts on station WNED Channel 17 in Buffalo. Again copies were made for Levine – although the recording of some episodes of 'The Ambassadors of Death' suffered from a persistent rainbow patterning fault. Later in 1978, Levine discovered that station KCET Channel 28 in Los Angeles was due to show 'The Dæmons' as a single two-hour compilation television movie, and so he arranged for a friend of his in LA to hire a Betamax video recorder for the weekend, and record the story for him on two one-hour tapes (the longest running time available for a blank Betamax tape at the time).

Levine had taken these NTSC Betamax recordings and transferred them all onto U-MATIC format tapes, again as 525-line recordings. Most U-MATIC machines could play back both PAL and NTSC tapes, so Levine was able to watch his recordings of these stories on his own machine, as long as it was hooked up to a multi-standard television monitor, which he also possessed.

Thanks to Levine, the few hundred fans lucky enough to squeeze into the video tent at the 1983 Longleat convention were able to watch 'Terror of the Autons' in colour for the first time since 1971.

Later the same year, the National Film Theatre in London hosted a retrospective run of old *Doctor Who* episodes, and elected to show 'The Dæmons'. Once again, Levine was able to provide them with a colour copy of the story for this purpose.

Copies of all of Levine's colour NTSC tapes were also placed in the BBC archive.

Ian Levine: I gave copies of them to Sue Malden; she had copies of them all. She bought me a set of blank tapes and I sat there with two U-MATIC machines making copies for the Library.

These domestic colour recordings were not up to broadcast standard, but at least were available to the BBC should there be any way of making use of them in the future.

By the end of 1983, the BBC's holdings for Jon Pertwee's *Doctor Who* adventures now looked like this:

CHAPTER 10

Story	Colour 625-line Two-inch Tape	Colour 525-line Two-inch Tape	Colour Converted 525-line to 625-line Two-inch tape	16mm Colour Film	16mm Black and White Film	Colour 525-line U-MATIC Tapes – Copies from Off-air
Spearhead from Space				1, 2, 3, 4		
Doctor Who and the Silurians					1, 2, 3, 4, 5, 6, 7	1, 2, 3, 4, 5, 6, 7
The Ambassadors of Death	1				1, 2, 3, 4, 5, 6, 7	1, 2, 3, 4, 5, 6, 7
Inferno		1, 2, 3, 4, 5, 6, 7	1, 2, 3, 4, 5, 6, 7		1, 2, 3, 4, 5, 6, 7	1, 2, 3, 4, 5, 6, 7
Terror of the Autons					1, 2, 3, 4	1, 2, 3, 4
The Mind of Evil					1, 2, 3, 4, 5, 6	
The Claws of Axos	1, 4	2, 3	2, 3		1, 2, 3, 4	1, 2, 3, 4
Colony in Space		1, 2, 3, 4, 5, 6	1, 2, 3, 4, 5, 6		1, 2, 3, 4, 5, 6	
The Dæmons	4				1, 2, 3, 4, 5	1, 2, 3, 4, 5
Day of the Daleks	1, 2, 3, 4					
The Curse of Peladon		1, 2, 4	1, 2, 3, 4		1, 2, 3, 4	
The Sea Devils	4, 5, 6	1, 2, 3	1, 2, 3		1, 2, 3, 4, 5, 6	1, 2, 3, 4, 5, 6
The Mutants	3, 4, 5, 6	1, 2	1, 2		1, 2, 3, 4, 5, 6	
The Time Monster		1, 2, 3, 4, 5, 6	1, 2, 3, 4, 5, 6		1, 2, 3, 4, 5, 6	
The Three Doctors	1, 2, 3, 4					

WIPED!

Carnival of Monsters	1, 2, 3, 4						
Frontier in Space	1, 2, 3, 4, 5, 6					1, 2, 3, 4, 5, 6	
Planet of the Daleks	1, 2, 4, 5, 6					1, 2, 3, 4, 5, 6	
The Green Death	1, 2, 3, 4, 5, 6						
The Time Warrior	1, 2, 3, 4						
Invasion of the Dinosaurs	2, 3, 4, 5, 6					1	
Death to the Daleks	2, 3, 4	1					
The Monster of Peladon	1, 2, 3, 4, 5, 6						
Planet of the Spiders	1, 2, 3, 4, 5, 6						

All 24 of Jon Pertwee's *Doctor Who* stories now existed in their entirety, 17 of them in a broadcast-standard colour format. Another 21 episodes were represented with an off-air colour domestic recording to show what they originally looked like, although the broadcast-standard copies were in black and white. Only eight episodes existed only in black and white, with no colour reference copy at all. Things were looking up.

THE FINAL JON PERTWEE RETURNS

The Film and Videotape Library were not averse to finding a home for duplicate material when it turned up. In May 1984, Basil Sands of the BBC Sydney office telexed Steve Bryant to tell him that TVNZ in New Zealand had just discovered that they held 16mm black and white film prints of the stories 'Spearhead from Space' and 'Doctor Who and the Silurians'. Did Windmill Road want the films returned? Bryant wasn't interested in 'Spearhead from Space', but did request that the seven films of 'Doctor Who and the Silurians' be sent back to London. Although the BBC already held all seven episodes as 16mm negatives, not every episode had a corresponding positive print, so a full set of prints was considered useful to have around. In September 1984, Bryant again contacted Sands, as he had heard a rumour that the ABC were about to show 'Doctor Who and the Silurians' and 'Terror of the Autons' in colour in a few weeks' time. This time, the rumour was unfounded.

Nearly a year later, in October 1985, Bryant contacted Sands once again, this time enquiring about the Pertwee story 'Death to the Daleks'. Bryant had heard that the

CHAPTER 10

whole story had recently been screened by ABC as a PAL 625-line recording, whereas the only copy of Part One that the Film and Videotape Library held at that point was a 525-line conversion returned from Canada in 1981. Sands replied at the end of October, confirming that ABC held Part One in 625-line PAL format, and arranged for a one-inch copy to be made and sent to London.

Upon the tape's arrival at Windmill Road, it was found that the episode was edited – the opening scene of the MSC astronaut being hit by a spear and falling into a lake had been removed from the ABC's copy by the Australian censors. Consequently, when the story was first released on VHS home video by BBC Enterprises in 1987, a PAL conversion of the complete 525-line copy of Part One was used, rather than the edited 625-line copy returned from the ABC.

In 1987, the BBC found it held Episode Six of 'The Time Monster' as a low band (i.e. black and white) 625-line two-inch recording. This was actually logged in the Windmill Road archive as a 'Television Sound Training' tape. According to the recording date on the spool, it had been made on 01/12/72. The tape contained other programmes as well as this *Doctor Who* episode, and the episode itself was edited into three discrete chunks. Although it was only in black and white, it was still 625-line, which meant it was of better resolution than the 525-line two-inch colour copy that had been returned from Canada.

We now jump forward to 1991, and David Stead re-enters the story. BBC Enterprises' offices at the huge Woodlands building in London had a number of loading bays at the back of the premises, and one day Stead noticed a pile of about 30 625-line two-inch videotapes stacked high on one of the bays – outside the building, and at the mercy of the elements.

Stead enquired about the tapes, and was informed they were a batch of old *Doctor Who* episodes recently returned to Enterprises from Dubai Radio & Colour Television. But no-one seemed to know what to do with them, so they had been left on the loading bay, presumably in the hope that they would eventually go away on their own!

Stead took it upon himself to look through the tapes. He discovered episodes of stories such as 'The Three Doctors', 'Planet of the Spiders', 'Genesis of the Daleks' and 'Pyramids of Mars', which all already existed in the archive. He also discovered tapes of the last three episodes of 'Planet of the Daleks', but annoyingly not the third episode, which the BBC held only as a 16mm black and white film print. But also in the batch was a two-inch tape of 'Death to the Daleks' Part One. Stead knew that the BBC's only complete copy of this episode was a 525-line conversion, so he grabbed the tape.

Stead realised that no-one at Enterprises had checked with the Film and Videotape Library what to do with the returned material, which was the proper procedure. However, as he was only on attachment to Enterprises, he didn't want to create any fuss. By this

WIPED!

point, two-inch videotape had been long superseded as the BBC's transmission format, and there weren't that many working two-inch machines left in the Corporation. By finding the 625-line two-inch tape of 'Death to the Daleks' Part One, Stead had created a problem for himself – how to get the episode returned to the Film and Videotape Library without revealing the circumstances of how it had come back from Dubai?

Stead contacted Paul Vanezis (the fan who had originally located the episodes of 'The Reign of Terror' in Cyprus), who by now was working for the BBC at their Pebble Mill studios in Birmingham. Stead removed all the labels from the tape and its box, and then sent it to Vanezis later that same day. When the tape arrived at Pebble Mill, Vanezis was able to book some 'training time' on one of the two-inch machines, where he attempted to play the tape. He found that the tape would not play for more than a few seconds at a time without the heads of the two-inch machine jamming up with gunk and oxide from the tape itself – similar to the problems displayed with the 525-line tape of 'The Curse of Peladon' a decade earlier. Vanezis managed to get a playback of the entire first scene, which was missing from the PAL copy of Part One that had been returned from the ABC. But he didn't have the time to go through the whole tape bit by bit, which he knew was the only way of salvaging the entire programme, so contacted a friend of his at an outside facilities house, who also had access to a two-inch machine. As his friend was something of a *Doctor Who* fan as well, Vanezis made up a story that he had been loaned the two-inch copy of the episode by a member of an amateur television society. This friend eventually took the two-inch tape to another colleague at Television Centre in London, who spent many hours getting partial replays from it, until all the scenes had been copied on to D3 videotape. The episode was then re-assembled from all these small segments, and a full D3 tape of 'Death to the Daleks' Part One was then sent to the Film and Videotape Library. The original two-inch tape that had come back from Dubai was then given to this writer[63].

The tally of Pertwee episodes and the various formats they are held on at the Film and Videotape Library in 1991 stood as follows:

---

63 It now serves as an unusual doorstop in my study!

CHAPTER 10

Story	Colour 625-line Two-inch Tape / D3 Dub	Black & White 625-line Two-inch Tape / D3 Dub	Colour 525-line Two-inch Tape	Colour Converted 525-line to 625-line Two-inch Tape	16mm Colour Film	16mm Black and White Film	Colour 525-line U-MATIC Tape
Spearhead from Space					1, 2, 3, 4		
Doctor Who and the Silurians						1, 2, 3, 4, 5, 6, 7	1, 2, 3, 4, 5, 6, 7
The Ambassadors of Death	1					1, 2, 3, 4, 5, 6, 7	1, 2, 3, 4, 5, 6, 7
Inferno			1, 2, 3, 4, 5, 6, 7	1, 2, 3, 4, 5, 6, 7		1, 2, 3, 4, 5, 6, 7	1, 2, 3, 4, 5, 6, 7
Terror of the Autons						1, 2, 3, 4	1, 2, 3, 4
The Mind of Evil						1, 2, 3, 4, 5, 6	
The Claws of Axos	1, 4		2, 3	2, 3		1, 2, 3, 4	1, 2, 3, 4
Colony in Space			1, 2, 3, 4, 5, 6	1, 2, 3, 4, 5, 6		1, 2, 3, 4, 5, 6	
The Dæmons	4					1, 2, 3, 4, 5	1, 2, 3, 4, 5
Day of the Daleks	1, 2, 3, 4						
The Curse of Peladon			1, 2, 4	1, 2, 3, 4		1, 2, 3, 4	
The Sea Devils	4, 5, 6		1, 2, 3	1, 2, 3		1, 2, 3, 4, 5, 6	1, 2, 3, 4, 5, 6

WIPED!

Story								
The Mutants	3, 4, 5, 6		1, 2	1, 2		1, 2, 3, 4, 5, 6		
The Time Monster		6	1, 2, 3, 4, 5, 6	1, 2, 3, 4, 5, 6		1, 2, 3, 4, 5, 6		
The Three Doctors	1, 2, 3, 4							
Carnival of Monsters	1, 2, 3, 4							
Frontier in Space	1, 2, 3, 4, 5. 6					1, 2, 3, 4, 5, 6		
Planet of the Daleks	1, 2, 4, 5, 6					1, 2, 3, 4, 5, 6		
The Green Death	1, 2, 3, 4, 5, 6							
The Time Warrior	1, 2, 3, 4							
Invasion of the Dinosaurs	2, 3, 4, 5, 6						1	
Death to the Daleks	1, 2, 3, 4		1					
The Monster of Peladon	1, 2, 3, 4, 5, 6							
Planet of the Spiders	1, 2, 3, 4, 5, 6							

AND FINALLY ...

A few more third Doctor-related goodies would turn up over the years. The BBC kept two 90-minute studio recordings from Pertwee's time in the series, on two-inch 625-line colour videotapes. The first was from 'The Claws of Axos', and was of the recording done in Studio TC3 between 8.30 pm and 10.00 pm on Friday 22 January 1971 (when the story was still being called 'The Vampire from Space'). The tape reference was VTC/6HT/63227/8. The second was from 'Death to the Daleks', and was the recording done in Studio TC3 between 10.30 am and midday on Tuesday 10 December 1973. This was on tape VTC/6HT/89269/A. A third Pertwee studio tape – for 'The Time Monster' – survived at the Film and Videotape Library for over ten years, but was wiped in 1985.

The original 35mm films of the opening and closing titles for all the Jon Pertwee episodes also survived, along with 16mm copies. A 16mm film copy of an unused

CHAPTER 10

version of the 'Spearhead from Space' title sequence was located in a private collection in the mid-1990s, along with the 16mm black and white film of all the build-up material for the sequence. These were subsequently loaned back to the BBC for archive copies to be made. The opening titles of 'Inferno', which saw the story and writer captions played over stock footage of lava and volcanic eruptions, also survived on 16mm colour film, as did the unique opening title sequences for 'The Ambassadors of Death' and 'The Claws of Axos'.

In addition, the BBC retained a copy of the 16mm location film sequences for 'Invasion of the Dinosaurs' Part One. However, this was only a black and white cutting copy print (i.e. a print assembled by the film editor which then is used by the negative cutter when assembling the master negative). It contains an early scene cut from the transmitted episode, of a looter being attacked by an unseen *something*. The 16mm colour A and B roll film sequences for Part Five of this story also reside in a private collection, although the BBC has subsequently taken copies.

In addition to the previously-mentioned pre-transmission versions of 'Inferno' Episode Five and 'Frontier in Space' Episode Five, the BBC retained a small number of other early edits of third Doctor episodes. These were 'Carnival of Monsters' Episode Two, 'The Green Death' Episode Five and 'Invasion of the Dinosaurs' Part Three, all held on 625-line two-inch colour videotape. The 105-minute repeat omnibus version of 'Planet of the Spiders' shown on BBC1 on the afternoon of Friday 27 December 1974 was also kept, and would later prove useful, as the BBC's master videotape copy of Part One of this story has a nasty scratch running throughout it. The scratch is also visible in the scenes from this episode in the repeat compilation (indicating that the damage must have occurred as long ago as in 1974), but is significantly less pronounced (meaning that it has been made worse over the years by the repeated playing of the tape). An edited version of Episode Four of 'Carnival of Monsters' from the 1981 *The Five Faces of Doctor Who* repeat season (cut at the request of producer Barry Letts, who was unhappy that the character Pletrac's false bald head looked a little too fake in a sequence toward the end) was retained on two-inch tape, as were the 50-minute compilations of 'The Curse of Peladon' from the *Doctor Who and the Monsters* repeat season of 1982.

A 1972 BBC documentary series called *Looking In* featured material shot behind the scenes during the making of 'Carnival of Monsters'. This was on 16mm colour film, and captured some of the events on the studio floor and in the gallery during the recording of the final battle scenes from Episode Four. This programme still exists in the Film and Videotape Library on 16mm colour film.

Private collectors have come forward over the years with a number of film sequences from the third Doctor's era, which have usually been made available for the BBC to take copies from. These include some mute 16mm colour location and model film from

WIPED!

'Colony in Space', 16mm colour film from 'The Curse of Peladon' of the fight scenes shot at Ealing, and some mute 16mm colour film of test sequences featuring the Drashig puppets from 'Carnival of Monsters'. Finally, the sound rushes for the film sequences for 'The Monster of Peladon' turned up on audio tape in private hands, although the actual films were junked by the BBC shortly after the story was screened in 1974.

In 1993, the BBC began transferring all of its two-inch tapes (which at the time numbered around 69,000) onto the digital D3 tape format for archival storage. Understandably, this took a number of years to complete, but once it was finished, all of the BBC's 625-line two-inch *Doctor Who* tapes (which included all the Jon Pertwee episodes extant in that format, plus all the Tom Baker and Peter Davison stories up to 'The Five Doctors') had been transferred to D3. These D3 tapes then became the BBC's master archive copies. To be strictly accurate, two D3 copies were made of each two-inch tape: one to be archived, one to be used as a viewing copy. The original two-inch tapes were then given to the National Film Archive, who placed them in storage, should the BBC ever need to access them again (which does happen from time to time). In 2007, the BBC decided to transfer all of its D3 tapes onto Digital Betacam, as well as making an MXF file[64] of the transfer. This project is still ongoing at the time of writing, but once it has been finished, MXF files will be the format on which the archive masters of these episodes are officially held.

---

64 Material Exchange Format (MXF) is a file format for the exchange of programme material between servers, tape streamers and digital archives. Its contents may be a complete programme as well as complete packages or sequences. MXF is self-contained, holding complete content without need of external material.

CHAPTER 11
RECOLOURISATION, REVERSE-STANDARDS AND CHROMA DOTS!

Since the recovery of a complete PAL copy of 'Death to the Daleks' Part One in 1991, the BBC's archive of Jon Pertwee episodes has remained the same to this day, with nothing further added. However, that's not to say that these copies of the third Doctor's episodes are still the best that there are. Beginning in 1992, the work of the *Doctor Who* Restoration Team has revolved around using these various disparate sources of archived material to present the stories in increasingly better quality for commercial release on VHS and latterly DVD and Blu-ray.

THE DOCTOR WHO RESTORATION TEAM

The Restoration Team was and is a loose collection of people interested in the preservation and restoration of old episodes of *Doctor Who*. It began life in 1992, when Ralph Montagu, who then worked in the BBC's Graphics department, and James Russell, from Rank Cintel, one of the leading manufacturers of film equipment, got together with Ian Levine to use his NTSC colour domestic recordings of Jon Pertwee stories to recolourise the BBC's 16mm black and white film prints. They were soon joined by Steve Roberts, who worked as a broadcast engineer at Television Centre. This team oversaw the colour Pertwee recolourisations in the early 1990s (see below for details). Paul Vanezis joined the team just after the recolourisations were completed, and would go on to produce the Special Edition of 'The Five Doctors' released on VHS in 1995.

Russell dropped out of the team's projects once the recolourisations had been completed, and Montagu took more of a back seat, while Roberts and Vanezis began looking at other potential projects. In 1997, the team was joined by Richard Molesworth (freelance researcher, and author of this very tome) and Mark Ayres (sound engineer and composer for 'The Greatest Show in the Galaxy', 'The Curse of Fenric' and 'Ghost Light') for a 1997 project to restore 'The War Machines' for VHS release. This utilised off-air audio recordings, the various 16mm prints that were held by the BBC, clips from *Blue Peter*, and the Australian censor clips (see Chapter 12) to rebuild the four episodes as far as was possible.

The team then oversaw the creation of the extended version of 'Battlefield' that was released on VHS in 1997. In 1998, quality issues with some of the BBC's other *Doctor Who* VHS releases led to the Restoration Team being put in charge of the

WIPED!

remastering of all future entries in the range. The team were responsible for the VHS box set of 'The Ice Warriors', which included a cut down photographic reconstruction of the still-missing Episodes Two and Three, a CD of the audios of Episodes Two and Three, and a documentary (produced by Roberts and directed by Vanezis) about the missing episodes, called *Doctor Who: The Missing Years*.

In 1999, the team were asked to oversee a planned BBC run of *Doctor Who* repeats, which began in the autumn of that year. Peter Finklestone joined the team in 2001, and developed a process called VidFIRE (Video Field Interpolation Restoration Effect), which restored a video 'look' to those *Doctor Who* episodes that survived as black and white film prints.

As well as supervising the BBC's *Doctor Who* VHS releases, the Restoration Team were asked to perform the same role on the DVD release of 'The Five Doctors – The Special Edition' in 1999, and then to look after the full classic *Doctor Who* DVD range, which launched in 2000. The team were responsible for remastering, scheduling and deciding the content of every classic *Doctor Who* DVD release until 2007. Since that point, they have been responsible for only the remastering of subsequent releases, with decisions on scheduling and content being made in-house at 2|entertain.

RECOLOURISATION

In 1992, the *Doctor Who* Restoration Team had a notion to try to restore colour to a number of Jon Pertwee episodes of which the only remaining broadcast-quality copies were 16mm black and white film prints. These colour-restored versions would then be available for either television broadcast or release on home video. The idea involved overlaying the colour part of the picture from the low-resolution 525-line domestic videotape copies of the episodes donated by Ian Levine in the mid-eighties onto the black and white pictures from the high-resolution film recordings. The episodes that were candidates for such a procedure were 'Doctor Who and the Silurians' Episodes One to Seven, 'The Ambassadors of Death' Episodes Two to Seven, 'Terror of the Autons' Episodes One to Four, and 'The Dæmons' Episodes One to Three, and Episode Five.

An early experiment in this process had taken place in 1986, when two BBC employees, Keith Hunter and Simon Anthony, had tried initiating a similar approach with 'Terror of the Autons', but had been unable to get funding to proceed with the project. The fledgling *Doctor Who* Restoration Team had better luck.

The new initiative was begun in 1992 by Ralph Montagu and James Russell. They were working with (what was for the BBC at that time) a new format of videotape called Betacam, one of the first broadcast-standard component videotape formats. A component video signal is one that is split into different parts, or components (as

CHAPTER 11

opposed to a composite signal, which has all the elements mixed together). Typically in component video, the signal is split into two parts; the luminance (basically the black and white part of the picture, which contains all the detail, plus the brightness of the picture) and the chroma (the colour information). When the off-air colour video recordings were copied onto Betacam, it was relatively easy to then split the chroma information away from poor-resolution luminance, and instead marry it with the high-resolution luminance from a Betacam copy of the 16mm black and white film recording of the same episode.

Of course, the chroma information didn't exactly match up with the luminance information. Some of the domestic recordings were from compilation repeats, which edited out material from the reprise at the start of each episode, and sometimes from the beginnings and ends of other scenes. Some (such as 'The Dæmons') were also missing portions of action because of simple things like tape-changes. But with a lot of tweaking and patience in an edit suite, the recordings could be made to marry up with one another.

The first episode to be tackled in this project was 'The Dæmons' Episode One. Montagu initially secured an agreement to access the 16mm black and white film print of the episode from the BBC Film and Videotape Library. He then approached the producer of *The Late Show*, a BBC2 arts strand that had recently overseen the production of a new documentary about *Doctor Who* ('Resistance is Useless') and a series of archive repeats. The producer, John Whiston, agreed to fund the trial recolourisation of the single episode.

Montagu and Russell borrowed Levine's original off-air Betamax recording of 'The Dæmons' from KCET's 1978 screening, and within a few days were able to show Whiston a near-fully colourised copy of the story's opening episode. Both Whiston and Archive Selector Adam Lee were impressed with the results, and between them, quickly came up with the funds for the recolourisation of Episodes Two, Three and Five of the story. (Episode Four didn't need doing, as it still survived in colour on its original two-inch transmission tape.) It was at this point that BBC engineer Steve Roberts independently asked Lee for permission to access the film prints of 'The Dæmons' to try some colourisation experiments of his own, and Lee referred him to Montagu. Montagu showed Roberts the initial results of his test, and Roberts was able to offer some suggestions on how to improve the process. And so the Restoration Team was born.

One of the main problems with marrying up the chroma and luminance components was the difference in size and shape of the two picture elements. The 16mm film recordings were slightly zoomed in – a common practice on all film recordings, not just limited to the Jon Pertwee stories, or to *Doctor Who* for that matter. This was done to ensure that the edges of the screen were never captured during the film recording process. And as each episode had been recorded on a different day, each one was zoomed in by a slightly different degree than the others.

To get around this problem, a handy piece of equipment was utilised. A Questech Charisma video effects processor was often used at the time on BBC programmes such as *Top of the Pops* and *The Clothes Show*, to manipulate pictures and fly them around the screen. This technique was adapted for the restoration work to resize and manipulate the chroma part of the picture so that it became a better match to the luminance signal (the only downside being that the outer edges of the picture were now lost altogether). Two in-synch Betacam SP machines were used to play the two different recordings, with the chroma signal fed through the Charisma machine, and the combined output was then recorded onto D3 to make the transmission master.

Recording would continue until one Betacam SP player went out of synch with the other – which would inevitably happen from time to time. The two players would then be stopped and re-synched, and the process restarted.

A second off-air colour NTSC copy of 'The Dæmons' (this time on VHS) was loaned to the team by Keith Hunter (one of the people who initially tried to get material recolourised in 1986). This was of a slightly poorer quality, but contained one section that Levine's omitted in the middle of Episode Three (due to the tapes being swapped over in the VCR at the time of the recording). This second off-air recording was good enough to be able to be used as the chroma source for this segment. (The exact US broadcast that this second recording was taken from isn't known.)

Finally, new opening and closing credits were made for the four recolourised episodes, using the original clean background 16mm colour films of the sequences (which were still retained by the Film and Videotape Library), married with the original captions, which were keyed from the 16mm black and white film recordings and then tinted to match the off-air colour.

The new, recolourised version of 'The Dæmons' was judged to be a complete success, so much so that it was given a screening on BBC2 between November and December 1992. It was released on VHS home video shortly after by BBC Video.

Montagu then successfully lobbied to be allowed to try to recolourise the three other *Doctor Who* stories that were candidates for this work – 'Doctor Who and the Silurians', 'The Ambassadors of Death' and 'Terror of the Autons'. This time, funding was split between three areas – the BBC Film and Videotape Library, BBC Home Video, and BBC Enterprises Programme Sales. Betacam copies of all the black and

CHAPTER 11

white episodes of these stories were made by Windmill Road for the team to begin work with, although this time new prints were made directly from the archived 16mm negatives (unlike with 'The Dæmons', which utilised copies from existing prints). Again, Levine supplied his colour domestic recordings for the team to use as the chroma picture source.

The first of these stories to be recolourised was 'Terror of the Autons', in September 1992. By this time, the Restoration Team had been joined by Paul Vanezis, based at BBC Pebble Mill. Vanezis had obtained his own off-air NTSC colour copy of 'Terror of the Autons' on U-MATIC some years previously, which had been originally recorded from WTTW Channel 11 in Chicago in 1977. He had then carried out a test recolourisation of Episode One on his own.

The Restoration Team approached the recolourisation of 'Terror of the Autons' using the same practices and procedures as they had utilised for 'The Dæmons'. Levine's domestic recordings of the story were episodic, which meant that this time there were no problems at the beginnings and ends of the episodes due to material being edited out. The only significant difficulty came in Episode Three, during the scene of the Doctor 'dissecting' the plastic troll doll. The 16mm black and white film recording suffered from a significant off-lock[65] in the picture. This resulted in a loss of picture for about 11 frames, lasting about half a second on screen. Various attempts to patch the gap, first with material from the domestic recordings and then with 'artificial' frames generated by applying the BBC's Gazelle image smoothing system, failed to achieve a convincing result. In the end, the picture from one of the domestic recordings was used, but put through an 'aperture corrector' to give a false impression of high resolution. There was still a drop in quality but, as this section lasted only about half a second, it was not too noticeable.

Early in October 1992, work began on getting 'Doctor Who and the Silurians' recolourised. The domestic colour recordings of this story suffered from the same intermittent rainbow patterning that plagued those of 'The Ambassadors of Death', but this was fortunately less noticeable and less frequent for this story. As with 'The Dæmons', the domestic recordings were all from compilation screenings, and so had small sections of action missing at the beginnings and ends of the episodes. One large section of action, bridging the end of Episode Five and the beginning of Episode Six and lasting for about 90 seconds, was missing from all the domestic colour recordings of the story to which the Restoration Team had access. A US company called American Film

---

65 Off-locks are usually the result of a bad physical splice in a videotape, which causes the machine replaying the tape to lose the sync-pulse needed to keep the picture stable. The upshot is that the picture rolls, or exhibits some other form of instability, for a few seconds, before restabilising.

WIPED!

Technologies Inc was found that specialised in recolourising black and white footage from scratch (i.e. without having a colour version as reference), and the 90-second section was sent to them. After they had rebuilt the colour on this segment – which they did for free, on a demonstration basis – the whole story was able to be completed. Both 'Terror of the Autons' and 'Doctor Who and the Silurians' were released in colour on VHS by BBC Video in 1993.

The colourisation of 'The Ambassadors of Death' was not so successful. Because of the locked-in rainbow pattern interference in the colour copy, only Episodes Five and Six could be fully recolourised. A one-minute section from the beginning of Episode Three was sent to American Film Technologies Inc, who successfully recolourised it as an experiment, but the cost of getting them to do the rest of the story was far more than the budget would allow, and so this was left partially unfinished.

In early 1994, Montagu used some of the budget originally allocated to the recolourisation of 'The Ambassadors of Death' to instead get new, higher-quality telecine transfers made of several 16mm black and white films of *Doctor Who* that had been found by private collectors over the years. These were the prints of 'The Moonbase' Episode Four, 'The Abominable Snowmen' Episode Two and 'Invasion of the Dinosaurs' Part One located by Roger Stevens in 1981; 'The Time Meddler' Episodes One and Three found by Ian Sheward; 'The Reign of Terror' Episodes Three and Six from Bruce Campbell; 'The Wheel in Space' Episode Three from David Stead; and 'The Faceless Ones' Episode Three and 'The Evil of the Daleks' Episode Two from Gordon Hendry.

The Restoration Team's recolourisation efforts didn't stop with the partial failure of 'The Ambassadors of Death'. In 1993, Vanezis used the same principle in another way. He had Betacam copies made of both the 625-line two-inch black and white tape of 'The Time Monster' Episode Six, and the 525-line colour two-inch tape of the same episode. He then edited the three sections of the black and white version seamlessly back together, and made an experimental recolourised Betacam copy using the luminance from that 625-line tape and the chroma from the 525-line colour conversion. The results were exceptional, although unfortunately one of the control cards was missing on the two-inch machine that he used to take a copy of the 625-line tape, making the picture rather smeary. He sent a copy of the recolourised episode to Windmill Road, but ensured it was archived as a non-transmission tape. He was therefore rather surprised to see it used for a repeat on UK Gold when they screened the series in the early 1990s! When the story was due to be released on VHS in 2001, Vanezis supervised a new transfer of the two-inch 625-line black and white tape, and redid his initial combination with the NTSC colour signal to make

CHAPTER 11

an episode that was of broadcast standard, and barely distinguishable from the lost original transmission tape.

In late 1999, BBC2 began screening a series of *Doctor Who* repeats, starting with 'Spearhead from Space' and originally intended to continue through all the surviving Jon Pertwee adventures, bar 'The Ambassadors of Death' and 'The Mind of Evil'. This gave Montagu the opportunity to revisit the restored versions of both 'Doctor Who and the Silurians' and 'Terror of the Autons' from 1992. He was able to reuse the pre-graded restoration master tapes of those two stories and enhance the general colour grading and apply better dirt reduction techniques to them.

As things transpired, after 'Doctor Who and the Silurians', the BBC2 repeats jumped on to Tom Baker's Doctor, starting with 'Genesis of the Daleks'. This decision was taken just the day after work had been finished on the new transmission tapes of 'Terror of the Autons', which have not been seen to date. Because of this change of plan, it wasn't possible to revisit the restoration of 'The Dæmons' at the time. Nor was it possible for Episode Three of 'Planet of the Daleks' to be fully recolourised by American Film Technologies Inc, as had been intended when that came up for transmission – although, given that BBC2 was screening an episode a week, this would have been about two years away.

'Doctor Who and the Silurians' was remastered by the Restoration Team a third time, for its release on DVD by 2|entertain in early 2008. First, digital copies were made of the 16mm negatives of all seven episodes, giving the best possible picture quality for this element of the new version. The Betacam copies of Levine's off-air NTSC recordings that had been made in 1992 for the original restoration were again used as the prime colour source (as it was felt that getting a better replay from the original off-air tapes nearly 15 years down the line was very unlikely).

The main difference for this restoration was the use of the VidFIRE process developed by freelance video technician Peter Finklestone some years previously. Briefly, this was a software-based system that took the 25-frames-a-second pictures from 16mm black and white film, and interpolated a new frame to sit between each existing frame of picture. This recreated the 50-fields-a-second motion unique to 625-line two-inch videotape-originated material. This process was applied to all the videotape-originated scenes in the seven episodes of 'Doctor Who and the Silurians'. The material in the story that was originally shot on 16mm film (mainly the exterior sequences) was left unprocessed. The overall result was to make the story visually much closer to how it would have originally looked in 1970. Also unlike the previous restorations of this story, a set of off-air domestic audio recordings was used as the basis for the new soundtrack, and not the optical soundtrack from the 16mm film recordings. Whenever the stories 'Terror of the Autons' and 'The Dæmons' come up for

WIPED!

release on DVD, the same new restoration principles will almost certainly be applied to them as well. (The VidFIRE process has also been applied to the vast majority of the William Hartnell and Patrick Troughton episodes when they have been restored for DVD release over the years.)

As a postscript to this section, it's worth first briefly mentioning the BBC Video VHS release of 'The Ambassadors of Death' in 2002. For this version, the off-air 525-line Betamax tapes of the story were again borrowed from Levine, and Episodes Five and Six were transferred to Digital Betacam in their entirety. The sections of usable colour from Episodes Two, Three, Four and Seven were also copied, and these recordings were then graded using the surviving colour two-inch tape of the first episode as a comparison. Digital Betacam copies of the 16mm film negatives of Episodes Two to Seven were also made, and both sets of picture elements were then cleaned up.

The 16mm black and white film recordings of Episodes Two to Seven were treated with the VidFIRE process for the studio-originated scenes, which restored the original video look of the material, and the colour sections were then added in from the cleaned up colour Digital Betacam transfer of the off-air material. Episodes Five and Six were recolourised entirely, but only a few sections of Episodes Two, Three, Four and Seven were presented in colour. Nevertheless, the eventual VHS release featured over half of the story in colour.

REVERSE STANDARDS CONVERSION

A new process called Reverse Standards Conversion (RSC) was specially developed in 2004 with the NTSC episodes of *Doctor Who* in mind, and was subsequently applied to all the Jon Pertwee episodes the BBC held as 525-line two-inch colour videotapes. These tapes had been supplied to BBC Canada via Time-Life Television in the USA in the mid 1970s. Prior to going to Time-Life, they had all been recorded in-house at the BBC using a piece of equipment known as a standards converter to change them from the UK's PAL format to the USA's NTSC format.

PAL AND NTSC

PAL (which stands for Phase Alternating Line) was the colour format adopted by both the BBC and ITV in the UK in the mid-1960s. It was also picked up for use in a number of other countries, including Australia and New Zealand. The system is based on a television picture being made up of a succession of images, or frames, formed from 625 lines of information – although only 576 of these contain active picture information; the other 49 carry information for subtitles, synch data etc. The speed of transition from one frame to the next gives the illusion of movement to the naked

CHAPTER 11

eye. To assist this illusion, the frames are refreshed in an interlaced manner, at a rate of 50 half-frames – or fields – a second (as described in Chapter 5). This refresh rate is dictated by the AC mains frequency of the British national grid, which supplies power at a frequency of 50 Hz. A video signal that runs at 50 Hz is ideally suited to producing 50 fields a second, as this helps prevent powerline hum and magnetic interference from causing visible beat frequencies in the television picture.

The American format, developed in the 1950s and also used by a number of other countries including Canada, is NTSC (which stands for National Television System Committee – although some cynics have suggested Never Twice the Same Colour or Never True Skin Colours as more accurate descriptions!) Like PAL, this system utilises interlaced pictures. It is based around America's 60 Hz power system, and so has a refresh rate of 60 fields a second (or, to be absolutely precise, 59.94 fields a second – see Chapter 5 for an explanation). NTSC differs from PAL in another way as well – it uses only 525 lines of picture information. Of these, 486 contain active picture information, with 39 used for subtitles and technical data.

So, in the UK, we have television pictures that are 625 lines of vertical resolution, refreshing themselves at a rate of 25 frames/50 fields a second. In the USA, they have television pictures of 525 lines of vertical resolution, refreshing at just less than 30 frames/60 fields a second.

PAL TO NTSC AND NTSC TO PAL STANDARDS CONVERSIONS

The BBC designed a piece of equipment called the CO6/508 Advanced Field Store Converter to convert between the two television formats. This bit of kit came in two forms. The MK2A was set up for converting programmes made in NTSC into PAL, for screening on British television. The MK2B worked in reverse, taking programmes made in PAL and converting them into NTSC for sale to the USA and Canada.

Until the development of the RSC process, the only way to convert NTSC copies of PAL programmes back into PAL was with normal standards conversion equipment. Because this was designed primarily for programmes made in NTSC in the first place, it interpolated certain lines from the 525-line material to give a 625-line picture, and also dropped 10 fields a second to get a 50 fields-a-second refresh rate. For old episodes of *Doctor Who* recovered as NTSC tapes from Canada, this produced results that didn't look too good. It introduced a number of visible picture problems – usually referred to as 'artefacts' in technical circles. In particular, the pictures looked very 'soft' (i.e. on-screen objects with hard edges looked a bit on the fuzzy side), and movement appeared very juddery.

WIPED!

The key to the success of RSC is its ability to unpick the precise method that the BBC MK2B equipment used to convert the PAL pictures into NTSC in the first place. To turn a video signal of 50 fields a second into one of 60 fields a second required 10 new picture fields to be created. This wasn't achieved randomly, but by applying a strict sequence that regularly either repeated a field or created a 'false' one based on a mix of two adjacent fields.

During a meeting with members of the BBC Research Department in 1993, Steve Roberts and Ralph Montagu put forward the idea that it might be possible to analyse the MK2B converter's output and unpick it to get back to something approaching the original PAL input. Jim Easterbrook of the research and development team took up the challenge and decided to look at the NTSC conversions of old BBC programmes, including *Doctor Who*, in an attempt to try to understand the original conversion sequence used in the 1970s.

The first step towards RSC was to make digital copies of the two-inch 525-line Jon Pertwee episodes held by the Film and Videotape Library onto D1 videocassette. (D1 was an early uncompressed digital 3/4" videocassette component format developed by Sony.) The NTSC footage was examined, and the composition of the 60 Hz field structure was analysed. It was found to follow a standard sequential pattern. The first and second NTSC fields were also the first and second PAL fields. The third NTSC field was a mixture of the second and third PAL fields. The fourth NTSC field was a mixture of the third and fourth PAL fields. The fifth NTSC field was a mixture of the fourth and fifth PAL fields. The sixth NTSC field was the full fifth PAL field. The seventh NTSC field was the full sixth PAL field. This sequence then repeated for 1001 fields, at which point there was a jump and it would start again. This 1001-field sequence was a direct consequence of the NTSC field frequency being 59.94 Hz rather than exactly 60 Hz. By locating the start of the 1001 field sequence, it was possible to automatically unpick the entire programme, allowing recreation of the original 50-field sequence from the 60-field conversions.

What couldn't be restored to these RSC pictures was the 625-line structure of the original recordings. The 1970s PAL to NTSC conversions had simply ditched 100 lines of original picture information, and there was no way to recreate this. Although the finished RSC tapes are in the 625-line format, the pictures are still made up of 525 upscaled lines.

Funding for the development of RSC was withdrawn by the BBC in 1994, but the principle had been proven. A few years later, a young BBC Research Department engineer named James Insell re-examined Jim Easterbrook's notes on the subject and decided to work on the project in his spare time. Collaborating with Ralph Montagu of the Restoration Team, he finally managed to get the process into a workable state.

CHAPTER 11

Some small funding was then given by BBC Worldwide, and Easterbrook returned to the project to oversee the development of the computer software being written to apply his algorithm of the original conversion into something that could be used practically.

The computer system that applies the RSC process to the 525-line footage takes about five hours to process a 25-minute episode of *Doctor Who*. The episodes to be converted were 'Inferno' Episodes One to Seven, 'The Claws of Axos' Episodes Two and Three, 'Colony in Space' Episodes One to Six, 'The Curse of Peladon' Episodes One to Four (the original two-inch tape of Episode Three was borrowed from Ian Levine for this purpose, and successfully replayed), 'The Sea Devils' Episodes One to Three, and 'The Time Monster' Episodes One to Five.

When 'The Claws of Axos' was released on DVD in 2005, it was the first RSC'd material to be commercially released by the BBC. There was a 90-minute 625-line two-inch studio tape also existing from this story, covering some of the material shot for Episodes One and Two. This was used as the source of certain scenes from Episode Two, which were dropped into this version of the episode in place of the equivalent RSC'd material.

The RSC process has since been applied to all of the Film and Videotape Library's holdings of other BBC shows of which the only copies are ones recovered from overseas on NTSC standards converted tapes.

However, the development of chroma dot colour recovery (see below), alongside improvements in the VidFIRE process, have since superseded RSC for improvements to some of the black and white Jon Pertwee episodes.

CHROMA DOT COLOUR RECOVERY

Just when there seemed to be nothing further that could be done to enhance the Jon Pertwee holdings of the BBC Film and Videotape Library, along came one further process.

In 2008, 2|entertain planned that the eventual release of 'Planet of the Daleks' on DVD should herald the long-awaited colourisation of Episode Three of this story. But with no off-air colour source to use as a basis for this, the colours would need to be created from scratch. American Film Technologies Inc had previously been sounded out about recolourising whole episodes from scratch back in the early 1990s, but the costs had proven too high. In 2008, American Film Technologies Inc no longer existed, but many of its key people were now working in a new company, Legend Films, based in California. The favourable currency exchange rate between British pounds and American dollars at that time meant that 2|entertain could afford to meet the (still quite high) cost of commissioning Legend Films to recolourise just the one

WIPED!

black and white episode of 'Planet of the Daleks'.

A Digital Betacam video transfer of the 16mm black and white film negative of the episode was made by the Film and Videotape Library and supplied to Legend Films for this purpose, along with colour copies of the other five episodes for them to use as a colour palette reference (so that things like the Spiridon jungle, the Daleks' casings, and the Doctor's jacket could be coloured in a manner that was consistent throughout the story). Legend Films worked on this footage for many months, before sending the fully re-colourised episode back to the BBC for grading.

At the same time, James Insell was about to put a long-held theory of his into practice. In the 1990s, Insell had watched old episodes of *Doctor Who* being repeated on UK Gold. For some of the Pertwee stories, UK Gold screened 16mm black and white film recordings, and Insell noticed that on his television set, small patches of colour would occasionally break through on the picture, for just a few seconds at a time. He speculated that colour information was somehow stored on the 16mm black and white film prints of episodes originally made in colour. But how was the colour information stored on black and white film?

Insell deduced that the film must have some sort of colour subcarrier signal captured on it. This was indeed the case, as a close examination of the prints of Episodes Two to Seven of 'The Ambassadors of Death', during remastering for its 2003 VHS release, revealed to him. When the episodes were transferred to composite videotape (in this case Digital Betacam) and viewed on a colour monitor, the pictures had green and magenta patches that flashed up occasionally. Looking at the film closely, Insell could see a pattern of very small dots – often referred to as chroma dots – burnt into every frame of the telerecording.

Most of the Pertwee 16mm black and white film prints were made at the time of each episode's transmission on BBC1, and the telerecording equipment that was used had been designed with a filter that *should* have been applied when making a recording from a colour source. This would have prevented the chroma dots from appearing in the captured film image. However, in most cases, this was not in fact done.

Insell was sure that there must be a way of obtaining the correct colour information for a programme from the chroma dots captured on the black and white film prints. He was unable to interest any of his Research Department colleagues in helping him with this, so instead set up an external internet-based working group to look at the problem. This Colour Recovery Working Group had some early partial successes. One member, Andrew Browne, developed a technique through which some colour elements of a picture could be recovered, and the resultant publicity attracted the attention of Andrew Steer, who joined the group and developed his own method,

CHAPTER 11

with markedly better results. However, even the best results were still a long way from resolving the full palette of colour information from the chroma dot patterns, with blues and purples proving difficult shades to retrieve.

Another member of the group was an ex-BBC Research Department employee, Richard Russell. He realised that there was a way to recover the full gamut of colour information. A computer programme was written that could apply his process to computer-captured footage, working at a rate of about 15 frames per minute (meaning it took about an hour to process 30 seconds of footage).

This method at last held out some prospect of recovering useable original colour information for the handful of Pertwee episodes that existed only in black and white. These were 'The Ambassadors of Death' Episodes Two to Four and Seven (for which, as discussed above, the colour signal from the domestic NTSC tapes suffers badly from interference), 'The Mind of Evil' Episodes One to Six, 'Planet of the Daleks' Episode Three and 'Invasion of the Dinosaurs' Part One. The 16mm black and white film prints of all these episodes were examined, in the hope they would all have chroma dots burnt into the pictures. They all did, apart from Episode One of 'The Mind of Evil'. The BBC engineer who made that particular telerecording in 1971 must have applied the correct filter, preventing the colour information from being captured.

The first successful implementation of Russell's colour recovery process was with some footage from *Top of the Pops*. Once the process had been successfully demonstrated, it was decided to apply it to a *Doctor Who* episode. This coincided with the colourisation of 'Planet of the Daleks' Episode Three by Legend Films, and so the process was attempted on the black and white film print of that episode.

The results were very good indeed, but not perfect. Variables such as the stability of the film as it went through the telecine equipment, the amount of spot-wobble applied, and the low saturation of particular colours in the original picture, all combined at times to limit the ability of the software to recover the correct colour information. But when the pictures obtained from this process were combined with those colourised from scratch by Legend Films, then an excellent, full colour version of the episode was the result. It still required a lot of manual tweaking to correct some errors, and to match the two colour sources together, but once coupled with the VidFIRE process, the end result was an episode that looked almost as good as the original two-inch 625-line transmission tape must once have done.

What the 'Planet of the Daleks' experiment demonstrated was that the best results were achieved by combining material hand-coloured by Legend Films with material retrieved using the chroma dot process. However, the costs of putting more episodes out to Legend Films are potentially extremely high – particularly as,

WIPED!

at the time of writing, the currency exchange rate has become much less favourable – and any further colourisations of these black and white Pertwee episodes might have to rely solely on information retrieved through the chroma dot process. Early experiments with Episodes Two to Six of 'The Mind of Evil' demonstrated that there was an enormous amount of work that needed to be done manually if the results were ever to be considered good enough for commercial release. For example, the film print of Episode Two produced quite a good colour palette albeit with oversaturated reds, whilst Episode Three didn't show any of these saturation problems, but had a noticeably worse colour palette. Further work has since been done manually to address these shortcomings, and the whole story is due to be released in colour on DVD in 2013, with the chroma dot recovery process forming the basis of the recolourisation of Episodes Two to Six. Episode One is being recoloured by hand.

'The Ambassadors of Death' was released on DVD in 2012, completely in colour. The black and white portions of the story that were left uncoloured after the VHS restoration were at last colourised using the chroma dot method.

For the opening monochrome episode of 'Invasion of the Dinosaurs', the chroma dot recovery process produced a result that was almost completely lacking in any blue in the final colour palette. As a result of this, the story's DVD release, also in 2012, saw the first episode being included in black and white as the default, but with an option to view the best colour version also. The results of the chroma dot method were enhanced by adding some of the blue colouring back into the pictures manually, with sympathetic grading then applied.

A refinement of the process was then used on the 16mm black and white Episodes Two and Three of 'The Claws of Axos', not to add colour but simply to remove the slight picture distortion that had been introduced when they were telerecorded. The film prints of the two episodes were scanned at HD quality, and VidFIRE was applied to the studio recorded scenes. Colour obtained from the NTSC recordings via the RSC process was then applied to the pictures, giving a far better overall result than the initial RSC'd video versions of the episodes. The remaining NTSC episodes of 'Inferno', 'Colony in Space', 'The Curse of Peladon', 'The Sea Devils', 'The Mutants' and 'The Time Monster' are all potential candidates for this treatment in the future.

THE THIRD DOCTOR—THE 'BEST' COPIES IN 2013

What exactly constitutes the 'best' copy of any of the Jon Pertwee episodes is perhaps a matter of opinion rather than of hard fact. For instance, as nice as the RSC'd episodes of 'Inferno' are, would better results have been forthcoming if the converted NTSC colour from the two-inch tapes had been overlaid onto a cleaned up and VidFIREd set

CHAPTER 11

of black and white 16mm film prints taken from the archived negatives?[66] Would the chromo dot colour recovery process as applied to 'Invasion of the Dinosaurs' Part One, variable as it is, be considered better than the monochrome version of the episode?

What is presented here is perhaps best described as a 'probable' list of the best copies of each of the third Doctor's episodes and stories. The criteria being: if any of them were to be dusted down and screened on BBC1, then which versions would be selected?

Story	*'Best' Copy*
Spearhead from Space	1, 2, 3, 4: 16mm colour film
Doctor Who and the Silurians	1, 2, 3, 4, 5, 6, 7: VidFIREd 16mm b&w film recolourised with domestic NTSC colour
The Ambassadors of Death	1: 2-inch colour PAL tape 2, 3, 4, 5, 6, 7: VidFIREd 16mm b&w film recolourised with domestic NTSC colour mixed with chroma dot colour recovery
Inferno	1, 2, 3, 4, 5, 6, 7: 2-inch colour NTSC -> PAL converted tape
Terror of the Autons	1, 2, 3, 4: VidFIREd 16mm b&w film recolourised with domestic NTSC colour
The Mind of Evil	1: VidFIREd 16mm b&w film with manually applied colour 2, 3, 4, 5, 6: VidFIREd 16mm b&w film recolourised by chroma dot colour recovery
The Claws of Axos	1, 4: 2-inch colour PAL tape 2, 3: VidFIREd 16mm b&w film recolourised with 2-inch NTSC->PAL converted colour
Colony in Space	1, 2, 3, 4, 5, 6: 2-inch colour NTSC -> PAL converted tape
The Dæmons	1, 2, 3, 5: VidFIREd 16mm b&w film recolourised with domestic NTSC colour 4: 2-inch colour PAL tape

---

[66] This latter process is to be used for a newly remastered Special Edition DVD of the story due for release in 2013, so fans will then have a chance to compare and contrast.

WIPED!

Day of the Daleks	1, 2, 3, 4: 2-inch colour PAL tape
The Curse of Peladon	1, 2, 3, 4: 2-inch colour NTSC -> PAL converted tape
The Sea Devils	1, 2, 3: 2-inch colour NTSC -> PAL converted tape 4, 5, 6: 2-inch colour PAL tape
The Mutants	1, 2: 2-inch colour NTSC -> PAL converted tape 3, 4, 5, 6: 2-inch colour PAL tape
The Time Monster	1, 2, 3, 4, 5: 2-inch colour NTSC -> PAL converted tape 6: 2-inch PAL b&w tape recolourised with 2-inch NTSC->PAL converted colour
The Three Doctors	1, 2, 3, 4: 2-inch colour PAL tape
Carnival of Monsters	1, 2, 3, 4: 2-inch colour PAL tape
Frontier in Space	1, 2, 3, 4, 5, 6: 2-inch colour PAL tape
Planet of the Daleks	1, 2, 4, 5, 6: 2-inch colour PAL tape 3: VidFIREd 16mm b&w film recolourised with chroma dot colour recovery plus manually applied colour
The Green Death	1, 2, 3, 4, 5, 6: 2-inch colour PAL tape
The Time Warrior	1, 2, 3, 4: 2-inch colour PAL tape
Invasion of the Dinosaurs	1: VidFIREd 16mm b&w film recolourised by chroma dot colour recovery 2, 3, 4, 5, 6: 2-inch colour PAL tape
Death to the Daleks	1, 2, 3, 4: 2-inch colour PAL tape
The Monster of Peladon	1, 2, 3, 4, 5, 6: 2-inch colour PAL tape
Planet of the Spiders	1, 2, 3, 4, 5, 6: 2-inch colour PAL tape

CHAPTER 12
RECOVERED FRAGMENTS—CLIPS AND AUDIOS

One of the more fascinating aspects of the whole missing episodes story is the sheer amount of material that still survives from the 106 lost episodes of *Doctor Who*. Over the years, an impressive archive of off-air photographs, audio recordings, and short clips have been unearthed, which help give us a flavour of what it is, exactly, that we are missing.

The stories of how this material was discovered, recorded or preserved are perhaps just as interesting as the material itself. This chapter will focus on those stories.

CLIPS AND OTHER VISUAL ODDITIES

The amount of clips and film footage that have surfaced over the years from the missing *Doctor Who* episodes is staggering. On odd occasions, these recoveries have proved to be almost as exciting as those of complete missing episodes. That so much footage has been located, and from such a wide variety of disparate sources, is something of a miracle in itself.

This section will attempt to recount these discoveries and recoveries in some sort of chronological order.

Episode	Clip Description / Duration
An Unearthly Child: Episode One ('An Unearthly Child')	Build-up material for title sequence Spool A (19 min 12 sec) Build-up material for title sequence Spool B (10 min 31 sec) Build-up material for title sequence Spool C (20 min 18 sec) Build-up material for title sequence Spool D (18 min 39 sec)
The Macra Terror: Episode One	Clean opening title sequence (0 min 39 sec) Unused Logo Caption (0 min 15 sec) Patrick Troughton's Face Caption (0 min 16 sec) Build-up material for title sequence (7 min 17 sec)

The BBC Film Library was always in possession of the filmed elements that Bernard Lodge created for *Doctor Who*'s first opening title sequence, which were shot in Studio TC5 at BBC Television Centre on Saturday 31 August 1963. All of the elements used to create the final sequence are present in this footage, apart from the initial 'rising finger of smoke', which was taken from another BBC programme, *Amahl and the Night Visitors*, broadcast on 24 December 1959. It was this earlier programme's use of the 'howlaround' technique, created by Ben Palmer, that actually inspired Lodge to adopt it for *Doctor Who*'s opening titles.[67] However, the BBC doesn't possess a clean print of the final, edited-together sequence. It exists only as part of the surviving 16mm black and white telerecordings of *Doctor Who* episodes from 'An Unearthly Child' through to 'The Moonbase'. Some of the build-up material was later used in episodes of 'The Daleks', seen on the screens of the Daleks' equipment in their city's control centre.

In 1967, Lodge was asked to create a new title sequence for *Doctor Who*, this time incorporating the face of the new Doctor, Patrick Troughton. He utilised the same 'howlaround' technique, incorporating a photo-caption of Troughton's face. This new sequence debuted with 'The Macra Terror', and continued in use until 'The War Games' in 1969.

All of the surviving sequences from these titles are on 35mm black and white film.

Episode	Clip Description / Duration
The Evil of the Daleks: Episode One	Kennedy is exterminated by a Dalek

This is mentioned only for completeness' sake. The clip of Kennedy being exterminated that was re-used at the end of 'The Wheel in Space' Episode Six (as the Doctor begins to tell Zoe about his last encounter with the Daleks) was taken from Episode One of 'The Evil of the Daleks'. It is just three frames longer than the clip of the same sequence that survives in the opening reprise of 'The Evil of the Daleks' Episode Two.

Episode	Clip Description / Duration
Fury from the Deep: Episode One	The TARDIS lands on the sea (0 min 19 sec)
The Wheel in Space: Episode One	The Wheel (0 min 04 sec)

As a budget-saving exercise, footage from three previous *Doctor Who* episodes was incorporated into Patrick Troughton's original swansong as the Doctor, 'The War Games' Episode Ten. In two cases, the footage is from episodes that are now lost[68]. First, a clip from the opening episode of 'Fury from the Deep', of the TARDIS coming

---

67 The 'howlaround' technique involves training a video camera on a screen showing its own output and capturing the resultant feedback patterns on film.

68 This episode also includes a clip from the extant opening episode of 'The Web of Fear', featuring the TARDIS, covered in web, hanging motionless in space.

CHAPTER 12

to land on the sea, was worked into the narrative, as the Doctor looks to evade capture by his people, the Time Lords. Secondly, a brief model shot of the Wheel from the opening episode of 'The Wheel in Space' was used to establish that Zoe had been returned to her correct point in time and space after the Doctor's trial. Both these clips survive in the 16mm film recording of 'The War Games' Episode Ten.

Episode	Clip Description / Duration
The Daleks Masterplan: Episode Three ('The Devil's Planet')	The Daleks in their control room (0 min 26 sec)
The Daleks Masterplan: Episode Four ('The Traitors')	Katarina's death (0 min 58 sec)
The Tenth Planet: Episode Four	The Doctor's first regeneration (0 min 27 sec)

The BBC's long-running children's programme *Blue Peter* ran a feature about *Doctor Who*'s tenth anniversary in the edition broadcast on 5 November 1973. This included clips from episodes that existed at the time at the BBC, but then subsequently went missing. Namely, Episodes Three and Four of 'The Daleks Masterplan', and Episode Four of 'The Tenth Planet'.

For this feature, the 16mm print of the 'The Daleks Masterplan' Episode Four was obtained from the BBC Film Library, while that of 'The Daleks Masterplan' Episode Three and 'The Tenth Planet' Episode Four both came from BBC Enterprises in Villiers House. These episodes were ordered by *Blue Peter*'s film editor, Justin Smith, who compiled the *Doctor Who* sequences to be used in the finished programme.

What happened to the films after this is something of a mystery. The Film Library chased Smith on a number of occasions for the return of the 'The Daleks Masterplan' Episode Four, to no avail. When Ian Levine visited the Film Library in 1977, he found that this was the only '60s *Doctor Who* episode that had an index card showing that it should exist, but was absent from the shelves. The information on the card showed that the episode had last left the Film Library in November 1973, and had not been returned by the *Blue Peter* team. It's been suggested that the same fate befell Enterprises' print of 'The Tenth Planet' Episode Four, but there's no evidence to back this up. Enterprises were still offering this story for sale in 1974, so if the print of 'The Tenth Planet' Episode Four loaned to *Blue Peter* was indeed lost at this time, it can't have been the only one that existed.

Years later, Smith was asked if he could recall what had happened to these episodes, but he had no memory of them – they were just two amongst the hundreds of films that regularly passed through the hands of the editors working in the BBC's East Tower cutting rooms. Although the clips were sourced from 16mm black and white film prints, this edition of *Blue Peter* was transmitted live, and was recorded on transmission on two-inch

WIPED!

625-line colour videotape, which survives to this day at the Film and Videotape Library.

Blue Peter recycled this feature again in 1978, with the presenters using largely the same script, with the same clips (sourced from the 1973 programme), for *Doctor Who*'s fifteenth anniversary. It was trotted out once again in 1980, this time to help introduce new Doctor Peter Davison.

Because this 1973 edition of *Blue Peter* was easy to pin down date-wise (and because the script and clips were reused in later years), the existence of the clips was always known about. Other later programmes and features would eventually use this episode of *Blue Peter* as their source material for them.

This 1973 edition of *Blue Peter* also featured a 26-second clip from 'The Daleks Masterplan' Episode Three ('Devil's Planet'), which featured the Daleks in their spaceship control room. This footage had newly-dubbed Dalek dialogue added to it, the origins of which remained a mystery for a long, long time. Nevertheless, for many years, this was the only source of this clip from a missing *Doctor Who* episode. (See below for details of the recovery of the longer sequence from which it was actually taken.)

This edition of *Blue Peter* also included a clip from 'An Unearthly Child' Episode Four that featured no dialogue, but had incidental music different from that in the transmitted episode. This was taken from an Arabic-dubbed print of the episode, which was held by BBC Enterprises at the time but now no longer survives at the BBC.

Episode	Clip Description / Duration
Galaxy 4: Episode One ('Four Hundred Dawns')	The Doctor argues with Maaga (0 min 30 sec)

This short clip was selected for inclusion in the 1977 documentary 'Whose Doctor Who'. It came from a 16mm film print of the episode that at the time was held by BBC Enterprises at Villiers House. The documentary's production team had a 16mm film copy made of a section of the episode lasting just under six minutes. The clip eventually chosen was from roughly half-way through this duplicate film, and was physically cut from it so that it could be spliced into the insert film used for 'Whose Doctor Who'. The two sections of film that came before and after the used clip were then meant to be junked, but at the last moment were instead given to the then-President of the Doctor Who Appreciation Society, Jan Vincent-Rudzki. The 30-second clip is preserved in the two-inch 625-line transmission videotape of 'Whose Doctor Who'.

Episode	Clip Description / Duration
The Evil of the Daleks: Episode Seven – Model Sequence	Two Daleks move through the wreckage in the Emperor's Chamber (0 min 03 sec)

CHAPTER 12

Michealjohn Harris was the BBC Visual Effects Department designer on this 1967 adventure. After his work on the story had been completed, he kept hold of a small reel of 35mm film of some of the model shots of the final battle scenes in the Emperor's chamber. This reel ended up in the drawer of his work desk, and occasionally he would tear off a strip of the film, a frame at a time, curl it up, and use it as an improvised toothpick. This continued for many years, with the film getting shorter week by week as frame after frame was ripped off and thrown away.

It was only the timely intervention of a couple of *Doctor Who* fans – who, when interviewing Harris in the mid-1970s, asked him if he'd kept any *Doctor Who* film – that stopped the film from being completely destroyed in the interests of his dental hygiene. The section that still survives lasts for approximately ten seconds, but is mostly made up of a shot of a pair of hands holding the Dalek models. This is followed by approximately three seconds of actual action. It is not known if this sequence was used in the transmitted episode or was just an outtake.

Episode	Clip Description / Duration
The Power of the Daleks: Episode Five	Daleks chanting 'Daleks conquer and destroy' (0 min 40 sec)

This clip is held by the BBC in two separate programmes in its archive.

The best version is to be found in the edition of *Whicker's World* shown on 27 January 1968. Entitled 'I Don't Like My Monsters To Have Oedipus Complexes', this featured an interview with Dalek creator Terry Nation conducted at his home. The clip from 'The Power of the Daleks' was used by way of illustration, and was transferred from the original 35mm film sequence, which still existed at the BBC in 1968.

Exactly the same sequence was used in the edition of *Blue Peter* screened on 27 November 1967, which launched a competition for its viewers to design a monster that could beat the Daleks. This time, the clip was sourced from a 16mm telerecording of the episode, and so wasn't as pristine as the *Whicker's World* version.

A third, shorter version of the same clip was later discovered in the *Perspectives:* 'C for Computer' film insert reel located in Australia in 1995 (of which, more below).

Episode	Clip Description / Duration
The Highlanders: Episode One – Film Trim	The TARDIS doors begin to open (10 seconds)

Fiona Cumming worked on this story as production assistant. As part of this job, she had to stand in front of the camera with the clapperboard at the beginning of each

WIPED!

take during location filming. This was the first time she had ever used a clapperboard; a fact she mentioned in passing to the film editor. A short time after the location work was concluded, the film editor sent her a small can of film marked 'Film for the Archive'. Inside was a short piece of film. This lasts for 10 seconds, and begins with Cumming in shot, beginning a take with a clapperboard, announcing it as 'Shot 80, take three'. The camera pans across to the TARDIS prop, the doors of which begin to open ... and then the film ends. So this is not strictly footage from a missing episode, but an off-cut from the location-shot film. The section *after* this, with the TARDIS doors actually opening, probably made it into the finished episode.

Cumming was amused by this gift, but left the film can behind in the office when she moved on to work on another programme. Two years later, she was sent the can, along with a very officious BBC memo telling her to keep better track of archive material.

Episode	Clip Description / Duration
The Daleks Masterplan: Episode Two ('Day of Armageddon') – Film Sequences	The Daleks light their pyroflames (0 min 38 sec)
	The Daleks begin to burn Kembel's jungle (0 min 47 sec)
	The Spar on its landing pad (0 min 12 sec)
	Smoke overlay (0 min 30 sec)

Until this episode's recovery in January 2004, all that existed from it was this spool of 35mm black and white film inserts, which had survived at the BBC Film Library since 1965. In fact, it came in two tins of film – one contained the mute 35mm pictures, and the second contained the corresponding soundtrack. Sometime during the late 1980s, the tin containing the pictures disappeared from the Windmill Road library. Attempts to locate it for the 1991 documentary *Resistance is Useless* proved unsuccessful – although this did lead to another find.

The missing film was eventually discovered in a private collection. The collector involved was quite horrified to discover that something he had purchased in good faith was essentially stolen property. He immediately handed it over to representatives of the *Doctor Who* Restoration Team, who were in turn able to hand it back to Adam Lee of the Film and Videotape Library at the 1993 Missing Believed Wiped conference at the National Film Theatre.

CHAPTER 12

Episode	Clip Description / Duration
The Daleks Masterplan: Episode One ('The Nightmare Begins') – Film Sequences	Kert Gantry is exterminated by a Dalek (0 min 54 sec)
	The TARDIS materialises (0 min 12 sec)
	The Spar lands on Kembel (0 min 28 sec)
	Dalek city lights (0 min 09 sec)

During the production of the 1991 BBC2 documentary *Resistance is Useless*, the production team ordered up the 35mm black and white film sequences that were known to exist for 'The Daleks Masterplan' Episode Two. The Film and Videotape Library duly delivered two tins of film; the first contained the soundtrack to the sequences, the second was mute 35mm film. It was only when both spools were loaded into a telecine machine that it became obvious that the pictures didn't match the soundtrack.

Luckily, on hand that day was Steve Roberts, who was advising the producers of the programme. He quickly realised that the pictures on the mute 35mm film were in fact from the first episode of 'The Daleks Masterplan'.

So what had gone on here, exactly?

Steve Roberts: Basically, the situation as I remember it is this. It turned out the Library held a mute 35mm print of the footage from Episode One, a mute 35mm negative also for the Episode One material, a mute 35mm print for the material for Episode Two and a 35mm magnetic soundtrack for the Episode Two footage. But all of this was logged as just Episode Two material. So the Library thought the negative was for Episode Two, and that they had two prints of it. At some point, someone had removed what they assumed to be the spare print of Episode Two, believing that there was another print, plus a negative, in the Library. When this was discovered, it meant that the Library now held just a print and a negative for Episode One's footage, and a sepmag soundtrack for Episode Two. I happened to know, through a friend of a friend, of a collector who had recently acquired a mute 35mm film of the Episode Two sequences, and when he realised what had gone on, he immediately handed over the film to me, and I gave it to Adam Lee at the Missing Believed Wiped event.

The existence of an off-air soundtrack eventually enabled the audio to be recombined with the pictures for these sequences from Episode One.

WIPED!

Episode	Clip Description / Duration
The Power of the Daleks: Episode Six	Daleks smoke and explode (0 min 06 sec)
The Abominable Snowmen: Episode Four	A zoom-in shot of a Yeti stood next to the TARDIS (0 min 02 sec)
	Three Yeti drag a man up a hillside (0 min 06 sec)

During pre-production for the 1993 documentary *Thirty Years in the TARDIS*, director Kevin Davies was keen to try to locate as much rare *Doctor Who* footage as possible for potential inclusion in the programme. He was assisted by researcher Andrew Pixley and BBC engineer Steve Roberts in attempting to track down old BBC programmes that might contain clips from now-missing episodes.

When *Doctor Who* sound effects creator Brian Hodgson was interviewed for the documentary, he presented Davies with a VHS videotape containing an old episode of a BBC programme called *Tom Tom*. This had included a feature on the BBC's Radiophonic Workshop, as part of which, a clip from the final episode of 'The Power of the Daleks' was used, showing the final destruction of the Daleks in a series of explosions. Davies discovered that the film insert for this edition of *Tom Tom* still existed in full on 16mm black and white film, not in the BBC's archives, but at BBC Bristol. This footage wasn't logged on Infax. Using this, he was able to source a transmission-standard copy of the missing clip. Roberts meanwhile found that the colour film inserts for the 25 November 1967 edition of the BBC2 series *Late Night Line-Up* also still existed in the BBC archive. This included a feature on *Doctor Who*'s special effects, which centred around an interview with Jack Kine of the Visual Effects Department. Newly-filmed colour footage was also featured, showing the Cybermats from 'The Tomb of the Cybermen' and a working Yeti gun prop. The feature also included two brief clips from Episode Four of 'The Abominable Snowmen'. The transmitted inserts existed on 16mm colour film, although the *Doctor Who* clips were naturally in black and white.

Episode	Clip Description / Duration
The Daleks Masterplan: Episode Three ('Devil's Planet)	The Spar is thrown off course/Daleks in their control room (1 min 38 sec)

While working on *Thirty Years in the TARDIS*, researcher Andrew Pixley began wondering if any other, long-forgotten BBC programmes might include clips from missing *Doctor Who* episodes. To help in his researches, he accessed the BBC's contributor files for the main actors from the series – the various Doctors and the

CHAPTER 12

companions – to see if there were any details of residual payments made to them for the use of *Doctor Who* clips in other BBC programmes.

From this, Pixley found details of a number of programmes that had used such clips in the 1960s and early 1970s. However, he soon discovered that the majority of these no longer existed themselves. One exception was an edition of *Blue Peter* from 25 October 1971, which had resulted in payments being made to both William Hartnell and Peter Purves. By the time Pixley discovered this, it was just too late for anything that might be found as a result to make it into the televised version of the documentary shown on BBC1 in November 1993. Early in 1994, the details of this edition of *Blue Peter* were passed to Davies, who in turn passed them on to Paul Vanezis at BBC Pebble Mill, who was at this time assisting Davies in the production of an extended version of the documentary, *More Than Thirty Years in the TARDIS*, for BBC Video. Vanezis ordered up the *Blue Peter* episode, and discovered that it contained a lengthy clip from 'The Daleks Masterplan' Episode Three. The clip began with the Doctor, Steven, Katarina and Brett in the control room of the Spar spaceship, and continued on to the next scene of the Daleks in their control room. This control room scene duplicated the material already known to exist from this episode in the 1973 edition of *Blue Peter*, only this time it had the correct soundtrack in place.

This 1971 *Blue Peter* feature concentrated on the Daleks themselves, and pondered if they could ever return to *Doctor Who*. The feature was presented by former companion and 'The Daleks Masterplan' cast member Peter Purves, who had joined the *Blue Peter* presenting team some years previously. Purves was joined by three Daleks in the studio, one of which was voiced (as well as operated) by John Scott Martin, in a rough approximation of a standard Dalek voice. It was this Dalek dialogue that had been lifted and overdubbed on to the 1973 version of the clip for the later *Blue Peter* feature. The feature enigmatically suggested that perhaps the Daleks might one day return to *Doctor Who* – and as the final studio session for 'Day of the Daleks' had been completed the previous week (and the Daleks were in the gunmetal and gold livery later seen in that story), then this stood a very good chance of being correct!

During his research, Pixley also discovered that Katy Manning had received a payment for *Doctor Who* footage used in a 1973 edition of the BBC's magazine programme *Nationwide*. Again the information was passed on to Vanezis, who ascertained that, although this edition of *Nationwide* didn't exist at the BBC, there was an insert spool for it still surviving, on two-inch 625-line videotape. When he ordered up the spool, he found that it was a pre-recorded introduction for a live interview that Manning had done on the programme, focusing on her imminent departure from *Doctor Who* after playing Jo Grant for three years. This pre-recorded section featured clips from three *Doctor Who* episodes, taken from their original 625-line two-inch colour videotapes. One of the clips was from 'Terror of the Autons' Episode One, showing Jo's first meeting with the Doctor, which no longer existed in its original colour form (although the black and white film prints had been recolourised using off-air NTSC colour in 1993). This clip ran to just over 30 seconds. (The other two clips featured were from 'Carnival of Monsters' and 'The Green Death'.)

Episode	Clip Description / Duration
The Power of the Daleks: Episode Four	Two Daleks pass through a sliding doorway (0 min 10 sec)
	Model shot of completed Daleks on a conveyer belt (0 min 7 sec)
The Power of the Daleks: Episode Five	A gunless Dalek glides up to the camera while talking (0 min 10 sec)
	Daleks gathering in their capsule (0 min 08 sec)

In the late 1980s and early 1990s there was a persistent rumour in *Doctor Who* fandom that the ABC in Australia once screened a programme called *C for Computer*, which featured many clips from the lost Patrick Troughton story 'The Power of the Daleks'. But when the ABC was contacted by the BBC about this, they could find no trace of having made a programme with this title.

Then in 1995, the BBC's Steve Roberts was contacted by an Australian fan, Robert Mammone, who was able to give him the transmission details of an *episode* of an ABC programme called *Perspectives*, which was titled 'C for Computer'. Steve Roberts decided to contact the ABC in an attempt to discover once and for all if this programme really did feature clips from 'The Power of the Daleks', and if so, to find out if ABC still had a copy of the programme.

ABC had screened this episode on 29 May 1974. The full programme didn't exist any more, but a 16mm insert film for it survived in the ABC archives, and when viewed, was indeed found to contain four clips from 'The Power of the Daleks'. The fan rumours had been more or less correct!

Roberts arranged for this insert film to be copied onto D3 videotape, which was then sent to him at the BBC in August 1995.

Some of these clips were duplicated in a 2005 find of a 16mm insert film from the 28 December 1966 edition of *Tomorrow's World* (see below).

CHAPTER 12

THE AUSTRALIAN CENSORS FILM CLIPS

Episode	Clip Description / Duration
The Smugglers: Episode One	Cherub throws a knife into Longfoot's back (0 min 23 sec)
The Smugglers: Episode Three	Jamaica talking to Pike (0 min 03 sec)
	Pike killing Jamaica, then wiping the blood from his hook (0 min 14 sec)
	Kewper is shot as Polly screams (0 min 04 sec)
The Smugglers: Episode Four	Pike kills Cherub with his sword (0 min 03 sec)
The Highlanders: Episode One	Alexander McLaren stabs a Redcoat soldier (0 min 02 sec)
	McLaren stabs the Redcoat again (0 min 01 sec)
	A Redcoat orders the hanging of the Doctor, Ben, Jamie and Colin McLaren (0 min 10 sec)
The Underwater Menace: Episode One	Polly is forced onto the operating table (0 min 14 sec)
The Underwater Menace: Episode Two	A syringe being filled from a bottle (0 min 02 sec)
	More shots of the syringe (0 min 03 sec)
	Polly cries as she is held down on the operating table (0 min 07 sec)
	Damon is interrupted as he is about to inject Polly (0 min 08 sec)
The Underwater Menace: Episode Four	Zaroff drowns as the waters rise (0 min 03 sec)
The Macra Terror: Episode Two	Polly is grabbed by a Macra, as Ben tries to free her (0 min 15 sec)
	Polly and Ben see another Macra approach (0 min 07 sec)
	Polly and Ben run straight into another Macra (0 min 03 sec)
	The Controller is attacked on the screen by a giant Macra claw (0 min 01 sec)
The Macra Terror: Episode Three	The Controller is attacked by a Macra (0 min 02 sec)
Fury from the Deep: Episode Two	Mr Oak and Mr Quill overpower Mrs Harris (0 min 54 sec)

WIPED!

Fury from the Deep: Episode Four	The Doctor and Jamie see something in the foam (0 min 03 sec)
	The Doctor and Jamie escape the Weed Creature (0 min 14 sec)
	Van Lutyens is sucked into the foam (0 min 14 sec)
Fury from the Deep: Episode Five	Robson overpowers a guard (0 min 17 sec)
	Robson's hands operate the helicopter controls (0 min 03 sec)
	Robson flies the helicopter, with a dazed Victoria beside him (0 min 11 sec)
The Wheel in Space: Episode Four	Duggan dying (0 min 01 sec)
	Duggan's final death throes (0 min 02 sec)

It was widely known that quite a few black and white episodes of *Doctor Who* were edited for censorship reasons prior to being screened in Australia in the 1960s and early 1970s. In 1984, Dallas Jones, the then-President of the Doctor Who Club of Australia, looked into the background to this, and was able to discover exactly what sections had been cut from which episodes. Sometime in early 1996, he discussed this research with fellow fan Damian Shanahan. This led Shanahan to wonder exactly what had happened to the material cut from the episodes.

Shanahan discovered that the cuts had all been made on the instruction of the Australian Film Censorship Board, which in January 1985 had been renamed the Office of Film and Literature Classification (OFLC). In each case, the 'offending' material had been physically removed from the 16mm film print supplied by BBC Enterprises to the ABC, and the print had then been spliced back together to cover the cut.

Shanahan began studying the website of the Australian Archives, the government body that acted as a repository for the storage of all documentation generated by the Australian Film Censorship Board in the 1960s and early 1970s, which therefore included all the paperwork relating to the *Doctor Who* edits. He identified a 'folder series number', C-3057, that appeared to be a general placement for everything related to television programmes. With this clue in hand, he decided to approach the OFLC to try to access further information. In order to give his enquiries a more official look, he asked his old friend and science fiction fan Ellen Parry, who at the time had recently begun studying for her Master's thesis at Griffith University, Brisbane, to write to the OFLC on his behalf. Although Parry's thesis had nothing to do with censorship, she agreed to write using her University's letterhead and introducing Shanahan to the OFLC as her research assistant. Shanahan's reasoning was that this would probably carry more weight than a letter from a fan – and he was proven correct!

With permission granted by the OFLC for him to access the folder series at the

CHAPTER 12

Australian Archives, Shanahan began an exhaustive trawl through the complete censorship files, discovering that the information Jones had been given in 1984 was only copied from a quick reference card series still held by the OFLC. Now, Shanahan was accessing the actual Certificates of Registration for the first time. Indeed it was revealed to him that no-one else had ever before even requested to view these old Certificates. Of course, there was no single file that related to *Doctor Who* specifically. As all television programmes screened in Australia at the time had to undergo Censorship Board acceptance, every one had its own Certificate, and these were all placed rather haphazardly, in rough chronological rather than alphabetical order. So dozens of heavy boxes of paperwork were transferred from the Board's holdings in Villawood, to the central Australian Archives Office in Sydney, and on his days off from his full-time work, Shanahan made his way through them. Slowly extracting the Certificates for *Doctor Who* episodes from the jumble, he discovered some highly detailed information, including the time and place of internal screening of each episode by the Censors, the rating given to each episode and, more interestingly, the rationale behind the cuts made. Clearly the Censors had to justify their actions under the strict guidelines of the Censors Act.

While Shanahan found all this fascinating, it was really only the answer to the question of whether or not the cut footage still existed that drove him to persist. He was undeterred by the repeated assertions by the Archive staff that there would be no way that the footage would still be around after all these years. He was acutely aware that in such a vast repository, staff couldn't possibly be aware of all their holdings, especially as that was not part of their job. What caught his attention specifically was that handwritten notes were occasionally added to the Certificates indicating what was done with the cut footage. He went back to the OFLC directly, having now established himself as a researcher in his own right, to see if anyone knew what could have happened to the excised footage. He was told, 'Look mate, everything we had then, we've sent to the Aussie Archives out at Villawood.'

Shanahan was convinced that there was a chance, however slim, that the censored footage might still be in existence at the Archives, as his research indicated that there was a statutory requirement for it to be kept indefinitely. Plus there were several references in the paperwork indicating that cut footage had been handed over by the ABC to the Australian Film Censorship Board – after all, this was the best way for the Board to ensure that the cuts had actually been made.

It was when he located another file series, listing the actual film holdings at Villawood, that Shanahan was able excitedly to direct the staff there to where the material might be found. This file series was alphabetical, so it didn't cause the staff too much trouble to go and check. Having been told virtually on which shelf to look and in which boxes, the previously sceptical staff began enthusiastically to draw out

WIPED!

tiny pieces of tightly-rolled-up film and splice them together in order to make a VHS viewing copy transfer. This was in early October 1996.

Before long, Shanahan was watching short bursts of lost *Doctor Who* episodes: Mr Oak and Mr Quill attacking Maggie Harris, Redcoats battling Highlanders, Polly being menaced by the Macra ... a whole selection of small segments. These included censored sections of episodes from stories such as 'The War Machines', 'The Dominators', and 'The Invasion', for which the BBC still held prints. And in the case of 'The War Machines' and 'The Dominators', the censored scenes were ones that were missing from the BBC's prints, and so could potentially be used to restore them to something closer to their original form.

One clip for which Shanahan had found details could not be traced initially. This was a brief sequence from 'The Underwater Menace' Episode Four, showing Professor Zaroff slipping under the rising water in his flooded laboratory. However, Shanahan had by this point established himself as a serious researcher, and had befriended several of the staff at the Villawood film repository. He was consequently able to negotiate time to enter the vaults himself and go through the boxes he'd identified earlier, holding all the rolled-up pieces of censored film footage. An unlabelled package caught his eye and, on inspection, revealed itself to be the missing clip in question. This discovery was announced in November 1996.

All the material located by Shanahan was then sent to the ABC to be transferred onto D3 videotape. This was because the Australian Archives possessed only rudimentary transfer facilities themselves. This tape was then forwarded to Steve Roberts at the BBC in London in late 1996.

The material located at the Australian Archives had all been cut from episodes that had arrived in Australia from 1967 onwards. Shanahan wanted to know what had become of the material from earlier stories, such as 'Marco Polo', 'The Reign of Terror' and 'Galaxy 4'. He discovered that the pre-1967 material had been transferred from the OFLC to the Australian Archives at the same time as the later material, in 1991. But for reasons of space, only the later material had been retained. The documentation for the earlier material was kept, but the physical film was disposed of at around the time of the move. 'We had a bonfire', Shanahan was told.

The Australian censor material also included all the scenes cut out of Episode Two of 'The Underwater Menace', which proved fortuitous in 2011 when the ex-ABC print of the episode was discovered. These sections were re-transferred at a very high resolution in 2011, so the episode could be fully restored.

Shanahan fully explored the possibilities of any other *Doctor Who* material existing at the Australian Archives – such as the 11 episodes of 'The Daleks Masterplan' that were sent to Australia but fell foul of the censors and were never shown – and was satisfied that no further material was held there.

CHAPTER 12

Episode	Clip Description / Duration
Galaxy 4: Episode One ('Four Hundred Dawns')	The Doctor, Steven and Vicki follow the Drahvins (2 min 31 sec)
	A Chumbley approaches the Drahvin ship (2 min 52 sec)

These off-cuts from the 16mm film of 'Galaxy 4' Episode One had sat safely in the collection of former DWAS President Jan Vincent-Rudzki since 1977. He had offered the film back to the BBC Film and Videotape Library in the 1980s, but his offer had been declined, on the basis that the Library was then only looking to recover complete programmes. Times change, however, and in 1997, BBC Video were making a feature about the missing *Doctor Who* episodes, to be included in a VHS box set along with the surviving episodes of 'The Ice Warriors' and 'The Underwater Menace'. This documentary, *Doctor Who: The Missing Years*, was being produced by Steve Roberts and directed by Paul Vanezis, who were keen to include as many clips from missing episodes as they could (although as things turned out, a couple were left out of the finished programme). Roberts knew that Vincent-Rudzki was in possession of this 'Galaxy 4' footage, and asked him if it would be possible to include it. Vincent-Rudzki agreed, and lent Roberts the 16mm black and white film so that it could be wet-gate telecined and copied onto D3 videotape by the BBC.

Once the two segments had been transferred, it was found that they could be recombined with the clip that was used in 'Whose Doctor Who' to make an almost-complete sequence running just short of six minutes.

THE 8MM FILM 'OFF-AIR' CLIPS

Episode	Clip Description / Duration
The Reign of Terror: Episode Four ('The Tyrant of France')	The Doctor in Robespierre's office (0 min 02 sec)
	Ian talking in Jules' house (0 min 03 sec)
	Ian talking in Jules' house the following morning (0 min 01 sec)
	Susan lying down in the surgery (0 min 01 sec)
	Susan looks worried (0 min 02 sec)
	Barbara tries to open the surgery door (0 min 01 sec)

WIPED!

The Reign of Terror: Episode Five ('A Bargain of Necessity')	Barbara in her cell, talking to the Doctor (0 min 04 sec)
	Barbara remarking on the Doctor's disguise (0 min 3 sec)
	Ian talking to Leon in the crypt (0 min 02 sec)
	The Doctor talking (0 min 01 sec)
	The Doctor talking (0 min 01 sec)
	Ian and Barbara in Jules' house (0 min 01 sec)
Galaxy 4: Episode One ('Four Hundred Dawns')	The Doctor operates the TARDIS controls (0 min 10 sec)
The Myth Makers: Episode One ('Temple of Secrets')	Steven and Vicki watch the TARDIS scanner (0 min 09 sec)
	Steven and Vicki talking (0 min 10 sec)
	Steven puts his cloak on (0 min 02 sec)
The Myth Makers: Episode Two ('Small Prophet, Quick Return')	Vicki looks worried as she watches the scanner (0 min 03 sec)
	More shots of Vicki looking at the scanner (0 min 03 sec)
	The Doctor and Steven talking on the plain (0 min 04 sec)
	More shots of the Doctor and Steven talking (0 min 04 sec)
	The Doctor talking (0 min 01 sec)
The Myth Makers: Episode Two ('Small Prophet, Quick Return')	Another shot of the Doctor talking (0 min 01 sec)
	Vicki leaving the TARDIS in Trojan dress (0 min 04 sec)
The Myth Makers: Episode Four ('Horse of Destruction')	The Doctor talking to Katarina (0 min 15 sec)
The Savages: Episode Three	Steven hears a noise and takes cover (0 min 05 sec)
	Steven and Dodo talking as they move along a corridor (0 min 03 sec)

CHAPTER 12

The Savages: Episode Four	Dodo talking to the Doctor, with Nanina and Steven (0 min 03 sec)	
	Dodo smashes lab equipment (0 min 06 sec)	
	Jano talking (0 min 01 sec)	
	Jano talking again (0 min 03 sec)	
	Steven looks surprised (0 min 01 sec)	
	Steven decides to stay, Dodo runs over to him (0 min 06 sec)	
	Steven says goodbye (0 min 03 sec)	
	Steven shakes hands with the Doctor (0 min 05 sec)	
	Steven looks back (0 min 01 sec)	
	The Doctor comforts Dodo (0 min 06 sec)	
	The Doctor and Dodo leave (0 min 01 sec)	
The Tenth Planet: Episode Four	The Doctor talking to Polly (0 min 04 sec)	
	More material of the Doctor talking to Polly (0 min 02 sec)	
	The Doctor addressing the Cyberleader (0 min 05 sec)	
	The Doctor talking again, same scene, slightly later (0 min 04 sec)	
	The Doctor talking again, same scene, slightly later (0 min 03 sec)	
	The Doctor talking again, same scene, slightly later (0 min 01 sec)	
	Polly being menaced by a Cyberman (0 min 02 sec)	
	Polly and the Doctor held prisoner on Cybership (0 min 03 sec)	
	Polly and the Doctor held prisoner on Cybership (0 min 01 sec)	
	Ben inside Cybership (0 min 01 sec)	
	Ben inside Cybership (0 min 01 sec)	
	The freed Doctor talking to Ben (0 min 02 sec)	
The Tenth Planet: Episode Four	The Doctor staggering towards the camera (0 min 03 sec)	
	The Doctor seen in silhouette, as the TARDIS lights pulsate (0 min 19 sec)	

WIPED!

The Power of the Daleks: Episode One	Ben and Polly discuss the 'new' Doctor (0 min 05 sec)
	Ben and Polly discuss the 'new' Doctor (0 min 01 sec)
	Ben and Polly discuss the 'new' Doctor (0 min 01 sec)
	The Doctor awakens, muttering to himself (0 min 03 sec)
	The Doctor feels his new face (0 min 01 sec)
	The Doctor turns and slumps on the TARDIS console (0 min 03 sec)
	Ben and Polly watch the Doctor rummage in a trunk (0 min 06 sec)
	The Doctor sees his 'old' face in a mirror (0 min 02 sec)
	The Doctor bites his finger (0 min 02 sec)
	The Doctor pulls on his tall hat (0 min 01 sec)
	The Doctor quickly walks out of the lab (0 min 07 sec)
	Ben and Polly with the cobwebbed Daleks (0 min 03 sec)
The Power of the Daleks: Episode Two	The Doctor talks while Ben and Polly look on (0 min 04 sec)
	Polly in Lesterson's lab (0 min 03 sec)
	The Doctor looks towards the ceiling (0 min 01 sec)
	Lesterson wheels out a Dalek (0 min 04 sec)
	The Doctor with his 500 year diary (0 min 01 sec)
	Resno is exterminated (0 min 02 sec)
	The Doctor looks on as a Dalek enters (0 min 01 sec)
	The Doctor backs away from the Dalek (0 min 04 sec)
	The Doctor and the Dalek (0 min 04 sec)
The Macra Terror: Episode Three	Opening titles (0 min 17 sec)
	The Doctor jokes about one of the colony's jingles (0 min 05 sec)
	The Doctor looks around (0 min 05 sec)
	The Doctor talking to the hypnotised Ben (0 min 06 sec)

CHAPTER 12

The Macra Terror: Episode Three	Polly in the mine (0 min 04 sec)
	Jamie in the mine (0 min 05 sec)
	Jamie looks around the mineshaft (0 min 01 sec)
	Polly and the Doctor talking (0 min 04 sec)
	The Doctor realises that there's 'something' in the mine (0 min 05 sec)
The Faceless Ones: Episode Two	The imposter Polly brushes the Doctor aside (0 min 03 sec)

Not much is known about the background to this footage, other than that it was made by an Australian fan in the mid-1960s by pointing a silent 8mm camera at a television screen. Because the clips are very short, yet usually cover key moments in the episodes in question, it seems likely that the film was shot during repeat screenings, when the unknown fan would have already known about their contents from the original ABC transmissions. The footage includes quite a few clips from existing episodes as well – such as 'Planet of Giants' and 'The Chase' – although a significant percentage is from missing episodes.

The footage was almost certainly filmed using a camera powered by a simple wind-up mechanism, which allowed for only brief sections of action to be recorded at any one time. Because of the mechanical nature of the equipment, the frame rate of the footage varies quite dramatically from one clip to another.

Video transfers of the footage were circulating amongst *Doctor Who* fans during the late 1980s and early 1990s, but a copy of the film itself surfaced only in 1998, when it was made available to the *Doctor Who* Restoration Team. Portions from it were used in *Doctor Who: The Missing Years*, slowed down to the correct speed in each case and married up with the relevant sections of off-air soundtrack.

All the 8mm clips were eventually showcased on the 'Lost in Time' DVD release of 2004.

THE NEW ZEALAND CENSORS FILM CLIPS

Episode	Clip Description / Duration
The Web of Fear: Episode Two	Two soldiers shoot at two Yeti (0 min 14 sec)
The Web of Fear: Episode Four	A Yeti strikes down Professor Travers, and then Anne (0 min 11 sec)
	Victoria discovers the cobwebbed dead soldiers (0 min 10 sec)
	The Web pulsates, and Private Evans clutches his ears, screaming (0 min 05 sec)

WIPED!

The Web of Fear: Episode Four	Two soldiers fire at two Yeti in the road; one recoils slightly (0 min 05 sec)
	Yeti smother two soldiers using their web guns (0 min 07 sec)
	Lethbridge-Stewart and a soldier hide on top of a market stall as a Yeti passes (0 min 03 sec)
The Web of Fear: Episode Five	Victoria and Professor Travers try to escape from a motionless Yeti, but it comes to life (0 min 03 sec)
The Wheel In Space: Episode Five	Flanagan fights with two Cyber-controlled members of the Wheel crew (0 min 07 sec)

New Zealand *Doctor Who* fan Graham Howard had spent a great deal of time and effort in the 1990s exploring every facet of New Zealand's screening of the Hartnell and Troughton episodes. It was by his diligent researches that he located and eventually gained access to the original programme traffic records held by TVNZ (previously NZBC) for *Doctor Who*. These showed that a lot of the 16mm film prints of the black and white episodes that had been sent to New Zealand had either been destroyed or forwarded on to other broadcasters at the BBC's request.

Howard also began contacting New Zealand film collectors, in the hope that they might be able to help locate any missing *Doctor Who* material existing in private hands. In early 2002, he was assisting one such collector in the cataloguing of his collection. Viewing one reel of 16mm black and white film identified as 'Television Extracts', he found it to contain a collection of clips from 1960s *Doctor Who*, lasting for about six minutes. Amongst all the material from existing episodes (mainly from 'The Ark') was just over a minute of footage from 'The Web of Fear', and a single sequence from 'The Wheel in Space'. All this footage was comprised of scenes that had been edited from the 16mm transmission prints of the episodes on the instruction of New Zealand censors.

The film extracts had originated at the NZBC, but had been discarded by them many years previously, and had been anonymously donated to the film collector in question. Up until the time of their discovery, there had been some debate within fan circles as to whether or not the NZBC had actually made its own censor cuts during the 1960s and early 1970s, since the programme traffic documentation revealed details of censor ratings and episodes rejected by the censor, but omitted to indicate whether or not cuts also were made. The only clue that there may have been cuts was that the episode durations listed in the records were sometimes shorter than they should be. The discovery of the censored material confirmed unequivocally that cuts to *Doctor Who* episodes had indeed been made in New Zealand.

In May 2002, Howard arranged with the film collector to send the entire 16mm film to Steve Roberts, who oversaw the telecine transfer of the material onto Digital

CHAPTER 12

Betacam tape. This was done after the film had been broken down into its component parts and then re-spliced with blank spacing frames added between the clips, and with the original editor's chinagraph marks removed from the surface of the film. The tape was then sent to the BBC Film and Videotape Library, while the 16mm film was returned to New Zealand.

Since the initial recovery of the clips, additional documentation has come to light. Late in 2002, the New Zealand Government's Department of Internal Affairs Censor Registers for 1960-1969 were located by Howard. These showed that prior to 1 April 1969, the NZBC's cuts to overseas-sourced television material were made at the request of Government censors. After that date, the system changed, and the NZBC began using its own in-house censors.

In 2004, another New Zealand *Doctor Who* fan, Jon Preddle, accessed some of the Government censors' records, which contained their notations relating to 'The Ark'. The following year he located the NZBC censors' viewing note books, which included notations for 'The Web of Fear' and 'The Wheel in Space'. This documentation indicated that a little more material may have been cut from 'The Web of Fear' than was recovered in 2002.

Episode	Clip Description / Duration
Fury from the Deep: Episode Six – Film Trims	The Weed Creature attacks (3 min 32 sec)

Andrew Martin was a one-time member of the Doctor Who Appreciation Society and co-author of the 1997 publication *Doctor Who: The Book of Lists*. However, his day job since 1989 had been working for the BBC Film and Videotape Library in Windmill Road. In his position as Senior Media Assistant, he was involved in a number of housekeeping projects at the Library, and in July 2003 he made a fantastic discovery.

BBC Ealing had always kept a stock of waste film for use as either filler or leader material.[69] Martin was at the time checking the whole film collection for acetate mag tracks, to preserve them onto polyester track and CD masters, and to dispose of spare copies. One mag track can that he examined contained two reels of 16mm film that had been used as filler or spacer material. When he viewed the reels, he discovered that they contained material from such old BBC shows as *Twice a Fortnight*, *The Dave Allen Show*, *The Forsyte Saga* and ... *Doctor Who*.

---

69 Mute (silent) waste film was often used as filler material when making a dubbing track for a programme, so that the track would run to the correct duration; the filler material would cover sections of the programme for which no new sounds had been created.

WIPED!

Being a fan of the series, Martin realised almost straight away that the footage had been shot during production of the missing Troughton-era story 'Fury from the Deep'. It was all mute, and was made up of film trims from the Ealing-staged sequence of the Weed Creature's attack on the refinery compound, featuring Patrick Troughton, Frazer Hines and Deborah Watling. These trims were what remained after the footage selected for inclusion in the finished programme was physically removed from the negative, so none of this material would have been seen on transmission. It did however include alternate takes of certain shots.[70]

Paul Vanezis was later able to edit this footage into a rough approximation of the transmitted sequence also using material from Tony Cornell's 8mm studio footage (see below), one of John Cura's Tele-snaps and the surviving off-air audio soundtrack. This sequence runs to just over a minute and was made available on the 'Lost in Time' Doctor Who DVD release in 2004.

Episode	Clip Description / Duration
The Power of the Daleks: Episode One	The Doctor, Ben and Polly find the inert Daleks (0 min 19 sec)

In October 2003, Andrew Martin was actively looking for 'extra' material, and was viewing a 16mm black and white film print of a BBC programme entitled *Beyond the Freeze – What Next?*, shown on BBC1 on Saturday 5 November 1966. The print was a PasB (Programme as Broadcast) recording, which meant that it was made at the time of transmission[71]. Whoever had made the PasB recording had started the film recorder early, immediately after the preceding programme had finished. They then stopped recordings, but then restarted it again and recorded the next couple of minutes of BBC1's output prior to the start of *Beyond the Freeze – What Next?* And that included a trailer for 'The Power of the Daleks' Episode One, the episode of *Doctor Who* due to be screened later that evening. Martin was surprised to realise that he'd discovered some previously lost footage from Patrick Troughton's debut episode.

Due to the stopping and starting of the film recorder, the very beginning of the trailer is missing, and the announcer's voice is initially distorted. However, this was

---

70 Among other things discovered during this examination of acetate mag tracks were three partial and one complete episode of *The Diary of Samuel Pepys* from 1958 starring Peter Sallis. The complete episode was effectively filler after the title music of a 1968 programme called *Personal Choice*, featuring Robert Kennedy – perhaps suggesting it was 'junked' after 10 years, or had been sitting around for a very long time!

71 Martin knew that PasB recordings were always a good place to look for 'extra' footage – the only known copy that exists of the original *Top of the Pops* opening titles comes from the end of a recording of an edition of *General Election Question Time*.

CHAPTER 12

over just a section of footage from the standard *Doctor Who* title sequence of the day. The main part of the trailer, which was captured perfectly, consists of a clip of the new Doctor introducing Ben and Polly to the static Daleks that they have just discovered in the mysterious capsule in Lesterson's lab.

Episode	Clip Description / Duration
The Space Pirates: Episode One – Film Sequences	Space-suited Pirates set charges on Alpha 1 (1 min 02 sec)
	The black dart ship undocks and Alpha 1 explodes (0 min 24 sec)

In 2004, Ralph Montagu was working on a project relating to the BBC comedy series *Dad's Army*, in preparation for the early episodes to be restored prior to release on DVD. He'd ordered up a tin of 35mm film that had been held in the Film and Videotape Library since the late 1960s, which was simply titled *Dad's Army – Old Titles*. He hoped it might contain footage to help restore the opening titles of the series, which looked very grainy and jumpy on the surviving prints. But when he viewed the footage, he realised straight away that it wasn't from *Dad's Army*. Instead, he suspected the mute 35mm footage of spacesuited figures and spaceships might be *Doctor Who* material, but wasn't entirely sure ...

Montagu had already booked some telecine time to have all his *Dad's Army* footage transferred to videotape just a few days after he had viewed it, and asked Andrew Martin to look at the footage on this particular spool, to see if he could determine what it actually was.

Martin duly watched the film, and realised that it was from the *Doctor Who* story 'The Space Pirates'. It had been known for some time that a tin of mute 35mm film sequences from (the existing) Episode Two of this story was held by the Library, and it was initially thought that perhaps this was what Montagu had been (wrongly) supplied with in the *Dad's Army* can. Further investigation revealed that it was actually two clips from the missing first episode of the story. Although mute, it has since been matched with the relevant section of off-air soundtrack. The first clip runs to 62 seconds, but only a portion of this was used in the transmitted episode, running to 41 seconds.

Episode	Clip Description / Duration
The Power of the Daleks: Episode Four	Daleks on the Production Line (0 min 08 sec)
	Daleks on the Production Line (0 min 06 sec)

On 11 September 2005, the BBC programme *Sunday Past Times* featured clips from 'The Power of the Daleks', which surprised some *Doctor Who* fans who were watching,

who suspected that they weren't amongst those previously known to exist. Within hours of the programme being transmitted, a couple of these fans had posted details on the forum section of the *Doctor Who* Restoration Team website. These were seen by Paul Vanezis of BBC Birmingham, who knew that that edition of *Sunday Past Times* had been made and edited there earlier that week.

When he arrived at work the next day, Vanezis tracked down the list of all the programmes that had been used as clip sources for *Sunday Past Times*, and found that all the relevant tapes were still at BBC Birmingham. The clips from 'The Power of the Daleks' were taken from a 16mm black and white film insert reel for an edition of the BBC's science magazine programme *Tomorrow's World* screened on BBC1 on Wednesday 28 December 1966. Vanezis discovered that the film had been transferred onto Digital Betacam for the *Sunday Past Times* programme, so he viewed the tape. It contained material from 'The Power of the Daleks' Episode Four that already existed in the 'C for Computer' film returned from Australia in 1995, plus two further brief scenes from the same episode, which hadn't been known to exist before. The *Tomorrow's World* programme had sourced all these clips from the episode's original 35mm film inserts (which had still existed in 1966), rather than from a 16mm telerecording, so even the one previously found in 'C for Computer' was of a higher picture quality here.

OFF-AIR AUDIO RECORDINGS

Almost as soon as *Doctor Who* began in 1963, it started attracting fans – people who liked the series so much that they wanted to try to preserve and capture as much of it as possible, so that they could re-live the adventures again and again and again. Nowadays, it's easy to record your favourite programme on tape or DVD or onto a hard-drive. And if you miss an episode, then chances are it'll be repeated later in the week, or show up a few months later on a satellite channel. And there's always the DVD box set to buy in a few months' time.

But in the 1960s, there were no video recorders, no hard-drives, no sell-thru home video market, and very few repeats. Once a programme had been shown, that was it. Gone!

Very quickly, a number of individuals all came up with the same idea – *Doctor Who* could be preserved in audio form. There was no practical way of recording the pictures at the time, but a lot of homes had reel-to-reel audio tape recorders. Suddenly, a lot of pocket money was being spent on audio tapes on which to record the soundtracks of *Doctor Who* episodes.

What is remarkable is that some of these recordings survive to this day, and that many are of a very respectable quality considering their age and the methods used to capture them.

CHAPTER 12

RICHARD LANDEN

Richard Landen's *Doctor Who* audio recordings became known about in *Doctor Who* fandom years before any of the others.

In the early 1980s, Landen was the main feature writer for *Doctor Who Magazine*, but in the 1960s, he was a schoolboy fan of *Doctor Who*. Like many others before and after him, he wanted to find a way of re-living episodes after they'd been shown on television. He began by writing copious notes on each episode in purloined school exercise books. However, after using a reel-to-reel tape recorder to play in sound effects for a school play, he decided to save up and purchase his own machine, so that he could make off-air recordings of *Doctor Who*. His initial motivation for this was simply to enable him to accurately transcribe the dialogue of each episode at his leisure after it had aired. The first recording he made was of Episode Three of 'The Myth Makers' ('Death of a Spy') in 1965. He listened to this a number of times over the following week, but then decided to record over it with the next episode, 'The Myth Makers' Episode Four ('Horse of Destruction').

Landen so enjoyed the soundtrack to this particular episode that he couldn't bring himself to tape over it the following week, and instead elected to keep the recording. He used a new tape to record the next week's episode, 'The Daleks Masterplan' Episode One ('The Nightmare Begins'), and from this point in time, began retaining soundtrack recordings of each and every episode of *Doctor Who*. He still watched *Doctor Who* with an exercise book in front of him, but now he used it for sketching out various scenes and drawing bits of equipment and scenery as seen on screen, rather than jotting down the dialogue. From these sketches and notes, he began making various models of props such as the TARDIS console, and the police box exterior of the ship.

To begin with, Landen used the simple method of placing the tape recorder's microphone next to his television speaker to obtain his recordings. But from around the time of 'The Ice Warriors', he managed to make direct line recordings from his television straight into his reel-to-reel tape recorder, producing better quality recordings.

Landen continued making soundtrack recordings of every single episode of *Doctor Who* right up to the final episode of 'Underworld' in 1978. He stopped at this point only because by then he'd purchased his first video recorder, and was able to videotape the episodes. But from Episode Four of 'The Myth Makers' in 1965 through to Part Four of 'Underworld' in 1978, Landen managed to record the soundtrack of every single episode of *Doctor Who*. He didn't miss one!

Richard Landen: In 1972, the miner's strike caused a three day week and

WIPED!

selected power cuts throughout the nation. Where I lived, in Surrey, the power usually went off at 6.00 pm. This was ten minutes into an episode of *Doctor Who*! This meant that, in our area, we saw only the first ten minutes of each episode of 'The Curse of Peladon' and also didn't see several episodes of 'The Sea Devils'. To counteract this I went out and bought a portable tape recorder and a then-vogue Russian television set (black and white, of course). These were both then connected up to my car battery, so the first ten minutes of an episode was normally seen indoors, while I watched the remainder outside, sat in the car. And it was cold!

Another panic was that my Gran's television broke down one Friday. I always recorded *Doctor Who* at my grandparents'. So I had to move my recorder over to my parent's house for Episode Five of 'The Mind Robber'. Now, my Mum was a real Philistine regarding *Doctor Who*. Not only that, but for one week I had to revert to microphone recording. I basically missed watching the episode as I frantically tried to keep everyone quiet for 20 minutes. No mean feat with my mother cooking, and a sister trying to play records, shouting, and my father aiding and abetting audio mayhem!

As an early member of the Doctor Who Appreciation Society, Landen was happy to make his soundtrack recordings available to others, and soon copies were being enthusiastically duplicated far and wide, albeit dropping many generations in the process, providing the fans of the late 1970s and 1980s with a way of reliving those long-forgotten stories.

In 1992, ex-*Doctor Who* producer John Nathan-Turner proposed an audio cassette range of missing stories to BBC Audiobooks, and was given the go-ahead to prepare an initial batch of releases. The first two were 'The Macra Terror' and 'The Evil of the Daleks', and Landen loaned Nathan-Turner copies of his off-air recordings to use as the basis for these. Linking narration was supplied by Colin Baker and Tom Baker respectively. 'The Tomb of the Cybermen' was also scheduled to be released, with linking narration by Jon Pertwee, but the unexpected return of the episodes from Hong Kong just weeks before the range was launched saw the title pulled, although it did eventually come out some months later.

Because Landen's audio collection began with the final episode of 'The Myth Makers', there was a period of time when audio copies of the missing episodes of 'Marco Polo', 'The Reign of Terror', 'The Crusade', 'Galaxy 4', 'Mission to the Unknown' and the rest of 'The Myth Makers' were not known to exist.

In recent years, the discoveries of Graham Strong's and David Holman's off-air recordings have made much of Landen's collection redundant. But it was his audios

CHAPTER 12

that were copied far and wide amongst *Doctor Who* fans in the early years of fandom, and that helped generate such interest in the missing episodes of the 1960s.

IAN LEVINE

Ian Levine, as readers will probably have gathered by now, was very enthusiastic about *Doctor Who* almost from the beginning. From the second story, 'The Daleks', he began keeping detailed notes about each episode after it was broadcast. Not long after that, he began recording the soundtracks. His only problem was that his first tape recorder used tapes that ran for only 15 minutes. So he would record the first 15 minutes of each episode, and make copious notes for the final ten minutes. He would then listen to his recording after the episode had aired, and make more notes. In this way, he could document a whole episode's action and dialogue.

> **Ian Levine**: I'd started recording my audios with little 15-minute tapes, as far back as 'The Reign of Terror' Episode Five. I didn't get a reel-to-reel tape machine that I could record a whole episode on until 'The Chase' Episode Six, which was the first one I taped properly. I'd taped lots of bits before then, but not full episodes. So from 'The Chase' Episode Six, there was an audio recording, with awful sound, along with the transcript and my full notes, the latter of which I've still got. Jan Vincent-Rudzki taped Episodes One and Two of 'The Daleks', but nothing else. I've still got some of my old reel-to-reel recordings of 'The Evil of the Daleks'.

JAMES RUSSELL

James Russell is the son of iconic film director Ken Russell, and also a big *Doctor Who* fan. In the mid 1970s, he got to know fellow fans Ian Levine and Richard Landen, and was particularly impressed with Landen's collection of audio recordings, which (as we have learnt) went back all the way to the final episode of 'The Myth Makers'. Russell was able to locate audio recordings of earlier episodes of *Doctor Who*, stretching all the way back to the very first episode. These included the soundtracks to the missing episodes of 'Marco Polo', 'The Reign of Terror', 'The Crusade', 'Galaxy 4', 'Mission to the Unknown' and 'The Myth Makers'.

Thanks to Russell, by the late 1970s, Landen and Levine now had a complete collection of missing *Doctor Who* episodes on audio. Soundtracks of stories such as 'Marco Polo' and 'Mission to the Unknown' began to be copied amongst fans for the first time, although those of 'The Crusade' and 'Galaxy 4' were purposely withheld from wider distribution. Landen and Levine reasoned that they had to keep some soundtracks 'rare', in case they were needed as bargaining materials to exchange for a missing episode.

It was from copies of Russell's recordings that the 1993 Tom Baker-narrated BBC audio cassette releases of 'The Power of the Daleks' and 'Fury from the Deep' originated.

The tapes in Russell's possession covered all of the William Hartnell and Patrick Troughton eras, and were copies of off-air recordings made by a third party. Russell was of the opinion that the originals were all direct line recordings made at the time of broadcast, although some of them also have characteristics of being microphone recordings.

Russell's tapes include no untransmitted material, e.g. from early edits of episodes, as some rumours have suggested over the years, and there are often sections missing from episodes due to tapes being turned over while either the play source or transmission continued. The quality of some recordings is excellent, and of others not very good at all. Like all off-air recordings, they all have some degree of background hiss. Some (though by no means all) are of better quality than those already in the audio archive, so there remains the possibility of them being used to produce improved restoration masters of selected episodes in the future.

In early 2010, Russell loaned his collection of ¼-inch audio tapes of *Doctor Who* episodes to Ralph Montagu and Mark Ayres for cataloguing and digitisation. However, before any substantial work had been done with them, Russell then offered to put Ayres and Montagu in touch with the person he originally got his copies from ...

JOHN DE RIVAZ

Mark Ayres takes up the story: 'At its simplest, James Russell made very early contact with an enthusiast who had recorded all the episodes of *Doctor Who* in the 1960s off-air from the very start of transmission. The recordist made copies for James, but there were often (as we have discovered) bits missing where tapes were exchanged. A couple of years ago, James lent all of his copies to Ralph Montagu and me – all of these have been transferred. However, when it became obvious that we might finally track down the original source, I stopped serious cataloguing as it seemed moot. Earlier this year, Ralph and I finally travelled to the tip of the country to meet John de Rivaz, whose wife fed us a very nice lasagne, before they sent us away with a car full (literally!) of tapes'.

> **John de Rivaz:** James originally wrote to me following my articles in *Television* magazine concerning modifying early Philips VCRs to record and play for more than the one hour per cassette,' recalls de Rivaz. 'He asked if I had any *Doctor Who* recordings purely by chance, and I was able to provide

CHAPTER 12

him with sound recordings I had made. I originally made them because of a fascination with the idea of time manipulation. Tape recording itself seemed that way in the 1950s and 1960s, as few people were capable of operating the machines when you had to thread a tape through a head block. The idea of recording radio plays (and subsequently TV sound) came from school, where teachers had been doing it since about 1955. The first machine I came across used in 1955 for educational purposes was a Phillips EL 3510, and then later the Phillips EL 3516. The first tape recorder I was given was pretty useless, a Geloso G255. It even had a two pin plug and a live chassis! But then I was given a Philips EL3541, and after that made my own recorder using first a Collaro deck and then a Wearite deck (a brand name of Ferrograph).

Mark Ayres continues: 'There are many hundreds of tapes, which we now have and are evaluating. I have started going through them, but there are issues with getting optimum playback due to the experimental nature of John's recording equipment. He used a classic Wearite (Ferrograph) chassis, but with Marriott heads on home-made mountings. He was constantly modifying his set-up, with the result that head height against the tape and azimuth (vertical angle of incidence of head to tape) frequently changed. Hence, to get decent playback from the tapes, the heads need to be adjusted before each tape is played – tiny adjustments can mean the difference between crystal clear reproduction and a muddy mess. Unfortunately, tape machines are designed to be aligned and then left alone – continual adjustment can only cause wear and unreliability. Therefore I am researching having a machine built that will itself be based around a classic Ferrograph chassis with original heads, but with robust mechanical adjustment controls. This is taking some time, but is worth getting right. Once that is done, I will be able to proceed apace.

'What we can tell is that John appears to have taped everything from 'An Unearthly Child' through to 'The War Games', at which point he took a break. His recordings pick up with the Christmas compilation version of 'The Dæmons', and then continue right through to 'Survival'. There are short breaks in some episodes where the tape was turned over during recording, but the full details aren't yet known on which episodes this occurs – this is all to be catalogued. There were even more breaks in James's copies, where John's tapes had themselves been turned over during copying – sometimes there is an overlap; sometimes not. Of course, unless there is major subsequent damage to one of John's tapes since James's copies were made, James's tapes are now irrelevant.

'The other point to note is that the *Doctor Who* recordings are a tiny proportion of the complete collection – we expect the final catalogue to be of enormous interest once fully explored. I have already used portions of John's recording of 'The Reign of

WIPED!

Terror' to improve the soundtrack on the forthcoming animated reconstruction of Episodes Four and Five for the 2013 DVD release of the story'.

GRAHAM STRONG

Graham Strong was 14 years old when *Doctor Who* began in 1963. He was interested in the show from its very first episode, but did not get his first audio tape recorder until Christmas 1963. His first machine was a second hand Elizabethan, complete with valves, a maximum capacity of five-inch reels, a fixed recording speed of 3.75 inches per second, and the ability to record two audio tracks on a single tape. As a schoolboy, Strong didn't have the money to purchase additional reels of tape, and so a single reel would be reused repeatedly.

Strong's early audio recordings of *Doctor Who* were performed by the common method of placing the microphone of the tape recorder close to the speaker of his television set. To start with, he would usually listen to each episode a few times and then re-use the tape to record something else. (Apart from *Doctor Who*, he also recorded documentaries and comedy programmes to listen to at his leisure.) However, he did keep a few of his early recordings for posterity, such as selected episodes of 'The Keys of Marinus', 'The Sensorites' and 'The Space Museum'.

By late 1965, the Elizabethan tape recorder was beginning to wear out, so Strong purchased a Philips EL3548. This new machine allowed seven-inch reels to be used (as long as the lid was removed), had four mono audio tracks (or two stereo tracks, depending on how the operator configured the recording settings) and two recording speeds.

Strong was ultimately dissatisfied with the results of making recordings just by using a microphone, and his interest in electronics led him to ponder the practicalities of linking his reel-to-reel recorder directly to the workings of his television set, in order to make direct line recordings[72]. He put his theory to the test over Christmas 1965, and successfully made a crystal clear recording of Episode Eight of 'The Daleks Masterplan'. These line recordings weren't susceptible to external noises (which meant that Strong no longer had to sit silently through episodes), and were of extremely high quality.

The success of this new recording method prompted Strong to retain his recordings rather than tape over them with other programmes. He did so – with a few exceptions – from Episode Eight of 'The Daleks Masterplan' all the way through to Episode Five of 'The Dominators' in 1968.

One early exception was the eleventh episode of 'The Daleks Masterplan', which Strong suspects he missed because he was out at the time – only very expensive reel-to-reel recorders had timers that could be set to record in advance. Then, towards the end

---

52 Do not *ever* attempt to emulate Strong! The inside of a TV set is not the place to go poking about with a screwdriver.

CHAPTER 12

of William Hartnell's time as the Doctor, he found some of the programme's offerings weren't to his taste. He recorded all four episodes of both 'The Celestial Toymaker' and 'The Gunfighters', but elected to erase them, as he didn't like either of the stories.

Using seven-inch reels running at the slowest recording speed of 1 ⅞ inches per second, Strong now had the ability to store as many as 32 episodes of *Doctor Who* on a single tape – but only if he was judicious with what he recorded. This meant that he omitted to record the opening and closing credits to most episodes, and occasionally skipped reprises from previous episodes as well.

By the time Strong stopped recording *Doctor Who* soundtracks in 1968, he had a collection of 115 episodes, stored on just four reels of audio tape. Of these, 71 were soundtracks to episodes that are still missing today.

There are a few problems with Strong's recordings. 'The Massacre' Episode Four suffers from interference from a French television station – this usually occurred every summer in Strong's area, causing the picture and sound on his television set to fluctuate randomly. 'Fury from the Deep' Episode Four has a large amount of background hum, which cannot be easily explained, but may have been caused by a poor connection between the television and the reel-to-reel machine at the time. The opening of 'The Enemy of the World' Episode Six is missing a few lines of dialogue, as Strong was slightly too late pressing the 'record' button on his machine.

In general, however, Strong's soundtracks are of excellent quality, In fact, his recordings of 'The Tenth Planet' are probably the best that exist – and that includes the optical soundtracks on the surviving 16mm film prints of Episodes One to Three. His recording of Episode Four of the story stops just before the crucial regeneration sequence (the tape ran out!), but fortunately this is at the point where the clip retained in the 1973 *Blue Peter* edition begins, so the soundtrack was eventually completed by combining the two sources.

Strong also recorded the repeat screening of 'The Evil of the Daleks' in 1968, including the newly-dubbed dialogue by Patrick Troughton at the start of Episode One, providing an excellent source for that.

Strong replaced his Philips EL3548 tape recorder in October 1974 with a transistor-operated Philips N4414, which he still has at time of writing and keeps in full working order.

In the early 1990s, BBC Audiobooks' release of audio cassette soundtracks of several missing *Doctor Who* stories prompted Strong to approach the BBC and offer them access to his own off-air recordings. His initial approach received a lukewarm response. Undeterred, he was persuaded by some friends to make a 'sampler' tape of some excerpts of his material, which was then eventually passed through to Paul Vanezis. Vanezis was immediately aware of the importance of Strong's recordings, and equally impressed by their excellent quality, and made arrangements to meet him.

The BBC's initial indifference was primarily down to the fact that Strong's recordings fell between two stools. Although they were audio recordings, they were of television programmes, and so were of little interest to the sound archive, which mainly dealt with radio material. The Film and Videotape Library, on the other hand, didn't usually store soundtracks of programmes for which there were no pictures remaining. However, Vanezis made the case to the BBC that one day in the future, missing *Doctor Who* material might turn up that had been dubbed into a foreign language, in which case the preservation of the original soundtracks could prove invaluable.

In April 1994, Strong met up with Vanezis at Television Centre in London and loaned him the four reels of audio tape that contained all his *Doctor Who* soundtrack recordings. Vanezis then spent many months getting the recordings copied to DAT audio tape in his spare time. Copies of these DAT tapes have since been digitally restored by Mark Ayres for use in the new range of BBC *Doctor Who* soundtrack releases, which launched on CD in 1999.

Strong's soundtracks have also proved beneficial for restoring sound to the mute off-air 8mm film footage from Australia, and in the restoration of 'The War Machines', where cut material has been re-inserted into the episode.

The four reels of *Doctor Who* episodes were subsequently returned to Strong at a further visit that he made to the BBC studios.

Graham Strong: The BBC have been kind enough to send me a copy of all the restored *Doctor Who* CDs where my original audio recordings were used. I am very pleased and grateful for this gesture, as I now have a better copy of my recordings that will last forever. I also particularly like the narration covering the parts where there is no original dialogue, and am grateful for the mention of my name in the CD sleeve credits as being a participant in their production.

Missing episodes of which Graham Strong has the best quality audio recordings:[73]

The Daleks Masterplan	8, 9, 12
The Massacre	1, 2, 3, 4
The Savages	1, 2, 3, 4
The Smugglers	1, 2, 3, 4
The Tenth Planet	4

---

73 Not including the John de Rivaz recordings, which are still being assessed at the time of writing.

CHAPTER 12

The Power of the Daleks	1, 2, 3, 4, 5, 6
The Highlanders	1, 2, 3, 4
The Underwater Menace	1, 4
The Moonbase	1, 3
The Macra Terror	1, 2, 3, 4
The Faceless Ones	2, 4, 5, 6
The Evil of the Daleks	1, 3, 4, 5, 6, 7
The Abominable Snowmen	1, 3, 4, 5, 6
The Ice Warriors	2, 3
The Enemy of the World	1, 2, 4, 5, 6
The Web of Fear	2, 3, 4, 5, 6
Fury from the Deep	1, 2, 3, 4, 5, 6
The Wheel in Space	1, 2, 4, 5

DAVID HOLMAN

David Holman also began watching *Doctor Who* from the very first story, 'An Unearthly Child'. By the time of the second story, 'The Daleks', he had begun to consider the idea of recording the soundtracks of the episodes. His technique was again the traditional one of placing the microphone of his reel-to-reel tape recorder next to his television loudspeaker, and urging everyone in the room to keep very quiet while the recording was in progress.

The first episode that Holman recorded in this manner was Episode One of 'Marco Polo'. Unlike Graham Strong, Holman kept all of his recordings, and continued to make them for every episode up to and including 'The Three Doctors' in 1973. However, Holman also elected not to record the opening and closing titles of each episode. He tried to begin each recording just at the point the reprise from the previous episode ended – a feat he managed with remarkable precision on most occasions. Utilising this method, he was able to record between four and six episodes on a reel of tape.

Holman kept his recordings throughout the 1970s and 1980s, and eventually his enthusiasm for all things science fiction led him to open a memorabilia shop. Conversing with one of his customers in the early 1990s, he mentioned he still had his *Doctor Who* soundtracks of early episodes, and his customer asked if he would mind making some copies for him. At the time, there were no copies of 'The Crusade' or 'Galaxy 4' in circulation (although Ian Levine, James Russell and Richard Landen had tapes of them), so these were amongst the first batch requested. Audio copies of these two stories soon came into the possession of fan Allan Groves, who alerted a number of other fans to their existence.

Eventually, Holman was put into contact with Paul Vanezis, and the two of them met up in April 1996, whereupon Holman loaned Vanezis his original reel-to-reel recordings. Although the quality of the recordings was extremely good, because they had been made with a microphone, they lacked some of the clarity of Graham Strong's. Nevertheless, Holman had retained episodes that Strong hadn't recorded and/or kept, and his were the best quality copies known to exist of most of those.

Again, these recordings were initially transferred to DAT by Vanezis, and then digitally restored by Mark Ayres for use in the BBC Audio soundtrack releases. For some episodes of which Strong's recording was generally the superior, Holman's was still useful in patching faults.

Holman's recordings do have occasional minor problems of their own. His tape of 'Marco Polo' Episode Seven is missing around ten seconds of material at the start, and that of 'The Reign of Terror' Episode Four is missing nearly a minute's worth of material, again at the beginning. And although he taped 'The Space Pirates' (as did Richard Landen), the quality of this is quite poor compared to his other recordings

Missing episodes of which David Holman has the best quality audio recordings:[74]

Story	Episodes
Marco Polo	1, 2, 3, 4, 5, 6, 7
The Reign of Terror	4, 5
The Crusade	2, 4
Galaxy 4	1, 2, 4
Mission to the Unknown	1
The Myth Makers	1, 2, 3, 4
The Daleks Masterplan	1, 3, 4, 6, 7, 11
The Celestial Toymaker	1, 2, 3, 4

OTHER RECORDINGS

Over the years, other audio recordings of missing *Doctor Who* episodes have come to light.

David Butler made recordings from Episode Four of 'The Web Planet' in 1965 through to the final episode of 'Logopolis' in 1981. However, as audio tape was expensive, he recorded only occasional episodes; generally the first and last of each story. Of the third season episodes, he recorded only 'Mission to the Unknown', Episode Eight of 'The Daleks Masterplan' and Episode One of 'The Ark'. Butler's recording of 'Mission to the Unknown' is regarded as on a par with David Holman's.

Butler generally recorded each episode complete with opening and closing credits. And as he usually recorded the last episode of a story, he would keep the

---

[74] Not including the John de Rivaz recordings, which are still being assessed at the time of writing.

CHAPTER 12

recording going after it concluded, to capture any trailer that might be aired for the following week's new adventure. Thus the soundtracks of trailers for 'The Abominable Snowmen', 'The Enemy of the World', 'The Web of Fear', 'Fury from the Deep' and 'The Wheel in Space' were preserved for posterity.

An unknown Australian fan recorded the soundtracks to 'The Invasion' and 'The Space Pirates' from their screenings on the ABC in the early 1970s (as evidenced by the continuity announcements preserved on them). Copies of these recordings were commonly distributed in *Doctor Who* fandom in the UK in the 1980s, and the clarity is extremely good. In fact, those of Episodes One and Four of 'The Invasion' were used as the basis for the re-mastered soundtrack of the animated versions included on that story's DVD release in 2006, while those of 'The Space Pirates' are better than both Holman's and Landen's.

Alternative off-air recordings have since been found of 'Galaxy 4' and 'The Daleks Masterplan', although they aren't quite as good, quality-wise, as the Strong and Holman ones. These were recorded off-air by Allen Wilson, along with Episode One of 'The Myth Makers', which includes material at the very start that is missing from Holman's copy.

TELE-SNAPS AND OFF-AIR PHOTOGRAPHS
JOHN CURA

For many missing episodes of *Doctor Who*, there at least remains a good photographic record of what was seen on screen. This is down to the work of one man – John Cura.

Cura was born in 1902, and developed early interests in both photography and electronics. He served as a photographer for the RAF in the Second World War, but left the service at the end of the War in 1945. He began working as a freelance photographer, but was interested in the newly restored television service that the BBC had started in 1946.

He hit upon the idea of taking photographs from the television screen as a way of making a record of programmes in the live, pre-videotape age, and wrote to the BBC in September 1947, outlining his ideas. His initial proposal was to approach the various actors who appeared in the BBC's television productions, to see if they wanted to keep a record of their performances, and then charge them a small fee for taking good quality off-air photographs of whichever programme they were appearing in. To enable him to do this, he had designed his own camera equipment, which was able to handle the demands of capturing an image generated on a 405-line cathode ray tube.

Cura's camera worked with 35mm film, but was adapted by him to use only half of the available frame for each picture, thus doubling the number of pictures he could take with a roll of film. But this meant that the size of the final, developed pictures was only 24mm x 18mm – roughly the size of a postage stamp. He also offered enlargements,

WIPED!

which were 60mm x 40mm – about the size of a standard business card.

After a bit of to-ing and fro-ing with the BBC's legal department, it was eventually agreed that Cura could offer his services to the actors who appeared in the BBC's programmes. He began taking off-air photographs with some degree of gusto, and found a ready stream of customers in the acting community, all willing to pay a small fee to have some record of their television performances.

In the early 1950s, Cura refined his business ideas. He approached the BBC once again. This time he offered to take, for a small fee, a set of between 40 and 80 high-quality off-air photographs of any given production, which he would then supply to the relevant BBC department as a way for them to keep a record of the programme.

By the end of the 1950s, Cura had taken over a quarter of a million off-screen pictures, and had built up a large client list of celebrities of the day, such as Benny Hill, and the Beverley Sisters, who went on to became good friends of the photographer. He coined the name 'Tele-snaps' to market his pictures and promote his business. If you wanted Tele-snaps, then John Cura was your man.

In the late 1950s, Cura set up a three-tiered service offer to the BBC. What he called Single Coverage would provide between 60 and 70 of the smaller size Tele-snaps of any given programme. At nearly double the cost was Double Coverage, which would provide between 130 and 140 Tele-snaps at the smaller size with 20 at the larger size. The final package was Triple Coverage, and would provide between 190 and 210 smaller size Tele-snaps and 30 enlargements. The BBC decided that production budgets would generally run to only Single Coverage for most programmes that decided to commission Cura.

By the time *Doctor Who* began in 1963, it was a fairly common practice for BBC programmes to have a set of Tele-snaps taken by Cura. This was down to the discretion of each individual BBC producer, and was paid for out of each programme's individual budget. Cura would also offer copies of the photos to the directors of the programmes and to the actors who appeared in them.

It would seem that Cura was a semi-regular chronicler of *Doctor Who* during Verity Lambert's time as producer. But when John Wiles took over from her, starting from 'Galaxy 4', it would appear that his services were dispensed with. No records exist of any payments being made to Cura during Wiles' time as producer, and no Tele-snaps from any of the episodes between 'Galaxy 4' and 'The Celestial Toymaker' have been discovered.

Cura was back with his camera to capture the first episode of 'The Gunfighters', as Innes Lloyd replaced Wiles at the programme's helm. Cura then stayed with *Doctor Who* until the third episode of 'The Mind Robber' in 1968, failing to take Tele-snaps of only two episodes during that period.

Cura supplied copies of his Tele-snaps to the *Doctor Who* production office, but

CHAPTER 12

most of these were not to be seen again for many years. He also sold copies to various people who worked on the series. Director Christopher Barry was one of Cura's occasional clients, purchasing copies of the Tele-snaps for 'The Daleks' Episodes One, Two and Five, 'The Rescue', 'The Romans', 'The Savages' and 'The Power of the Daleks', all of which stories he directed. Other customers included director Richard Martin ('The Daleks'), director Hugh David ('The Highlanders'), director John Davies ('The Macra Terror') and actor Michael Wolf (who played Nils Jensen in 'The Moonbase'). Both Wolf and Barry also ordered enlargements of certain images – in Wolf's case, of scenes in which his character was featured.

It's unclear why Cura stopped photographing *Doctor Who* after the third instalment of 'The Mind Robber', transmitted on Saturday 28 September 1968, but one possibility is that his health was declining. He died just a few months later, on Monday 21 April 1969, having been suffering with cancer of the colon for some time.

It wasn't until the early 1980s that Cura's *Doctor Who* Tele-snaps were rediscovered, in a very piecemeal fashion. Writer Jeremy Bentham, when doing research for his book *Doctor Who – The Early Years* (WH Allen, 1984), had arranged to meet up with Christopher Barry to talk to him about the early days of the programme. Barry happened to show Bentham his collection of Tele-snaps from various stories, which ultimately led to the full set of Tele-snaps from Episode One of 'The Power of the Daleks' being reproduced as an endpiece to Bentham's book.

In 1986, writer Patrick Mulkern visited Hugh David to interview him for that year's *Doctor Who Magazine* Summer Special, and during their conversation, David produced his copies of the Tele-snaps from 'The Highlanders'. Mulkern arranged to borrow them, and a selection of them accompanied the printed interview in the magazine.

December 1986 saw the DWAS newsletter *Celestial Toyroom* print a selection of Christopher Barry's Tele-snaps from Episode Two of 'The Power of the Daleks', with Episodes Three to Six appearing in the following months. At the same time, the fanzine *DWB* also ran a selection of 'The Power of the Daleks' Tele-snaps to accompany an interview they had done with Barry. Barry also did an interview with the fanzine *The Frame* in early 1987, which again featured some of 'The Power of the Daleks' Tele-snaps. Later issues of *The Frame* would run a selection of Barry's Tele-snaps from 'The Savages' as a photonovel, covering an episode an issue.

Fan Richard Landen experimented with his video editing skills in early 1987, synching up his off-air soundtrack of Episode Two of 'The Power of the Daleks' with a selection of Barry's Tele-snaps, to create a reconstruction of the episode. This was shown at the first TellyCon convention in April 1987.

Over the next few years, *DWB* was heavily involved in tracking down and printing more *Doctor Who* Tele-snaps. It published a full photonovel of 'The Power of the

WIPED!

Daleks' in 1988, and in 1991 located and published in the same form Michael Wolf's Tele-snaps of all four episodes of 'The Moonbase'. Later that year, it printed 36 Tele-snaps from 'The Macra Terror', which were all that director John Davies had retained from that story. *DWB* photonovels of 'The Savages' (sourced from Christopher Barry's collection) and 'The Highlanders' (from Hugh David's) soon followed.

In 1993, Marcus Hearn was the assistant editor of *Doctor Who Magazine*, and was researching the early days of *Doctor Who* for a series of articles he was planning to write as part of the publication's celebration of the show's thirtieth anniversary. He was visiting the BBC's Written Archives Centre at Caversham, which was the repository of many decades' worth of BBC paperwork and documentation, and the home of many files from the *Doctor Who* production office dating back to 1963.

Hearn had asked the BBC Caversham staff to produce for him a computer print-out detailing all of the files they had relating to *Doctor Who*. Most of the files listed were for specific stories, but at the end was an entry for two that simply stated 'Tele-snaps: Series Z – UU'. Hearn asked to inspect the files, and after a short wait, was presented with two old folders. Inside were bound page after page of Cura's Tele-snaps; a complete run from 'The Gunfighters' (story 'Z') through to 'The Mind Robber' (story 'UU'). The only episodes not covered were Episode Four of 'The Enemy of the World', Episode Five of 'The Dominators' and the final two episodes of 'The Mind Robber'. Each page was devoted to a single episode, and had every one of Cura's postage-stamp-sized photographs of that episode glued onto it in strips, alongside a cutting of the relevant *Radio Times* billing.

Hearn contacted his editor at *Doctor Who Magazine*, Gary Russell, and they made arrangements with Caversham for professional photographic negatives to be made of all the Tele-snaps.

By a startling coincidence, during exactly the same period that Hearn was visiting the Written Archives Centre, *Doctor Who* writer and historian Stephen James Walker was also conducting research there for a series of books being co-written with David J Howe and Mark Stammers for publication by Virgin Publishing. Like Hearn, Walker discovered the files of Tele-snaps, and immediately realised their importance. He had a photocopy made of each page in the files, and explored with the Written Archives Centre staff the possibility of getting proper photographic copies produced. He quickly realised, however, that the cost of this would far exceed the budget he had available. After discussing the matter with fellow researcher Andrew Pixley, he contacted Russell at *Doctor Who Magazine* and informed him of the find. Russell told Walker that Hearn had also been in touch the same week with the same news!

The Tele-snap discovery was announced in the November 1993 edition of *Doctor Who Magazine*, which also printed all of the Tele-snaps for 'The Tenth Planet' Episode Four for the first time. Over the next two years, *Doctor Who Magazine*, and its sister

CHAPTER 12

publication *Doctor Who Classic Comics*, would print a Tele-snap Archive in each issue, showcasing all of the Cura Tele-snaps of one particular episode per issue. This feature was alternated between the two publications, and would run through whole stories at a time. Eventually, the Tele-snaps of 'The Smugglers', 'The Highlanders', 'The Underwater Menace', 'The Macra Terror', 'The Faceless Ones', 'The Evil of the Daleks', 'The Ice Warriors', 'The Enemy of the World', 'The Web of Fear', 'Fury from the Deep' and 'The Wheel in Space' were all printed in this way. (Those for 'The Savages', 'The Power of the Daleks' and 'The Moonbase' weren't printed due to the exposure that they had already been given by *DWB*.)

In 1999, just months after the 16mm film print of the first episode of 'The Crusade' was found in New Zealand, former *Doctor Who* production assistant/production manager George Gallaccio was being interviewed by Peter Griffiths for *Doctor Who Magazine*. During the interview, Gallaccio mentioned that he had a number of Tele-snaps of old *Doctor Who* episodes, which he had obtained when the *Doctor Who* production office was having a bit of a clear-out in the mid-1970s. Gallaccio just happened to be in the office at the time, and was told he could help himself to anything that was going to be thrown in the skip. He took a shine to a batch of Cura's Tele-snaps that had been deemed surplus to requirements, and took them home with him. This collection included all four episodes of 'The Time Meddler' and 'The Tenth Planet', 'The Moonbase' Episodes One to Three, 'The Evil of the Daleks' Episodes Three, Five and Seven, and all four episodes of 'The Crusade'. This was the first time that Tele-snaps for 'The Crusade' (and for 'The Time Meddler', which wasn't a missing story) had been located.

Unfortunately, Gallaccio's Tele-snaps were discovered just too late to be used as visual material in BBC Video's VHS release of 'The Crusade', which instead featured newly-recorded links by William Russell (playing Ian Chesterton for the first time since 1965) to cover the events in the missing second and fourth episodes. The Tele-snaps were eventually published by *Doctor Who Magazine* a few months later. Gallaccio also held a few enlargements of selected Tele-snaps from 'The Smugglers', 'The Tenth Planet', 'The Highlanders' and 'The Underwater Menace'.[75]

---

[75] This poses the question – if Gallaccio's Tele-snaps were once part of the collection held by the *Doctor Who* production office, then do the ones in the Caversham files originate from another source within the BBC? Did another department, for whatever reason, and possibly unbeknownst to the *Doctor Who* production office, also arrange with Cura to purchase Tele-snaps of *Doctor Who* episodes? If so, could there perhaps have been a now-missing file covering serials 'A' ('An Unearthly Child') through to 'Y' ('The Celestial Toymaker'), despite the paperwork suggesting that none was taken during John Wiles' period as producer? Well, if there was such a file, then there is no record of it at the Written Archives Centre, and Tele-snaps from the episodes that aren't known to have been photographed by Cura have yet to surface.

WIPED!

The final discovery of Cura's *Doctor Who* work occurred in June 2003, and came about due to director Waris Hussein attending a signing session at the 10th Planet science fiction memorabilia shop in Barking. One person in attendance that day was Derek Handley, a fan with a keen interest in the Tele-snaps of missing *Doctor Who* episodes. He knew that the surviving production paperwork at Caversham indicated that Cura had taken Tele-snaps of 'Marco Polo', a story of which Hussein had directed six out of seven episodes. Hussein distinctly remembered being given a set of Tele-snaps for each of those six episodes. A few months later, he located his copies of them, and *Doctor Who Magazine* was able to print them over six issues in 2004.

In total, 71 of the missing 106 episodes of *Doctor Who* have Tele-snaps that survive to give some visual record of the on-screen action. They can show us how sets looked and how characters appeared, and can give a real feel for the style and content of each of the episodes they document.

The word 'Tele-snap' has, in recent times, become interchangeable with the phrase 'off-air photograph' to describe a picture taken from a television set's screen. But strictly speaking, the word was coined by Cura to describe and differentiate his work from any other off-air photographs. In fairness to Cura, it is perhaps best to assign the descriptor 'Tele-snap' *only* to those photos he took. Any off-screen photos taken by other people over the years are not 'Tele-snaps' in the truest sense.

The *Doctor Who* production paperwork that survives at the Written Archives Centre shows that Cura photographed some early William Hartnell episodes for which no Tele-snaps are currently known to exist. However, only one of these is a missing episode.

The following table indicates which episodes we know Cura to have photographed:

Story	Existing Tele-snaps (numbers in brackets indicate how many Tele-snaps from each episode were taken)	Missing Tele-snaps (Where production paperwork indicates that Cura was paid to photograph an episode, but no actual pictures are known to survive)
An Unearthly Child		1
The Daleks	1 (76), 2 (76), 5(76)	3, 6, 7
The Edge of Destruction		1, 2
Marco Polo	1 (72), 2 (78), 3 (75), 5 (70), 6 (69), 7 (80)	4

CHAPTER 12

The Keys of Marinus		1, 2
The Aztecs		
The Sensorites		1, 2, 6
The Reign of Terror		
Planet of Giants		1, 2, 3
The Dalek Invasion of Earth		
The Rescue	1 (78), 2 (72)	
The Romans	1, (76), 2 (76), 3, (76), 4 (77)	
The Web Planet		1, 2, 3, 4, 5, 6
The Crusade	1 (?), 2 (72), 3 (?), 4(67)	
The Space Museum		
The Chase		1, 2, 3, 4, 5, 6
The Time Meddler	1 (?), 2 (?), 3 (?), 4 (?)	
Galaxy 4		
Mission to the Unknown		
The Myth Makers		
The Daleks Masterplan		
The Massacre		
The Ark		
The Celestial Toymaker		
The Gunfighters	1 (68), 2 (71), 3 (72), 4 (73)	
The Savages	1 (70), 2 (65), 3 (70), 4 (73)	
The War Machines	1 (69), 2 (67), 3 (67), 4 (75)	
The Smugglers	1 (71), 2 (67), 3 (71), 4 (71)	
The Tenth Planet	1 (72), 2 (66), 3 (67), 4 (76)	
The Power of the Daleks	1 (70), 2 (69), 3 (67), 4 (68), 5 (66), 6 (75)	
The Highlanders	1 (64), 2 (71), 3 (71), 4 (69)	
The Underwater Menace	1 (66), 2 (73), 3 (72), 4 (68)	
The Moonbase	1 (71), 2 (71), 3 (78), 4 (71)	
The Macra Terror	1 (62), 2 (64), 3 (64), 4 (57)	
The Faceless Ones	1 (64), 2, (68), 3 (62), 4 (64), 5 (63), 6 (61)	
The Evil of the Daleks	1 (63), 2 (64), 3 (61), 4 (63), 5 (67), 6 (65), 7 (64)	
The Tomb of the Cybermen	1 (62), 2 (63), 3 (67), 4 (64)	
The Abominable Snowmen	1 (62), 2 (66), 3 (60), 4 (63), 5 (63), 6 (59)	
The Ice Warriors	1 (62), 2 (64), 3 (66), 4 (71), 5 (63), 6 (60)	

WIPED!

The Enemy of the World	1 (64), 2 (64), 3 (64), 5 (61), 6 (63)	
The Web of Fear	1 (64), 2 (63), 3 (59), 4 (62), 5 (60), 6 (62)	
Fury from the Deep	1 (59), 2 (63), 3 (60), 4 (63), 5 (60), 6 (62)	
The Wheel in Space	1 (60), 2 (63), 3 (62), 4 (62), 5 (62) 6 (66)	
The Dominators	1 (60), 2 (60), 3 (60), 4 (63)	
The Mind Robber	1 (62), 2 (63) 3 (63)	
The Invasion		
The Krotons		
The Seeds of Death		
The Space Pirates		
The War Games		

OTHER OFF-AIR PHOTOGRAPHS

John Cura wasn't the only person to take off-screen photographs from episodes of *Doctor Who* in the 1960s. There are a handful of other known examples that survive to give us a glimpse of what the missing episodes actually looked like.

'MARCO POLO'

During the 1965 screenings of 'Marco Polo' and 'The Aztecs' in Australia, a young fan used his camera to take a selection of off-screen photographs. In total, two photos from 'Marco Polo' Episode Six ('Mighty Kublai Khan'), six photos from Episode Seven ('Assassin at Peking') and a single photo from Episode Four of 'The Aztecs' ('Day of Darkness') were taken by the unknown fan. The photos were unearthed in 1988 by Australian fans Dallas Jones and Antony Howe, and the 'Marco Polo' ones were published in the fanzine *DWB* later that same year.

'THE DALEKS MASTERPLAN'

DWB editor Gary Leigh visited Australia in 1986, and took the opportunity to meet up with the actor Robert Jewell, in order to interview him for the magazine. Jewell had been a Dalek operator for all of their appearances in *Doctor Who* in the 1960s, and had also played a Zarbi in 'The Web Planet' and a Macra in 'The Macra Terror'. He had moved to Australia in the early 1970s. On Christmas Day 1965, Jewell himself had taken 20 off-screen photographs of his appearance as the clown in Episode Seven of 'The Daleks Masterplan' ('The Feast of Steven') – his one role in the series when he wasn't enveloped by a monster costume. During the course of his chat with Leigh,

CHAPTER 12

Jewell mentioned these photos, and that he still had them. Leigh borrowed the prints, and they were published in *DWB* later in 1986.

'THE EVIL OF THE DALEKS'

Aside from the John Cura Tele-snaps, a few other off-screen photos from this story have cropped up over the years. DWAS artist Gordon 'Drog' Lengden took two photos during the story's 1968 repeat of the scene at the beginning of Episode Six where the Doctor is playing 'trains' with the humanised Daleks. Fan Terry Reason took one off-screen photo from Episode Four and two from Episode Five. The story's designer, Christopher Thompson, also took 26 off-screen photographs during Episode One's transmission. All of these various photos from 'The Evil of the Daleks' have been published in issue three of the fanzine *Nothing At The End of the Lane*.

'THE WEB OF FEAR'

Fan Terry Reason took two off-screen photos from this story, but these have never been published to date.

BEHIND-THE-SCENES FILM

A number of people who were present when *Doctor Who* was being made in the 1960s and 1970s kept a record of the occasion. 8mm film cameras were a fairly common accessory in the decades before video cameras were invented.

Standard 8mm film was developed by Eastman Kodak in the early 1930s, and was first available for purchase in 1932. 8mm was actually a spool of 16mm film with double the amount of perforations along each edge, which was then passed through the camera in such a way that only half of the film was exposed. When one half of the film had been used, the camera was opened, and the spool flipped over. The other half was then exposed. During processing, the film was split down the middle, giving two lengths of 8mm film. This enabled four times as many frames to be shot on 8mm film as on the same length of 16mm film.

In 1965, Super-8 film was introduced. This was an easier system to use, as the film was contained in a cartridge that didn't require reloading and re-threading halfway through. Most 8mm film cartridges contained 50 feet of film, which was usually run at either 24 frames a second (which meant the cartridge could record roughly two-and-a-half minutes of material) or 18 frames a second (which would then run to three minutes and 20 seconds).

The earliest known example of behind-the-scenes 8mm film footage from *Doctor Who* was shot by actress Carole Ann Ford (who played Susan) on Friday 23 October 1964, during her final day of work on the series. She captured one minute and 50

WIPED!

seconds of material showing her co-stars rehearsing on set during the studio day for the final episode of 'The Dalek Invasion of Earth'. This was on standard colour 8mm stock, and was silent. Later, Ford re-used the film to record a family function, and accidentally double-exposed it. This meant that both sets of images were permanently imprinted on it. This double-exposed film is included as an extra on the DVD release of 'The Dalek Invasion of Earth'.

The penultimate William Hartnell story, 'The Smugglers', is the next from which behind-the-scenes film is known to exist. In this instance it was 16mm mute colour film that was used to record the proceedings. Two minutes and 37 seconds was shot during the location filming done for this story on Wednesday 22 June 1966 at Trethewey Farm in Cornwall. This included sequences of William Hartnell's stunt double, Gordon Craig, being carried away and bundled onto the back of a handcart, Cherub (George A Cooper) watching proceedings from behind some bushes, and shots of the Squire (Paul Whitsun-Jones) on horseback.

Tony Cornell was a designer based at the BBC's Ealing Film Studios in the mid-1960s, and regularly worked on *Doctor Who* when filming was done there. The stories he worked on included 'The Tenth Planet', 'The Evil of the Daleks', 'The Web of Fear' and 'Fury from the Deep'. During the making of 'The Evil of the Daleks', he took his 8mm camera (loaded with black and white silent film) along to several of the filming days. On Wednesday 26 April 1967, he filmed the Visual Effects Department's designers Michealjohn Harris and Peter Day working on the modelwork for some of the Dalek city scenes for the latter episodes of the story. On Tuesday 16 and Wednesday 17 May 1967, he returned to film material on the studio floor of the Emperor Dalek's control room. This time, full-sized sets were utilised, along with full-sized Dalek props. These were used to pre-film some effects sequences of exploding Daleks, and the final destruction of the Emperor for the last episode of the story. Cornell then edited all this footage down into a short film he called *The Last Dalek*, which ran to nine minutes and 35 seconds.

Cornell next filmed material during production of 'Fury from the Deep'. Only this time, his camera was loaded with mute colour 8mm film. On Tuesday 5 and Wednesday 6 March 1968, he recorded four minutes and five seconds of footage of the final attack of the seaweed creature from Episode Six of this story.

The location filming for 'The Abominable Snowmen', which took place in North Wales between Monday 4 and Saturday 9 September 1967, was covered by two members of the *Doctor Who* team, who each took along an 8mm camera. One was director Gerald Blake, who shot three minutes and 26 seconds of colour mute film of the cast relaxing between takes. The other was Jamie actor Frazer Hines, who shot just over a minute-and-a-half of silent colour footage of his behind-the-scenes antics.

CHAPTER 12

During the 1970s and 1980s, colour 8mm footage was shot during the location filming of 'The Dæmons', 'The Sea Devils', 'Shada', 'The Leisure Hive' and 'Full Circle', although all of these stories survive at the BBC to this day.

One final 8mm film of note was discovered in 2009. In 1967, Gerry Irwin of the Ealing and Boston Manor Cine Club took his colour 8mm camera to the workshops of Shawcraft models in Uxbridge, who used to provide many and varied props for *Doctor Who* at the time. Colour footage was recorded of the Dalek props (circa 'The Evil of the Daleks'), the Macra, various model TARDISes and the Chameleon Tours plane from 'The Faceless Ones', amongst other items of note. This film was included as an extra on the DVD release of 'The Chase'/'The Space Museum' in 2010.

There are bound to have been other instances during the 1960s and 1970s of *Doctor Who* location work being captured on 8mm film by members of the public. Indeed, still photographs taken on location for some stories, including 'The Invasion' and 'The Mutants', show onlookers holding 8mm cameras. To date, however, no other surviving films of this nature have surfaced.

WIPED!

CHAPTER 13
MISSING *DOCTOR WHO* ABROAD IN THE 1960S AND 1970S: THE HARTNELL AND TROUGHTON YEARS

A large number of countries have purchased *Doctor Who* over the years, and a detailed listing of transmission information for all known overseas broadcasts of missing episodes is given in Appendix (i) of this book. But in this section, we'll look a bit more closely at the situation in some of the countries that purchased the Hartnell and Troughton stories, simply because this is the era of the programme that all the missing episodes are from.

Most of the obvious markets for *Doctor Who* in the 1960s and 1970s – such as Canada, Australia and New Zealand – have been thoroughly investigated over the years, to the point that it's now almost certain that no missing episodes reside in their television archives. Broadcasters in other countries, such as Cyprus, Singapore and Mexico, have been contacted numerous times over the years, and have convinced most interested observers that there is nothing more to be found there. More recently, a thorough investigation of African stations was instigated, and early reports indicate that nothing further exists there either.

SALES IN THE 1960S AND 1970S

All early overseas sales of Hartnell and Troughton *Doctor Who* episodes were on 16mm film. (It was not until the mid-1980s, when Australia and America began purchasing stories from the series' back catalogue, that black and white episodes were supplied on videotape.) Many of these sales were to countries that had close cultural, colonial and economic ties to Great Britain. Where appropriate, these ties have been highlighted to help explain why *Doctor Who* was sold to those countries in the first place.

An early indication of *Doctor Who*'s success in overseas markets can be found in an internal BBC Enterprises memo dated 7 July 1965, which rounded up the details of where the series had been offered and successfully sold up to that point in time. ABC in Australia had purchased 53 episodes ('An Unearthly Child' through to 'The Rescue'), Associated Rediffusion in Malta, CBC in Canada, the Nigerian Television Service in Lagos and RTS in Singapore had all purchased 26 episodes ('An Unearthly Child' through to 'The Keys of Marinus'), while NZBC in New Zealand had purchased 13 episodes ('An Unearthly Child' through to 'The Edge of Destruction'). Additionally, a distribution company called Television International Enterprises Ltd had purchased 26 episodes, from 'An Unearthly Child' through to 'The Keys of Marinus', for screening

WIPED!

in Gibraltar, Aden, Trinidad and Tobago and Bermuda. Together, these sales had generated an income just short of £36,000 for BBC Enterprises, at a time when the average budget for an episode of *Doctor Who* was around £2,500.

WHAT WAS TELEVISION INTERNATIONAL ENTERPRISES?

Television International Enterprises Ltd (TIE) was a company representing a large number of radio and television stations around the world that were looking to sell their programmes to European markets.

In 1966, TIE advertised that the territories they represented were as follows. In Africa, Ethiopia (EBS, soon to become ETV), Kenya (Voice of Kenya), Malawi (MBC – radio only), Mauritius (MBC), Nigeria (NTS – television only, NBC – radio only), Sierra Leone (SLBS and SLTV), Sudan (SBS and STV) and Uganda (Radio Uganda – radio only). In the Caribbean and Western Atlantic, Barbados (CBC), Bermuda (ZFB1 and ZFB-TV), Jamaica (JBC), Trinidad and Tobago (TTT – television only) and the Virgin Islands (WBNB and WBNB-TV). In the Middle East, the Federation of South Arabia (SABS and SATV).

Another advert for TIE in 1969 shows a few changes. In Africa, Malawi and Sudan had been dropped altogether, while in Nigeria TIE now represented only NBC-TV, but this time for television only. In the Caribbean, Bermuda and the Virgin Islands had been dropped, but Guyana (GBS – radio only) had been added. TIE advertised its presence in Asia for the first time, representing Pakistan (PTC), and also in the Far East, representing Hong Kong (HK-TVB – not to be confused with RTV). In the Middle East, it now claimed to represent only the People's Republic of South Yemen (PROSYBS), which was more of a change of name for the region than anything else.

By 1972, TIE had increased the number of radio stations it represented enormously. Its television representation remained largely the same though. In Africa, Sudan had returned to the fold, but Ethiopia had departed. In the Caribbean, the Virgin Islands were back, and a new market of Surinam (SRS and STVS) had been added. In the Middle East, Aden (PDRY BS) was listed for the first time.

TIE nominally looked to find overseas markets for material produced by these stations through its offices in London and New York, or through its European offices in Amsterdam, Paris and Geneva.

However, through its division TIE (Programmes) Ltd, the company also acted as a purchasing agent for some of the above-mentioned stations, plus the Gibraltar Broadcasting Corporation, which it listed separately. This meant it acquired programmes from television stations such as the BBC, and then sold them on to its select group of foreign television broadcasters.

CHAPTER 13

From the previously-mentioned BBC Enterprises document, we know that TIE handled sales of 'An Unearthly Child', 'The Daleks', 'The Edge of Destruction', 'Marco Polo' and 'The Keys of Marinus' to television stations in Gibraltar, Aden, Trinidad and Tobago and Bermuda at some point prior to July 1965. But it's not known if the company was involved in any later sales to any of these four countries, or in sales of *Doctor Who* to any of the other countries that it also represented. Chances are, it probably was.

Behind the scenes at TIE, things were not entirely what they appeared to be. The company chairman was one Sir David Stirling, who in 1942, during the Second World War, founded the Special Air Service, or SAS as it's now usually known. He was captured by the Germans in 1943, and spent most of the rest of the War as a captive in the Colditz prisoner-of-war camp. Some years after hostilities ceased, Stirling set up TIE as a legitimate business. However, he also set up a company called Watchguard International Ltd, which sold arms and ammunition overseas and operated from the same offices as TIE, and KAS Enterprises, a private military company that hired out ex-SAS (and sometimes current SAS) members for clandestine work, supported at times by the British Government's various security services. As a result, TIE was sometimes used as a front for some of Stirling's more… *unorthodox* work; most significantly, the funding and fighting of a counter-revolution in Yemen in 1963, which was backed by MI6.

However, TIE did undoubtedly have legitimate television interests, as can be seen from its adverts in the World Radio TV Handbooks between 1966 and 1972. Amongst other things, it was the company responsible for bringing the American series *Sesame Street* to the UK, and later worked with Jim Henson to create *The Muppet Show*.

MORE OVERSEAS INTEREST

Further sales of *Doctor Who* were anticipated by BBC Enterprises. The July 1965 report noted that NZBC in New Zealand had been offered 'Marco Polo', 'The Keys of Marinus', 'The Reign of Terror' and all the stories from 'The Dalek Invasion of Earth' through to 'The Crusade'. CBC in Canada had been offered 'The Aztecs' through to 'The Reign of Terror', and then 'The Dalek Invasion of Earth' through to 'The Crusade'. Singapore had been offered the complete run of stories from 'The Aztecs' through to 'The Rescue'. Not all of these sales ultimately happened, however.

Most interestingly, the report goes on to detail the countries that had been offered *Doctor Who* but had not accepted it at that point: Japan (offered 'An Unearthly Child' through to 'The Keys of Marinus'), Yugoslavia (offered 'An Unearthly Child' and 'The Daleks'), Italy (offered 'An Unearthly Child' through to 'Marco Polo'), USA (offered 'The Daleks' through to 'The Crusade', barring 'Planet of Giants'), Finland, Switzerland,

WIPED!

and Sweden (all offered 'The Daleks', 'The Edge of Destruction' and 'The Dalek Invasion of Earth'), Holland (offered 'The Daleks', 'The Aztecs' and 'The Sensorites'), Lebanon (offered 'The Daleks' and 'The Dalek Invasion of Earth'), Germany (offered 'Marco Polo', 'The Aztecs' and 'The Dalek Invasion of Earth'), and Cyprus (offered 'The Dalek Invasion of Earth'). The report also noted that Associated London Scripts Management, who represented writer Terry Nation, had purchased four episodes of 'The Dalek Invasion of Earth'.

THE RELIABILITY OF BBC PAPERWORK!

A word of warning … Much of the following information comes from old BBC documentation of varying reliability, and some of the dates quoted make no real sense. For example, the sale of a story to a particular country might be logged on one piece of paperwork as having taken place on a certain date, but transmission or programme traffic records from the country itself might show that the foreign broadcaster actually received or screened the episodes some months prior to that date. The writer of the story – who would always receive a residual payment for each sale – would often have the sale notified to him on a later date still, and sometimes this is the only remaining record in the BBC's files of a story being sold to a particular country. So sometimes we have a date for a story being purchased by a foreign station that comes *after* that of the story's known transmission on that station.

The main source of the following information is a type of internal BBC paperwork called Clearance History Sheets. Each story is logged on its own A4 sheet of paper, with its production code (A, B, etc), the number of episodes, and the BBC1 transmission date of each episode typed on it. Sometimes a story title has also been written on by hand. Each story is then assigned an internal BBC sales code, with a second code listed if a foreign language version was also detailed as available.

So, for example, the Clearance History Sheet for 'DR. WHO: SERIES 'W'' has 'Dr Who and the Massacre of Bartholomew' written on it, along with 'War of God'. 'NO. IN SERIES' is given as '4', and the BBC1 transmission dates of all four episodes have been typed underneath. The 'CODE' for this story is given as '44704', which has been typed onto the form, but written next to this is '45699 (SPANISH VERSION CODE NO.)'. The form is then divided into eight columns:

Sale to	Inv. No.	Prog. Contr. Advised	Music Copyright Advised	Copyright Script Advised	O/S Film Purchaser Advised	Stills Tel. Accts. Advised	Misc.

CHAPTER 13

Under 'Sale to', the name of each country to which the story was sold has been written in by hand. Under 'Inv. No', an invoice number is logged, presumably ensuring that the sale has been charged. Then a series of dates are logged in the next three columns, showing if and when other BBC departments were notified of the sale. The final three columns are invariably left blank on all the *Doctor Who* sales sheets.

For example, the exact details on the sheet for 'The Massacre' are as follows:

Sale to	Inv. No.	Prog. Contr. Advised	Music Copyright Advised	Copyright Script Advised	O/S Film Purchaser Advised	Stills Tel. Accts. Advised	Misc.
Australia	15669	13.4.67 Paid 24.4.67 Inc 2 M/CWLTH	13.4.67	19.4.67 107 CVP	-	-	-
Barbados	17115	16.8.67 1 M/CWLTH IN HAND	16.8.67	18.8.67 222 CVP	-	-	-
Zambia	19320	25.3.68	25.3.68	2.4.68 461 CVP	-	-	-
New Zealand	TE/3877	18.12.68	18.12.68	20.12.68 763 CVP	-	-	-
Sierra Leone	TE/11612	12.8.70 Paid 14.9.70 + 1 M/CWLTH	12.8.70	20.10.70 2348 CVP	-	-	-
Singapore (1 TX)	TE/20121	18/12/72	18/12/72	19.12.72 6345 CVP	-	-	-

Some of these annotations are self explanatory. The '1TX' next to Singapore means that they purchased the rights to screen the story only once, as opposed to the usual two screenings that sales contracts allowed. (This might have had something to do with the sale taking place after the initial five-year rights period had expired.) Some annotations refer to the sale being made to a Commonwealth country (M/CWLTH), which probably had a bearing on the amount that the BBC had then to pay writers, musicians, etc. The 'CVP' annotation is probably the initials of the person who filled in this information on the sheets at the time.[76]

For the information presented in this chapter, I have tended to take the date of a sale as the date logged in the BBC's paperwork for 'Prog. Contr. Advised' (which *probably* stands for Programme Contributors Advised – i.e. writers, musicians, actors or anyone that worked on the programme but wasn't BBC staff) – but where that date is inconclusive, other known dates from a foreign station's paperwork or from programme traffic records have been used. I've tried to indicate where this has been done in most cases. But don't try to read too many patterns into the various dates quoted in this section …

ADEN

The port of Aden in Yemen was owned by the British Crown from 1838 to 1963, and was part of the British Commonwealth during this time. It was located in a very strategic position for the British Empire, close to the Suez Canal, Bombay and Zanzibar, which were all also under British rule. The port became the state of Aden on its independence from Britain in 1963, becoming in turn part of the Federation of South Arabia, which was then renamed the People's Republic of South Yemen in November 1967.

Partly because of Aden's close links to Britain, the BBC was able to sell a number of its programmes to the country, via distributor TIE. There were two batches of *Doctor Who* sales, both in 1965, to the South Arabian Television Service (SATS). The first batch, in May 1965, consisted of 'An Unearthly Child', 'The Daleks', 'The Edge of Destruction', 'Marco Polo' and 'The Keys of Marinus', all sold through TIE. This was followed in November 1965 by 'The Aztecs', 'The Sensorites', 'The Reign of Terror', 'Planet of Giants', 'The Dalek Invasion of Earth' and 'The Rescue', although it's not known if these were also procured through TIE. On the BBC's sales sheets, it appears that Aden's purchase of this second batch of episodes was tied in to the sale of the same stories to Hong Kong, suggesting that for these stories at least, prints were perhaps shared between the two markets.

SATS began screening the series on Sunday 4 July 1965 with the opening episode of 'An Unearthly Child' and kept showing episodes weekly (albeit in differing time slots) until it screened the final episode of 'The Rescue' on Sunday 3 July 1966.

---

76 Clearance History Sheets have been found for most of the Hartnell and Troughton stories; however there are exceptions. No sheets have been located to date for 'The Chase', 'Mission to the Unknown', 'The Daleks Masterplan', 'The Wheel in Space', or 'The Invasion'. Information on the sales of these stories has therefore had to come from other sources. Also, some of the sheets that do survive have suffered from general wear and tear over the years – the sheet for 'An Unearthly Child' is particularly tatty – and some missing information has had to be interpolated from adjacent story sales.

CHAPTER 13

ALGERIA

Algeria is one of the largest countries in Northern Africa, located on the coast of the Mediterranean Sea. A mainly Arabic-speaking country, it was a French colony between 1830 and 1962, before it gained its independence later that same year. Television broadcasts first began there in December 1956.

Radiodiffusion Television Algerienne (RTA) purchased a batch of Hartnell episodes in July 1973, consisting of 'An Unearthly Child' (the surviving paperwork suggests that only the first episode of this story was screened), 'The Daleks', 'The Edge of Destruction', 'The Keys of Marinus', 'The Aztecs', 'The Sensorites', 'Planet of Giants', 'The Dalek Invasion of Earth' and 'The Rescue'. BBC documentation shows that these were for one transmission only; sales to other countries were nearly always for one screening *plus* one repeat. As Algeria is an Arabic-speaking country, the series was almost certainly dubbed into Arabic here.

Le Docteur Who debuted on RTA on Monday 31 December 1973 at 7.30 pm, with the opening episode of 'An Unearthly Child', given the title 'Suzane' in the television listings. This was followed on Tuesday 1 January 1974 with the first episode of 'The Daleks', 'The Dead Planet' ('La Planete'), again at 7.30 pm. Subsequent episodes were shown daily, even over weekends, in the same time slot. The final story shown, 'The Rescue', had its opening episode screened on Wednesday 6 February 1974.

Conjecture time here. The list of *Doctor Who* holdings prepared for 'Whose Doctor Who' in November 1976 shows that BBC Enterprises at Villiers House at that point held 16mm Arabic film prints of all of these – and only these – nine stories. Had the films supplied to Algeria in 1973 been returned to the UK at some point prior to November 1976, complete with Arabic soundtracks? And, if so, did these episodes also have their English soundtracks as well as the Arabic ones? The 'Whose Doctor Who' list seemingly indicates that the answer to the latter question is negative, but perhaps it was wrong on this point for some reason? For RTA to have shown the stories in Arabic, they would probably have needed to be supplied with three components by BBC Enterprises: a 16mm film print of each episode, a 16mm film negative of the same episode, and an M&E (music and effects) soundtrack, which would contain every element of sound *apart* from the dialogue. With all these elements, a new 16mm copy of the episode dubbed into Arabic could be originated, which would then become BBC copyright under the terms of the sale. When the rights to the material expired, then not only the positive and negative 16mm copies of the episodes but also the M&E tracks and the 16mm Arabic versions would have had to have been returned to Enterprises. So, for a seven-part story such as 'The Daleks', 28 tins of material would have had to have been returned. Does this start to sound familiar …?

If this is the case – and we can only guess – then this sale to Algeria and the

WIPED!

subsequent return of the English and Arabic film prints to BBC Enterprises might be the *only* reason why these nine stories from the first two seasons of *Doctor Who* were still held at BBC Enterprises in 1978.

In an interview that former Archive Selector Sue Malden gave to fan Douglas Wulf for the *Lost Doctor Who* website in 2007, she said of the recovery of 'The Daleks':

> '... the [prints] that Ian [Levine] and I found in Enterprises were a set that had come back, well, I can't remember where from, but the complete seven had come back from another country for destruction .... Enterprises were going to destroy the negatives, because they had finished selling the programme, thought there was no more value in the negatives, and had assumed that the master was still in the BBC archive.'

This seems to indicate that the film prints of 'The Daleks' found at Enterprises in 1978 had indeed recently been returned from another country.

AUSTRALIA

Australia was claimed by James Cook as part of the British Empire in 1770, although its pre-colonial roots go back tens of thousands of years before then. The British Crown Colony of New South Wales was established in 1788, and Britain went on to claim the rest of Western Australia in 1829.

Australia stayed as part of the British Empire until 1931, when the Statute of Westminster formally ended most of the constitutional links with the country. What few ties were left were finally severed by the Australia Act of 1986. However, Queen Elizabeth II is still the country's monarch, and Australia remains part of the British Commonwealth.

The country today is divided into six states and two mainland territories. The states are: New South Wales (with Sydney as its capital), Queensland (capital: Brisbane), South Australia (capital: Adelaide), Tasmania (capital: Hobart), Victoria (capital: Melbourne) and Western Australia (capital: Perth). The two territories are the Northern Territory (which is the size of a state, and has Darwin as its capital) and Australian Capital Territory (which is actually an enclave of New South Wales, and has Canberra as its capital).

The first Australian television test broadcasts took place in 1929 in Melbourne, but a full television service didn't begin until 1956. The catalyst for this being set up was the 1956 Olympics, which were due to be held in Melbourne. The country's initial channels were TCN-9 in Sydney (which began on 16 September 1956), GTV-9 in Melbourne (27 September 1956), HSV-7 in Melbourne (4 November 1956), ABN-2

CHAPTER 13

in Sydney (5 November 1956) and ABV-2 also in Melbourne (19 November 1956). By the end of the 1950s, the service had expanded to cover Brisbane, Adelaide and Perth, even though fewer than 5% of people in Melbourne and 1% of people in Sydney actually owned television sets.

During the 1960s, more stations began to emerge in the state and territory capitals, and these began to form into networks: the National Television Network (forerunner to the Nine Network), the Australian Television Network (later to become the Seven Network) and the Australian Broadcasting Commission, latterly renamed the Australian Broadcasting Corporation (ABC). It was the ABC that purchased *Doctor Who* from BBC Enterprises.

The ABC's first two channels were the aforementioned ABN-2 Sydney and ABV-2 Melbourne. More channels were added in the 1950s and 1960s:

State / Territory	Station	On-Air Date
New South Wales	ABN-2 Sydney	05/11/56
Victoria	ABV-2 Melbourne	19/11/56
Queensland	ABQ-2 Brisbane	02/11/59
Western Australia	ABW-2 Perth	07/05/60
Tasmania	ABT-2 Hobart	04/06/60
South Australia	ABS-2 Adelaide	11/03/62
Australian Capital Territory	ABC-3 Canberra	18/12/62

Direct microwave relays between Sydney, Melbourne and Canberra were established in 1961, which allowed for simultaneous broadcasts on these three stations, and in *Doctor Who*'s case, this happened a great deal for broadcasts in Sydney and Canberra. Brisbane, Adelaide, Perth and Hobart had to rely on programmes being physically sent on to them after another region had broadcast them. *Doctor Who* was shown in Australia in this manner, up until the mid-1970s, with different regions showing different episodes in different weeks. Although capital of its own territory, Canberra's television station came under the auspices of New South Wales's transmitters, and many of its *Doctor Who* transmissions were relays from Sydney.

The BBC at the time had a large office in Sydney, from where it would co-ordinate sales of its programmes to Australia, New Zealand and various other Southern Hemisphere countries. In the case of *Doctor Who*, BBC Sydney would receive a set of audition prints of all the episodes of a story from the BBC in London, and would then

WIPED!

arrange for the purchasing executives at ABC to view the material with a view to them buying the programme. This seemed to happen with all the *Doctor Who* stories sold to ABC in Australia in the first ten years or so, with every new story being auditioned prior to being purchased. Sales weren't taken for granted.

All programmes then purchased by the ABC for screening on its channels had to first be vetted by the Australian Film Censorship Board, which would assign a rating to each. Programmes were rated as either 'G' (General Audience), which meant that they could be shown at any time, or 'A' (Unsuitable for Children), which meant they could be shown only after 7.30 pm. For the vast majority of *Doctor Who* episodes, one single film print would be the audition print (shown by BBC Sydney to ABC), the purchased print (handed over to ABC), the viewing print for the censors (which would be cut if required), and the country-wide cycled transmission print (going round all the states and territories).

When the ABC purchased its first batch of 13 *Doctor Who* episodes from the BBC, from 'An Unearthly Child' through to 'The Edge of Destruction', it anticipated them receiving a 'G' rating, and so had early evening transmission slots lined up, beginning in May 1964. However, on 14 April 1964, the Australian Film Censorship Board rated the first two episodes of 'An Unearthly Child' as 'A', so a re-think was called for.

One option would have been for the ABC to edit the episodes, removing any material that the censors had deemed unsuitable for a 'G' rating, and then re-submit them for classification. But in this instance, the decision was taken to hold back transmission of *Doctor Who* until a later evening slot could be found. *Doctor Who* therefore didn't begin in Australia until Tuesday 12 January 1965, when ABW-2 Perth screened the first episode of 'An Unearthly Child' at 7.30 pm.

The episode was then shown in the same time slot on both ABN-2 Sydney and the Canberra station on Friday 15 January, on ABQ-2 Brisbane on Friday 22 January, and on ABV-2 Melbourne on Saturday 20 February. Viewers of ABS-2 Adelaide had to wait until 15 March for the series to begin, while those of ABT-2 Hobart had to wait even longer, until 11 June.

By this time, many of the states and territories had transmitter relay stations that could carry the signals from the main stations, allowing them to be viewed over a wider area. New South Wales had four transmitters as well as the stations at Sydney and Canberra;. Queensland and Victoria both had three; and Tasmania had one. However – and this is where things get really complicated – not every relay station screened *Doctor Who* at the same time as the parent stations. A *Doctor Who* film print had to travel between states and territories, and sometimes would have to come back on itself.

For example, for the first episode of 'An Unearthly Child' we have transmission dates as follows:

CHAPTER 13

State / Territory	Station / Transmitter	Transmission Date
Western Australia	ABW-2 Perth	12/01/65
New South Wales	ABN-2 Sydney	15/01/65
	ABC-3 Canberra	
	ABH N-5 Newcastle	
	ABC N-1 Orange	
	ABW N-5A Wollongong	
	ABR N-6 Lismore	
Queensland	ABQ-2 Brisbane	22/01/65
	ABD Q-3 Toowoomba	
Victoria	ABV-2 Melbourne	22/02/65
	ABL V-4 Traralgon	
	ABG V-3 Shepparton	
	ABE V-1 Bendigo	
Queensland	ABT Q-3 Townsville	04/03/65
South Australia	ABS-2 Adelaide	15/03/65
Queensland	ABR Q-3 Rockhampton	18/03/65
Tasmania	ABT-2 Hobart	11/06/65
	ABN T-3 Launceston	

Most of these stations transmitted a full run of stories from 'An Unearthly Child' through to 'The Crusade', although at least one region – Victoria – didn't screen 'The Dalek Invasion of Earth' or 'The Rescue'. This weekly run of episodes went through to April 1966, by which time more relay stations had been set up throughout Australia by the ABC. By the time ABC was screening 'The Crusade' it had the following stations and transmitters:

Western Australia	ABW-2 Perth	Station
	ABS W-5 Bunbury	Transmitter
	ABG W-4 Northam/York	Transmitter
	ABA W-2 Albany	Transmitter

WIPED!

	ABN-2 Sydney	Station
	ABM N-0 Wagga	Transmitter
	ABG N-7 Griffith	Transmitter
	ABH N-5 Newcastle	Transmitter
	ABT N-1 Taree	Transmitter
	ABD N-2 Grafton	Transmitter
New South Wales	ABU N-7 Upper Namoi	Transmitter
	ABC N-1 Orange	Transmitter
	ABQ N-3 Dubbo	Transmitter
	ABW N-5A Wollongong	Transmitter
	ABS N-0 Bega	Transmitter
	ABR N-6 Lismore	Transmitter
	ABC-3 Canberra	Station
	ABQ-2 Brisbane	Station
	ABM Q-6 Maryborough	Transmitter
	ABA Q-4 Mackay	Transmitter
Queensland	ABN Q-9 Cairns	Transmitter
	ABD Q-3 Toowoomba	Transmitter
	ABS Q-1 Warwick	Transmitter
	ABT Q-3 Townsville	Transmitter
	ABR Q-3 Rockhampton	Transmitter
	ABV-2 Melbourne	Station
	ABL V-4 Traralgon	Transmitter
	ABG V-3 Shepparton	Transmitter
	ABA V-1 Albury	Transmitter
Victoria	ABE V-1 Bendigo	Transmitter
	ABR V-3 Ballarat	Transmitter
	ABS V-4 Mildura	Transmitter
	ABV M-2 Swan Hill	Transmitter
	ABS-2 Adelaide	Station
South Australia	ABG S-1 Mount Gambier	Transmitter
	ABN S-1 Port Pirie	Transmitter
	ABL N-2 Broken Hill	Transmitter

CHAPTER 13

Tasmania	ABT-2 Hobart	Station
	ABN T-3 Launceston	Transmitter

Doctor Who returned to the ABC in October 1966, this time screening four nights a week in most regions, from Monday to Thursday. While some regions picked up the series where they had left off, with 'The Space Museum', others skipped ahead and showed 'The Time Meddler' and 'Galaxy 4' first, before returning to the earlier Season Two tales. This was probably due to the logistics of getting one set of prints around all the stations and transmitters within the space of a few weeks.

This weekly screening of episodes continued up until 'The Myth Makers' in most regions, before switching to the first Australian repeats of the series. Stories rated 'A' weren't included in these repeats, so that meant no 'An Unearthly Child', 'The Daleks', 'The Edge of Destruction', 'The Keys of Marinus' 'The Sensorites' or 'The Dalek Invasion of Earth'. 'The Rescue' was also omitted, and 'Marco Polo' was repeated only in Adelaide. But the remaining stories from the initial run, up to 'The Crusade', were all repeated in the weekly slots. Once these had finished, new stories began from 'The Massacre', and continued into 1967, ending with 'The Gunfighters'.

Within a few months, *Doctor Who* returned with 'The Savages', beginning in most areas in March/April 1967. The series was back to screening an episode a week, and this run went through to 'The Faceless Ones' in most areas, ending in January 1968. A few weeks later, and more repeats began, again going out four nights a week, from Monday through to Thursday. These began with either 'The Space Museum' or 'The Chase' (depending on region), and continued through to 'The Faceless Ones'.

'The Evil of the Daleks' was skipped over at this point, and instead Season Five began on most ABC regions a little over a week after the repeats concluded, 'The Tomb of the Cybermen' screening in July/August 1968 in most regions. Stories were then shown in order, until 'The Web of Fear', which was followed by 'The Evil of the Daleks'. After viewers had witnessed Victoria join the TARDIS crew, they could quickly see her leave, as 'Fury from the Deep' came next, and then 'The Wheel in Space' in April/May 1969.

Further repeats also began at around this time, but were a lot more varied between the ABC regions. For example, in May 1969, Brisbane repeated 'The Tomb of the Cybermen', Sydney repeated 'The Evil of the Daleks', Perth showed 'The Abominable Snowmen', Melbourne repeated 'The Faceless Ones', and Adelaide screened both 'The Tomb of the Cybermen' and 'The Abominable Snowmen'.

These runs of daily repeats tended to coincide with Australian school holidays two or three time a year, and would continue from 1969 through to 1973, encompassing the Troughton stories from 'The Evil of the Daleks' through to 'The War Games'.

WIPED!

First-run *Doctor Who* returned in April/May 1970, again screening weekly, with a batch of stories from 'The Dominators' through to 'The Seeds of Death', concluding in November 1970. The next batch of new episodes started in April/May 1971, again screening weekly. This run went from 'The Space Pirates' through to 'The Ambassadors of Death'. Most regions saw Troughton's final story, 'The War Games' in July/August 1971.

On 13 August 1971, the ABC came to the Northern Territory for the first time, with the opening of a new station (ABD-6) in the capitol city, Darwin. Two days later, on 15 August 1971, it began screening *Doctor Who* weekly on Sunday afternoons, beginning with 'Fury from the Deep', before moving on to 'The Dominators' and then screening the rest of the sixth season, ending with 'The War Games' in July 1972.

The ABC is unique out of all the foreign stations that showed *Doctor Who* in that, between June 1964 and October 1971, it purchased every single Hartnell and Troughton story, from 'An Unearthly Child' right through to 'The War Games'. The only two stories it didn't screen, despite being offered them, were 'Mission to the Unknown' and 'The Daleks Masterplan'. And this was down to the Australian censors rejecting them outright, not from any lack of desire from the ABC. In the case of 'Mission to the Unknown', this was largely because of its depiction of Jeff Garvey falling victim to a Varga plant. In the case of 'The Daleks Masterplan', which was sold to the ABC only as an 11-part serial – Episode Seven ('The Feast of Steven') was never offered for sale by BBC Enterprises – the censors concluded that it wasn't possible to edit the material in any way to enable it to be given a 'G' rating.

Many of the Troughton episodes required cuts before they could be awarded a 'G' rating. 'The Tomb of the Cybermen' was originally rated 'A', but this was successfully appealed on 16/04/68, and altered to 'G' without the need for any cuts.

Full details of the cuts the Australian Film Censorship Board made to *Doctor Who* episodes are as follows:

Episode	Details of Cuts & Censors' Comments[77]
Marco Polo: Episode 5	'Cuts 5ft' 'At end of reel delete chop to guard's back'
Marco Polo: Episode 7	'Cuts 4ft' 'At 2 mins – delete knife in thief's back'
The Keys of Marinus: Episode 2	'Cuts 8ft'. 'Near end remove sequence in which girl smashes brain creatures. A brief flash or two may be seen, but remove all screams and close-up shots of creatures'

---

[77] Spellings (or mis-spellings!) and punctuation as are in the original documentation.

CHAPTER 13

The Sensorites: Episodes 1 & 2	Originally rated 'A' but reclassified 'G' and with the following handwritten note: 'Reclass G & cut. See files'. Small cuts were made to the first two episodes. A latter memo dated 09.12.66 reads, 'The Sensorites. 6 episodes, reviewed by Mrs Stuckey and Mr Robin and reclassified as G'
The Reign of Terror: Episode 5	'Cuts 3ft'. 'At 19 mins delete shots of Dr Who picking up a bottle and following Gaoler to cell whilst bottle is still visible as weapon-threat'
Planet of Giants: Episode 2	'Cuts 18ft'. 'At 4 mins delete shots of man turning over body and displaying blood-stained face and chest' 'At 7 mins delete shots of 2 men turning over body and dragging it away'
The Dalek Invasion of Earth: Episode 1	'Cuts 4ft'. 'At 13 mins – delete dagger sticking out of man's body'
The Dalek Invasion of Earth: Episode 4	'Cuts 17ft'. 'At 13 mins – delete monster wherever appearing from here to end of episode (2 mins)'
The Dalek Invasion of Earth: Episode 5	'Cuts 3ft'. 'At start delete shot of slyther'
The Chase: Episode 2	'Cuts 16ft'. 'At 6 mins delete underlined words in 'What do they feed on? They are flesheaters. They eat humans? Yes.'' 'At 7 mins, delete shot of girl seized around throat by trench or tail of monster.' 'At 13 mins, delete shot of Darleks blasting the Indians' 'At 17 mins, delete close-up of monster'
Galaxy 4: Episode 4	'Cuts 7ft'. 'At end delete item by newcomer – 'I must kill' 3 times'
Mission to the Unknown	The person reviewing this episode on 13 September 1966 made numerous notes regarding the mutation of Garvey into a Varga plant, his subsequent death and Lowery's infection by a Varga, and cited numerous examples of questionable dialogue that dealt with these subjects. The episode was rejected on 28 September 1966, with the handwritten note. 'Entered into Reject Book 19/10/66 – Rejected 13 (d) – Horror.'

WIPED!

The Daleks Masterplan	The 11 episodes of this story were reviewed by two officials of the Censor's office on 13 September 1966. Episodes One, Two, Three, Four, Five and Six were rated 'A' by both censors on the proviso that cuts were made. Episode Seven was not sent to the ABC at all. Only one censor rated Episode Eight as an 'A' if cuts were made, while the other thought it would achieve a 'G' with cuts. Episode Nine was rated 'A' as it stood by one censor, while the other though it would make a 'G' rating with cuts. Episode Ten was rated (strangely) both 'A' and 'G' by one censor, while the other suggested cuts in order to apply a 'G' rating. Episode Eleven was rated 'A' by one censor, while the other suggested cuts to enable a 'G' rating. Episode Twelve was rated 'A' by both censors. The full details of the cuts suggested by both censors to all the episodes are too lengthy to list here. The ABC were advised on 26 September 1966 what cuts to the episodes were required to enable 'The Daleks Masterplan' to at least get an 'A' classification, and invited the ABC to 'reconstruct and resubmit' the story. It seems that the ABC were keen to get the story a 'G' rating, but decided that the episodes classed as 'A' did not lend themselves to further cutting in order to achieve this. This seemingly prompted further discussions between the ABC and BBC Enterprises, which resulted in Basil Sands of BBC Sydney writing to the Censor's office on 13 March 1967: 'I feel that in the circumstances it would not be warranted to attempt the editing of the 12 episodes ... since I understand the main problem is the story line rather than specific scenes in each episode. There is not much point,
The Daleks Masterplan	therefore, in pursuing the matter.' A further note on the paperwork reads, 'These episodes were all considered unsuitable for TV rated "G", not because of specific scenes but because of their storylines. The importer therefore elected not to attempt reconstruction, and the episodes were not registered.'
The Ark: Episode 1	'At 1 minute delete close up shot of one-eyed creature'
The Ark: Episode 3	'Cuts 2ft' 'Reduce close-up shots of Monoid faces'

CHAPTER 13

The Ark: Episode 4	'Cuts 39ft'	
	'Reduce number of close-up shots of Monoid face and reduce killing of Monoids with beat rods. In particular reduce to minimum screams of victims'	
The Gunfighters: Episode 3	'Cuts 31 ft' 'At 20 mins where marked delete shot of barman's body lying across counter'	
The Gunfighters: Episode 4	'Cuts 13ft' 'Delete shot of bodies strewn over street'	
The War Machines: Episode 3 (*)	'Cuts 55ft' 'At 8 min delete sentence 'All human beings who break down will be eliminated' and accompanying shot of man knocked down with blow to neck' '16min reduce by about half hand-to-hand fighting and delete shot of soldier killed by spray from machines'.	
The War Machines: Episode 4 (*)	'Cut 10ft' 'Reduce writhing and delete fall of scientist after he is sprayed by machine'	
The Smugglers: Episode 1 (*)	'Cut 14ft' 'Delete shot of knife being thrown, shot of it protruding from mans back and his final groans and fall'	
The Smugglers: Episode 3 (*)	'Cut 12ft' 'At 13 mins delete dialogue 'but not for you' and subsequent wiping of blood from hook and dropping of bloodied handkerchief' 'Also shot of Jamaica's dead body' 'Delete scream of Kecoper as he is struck in back with knife'	
The Smugglers: Episode 4 (*)	'Cut 2ft' '7 mins delete shot of sword being withdrawn from Cherub's body'	
The Highlanders: Episode 1 (*)	'Cut 8ft' 'At 2 mins delete the grunt of man after stabbing in two instances' 'At 17 mins remove sight of feet of men about to be hanged and the officers words 'Take the chair''	
The Underwater Menace: Episode 1 (*)	'Cut 8ft' 'At 23 mins reduce sequence in which Polly struggles against Atlantians who are preparing her for artificial gill operation'	

WIPED!

The Underwater Menace: Episode 2 (*)	'Cut 13ft' 'At 21 mins reduce sequence in which Polly is prepared for artificial fish gill operation – deletions to include close-ups of her arm as it is held for injection and reduce her sobs'
The Underwater Menace: Episode 3 (*)	'Cut 9ft' 'At 16 mins reduce throttling of Ando by Zaroff with spearshaft and delete off-screen stabbing of Ando and girls screams'
The Underwater Menace: Episode 4 (*)	'Cut 3ft' 'At 18 mins delete second shot of Zaroff behind bars as his head goes under water'
The Macra Terror: Episode 2 (*)	'Cut 18ft' 'At 18 mins reduce considerably shots of Polly being attacked by clawed creatures – also reduce sound of her cries' 'Reduce subsequent sequence as above' 'At 23 mins reduce attack on man on screen with clawed arm'
The Macra Terror: Episode 3 (*)	'Cut 1ft' 'At 1 min reduce attack on man on screen with clawed arm'
The Faceless Ones: Episode 1	'Cut 18ft' 'At 4 mins allow ray gun to be aimed and cut to body on floor' 'At 16 mins reduce shots of hand emerging from cupboard' 'At 20 mins reduce close-up shots of faceless creature'
The Tomb of the Cybermen	Originally rated 'A'. Rating revised to 'G' on appeal 16 April 1968
Fury from the Deep: Episode 2 (*)	'From 10 mins. Allow Mr Oak and Mr Quill to enter Mrs Harris's flat and tinker with the gas plant, then delete the sequence in which they enter her bedroom and approach her with staring eyes and open mouths, breathing out toxic fumes that cause her collapse'

CHAPTER 13

Fury from the Deep: Episode 4 (*)	'Cut 19ft' 'At 9 mins, reduce scene in which Van Luytens is attacked by weeds in the bottom of the shaft and his screams' 'At 15 mins, delete the shot of body on the floor surrounded by the pulsating mass'
Fury from the Deep: Episode 5 (*)	'Cut 19ft' 'From 11-12 mins delete close-up shot of Robson's hand covered with seaweed growth' 'From 16-17 mins reduce emphasis on Robson's seaweed hands'
The Wheel in Space: Episode 4 (*)	'Cut 2ft' 'At 23 mins reduce to minimum attack on man with laser beam. Reductions will include man's groans'
The Dominators: Episode 4 (*)	'Cut 12ft' 'At 19 mins reduce to minimum killing of Tensor in Senate' 'At 21 mins reduce to minimum punishment of young man at drill site by robots with invisible force' 'At 23 min reduce to minimum killing of Senator and accompanying cries'
The Dominators: Episode 5 (*)	'Cut 2ft' 'Prologue – repeat of killing of Senator (as in ep 4). Reduce to minimum'
The Invasion: Episode 5 (*)	Originally classified as 'A' but revised to 'G' after the cutting of 3ft.
The Invasion: Episode 6 (*)	Originally classified as 'A' but revised to 'G' after the cutting of 11ft.
The Invasion: Episode 7 (*)	Originally classified as A but revised to 'G' after the cutting of 6ft.
The War Games: Episode 4	(No specific details)

When much of the cut footage – all the sequences marked with a (*) – was located years later in the Australian Archives by Damian Shanahan, it was discovered that for some stories there were two copies of each excised section. This demonstrates that – for some stories at least – two sets of prints were supplied to the ABC.

Partial programme traffic records exist in Australia showing the movements of some of the 16mm film prints of the Hartnell and Troughton episodes. The dates given in the ABC records for the purchase of each story differ wildly from those listed in the BBC records for the corresponding sale.

WIPED!

Story Title	ABC Arrival Information	Censor Rating	ABC Departure/Destruction Information
An Unearthly Child	Purchased 14/04/64	A	
The Daleks	Purchased 05/05/64	A	
The Edge of Destruction	Purchased 05/05/64	A	
Marco Polo	Purchased 28/10/64	G	
The Keys of Marinus	Purchased 25/11/64	A	
The Aztecs	Purchased 30/12/64	G	
The Sensorites	Purchased 22/12/64	A/G	
The Reign of Terror	Purchased 27/04/65	G	Films sent 28/07/67 to NZBC New Zealand
Planet of Giants	Purchased 29/06/65	A/G	Films sent 28/07/67 to NZBC New Zealand
The Dalek Invasion of Earth	Purchased 09/09/65	A	Films sent 28/07/67 to NZBC New Zealand
The Rescue	Purchased 11/11/65	G	Films sent 28/07/67 to NZBC New Zealand
The Romans	Purchased 13/10/65	G	Films sent 28/07/67 to NZBC New Zealand
The Web Planet	Purchased 16/12/65	G	
The Crusade	Purchased 26/01/66	G	
The Space Museum	Purchased 22/03/66	G	Returned to the BBC 04/06/75
The Chase	Purchased 11/05/66	G	Returned to the BBC 04/06/75 (only eps 2-6; ep 1 acquired by a private collector)
The Time Meddler	Purchased 24/05/66	G	ABC had two sets of prints – both returned to the BBC 04/06/75
Galaxy 4	Purchased 25/08/66	G	
Mission to the Unknown	Purchased 13/09/66		

CHAPTER 13

The Myth Makers	Purchased 01/09/66	G	Episodes One, Three and Four returned to the BBC 04/06/75. No record of Episode Two.
The Daleks Masterplan (bar Episode Seven)	Purchased 13/09/66		
The Massacre	Purchased 06/10/66	G	
The Ark	Purchased 27/09/66	G	Returned to the BBC 04/06/75
The Celestial Toymaker	Purchased 29/10/66	G	Episode Four destroyed/returned to the BBC (records differ). No record of Episodes One, Two and Three.
The Gunfighters	Purchased 03/11/66	G	
The Savages	Purchased 28/11/66	G	No records for any of the four episodes being destroyed/returned to the BBC
The War Machines	Purchased 31/01/67	G	
The Smugglers	Purchased 18/01/67	G	Returned to the BBC 04/06/75. However a duplicate print of Episode Two was sent to ABC in 1967, and may not have been returned
The Tenth Planet	Purchased 31/05/67	G	Returned to the BBC 04/06/75
The Power of the Daleks	Purchased 07/06/67	G	Returned to the BBC 04/06/75
The Highlanders	Purchased 13/06/67	G	ABC destroyed all four episodes 26/07/76
The Underwater Menace	Purchased 20/06/67	G	Returned to the BBC 04/06/75
The Moonbase	Purchased 21/09/67	G	Returned to the BBC 04/06/75
The Macra Terror	Purchased 12/10/67	G	ABC destroyed all four episodes 26/07/76
The Faceless Ones	Purchased 30/10/67	G	Returned to the BBC 04/06/75 (only eps 2-6; ep 1 acquired by a private collector)
The Evil of the Daleks	Purchased 01/11/68	G	Returned to the BBC 04/06/75

WIPED!

The Tomb of the Cybermen	Purchased 10/01/68	A	Returned to the BBC 04/06/75
The Abominable Snowmen	Purchased 05/03/68	G	Returned to the BBC 04/06/75
The Ice Warriors	Purchased 13/03/68	G	Returned to the BBC 04/06/75
The Enemy of the World	Purchased 18/06/68	G	Returned to the BBC 04/06/75
The Web of Fear	Purchased 11/06/68	G	Returned to the BBC 04/06/75
Fury from the Deep	Purchased 22/01/69	G	No records for any of the six episodes being destroyed or returned to the BBC
The Wheel in Space	Purchased 13/03/69	G	Episode One destroyed 26/07/76. No records for Episodes Two to Six
The Dominators	Purchased 10/04/69	G	Returned to the BBC 04/06/75
The Mind Robber	Purchased 26/08/69	G	Returned to the BBC 04/06/75
The Invasion	Purchased 24/02/70	A	Returned to the BBC 04/06/75
The Krotons	Purchased 12/03/70	G	Returned to the BBC 09/06/75
The Seeds of Death	Purchased 16/06/70	G	Returned to the BBC 04/06/75
The Space Pirates	Purchased 25/08/70	G	Episodes One to Three, Five and Six returned to the BBC 04/06/75. No records for Episode Four.
The War Games	Purchased 22/09/70	G	Returned to the BBC 04/06/75

One slight oddity worth mentioning: when 'The Keys of Marinus' was repeated by ABC in 2003, it was screened from Suppressed Field 16mm film prints. These could well have been the very same films that ABC purchased in 1964, nearly 40 years previously. They weren't films that had been supplied by the BBC at any point after 1978, as the BBC only had Stored Field prints of the story from this point onwards.

BARBADOS

Historically one of Britain's main colonies in the Caribbean Sea, Barbados was granted independence in November 1966. However, its strong cultural links with Britain made it an important market for BBC Enterprises. Nearly all of the Hartnell *Doctor Who*

CHAPTER 13

stories were sold to the government-owned Caribbean Broadcasting Corporation (CBC) in the 1960s. At the time, this was the only television station in Barbados, which had begun broadcasting in December 1964.

The stories known to have been purchased by Barbados were sold in several batches. The first batch consisted of 'An Unearthly Child', 'The Daleks', 'The Edge of Destruction', 'Marco Polo' and 'The Keys of Marinus', which were all sold in September 1965. The second, comprising 'The Aztecs', 'The Sensorites', 'The Reign of Terror', 'Planet of Giants', 'The Dalek Invasion of Earth' and 'The Rescue', was sold in November 1966.

A third batch, sold in June 1967, consisted of 'The Romans', 'The Web Planet', 'The Crusade', 'The Space Museum', 'The Chase' and 'The Time Meddler'. A final batch was sold in August 1967, comprising 'Galaxy 4', 'The Myth Makers', 'The Massacre', 'The Ark', 'The Celestial Toymaker', 'The Gunfighters', 'The Savages', 'The War Machines' and 'The Smugglers'.

Doctor Who began on the CBC on Monday 25 April 1966, when Episode One of 'An Unearthly Child' was shown at 6.20 pm. The series then continued weekly at this day and time, until Episode Three of 'Marco Polo', when it moved to Tuesday evenings at 6.00 pm instead. It remained in that same weekly slot for nearly two years, until the final episode of 'The Smugglers' was screened on Tuesday 16 July 1968. This is perhaps the longest uninterrupted run the programme has *ever* had on *any* television station in the world.

BERMUDA

Still a British Overseas Territory to this day, Bermuda (actually a collective name for a group of approximately 138 islands) sits in the North Atlantic Ocean, just over 1,000 miles off the east coast of the USA. All of Bermuda's television stations operate from the city of Hamilton on the largest island in the group. Capital Broadcasting Co Ltd, also known as ZFB-TV was the station that purchased *Doctor Who*, and the series was shown on Channel 8.

A total of five Hartnell stories are known to have been sold to Bermuda, via distributor TIE. 'An Unearthly Child', 'The Daleks' and 'The Edge of Destruction' were purchased in June 1965, followed by 'Marco Polo' and 'The Keys of Marinus' in July 1966.

Curiously, these are exactly the same five stories screened by another of America's neighbours, Canada. Perhaps there was some connection between these two markets …?

Episode One of 'An Unearthly Child' debuted at 6.30 pm on Monday 13 December 1965. The series was shown weekly, in the same Monday night slot, until the final

WIPED!

episode of 'The Keys of Marinus' was transmitted on Monday 6 June 1966.

CANADA

Canada was, historically, one of Britain's biggest colonies. The North American country gained its independence in 1982, although it still maintains its place in the British Commonwealth, with Queen Elizabeth II remaining as its head of state.

The Canadian Broadcasting Corporation (CBC) was one of the first stations to which BBC Enterprises sold *Doctor Who* in the 1960s, although its dalliance with the series was quite short-lived.

'An Unearthly Child', 'The Daleks', 'The Edge of Destruction', 'Marco Polo', 'The Keys of Marinus', 'The Aztecs' and 'The Sensorites' were all sold to the CBC in November 1964. (Some BBC paperwork seems to indicate that Episode One of 'The Daleks' wasn't included in the sale, only Episodes Two to Seven, but this doesn't seem likely.) Although Canada is a huge country (stretching across five time zones), the CBC was an innovator in the field of country-wide broadcasting, and by the mid-1950s had developed a microwave transmitter system that allowed simultaneous broadcasts to all its regions. This side-stepped the problem faced by stations in other large countries such as Australia and New Zealand, who had to move their film prints of *Doctor Who* from region to region. Nevertheless, *Doctor Who* was not shown simultaneously on all the CBC's regional channels, so film copies of the episodes might also have been moved around the country. Alternatively, an affiliate station might have videotaped each episode via the microwave transmission, and then used that recording to show at a later date.

'An Unearthly Child' debuted on CBLT in Toronto at 5.00 pm on Saturday 23 January 1965. Subsequent episodes then followed on a weekly basis. CKVR in Barrie showed the same episodes exactly one week behind the rest of the country. 'The Daleks' was then shown in the same weekly Saturday slot.

On 21 April 1965, the series was moved from its Saturday slot on CBLT and instead shown at 5.00 pm on Wednesdays, beginning with Episode One of 'The Edge of Destruction'. 'Marco Polo' and 'The Keys of Marinus' were also shown, and then the series was taken off the air altogether. 'The Aztecs' and 'The Sensorites' never were screened in Canada. The CBC were offered the chance to purchase further Hartnell stories – specifically, 'The Reign of Terror', 'The Dalek Invasion of Earth', 'The Rescue', 'The Romans' and 'The Crusade' – but declined. So the series disappeared from Canada's screens for the remainder of the 1960s.

The CBC have since confirmed that they no longer hold any of the black and white *Doctor Who* episodes that they purchased in 1964 and screened in 1965.

It has been rumoured in recent years that another, unknown television station

CHAPTER 13

in Canada screened other black and white *Doctor Who* stories, such as 'The Celestial Toymaker', 'The Evil of the Daleks' and 'The Wheel in Space', during the late '60s or early '70s. There is no evidence whatsoever in any BBC sales records or documentation to back this up.

CYPRUS

The third-largest island in the Mediterranean Sea, Cyprus was a British Colony until it gained independence in 1960, although it joined the British Commonwealth in 1961. The Cyprus Broadcasting Corporation (CBC) first went on air in October 1957, bringing television to the country for the first time.

In September 1965, the CBC purchased 'An Unearthly Child', 'The Daleks', and 'The Edge of Destruction', for screening sometime during 1966. This was followed in May 1966 by 'Marco Polo' and 'The Keys of Marinus', and in October 1966 by 'The Aztecs' and 'The Sensorites'. 'The Reign of Terror' was also sent to Cyprus, although this story doesn't appear on the BBC's sales paperwork. From the material that was recovered from the CBC in 1984, it seems that these were all Stored Field telerecordings.

There is a reference to the sale of 'The Dalek Invasion of Earth' to Cyprus at this time in one obscure piece of BBC paperwork, although an examination of the CBC's programme traffic records by Paul Vanezis confirmed that they were never sent this story. However, sometime prior to July 1965, they were at least offered the opportunity to purchase it.

Episode One of 'An Unearthly Child' was shown at 7.55 pm on Saturday 12 March 1966. The series then continued weekly on Saturdays until the final episode of 'The Edge of Destruction' on 4 June. Episode One of 'Marco Polo' was then shown on Friday 10 June 1966, and Fridays became the series' regular home, right through to the final episode of 'The Sensorites', which was shown on Friday 25 November 1966. 'The Reign of Terror' was never screened by the CBC.

Subsequently, BBC Enterprises asked the CBC to forward some of the *Doctor Who* film prints they had to other overseas television stations. All the episodes of 'An Unearthly Child', 'The Daleks' and 'The Edge of Destruction' went to UTV in Uganda[78], while all those of 'Marco Polo' and 'The Keys of Marinus' went to Hong

---

78 This is something Paul Vanezis is very definite about from his recollection of the Programme Traffic Records he saw in Cyprus in 1989. However, Uganda actually screened these three stories between January and April 1966, which was some weeks *before* the stories were screened in Cyprus. Why would the BBC ask Cyprus to send its prints of these stories to a station that had already screened the episodes? Maybe Uganda had already sent its original prints of these stories elsewhere, and then decided to repeat them, needing another set of prints? There is no record of any repeats in Uganda, so if this was the case, then the repeats never happened. Yet another mystery ...

WIPED!

Kong Rediffusion in 1966[79]. All the episodes of 'The Aztecs', 'The Sensorites' and 'The Reign of Terror' remained in Cyprus in the CBC's archive.

There was an unsuccessful coup in Cyprus in 1974, and during the civil war, one of the buildings used by the CBC as a film storage vault was blown up, its contents completely destroyed. It was later discovered that this storage depot had contained the CBC's prints of 'The Aztecs' Episode Two and 'The Reign of Terror' Episodes Four and Five.

The CBC's copies of Episodes One, Three and Four of 'The Aztecs', all six episodes of 'The Sensorites', and Episodes One, Two, Three and Six of 'The Reign of Terror' were discovered by researcher Paul Vanezis in 1984, and then a few weeks later by the BBC themselves. The films were all quickly returned to the BBC Film and Videotape Library.

Vanezis later visited the CBC in 1989 and examined all their paperwork and programme traffic records relating to *Doctor Who*, in order to confirm that nothing further remained in the country. He also checked for other BBC material that the CBC might hold, and found about two hundred 16mm black and white films of programmes that were still missing from the BBC at that time, including the first seven episodes of *Z Cars*. He arranged for this material to be returned to the BBC in England.

ETHIOPIA

Ethiopia is a large, landlocked country located on the Somali Peninsula in Eastern Africa. Television was first introduced there in November 1964. The station Ethiopian Television Service (ETV) purchased a large selection of Hartnell episodes, in two distinct batches, in the early 1970s.

In October 1970, they purchased 'An Unearthly Child', 'The Daleks', 'The Edge of Destruction', 'Marco Polo', 'The Keys of Marinus', 'The Aztecs', 'The Sensorites', 'The Reign of Terror', 'Planet of Giants', 'The Dalek Invasion of Earth' and 'The Rescue'. In October 1971, they followed this up with 'The Romans', 'The Web Planet', 'The Crusade', 'The Space Museum' and 'The Chase'.

Doctor Who began on the ETV on Thursday 22 October 1970, with the first episode of 'An Unearthly Child'. The series was shown weekly, and usually went out sometime between 7.00 pm and 7.30 pm. The stories were screened in an unbroken run, although mid-way through 'The Dalek Invasion of Earth', the programme moved to Wednesday evenings. This run concluded with the final episode of 'The Chase' on Wednesday 5 April 1972.

---

79 Hong Kong screened these two stories between July and October 1966, some weeks after the Cyprus transmission dates, so this at least seems consistent with the evidence.

CHAPTER 13

GHANA

Another former British colony, Ghana was one of the first African countries to gain its independence, in 1957. Like many former colonies, it retained close ties with Britain thereafter. Television first began in Ghana in July 1965.

In January 1966, the Ghana Radio and Television Corporation purchased 'An Unearthly Child', 'The Daleks', 'The Edge of Destruction', 'Marco Polo' and 'The Keys of Marinus'. These were the only *Doctor Who* stories ever sold to this country.

Doctor Who's on-air debut in Ghana came on Monday 11 July 1966, when the first episode of 'An Unearthly Child' was shown. The series was screened weekly, until the final episode of 'The Keys of Marinus' on Monday 2 January 1967.

A popular fan rumour doing the rounds in the early 1990s told how a mystery television station in Ghana was still screening old stories such as 'The Power of the Daleks' in 1986, only for the film archive of the station to be completely destroyed in a fire in 1989, incinerating its stockpile of missing *Doctor Who* prints. Like most fan rumours, there is no truth in this whatsoever!

GIBRALTAR

The small peninsula that is Gibraltar is located at the southernmost tip of Spain, and is yet another British overseas colony, and has been ever since 1713. Strategically, it is of great importance to Britain, as it overlooks the Strait of Gibraltar – the narrow stretch of sea that connects the Atlantic Ocean to the Mediterranean Sea, and which separates Spain from Morocco. Here, the continents of Europe and Africa are only just over 14 kilometres (about eight nautical miles) apart from each other, and any shipping that enters the Mediterranean has to pass through the Strait of Gibraltar. Television first began in Gibraltar in October 1962.

The Gibraltar Broadcasting Corporation (GBC) purchased a considerable number of *Doctor Who* stories over the years. The first batch it acquired, via distributor TIE, consisted of 'An Unearthly Child', 'The Daleks', 'The Edge of Destruction', 'Marco Polo' and 'The Keys of Marinus' in May 1965. This was followed by a second batch, 'The Aztecs', 'The Sensorites', 'The Reign of Terror', 'Planet of Giants' and 'The Rescue', in August 1965, although it's unknown if TIE played any part in this or other subsequent sales. The third and final batch of sales of Hartnell stories took place in May 1966, with 'The Romans', 'The Web Planet', 'The Crusade', 'The Space Museum', 'The Chase' and 'The Time Meddler'.

In 1972, after a gap of around six years, the GBC next purchased a batch of Troughton stories, which consisted of 'The Dominators' and 'The Mind Robber' in May, and 'The Invasion', 'The Krotons', 'The Seeds of Death', 'The Space Pirates' and 'The War Games' in August.

WIPED!

Finally, in April 1973, the GBC purchased another selection of Troughton adventures, although this meant that they would now be showing the series out of sequence. The stories sold this time around were 'The Abominable Snowmen', 'The Ice Warriors', 'The Enemy of the World', 'The Web of Fear', 'Fury from the Deep' and 'The Wheel in Space'.

It would appear that the series was first screened by GBC on Thursday 8 April 1965, beginning with the first episode of 'An Unearthly Child'. The series then moved to Tuesday evenings with the third episode of this story, and continued airing weekly in this slot until the final episode of 'Planet of Giants' was shown on Tuesday 15 February 1966. The series then switched to a Saturday slot with the first episode of 'The Dalek Invasion of Earth' on 5 March 1966, and continued until the final episode of 'The Time Meddler' was screened on Saturday 12 November 1966.

The series returned six years later, with the first episode of 'The Dominators' screening on Monday 14 February 1972. *Doctor Who* would generally stay in this weekly Monday slot for the rest of the year, right through to the final episode of 'The War Games', which was shown on Monday 11 December 1972. The first three Jon Pertwee stories were then screened weekly through to April 1973, and then the second Doctor returned with the first episode of 'The Abominable Snowmen' screening on Mon 23 April 1973. This run of six Patrick Troughton stories saw the series move to Saturday transmissions halfway through 'Fury from the Deep' in October, and concluded with the final episode of 'The Wheel in Space' on Saturday 22 December 1973. Jon Pertwee's Doctor than re-appeared the following week, as 'Terror of the Autons' began a run of more third Doctor stories.

HONG KONG

Hong Kong, located on the Pearl River delta in China, was a British Colony from 1842 until 1997. In 1997, its sovereignty was transferred back to China, who had leased the territory to Britain for the previous 99 years.

The main television station in Hong Kong in the 1960s was Rediffusion Television (or Hong Kong Rediffusion as it was sometimes known), which launched in 1957 as a subscription cable channel, becoming the very first television station to appear in any of the British colonies. It was a subsidiary of Associated Rediffusion, the British-based ITV broadcaster. RTV would broadcast four hours of English-language programmes a day, and from 1963, a second, Chinese-language channel was added. By 1967, RTV had 67,000 subscribers in Hong Kong, and in April 1973, it was offered a free-to-air broadcast licence, which it took up. It changed its name to Rediffusion Television Ltd in December 1973, and again to Asia Television Ltd in 1982.

The following batch of Hartnell stories were sold to RTV in November 1965: 'An

CHAPTER 13

Unearthly Child', 'The Daleks', 'The Edge of Destruction', 'Marco Polo', 'The Keys of Marinus', 'The Aztecs', 'The Sensorites', 'The Reign of Terror', 'Planet of Giants', 'The Dalek Invasion of Earth' and 'The Rescue'. The prints of all the episodes of 'Marco Polo' and 'The Keys of Marinus' were supplied to RTV from the CBC in Cyprus, at the request of BBC Enterprises. All of the stories between 'The Aztecs' and 'The Rescue' were supplied on the same BBC invoice number as the sale of the same stories to Aden, suggesting that there might have been a connection between the two stations at this point in time.

The next batch of sales took place in April 1969, and comprised the Patrick Troughton stories 'The Highlanders', 'The Underwater Menace', 'The Moonbase', 'The Macra Terror' and 'The Faceless Ones'. This was quickly followed in November 1969 by sales of 'The Evil of the Daleks', 'The Tomb of the Cybermen', 'The Abominable Snowmen', 'The Ice Warriors' and 'The Enemy of the World'.

Further sales of Troughton stories were a bit patchier in the years that followed. 'The Web of Fear' and 'Fury from the Deep' were sold in March 1970, 'The Wheel in Space' in May 1970, 'The Dominators', 'The Mind Robber' and 'The Invasion' in August 1970, 'The Krotons' in October 1970, 'The Seeds of Death' and 'The Space Pirates' in May 1971 and 'The War Games' in October 1972.

The initial run of *Doctor Who* on RTV began with the first episode of 'An Unearthly Child' on Tuesday 26 April 1966. The series was shown weekly at 6.30pm, until the final episode of 'The Rescue', which went out on Tuesday 16 May 1967.

Doctor Who returned on Friday 7 March 1969, with the first episode of 'The Highlanders', which was screened at 6.05pm. RTV then went on to screen all the subsequent Patrick Troughton stories on a weekly basis in this time slot, culminating with the final episode of 'The War Games' on Friday 21 May 1971. However, it would appear that some stories were shown out of sequence: 'The Abominable Snowmen' was shown straight after 'The Evil of the Daleks', 'The Wheel in Space' was shown before 'The Web of Fear', and 'The Tomb of the Cybermen' was screened after 'Fury from the Deep'.

Asia Television returned 16mm film prints of all four episodes of 'The Tomb of the Cybermen' to BBC Enterprises in January 1992. They have been contacted many times in the years after the return of 'The Tomb of the Cybermen' to see if they have any other *Doctor Who* material, and have repeatedly replied that they hold no further episodes – although in a letter sent to this writer in late 1992, they confessed that all their film archive records had been destroyed in a fire some years previously, and until their re-cataloguing was complete, they couldn't be entirely sure that they had checked through everything.

Hong Kong returned to Chinese sovereignty in 1997, and Asia Television has since moved out of its old headquarters in Kowloon to a new facility in Tai Po.

WIPED!

IRAN

Despite having a very frosty relationship with Britain in the 1950s, a new regime in Iran under the ruling monarch (or Shah, as he was known) saw rapid modernisation and an influx of Western ideas and values during the 1960s. And this influx included television.

Iran's first television station, National Iranian Radio and Television (NIR&T), went on-air in 1966. In July 1968, it purchased the following William Hartnell stories from BBC Enterprises: 'An Unearthly Child', 'The Daleks', 'The Edge of Destruction', 'The Keys of Marinus', 'The Aztecs', 'The Sensorites', 'Planet of Giants', 'The Dalek Invasion of Earth', 'The Rescue', 'The Web Planet', 'The Space Museum' and 'The Chase'. These stories were all dubbed into Arabic.

Transmission details for *Doctor Who* in Iran are very sketchy, although it is known that some unidentified episodes were screened weekly on Tuesday evenings between May and October 1969.

Programme traffic records in New Zealand show that, in addition to the stories listed above, the first two episodes of 'Marco Polo' were sent to National Iranian Radio and Television by NZBC in October 1967, at the request of BBC Enterprises. However, no sale of this story to Iran is logged in BBC records, so it's possible that these two episodes were sent for viewing and assessment only, and a decision was taken not to buy the serial as a result, probably as no Arabic dubbed prints of this story were available. Or it possibly could indicate that the story *was* sold, but the sale was not recorded by the BBC for some reason.

After the 1979 revolution and the founding of the Islamic state that now governs Iran, the television station was re-named Islamic Republic of Iran Broadcasting, and programming became tightly centred on the Islamic criteria that the new rulers of the country were advocating. In 1984, the station was contacted by Roger Brunskill of BBC Enterprises, who enquired if it still had any *Doctor Who* episodes in its archives. The reply he reportedly received – 'In the name of Allah, what are you talking about?' – has since passed into fan legend, perhaps somewhat unfairly.

Paul Vanezis, with the help of Sue Malden (in her position at Fédération Internationale des Archives de Télévision/The International Federation of Television Archives), had a long correspondence with the archivists at NIR&TV in 2010 in the hope of discovering the fate of the two 'Marco Polo' episodes, and was at least able to conclude that the films – or any other episodes of Doctor Who - were no longer at the station.

JAMAICA

Located 90 miles south of Cuba in the Caribbean Sea, Jamaica is a former British colony, which was granted independence in 1962, although it still remains a member of the British Commonwealth to this day. Television was first introduced to Jamaica in August 1963.

Between 1966 and 1969, the Jamaica Broadcasting Corporation (JBC) purchased a large selection of Hartnell stories, in three distinct batches. First, 'An Unearthly Child', 'The Daleks', 'The Edge of Destruction', 'Marco Polo' and 'The Keys of Marinus' were sold in March 1966. This was followed by sales of 'The Aztecs', 'The Sensorites', 'The Reign of Terror', 'Planet of Giants', 'The Dalek Invasion of Earth' and 'The Rescue' in October 1966. Finally, 'The Romans', 'The Web Planet', 'The Crusade', 'The Space Museum', 'The Chase' and 'The Time Meddler' were sold in March 1969.

Doctor Who began on JBC on Thursday 3 March 1966, with the first episode of 'An Unearthly Child'. The series ran on a weekly basis, but episodes were often postponed to make way for coverage of cricket matches. By the time the station was showing 'The Keys of Marinus' in August 1966, the schedules were also being disrupted by coverage of the Commonwealth Games. By the time 'The Aztecs' began, the series had switched to a Saturday evening slot. 'The Sensorites' was shown in the space of just three weeks, as two episodes each Saturday evening were screened. *Doctor Who* continued until Saturday 25 March 1967, when the final episode of 'The Romans' was screened, to be replaced by episodes of *Batman* in JBC's schedules.

Doctor Who returned on Sunday 2 February 1969, with the first episode of 'The Web Planet'. The series was again shown weekly, through to the final episode of 'The Time Meddler' on Sunday 20 July 1969.

KENYA

Located on the coast of East Africa, Kenya is another former British colony, which gained independence in December 1953. The Kenya Broadcasting Corporation was formed in 1961, and took over the existing radio networks owned by the government. Its early broadcasts were mainly aimed at the minority white settlers in the country. Television was introduced in October 1962, with the country's first transmitting station operating from a farm house in Limuru and covering a radius of just 15 miles. In July 1965, the station was renamed Voice of Kenya (VoK), but this reverted to Kenya Broadcasting Corporation (KBC) in 1969.

A number of Hartnell stories were sold to Voice of Kenya in two distinct batches. The first batch, sold in July 1966, contained 'An Unearthly Child', 'The Daleks', 'The Edge of Destruction', 'Marco Polo' and 'The Keys of Marinus'. The second batch, sold in January 1967, comprised 'The Aztecs', 'The Sensorites', 'The Reign of Terror', 'Planet of Giants', 'The Dalek Invasion of Earth' and 'The Rescue'.

The debut of *Doctor Who* on VoK appears to have been delayed a number of times. The first episode of 'An Unearthly Child' was due to air at 6.00 pm on Thursday 16

WIPED!

June 1966, but the same episode was then billed the following week in the same time slot, and then again a week later on Thursday 30 June 1966. It would appear, then, that film prints of the series were delayed in transit *en route* to Kenya – see also Zambia.

After this shaky start, *Doctor Who* was screened weekly in Nairobi on Thursday evenings, until the final episode of 'The Rescue' went out at 6.00 pm on Thursday 13 July 1967.

MALTA

The island nation of Malta, located in the Mediterranean Sea, was part of the British Empire from 1814 until its independence in September 1964, and is still a member of the British Commonwealth.

The history of television in Malta is quite convoluted. Associated Rediffusion, the London and East Midlands ITV broadcaster in Britain, operated a radio service in Malta as early as 1935 (as it also later did in Hong Kong). The company was given a television licence in the early 1960s, and launched the station Rediffusion Malta in September 1962, although due to the relatively high prices of television sets, radio remained the dominant form of broadcasting in Malta well into the 1970s. Rediffusion's television operations were later taken over by a company called Xandir Malta. Colour television launched in July 1981, and Xandir Malta eventually changed its name to Public Broadcasting Services Ltd.

There are two distinct periods of *Doctor Who* sales to Malta recorded in the BBC paperwork in the 1960s. In December 1964, 'An Unearthly Child', 'The Daleks', 'The Edge of Destruction', 'Marco Polo' and 'The Keys of Marinus' were sold. This was followed in August 1965 by 'The Aztecs', 'The Sensorites', 'The Reign of Terror', 'Planet of Giants', 'The Dalek Invasion of Earth' and 'The Rescue'.

Doctor Who began in Malta with the first episode of 'An Unearthly Child' at 6.30 pm on Monday 24 May 1965. The series was shown weekly in this time slot in an unbroken run, which ended with the final episode of 'The Rescue' on Monday 23 May 1966.

Doctor Who wasn't seen again on Maltese television until Jon Pertwee's stories began screening in colour over a decade later, in April 1979. However, the series evidently became reasonably popular in Malta in the early 1970s – the early editions of the Target range of *Doctor Who* books all had prices printed in Maltese dollars included on the reverse.

MAURITIUS

Yet another former British colony, the island of Mauritius lies off the southern coast of Africa in the Indian Ocean. Television broadcasts began there in February 1965. It gained its independence from Britain in 1968, although it remains a Commonwealth member to this

CHAPTER 13

day. All of its known purchases of *Doctor Who* pre-date the declaration of independence.

Mauritius Broadcasting Corporation (MBC) purchased *Doctor Who* in three separate batches. The first was of 'An Unearthly Child', 'The Daleks', 'The Edge of Destruction', 'Marco Polo' and 'The Keys of Marinus', all in January 1967. This was followed by 'The Aztecs', 'The Sensorites', 'The Reign of Terror', 'Planet of Giants', 'The Dalek Invasion of Earth' and 'The Rescue' in April 1967. Finally, 'The Romans', 'The Web Planet', 'The Crusade', 'The Space Museum', 'The Chase', and 'The Time Meddler' were sold in November 1967.

Doctor Who began screening on MBC on Friday 21 October 1966, when the first episode of 'An Unearthly Child' was shown at 6.30 pm. The series then went out weekly in this time slot, right through to the final episode of 'The Time Meddler' on Friday 29 March 1968. It would appear that stories were screened out of sequence, with 'The Rescue' following 'The Reign of Terror', 'The Aztecs' then following 'The Rescue', and 'Planet of Giants' slipping between 'The Web Planet' and 'The Crusade'. It would also appear that 'The Chase' wasn't screened at all (possibly because of the restriction of the sale of Dalek stories due to the negotiations that were going on between the BBC and Terry Nation's representatives about the Dalek spin-off series at this time).

NEW ZEALAND

The islands of New Zealand were first discovered by Dutch explorers in the 17th Century, but Britain's James Cook was the first to map the coastline, in 1769. Britain claimed sovereignty over the islands in 1840, although New Zealand would become an independent dominion of the British Crown in 1907, and a fully independent nation in 1947. However, Queen Elizabeth II is still the head of state, and New Zealand remains in the British Commonwealth.

Television was introduced to New Zealand in 1960. The country's first channel was AKTV-2, which took to the air in Auckland on 1 June 1960, transmitting for two hours a day, two days a week. CHTV-3 in Christchurch was launched in June 1961; WNTV-1 in Wellington in July 1961; and finally DNTV-2 in Dunedin in July 1962. All the stations were owned and operated by the New Zealand Broadcasting Service (NZBS), which became the New Zealand Broadcasting Corporation (NZBC) in 1962.

NZBC's purchase of black and white *Doctor Who* stories was – according to BBC records – quite piecemeal; at least when the acquisition dates and story selections are scrutinised. Detailed programme traffic records also exist in New Zealand. These show on which dates stories were physically acquired and differ from the dates on the BBC's own documentation.

The first batch of stories – 'An Unearthly Child', 'The Daleks' and 'The Edge of Destruction' – were purchased in June 1964. These had to be assessed by the New Zealand government film and television censors, who operated a rating system similar

WIPED!

to that of nearby Australia. Stories were viewed and given ratings; a 'G' (for 'General') meant that the programme could be shown at any time of the day, while a 'Y' meant that it could be shown only in a later time slot, believed to be after 7.30 pm.

The first three *Doctor Who* stories were all rated 'Y', and so could be shown only after 7.30 pm. Once these three stories had been screened unedited in evening slots in late 1964/early 1965, the NZBC decided that all subsequent stories had to meet the 'G' rating if they were to be broadcast. This meant that edits sometimes needed to be made to individual episodes in order to achieve this. However, some stories that were given a 'Y' rating were not edited to try to get a 'G' certificate. These ended up not being screened at all in New Zealand.

The next sale to NZBC was the lone adventure 'Marco Polo' in November 1965, although this wasn't actually screened until 1967.

It was not until over two years later, in February 1968 that more stories were purchased. These were 'The Reign of Terror', 'Planet of Giants', 'The Dalek Invasion of Earth' and 'The Rescue'. By this time, the NZBC was having its prints of the episodes sent to it by the ABC in Australia, so this batch would have been subject to any cuts already made by the Australian censors. 'The Romans', 'The Web Planet' and 'The Crusade' followed in May 1968. All these films still had to pass through the hands of the New Zealand censors as well, however, and 'The Dalek Invasion of Earth' and 'The Web Planet' were both awarded 'Y' ratings, and so were never screened. 'The Crusade', according to some sources, was given a 'G' rating, but it was never screened either, leading credence to other reports that it too got a 'Y' rating. Regardless, all the episodes of all of these unscreened stories were kept by the NZBC for many years.

The next batch of purchases came in October 1968, consisting of 'The Space Museum', 'The Time Meddler', 'Galaxy 4' and 'The Myth Makers'. These were quickly followed in December 1968 by 'The Massacre', 'The Ark', 'The Celestial Toymaker', 'The Savages', 'The War Machines', 'The Smugglers' and 'The Tenth Planet'.

From this point on, the NZBC's purchases of stories were sporadic, rather than coming in large batches as previously. Between May 1969 and June 1970, all the Troughton adventures from 'The Power of the Daleks' through to 'The Evil of the Daleks' were acquired. By this time, NZBC were being supplied prints sent to them from BBC Sydney in Australia. Sales of all the fifth season stories, from 'The Tomb of the Cybermen' through to 'The Wheel in Space', took place between September 1970 and February 1972. From this batch, 'The Faceless Ones', 'The Ice Warriors', and 'Fury from the Deep' were all awarded the dreaded 'Y' rating by the censors, and so were not broadcast. 'The Web of Fear' was specifically purchased for two screenings, but the NZBC never took up the option of a second screening. Not a single story from the programme's sixth season was purchased by the NZBC. 'The Wheel in Space' was thus

CHAPTER 13

the last Troughton story to be screened in New Zealand in 1971[80]. When the series eventually returned to the NZBC in 1975, it was with Jon Pertwee's Doctor.

As previously mentioned, the 16mm film prints of all the William Hartnell and Patrick Troughton stories that were sent to New Zealand had to be reviewed by the country's film censors prior to the stories being screened (or not), and sometimes material was cut from the physical films in order for the episodes to achieve the necessary rating for transmission (similar to the system that also existed in Australia).

The details of the ratings/cuts are as follows:

Story Title	*Rating*	*Editing Details (Episode / Duration)*[81]
An Unearthly Child	Y	
The Daleks	Y	
The Edge of Destruction	Y	1 (duration n/k) 'Delete views of Susan stabbing couch repeatedly with scissors & later picking up scissors, Barbara taking them off her'.
Marco Polo	G	3 (34 secs) 'Delete woman's screams as she is grabbed by Tegana. Delete threat to bound woman prisoner. Delete close up view of mask face. Delete view of woman with knife at throat.' 4 (18 secs) 'Delete scream & close view of mask face. Delete scream of girl. Delete view of dagger in man's back.' 5 (22 secs) 'Delete view of dagger in man's back. Delete view of knife in man's chest & throttling of man in tent.' 6 (19 secs) 'Delete or reduce screaming of girl and holding of knife at girl's throat. Delete scream of girl and knife attack.' 7 (14 secs) 'Reduce knife attack.'

---

80 That is until many years later, when selected surviving Patrick Troughton stories from the series were repeated in the 1980s.

81 These cut durations have been worked out by comparing the durations of the episodes as per the BBC's PasB paperwork with the durations of the episodes as noted by the NZBC's own paperwork. Spellings (or mis-spellings!) and punctuation as are in the original documentation.

WIPED!

The Reign of Terror	G	
Planet of Giants	G	
The Dalek Invasion of Earth	Y	Not Screened
The Rescue	G	
The Romans	G	4 (14 secs) 'Delete view of lighted torch being jabbed into man's face & later view of others bending over body.'
The Web Planet	Y (1 – 4) G (5 – 6)	Not Screened
The Crusade	Y (1) G (2 – 4)	Not Screened
The Space Museum	G	3 (18 secs) 'Reduce fight deleting kick & rabbit chop etc. Delete remarks to "wanting to see Morogs dead". Delete remark "Don't kill me". Delete u/lined words "possibly but it (killing Morog) would be enjoyable".' 4 (1 min 0 secs) 'Delete remark "Kill them".'
The Time Meddler[82]	G	2 (31 secs) 'Reduce or delete threat with knife (twice). Reduce battle particularly close stabbings axe blows etc.' 3 (10 secs) 'Delete threat with knife & remark "Go on kill me"' 4 (13 secs) 'Delete killing of Vikings after they surrender.'

---

82 No cuts are noted for the first episode of this story, and the NZBC-listed duration matches the BBC's PasB records. And yet, strangely, the ex-NZBC print of the first episode of this story that was located in Nigeria in 1984 was missing a fair few minutes of material from the opening of the episode.

CHAPTER 13

Galaxy 4	G	1 (16 secs) 'Delete remarks "They kill"; "Do you want to be killed" and "You want to kill us".' 2 (45 secs) 'Delete remark "Very well we will kill the girl". Delete remarks about "killing Steven". Delete scream of girl & delete or reduce to flash views of master face.' 3 (49 secs) 'Delete scream & reduce or delete horror face. Reduce views of horror face consistent with dialogue. Delete chop by Steven to Dravhin woman. Delete remark u/lined "<u>Kill me now</u> I have failed in my duty".' 4 (2 mins 4 secs) 'Delete u/lined words "After them <u>and kill</u>". Delete all close views of monsters consistent with dialogue. Delete remarks by man "Kill Kill" etc.'
The Myth Makers	G	1 (21 secs) 'Delete reference to wife being unfaithful & reply. Delete reference to "knife between ribs" & reduce threat with sword. Delete reference to "cut out his tongue for insolence".' 2 (1 min 19 secs) 'Delete remarks about "<u>cutting throats</u>". Delete references to "killing girl" and "she shall die" & reduce threat. Delete remarks "Kill them Kill them".' 3 (39 secs) 'Delete remarks "Kill her Kill all of them". Delete view of Stephen hitting guard & return blow.' 4 (2 mins 43 secs) 'Delete remarks "I shall kill you" etc. Reduce or delete killing of Trojans. Reduce sword fight between Troilus & Achilles particularly final views. Reduce sacking of city, screams & remarks "Kill them".'
The Massacre	G	3 (30 secs) 'Delete loading of gun and reduce views of attempted assassination.' 4 (45 secs) 'Reduce or delete views of massacre, particularly detailed views of killings.'

WIPED!

The Ark	G	1 (38 secs) 'Reduce or delete views of one eyed creature.' 3 (1 min 26 secs) 'Reduce views of Monoids particularly close views. Reduce or delete use of heat gun on man. Delete remark about destroying population or reduce. Reduce killing of man deleting screaming.' 4 (3 min 12 secs) 'Reduce or delete close views of Monoids. Delete remark "They will die". Reduce view of Monoids but retain dialogue about hiding place of bomb. Delete close views of Monoids and reduce views of battle & killing of Monoids particularly close views.'
The Celestial Toymaker	G	2 (13 secs) 'Delete remark "does he really mean to kill us".' 4 (40 secs)[83] 'Delete words "and you will be killed".'
The Savages	G	
The War Machines	G	2 (1 min 17 secs) 'Delete view of bottle & pad held in man's hand in kidnap attempt. Reduce or delete sequence of tramp being killed in factory. Delete demonstration of killing of man & delete later view on floor if necessary.' 3 (2 min 14 secs) 'Delete remarks "Machines programmed to attack all forms of human life" & "all human beings will be eliminated". Reduce attack on troops.' 4 (18 secs) 'Delete killing of man in phone box and delete remarks to Polly about being killed by Voltan.'

---

83 If, as seems the case, the recovered print we have of Episode Four of this story is indeed this print (having travelled from New Zealand to Singapore and then on to Australia), then there isn't 40 seconds' worth of material missing from it. However, sometimes cut durations are listed when only dialogue needed removing from the episodes, and one way this would have been done was to simply cover sections of the optical soundtrack of the film print with sellotape, rendering portions of the soundtrack mute. Perhaps this was what happened in this instance ...?

CHAPTER 13

The Smugglers	G	1 (1 min 46 secs) 'Reduce threat to Joseph with knife.' 2 (43 secs) 'Delete Cherub's physical & verbal threats with knife. Delete Captain's remarks "I'll slit your gizzard".' 3 (9 secs) 'Delete view of Cherub holding knife across Tom's throat.' 4 (20 secs) 'Delete views of Captain thrusting & withdrawing sword from Cherub's body.'
The Tenth Planet	G	4 (37 secs) 'Delete scream in girl. Delete view of her being rendered unconscious.'
The Power of the Daleks	G	5 (26 secs) 'Reduce to minimum chanting of Daleks vowing to kill human beings.' 6 (1 min 16 secs) 'Reduce to minimum chanting of Daleks vowing to kill humans & throughout episode reduce to minimum shootings & killings by Daleks.'
The Highlanders	G	
The Underwater Menace	G	
The Moonbase	G	
The Macra Terror	G	
The Faceless Ones	Y	Not Screened
The Evil of the Daleks	G	4 (duration n/k) 5 (duration n/k)
The Tomb of the Cybermen	G	
The Abominable Snowmen	G	
The Ice Warriors	G (1) Y (2 – 6)	Not Screened
The Enemy of the World	G	4 (33 secs) 5 (30 secs)

WIPED!

The Web of Fear	G	1 (4 secs) 2 (18 secs) 3 (2 secs) 4 (41 secs) 5 (2 secs) 6 (16 secs)
Fury from the Deep	Y	Not Screened
The Wheel in Space	G	3 (3 secs) 5 (8 secs) 6 (14 secs)

In 2002, a reel of 16mm film containing most of the material edited from 'The Ark', 'The Web of Fear' and Episode Five of 'The Wheel in Space' was found in a private collection in New Zealand.

New Zealand has the honour of being the first country to screen *Doctor Who* outside the UK. The first episode of 'An Unearthly Child' debuted on Friday 18 September 1964 in Christchurch. As it was unable to transmit country-wide, the NZBC had no alternative but to send the 16mm film print of each episode to each of its four regions in turn, so each region showed the series on a different day.

For the first batch of stories shown in New Zealand, from 'An Unearthly Child' through to 'The Edge of Destruction', the episodes went from CHTV-3 in Christchurch, to AKTV-2 in Auckland, to WNTV-1 in Wellington and finally to DNTV-2 in Dunedin. This was in late 1964/early 1965.

'Marco Polo' was then screened in 1967, only this time AKTV-2 in Auckland got to have it first. The prints then went to WNTV-1 in Wellington, DNTV-2 in Dunedin, and finally CHTV-3 in Christchurch.

A run of four stories from 'The Reign of Terror' through to 'The Romans' took place in early 1968, and again CHTV-3 got to see each episode first. WNTV-1 came second, DNTV-2 third and AKTV-2 last.

The next run, from 'The Space Museum' through to 'The Macra Terror', took place between 1968 and 1970, and CHTV-3 in Christchurch got to screen the episodes first again. WNTV-1 was second, AKTV-2 third and DNTV-2 last.

The two final runs of Troughton adventures occurred in 1970 and 1971. In both instances, WNTV-1 got to debut the episodes for the first time, AKTV-2 got them second, CHTV-3 third, and again DNTV-2 came last.

After the broadcast of all of these black and white stories by whichever of the four New Zealand television regions had them last, all the 16mm film prints were returned to the NZBC's head office in Wellington, from where they were sent on to the NZBC

CHAPTER 13

film store in Harriett Street in the Thorndon district of Wellington.

As mentioned earlier in this book, diligent research by New Zealand fan Graham Howard later unearthed full details of the programme traffic records for the country. These detail when the 16mm film prints of each story physically arrived in New Zealand and, more intriguingly, what happened to them after they had been screened and returned to the NZBC's head office. Every year on 1 April, the NZBC undertook a stock-take of their film holdings at Harriett Street. These holdings were recorded as '(HS)' in the programme traffic records, alongside the date of the last audit in which they were present. The records for the black and white *Doctor Who* episodes are as follows (the dates quoted in the 'Arrival Information' column below are sometime often not simply the actual dates that the films arrived in New Zealand, but the dates from which the rights period commenced):

Story Title	*Arrival Information*	*Departure / Destruction Information*
An Unearthly Child	Films arrived --/08/67	All 4 episodes sent on to Denmark 20/03/68
The Daleks	Films arrived --/08/67	All 7 episodes sent on to Denmark 20/03/68
The Edge of Destruction	Films arrived --/08/67	Both episodes sent on to Denmark 20/03/68
Marco Polo	n/k	Episodes One and Two sent to Iran --/10/67. Episodes Three to Seven in Harriett Street store as of 01/04/70
The Reign of Terror	Films sent 28/07/67 from ABC Australia	All six episodes destroyed 18/06/71
Planet of Giants	Films sent 28/07/67 from ABC Australia	All three episodes destroyed 14/07/71
The Dalek Invasion of Earth	Films sent 28/07/67 from ABC Australia	In Harriett Street store as of 01/04/70
The Rescue	Films sent 28/07/67 from ABC Australia	In Harriett Street store as of 01/04/70
The Romans	Films arrived 19/09/67	In Harriett Street store as of 01/04/70
The Web Planet	Films arrived 19/09/67	In Harriett Street store as of 01/04/70
The Crusade	Films arrived 19/09/67	In Harriett Street store as of 01/04/70. All four episodes junked in early 1974. Episode One rescued by private collector, and returned to the BBC in 1999

WIPED!

The Space Museum	Films arrived 23/09/68	In Harriett Street store as of 01/04/70
The Time Meddler	Films arrived 23/09/68	All four episodes sent to Nigeria 02/03/73
Galaxy 4	Films arrived 23/09/68	All four episodes sent to Singapore 20/09/72
The Myth Makers	Films arrived 23/09/68	All four episodes sent to Singapore 20/09/72
The Massacre	Films arrived 23/09/68	All four episodes sent to Singapore 20/09/72
The Ark	Films arrived 23/09/68	All four episodes sent to Singapore 20/09/72
The Celestial Toymaker	Films arrived 23/09/68	All four episodes sent to Singapore 20/09/72
The Savages	Films arrived 23/09/68	All four episodes sent to Singapore 10/01/72
The War Machines	Films arrived 23/09/68	All four episodes sent to Singapore 10/01/72
The Smugglers	Films arrived 23/09/68	All four episodes sent to Singapore 10/01/72
The Tenth Planet	Films arrived 23/09/68	All four episodes sent to Singapore 10/01/72
The Power of the Daleks	Films arrived 20/03/69	All six episodes sent to Singapore 10/01/72
The Highlanders	Films arrived 24/03/69	The fate of these films is unclear, but they were probably destroyed. Episode One is listed as destroyed, whilst episodes Two – Four have marks which look to be 'ditto' marks next to them
The Underwater Menace	Films arrived 11/04/69	The fate of these films is unclear, but they were probably destroyed. Similar (but not identical) 'ditto' marks follow on from the listing of 'The Highlanders' for episodes One – Three of the story. However, the story is also listed as being in the Harriett Street store as of 01/04/70
The Moonbase	n/k	Listed as 'AK 01/04/70', which probably meant that the films were at station AKTV-2 waiting to be transmitted at the time of the stocktake
The Macra Terror	n/k	All four episodes destroyed 24/06/74

CHAPTER 13

The Faceless Ones	Films arrived 12/08/69	Censors rejected – returned to London 03/07/70
The Evil of the Daleks	Films arrived 15/09/69	All seven episodes listed as destroyed, date not recorded
The Tomb of the Cybermen	Films arrived 13/10/69	Records unclear. Possibly destroyed, date not recorded
The Abominable Snowmen	Films arrived 21/10/69	Note in file says 'Exp 31/08/73'. Possibly means the episodes were sent on (if 'Exp' = Exported) elsewhere on this date. Alternatively, it could also just be the Expiry date of the rights to show this story.
The Ice Warriors	Films arrived 28/10/70	Censors rejected – no other records
The Enemy of the World	Films arrived 04/11/70	No records
The Web of Fear	Films arrived 09/11/70	No records
Fury from the Deep	Films arrived 01/12/70	Censors rejected – no other records
The Wheel in Space	Films arrived 19/11/70	No records

By early 1973, NZBC in Wellington was preparing to relocate to a new television centre being built in Avalon, Lower Hutt. While the studios and other facilities were not due to be completed until March 1975, some of the other departments were able to move much earlier. One of these departments was the NZBC film store. The store at the new Avalon building was a lot smaller than the one that NZBC used at Harriett Street (which had begun operations in late 1964), mainly because more programmes were now being purchased and transmitted on videotape rather than film. To avoid having to move all the films from Harriett Street, a final stock-take of holdings was done, and materials to which NZBC's rights had expired were prime candidates for destruction, This meant that NZBC's remaining stock of black and white Hartnell and Troughton *Doctor Who* episodes would now be junked.

By early 1975, all their remaining 16mm film prints of '60s *Doctor Who* had been officially destroyed by NZBC. In the main, the films were taken out of their tins, and fed through a band saw that cut the spools neatly in half, leaving thousands of short strips of film. These strips were then thrown into a skip bound for the nearest landfill site for burial. This is the fate that befell certainly the films marked as destroyed in the New Zealand programme traffic records, and almost certainly the remainder of the unaccounted-for episodes as well. It was during these junkings that NZBC's 16mm film print of 'The Crusade' Episode One ('The Lion'), managed somehow to escape destruction and be intercepted by a film collector (see the chapter on the returned

WIPED!

episodes for more details).

More intriguing is the possibility that other episodes might have escaped the purge. One of the fans who eventually discovered the film of 'The Lion', Neil Lambess, recalls watching two episodes of 'The Macra Terror' projected from 16mm film onto a screen during a cancelled sports day at his school sometime in 1972 or 1973. He has since ascertained that in the 1970s, if schools asked nicely enough, the NZBC were perfectly happy to send them a few film prints of programmes to which the rights had expired, which they could then '... splice, dice and play around with, as long as they didn't screen them ...' Obviously, this practice was never 'official' in any way, but apparently it did happen. However, as 'The Macra Terror' has a junking date of 24/06/74 attributed to it by the NZBC, it's possible they could have recalled any prints that they had loaned to schools in previous years, and then seen to it that they were destroyed.

As happened at BBC Enterprises in London (according to Ian Levine's recollection), the metal film cans that previously held the junked *Doctor Who* prints were sometimes kept and reused by the NZBC. In 1990, two such cans were discovered at the TVNZ regional office in Wellington, labelled as 'The Moonbase' Episode Three and 'Assassin at Pekin'[84] ('Marco Polo' Episode Seven). The contents were checked, and turned out not to be episodes of *Doctor Who* at all.

NIGERIA

Situated on the west coast of Africa, Nigeria became part of the British Empire in 1901, and gained its independence in October 1960. Television began there in 1959, with the launch of Western Nigeria Television (WNTV). A year later, Eastern Nigerian Television (ENTV) began broadcasting, followed in 1962 by Radio Kaduna Television (RKTV), and the government-owned Nigerian Television Service (NTS) in Lagos, which later became the Nigerian Broadcasting Corporation (NBC) Channel 10. Midwest Television (MTS) began broadcasting in Benin in 1973, and the Benue Plateau Broadcasting Corporation (BPBC) went on air for the first time in 1974 (and was first African TV station to screen colour programmes). *Doctor Who* was initially purchased and shown in Nigeria by RKTV.

'An Unearthly Child', 'The Daleks', 'The Edge of Destruction', 'Marco Polo' and 'The Keys of Marinus' were all sold to this station in June 1965. They were followed in August 1965 by 'The Aztecs', 'The Sensorites', 'The Reign of Terror', 'Planet of Giants', 'The Dalek Invasion of Earth' and 'The Rescue'. A third batch of stories was then sold, consisting of 'The Romans', 'The Web Planet', 'The Crusade', 'The Space Museum', 'The Chase and 'The Time Meddler', in July 1966.

---

84 That's how it was spelt on the label!

CHAPTER 13

The series debuted on RKTV on Tuesday 3 August 1965, when the first episode of 'An Unearthly Child' went out at 6.35 pm. *Doctor Who* was then screened on a weekly basis on Tuesday evenings throughout the rest of 1965 and 1966, until the final episode of 'The Time Meddler' in April 1967.

There then was a gap of seven years before Nigeria started buying *Doctor Who* episodes again. 'The Web Planet' and 'The Time Meddler' were re-sold to the country in July 1973, along with 'The War Machines' for the first time. This time, *Doctor Who* was shown by the station Midwest TV. Episodes went out weekly on Monday evenings, under the banner *Children's Time*, between April and July 1973. For this sale, the film prints of 'The Time Meddler' were sent to Nigeria directly from New Zealand. The prints of 'The War Machines' screened in Nigeria were also later found to have originated in New Zealand, although they had been initially sent to Singapore in 1972 by the NZBC.

A batch of Patrick Troughton episodes was sold to Nigeria in 1974. Three stories – 'The Abominable Snowmen', 'The Enemy of the World' and 'The Web of Fear' – were purchased in October of that year. 'The Wheel in Space' was also sold, but the BBC sales records are missing, so the exact date isn't known – although it seems almost certain that it was at the same time as the other three Troughton tales. Records at the NTA indicate that these episodes were screened weekly by the Benue Plateau Broadcasting Corporation (BPBC) between March and August 1975, on Tuesday evenings.

Almost as an afterthought, the story 'The Dominators' was sold to Nigeria in November 1975. No details have been found (to date) on where and when this story was screened[85].

Finally, 'The Krotons' was sold to Nigeria in February 1976. This single story was screened by NBC Channel 10, going out weekly on Monday evenings in December 1975 (which was some months before the BBC 'officially' recorded the sale). Oddly, in newspaper television listings, the series was called *Son of Dr Who*. This was the last Nigeria saw of *Doctor Who* until the station NTV-Kano purchased a batch of Tom Baker stories in colour in 1979.

The Nigerian Television Authority (NTA) Decree 27 of 1976 brought the existing regional and state television stations under the control of the Federal Government, resulting in the single network of stations known as the NTA. This came into effect early in 1977.

As a result of this, RKTV became NTA Kaduna, Midwest Television became NTA Benin, BPBC became NTA Jos and NBC Channel 10 became NTA Channel 10 Lagos.

The NTA were contacted by Ian Levine and the BBC in 1984, and this resulted

---

85 'The Dominators' certainly wasn't purchased by RKTV, Midwest TV or BPBC. It's possible that the station could have been NBC Channel 10, although (to date) no newspaper television listings have been found to support this theory.

WIPED!

in the film prints of the three William Hartnell stories that were shown by Midwest Television in 1973 being recovered from NTA Benin and returned to the BBC in early 1985.

The prints of the first two William Hartnell seasons held by NTA Kaduna were all destroyed.

RHODESIA

The former Rhodesia, now called Zimbabwe, is a landlocked country in Southern Africa with a convoluted and contentious history. The country as it is today was formed out of a number of territories located between the Zambezi and Limpopo rivers, then known as Zambesia. In 1888, the British colonialist Cecil Rhodes negotiated the mining rights for the region with King Lobengula, and a Royal Charter was granted to the country, which was renamed Rhodesia in honour of Rhodes. The land was then split into two regions; Northern Rhodesia would eventually change its name again to Zambia, while Southern Rhodesia would eventually become known as Zimbabwe.

Southern Rhodesia became a British colony in October 1923, but relations soured in the 1950s when Britain tried to consolidate the territory with that of Northern Rhodesia and Nyasaland (since renamed Malawi). African opposition to this move forced Britain to dissolve the union in 1963.

The government of Southern Rhodesia made a unilateral declaration of independence from Britain in November 1965, at which point the country became known simply as Rhodesia. The British government ruled that this was as an act of rebellion, and imposed economic sanctions, although it didn't move to re-establish control.

The country was renamed again in 1979 as Zimbabwe Rhodesia, and temporarily came back under British control until elections the following year. 1980 saw the country granted full independence from Britain, and its name changed to Zimbabwe.

Television came to Southern Rhodesia in 1960, with the advent of the Rhodesia Broadcasting Corporation (RBC). Although a television licence fee was required to be paid, the RBC also ran adverts. Television reception was initially confined mainly to the larger cities, and programmes catered mainly for the white minority in the country. In 1979, the Rhodesia Broadcasting Corporation became the Zimbabwe Rhodesia Broadcasting Corporation (ZRBC), and in 1980, the name changed again to the Zimbabwe Broadcasting Corporation (ZBC). Colour television didn't arrive in Zimbabwe until 1984.

Sales of *Doctor Who* to the RBC occurred in two batches. The first was in September 1965, and comprised 'An Unearthly Child', 'The Daleks', 'The Edge of Destruction', 'Marco Polo' and 'The Keys of Marinus'. The second batch came in December 1966, consisting of 'The Aztecs', 'The Sensorites', 'The Reign of Terror', 'Planet of Giants', 'The

CHAPTER 13

Dalek Invasion of Earth' and 'The Rescue'.

Doctor Who was due to begin on Sunday 5 September 1965 on RBC, as newspaper television listings from the time confirm. The 16mm film prints must have been delayed in transit, however, as the series failed to screen. It was listed for the following week, but was not screened then either. On Sunday 19 September, the programme *Forest Rangers* was listed as being screened in the *Doctor Who* slot (this was the programme that had previously occupied this time slot). The series finally began on the RBC on Sunday 26 September 1965, when the first episode of 'An Unearthly Child' was screened at 5.40 pm – the film prints had obviously finally arrived in the country. The series was shown weekly, through to the final episode of 'The Rescue' in September 1966.

After screening the series, RBC sent its prints of *Doctor Who* on to ZNBC in Zambia.

SIERRA LEONE

Sierra Leone is to be found on the West Coast of Africa, and was a British colony from 1808 through to 1961, after which it gained its independence. Television began in April 1963 with the Sierra Leone Broadcasting Service (SLBS), which was the sole network until ABC Television-Africa was launched in 2005.

Doctor Who stories were purchased by the SLBS in a number of distinct batches. The first, in April 1967, comprised 'An Unearthly Child', 'The Daleks', 'The Edge of Destruction', 'Marco Polo', and 'The Keys of Marinus'. This was followed in February 1968 by 'The Aztecs', 'The Sensorites', 'The Reign of Terror', 'Planet of Giants', 'The Dalek Invasion of Earth' and 'The Rescue'. In August 1968, more stories followed: 'The Romans', 'The Web Planet', 'The Crusade', 'The Space Museum', 'The Chase' and 'The Time Meddler'.

The final batch of Hartnell stories were all sold in August 1970. These were: 'Galaxy 4', 'The Myth Makers', 'The Massacre', 'The Ark', 'The Celestial Toymaker', 'The Gunfighters', 'The Savages', 'The War Machines' and 'The Smugglers'.

The SLBS's next dalliance with *Doctor Who* occurred in September 1979, when it purchased the Pertwee stories 'Spearhead from Space', 'The Three Doctors', 'The Time Monster' and 'The Monster of Peladon'.

Transmission details for the SLBS are somewhat sketchy. There was a block of unknown *Doctor Who* episodes shown weekly on Wednesday evenings between 12 April and 18 October 1967. This probably accounts for the stories from 'An Unearthly Child' through to 'The Keys of Marinus'. The series then returned on 13 November 1967, only it had now switched to Monday evening screenings. This run lasted until Monday 23 December 1968, and probably accounts for the stories from 'The Aztecs'

WIPED!

to 'The Time Meddler'.

A third run of stories began on Friday 24 July 1970, again shown weekly, this time on Friday evenings. It appears that at least some of these screenings may have been scheduled by applying a mistaken alphabetical logic to the story codes. So for the batch of stories purchased in August 1970, the screening order was 'The Savages' (story code AA), 'The War Machines' (BB), 'The Smugglers' (CC), 'Galaxy 4' (T) 'The Myth Makers' (U), 'The Massacre' (W), 'The Ark' (X), 'The Celestial Toymaker' (Y) and 'The Gunfighters' (Z). This final run of episodes concluded on Friday 26 March 1971.

There are very credible reports that some Hartnell episodes may have been screened again in Sierra Leone without the BBC's consent some years later. It's almost certain that at least 'The Savages' was screened in 1984.

Many of the Hartnell episodes that SLBS purchased in the 1960s were still in the SLBS film vault in the 1990s. However, civil war broke out in the country in 1991, and peace wasn't resumed until 2001. During the war, SLBS's television station, including its film vault, was totally destroyed in 1999. Paperwork indicates that it still held film prints of 'Galaxy 4', 'The Myth Makers', 'The Massacre', 'The Savages' and 'The Celestial Toymaker' at the time.

SINGAPORE

Located at the very tip of Malaysia, the island of Singapore is a remarkably small country, covering just 273 square miles. The British East India Company established a trading post there in 1819, and it soon became the cornerstone outpost of the British Empire in Southeast Asia. It was occupied by the Japanese army during the Second World War, but reverted to British rule in 1945. The country was granted independence in 1963, although it remains a member of the British Commonwealth to this day.

Television began in Singapore in February 1963, with the station Radio & Television of Singapore (RTS) broadcasting 90 minutes of material a day on Channel 5 (oddly named, as this was the only channel!) The programmes shown were all in the English language. Broadcasts increased to four hours a day from April 1963. In November 1963, a second channel – Channel 8 – was launched, for Chinese-language programmes. Colour transmissions began in 1974, and the station changed its name in 1980 to the Singapore Broadcasting Corporation (SBC), in 1994 to Television Corporation of Singapore (TCS) and finally in 2004 to Media Corporation of Singapore (MCS).

An initial batch of *Doctor Who* stories was sold to RTS in April 1965. This consisted of: 'An Unearthly Child', 'The Daleks', 'The Edge of Destruction', 'Marco Polo' and 'The Keys of Marinus'. In November 1965 there followed sales of: 'The Aztecs', 'The

CHAPTER 13

Sensorites', 'The Reign of Terror', 'Planet of Giants', 'The Dalek Invasion of Earth' and 'The Rescue'. More Hartnell stories were purchased in May 1966: 'The Romans', 'The Web Planet', 'The Crusade', 'The Space Museum', 'The Chase', and 'The Time Meddler'.

RTS began screening *Doctor Who* on Wednesday 7 April 1965, with the first episode of 'An Unearthly Child'. The series was shown weekly, with episodes going out between 6.30 pm and 7.00 pm, through to the final episode of 'The Romans' on 11 May 1966. The series returned on Saturday 9 July 1966, with the first episode of 'The Web Planet', which went out at 6.05 pm. *Doctor Who* continued being shown weekly, but was briefly switched to Fridays, beginning with the last episode of 'The Crusade'. It then moved to Sunday afternoons from the second episode of 'The Space Museum', and remained in that slot until the final episode of 'The Time Meddler', which was shown on Christmas Day 1966.

The next batch of *Doctor Who* sales to RTS came in March 1969 and jumped forward to Patrick Troughton's Doctor. This consisted of 'The Highlanders', 'The Underwater Menace', 'The Moonbase', 'The Macra Terror' and 'The Faceless Ones'. Transmission of these stories began on Thursday 13 February 1969 with 'The Highlanders' Episode One. *Doctor Who* was again shown once a week, and this run concluded with the final episode of 'The Faceless Ones' on Thursday 10 July 1969.

In January 1970, RTS bought 'The Evil of the Daleks' and 'The Tomb of the Cybermen'. These were followed in May 1970 by sales of 'The Abominable Snowmen', 'The Ice Warriors', 'The Enemy of the World', 'The Web of Fear', 'Fury from the Deep' and 'The Wheel in Space'. The next batch of stories, sold in February 1971, consisted of 'The Dominators', 'The Mind Robber', 'The Invasion' and 'The Krotons'. This was followed in October 1971 by sales of 'The Seeds of Death', 'The Space Pirates', 'The War Games' and the first three Jon Pertwee stories.

Then, in February 1972, a batch of earlier *Doctor Who* stories was sold to RTS for the first time. These were 'The Savages', 'The War Machines', 'The Smugglers', 'The Tenth Planet' and 'The Power of the Daleks'. The film prints of these episodes weren't supplied direct to Singapore by BBC Enterprises in this instance. Programme traffic records in New Zealand show that they were all sent from the NZBC to Singapore at Enterprises' request on Monday 10 January 1972, which was the month before the sales were actually recorded in the BBC's own documentation.

RTS began showing *Doctor Who* again from Thursday 4 December 1969, at 6.00 pm. This weekly run continued through to Thursday 15 June 1972, and included all the Troughton stories from 'The Evil of the Daleks' to 'The War Games', and perhaps even the first Pertwee season as well. These stories were followed by screenings of the episodes sent from New Zealand, which took up the final six months of this run, between January and June 1972. Sometime around July 1973, RTS sent its film prints of all four episodes

WIPED!

of 'The War Machines' on to Nigeria.

The next batch of *Doctor Who* sales to RTS took place in December 1972, according to BBC records. Seemingly working in reverse again, the stories sold this time were 'Galaxy 4', 'The Myth Makers', 'The Massacre', 'The Ark', 'The Celestial Toymaker' and 'The Gunfighters'. Once again, prints of most of these episodes were sent to RTS from the NZBC in New Zealand at BBC Enterprises' behest. These were sent on Wednesday 20 September 1972, again some weeks prior to the dates recorded for the sales in the BBC's own documentation. The only story in this batch of sales to Singapore not sent from New Zealand was 'The Gunfighters', as it was never sold to the NZBC in the first place. Where RTS got its film prints of this story from isn't known.

Doctor Who returned to RTS on Monday 9 October 1972, and again was shown weekly. This run concluded on Monday 26 March 1973, and was *probably* made up of the final batch of Hartnell episodes to be purchased, although transmission details are sketchy. The series then continued screening on a weekly basis, with Jon Pertwee episodes from 'Terror of the Autons' onwards, until the final *Doctor Who* story screened in Singapore, 'Planet of the Daleks', was shown in May and June 1974.

SBC (the new name for RTS) were contacted in the early 1990s, and stated that they no longer held any episodes of *Doctor Who* in their archives.

THAILAND

Sitting at the heart of Southeast Asia, Thailand is bordered by Cambodia, Malaysia and Laos. Television was first introduced to Thailand in 1955. HSA-TV (Channel 7) purchased two batches of Hartnell episodes. The first, in October 1966, consisted of 'An Unearthly Child', 'The Daleks', 'The Edge of Destruction', 'Marco Polo' and 'The Keys of Marinus'. The second, in April 1967, consisted of 'The Aztecs', 'The Sensorites', 'The Reign of Terror', 'Planet of Giants', 'The Dalek Invasion of Earth' and 'The Rescue'.

Doctor Who began on HSA-TV (Channel 7) on Saturday 20 August 1966, when the first episode of 'An Unearthly Child' was shown at 5.30 pm. The series was shown weekly (although it did skip the occasional week) until the final episode of 'The Rescue' was screened on Saturday 2 December 1967.

TRINIDAD AND TOBAGO

This group of islands lies in the southern Caribbean Sea, north-east of Venezuela and south of Grenada. Trinidad became a British colony in 1802, while Tobago regularly changed hands between the British, French and Dutch up until 1814, when it too became a British property. In 1889, Trinidad and Tobago were united as a single colony, and they have remained as a single nation ever since. They gained independence from Britain in 1962, the year that the Trinidad and Tobago Television Company (TTT)

CHAPTER 13

began broadcasting.

TTT purchased two batches of Hartnell stories. The first, in May 1965, was via the distributor TIE and comprised 'An Unearthly Child', 'The Daleks', 'The Edge of Destruction', 'Marco Polo' and 'The Keys of Marinus'. The second, in March 1966, consisted of 'The Aztecs', 'The Sensorites', 'The Reign of Terror', 'Planet of Giants', 'The Dalek Invasion of Earth', and 'The Rescue'. It's not known if TIE played any part in the sale of these stories.

Doctor Who began on TTT on Sunday 31 October 1965, when the first episode of 'An Unearthly Child' was shown at 6.30 pm. The series then continued being screened in this time slot on a weekly basis, until the final episode of 'The Rescue' was shown on Sunday 30 October 1966.

In 1990, during a failed coup on the island, TTT was taken over by a group of rebels, who surrendered to the army after a six-day stand-off. In 1994, the station was merged with the state-owned radio company, the National Broadcasting Service, and became known as the National Broadcasting Network. However, on 14 January 2005, the National Broadcasting Network was shut down for good by the government.

UGANDA

Uganda is a landlocked country in East Africa. It became a British colony in 1888 and gained its independence in October 1962. A year later, in October 1963, television transmissions began there.

Uganda Television (UTV) was the country's first television station, which opened in Kampala, the capital city. UTV began purchasing *Doctor Who* from BBC Enterprises in November 1965, with 'An Unearthly Child', 'The Daleks', 'The Edge of Destruction', 'Marco Polo' and 'The Keys of Marinus'. In the case of the first three stories, the film prints weren't sent direct to UTV from London. Instead, CBC in Cyprus forwarded their copies to UTV at BBC Enterprises' request.

More Hartnell adventures were then sold to UTV in April 1966: 'The Aztecs', 'The Sensorites', 'The Reign of Terror' 'Planet of Giants', 'The Dalek Invasion of Earth' and 'The Rescue'. This was followed in November 1968 by a batch of Troughton stories: 'The Highlanders', 'The Underwater Menace', 'The Moonbase', 'The Macra Terror' and 'The Faceless Ones'.

Doctor Who began on UTV on Tuesday 18 January 1966, when the first episode of 'An Unearthly Child' was screened. The series was then shown weekly on Tuesday evenings, until the final episode of 'The Rescue' went out on Tuesday 17 January 1967. The series returned on Sunday 28 September 1968 with the first episode of 'The Highlanders', shown at 7.00 pm. *Doctor Who* was again screened weekly, right through to the final episode of 'The Faceless Ones' in March 1969.

WIPED!

ZAMBIA

Zambia is a landlocked country in the middle of Southern Africa. In the 18th Century, the territory was gradually claimed by British explorers as part of the British Empire, and was given the name Northern Rhodesia. On its independence from Britain in October 1964, Northern Rhodesia was renamed the Republic of Zambia. Television came to Zambia in 1961, with the formation of the Zambia National Broadcasting Corporation (ZNBC), a single-channel station.

There appear to have been a number of discrete blocks of sales of *Doctor Who* episodes to the ZNBC over the years. In March 1966, 'An Unearthly Child', 'The Daleks', 'The Edge of Destruction', 'Marco Polo', 'The Keys of Marinus', 'The Aztecs', 'The Sensorites', 'The Reign of Terror', 'Planet of Giants', 'The Dalek Invasion of Earth' and 'The Rescue' were all sold. These stories were followed in October 1966 by sales of 'The Romans', 'The Web Planet', 'The Crusade', 'The Space Museum', 'The Chase' and 'The Time Meddler'. In March 1968, a further batch of Hartnell stories was sold: 'Galaxy 4', 'The Myth Makers', 'The Massacre', 'The Ark', 'The Celestial Toymaker', 'The Gunfighters', 'The Savages', 'The War Machines' and 'The Smugglers'.

Exactly two years later, in March 1970, the following Troughton stories were sold: 'The Highlanders', 'The Underwater Menace', 'The Moonbase', 'The Macra Terror' and 'The Faceless Ones'. Another batch of *Doctor Who* sales to ZNBC took place in October 1973. This comprised 'The Abominable Snowmen', 'The Ice Warriors', 'The Enemy of the World' and 'The Web of Fear'.

Finally, the ZNBC purchased 'The Seeds of Death' in February 1976, 'The Space Pirates' in April 1976 and 'The War Games' in May 1976. As 'The Space Pirates' had been junked by BBC Enterprises in 1974, prints for this 1976 sale would have had to have been supplied to the ZNBC from another overseas station. BBC Enterprises still had copies of 'The Seeds of Death' and 'The War Games' at this point in time.

Doctor Who's screenings on the ZNBC are difficult to pin down with any certainty. The series was due to begin in Kitwe on Sunday 19 September 1965, but the prints that ZNBC were relying on showing were still in transit to them from RBC in Rhodesia. The series was then scheduled to begin the following week, on Sunday 26 September, but again the prints didn't arrive.

Finally, after four weeks of delays, the series began screening in the district of Kitwe on Sunday 17 October 1965, and was then shown on weekly basis. The region of Lusaka followed, screening episodes exactly one week behind their Kitwe debut. By September 1966, Kitwe and Lusaka had both moved the programme's time slot and were now screening episodes weekly on Tuesday evenings, with Lusaka still one week behind Kitwe. So, for example, on Tuesday 11 October 1966, Kitwe screened the first episode of 'The Rescue', while Lusaka showed the final episode of 'The Dalek Invasion of Earth'. The series continued to be screened in this manner until June 1967, when the final episode of 'The Time Meddler' was shown on both stations, albeit a week later in Lusaka.

Doctor Who returned to Zambian television in January 1968. Only television listings for Lusaka have been found (to date) for this and subsequent runs, although presumably they were still showing episodes a week behind Kitwe. The first episode of 'Galaxy 4' went out on Tuesday 30 January 1968 in Lusaka, and the series continued through the rest of the William Hartnell stories up to 'The Smugglers', which was shown in November 1968.

Doctor Who was next seen in Lusaka on Wednesday 8 April 1970, and ran weekly through to Wednesday 29 July 1970. This block of episodes would have been for the stories from 'The Highlanders' to 'The Macra Terror'.

The series was back after a lengthy gap, again in Lusaka, on Monday 11 June 1973, and then ran weekly through to Monday 31 December 1973. This would have encompassed the stories from 'The Faceless Ones' to 'The Web of Fear'.

The final batch of episodes was shown weekly between Thursday 5 February and Thursday 1 July 1976. This would have comprised 'The Seeds of Death', 'The Space Pirates' and 'The War Games'.

It would appear that only stories from the Hartnell and Troughton era were ever shown in Zambia, as no further sales are recorded after this point. Perhaps the main reason was that Zambia's economy began to decline in the 1970s, as the price of copper – Zambia's principal export – fell sharply in the world markets, and remained at low levels in the decades that followed.

A report by the Fédération Internationale des Archives de Télévision/The International Federation of Television Archives (FIAT/IFTA) in 2003 into the state of the Radio and Television Archive of ZNBC revealed that between five and ten thousand boxes of 16mm film, mostly uncatalogued and unlabeled, were still held by the Archive. Most of the film was affected by 'vinegar syndrome', meaning it would soon become unsalvageable, if it wasn't already. A number of *Doctor Who* fan websites seized on this report as evidence that some old *Doctor Who* films might still exist in Zambia … However, all the Zambian film archives have now been thoroughly checked, and no *Doctor Who* material was found in them.

THOSE WILLIAM HARTNELL & PATRICK TROUGHTON OVERSEAS SALES IN FULL

Below is a tabulated list of all the BBC sales of William Hartnell and Patrick Troughton Doctor Who stories in the 1960s and 1970s.

The list is presented in Invoice Number order, rather than in any date order from

WIPED!

the Prog Contr Advised column, or any other similar date columns on the sheets. This is based on the assumption that the BBC would have a sequential invoice numbering system (i.e. they would issue invoice no. 00002 only after they had already issued invoice no 00001).

The problem with this is that there would appear to have been several different invoice number systems used by the BBC between 1964 and 1976.

The first sequence, used from 1964, was a simple four-figure numerical progression invoice number. This became a five-figure number in 1965, and this also usually included a w/e date as well (presumably the week ending date for the week in which the relevant invoice run was done). In early 1966, the w/e date briefly took precedence, although the system reverted back to the five-figure number soon after.

This continued until the middle of 1968, when the sale to Iran was given both a five-figure invoice number and a TE/xxxx reference (where the xxxx was a four-figure number). From this point in time, the five-figure invoice number was dropped, and the TE/xxxx sequence continued, in ascending numerical order. This continued until the number sequence increased to five digits in 1970, and then carried on until 1973, by which time the five-figure number was in the 20000+ region.

In the middle of 1973, a new TE/ number sequence began, staying at five figures, but resetting itself down to 02000, then this sequentially increased over time, through to the last invoice listed here in 1976.

This list also includes only 'actual' sales. So where we know that episodes were sent to a particular country but did not screen (for whatever reason) these are not shown, as they do not appear on the BBC's Clearance History Sheets at all. So there is no listing for 'The Reign of Terror' against Cyprus, 'The Crusade' against New Zealand, 'An Unearthly Child' against Denmark, etc.

Inv No.	Country	Story	Prog Contr. Advised	Music Copyright Advised	Script Copyright Advised
5306	Australia	An Unearthly Child	24.06.64	24.06.64	07.08.64
		The Daleks	24.06.64	24.06.64	07.06.64
		The Edge of Destruction	24.06.64	24.06.64	07.08.64
5312	New Zealand	An Unearthly Child	24.06.64	24.06.64	07.08.64
		The Daleks	24.06.64	24.06.64	07.08.64
		The Edge of Destruction	24.06.64	24.06.64	07.08.64

CHAPTER 13

6355	Malta	An Unearthly Child	07.12.64	13.04.65	12.04.65
		The Daleks	07.12.64	13.04.65	12.04.65
		The Edge of Destruction	07.12.64	13.04.65	12.04.65
		Marco Polo	07.12.64	13.04.65	12.04.65
		The Keys of Marinus	07.12.64	13.04.65	12.04.65
6564	Australia	Marco Polo	18.08.64	13.04.65	18.08.64
		The Keys of Marinus	18.08.64	-	18.08.64
		The Aztecs	21.01.65	13.04.65	22.02.65
		The Sensorites	21.01.65	-	22.02.65
		The Reign of Terror	21.01.65	13.04.65	22.02.65
		Planet of Giants	21.01.65	13.04.65	22.02.65
		The Dalek Invasion of Earth	21.01.65	13.04.65	22.02.65
		The Rescue (Ep 1 only)	21.01.65	-	22.02.65
6778	Canada	An Unearthly Child	18.11.64	-	18.11.64
		The Daleks	18.11.64	-	18.1164
6984	Singapore	An Unearthly Child	13.04.65	13.04.65	12.04.65
		The Daleks	13.04.65	13.04.65	12.04.65
		The Edge of Destruction	13.04.65	13.04.65	12.04.65
		Marco Polo	13.04.65	13.04.65	12.04.65
		The Keys of Marinus	13.04.65	13.04.65	12.04.65
7243	Canada	The Edge of Destruction	18.11.64	13.04.65	16.11.64

WIPED!

7425 w/e 08.05.65	Gibraltar Aden Trinidad	An Unearthly Child	14.05.65	-	14.05.65
		The Daleks	14.05.65	-	14.05.65
		The Edge of Destruction	14.05.65	-	14.05.65
		Marco Polo	14.05.65	-	14.05.65
		The Keys of Marinus	14.05.65	-	14.05.65
w/e 22.05.65	Australia	The Rescue (Ep 2 only)	24.05.65	24.05.65	24.05.65
7572	Bermuda	An Unearthly Child	14.06.65	-	14.06.65
		The Daleks	14.06.65	-	14.06.65
		The Edge of Destruction	14.06.65	-	14.06.65
7575	Canada	Marco Polo	18.11.64	-	18.11.64
7647 w/e 12.06.65	Nigeria	An Unearthly Child	Not on Sales Sheet – Sheet Damaged		
		The Daleks	14.06.65	-	14.06.65
		The Edge of Destruction	14.06.65	-	14.06.65
		Marco Polo	14.06.65	-	14.06.65
		The Keys of Marinus	14.06.65	-	14.06.65
7766	Canada	The Keys of Marinus	18.11.64	13.04.65	18.11.64
ADV INV	Canada	The Aztecs	18.11.64	13.04.65	18.11.64
		The Sensorites	18.11.64	13.04.65	18.11.64
10243 w/e 21.08.65	Gibraltar	The Aztecs	29.08.65	-	28.08.65
		The Sensorites	23.08.65	-	23.08.65
		The Reign of Terror	23.08.65	-	23.08.65
		Planet of Giants	23.08.65	-	23.08.65
		The Dalek Invasion of Earth	23.08.65	-	23.08.65
		The Rescue	23.08.65	-	23.08.65

CHAPTER 13

10288 w/e 28.08.65	Malta	The Aztecs	31.08.65	-	31.08.65
		The Sensorites	31.08.65	-	31.08.65
		The Reign of Terror	31.08.65	-	31.08.65
		Planet of Giants	31.08.65	-	31.08.65
		The Dalek Invasion of Earth	31.08.65	-	31.08.65
		The Rescue	31.08.65	-	31.08.65
10320 w/e 04.09.65	Rhodesia	An Unearthly Child	06.09.65	-	06.09.65
		The Daleks	06.09.65	-	06.09.65
		The Edge of Destruction	06.09.65	-	06.09.65
		Marco Polo	06.09.65	-	06.09.68
		The Keys of Marinus	06.09.65	-	09.09.65
10386 w/e 11.09.65	Cyprus Barbados	An Unearthly Child	09.09.65	-	21.09.65
		The Daleks	06.09.65	-	06.09.65
		The Edge of Destruction	21.09.65	-	21.09.65
w/e 11.09.65	Barbados	Marco Polo	21.09.65	-	21.09.65
		The Keys of Marinus	21.09.65	-	21.09.65
10390 w/e 28.08.65	Nigeria	The Aztecs	Not on Sales Sheet – Sheet Damaged		
		The Sensorites	31.08.65	-	31.08.65
		The Reign of Terror	31.08.65	-	31.08.65
		Planet of Giants	31.08.65	-	31.08.65
		The Dalek Invasion of Earth	31.08.65	-	31.08.65
		The Rescue	31.08.65	-	31.08.65
w/e 06.11.65	New Zealand	Marco Polo	30.11.65	-	30.11.65

WIPED!

10917	Singapore	The Aztecs	30.11.65	-	30.11.65
		The Sensorites	30.11.65	-	30.11.65
		The Reign of Terror	30.11.65	-	30.11.65
		Planet of Giants	30.11.65	-	31.11.65
		The Dalek Invasion of Earth	30.11.65	-	31.11.65
		The Rescue	30.11.65	-	30.11.65
10958 w/e 27.11.65	Uganda	An Unearthly Child	30.11.65	-	30.11.65
		The Daleks	30.11.65	-	30.11.65
		The Edge of Destruction	30.11.65	-	30.11.65
		Marco Polo	30.11.65	-	30.11.65
		The Keys of Marinus	30.11.65	-	30.11.65
11037 w/e 20.11.65	Hong Kong	An Unearthly Child	23.11.65	-	23.11.65
		The Daleks	23.11.65	-	23.11.65
		The Edge of Destruction	23.11.65	-	23.11.65
		Marco Polo	23.11.65	-	23.11.65
		The Keys of Marinus	23.11.65	-	23.11.65
11268	Australia	The Romans	13.01.66	13.01.66	13.01.66
		The Web Planet	13.01.66	13.01.66	13.01.66
		The Crusade	13.01.66	13.01.66	13.0166
11615 w/e 20.11.65	Hong Kong Aden	The Aztecs	23.11.65	-	23.11.65
		The Sensorites	23.11.65	-	23.11.65
		The Reign of Terror	23.11.65	-	23.11.65
		Planet of Giants	23.11.65	-	23.11.65
		The Dalek Invasion of Earth	23.11.65	-	23.11.65
		The Rescue	23.11.65	-	23.11.65

CHAPTER 13

w/e					
w/e 22.01.66	Ghana	An Unearthly Child	Not on Sales Sheet – Sheet Damaged		
		The Daleks	26.01.66	-	26.01.66
		The Edge of Destruction	26.01.66	-	26.01.66
		Marco Polo	26.01.66	-	26.01.66
		The Keys of Marinus	26.01.66	-	26.01.66
w/e 05.02.66	Zambia	An Unearthly Child	Not on Sales Sheet – Sheet Damaged		
		The Daleks	07.03.66	-	07.03.66
		The Edge of Destruction	07.03.66	-	07.03.66
		Marco Polo	07.03.66	-	07.03.66
		The Keys of Marinus	07.03.66	-	07.03.66
w/e 05.02.66	Gibraltar	The Romans	16.05.66	05.08.66	16.05.66
		The Web Planet	16.05.66	16.05.66	16.05.66
		The Crusade	16.05.66	16.05.66	16.05.66
		The Space Museum	16.05.66	16.05.66	16.05.66
		The Chase	No BBC Sales Sheet		
		The Time Meddler	16.05.66	16.05.66	16.05.66
w/e 12.02.66	Jamaica	An Unearthly Child	Not on Sales Sheet – Sheet Damaged		
		The Daleks	07.03.66	-	07.03.66
		The Edge of Destruction	07.03.66	-	07.03.66
		Marco Polo	07.03.66	-	07.03.66
		The Keys of Marinus	07.03.66	-	07.03.66

WIPED!

11710 w/e 12.02.66	Trinidad	The Aztecs	07.03.66	-	07.03.66
		The Sensorites	07.03.66	-	07.03.66
		The Reign of Terror	07.03.66	-	07.03.66
		Planet of Giants	07.03.66	-	07.03.66
		The Dalek Invasion of Earth	07.03.66	-	07.03.66
		The Rescue	07.03.66	-	07.03.66
11735 w/e 19.02.66	Zambia	The Aztecs	07.03.66	-	07.03.66
		The Sensorites	07.03.66	-	07.03.66
		The Reign of Terror	07.03.66	-	07.03.66
		Planet of Giants	07.03.66	-	07.03.66
		The Dalek Invasion of Earth	07.03.66	-	-
		The Rescue	07.03.66	-	07.03.66
w/e 23.04.66	Uganda	The Aztecs	25.04.66	-	25.04.66
		The Sensorites	25.04.66	-	25.04.66
		The Reign of Terror	25.04.66	-	25.04.66
		Planet of Giants	25.04.66	-	25.04.66
		The Dalek Invasion of Earth	25.04.66	-	25.04.66
		The Rescue	25.04.66	-	25.04.66
w/e 30.04.66	Singapore	The Romans	16.05.66	05.08.66	16.05.66
		The Web Planet	16.05.66	16.05.66	16.05.66
		The Crusade	16.05.66	16.05.66	16.05.66
		The Space Museum	16.05.66	16.05.66	16.05.66
		The Chase	No BBC Sales Sheet		
		The Time Meddler	16.05.66	16.05.66	16.05.66
12370	Cyprus	Marco Polo	26.05.66	-	26.05.66
		The Keys of Marinus	26.05.66	-	26.05.66

CHAPTER 13

12630	Nigeria	The Romans	07.07.66	-	04.07.66
		The Web Planet	04.07.66	-	04.07.66
		The Crusade	04.07.66	-	04.07.66
		The Space Museum	04.07.66	-	04.07.66
		The Chase	No BBC Sales Sheet		
		The Time Meddler	04.07.66	-	04.07.66
12734	Kenya	An Unearthly Child	Not on Sales Sheet – Sheet Damaged		
		The Daleks	04.07.66	-	04.07.66
		The Edge of Destruction	04.07.66	-	04.07.66
		Marco Polo	04.07.66	-	04.07.66
		The Keys of Marinus	04.07.66	-	04.07.66
12947	Bermuda	Marco Polo	11.07.66	-	11.07.66
		The Keys of Marinus	11.07.66	-	11.07.66
13346	Cyprus	The Aztecs	18.10.66	-	18.10.66
		The Sensorites	18.10.66	-	18.10.66
13350	Jamaica	The Aztecs	18.10.66	-	18.10.66
		The Sensorites	18.10.66	-	18.10.66
		The Reign of Terror	18.10.66	-	18.10.66
		Planet of Giants	18.10.66	-	18.10.66
		The Dalek Invasion of Earth	18.10.66	-	-
		The Rescue	18.10.66	-	18.10.66
13648	Australia	Galaxy 4	24.10.66	24.10.66	13.09.66
13649	Australia	The Space Museum	24.10.66	24.10.66	24.10.66
		The Chase	No BBC Sales Sheet		
		The Time Meddler	24.10.66	24.10.66	24.10.66

WIPED!

13813	Thailand	An Unearthly Child	20.10.66	21.10.66	21.10.66
		The Daleks	20.10.66	21.10.66	21.10.66
		The Edge of Destruction	20.10.66	21.10.66	21.10.66
		Marco Polo	20.10.66	21.10.66	21.10.66
		The Keys of Marinus	20.10.66	21.10.66	21.10.66
13820	Zambia	The Romans	21.10.66	21.10.66	21.10.66
		The Web Planet	21.10.66	-	21.10.66
		The Crusade	21.10.66	-	21.10.66
		The Space Museum	21.10.66	-	21.10.66
		The Chase	No BBC Sales Sheet		
		The Time Meddler	21.10.66	-	21.10.66
13865	Venezuela	An Unearthly Child	18.01.67	18.01.67	18.01.67
		The Daleks	18.01.67	18.01.67	18.01.67
		The Edge of Destruction	18.01.67	18.01.67	18.01.67
		Marco Polo	18.01.67	-	-
		The Keys of Marinus	18.01.67	18.01.67	18.01.67
		The Aztecs	18.01.67	18.01.67	18.01.67
		The Sensorites	12.10.66	-	-
		The Sensorites	18.01.67	-	-
		The Reign of Terror	18.01.67	-	-
		Planet of Giants	18.01.67	18.01.67	18.01.67
		The Dalek Invasion of Earth	18.01.67	18.01.67	18.01.67
13914	Mauritius	An Unearthly Child	18.01.67	18.01.67	18.01.67
		The Daleks	18.01.67	18.01.67	18.01.67
		The Edge of Destruction	18.01.67	18.01.67	18.01.67
		Marco Polo	18.01.67	18.01.67	18.01.67
		The Keys of Marinus	18.01.67	18.01.67	18.01.67

CHAPTER 13

13918	Barbados	The Aztecs	11.11.66	-	11.11.66
		The Sensorites	11.11.66	-	-
		The Reign of Terror	11.11.66	-	11.11.66
		Planet of Giants	11.11.66	-	11.11.66
		The Dalek Invasion of Earth	11.11.66	-	11.11.66
		The Rescue	11.11.66	-	11.11.66
14286	Rhodesia	The Aztecs	13.12.66	-	13.12.66
		The Sensorites	13.12.66	-	13.12.66
		The Reign of Terror	13.12.66	-	13.12.66
		Planet of Giants	13.12.66	-	13.12.66
		The Dalek Invasion of Earth	13.12.66	-	13.12.66
		The Rescue	13.12.66	-	13.12.66
14679	Kenya	The Aztecs	18.01.67	18.01.67	18.01.67
		The Sensorites	18.01.67	-	-
		The Reign of Terror	18.01.67	18..01.67	18.01.67
		Planet of Giants	18.01.67	18.01.67	18.01.68
		The Dalek Invasion of Earth	18.01.67	18.01.67	18.01.67
		The Rescue	18.01.67	18.01.67	18.01.67
14972	Venezuela	The Rescue	18.01.67	18.01.67	18.01.67
		The Web Planet	24.02.67	24.02.67	24.02.67
		The Space Museum	24.02.67	24.02.67	26.02.67
15550	Mauritius	The Aztecs	06.04.67	-	06.04.67
		The Sensorites	06.04.67	-	06.04.67
		The Reign of Terror	06.04.67	-	06.04.67
		Planet of Giants	06.04.67	-	06.04.67
		The Dalek Invasion of Earth	06.04.67	-	06.04.67
		The Rescue	06.04.67	-	06.04.67

WIPED!

15587	Sierra Leone	An Unearthly Child	06.04.67	-	06.04.67
		The Daleks	06.04.67	-	06.04.67
		The Edge of Destruction	06.04.67	-	06.04.67
		Marco Polo	06.04.67	-	06.04.67
		The Keys of Marinus	06.04.67	-	06.04.67
15621	Thailand	The Aztecs	26.04.67	26.04.67	26.04.67
		The Sensorites	26.04.67	26.04.67	26.04.67
		The Reign of Terror	26.04.67	26.04.67	26.04.67
		Planet of Giants	26.04.67	26.04.67	26.04.67
		The Dalek Invasion of Earth	26.04.67	26.04.67	26.04.67
		The Rescue	26.04.67	26.04.67	26.04.67
15669	Australia	The Myth Makers	13.04.67	13.04.67	13.04.67
		The Massacre	13.04.67	13.04.67	19.04.67
15670	Australia	The Ark	14.04.67	14.04.67	19.04.67
		The Celestial Toymaker	14.04.67	14.04.67	19.04.67
		The Gunfighters	14.04.67	14.04.67	19.04.67
15671	Australia	The Savages	14.04.67	19.04.67	19.04.67
		The War Machines	14.04.67	19.04.67	19.04.67
		The Smugglers	14.04.67	-	16.04.67
16244	Barbados	The Romans	14.06.67	14.06.67	14.06.67
		The Web Planet	14.06.67	-	14.06.67
		The Crusade	14.06.67	-	14.06.67
		The Space Museum	14.06.67	-	14.06.67
		The Chase	No BBC Sales Sheet		
		The Time Meddler	14.06.67	-	14.06.67

CHAPTER 13

17115	Barbados	Galaxy 4	16.08.67	16.08.67	16.08.67
		The Myth Makers	16.08.67	16.08.67	16.08.67
		The Massacre	16.08.67	16.08.67	16.08.67
		The Ark	16.08.67	16.08.67	18.08.67
		The Celestial Toymaker	16.08.67	16.08.67	18.08.67
		The Gunfighters	16.08.67	16.08.67	18.08.67
		The Savages	16.08.67	16.08.67	18.08.67
		The War Machines	16.08.67	16.08.67	18.08.67
		The Smugglers	16.08.67	-	18.08.67
17194	Australia	The Underwater Menace	21.08.67	21.08.67	08.09.67
17195	Australia	The Highlanders	21.08.67	-	08.09.67
17196	Australia	The Tenth Planet	23.08.67	23.08.67	25.08.67
17399	Australia	The Power of the Daleks	09.10.67	-	05.10.67
17725	Tunisia	An Unearthly Child	25.10.67	25.10.67	25.10.67
		The Daleks	25.10.67	25.10.67	25.10.67
		The Edge of Destruction	25.10.67	25.10.67	25.10.67
17972	Mauritius	The Romans	14.11.67	14.11.67	14.11.67
		The Web Planet	14.11.67	14.11.67	14.11.67
		The Crusade	14.11.67	14.11.67	14.11.67
		The Space Museum	14.11.67	14.11.67	14.11.67
		The Chase	No BBC Sales Sheet		
		The Time Meddler	14.11.67	14.11.67	14.11.67
18097	Tunisia	The Aztecs	20.11.67	20.11.67	20.11.67
		The Sensorites	20.11.67	20.11.67	20.11.67
		Planet of Giants	20.11.67	20.11.67	20.11.67
18268	Tunisia	The Keys of Marinus	12.12.67	12.12.67	12.12.67

WIPED!

18475	Sierra Leone	The Aztecs	16.02.68	20.11.67	20.11.67
		The Sensorites	16.02.68	-	16.02.68
		The Reign of Terror	16.02.68	-	16.02.68
		Planet of Giants	16.02.68	-	16.02.68
		The Dalek Invasion of Earth	Not on Sales Sheet – No Explanation		
		The Rescue	16.02.68	-	16.02.68
18546	Australia	The Moonbase	16.02.68	16.02.68	10.01.68
18547	Australia	The Macra Terror	16.02.68	16.02.68	10.01.68
18548	Australia	The Faceless Ones	16.02.68	16.02.68	10.01.68
18903	New Zealand	Planet of Giants	08.02.68	-	-
18904	New Zealand	The Reign of Terror	08.02.68	-	-
18914	New Zealand	The Rescue	08.02.68	-	-
19057	Morocco	An Unearthly Child (Ep 1 only)	06.05.68	27.05.68	27.05.68
		The Daleks	06.05.68	06.05.68	06.05.68
		The Edge of Destruction	06.05.68	06.05.68	06.05.68
		The Keys of Marinus	06.05.68	06.05.68	06.05.68
		The Aztecs	06.05.68	06.05.68	06.05.68
		The Sensorites	06.05.68	06.05.68	06.05.68
		Planet of Giants	06.05.68	06.05.68	06.05.68
		The Dalek Invasion of Earth	06.05.68	06.05.68	06.05.68
		The Rescue	06.05.68	06.05.68	06.05.68

CHAPTER 13

19320	Zambia	Galaxy 4	25.03.68	25.03.68	25.03.68
		The Myth Makers	25.03.68	25.03.68	25.03.68
		The Massacre	25.03.68	25.03.68	02.04.68
		The Ark	25.03.68	25.03.68	02.04.68
		The Celestial Toymaker	25.03.68	25.03.68	02.04.68
		The Gunfighters	25.03.68	25.03.68	02.04.68
		The Savages	25.03.68	25.03.68	02.04.68
		The War Machines	25.03.68	25.03.68	02.04.68
		The Smugglers	25.03.68	-	02.04.68
19471	Mexico	An Unearthly Child	27.05.68	27.05.68	27.05.68
		The Daleks	27.05.68	27.05.68	27.05.68
		The Edge of Destruction	27.05.68	27.05.68	27.05.68
		The Keys of Marinus	27.05.68	27.05.68	27.05.68
		The Aztecs	28.05.68	28.05.68	28.05.68
		The Sensorites	28.05.68	28.05.68	28.05.68
		Planet of Giants	28.05.68	28.05.68	28.05.68
		The Dalek Invasion of Earth	28.05.68	28.05.68	-
		The Rescue	28.05.68	28.05.68	28.05.68
		The Web Planet	28.05.68	28.05.68	28.05.68
		The Space Museum	28.05.68	28.05.68	28.05.68
		The Chase	No BBC Sales Sheet		
19757	New Zealand	The Romans	Not on Sales Sheet – No Explanation		
		The Web Planet	27.05.68	-	27.05.68

WIPED!

20330	Saudi Arabia	An Unearthly Child	27.05.68	-	-
		The Daleks	27.05.68	27.05.68	27.05.68
		The Edge of Destruction	27.05.68	27.05.68	27.05.68
		The Keys of Marinus	27.05.68	-	-
		The Aztecs	28.05.68	28.05.68	28.05.68
		The Sensorites	28.05.68	28.05.68	28.05.68
		Planet of Giants	28.05.68	28.05.68	28.05.68
		The Dalek Invasion of Earth	28.05.68	28.05.68	-
		The Rescue	28.05.65	28.05.68	28.05.68
20364	Australia	The Ice Warriors	20.08.68		16.08.68
20366	Australia	The Abominable Snowmen	16.08.68	-	13.06.68
20726 TE/2000	Iran	An Unearthly Child	11.07.68	-	-
		The Daleks	11.07.68	11.07.68	-
		The Edge of Destruction	11.07.68	11.07.68	-
		The Keys of Marinus	11.07.68	11.07.68	-
		The Aztecs	11.07.68	11.07.68	-
		The Sensorites	11.07.68	11.07.68	-
		Planet of Giants	11.07.68	11.07.68	-
		The Dalek Invasion of Earth	11.07.68	11.07.68	-
		The Rescue	11.07.68	11.07.68	-
		The Web Planet	11.07.68	11.07.68	11.07.68
		The Space Museum	11.07.68	11.07.68	11.07.68
		The Chase	No BBC Sales Sheet		
TE/2154	Australia	The Tomb of the Cybermen	13.08.68	13.08.69	16.08.68

CHAPTER 13

TE/2444	Sierra Leone	The Romans	13.08.68	-	13.08.68
		The Web Planet	13.08.68	-	13.08.68
		The Crusade	13.08.68	-	13.08.68
		The Space Museum	13.08.68	-	13.08.68
		The Chase	No BBC Sales Sheet		
		The Time Meddler	13.08.68	-	13.08.68
TE/2725	Australia	The Enemy of the World	08.11.68	08.11.68	27.11.68
TE/2958	New Zealand	The Space Museum	22.10.68	22.10.68	22.10.68
		The Time Meddler	22.10.68	22.10.68	22.10.68
TE/2972	New Zealand	Galaxy 4	22.10.68	22.10.68	22.10.68
		The Myth Makers	22.10.68	22.10.68	22.10.68
TE/3320	Chile	An Unearthly Child	22.10.68	-	-
		The Daleks	22.10.68	22.10.68	-
		The Edge of Destruction	22.10.68	22.10.68	-
		The Keys of Marinus	22.10.68	22.10.68	-
		The Aztecs	22.10.68	22.10.68	-
		The Sensorites	22.10.68	22.10.68	-
		Planet of Giants	22.10.68	22.10.68	-
		The Dalek Invasion of Earth	22.10.68	22.10.68	-
		The Rescue	22.10.68	22.10.68	-
		The Web Planet	22.10.68	22.10.68	22.10.68
		The Space Museum	22.10.68	22.10.68	22.10.68
		The Chase	No BBC Sales Sheet		
TE/3364	Uganda	The Highlanders	08.11.68	-	12.03.69
		The Underwater Menace	08.11.68	08.11.68	12.03.69
		The Moonbase	08.11.68	08.11.68	12.03.69
		The Macra Terror	08.11.68	-	12.03.69
		The Faceless Ones	08.11.68	08.11.68	12.03.69

WIPED!

TE/3465	Dominica	An Unearthly Child	03.12.68	03.12.68	-
		The Daleks	03.12.68	03.12.68	-
		The Edge of Destruction	03.12.68	03.12.68	-
		The Keys of Marinus	03.12.68	13.12.68	-
		The Aztecs	03.12.68	03.12.68	-
		The Sensorites	03.12.68	03.12.68	-
		Planet of Giants	03.12.68	03.12.68	-
		The Dalek Invasion of Earth	03.12.68	03.12.68	-
		The Rescue	03.12.68	03.12.68	03.12.68
		The Web Planet	03.12.68	03.12.68	03.12.68
		The Space Museum	03.12.68	03.12.68	03.12.68
TE/3704	Australia	The Web of Fear	07.01.69	07.01.69	05.11.68
TE/3730	Hong Kong	The Highlanders	09.04.69	-	08.04.69
		The Underwater Menace	09.04.69	09.04.69	08.04.69
		The Moonbase	09.04.69	09.04.69	08.04.69
		The Macra Terror	09.04.69	-	08.04.69
		The Faceless Ones	09.04.69	06.03.70	06.03.70
TE/3877	New Zealand	The Massacre	18.12.68	18.12.68	20.12.68
TE/3878	New Zealand	The Ark	18.12.68	18.12.68	20.12.68
TE/3879	New Zealand	The Celestial Toymaker	18.12.68	18.12.68	20.12.68
TE/3880	New Zealand	The Savages	18.12.68	18.12.68	20.12.68
TE/3881	New Zealand	The War Machines	18.12.68	18.12.68	20.12.68
TE/3883	New Zealand	The Smugglers	18.12.68	18.12.68	20.12.68
		The Tenth Planet	18.12.68	18.12.68	20.12.68

CHAPTER 13

TE/3924	Singapore	The Highlanders	12.03.69	-	-
		The Underwater Menace	12.03.69	12.03.69	-
		The Moonbase	12.03.69	12.03.69	-
		The Macra Terror	12.03.69	-	-
		The Faceless Ones	12.03.69	12.03.69	-
TE/4299	Libya	An Unearthly Child	17.12.69	12.12.69	-
		The Daleks	17.12.69	-	-
		The Edge of Destruction	17.12.69	-	-
		The Keys of Marinus	17.12.69	-	-
		The Aztecs	17.12.69	-	-
		The Sensorites	17.12.69	-	-
		Planet of Giants	17.12.69	17.12.69	-
		The Dalek Invasion of Earth	17.12.69	17.12.69	-
		The Rescue	17.12.69	17.12.69	-
TE/4800	Australia	The Evil of the Daleks	10.03.69	10.03.69	07.03.69
TE/5273	Jamaica	The Romans	18.03.69	-	18.03.69
		The Web Planet	18.03.69	-	18.03.69
		The Crusade	18.03.69	-	18.03.69
		The Space Museum	18.03.69	-	18.03.69
		The Chase	No BBC Sales Sheet		
		The Time Meddler	18.03.69	-	18.03.69
TE/5353	Australia	Fury from the Deep	09.04.69	09.04.69	08.04.69
		The Wheel in Space	No BBC Sales Sheet		
TE/5753	New Zealand	The Power of the Daleks	20.05.69	-	19.05.69

WIPED!

TE/6059	Chile	An Unearthly Child	27.05.69	-	-
		The Daleks	27.05.69	-	-
		The Edge of Destruction	27.05.69	-	-
		The Keys of Marinus	28.05.69	-	-
		The Aztecs	28.05.69	-	-
		The Sensorites	28.05.69	-	-
		Planet of Giants	28.05.69	-	-
		The Dalek Invasion of Earth	28.05.69	-	-
		The Rescue	28.05.69	29.05.69	27.05.69
		The Web Planet	28.05.69	-	27.05.69
		The Space Museum	28.05.69	-	27.05.69
		The Chase	No BBC Sales Sheet		
TE/6095	Jordan	An Unearthly Child	28.05.69	29.05.69	-
		The Daleks	28.05.69	29.05.69	-
		The Edge of Destruction	28.05.69	28.05.69	-
		The Keys of Marinus	28.05.69	29.05.69	-
		The Aztecs	28.05.69	29.05.69	-
		The Sensorites	28.05.69	29.05.69	-
		Planet of Giants	28.05.69	29.05.69	-
		The Dalek Invasion of Earth	28.05.69	29.05.69	27.05.69
		The Rescue	28.05.69	29.05.69	27.05.69
TE/6309	New Zealand	The Highlanders	24.06.69	24.06.69	23.06.69
		The Underwater Menace	24.06.69	24.06.69	23.06.69
TE/7166	Australia	The Dominators	28.11.69	-	17.12.69
TE/7187	New Zealand	The Moonbase	11.08.69	11.08.69	19.08.69

CHAPTER 13

TE/7188	New Zealand	The Macra Terror	11.08.69	-	19.08.69
TE/8269	Hong Kong	The Evil of the Daleks	25.11.69	25.11.69	08.12.69
		The Tomb of the Cybermen	25.11.69	25.11.69	08.12.69
		The Abominable Snowmen	25.11.69	-	08.12.69
		The Ice Warriors	25.11.69	-	08.12.69
		The Enemy of the World	25.11.69	25.11.69	08.12.69
TE/8354	Australia	The Mind Robber	22.12.69	22.12.69	19.12.69
		The Invasion	No BBC Sales Sheet		
TE/8429	Singapore	The Evil of the Daleks	06.01.70	06.01.70	06.03.70
		The Tomb of the Cybermen	06.01.70	06.01.70	06.03.70
TE/8970	Hong Kong	The Web of Fear	06.03.70	06.03.70	06.03.70
		Fury from the Deep	06.03.70	-	06.03.70
		The Wheel in Space	No BBC Sales Sheet		
TE/9437	Zambia	The Highlanders	06.03.70	-	06.03.70
		The Underwater Menace	06.03.70	-	06.03.70
		The Moonbase	06.03.70	06.03.70	06.03.70
		The Macra Terror	06.03.70	-	06.03.70
		The Faceless Ones	06.03.70	06.03.70	06.03.70
TE/10380	Singapore	The Abominable Snowmen	04.05.70	-	01.07.70
		The Ice Warriors	04.05.70	-	01.07.70
		The Enemy of the World	04.05.70	04.05.70	01.07.70
		The Web of Fear	04.05.70	04.05.70	01.07.10
		Fury from the Deep	04.05.70	-	01.07.70
		The Wheel in Space	No BBC Sales Sheet		

WIPED!

TE/ 10889	Australia	The Krotons	10.08.70	-	25.09.70
TE/ 11319	New Zealand	The Tomb of the Cybermen	25.09.70	25.09.70	14.08.70
TE/ 11328	New Zealand	The Abominable Snowmen	06.10.70	-	28.10.70
TE/ 11329	New Zealand	The Evil of the Daleks	24.07.70	24.07.70	28.07.70
TE/ 11362	Hong Kong	The Dominators	12.08.70	-	20.10.70
		The Mind Robber	12.08.70	12.08.70	20.10.70
		The Invasion	No BBC Sales Sheet		
TE/ 11485	Australia	The Seeds of Death	07.10.70	07.10.70	05.05.71
TE/ 11612	Sierra Leone	Galaxy 4	12.08.70	12.08.70	12.08.70
		The Myth Makers	12.08.70	12.08.70	12.08.70
		The Massacre	12.08.70	12.08.70	20.10.70
		The Ark	12.08.70	12.08.70	20.10.70
		The Celestial Toymaker	12.08.70	12.08.70	20.10.70
		The Gunfighters	12.08.70	12.08.70	20.10.70
		The Savages	12.08.70	12.08.70	20.10.70
		The War Machines	12.08.70	12.08.70	20.10.70
		The Smugglers	12.08.70	-	20.10.70
TE/ 11988	Hong Kong	The Krotons	14.10.70	-	23.10.70

CHAPTER 13

TE/12362	Ethiopia	An Unearthly Child	26.10.70	26.10.70	-
		The Daleks	26.10.70	26.10.70	-
		The Edge of Destruction	26.10.70	26.10.70	-
		Marco Polo	26.10.70	26.10.70	26.10.70
		The Keys of Marinus	26.10.70	26.10.70	-
		The Aztecs	26.10.70	26.10.70	-
		The Sensorites	26.10.70	26.10.70	-
		The Reign of Terror	26.10.70	26.10.70	-
		Planet of Giants	26.10.70	26.10.70	-
		The Dalek Invasion of Earth	26.10.70	26.10.70	-
		The Rescue	26.10.70	26.10.70	-
TE/12533	Australia	The Space Pirates	13.05.71	-	-
TE/12799	Hong Kong	The Seeds of Death	13.05.71	-	05.05.71
		The Space Pirates	13.05.71	-	-
TE/13159	Singapore	The Dominators	12.02.71	-	05.02.71
		The Mind Robber	12.02.71	12.02.71	05.02.71
		The Invasion	No BBC Sales Sheet		
		The Krotons	12.02.71	-	05.02.70
TE/13483	Hong Kong	The War Games	01.10.71	-	27.09.71
TE/14106	New Zealand	The Enemy of the World	13.05.71	13.05.71	05.05.71
TE/14610	Australia	The War Games	01.10.71	-	-
TE/14848	Singapore	The War Games	01.10.71	-	-
TE/15913	Singapore	The Seeds of Death	27.10.71	-	25.10.71
		The Space Pirates	29.10.71	-	25.10.71

WIPED!

TE/ 15991	Ethiopia	The Romans	22.10.71	22.10.71	22.10.71
		The Web Planet	22.10.71	22.10.71	22.10.71
		The Crusade	22.10.71	22.10.71	22.10.71
		The Space Museum	22.10.71	22.10.71	22.10.71
		The Chase	No BBC Sales Sheet		
TE/ 17391	New Zealand	The Web of Fear	22.02.72	22.02.72	30.03.72
		The Wheel in Space	No BBC Sales Sheet		
TE/ 17540	Singapore	The Savages	24.02.72	24.02.72	24.03.72
		The War Machines	24.02.72	24.02.72	24.03.72
		The Smugglers	24.02.72	-	24.03.73
		The Tenth Planet	24.02.72	24.02.72	24.03.72
		The Power of the Daleks	24.02.72	-	24.03.72
TE/ 18094	Gibraltar	The Mind Robber	16.05.72	16.05.72	21.09.72
		The Invasion	No BBC Sales Sheet		
TE/ 19074	Gibraltar	The Krotons	09.08.72	-	02.08.72
TE/ 19075	Gibraltar	The Seeds of Death	09.08.72	-	02.08.72
TE/ 19076	Gibraltar	The War Games	09.08.72	-	03.08.72
TE/ 19079	Gibraltar	The Space Pirates	09.08.72	-	02.08.72
TE/ 20121	Singapore	Galaxy 4	18.12.72	18.12.72	27.11.72
		The Myth Makers	18.12.72	18.12.72	27.11.72
		The Massacre	18.12.72	18.12.72	19.12.72
		The Ark	18.12.72	18.12.72	12.12.72
		The Celestial Toymaker	18.12.72	18.12.72	12.12.72
		The Gunfighters	19.12.72	18.12.72	12.12.72

CHAPTER 13

TE/ 21478	Gibraltar	The Abominable Snowmen	18.04.73	-	19.04.73
		The Ice Warriors	18.04.73	-	19.04.73
		The Enemy of the World	19.04.73	19.04.73	19.04.73
		The Web of Fear	19.04.73	19.04.73	19.04.73
		Fury from the Deep	19.04.73	-	19.04.73
		The Wheel in Space	No BBC Sales Sheet		
		The Dominators	19.04.73	-	19.04.73
TE/ 02050	Nigeria	The Web Planet	25.07.73	-	31.07.73
		The Time Meddler	25.07.73	-	31.07.73
TE/ 02508	Nigeria	The War Machines	10.07.73	10.07.73	12.07.73
TE/ 03020	Algeria	An Unearthly Child	24.07.73	24.07.73	-
		The Daleks	24.07.73	24.07.73	-
		The Edge of Destruction	24.07.73	24.07.73	-
		The Keys of Marinus	24.07.73	24.07.73	-
		The Aztecs	24.07.73	24.07.73	-
		The Sensorites	24.07.73	24.07.73	-
		Planet of Giants	24.07.73	24.07.73	-
		The Dalek Invasion of Earth	24.07.73	24.07.73	-
		The Rescue	24.07.73	24.07.73	-
TE/ 03183	Zambia	The Abominable Snowmen	04.10.73	-	05.10.73
		The Ice Warriors	04.10.73	-	05.10.73
		The Enemy of the World	04.10.73	24.10.74	05.10.73
		The Web of Fear	04.10.73	04.10.73	05.10.73

WIPED!

TE/ 08711	Nigeria	The Abominable Snowmen	24.10.74	-	-
		The Enemy of the World	24.10.74	24.10.74	-
		The Web of Fear	24.10.74	24.10.74	-
		The Wheel in Space	No BBC Sales Sheet		
TE/ 14563	Nigeria	The Dominators	20.11.75	-	12.11.75
TE/ 15070	Nigeria	The Krotons	06.02.76	-	-
TE/ 16101	Zambia	The Seeds of Death	19.02.76	-	11.02.76
TE/ 16652	Zambia	The Space Pirates	01.04.76	-	-
TE/ 17358	Zambia	The War Games	17.05.76	-	11.05.76

CHAPTER 14
THE OVERSEAS SALES OF THE JON PERTWEE EPISODES

Whereas all the overseas sales of Hartnell and Troughton episodes in the 1960s and 1970s were on 16mm black and white film, with the Pertwee episodes matters become more complex.

All of the BBC's surviving sales information for the Pertwee stories simply records *where* a sale was made, and sometimes *when*. But the *format* on which the sale was made is not recorded at all. The Clearance History Sheets simply retain the same layout as for the Hartnell and Troughton episodes. Therefore, a lot of detective work, backed up by anecdotal evidence, and finished off with a large dollop of reasonable assumption, is required to try to work these details out.

All the initial overseas sales of Pertwee stories in 1970 and 1971 were almost certainly on 16mm black and white film. No black and white episodes of *Doctor Who* were sold on videotape until the 1980s.

In 1972, the BBC tried to crack the US market with *Doctor Who* for the first time since the unsuccessful attempt of the mid-1960s, making all of Pertwee's stories from 'Doctor Who and the Silurians' through to 'The Time Monster' available as 525-line NTSC colour conversions. This was possibly the first time that colour episodes of *Doctor Who* were ever offered for sale overseas. The established main markets for *Doctor Who* in the early 1970s – New Zealand, Australia, Gibraltar, Singapore, Hong Kong – were still buying the series in black and white. Certainly Hong Kong and Singapore bought Seasons Seven through to Ten only as 16mm black and white film prints, and only the stories that were initially bought by ABC in Australia were also sold to these two countries.

One thing is certain – 'Invasion of the Dinosaurs' was *never* sold abroad by the BBC in the 1970s. Sales of this story happened for the first time only in the early 1980s, *after* Part One was returned as a 16mm black and white film print. A colour copy of Part One of this story has *never* been sold abroad, so the chances of obtaining an off-air colour recording of it are nil.

While not quite hitting as many markets as the early Hartnell adventures had (30+ countries), the Pertwee stories sold to rather more countries in the early-to-mid 1970s than the half-a-dozen or so that the Troughton tales had reached. A number of interesting patterns emerge from looking at what was sold when and where. The purchase by the ABC in Australia of seasons seven through to ten, minus four 'banned'

WIPED!

stories, on 16mm black and white film was exactly matched by sales to Gibraltar, Hong Kong and Singapore, strongly suggesting that these stations were in some kind of bicycling chain at the time. Later in the decade, colour sales to New Zealand seem to have resonated with almost identical sales to Dubai, Malta and Brunei, suggesting another bicycling chain. However, in the NTSC market, there seems to have been no correlation between what the USA purchased (via Time-Life distributors) and what was sold to Canada or other countries.

The *key* overseas sales of the Pertwee episodes of *Doctor Who* were as follows:

AUSTRALIA

On the face of it, the Pertwee sales to Australia should be amongst the easiest to document, but when the details are closely scrutinised, a number of questions arise …

The ABC purchased all the Pertwee stories from Seasons Seven through to Ten ('Spearhead from Space' through to 'The Green Death') as 16mm black and white film prints. These were supplied via BBC Sydney. It's possible that BBC Sydney were also sent 625-line two-inch colour tapes of at least some of the later stories from this batch, but if so, these were never passed on to the ABC.

Just like the Hartnell and Troughton ones, the Pertwee stories had to be submitted to the Australian Film Censorship Board. Four were given the dreaded 'A' rating, and so weren't screened in Australia during the programme's initial run. These 'banned' stories were 'Inferno', 'The Mind of Evil', 'The Dæmons' and 'The Green Death'. Other stories were cut in order to obtain a 'G' rating. A consequence of this was that subsequent black and white sales of these Pertwee stories to Hong Kong, Singapore and Gibraltar were also missing these four 'problematical' stories.

The ABC were still doing regional screenings in the 1970s, and the 16mm black and white film prints of Pertwee's first four seasons ran on the various Australian regional stations between 1971 and 1975, with occasional repeats thrown in for good measure.

Doctor Who was seen in colour for the first time in Australia when the eleventh season opened in Sydney with 'The Time Warrior' Part One on Friday 7 March 1975. The ABC were now buying the programme on 625-line two-inch tape. The story was shown a week later in Melbourne, and then in Adelaide and Brisbane on separate later dates, and there is a suggestion that some of these regional screenings may not have been in colour, but still in black and white from 16mm film prints. As 'Invasion of the Dinosaurs' was not offered for sale, the ABC then skipped to 'Death to the Daleks', and the staggered regional screenings continued with 'The Monster of Peladon' and 'Planet of the Spiders'.

These eleventh season stories were all submitted to the censors on two-inch

CHAPTER 14

videotape rather than 16mm black and white film. It's believed that the cuts requested by the censors were physically spliced from the two-inch tapes (in the same way that the BBC used to edit two-inch tapes in the 1960s) prior to the episodes being screened.

Tom Baker's Doctor debuted on the ABC with 'Robot' in 1976, and screenings of his stories would continue intermittently until 1978. However, in 1978, the ABC also decided to repeat a number of Pertwee stories, and for many of them, it would be the first time they would be seen in colour down under, as new 625-line two-inch tape copies were supplied by BBC Enterprises. These repeats were of 'Spearhead from Space' (almost certainly supplied on 16mm colour film), 'Day of the Daleks', 'The Three Doctors' and 'Carnival of Monsters', plus the four stories from Season 11 that the ABC had already screened in colour some years previously. It's probably at this point that that ABC were accidentally supplied with the pre-transmission edit of 'Carnival of Monsters' Episode Two that they screened a number of times in the years that followed. (This version had a couple of extra scenes, and the abandoned 'Delaware' arrangement of the theme tune dubbed onto its opening and closing titles.) Amongst these repeats, a debut Australian colour airing was given to 'The Green Death', which had been re-submitted to the censors on Thursday 18 May 1978 and re-classified with a 'G' rating after a single cut had been made to Episode Three ('Delete shot of body on ground at approx. 18mins'). These nine colour Pertwee stories were then repeated again in 1979.

In 1981, BBC Enterprises in Sydney offered the ABC the option to buy three more Pertwee stories in colour for the first time. These were 'The Ambassadors of Death', 'The Mind of Evil' and 'Frontier in Space'. The ABC were encouraged to have a look at a U-MATIC viewing copy of at least one of the episodes from this selection. It's uncertain which episode(s) they viewed, but the only story they chose to buy was 'Frontier in Space'. Later correspondence shows that the other two stories had been offered by BBC Sydney in the NTSC colour 525-line format, but that the tapes had been wiped subsequently, and were 'no longer available'. Where exactly BBC Sydney got the 625-line colour two-inch tapes of 'Frontier in Space' from is something of a mystery, as the BBC in London held only Episodes Four and Five in colour at the time. But it's clear that the other two stories, being specified as 525-line copies, would have come from Time-Life in America. This was probably arranged between Time-Life and BBC Sydney without any reference to BBC Enterprises in London, and *probably* involved a good deal of assumption about what Time-Life had actually still got access to, *Doctor Who*-wise, at this point in time. Although, given that BBC Sydney managed to magic-up copies of 'Frontier in Space', perhaps the 525-line tapes were indeed still in existence, at least when the offer was originally made to the ABC.

WIPED!

BRUNEI

Talivishen Brunei (TVB) was the fourth station to start buying *Doctor Who* in PAL colour in the 1970s (after Australia, New Zealand and Dubai). In 1976, the station purchased 'Day of the Daleks', 'The Three Doctors', 'Carnival of Monsters', 'Frontier in Space', 'The Time Warrior', 'Death to the Daleks', 'The Monster of Peladon' and 'Planet of the Spiders'.

This sale of these stories isn't that remarkable, apart from the fact that this is the last time 'Frontier in Space' was sold abroad be the BBC in PAL colour during the 1970s (and prior to this, Dubai was the only other country this story was sold to in PAL). Perhaps the two-inch PAL tapes of 'Frontier in Space' that were eventually returned to the BBC from Australia in June 1983 had originated in Brunei ...?

CANADA

After the sale of a batch of early Hartnell episodes to the CBC in 1964, *Doctor Who* disappeared from Canadian television screens for over a decade. On 4 September 1976, an independent television station called CKVU took to the air for the first time, transmitting in Vancouver, British Columbia. It purchased 14 Jon Pertwee stories between February 1977 and March 1978, which were supplied by BBC Enterprises as colour 525-line two-inch videotapes, converted into NTSC from the UK's 625-line PAL format. The stories shown, in a pretty random sequence, were 'Inferno', 'The Claws of Axos', 'Colony in Space', 'Day of the Daleks', 'The Curse of Peladon', 'The Sea Devils', 'The Mutants', 'The Time Monster', 'The Three Doctors', 'The Green Death', 'The Time Warrior', 'Death to the Daleks', 'The Monster of Peladon' and 'Planet of the Spiders'. Although the BBC records these sales as having taken place in 1977 and 1978, CKVU actually began showing *Doctor Who* on Saturday 18 September 1976.

CKVU continued screening and re-screening these same stories right up until the end of 1982, when its rights expired on 31 December. All of the tapes were then dispatched back to the BBC's Canadian office in Toronto. The last batch sent, at the end of 1982, consisted of 55 episodes, including all six of 'The Mind of Evil' – which was never actually purchased or screened by CKVU. Some of the tapes, including what were, at that point, the only surviving broadcast-standard colour copies of 'Colony in Space' and 'The Sea Devils' Episodes One to Three, were eventually returned to the BBC Film and Videotape Library in Brentford in June 1983. But those of 'The Mind of Evil' were apparently either lost or destroyed by BBC Toronto very soon after they received them. Certainly, neither CKVU nor BBC Toronto still hold any remaining *Doctor Who* episodes from this point in time.

CKVU wasn't the only station screening colour Pertwee stories in Canada in 1976. TV Ontario in Toronto had also purchased a batch of 11 stories on 525-line two-

CHAPTER 14

inch videotape, again via BBC Toronto. The first run of adventures it screened were shown weekly between Saturday 18 September 1976 and Saturday 12 March 1977, and consisted of (in order of transmission) 'The Three Doctors', 'Day of the Daleks', 'The Curse of Peladon', 'The Claws of Axos', 'The Mutants' and 'The Time Warrior'. All of these bar 'The Claws of Axos' and 'The Time Warrior' were repeated in 1979.

A second batch of Pertwee stories was shown weekly by TV Ontario between Saturday 17 September 1977 and Saturday 25 March 1978. These were 'The Time Monster', 'The Green Death', 'Death to the Daleks', 'The Monster of Peladon' and 'Planet of the Spiders'. The screening of 'The Green Death' was the first time the story had been seen anywhere outside of the UK. All bar 'Death to the Daleks' and 'Planet of the Spiders' were repeated in 1980.

This was followed over the next few years by regular runs of Tom Baker stories, although these were often screened in a bizarre order, and missed out 'The Talons of Weng-Chiang', 'Image of the Fendahl', 'The Sunmakers' and 'Underworld'. All of the Peter Davison stories were then aired, and a fair few Colin Baker ones too.

The TV Ontario repeat screenings of some of the Pertwee episodes in 1979 and 1980 eventually resulted in this batch of 525-line NTSC colour Pertwee episodes being returned to BBC Toronto in 1981. This is probably why, when they were first contacted by Sue Malden and Ian Levine in 1981, BBC Toronto had only TV Ontario's transmission tapes – CKVU's tapes hadn't yet been sent back to them. In early 1981, BBC Toronto were able to return to the BBC in London the 525-line colour copies of 'The Claws of Axos' Episodes Two and Three, all four episodes of 'The Curse of Peladon', 'The Mutants' Episodes One and Two and 'Death to the Daleks' Part One. At some point in the early 1980s (certainly before 1982), colour copies of 'The Time Monster', which had originated at TV Ontario, were also returned to the BBC in London.

All seven episodes of 'Inferno' on 525-line colour two-inch videotape were returned to the Film and Videotape Library from BBC's Ontario office in 1983, quite some time after the other material from CKVU and TV Ontario. These tapes would have almost certainly originated at CKVU, as TV Ontario never screened this story.

Three NTSC Jon Pertwee stories were also sold to the Co-Operative Programming Network (CPN) in the province of Saskatchewan in February 1979. These were 'The Claws of Axos', 'Day of the Daleks' and 'The Mutants'.

Canada is the only NTSC country that purchased 525-line colour copies of selected stories from Seasons Ten and Eleven (although 'Carnival of Monsters', 'Frontier in Space', 'Planet of the Daleks' and 'Invasion of the Dinosaurs' were omitted from these sales).

In the late 1980s, other Canadian broadcasters such as YTV Canada in Toronto

WIPED!

bought episodes of *Doctor Who* from the BBC via the distributor Time-Life, but these were now copies of the archived materials in the Film and Videotape Library. WTVS-TV in Michigan, on the American–Canadian border, also ran the series in later years.

DUBAI

Dubai is one of the seven emirates in the Persian Gulf that make up the United Arab Emirates, and one of its two major cities, the other being Abu Dhabi. Dubai was a British protectorate up until 1971, when Britain pulled its forces out of the countries of the Persian Gulf and the area around the Suez canal. Britain's withdrawal led the leaders of Dubai and Abu Dhabi to form the United Arab Emirates, and they were soon joined by five other neighbouring emirates. However, Dubai retained its close links with Britain throughout the rest of the decade.

Dubai was the second country (after Australia) to purchase Jon Pertwee stories in 625-line PAL colour – the broadcast standard in Dubai – beginning in March 1975. The stories sold were 'Spearhead from Space', 'Day of the Daleks', 'The Three Doctors', 'Carnival of Monsters', 'Frontier in Space', 'Planet of the Daleks' (almost certainly the only time this story was sold abroad in colour), 'The Time Warrior', 'Death to the Daleks', 'The Monster of Peladon' and 'Planet of the Spiders'.

This batch of episodes was then shipped around various television stations in Jordan and Kuwait (and possibly Brunei) over the next ten to 12 years or so.

In 1991, a batch of around 30 of these tapes was returned to BBC Enterprises from Dubai Radio and Colour TV. This included Part One of 'Death to the Daleks' and Episodes Four, Five and Six of 'Planet of the Daleks' (although sadly not Episode Three). The tapes were not thoroughly checked at the time of arrival, and were left outside on an external loading bay. Eventually, they were found and examined by David Stead, and Part One of 'Death to the Daleks' was rescued.

Contact was later made with Dubai Radio and Colour TV, to see if they still had any other *Doctor Who* tapes – perhaps even Episode Three of 'Planet of the Daleks'. They confirmed that they hadn't.

GIBRALTAR

The Gibraltar Broadcasting Corporation (GBC) had purchased a number of William Hartnell's and Patrick Troughton's *Doctor Who* stories from 1965 through to 1972. Sales continued from 1972 through to 1974, with stories featuring Jon Pertwee's Doctor. These early Pertwee sales were on 16mm black and white film and were of the stories 'Spearhead from Space', 'Doctor Who and the Silurians', 'The Ambassadors of Death', 'Terror of the Autons', 'The Claws of Axos', 'Colony in Space', 'Day of the Daleks', 'The Curse of Peladon', 'The Mutants' and 'The Time Monster'. These are exactly the same

CHAPTER 14

stories from Seasons Seven through to Nine that were shown by ABC in Australia (as well as RTS in Singapore and RTV in Hong Kong).

There then appears to have been a gap of about three years before *Doctor Who* returned to Gibraltar's TV screens with another batch of stories in 1977, but the BBC's records don't indicate if these were supplied in colour or (as is more likely) black and white. These stories were (in transmission order) 'Planet of the Daleks', 'The Sea Devils', 'Carnival of Monsters', 'Frontier in Space', 'The Three Doctors' and 'The Time Warrior'. In 1978, the station began showing stories featuring Tom Baker's Doctor.

JAPAN

There was a small sale of Jon Pertwee episodes to Japan in March 1978. As Japan broadcasts in NTSC, there is a good chance that this sale was in 525-line colour.

The three stories sold were 'Doctor Who and the Silurians', 'The Ambassadors of Death' and 'Terror of the Autons'. However, the station that purchased the stories was JCTV-2, which was a closed-circuit English language TV service that operated in Tokyo only, and could be seen only by subscription to apartments and hotels. It's possible that the stories were supplied on U-MATIC cassette rather than two-inch tape.

KOREA

BBC sales records show that Korea (presumably South Korea) purchased a handful of Jon Pertwee *Doctor Who* stories in early 1978. However, a number of the sales are marked as cancelled, so it is not known if any of these purchases actually went ahead or not.

The stories involved were: 'Doctor Who and the Silurians', 'The Ambassadors of Death' (both marked as cancelled), 'Terror of the Autons', 'The Mind of Evil' and 'The Dæmons'.

Korean TV at the time would have broadcast in 525-line NTSC colour, so *if* these sales did actually happen, chances are that this is the format these stories would have been supplied in. No transmission dates have been found for *Doctor Who* in this country at this time, which does suggest that the whole sale was indeed cancelled...

PHILIPPINES

The television station Radio Control Office (RCO) in the Philippines began purchasing 525-line NTSC colour copies of selected Jon Pertwee stories in March 1976. The stories sold were 'Doctor Who and the Silurians', 'The Ambassadors of Death', 'Inferno', 'Terror of the Autons', 'The Claws of Axos', 'Colony in Space', 'Day of the Daleks', 'The Curse of Peladon', 'The Sea Devils', 'The Mutants' and 'The Time Monster'.

WIPED!

SAUDI ARABIA

This particular sale is noteworthy partly because it's impossible to tell from the paperwork if these stories were supplied in black and white or colour ...

The Arabian American Oil Company (ARAMCO) set up a television station HZ-22 (known as Dhahran TV) in 1957, broadcasting English and Arabic programming. In 1976, Dhahran TV became a 525-line NTSC colour service. In 1977, it purchased *Doctor Who* for the first time, buying every single story from Seasons Seven, Eight Nine and Ten (apart from 'The Green Death'),[86] plus 'The Time Warrior' from Season Eleven.

If these stories were sold in black and white, then they would be the only 16mm black and white film sales of 'Inferno', 'The Mind of Evil' and 'The Dæmons' in the 1970s – which doesn't seem likely. However, if these stories were sold in colour, then they would have been 525-line NTSC, and would therefore have included the only known NTSC sales of 'Spearhead from Space', 'Carnival of Monsters, 'Frontier in 'Space' and 'Planet of the Daleks' – which seems even less likely! So chances are that these stories were shown in black and white on Dhahran TV.

In 1979, Dhahran TV switched over to broadcasting in PAL, bringing it into line with stations in neighbouring gulf states such as Bahrain, Dubai and Kuwait. In 1981, the station purchased *Doctor Who* again, buying 'Death to the Daleks', 'The Monster of Peladon' and 'Planet of the Spiders', this time on 625-line two-inch tapes.

UNITED STATES OF AMERICA

No Hartnell or Troughton episodes were screened in the USA until 1986, when a package of their surviving stories was sold to the PBS (Public Broadcasting Service) networks. America's first exposure to the good Doctor came in 1972, with the sale in NTSC colour of a package of 13 Pertwee stories through the distributor Time-Life.

These 13 stories comprised a full run from the seventh season's 'Doctor Who and the Silurians' through to the ninth season's finale, 'The Time Monster'. The PAL 625-line two-inch videotape masters were copied via a standards converter to make the NTSC 525-line two-inch tapes needed for compatibility with American television (see Chapter 11 for further details). ('Spearhead from Space' may have been omitted from this package because it had no colour videotape masters available for standards conversion. Or perhaps it was felt that the story posed too many questions about the Doctor's origins and back-story.)

These 13 stories screened on a small number of channels across America between

---

86 Theorising again, but maybe this story was excluded from sale to ARAMCO's TV station because of its environmental stance and anti-oil pollution message ...?

CHAPTER 14

the years 1972 and 1978. The sales dates are recorded in the BBC's paperwork as follows:

Channel	Purchase Date	No. of screenings
WPHL – Philadelphia, Pennsylvania	22/09/72	4
WFTV – Orlando, Florida	03/11/72	1
WPLG – Miami, Florida	03/11/72	2
WJXT – Jacksonville, Florida (incorrectly noted as WJKT on BBC sales sheets)	03/11/72	2
WTOP – Washington, D.C.	03/11/72	2
KVOA – Tuscon, Arizona	25/02/74	2
KPHO – Phoenix, Arizona	06/03/74	2
KIMO – Anchorage, Alaska	06/03/74	2
KGTF - Guam (incorrectly noted as KGTV on BBC sales sheets)	06/03/74	1
KRON – San Francisco, California	06/03/74	2
KHOL – Kearny / Hastings, Nebraska	10/04/74	Unrecorded
KCET – Los Angeles, California	22/12/75	Unrecorded
WVIA – Scranton, Pennsylvania	01/03/76	2
WTTW – Chicago, Illinois	01/03/76	1
WGBH – Boston, Massachusetts	01/03/76	1
WXXI – Rochester, New York	20/02/77	2
KDIN – Des Moines, Iowa	03/07/78	2

What's odd about this list is that no sale is recorded for WNED Channel 17 Buffalo, and yet it's from a 1970s broadcast by that station that the only surviving colour off-air copy of 'The Ambassadors of Death' derives. And that's not the only anomaly: the BBC Enterprises summary sales document for July-September 1972 records sales to WFTV and KPHO of all 13 NTSC Pertwee stories, yet the sales sheets for these stories have the WFTV sale taking place in November 1972 and the KPHO sale in March 1974.

A few US screening details of this batch of 13 stories have been traced over the years[87]. *Doctor Who* debuted on US screens for the first time on 21 August 1972, on WPHL Channel 17 in Philadelphia with the opening episode of 'Doctor Who and the Silurians'. As can be seen in the table on the following page, the first screening dates of the series on the various regional PBS stations don't really correlate to the sales dates noted in the BBC's paperwork:

---

87 With thanks to Jon Preddle and the www.broadwcast.org website.

WIPED!

Channel	Earliest Screening Date	Purchase Date
WPHL – Philadelphia, Pennsylvania	21/08/72	22/09/72
WFTV – Orlando, Florida	15/09/72	03/11/72
KPHO – Phoenix, Arizona	23/09/72	06/03/74
WPLG – Miami, Florida	c1972	03/11/72
KGTF – Guam (incorrectly noted as KGTV on BBC sales sheets)	27/11/72	06/03/74
WTOP – Washington, D.C.	04/06/73	03/11/72
WJXT – Jacksonville, Florida (incorrectly noted as WJKT on BBC sales sheets)	16/07/73	03/11/72
KVOA – Tuscon, Arizona	21/09/73	25/02/74
KRON – San Francisco, California	22/09/73	06/03/74
KIMO – Anchorage, Alaska	03/12/73	06/03/74
KDIN – Des Moines, Iowa	06/04/74	03/07/78
KHOL – Kearny / Hastings, Nebraska	30/06/75	10/04/74
KCET – Los Angeles, California	01/07/75	22/12/75
WVIA – Scranton, Pennsylvania	06/07/77	01/03/76
WTTW – Chicago, Illinois	29/09/75	01/03/76
WGBH – Boston, Massachusetts	05/01/76	01/03/76
WXXI – Rochester, New York	11/10/76	20/02/77
WNED – Buffalo, New York	25/10/77	Not Listed

It is only because of these American screenings that some domestic colour videotapes of the episodes now survive. A number of Pertwee stories were recorded by American fan Tom Lundie from WTTW Channel 11 in the late 1970s. He also obtained copies of stories shown on WNED Channel 17, including 'The Ambassadors of Death'. Ian Levine meanwhile obtained material recorded from KCET Channel 28 in Los Angeles. Betamax copies of these recordings were used in the subsequent recolourisation of 'Doctor Who and the Silurians', 'Terror of the Autons' and 'The Dæmons'. Another off-air copy has since been located of 'Terror of the Autons', recorded from KERA Channel 13 in North Texas.

CHAPTER 14

As none of the tenth or eleventh season stories was sold to America in the 1970s, no NTSC colour copies of 'Planet of the Daleks' Episodes Three or 'Invasion of the Dinosaurs' Part One were ever sent there.

The sales of these 13 Pertwee stories were moderate at best. However, the advent of the film *Star Wars* in 1977 saw a resurgence of interest in all things science fiction, and the BBC used this to their advantage in February 1978, when they announced that a new package of *Doctor Who* episodes, featuring Tom Baker's Doctor, would be made available to the American market, again via Time-Life.

TIME-LIFE, LIONHEART AND THE USA

Time-Life Television was a division of a much larger company, Time Inc, and handled the distribution of the BBC's television programmes throughout the USA during the 1970s. Apart from *Doctor Who*, it scored a notable early success with the comedy series *Monty Python's Flying Circus*.

Time Inc sold Time-Life in 1982, when it was acquired as a joint venture between the US network HBO and BBC Enterprises. The company was then renamed Lionheart Television International. In 1987, the BBC purchased Lionheart outright, making it their sole North American distributor, and it was eventually rebranded as BBC Worldwide Americas.

As detailed above, Time-Life was responsible for the distribution of the initial batch of 13 Jon Pertwee *Doctor Who* stories in the USA in the early to mid-1970s. The second batch in 1978 consisted of 23 Tom Baker stories ('Robot' through to 'The Invasion of Time'), sold to PBS stations again as colour 525-line two-inch conversions. To aid the viewer in following the plot, a newly-scripted introduction was recorded for each episode, voiced by actor Howard Da Silva.

These Tom Baker stories garnered far more sales than the earlier Pertwee ones. *Doctor Who* began to be screened weekly in the US by many different stations, and on each, once the final episode of 'The Invasion of Time' was shown, the run of stories would usually begin again the following week with the first episode of 'Robot'. With this intense rotation and exposure, *Doctor Who* at last began to take off in America towards the end of the 1970s. The impact of the film *Star Wars* in 1977, and the associated demand it generated for all things sci-fi, cannot be overestimated in helping *Doctor Who* gain a foothold in American culture. This success saw the remainder of the Tom Baker stories purchased for distribution in the early 1980s, followed by Peter Davison's run.

When the company was re-launched as Lionheart in 1982, it began phasing out the Da Silva versions of the episodes and syndicating new copies without the introductions. Stories were also made available to some PBS channels as 'television

WIPED!

movies' – i.e. with the episodes edited together, removing the cliffhangers, reprises and title sequences.

Lionheart began offering the Peter Davison stories in the early 1980s. Then, in 1983, as *Doctor Who*'s popularity was beginning to peak in America, the BBC's back-catalogue of Pertwee stories were sold to the PBS stations, this time as a mix of colour and black and white episodes. Both 'Planet of the Daleks' and 'Invasion of the Dinosaurs' were re-edited as five-part colour stories, with no explanation given as to what went on in the missing instalments. American viewers got to see 'The Five Doctors' on Wednesday 23 November 1983, the exact date of the programme's twentieth anniversary, and two days prior to the story's screening on BBC1 back in England.

In 1985/6, the surviving Hartnell and Troughton stories were sold to America, alongside Colin Baker's stories from Seasons 21 and 22. By now, the whole surviving run of *Doctor Who* stories was in rotation in America. However, demand for new material was starting to outstrip supply, especially as, back in England, the BBC had cut *Doctor Who*'s annual run down to 14 episodes. The remainder of Colin Baker's stories, plus all of Sylvester McCoy's, eventually screened in America toward the end of the 1980s, but interest in *Doctor Who* was waning. In the 1990s, with no new episodes to keep the PBS stations happy, repeats of *Doctor Who* slowly began to disappear.

CHAPTER 15
THE MYTH OF THE MISSING EPISODES

Since 1981, when details of the BBC's *Doctor Who* archive holdings were published for the first time in the *Doctor Who Monthly* Winter Special, fans have had to come to terms with the fact that a large proportion of the programme's past has been lost. Over the years since then, the odd recovery here and there has seen the number of missing episodes reduced by around 20% (a remarkable achievement nevertheless), but there appears to be little sign that the total will ever drop much below the current 106.

Is there something to be gained from this situation? Does the fact that there *are* missing episodes of *Doctor Who* make the series unique in some way? I would argue that it does. Most other classic genre shows such as *Star Trek*, *Blake's 7*, *Thunderbirds*, *The Prisoner*, *Batman* and *Lost in Space* (to name but a handful) have a full complement of episodes to keep their respective fans happy. Those that do have missing episodes, such as *Adam Adamant Lives!*, *The Avengers* and *Doomwatch*, all lack the mystique that *Doctor Who* holds. The only other genre show that perhaps comes close is *The Quatermass Experiment*. There is something legendary about this pioneering first Quatermass serial from 1953, and the fact that four of its six episodes were never recorded is perhaps a greater pity than the loss of any *Doctor Who* material. But such things are conjecture and opinion.

But ponder this. Would *Doctor Who* have become such a significant television institution, and have attracted such a wide and loyal fanbase if it weren't for the missing episodes? Well, if it wasn't for the successful relaunch of the series in 2005, then I would say that this was almost certainly the case. Ever since the mid-1980s, talk at convention bars and at local group meetings has always, sooner or later, turned to the subject of the missing episodes. The topic has regularly filled fanzine letters pages, and more recently, internet forums and message boards. Put simply, the missing episodes have made *Doctor Who* much, much more interesting.

RUMOURS AND HOAXES

The downside to all this interest in lost *Doctor Who* episodes has been the number of unsubstantiated rumours and hoaxes that the subject has attracted. Twenty years or so ago, this would manifest itself in any number of anonymous phone calls or letters between fans. Nowadays, the internet has made the life of the hoaxer much simpler, with false claims occasionally posted on websites, or fake auctions planted on eBay. But what *always* happens in these cases is that when proof is requested, none is ever produced, and the hoaxer scuttles away leaving disinformation and dissention in his or her wake. And this is nearly always the desired result, for the hoaxer at least.

Before pouring too much scorn on those who offer false leads and unsubstantiated claims, I have to hold my own hands up a little. At the time, walking around the sales room of the 1988 PanoptiCon convention with a 16mm film tin labelled '"The Tenth Planet" Episode Four' seemed to me to be a fairly innocuous, if rather silly, exercise. The film was actually a 16mm copy of a 1960s *Coronation Street* episode that belonged to a friend of mine, and had previously been loaned to a member of the convention's audio-visuals team to be transferred to videotape. They'd handed it to me earlier that day, to pass back to my friend, and somewhere along the line, someone thought that it'd be a nice touch to slap the prominent '"The Tenth Planet" Episode Four' label on it. But later, in the convention dealers' room, I made sure that the tin was spotted by Gary Leigh, then editor of the fanzine *DWB*. News items and articles about the episode's apparent existence cropped up in its pages in the months after the event.

Episode Four of 'The Tenth Planet' is probably the most high-profile missing episode of *Doctor Who* – it has even featured in a British Film Institute list of the most-wanted missing British television programmes. It features the Doctor's first regeneration, is the final episode of the first Cyberman adventure, and its return would complete a story of which the opening three episodes already exist. For these reasons, it seems to crop up as the hoaxer's episode-of-choice more often than any of the other 105 missing episodes.

One notable hoaxer from the 1980s and early 1990s went under the pseudonym Roger Barrett. He was in contact with various people and groups over the years, from *DWB*, to the organisers of the TellyCon conventions, to individuals such as Mark Gatiss in his pre-*The League of Gentleman* days. Barrett was always claiming to have a copy of 'The Tenth Planet' Episode Four, but was seemingly reluctant to agree on what he wanted in exchange for it, and ever ready with an implausible excuse whenever required to produce any proof of his claims. He even tried to sell a supposed film print of the episode to a large number of people over the years, and in the early 1990s, this drew the attention of the BBC. At this point, Barrett claimed not to have the print any longer. Instead, he handed over to the BBC a Shibaden videotape, on which he said the episode was recorded. However, the tape turned out to be completely blank. Oh, what a hoot!

In 1993, Barrett was even interviewed by the BBC for a five-minute programme on missing *Doctor Who* episodes – one of a strand of mini-documentaries shown alongside a BBC1 repeat of 'Planet of the Daleks' to mark the series' thirtieth anniversary – in which he mocked those gullible enough to be taken in by his wild stories. This programme, entitled *Missing in Action*, gave a rather one-sided view of the whole missing episode situation, and made the wildly inaccurate and unhelpful

CHAPTER 15

claim that film prints had in the past changed hands for huge sums of money.

Another vigorous scamp, based in Blackpool, would regularly place adverts in *Loot* or *Exchange and Mart*, offering the likes of 'The Tenth Planet' Episode Four (again!), various episodes of 'Fury from the Deep' or 'The Singing Sands' (Episode Two of 'Marco Polo') for sale or for swap. But whenever he was pressed for proof – surprise, surprise! – nothing was ever forthcoming.

In more recent years, hoaxers have used the internet to spread claims of the discovery of colour copies of 'The Mind of Evil' or episodes of 'Marco Polo' (another popular choice of story for the wind-up merchants). And in each and every instance, excuses have been lamely put forward whenever proof has been requested. Nothing ever comes of these claims.

In another corner of missing episode mythology sit the rumours. These are subtly different from the hoaxes, as they seem to percolate through fandom in a series of Chinese Whispers. Fans love to recount rumours, but usually have no idea from where they originally sprang.

Most fans hear these types of stories at a convention bar, drinking in the Fitzroy Tavern (the venue for a monthly London meeting of fans), posting on an internet bulletin board, attending a local group meeting or socialising with friends with a common interest. Every now and then, someone will claim that they know someone, who knows someone else, who has a copy of a missing episode of *Doctor Who*. The same stories get re-told, corrupted and turned into new variations of a familiar theme. Debunking these wild rumours became something of a tedious pastime for members of the *Doctor Who* Restoration Team over the years, to the point where they just weren't even commented upon any more.

Some of the stories are harmless, and are started with purely innocent motives. Most have been discredited. But some steadfastly refuse to die.

For example, there is an issue of the fanzine *Skaro* (Vol III, No.3), published in early 1983, in which the editor, Simon M Lydiard, wrote a lead article on the 'Scandal of the Lost and Found Episodes', alleging that the final episode of 'The Tenth Planet' and all four episodes of 'The Macra Terror' (amongst others) were being held by a private collector who was 'unlikely to return them to the BBC'. This was the first public 'outing' of a supposed hoarding of missing episodes, putting into print an allegation of the type that had served fandom so well at convention bars over the previous years. But Lydiard claimed he knew *for a fact* that at least five missing episodes existed in one person's collection. This person, the name of whom he was withholding for the moment, was obviously a fan of the series, and one he stated that many other fans at the time would know of.

What had actually happened in this case was this. Someone that Lydiard knew

WIPED!

well had been shown the 8mm off-air film that had been shot in Australia in the 1960s, featuring clips from 'The Tenth Planet' Episode Four and 'The Macra Terror' amongst others, and had made some gross assumptions about what the existence of these clips might mean. I contacted Lydiard about his article, and asked if the intervening years had given him some perspective on events:

> **Simon M Lydiard**: The truth is, I never had any hard evidence about people having copies of missing episodes. I was aware of a number of allegations, from people I trusted, about certain individuals. There were suggestions that some people were 'hoarding' missing material. This was at a time when there was no legitimate means for even possessing video copies of stories that had not recently been aired. There was a kind of clandestine world in which videos were sold and exchanged. And one was frequently made aware of suggestions that there were copies of 'rare' or 'missing' material being circulated. I never actually saw any of this material.
>
> My article was intended to flush out those fans who I thought were hoarding missing material. I suspect I probably phrased the article rather more strongly than I should have, leading people to believe that I had more definite information than, in fact, I did. This resulted in a number of phone calls, often rather uncomfortable. Quite honestly, the reaction was unpleasant, and that was why I went quiet about it.
>
> I have just re-read the article in question and I am surprised how strongly I phrased it. The manner in which I handled this was not necessarily wise. But it was intended to provoke a response.
>
> I have had the opportunity over the past few weeks to discuss this with Julian Chislett – Julian and I worked closely on *Skaro*. He has the same recollection as me – there were strong rumours that certain episodes missing from the archives were held by private collectors. Indeed, the claims that were made to us were pretty definite. In retrospect, I suspect our 'sources' had put two and two together to make 98!

The 8mm film arrived in the UK in the late 1970s after former DWAS President Jan Vincent-Rudzki got in contact with the Australian fan who had shot it in the 1960s, and acquired it in exchange for a mint copy of the 1973 *Radio Times Doctor Who* tenth anniversary special. He then made a copy for Ian Levine. Either Levine or Vincent-Rudzki – both big names in '80s fandom – then showed the footage to someone who then told Lydiard that he had seen proof that 'The Tenth Planet' Episode Four and 'The Macra Terror' still existed.

CHAPTER 15

It seemed that barely a month would go by in the 1980s without *DWB* announcing the rumoured return of specific missing episodes, which always came to nothing. Nowadays, fans take a dimmer view of such rumour-mongering, as demonstrated by the backlash that a certain website received after making unfounded claims about the imminent return of 'The Web of Fear' a few years back.

After the death of actor and writer Ian Marter in late 1986, his friend and colleague Nicholas Courtney wrote an obituary for him, which was printed in *Doctor Who Magazine* Issue 121, published in February 1987. This read in part: 'When he was novelising the *Doctor Who* story "The Invasion", he was *chez moi* one afternoon to view my video tape of the adventure that had been given to me by a fan. He wanted to compare the film version with the script he had been given. Imagine the difficulty he encountered when he discovered – as I had not, since the tape was a recent gift – that the first two episodes had no sound on my copy! Still … he duly wrote the book.'

Such innocent words gave rise to the rumour that Courtney was in possession of a silent copy of the missing first episode of 'The Invasion'. In fact, Courtney had been given a copy of the extant episodes, and the first two on the tape – Episodes Two and Three – were the mute copies.

All the examples I've quoted, and probably all the ones I've not, have one thing in common. There were no missing episodes waiting to be discovered behind any of the stories that were spun out, either deliberately or by misconstruction. And yet some fans still believe that there's a huge conspiracy somewhere. The truth is, there isn't.

THE MISSING EPISODE LEGACY

Over the years, the missing episodes themselves have taken on a legendary status. This is not an entirely good thing, as the 1992 recovery of 'The Tomb of the Cybermen' demonstrated in some quarters. Until that point, the story had been lauded as something way above average by those fortunate enough to have seen the four episodes on their original transmission in the 1960s. A pinnacle, perhaps, of the quality the series could offer. It was, put simply, the best *Doctor Who* story ever. But as it was absent from the archives, this was an opinion that was completely unimpeachable. It was a brave soul who might suggest otherwise. The only evidence to back up the story's apparent quality was Gerry Davis's moody Target novelisation, the surviving camera script, a copy of an off-air audio recording, and about a dozen eerie black and white BBC publicity photographs, all of which seemed to support the assertions of the elder statesmen fans who gushed about the story.

And then the episodes were found. Suddenly, the eerie Cyber-tomb of the Target book was seen as a cramped BBC plywood set. The spooky Cybermats were dodgy clockwork toys. The Cybermen were lumbering extras in silver suits. And – shock!

WIPED!

horror! – the epic fight between Toberman and the Cyber Controller was performed by a man on a Kirby wire, and featured a wrestling contest with an empty suit. Fans who'd been used to getting their kicks from slicker '80s stories such as 'Earthshock', 'The Caves of Androzani' and 'Remembrance of the Daleks' watched in some degree of puzzlement. It was as if they had just realised that the Emperor was in fact wearing no clothes. The backlash began.

The problem was the lack of context. People who grew up with '60s television could still watch programmes from that era with the same contextual filters that they had subconsciously used at the time. People who grew up with '80s television found it much harder to watch 'The Tomb of the Cybermen' on its own terms.

Twenty years later, in the early 21st Century, '60s programmes have an even harder fight on their hands to engage the modern viewer. And yet, as it approaches its fiftieth anniversary, *Doctor Who* is one of the few shows that can arguably still do this.

Even before the series' successful return in 2005, old *Doctor Who* episodes were still widely regarded as being of high cultural significance. Their sales on VHS and DVD were extremely healthy, and unmatched by those of other BBC programmes of the same era. And when missing episodes did occasionally surface – as in the case of 'The Crusade' Episode One in 1999, and 'The Daleks Masterplan' Episode Two in 2004 – then it was worthy of coverage on the national television news bulletins and in the national media. And this was *before* Christopher Eccleston, David Tennant and Matt Smith. The return in 2011 of two further missing episodes showed that the enhanced profile of the new series ensures that *Doctor Who*'s past remains very newsworthy indeed.

The fact that the BBC still has a 106-episode gap in its collection of *Doctor Who* is something that some people can never forgive, or come to terms with. And yet, those missing episodes have achieved some degree of immortality by dint of the fact that they *are* missing.

In the 1970s, 1980s and 1990s, novelisations were published of all of the 1960s *Doctor Who* stories, many of them authored by the original television scriptwriters. Although these are now out of print, some are being released as talking books by BBC Audiobooks, and most of the others are also worth hunting down and reading. Victor Pemberton's novelisation of 'Fury from the Deep' and Gerry Davis's of 'The Moonbase' (titled *Doctor Who and the Cybermen*) are particularly worthy of note, in this author's estimation.

Thanks to the fans who made off-air audio recordings of *Doctor Who* in the 1960s, the soundtracks of all 106 missing episodes survive. These have been painstakingly remastered, and are all available in CD form from the BBC, complete with accompanying narration to let listeners know what was happening on-screen.

CHAPTER 15

Today, you can't re-watch a missing episode, but you can at least listen to it.

And in a few cases, you can watch something too. When 'The Ice Warriors' was released on VHS in 1998, a partial reconstruction of the missing second and third episodes was attempted, using John Cura's Tele-snaps, frame-grabs from the surviving four episodes and BBC publicity photographs, all matched up to an off-air soundtrack recording. Similarly, when 'The Tenth Planet' came out on VHS in 2000, a version of the missing final episode was included, reconstructed in the same way, and also incorporating the surviving 8mm and *Blue Peter* clips. These reconstructions are perhaps little more than slideshows with sound, but do give an excellent indication of what the episodes *would* have looked like.

Other examples of this sort of thing have included a CD-rom release of 'The Power of the Daleks' in 2005, marrying the soundtrack of the six episodes with appropriate Tele-Snap images, and a cutdown version of 'Marco Polo' included on the DVD box set 'The Beginning' in 2006.[88] Again, these are essentially just successions of still photographs set to the relevant soundtrack, but do give an impression of how the episodes would originally have appeared.

BBCi – the people behind the BBC's *Doctor Who* website – decided that they would try a different approach in 2005, and used the animation company Cosgrove Hall to create visuals to match the off-air audio recordings of 'The Invasion' Episodes One and Four. These did not actually appear on the *Doctor Who* website as originally intended, but were instead included on the DVD release of 'The Invasion' in 2006. The animation was generally acclaimed by fans, but due to the relatively high costs involved, it was an experiment that looked unlikely to be repeated anytime soon. But then, in 2011, 2|entertain announced that animations of the missing fourth and fifth episodes of 'The Reign of Terror' were being commissioned for the DVD release of this story, and if sales were good enough, more missing episodes could possibly benefit from the same treatment.

But all this is trying to make the best out of what remains of the *Doctor Who* archive. What people will always be more interested in are the lost episodes themselves. Will any of the 106 still-missing *Doctor Who* episodes ever be found?

ARE THERE STILL MISSING EPISODES OUT THERE?

As any statistician will tell you, anything is possible. But we are now in the area of diminishing returns when it comes to the recovery of missing *Doctor Who* material. All of the obvious areas of research have been explored, and most of the unobvious

---

88 Groups of fans have also, over the years, attempted their own unofficial reconstructions of all the missing episodes, using similar techniques.

WIPED!

ones as well! And, as I mentioned statistics, let's look at the hard facts. Since the plight of the missing episodes was first publicly revealed in late 1981, the recoveries have come as follows:

1982 – 2 missing episodes found/returned
1983 – 3 missing episodes found/returned
1984 – 13 missing episodes found/returned
1985
1986
1987 – 2 missing episodes found/returned
1988 – 4 missing episodes found/returned
1989
1990
1991
1992 – 4 missing episodes found/returned
1993
1994
1995
1996
1997
1998
1999 – 1 missing episode found/returned
2000
2001
2002
2003
2004 – 1 missing episode found/returned
2005
2006
2007
2008
2009
2010
2011 – 2 missing episodes found/returned
2012

If this demonstrates anything, it's that any future recoveries will probably be few and far between. The reduction of missing episodes from 136 to 106 has taken 30 years,

CHAPTER 15

and 26 of the 30 recovered episodes were found inside of the first ten years.

But *if* material is still out there, waiting to be recovered, then where could it be?

The first and most obvious answer is *perhaps* at foreign television stations. However, all of the major overseas broadcasters that purchased *Doctor Who* in the 1960s and 1970s have been contacted a number of times over the last 30 years, to see if they might retain anything. Nearly all of them have replied in the negative. One or two have been a little more equivocal. Asia Television (formally RTV) in Hong Kong had a fire in 1988 that destroyed a lot of its film library records, leading to some uncertainly over its holdings as its documentation had to be re-written from scratch. Then there was the Iranian television authorities' infamous 'In the name of Allah, what are you talking about?' reply to the BBC's 1984 request for information about *Doctor Who* episodes. Perhaps surprisingly, however, those authorities have since tried their best to discover exactly what happened to the two episodes of 'Marco Polo' that were sent to them by the NZBC in 1967, to no avail.

At the time of writing, members of the *Doctor Who* Restoration Team, working in conjunction with the BBC Film and Videotape Library and the Fédération Internationale des Archives de Télévision/The International Federation of Television Archives (FIAT/IFTA), are still re-examining many of the foreign sales of the series from the 1960s, and re-establishing dialogue with many of the stations that purchased episodes, to finally determine the fate of the many film prints that were sent overseas by BBC Enterprises. But the chances of anything turning up are very slim. When the BBC first began looking for old *Doctor Who* material overseas in 1978, 'The Space Pirates' had been screened on BBC1 only nine years previously. It's now over 45 years since 'Marco Polo' was shown. Most prints would have been destroyed by overseas stations within two years of them purchasing the programmes in the first place. If any survived at that point, there have been plenty of opportunities for them to have been junked in the intervening years.

Another factor is that there was a sharp decline in overseas interest in the series after the second season. While many countries screened 'Marco Polo', 'The Reign of Terror' and 'The Crusade', the number that bought the stories from 'Galaxy 4' onwards fell into single figures, perhaps with as few as four 16mm film prints of each episode ever in circulation. The relatively large number of sales of the relatively few missing episodes of Seasons One and Two does offer more hope that they may still survive somewhere, but this is tempered by the knowledge that the number of prints needed to service all those sales might still have been relatively small – perhaps fewer than half-a-dozen copies of each episode – as they were probably just bicycled from country to country as needs dictated.

The stories with the smallest number of overseas sales can almost certainly be

WIPED!

written off as missing for good. 'Mission to the Unknown' and 'The Daleks Masterplan' had only one abortive sale apiece, to Australia. This almost certainly equates to only a single print of each of these episodes being produced. 'The Tenth Planet' and 'The Power of the Daleks' had only three overseas sales apiece; and we know that at least two of the stations involved shared the same set of prints, so only two copies (at most) of these two stories were ever in circulation. The markets they were sold to have been fully investigated, and the prints haven't survived.

These four stories top the list of material that will probably never see the light of day again. The ultimate lost episode is Episode Seven of 'The Daleks Masterplan'. With no telerecording ever having been made of this one episode, there is just no scope for a copy to have survived at all. Certainly not overseas, at any rate.

If overseas television stations have junked whatever *Doctor Who* material they might have possessed, then could some of the 16mm films have evaded destruction, and ended up in the hands of private collectors? Well, the recovery of Episode Two of 'The War Machines' from a collector in Australia in the 1970s, and Episode One of 'The Crusade' from a collector in New Zealand in the 1990s, would suggest that there is always a chance of this sort of thing happening again. However, the ability of those seeking the missing episodes to actually do anything proactive about hunting them down from such sources is practically non-existent. And Australia and New Zealand both have thriving *Doctor Who* fan networks. What chance then of finding – say – a missing episode in private hands in places such as Uganda or Zambia? Nevertheless, over the years, there have been credible reports of episodes of 'The Macra Terror' being shown (with the use of a 16mm projector) during a cancelled sports day at a school in New Zealand in the early 1970s, and of episodes of a Patrick Troughton Yeti story being screened in the same manner in Africa in the mid-1970s.

But if missing *Doctor Who* episodes are going to be returned from overseas, then they will almost certainly come from television stations, not private individuals. And most of the television stations that purchased *Doctor Who* have been fully explored and ruled out. And as the search rules more and more overseas stations out, then the scope for possible returns from this route narrows and narrows.

If there are fewer and fewer credible avenues for missing episodes to be found overseas, what are the chances that any still reside in the UK?

Miracles do sometimes happen within the BBC. In 2003, the missing final episode of the first season of *Adam Adamant Lives!* was discovered in the BBC Film and Videotape Library, inside a mislabelled 16mm film can. But instances like this are few and far between, and if there is any other missing *Doctor Who* material in the UK, it is very unlikely to be lurking unnoticed in the BBC archive.

The history of recovered *Doctor Who* episodes is full of instances of prints coming

CHAPTER 15

from UK film collectors. Throughout the 1960s, 1970s and 1980s, film collecting was a way for genre enthusiasts to obtain and re-watch material in their own homes. As a rule, film collectors usually concentrated on obtaining copies of movies, with television programmes relegated to a niche sideline. The huge impact of VHS as a format to re-watch material in the 1980s saw film collecting dwindle as a hobby in the UK, but nevertheless, a hard-core community of collectors still exists today.

The high profile that *Doctor Who* has enjoyed over the years has meant that most if not all UK film collectors are now well aware of the issue of missing episodes. *Doctor Who* continues to be at the forefront of any discussion of missing material in a wider television context, despite the fact that there are many other shows from the 1950s, 1960s and 1970s that have episodes absent from the archives. In fact, there is a certain degree of disgruntlement in the wider television community that *Doctor Who* manages to dominate any discussion of the subject, possibly to the detriment of other programmes. The only realistic hope is that a non-collector, somewhere, might have prints of a couple of missing episodes, and just not realise their importance. This is exactly what happened in 2011, with the return of 'Galaxy Four' Episode Three and 'The Underwater Menace' Episode Two.

There were a small number of *Doctor Who* 16mm film prints regularly doing the rounds in film collector circles in the 1970s and 1980s, all of which were duplicates of episodes that already existed at the BBC at the time. One by one, these were bought up by people with a specific interest in missing *Doctor Who* episodes, not necessarily because they particularly wanted them for their own collections, but because it took them out of circulation. If you're looking for missing material on 16mm film, then you can spend months and months following up a lead, only to find eventually that it takes you to a copy of an existing episode. Then, a few years later, another lead is followed up, only for you to find the self-same film print sitting at the end of the chase. Better to buy the print, take it out of circulation and know you won't end up spending time and resources tracking it down again. Nowadays, there are very few 16mm episodes of *Doctor Who* doing the rounds. A rare exception came to light in August 2011, when the BBC were contacted by a family in Essex who had found a collection of old films in a makeshift shed-cum-cinema at the bottom of the garden in their new house. One of the films was a *Doctor Who* episode, which turned out to be a copy of the (extant) third episode of 'The Romans'. A few months later, a hitherto previously unknown 16mm print of 'The Reign of Terror' Episode One was sold on eBay. All of which shows that material can still turn up in the most unexpected places.

However, it's worth pondering for a moment the origins of the prints that found their way into private collections. Significantly, they were always 16mm prints, never

WIPED!

35mm. Black and white BBC transmission prints for *Doctor Who* were always 35mm[89], while overseas sales prints from BBC Enterprises were 16mm. All the 16mm *Doctor Who* telerecordings that were ever made were made by BBC Enterprises. And so every single *Doctor Who* 16mm film that has been found in private hands originated at some point at BBC Enterprises.

Only it's not as simple as that. In the 1960s and 1970s, the BBC was awash with 16mm film. The BBC Film Library and BBC Enterprises both kept their own films in a reasonably organised system, but (prior to 1978 and Sue Malden becoming Archive Selector, leastways) there were a huge number of films that existed outside of these two systems at the BBC. Most of them were originally duplicate prints, although as the years went by, many of the originals were destroyed, leaving them as the only copies. But no-one was really aware of this at the time. Francis Watson worked at the BBC's Ealing studios in the early 1970s, and was able to take home 16mm prints of 'The Daleks' Episode Five and 'The Daleks Masterplan' Episode Two when they were no longer wanted. Roger Stevens and Ian Sheward (both BBC employees) also both knew people at the BBC who had also taken home 16mm episodes of *Doctor Who* ('The Abominable Snowmen' Episode Two, 'Invasion of the Dinosaurs' Part One and 'The Time Meddler' Episodes One and Three amongst others). These weren't films taken from the BBC Film Library without permission, or swiped from the shelves of Villiers House. These were unaccounted for, uncatalogued and unwanted spares. Could this be the way that all the other episodes recovered from private collections ended up outside the BBC?

Consider this recollection by Graham Walker[90], a former film editor at the BBC's Ealing Studios between 1970 and 1986:

> Ealing had a large maintenance department which had a constant need for spare and redundant prints for use in testing various items of film equipment. Whenever the film library or whoever had a clear-out, a certain number of these prints would be sent to maintenance. A few years before I left the BBC, to pursue my freelance career, the maintenance department at Ealing closed as the first phase of moving the whole of film department to White City. To make the move easier all the prints in maintenance were to be thrown away. One day one of the maintenance guys whom I knew well and who knew I was a film collector and fan of *Till Death Us Do Part* came into my cutting

---

[89] With the notable exception of the repeats of 'An Unearthly Child' and 'The Krotons' during the 1981 repeat season 'The Five Faces of Doctor Who', which were transmitted from 16mm film.

[90] Interviewed on www.wipednews.com.

CHAPTER 15

room with three *Till Death Us Do Part* prints and said 'It seems such a shame to throw these into the skip – would you like to keep them?' I had no idea at the time that at least two of these prints were to become, possibly, the only surviving copies of these episodes ...

Roger Stevens (who worked at the BBC in the 1970s and 1980s) has his own thoughts on how material might have 'escaped' from the Corporation:

> One thing that comes to mind is the (perhaps overlooked) role of Film Despatch, who were responsible for sending film (but not videotape) round the BBC. Since they were based at Ealing, Windmill Road, Television Centre, Lime Grove, Kensington House et al they were the guys who physically handled all the film. Thus in 1973, episodes like 'The Tenth Planet' Episode Four would have gone to the *Blue Peter* offices via the East Tower Film Despatch, and then back to wherever it was sent from (or not!). Of course, the departments are all now long gone, and whatever records they had have probably also been destroyed, but it was a way of getting your hands on stuff, simply by taking it off the shelves, as the checks were non-existent, and also a way of 'smuggling' films in and out of the BBC itself.

Another ex-BBC employee, Barry Littlechild, also recalls that the Film Despatch department was something of a weak link in security when it came to the films for which it was responsible:

> Film Despatch at BBC Ealing Film Studios was *the* place in the '60s. As home video was a thing of the future, keeping 16mm telerecordings and prints was a costly business for the Beeb. Every so often skips would arrive at Ealing and they were filled with cans of film ... everything from *The Black & White Minstrel Show* to *Panorama*!
>
> At the time it was so easy to get prints that most of us collectors didn't bother to sort out these prize gems ... I can remember 30 copies of *This Is The BBC* being junked ... This lasted for several years, but then I think they must have realised money was being thrown away and the practice stopped. Most cutting rooms had stacks of cans that the editor just hung onto ... I expect they are now hidden in lofts awaiting someone to find them.
>
> Another way of getting a copy of a film was to bribe the lab inspectors who turned up each day to view rushes or bribe a telerecording operator for a copy of a live show, as Galton and Simpson did for *Hancock's Half Hour* and

WIPED!

Steptoe and Son. Dudley Moore told me they tried to get *Not Only But Also* prints properly through the BBC but were turned down, saying they wouldn't be able to clear all copyrights .... all those shows are now lost! If only they had nicked 'em!

Despite all the good efforts that went on in the 1970s and 1980s to make sure that all film and videotape material was catalogued at the BBC, things were still being thrown away without any proper checks.

What makes this all the more interesting, and perhaps relevant, is the recovery of the Australian ABC prints of Episode Three of 'Galaxy 4' and Episode Two of 'The Underwater Menace' from a private collector in England in 2011. Let's speculate for a moment on the path that these episodes might have taken. The prints were made by BBC Enterprises and sold to ABC. They were screened twice in each of the ABC broadcast areas in the late 1960s. They were then sent back to BBC Enterprises in June 1975, along with many, many more episodes of *Doctor Who*. As they were returned sales prints, they were deemed surplus to requirements, and all these ABC prints were junked ... but not before someone with access to the films took a shine to some of them, and rather than see them thrown in a skip, decided to take at least two home with them. Perhaps this happened a lot in the early 1970s? Perhaps all the 16mm *Doctor Who* films recovered from private collectors in the UK are duplicate prints that were returned to the BBC from foreign broadcasters over the years, and not merely those that were Withdrawn, Accessioned and Junked by Villiers House from its own sales vault? If so, the number of potential films 'out there' in the UK could be far greater than first thought ...

None of the 16mm *Doctor Who* films located in private collections over the years has had an Enterprises catalogue number label on it. This proves nothing, as labels can be removed, and anyone 'liberating' films from the BBC might think that removing such labels would be a very good move when it came to covering the tracks of the origins of the films in question. And the prints of the 'Galaxy 4' and 'The Underwater Menace' episodes are the first returned prints of missing episodes from a UK private collector that we can say with any degree of certainty originated at a foreign broadcaster. But it does at least *suggest* that these aren't films that escaped destruction after being officially 'Withdrawn, De-accessioned and Junked' at Villiers House.

When the 16mm film prints of 'The Ice Warriors' Episodes One, Four, Five and Six were found in the basement of the empty Villiers House in 1988, the film cans still had their original BBC Enterprises catalogue number labels attached, as would any films that had been in the BBC Enterprises system. This would include all the 16mm films that BBC Enterprises junked in previous decades.

CHAPTER 15

What isn't known is just how many *Doctor Who* films found their way out of the BBC in the 1960s and 1970s. The figure can't even be guessed at. But there will inevitably come a time when each and every film that still survives has been found. We may well have already reached that point (although there were 108 missing *Doctor Who* episodes when the first edition of this book was published, and now there are only 106 ...). But whenever we do reach it, we will never know that we *have* reached it. You can't prove a negative!

If there are no more 16mm films to be found, then there is one other possibility for finding missing *Doctor Who* episodes, albeit an extremely remote one. Sony marketed what is recognised as the world's first domestic video recorder, the CV-2000, in 1965. This used ½-inch open-reel videotapes, which ran for 60 minutes. Prior to that, there were a few older, more obscure video recorders, such as the Philips EL3400 and the Peto Scott E2770 (which was a 'clone' of the Philips machine). These both came out in 1964, but used one-inch tape reels and were not really designed for domestic use. But the CV-2000 was a domestic machine. At least, for those who could afford such things – it would have cost around £500 at the time, when the weekly wage was just under £10. Blank tapes were around the £25 mark, so it was not a cheap thing to own or use.

In 1998, members of the *Doctor Who* Restoration Team were put in touch with someone who had purchased a CV-2000 in the summer of 1967, and recalled recording episodes of *Doctor Who* off-air in the 1960s and 1970s. When they visited his house, they discovered that he also owned a Sony CV-2100 (the 625-line replacement for the CV-2000) and a colour Shibaden machine. He hadn't been able to afford the correct Sony ½-inch videotapes at the time, and so had devised a way of using other, wider, magnetic tapes, and cutting them down to a width of ½ an inch using a system he had constructed himself out of the children's building toy Meccano.

He had recorded a number of television programmes in the 1960s and 1970s, including *Doctor Who*, and had boxes and boxes of tapes in his attic, totalling around 300 spools. He had located in his collection some black and white recordings of episodes of 'Carnival of Monsters', plus colour recordings of episodes of 'Frontier in Space'. But while going through a box of some older recordings, a number of tapes were found from 1968 and 1969, which also appeared to have *Doctor Who* episodes on them. One of them was found to hold an off-air recording of Episode Two of 'The Space Pirates' – ironically the only episode of that story that already survived at the BBC. Others had recording dates written on them that corresponded with the BBC1 repeat of 'The Evil of the Daleks' in 1968. When these tapes were played, it was discovered that the original contents had been recorded over with episodes of *The Forsyte Saga*, which had been repeated on BBC1 in late 1968. So near, and yet so far.

WIPED!

There is one other example I know of relating to episodes of *Doctor Who* being recorded on video off-air in the 1960s. An old and trusted friend of mine used to avidly watch *Doctor Who* in the 1960s. His father worked for a company that had a reel-to-reel video recorder (possibly a Sony CV-2000, although it's difficult to be certain after so many years), and would occasionally record programmes for his son to watch later. These included all six episodes of the Troughton story 'The Ice Warriors', recorded off-air from BBC1 in November/December 1967. My friend's father retained the tapes for him to watch during the school summer holiday of 1968, which he did a number of times. But as soon as term time came around, his father wiped the tapes and returned them to his company's library.

So the possibility exists, however small, that other episodes of *Doctor Who* might have been recorded off-air on CV-2000 tapes from 1965 onwards. However, CV-2000 tapes are notoriously difficult to replay, and working machines are hard to come by these days. The day will soon come when any such recordings, should they exist, will be completely unplayable.

The final truth is simply this. There are 106 episodes of *Doctor Who* that are missing. As much as we wish that some or all of them might survive out there, somewhere, the fact of the matter is that they probably don't. We could have already reached the point where everything that can be found, has been found. But we will never know for certain. And that is why we keep on hoping and dreaming and wishing. And perhaps, one day I'll get to write a third edition of this very book, with wildly differing conclusions in the final chapter …

APPENDIX I

THE MISSING EPISODES: OVERSEAS SALES AND TRANSMISSIONS

Earlier in the book, some of the sales of the Hartnell and Troughton episodes of *Doctor Who* were detailed on a per-country basis. In this section, we'll look only at the missing episodes. I'll attempt to put all that information into a timeline for each story, showing the order of overseas sales, the transmission details in each country (where known), plus any known information about what happened to the 16mm film prints of the episodes after they were screened.[91]

A lot of information has been unearthed that shows when episodes were sent to other countries from those that originally screened them, but equally a lot of details are annoyingly sparse, despite the best efforts of researchers over the last 20-odd years.

The one hundred million dollar question that has to be asked is this: *do the film prints of any of these episodes still exist at overseas television stations?* In nearly all the cases, the answer is definitely not. Most of the main markets for *Doctor Who* – such as Australia, New Zealand, Hong Kong and Singapore – have been contacted a number of times over the years, and each time they have checked their archives and found nothing. In fact, the ABC in Australia has had so many requests over the years from fans asking if they still have any of the missing stories that they can no longer reply to such letters. So please don't write to the ABC!

A number of the smaller markets – such as Canada and Cyprus – have also been extensively checked for missing material. So much so, that it can be said with complete confidence that no missing *Doctor Who* material still exists at the relevant stations.

Most of the other overseas stations that bought now-missing episodes have been contacted by the BBC or by individuals (such as members of the *Doctor Who* Restoration Team) over the years, and nothing has been found that would indicate that the episodes might still exist at those stations. In recent years, an official initiative, utilising the joint knowledge of the BBC, the *Doctor Who* Restoration Team and Fédération Internationale des Archives de Télévision/The International Federation of Television Archives (FIAT/IFTA), has begun approaching many stations directly to

---

91 My thanks to Jon Preddle and the website broadcast.org, which has unearthed a lot of valuable information of the overseas transmission of *Doctor Who* in the 1960s, 1970s and 1980s since the first edition of this book was published in 2010.

WIPED!

try to get definitive answers to any outstanding questions, and this is still ongoing at the time of writing.

In truth, there will never be a 100% certain answer to the question of what happened to all the prints of these episodes. We can only guess. But the best-guess answer is that once the episodes were finished with by these overseas stations, they were:

a) destroyed
b) sent on to another foreign broadcaster at BBC Enterprises' request, or
c) sent back to BBC Enterprises as per the terms of their original sales contract.

There exists the teeniest, tiniest chance that material might have survived beyond any certified destruction orders, either inside the various television stations, or in private collections. The recovery of the print of 'The Crusade' Episode One in New Zealand in 1999 proves that weird things can happen.

But at the end of the day, you can't prove a negative. The film prints no longer exist. What remains is just their trail.

MARCO POLO (7 EPISODES)
EPISODES 1, 2, 3, 4, 5, 6 & 7 MISSING

Country / TV Station	BBC Sales Date	Transmission Dates	Notes	What Happened to the 16mm Prints...?
Australia / ABC	18/08/64	Perth 12/04/65 – 24/05/65 Canberra 16/04/65 – 28/05/65 Sydney 16/04/65 – 28/05/65 Brisbane 23/04/65 – 04/06/65 Adelaide 14/06/65 – 26/07/65 Melbourne 05/07/65 – 16/08/65 Hobart 10/09/65 – 22/10/65 Sydney 20/12/65 – 28/12/65 Melbourne 30/12/65 – 07/01/66 Perth 12/01/66 – 20/01/66 Adelaide 09/11/66 – 21/11/66 Hobart 23/11/66 – 05/12/66	ABC records show that the story was purchased on 28/10/64 ABC records show that censors made edits to Episodes Five & Seven	ABC confirm they no longer have the episodes

APPENDIX I

Canada / CBC	18/11/64	Toronto 05/05/65 -16/06/65 Barrie 12/05/65 – ??/06/65	Series cancelled on CBC after 'The Keys of Marinus'	CBC confirm they no longer have the episodes
Malta / Xandir Malta	07/12/64	23/08/65 – 04/10/65		
Singapore / RTS	18/04/65	07/07/65 – 18/08/65		RTS confirm they no longer have the episodes
Gibraltar / GBC	14/05/65	13/07/65 – 24/08/65	Story purchased through TIE Ltd	As TIE distributed this story, the same prints probably serviced Aden, Trinidad & Tobago and Bermuda
Aden / SATS	14/05/65	03/10/65 – 14/11/65	Story purchased through TIE Ltd	As TIE distributed this story, the same prints probably serviced Gibraltar, Trinidad & Tobago and Bermuda
Trinidad & Tobago / TTT	14/05/65	30/01/66 – 13/03/66	Story purchased through TIE Ltd	As TIE distributed this story, the same prints probably serviced Aden, Gibraltar and Bermuda
Nigeria / RKTV	14/06/65	02/11/65 – 12/12/65		RKTV confirm that all seven episodes were destroyed
Rhodesia / RBC	06/09/65	26/12/65 – 06/02/66		RBC sent their prints onto ZNBC in Zambia after transmission
Barbados / CBC	21/09/65	25/07/66 – 06/09/66		CBC confirm that they no longer have the episodes
Hong Kong / RTV	23/11/65	26/07/66 – 06/09/66	RTV had to wait for prints to be sent from CBC in Cyprus in 1966	RTV confirm they no longer have the episodes
Uganda / UTV	30/11/65	19/04/66 – 31/05/66		UTV confirm they no longer have the episodes

WIPED!

New Zealand / NZBC	30/11/65	Auckland 27/10/66 – 08/12/66 Wellington 01/11/66 – 13/12/66 Dunedin 15/12/66 – 26/01/67 Christchurch 20/03/67 – 01/05/67	NZBC records show that censors made edits to Episodes Three, Four, Five, Six & Seven	Episodes One & Two sent to NIR&T Iran in October 1967 Episodes Three – Seven sent to Harriett Street store, and were still there on 01/04/70 Episodes Three – Seven junked c1975 Original 16mm film tin for Episode Seven found in Wellington in 1990
Ghana / GRTC	26/01/66	10/10/66 – 21/10/66		GRTC confirm they no longer have the episodes
Zambia / ZNBC	07/03/66	Kitwe 16/01/66 – 27/02/66 Lusaka 23/01/66 – 06/03/66	Prints sent from RBC in Rhodesia	ZNBC confirm they no longer have the episodes
Jamaica / JBC	07/03/66	02/06/66 – 28/07/66		
Cyprus / CBC	26/05/66	10/06/66 – 29/07/66		Prints of all seven episodes sent to RTV in Hong Kong in 1966
Kenya / VoK	04/07/66	29/09/66 – 10/11/66		VoK confirm they no longer have the episodes
Bermuda / ZFB-TV	11/07/66	14/03/66 – 25/04/66	Story purchased through TIE Ltd	As TIE distributed this story, the same prints probably serviced Aden, Gibraltar and Trinidad & Tobago
Thailand / HSA-TV	20/10/66	19/11/66 – 31/12/66		
Mauritius / MBC	18/01/67	20/01/67 – 03/03/67		
Venezuela / RCT	27/01/67	Not shown	Sale cancelled	Prints probably not ever sent
Sierra Leone / SLBS	06/04/67	12/07/67 – 23/08/67		SLBS confirm that they no longer have the episodes

APPENDIX I

Country / TV Station	BBC Sales Date	Transmission Dates	Notes	What Happened to the 16mm Prints...?
Iran / NIR&T	Not purchased	Not shown	Prints of Episodes One & Two received from NZBC in New Zealand in October 1967, but whole story never purchased	NIR&T confirm that they no longer have Episodes One & Two
Ethiopia / ETV	26/10/70	21/01/71 – 04/03/71		

THE REIGN OF TERROR (6 EPISODES)
EPISODES 4 & 5 MISSING

Country / TV Station	BBC Sales Date	Transmission Dates	Notes	What Happened to the 16mm Prints...?
Australia / ABC	21/01/65	Perth 20/09/65 – 25/10/65 Canberra 24/09/65 – 29/10/65 Sydney 24/09/65 – 29/10/65 Brisbane 01/10/65 – 05/11/65 Adelaide 22/11/65 – 27/12/65 Melbourne 13/12/65 – 17/01/66 Hobart 25/02/66 – 01/04/66 Brisbane 02/11/66 – 10/11/66 Sydney 09/11/66 – 17/11/66 Melbourne 16/11/66 – 24/11/66 Canberra 22/11/66 – 05/12/66 Perth 30/11/66 – 08/12/66 Adelaide 15/12/66 – 26/12/66	ABC records show that the story was purchased on 27/04/65 ABC records show that censors made edits to Episode Five	Prints of all six episodes sent to NZBC in New Zealand in September 1967 ABC confirm they no longer have the episodes
Gibraltar / GBC	23/08/65	21/12/65 – 25/01/66		
Malta / Xandir Malta	31/08/65	31/01/66 – 07/03/66		
Nigeria / RKTV	31/08/65	12/04/66 – 17/05/66		RKTV confirm that all six episodes were destroyed

WIPED!

Country / Broadcaster	Sale Date	Screening Dates	Notes	Status
Hong Kong / RTV	23/11/65	03/01/67 – 07/02/67		RTV confirm they no longer have the episodes
Aden / SATS	23/11/65	13/03/66 – 17/04/66		
Singapore / RTS	30/11/65	15/12/65 – 26/01/66		RTS confirm they no longer have the episodes
Trinidad & Tobago / TTT	07/03/66	10/07/66 – 14/08/66		
Zambia / ZNBC	07/03/66	Kitwe 21/06/66 – 26/07/66 Lusaka 28/06/66 – 02/08/66		ZNBC confirm they no longer have the episodes
Uganda / UTV	25/04/66	27/09/66 – 01/11/66		UTV confirm they no longer have the episodes
Jamaica / JBC	18/10/66	05/11/66 – 10/12/66		
Barbados / CBC	11/11/66	03/01/67 – 07/02/67		CBC confirm that they no longer have the episodes
Rhodesia / RBC	13/12/66	05/06/66 – 10/07/66		
Cyprus / CBC	Sale not recorded by the BBC	Not shown	There is no sale or screening information for this story on CBC Why they were sent prints of this story isn't known	Prints of Episodes One, Two, Three & Six returned to the BBC in 1984. Prints of Episodes Four & Five destroyed in 1974
Venezuela / RCT	18/01/67	Not shown	Sale cancelled	Prints probably not sent
Kenya / VoK	18/01/67	09/03/67 – 13/04/67		VoK confirm they no longer have the episodes
Mauritius / MBC	06/04/67	09/06/67 – 14/07/67		MBC confirm that they no longer have the episodes
Thailand / HSA-TV	26/04/67	13/05/67 – 17/06/67		
New Zealand / NZBC	08/02/68	Wellington 08/03/68 – 12/04/68 Dunedin 29/03/68 – 03/05/68 Auckland 24/05/68 – 28/06/68 Christchurch 26/01/68 – 01/03/68	NZBC records show that the film prints arrived in the country from ABC in Australia on 19/09/67	Prints of all six episodes destroyed on 18/06/71

APPENDIX I

Sierra Leone/ SLBS	16/02/68	29/01/68 – 04/03/68		SLBS confirm that they no longer have the episodes
Ethiopia / ETS	26/10/70	01/07/71 – 05/08/71		

THE CRUSADE (4 EPISODES)
EPISODES 2 & 4 MISSING

Country / TV Station	BBC Sales Date	Transmission Dates	Notes	What Happened to the 16mm Prints…?
Australia / ABC	13/01/66	Perth 28/03/66 – 18/04/66 Canberra 01/04/66 – 22/04/66 Sydney 01/04/66 – 22/04/66 Brisbane 08/04/66 – 29/04/66 Melbourne 02/05/66 – 23/05/66 Adelaide 16/05/66 – 06/06/66 Hobart 08/07/66 – 29/07/66 Brisbane 01/12/66 – 07/12/66 Sydney 13/12/66 – 19/12/66 Melbourne 20/12/66 – 26/12/66 Perth 27/12/66 – 02/01/67 Canberra 04/01/67 – 11/01/67 Hobart 09/01/67 – 12/01/67 Adelaide 26/02/68 – 29/02/68	ABC records show that the story was purchased on 26/01/66	ABC confirm they no longer have the episodes
Gibraltar / GBC	16/05/66	09/07/66 – 06/08/66		
Singapore / RTS	16/05/66	20/08/66 – 09/09/66		RTS confirm they no longer have the episodes
Nigeria / RKTV	04/07/66	18/10/66 – 08/11/66		RKTV confirm that all four episodes were destroyed

WIPED!

Country / TV Station	BBC Sales Date	Transmission Dates	Notes	What Happened to the 16mm Prints...?
Zambia / ZNBC	21/10/66	Kitwe 03/01/67 – 24/01/67 Lusaka 10/01/67 – 31/01/67		ZNBC confirm they no longer have the episodes
Barbados / CBC	14/06/67	11/07/67 – 01/08/67		CBC confirm that they no longer have the episodes
New Zealand / NZBC	Sale not recorded by the BBC	Not shown	NZBC records show that the film prints arrived in the country on 19/09/67	All four episodes sent to Harriett Street store, and were still there on 01/04/70 Episodes junked c1975 Episode One saved by a collector, and eventually returned to the BBC in 1999
Mauritius / MBC	14/11/67	12/01/68 – 02/02/68		MBC confirm that they no longer have the episodes
Sierra Leone / SLBS	13/08/68	29/07/68 – 26/08/68		SLBS confirm that they no longer have the episodes
Jamaica / JBC	18/03/69	16/03/69 – 13/04/69		
Ethiopia / ETV	22/10/71	05/01/72 – 26/01/72		

GALAXY 4 (4 EPISODES)
EPISODES 1, 2 & 4 MISSING

Country / TV Station	BBC Sales Date	Transmission Dates	Notes	What Happened to the 16mm Prints...?
Australia / ABC	24/10/66	Hobart 10/10/66 – 13/10/66 Perth 17/10/66 – 20/10/66 Brisbane 26/10/66 – 01/11/66 Sydney 26/10/66 – 01/11/66 Adelaide 02/11/66 – 08/11/66 Canberra 02/11/66 – 09/11/66 Melbourne 09/11/66 – 15/11/66 Canberra 28/02/68 – 05/03/68 Sydney 28/02/68 – 05/03/68	ABC records show that the story was purchased on 25/08/66	ABC returned all four episodes to the BBC on 04/06/75 The BBC junked all four prints, but the 16mm film of Episode Three survived and passed into the hands of a private collector Episode Three returned to the BBC in 2011

APPENDIX I

Country / TV Station	BBC Sales Date	Transmission Dates	Notes	What Happened to the 16mm Print...?
Australia / ABC	24/10/66	Melbourne 06/03/68 – 12/03/68 Brisbane 13/03/68 – 19/03/68 Perth 20/03/68 – 26/03/68 Adelaide 27/03/68 – 02/04/68 Hobart 03/04/68 – 09/04/68	ABC records show that the story was purchased on 25/08/66	ABC returned all four episodes to the BBC on 04/06/75 The BBC junked all four prints, but the 16mm film of Episode Three survived and passed into the hands of a private collector Episode Three returned to the BBC in 2011
Barbados / CBC	16/08/67	14/11/67 – 05/12/67		CBC confirm that they no longer have the episodes
Zambia / ZNBC	23/03/68	Kitwe ??/??/68 – ??/??/68 Lusaka 06/02/68 – 27/02/68		ZNBC confirm they no longer have the episodes
New Zealand / NZBC	22/10/68	Christchurch 22/12/68 – 12/01/69 Wellington 19/01/69 – 09/02/69 Auckland 02/03/69 – 23/03/69 Dunedin 09/03/69 – 30/03/69	NZBC records show that the film prints arrived in the country on 23/09/68 NZBC records show that censors made edits to all four episodes	All four episodes sent to RTS in Singapore on 20/09/72
Sierra Leone / SLBS	12/08/70	16/10/70 – 06/11/70		
Singapore / RTS	18/12/72	09/10/72 – 30/10/72	All four episodes received from NZBC in New Zealand on 20/09/72	RTS confirm they no longer have the episodes

MISSION TO THE UNKNOWN (1 EPISODE)
EPISODE 1 MISSING

Country / TV Station	BBC Sales Date	Transmission Dates	Notes	What Happened to the 16mm Print...?
Australia / ABC	Sale not recorded by the BBC	Not shown due to problems with Australian censors	ABC records show that the story was purchased on 13/09/66. This is also the date that the episode was reviewed by the Australian Film Censorship Board	ABC confirm they no longer have the episode

WIPED!

THE MYTH MAKERS (4 EPISODES)
EPISODES 1, 2, 3 & 4 MISSING

Country / TV Station	BBC Sales Date	Transmission Dates	Notes	What Happened to the 16mm Prints...?
Australia / ABC	13/04/67	Melbourne 26/10/66 – 01/11/66 Sydney 02/11/66 – 08/11/66 Hobart 09/11/66 – 15/11/66 Canberra 14/11/66 – 21/11/66 Brisbane 17/11/66 – 23/11/66 Perth 23/11/66 – 29/11/66 Adelaide 08/12/66 – 14/12/66 Canberra 06/03/68 – 12/03/68 Sydney 06/03/68 – 12/03/68 Melbourne 13/03/68 – 19/03/68 Brisbane 20/03/68 – 26/03/68 Perth 27/03/68 – 02/04/68 Adelaide 03/04/68 – 09/04/68 Hobart 10/04/68 – 16/04/68	ABC records show that the story was purchased on 01/09/66	ABC returned all four episodes to the BBC on 04/06/75 However, there is conflicting paperwork regarding the fate of Episode Two ABC confirm they no longer have the episodes
Barbados / CBC	16/08/67	12/12/67 – 02/01/68		CBC confirm that they no longer have the episodes
Zambia / ZNBC	25/03/68	Kitwe ??/??/68 - ??/??/68 Lusaka 05/03/68 – 26/03/68		ZNBC confirm they no longer have the episodes
New Zealand / NZBC	22/10/68	Christchurch 19/01/69 – 09/02/69 Wellington 16/02/69 – 09/03/69 Auckland 30/03/69 – 20/04/69 Dunedin 06/04/69 – 27/04/69	NZBC records show that the film prints arrived in the country on 23/09/68 NZBC records show that censors made edits to all four episodes	All four episodes sent to RTS in Singapore on 20/09/72

APPENDIX I

Country / TV Station	BBC Sales Date	Transmission Dates	Notes	What Happened to the 16mm Prints...?
Sierra Leone / SLBS	12/08/70	13/11/70 – 04/12/70		SLBS confirm that all four episodes were destroyed in 1999
Singapore / RTS	18/12/72	06/11/72 – 27/11/72	All 4 episodes received from NZBC in New Zealand on 20/09/72	RTS confirm they no longer have the episodes

THE DALEKS MASTERPLAN (12 EPISODES)
EPISODES 1, 3, 4, 6, 7, 8, 9, 11 & 12 MISSING

Country / TV Station	BBC Sales Date	Transmission Dates	Notes	What Happened to the 16mm Prints...?
Australia / ABC	Sale not recorded by the BBC	Not shown due to problems with Australian censors	ABC records show that the story (apart from Episode Seven) was purchased on 13/09/66. This is also the date that Episodes One - Six and Eight - Twelve were reviewed by the Australian Film Censorship Board	ABC confirm they no longer have the eleven episodes

THE MASSACRE (4 EPISODES)
EPISODES 1, 2, 3 & 4 MISSING

Country / TV Station	BBC Sales Date	Transmission Dates	Notes	What Happened to the 16mm Prints...?
Australia / ABC	13/04/67	Sydney 20/12/66 – 26/12/66 Brisbane 27/12/66 – 02/01/67 Melbourne 27/12/66 – 02/01/67 Perth 03/01/67 – 09/01/67 Adelaide 09/01/67 – 12/01/67 Canberra 16/01/67 – 23/01/67 Hobart 16/01/67 – 19/01/67 Canberra 13/03/68 – 19/03/68	ABC records show that the story was purchased on 06/10/66	ABC have records of destroying all four episodes on 27/07/76 ABC confirm they no longer have the episodes

WIPED!

Australia / ABC	13/04/67	Sydney 13/03/68 – 19/03/68 Melbourne 20/03/68 – 26/03/68 Brisbane 27/03/68 – 02/04/68 Perth 03/04/68 – 09/04/68 Adelaide 10/04/68 – 16/04/68 Hobart 17/04/68 – 23/04/68	ABC records show that the story was purchased on 06/10/66	ABC have records of destroying all four episodes on 27/07/76 ABC confirm they no longer have the episodes
Barbados / CBC	16/08/67	09/01/68 – 30/01/68		CBC confirm that they no longer have the episodes
Zambia / ZNBC	25/03/68	Kitwe ??/??/68 - ??/??/68 Lusaka 09/04/68 – 30/04/68		ZNBC confirm they no longer have the episodes
New Zealand / NZBC	18/12/68	Christchurch 16/02/69 – 09/03/69 Wellington 16/03/69 – 06/04/69 Auckland 27/04/69 – 18/05/69 Dunedin 04/05/69 – 25/05/69	NZBC records show that the film prints arrived in the country on 23/09/68 NZBC records show that censors made edits to Episodes Three and Four	All four episodes sent to RTS in Singapore on 20/09/72
Sierra Leone / SLBS	12/08/70	11/12/70 – 01/01/71		SLBS confirm that all four episodes were destroyed in 1999
Singapore / RTS	18/12/72	04/12/72 – 01/01/73	All 4 episodes received from NZBC in New Zealand on 20/09/72	RTS confirm they no longer have the episodes

APPENDIX I

THE CELESTIAL TOYMAKER (4 EPISODES)
EPISODES 1, 2 & 3 MISSING

Country / TV Station	BBC Sales Date	Transmission Dates	Notes	What Happened to the 16mm Prints...?
Australia / ABC	14/04/67	Sydney 03/01/67 – 09/01/67 Brisbane 10/01/67 – 16/01/67 Melbourne 10/01/67 – 16/01/67 Perth 17/01/67 – 23/01/67 Adelaide 23/01/67 – 26/01/67 Hobart 31/01/67 – 06/02/67 Canberra 01/02/67 – 08/02/67 Canberra 27/03/68 – 02/04/68 Sydney 27/03/68 – 02/04/68 Melbourne 03/04/68 – 09/04/68 Brisbane 10/04/68 – 16/04/68 Perth 17/04/68 – 23/04/68 Adelaide 24/04/68 – 30/04/68 Hobart 01/05/68 – 07/05/68	ABC records show that the story was purchased on 29/10/66	ABC have records of destroying Episode Four on 27/07/76 There is no record of them destroying Episodes One, Two or Three ABC confirm they no longer have the episodes Episode Four returned to the BBC by ABC in 1984, although this is thought to have been a print sent back from TVS in Singapore
Barbados / CBC	16/08/67	05/03/68 – 26/03/68		CBC confirm that they no longer have the episodes
Zambia / ZNBC	25/03/68	Kitwe ??/??/68 – ??/??/68 Lusaka 04/06/68 – 25/06/68		ZNBC confirm they no longer have the episodes
New Zealand / NZBC	18/12/68	Christchurch 13/04/69 – 04/05/69 Wellington 11/05/69 – 01/06/69 Auckland 22/06/69 – 13/07/69 Dunedin 29/06/69 – 20/07/69	NZBC records show that the film prints arrived in the country on 23/09/68 NZBC records show that censors made edits to Episodes Two and Four	All four episodes sent to RTS in Singapore on 20/09/72

WIPED!

Country / TV Station	BBC Sales Date	Transmission Dates	Notes	What Happened to the 16mm Prints...?
Sierra Leone / SLBS	12/08/70	05/02/71 – 26/02/71		SLBS confirm that all four episodes were destroyed in 1999
Singapore / RTS	18/12/72	05/02/73 – 26/02/73	All four episodes received from NZBC in New Zealand on 20/09/72	Episode Four sent to BBC Sydney in mid-1970s, where it ended up at ABC by mistake – ABC returned the print in 1984 RTS confirm they no longer have the episodes

THE SAVAGES (4 EPISODES)
EPISODES 1, 2, 3 & 4 MISSING

Country / TV Station	BBC Sales Date	Transmission Dates	Notes	What Happened to the 16mm Prints...?
Australia / ABC	14/04/67	Adelaide 24/03/67 – 14/04/67 Brisbane 24/03/67 – 14/04/67 Hobart 24/03/67 – 14/04/67 Perth 24/03/67 – 14/04/67 Sydney 31/03/67 – 21/04/67 Canberra 07/04/67 – 28/04/67 Melbourne 19/05/67 – 09/06/67 Canberra 10/04/68 – 16/04/68 Sydney 10/04/68 – 16/04/68 Melbourne 18/04/68 – 24/04/68 Brisbane 24/04/68 – 30/04/68 Perth 01/05/68 – 07/05/68 Adelaide 08/05/68 – 14/05/68 Hobart 15/05/68 – 21/05/68	ABC records show that the story was purchased on 28/11/66	ABC's rights to screen this story expired on 11/02/74 Film can references: 191/77 191/78 191/79 191/80 ABC have no records of them destroying/returning to the BBC any of the four episodes of this story However, ABC confirm they no longer have the episodes
Barbados / CBC	16/08/67	30/04/68 – 21/05/68		CBC confirm that they no longer have the episodes

APPENDIX I

Country / TV Station	BBC Sales Date	Transmission Dates	Notes	What Happened to the 16mm Prints...?
Zambia / ZNBC	25/03/68	Kitwe ??/??/68 - ??/??/68 Lusaka 06/08/68 – 27/08/68		ZNBC confirm they no longer have the episodes
New Zealand / NZBC	18/12/68	Christchurch 11/05/69 – 01/06/69 Wellington 08/06/69 – 29/06/69 Auckland 20/07/69 – 10/08/69 Dunedin 27/07/69 – 17/08/69	NZBC records show that the film prints arrived in the country on 23/09/68	All four episodes sent to RTS in Singapore on 10/01/72
Sierra Leone / SLBS	12/08/70	24/07/70 – 14/08/70		SLBS confirm that all four episodes were destroyed in 1999
Singapore / RTS	24/02/72	20/01/72 – 10/02/72	All four episodes received from NZBC in New Zealand on 10/01/72	RTS confirm they no longer have the episodes

THE SMUGGLERS (4 EPISODES)
EPISODES 1, 2, 3 & 4 MISSING

Country / TV Station	BBC Sales Date	Transmission Dates	Notes	What Happened to the 16mm Prints...?
Australia / ABC	14/04/67	Adelaide 19/05/67 – 09/06/67 Brisbane 19/05/67 – 09/06/67 Hobart 19/05/67 – 09/06/67 Perth 19/05/67 – 09/06/67 Sydney 26/05/67 – 16/06/67 Canberra 02/06/67 – 23/06/67 Melbourne 14/07/67 – 04/08/67 Canberra 24/04/68 – 30/04/68 Sydney 24/04/68 – 30/04/68 Melbourne 06/05/68 – 09/05/68 Brisbane 08/05/68 – 14/05/68 Perth 15/05/68 – 21/05/68	ABC records show that the story was purchased on 18/01/67 ABC records show that censors made edits to Episodes One, Three & Four	ABC had a duplicate print of Episode Two of this story ABC returned all four episodes of this story to the BBC on 04/06/75 It's possible that both copies of Episode Two were not returned in this batch However, ABC confirm they no longer have any episodes of this story

453

WIPED!

Australia / ABC	14/04/67	Adelaide 22/05/68 – 28/05/68 Hobart 29/05/68 – 04/06/68	ABC records show that the story was purchased on 18/01/67 ABC records show that censors made edits to Episodes One, Three & Four	ABC had a duplicate print of Episode Two of this story ABC returned all four episodes of this story to the BBC on 04/06/75 It's possible that both copies of Episode Two were not returned in this batch However, ABC confirm they no longer have any episodes of this story
Barbados / CBC	16/08/67	25/06/68 – 16/07/68		CBC confirm that they no longer have the episodes
Zambia / ZNBC	25/03/68	Kitwe ??/??/68 – ??/??/68 Lusaka 15/10/68 – 05/11/68		ZNBC confirm they no longer have the episodes
New Zealand / NZBC	18/12/68	Christchurch 06/07/69 – 27/07/69 Wellington 03/08/69 – 24/08/69 Auckland 14/09/69 – 05/10/69 Dunedin 21/09/69 – 12/10/69	NZBC records show that the film prints arrived in the country on 23/09/68 NZBC records show that censors made edits to all four episodes	All four episodes sent to RTS in Singapore on 10/01/72
Sierra Leone / SLBS	12/08/70	18/09/70 – 09/10/70		SLBS confirm that all four episodes were destroyed in 1999
Singapore / RTS	24/02/72	16/03/72 – 06/04/72	All four episodes received from NZBC in New Zealand on 10/01/72	RTS confirm they no longer have the episodes

APPENDIX I

THE TENTH PLANET (4 EPISODES)
EPISODE 4 MISSING

Country / TV Station	BBC Sales Date	Transmission Dates	Notes	What Happened to the 16mm Prints...?
Australia / ABC	23/08/67	Adelaide 16/06/67 – 07/07/67 Hobart 16/06/67 – 07/07/67 Perth 16/06/67 – 07/07/67 Brisbane 23/06/67 – 14/07/67 Sydney 23/06/67 – 14/07/67 Canberra 30/06/67 – 21/07/67 Melbourne 11/08/67 – 01/09/67 Canberra 01/05/68 – 07/05/68 Sydney 01/05/68 – 07/05/68 Melbourne 13/05/68 – 16/05/68 Brisbane 15/05/68 – 21/05/68 Perth 22/05/68 – 28/05/68 Adelaide 29/05/68 – 04/06/68 Hobart 05/06/68 – 11/06/68	ABC records show that the story was purchased on 31/05/67	ABC returned all four episodes of this story to the BBC on 04/06/75 ABC confirm they no longer have the episodes
New Zealand / NZBC	18/12/68	Christchurch 03/08/69 – 24/08/69 Wellington 31/08/69 – 21/09/69 Auckland 13/10/69 – 03/11/69 Dunedin 19/10/69 – 10/11/69	NZBC records show that the film prints arrived in the country on 23/09/68 NZBC records show that censors made edits to Episode Four	All four episodes sent to RTS in Singapore on 10/01/72
Singapore / RTS	24/02/72	13/04/72 – 04/05/72	All four episodes received from NZBC in New Zealand on 10/01/72	RTS confirm they no longer have the episodes

WIPED!

THE POWER OF THE DALEKS (6 EPISODES)
EPISODES 1, 2, 3, 4, 5 & 6 MISSING

Country / TV Station	BBC Sales Date	Transmission Dates	Notes	What Happened to the 16mm Prints...?
Australia / ABC	09/10/67 BBC Sales sheet is crossed through and annotated: 'Although programme withdrawn pay when invoiced – no other sales permitted 18/08/67'	Adelaide 14/07/67 – 18/08/67 Hobart 14/07/67 – 18/08/67 Perth 14/07/67 – 18/08/67 Brisbane 21/07/67 – 25/08/67 Sydney 21/07/67 – 25/08/67 Canberra 28/07/67 – 01/09/67 Melbourne 08/09/67 – 13/10/67 Canberra 08/05/68 – 16/05/68 Sydney 08/05/68 – 16/05/68 Melbourne 20/05/68 – 28/05/68 Brisbane 22/05/68 – 30/05/68 Perth 29/05/68 – 06/06/68 Adelaide 05/06/68 – 13/06/68 Hobart 12/06/68 – 20/06/68	ABC records show that the story was purchased on 07/06/67 The BBC's Sales Sheet notes that: 'Programme withdrawn – no other sales permitted 18/08/67'	ABC returned all six episodes of this story to the BBC on 04/06/75 ABC confirm they no longer have the episodes
New Zealand / NZBC	20/05/69 BBC Sales sheet is re-raised and 'Withdrawn' has been crossed through	Christchurch 31/08/69 – 05/10/69 Wellington 28/09/69 – 03/11/69 Auckland 10/11/69 – 15/12/69 Dunedin 17/11/69 – 22/12/69	NZBC records show that the film prints arrived in the country on 20/03/69 NZBC records show that censors made edits to Episodes Five and Six	All six episodes sent to RTS in Singapore on 10/01/72
Singapore / RTS	24/03/72	11/05/72 – 15/06/72	All 6 episodes received from NZBC in New Zealand on 10/01/72	RTS confirm they no longer have the episodes

APPENDIX I

THE HIGHLANDERS (4 EPISODES)
EPISODES 1, 2, 3 & 4 MISSING

Country / TV Station	BBC Sales Date	Transmission Dates	Notes	What Happened to the 16mm Prints...?
Australia / ABC	21/08/67	Adelaide 25/08/67 – 15/09/67 Hobart 25/08/67 – 15/09/67 Perth 25/08/67 – 15/09/67 Brisbane 01/09/67 – 22/09/67 Sydney 01/09/67 – 22/09/67 Canberra 08/09/67 – 29/09/67 Melbourne 20/10/67 – 10/11/67 Canberra 20/05/68 – 23/05/68 Sydney 20/05/68 – 23/05/68 Melbourne 29/05/68 – 04/06/68 Brisbane 03/06/68 – 06/06/68 Perth 10/06/68 – 13/06/68 Adelaide 17/06/68 – 20/06/68 Hobart 24/06/68 – 27/06/68	ABC records show that the story was purchased on 13/06/67 ABC records show that censors made edits to Episode One	ABC have records of destroying all four episodes on 27/07/76 ABC confirm they no longer have the episodes
Uganda / UTV	08/11/68	28/09/68 – 19/10/68		UTV confirm they no longer have the episodes
Singapore / RTS	12/03/69	13/02/69 – 06/03/69		RTS confirm they no longer have the episodes
Hong Kong / RTV	09/04/69	07/03/69 – 28/03/69		RTV confirm they no longer have the episodes
New Zealand / NZBC	24/06/69	Christchurch 12/10/69 – 03/11/69 Wellington 10/11/69 – 01/12/69 Auckland 22/12/69 – 12/01/70 Dunedin 29/12/69 – 19/01/70	NZBC records show that the film prints arrived in the country on 24/03/69	The fate of these films is unclear, but they were probably destroyed. Episode One is listed as destroyed, whilst episodes Two – Four have marks which look to be 'ditto' marks next to them

WIPED!

Country / TV Station	BBC Sales Date	Transmission Dates	Notes	What Happened to the 16mm Prints...?
Zambia / ZNBC	06/03/70	Kitwe ??/??/70 – ??/??/70 Lusaka 08/04/70 – 29/04/70		ZNBC confirm they no longer have the episodes

THE UNDERWATER MENACE (4 EPISODES)
EPISODES 1 & 4 MISSING

Country / TV Station	BBC Sales Date	Transmission Dates	Notes	What Happened to the 16mm Prints...?
Australia / ABC	21/08/67	Adelaide 22/09/67 – 13/10/67 Hobart 22/09/67 – 13/10/67 Perth 22/09/67 – 13/10/67 Brisbane 29/09/67 – 20/10/67 Sydney 29/09/67 – 20/10/67 Canberra 06/10/67 – 27/10/67 Melbourne 17/11/67 – 08/12/67 Canberra 27/05/68 – 30/05/68 Sydney 27/05/68 – 30/05/68 Melbourne 05/06/68 – 11/06/68 Brisbane 10/06/68 – 13/06/68	ABC records show that the story was purchased on 20/06/67 ABC records show that censors made edits to all four episodes	ABC returned all four episodes to the BBC on 04/06/75 The BBC junked all four prints, but the 16mm film of Episode Two survived and passed into the hands of a private collector Episode Two returned to the BBC in 2011
Australia / ABC	21/08/67	Perth 17/06/68 – 20/06/68 Adelaide 24/06/68 – 27/06/68 Hobart 01/07/68 – 04/07/68	ABC records show that the story was purchased on 20/06/67	ABC records show that the story was purchased on 20/06/67
Uganda / UTV	08/11/68	26/10/68 – 16/11/68		UTV confirm they no longer have the episodes
Singapore / RTS	12/03/69	13/03/69 – 03/04/69		RTS confirm they no longer have the episodes
Hong Kong / RTV	09/04/69	04/04/69 – 25/04/69		RTV confirm they no longer have the episodes

APPENDIX I

Country / TV Station	BBC Sales Date	Transmission Dates	Notes	What Happened to the 16mm Prints...?
New Zealand / NZBC	24/06/69	Christchurch 10/11/69 – 01/12/69 Wellington 08/12/69 – 29/12/69 Auckland 19/01/70 – 09/02/70 Dunedin 26/01/70 – 16/02/70	NZBC records show that the film prints arrived in the country on 11/04/69	The fate of these films is unclear, but they were probably destroyed. However, the story is also listed as being in the Harriett Street store as of 01/04/70
Zambia / ZNBC	06/03/70	Kitwe ??/??/70 - ??/??/70 Lusaka 06/05/70 – 27/05/70		ZNBC confirm they no longer have the episodes

THE MOONBASE (4 EPISODES)
EPISODES 1 & 3 MISSING

Country / TV Station	BBC Sales Date	Transmission Dates	Notes	What Happened to the 16mm Prints...?
Australia / ABC	16/02/68	Adelaide 20/10/67 – 10/11/67 Hobart 20/10/67 – 10/11/67 Perth 20/10/67 – 10/11/67 Brisbane 27/10/67 – 17/11/67 Sydney 27/10/67 – 17/11/67 Canberra 03/11/67 – 24/11/67 Melbourne 15/12/67 – 05/01/68 Canberra 03/06/68 – 06/06/68 Sydney 03/06/68 – 06/06/68 Melbourne 12/06/68 – 18/06/68 Brisbane 17/06/68 – 20/06/68 Perth 24/06/68 – 27/06/68 Adelaide 01/07/68 – 04/07/68 Hobart 08/07/68 – 11/07/68	ABC records show that the story was purchased on 21/09/67	ABC returned all four episodes to the BBC on 04/06/75 ABC confirm they no longer have the episodes
Uganda / UTV	08/11/68	23/11/68 – 14/12/68		UTV confirm they no longer have the episodes

WIPED!

Country / TV Station	BBC Sales Date	Transmission Dates	Notes	What Happened to the 16mm Prints...?
Singapore / RTS	12/03/69	10/04/69 – 01/05/69		RTS confirm they no longer have the episodes
Hong Kong / RTV	09/04/69	02/05/69 – 23/05/69		RTV confirm they no longer have the episodes
New Zealand / NZBC	11/08/69	Christchurch 08/12/69 – 29/12/69 Wellington 05/01/70 – 26/01/70 Auckland 26/06/70 -17/07/70 Dunedin 10/07/70 – 31/07/70		All four episodes almost certainly sent to Harriett Street store Junked c1975 Original 16mm film tin for Episode Three found in TVNZ in 1990
Zambia / ZNBC	06/03/70	Kitwe ??/??/70 - ??/??/70 Lusaka 10/06/70 – 01/07/70		ZNBC confirm they no longer have the episodes

THE MACRA TERROR (4 EPISODES)
EPISODES 1, 2, 3 & 4 MISSING

Country / TV Station	BBC Sales Date	Transmission Dates	Notes	What Happened to the 16mm Prints...?
Australia / ABC	16/02/68	Adelaide 17/11/67 – 08/12/67 Hobart 17/11/67 – 08/12/67 Perth 17/11/67 – 08/12/67 Brisbane 24/11/67 – 15/12/67 Sydney 24/11/67 – 15/12/67 Canberra 01/12/67 – 22/12/67 Melbourne 12/01/68 – 02/02/68 Sydney 10/06/68 – 13/06/68 Canberra 10/06/68 – 13/06/68 Melbourne 19/06/68 – 25/06/68 Brisbane 24/06/68 – 27/06/68 Perth 01/07/68 – 04/07/68	ABC records show that the story was purchased on 12/10/67 ABC records show that censors made edits to Episodes Two & Three	ABC have records of destroying all four episodes on 27/07/76 ABC confirm they no longer have the episodes

APPENDIX I

Country / TV Station	BBC Sales Date	Transmission Dates	Notes	What Happened to the 16mm Prints...?
Australia / ABC	16/02/68	Adelaide 08/07/68 – 11/07/68 Hobart 15/07/68 – 18/07/68	ABC records show that the story was purchased on 12/10/67 ABC records show that censors made edits to Episodes Two & Three	ABC have records of destroying all four episodes on 27/07/76 ABC confirm they no longer have the episodes
Uganda / UTV	08/11/68	28/12/68 – 18/01/69		UTV confirm they no longer have the episodes
Singapore / RTS	12/03/69	08/05/69 – 29/05/69		RTS confirm they no longer have the episodes
Hong Kong / RTV	09/04/69	30/05/69 – 20/06/69		RTV confirm they no longer have the episodes
New Zealand / NZBC	11/08/69	Christchurch 05/01/70 – 26/01/70 Wellington 02/02/70 – 23/02/70 Auckland 24/07/70 – 14/08/70 Dunedin 07/08/70 – 28/08/70		All four episodes destroyed 24/06/74
Zambia / ZNBC	06/03/70	Kitwe ??/??/70 - ??/??/70 Lusaka 08/07/70 – 29/07/70		ZNBC confirm they no longer have the episodes

THE FACELESS ONES (6 EPISODES)
EPISODES 2, 4, 5 & 6 MISSING

Country / TV Station	BBC Sales Date	Transmission Dates	Notes	What Happened to the 16mm Prints...?
Australia / ABC	16/02/68	Adelaide 15/12/67 – 19/01/68 Hobart 15/12/67 – 19/01/68 Perth 15/12/67 – 19/01/68 Brisbane 22/12/67 – 26/01/68 Sydney 22/12/67 – 26/01/68 Canberra 29/12/67 – 02/02/68	ABC records show that the story was purchased on 30/10/67 ABC records show that censors made edits to Episode One	ABC returned Episodes Two, Three, Four, Five & Six to the BBC on 04/06/75 The Ex-ABC 16mm edited print of Episode One held by a private collector, c1968 Print passed to David Gee in 1970 ABC confirm they no longer have the episodes

461

WIPED!

Country / TV Station	BBC Sales Date	Transmission Dates	Notes	What Happened to the 16mm Prints...?
Australia / ABC	16/02/68	Melbourne 26/06/68 – 04/07/68 Canberra 17/06/68 – 25/06/68 Sydney 17/06/68 – 25/06/68 Brisbane 01/07/68 – 09/07/68 Perth 08/07/68 – 16/07/68 Adelaide 15/07/68 – 23/07/68 Hobart 22/07/68 – 30/07/68 Melbourne 12/05/69 – 16/05/69	ABC records show that the story was purchased on 30/10/67 ABC records show that censors made edits to Episode One	ABC returned Episodes Two, Three, Four, Five & Six to the BBC on 04/06/75 The Ex-ABC 16mm edited print of Episode One held by a private collector, c1968 Print passed to David Gee in 1970 ABC confirm they no longer have the episodes
Uganda / UTV	08/11/68	25/01/69 – 08/03/69		UTV confirm they no longer have the episodes
Singapore / RTS	12/03/69	05/06/69 – 10/07/69		RTS confirm they no longer have the episodes
Hong Kong / RTV	09/04/69	27/06/69 – 01/08/69		RTV confirm they no longer have the episodes
New Zealand / NZBC	Sale not recorded by the BBC	Not shown	NZBC records show that the film prints arrived in the country on 12/08/69	Censors rejected – the films were returned to London 03/07/70
Zambia / ZNBC	06/03/70	Kitwe ??/??/73 - ??/??/73 Lusaka 11/06/73 – 16/07/73		ZNBC confirm they no longer have the episodes

THE EVIL OF THE DALEKS (7 EPISODES)
EPISODES 1, 3, 4, 5, 6 & 7 MISSING

Country / TV Station	BBC Sales Date	Transmission Dates	Notes	What Happened to the 16mm Prints...?
Australia / ABC	10/03/69	Canberra 12/01/69 – 23/02/69 Sydney 12/01/69 – 23/02/69 Melbourne 19/01/69 – 02/03/69 Brisbane 26/01/69 – 09/03/69	ABC records show that the story was purchased on 01/11/68	ABC returned all seven episodes to the BBC on 04/06/75 ABC confirm they no longer have the episodes

APPENDIX I

Australia / ABC	10/03/69	Perth 02/02/69 – 16/03/69 Adelaide 09/02/69 – 23/03/69 Hobart 16/02/69 – 30/03/69 Canberra 08/05/69 – 16/05/69 Sydney 08/05/69 – 16/05/69 Hobart 22/08/69 – 01/09/69 Perth ??/??/69 – ??/?/69 Brisbane 08/12/69 – 29/12/69 Adelaide 22/12/69 – 12/01/70 Melbourne 02/01/70 – 12/01/70	ABC records show that the story was purchased on 01/11/68	ABC returned all seven episodes to the BBC on 04/06/75 ABC confirm they no longer have the episodes
Hong Kong / RTV	25/11/69	08/08/69 – 26/09/69		RTV confirm they no longer have the episodes
Singapore / RTS	06/01/70	04/12/69 – 15/01/70		RTS confirm they no longer have the episodes
New Zealand / NZBC	24/07/70	Wellington 19/06/70 – 31/07/70 Christchurch 03/07/70 – 14/08/70 Auckland 21/08/70 – 02/10/70 Dunedin 04/09/70 – 16/10/70	NZBC records show that the film prints arrived in the country on 15/09/69 NZBC records show that censors made edits to Episodes Four & Five	NZBC destroyed all seven episodes, date not recorded

The first overseas sale of 'The Evil of the Daleks' was to ABC in Australia, and this was some *seven months* after the following two stories 'The Tomb of the Cybermen' and 'The Abominable Snowmen' were sold to ABC (and over a year *after* the sale of the preceding story, 'The Faceless Ones' to ABC). Consequently, the first ABC screenings of this story in Australia confusingly positioned it between 'The Web of Fear' and 'Fury from the Deep' in transmission order.

Details of the story's transmission dates in Singapore and Hong Kong are partially incomplete, but what is known suggests that those countries' stations were able to slot 'The Evil of the Daleks' into its correct position in the story transmission order.

The various NZBC regions in New Zealand were running stories much later

WIPED!

than the rest of the world, and so were able to screen 'The Evil of the Daleks' after 'The Macra Terror' (as 'The Faceless Ones' wasn't screened at all), and then continue through to the fifth season with 'The Tomb of the Cybermen'.

THE ABOMINABLE SNOWMEN (6 EPISODES)
EPISODES 1, 3, 4, 5 & 6 MISSING

Country / TV Station	BBC Sales Date	Transmission Dates	Notes	What Happened to the 16mm Prints…?
Australia / ABC	16/08/68	Canberra 02/08/68 – 06/09/68 Sydney 02/08/68 – 06/09/68 Melbourne 10/08/68 – 13/09/68 Brisbane 16/08/68 – 20/09/68 Perth 23/08/68 – 27/09/68 Adelaide 30/08/68 – 04/10/68 Hobart 06/09/68 – 11/10/68 Perth 05/05/69 – 12/05/69 Adelaide 22/05/69 – 26/05/69 Brisbane 11/08/69 – 15/08/69 Canberra 28/08/69 – 04/09/69 Sydney 28/08/69 – 04/09/69 Melbourne 13/01/70 – 20/01/70 Hobart 01/05/70 – 08/05/70	ABC records show that the story was purchased on 05/03/68	ABC returned all six episodes to the BBC on 04/06/75 ABC confirm they no longer have the episodes
Hong Kong / RTV	25/11/69	03/10/69 – 07/11/69		RTV confirm they no longer have the episodes
Singapore / RTS	04/05/70	05/03/70 – 09/04/70		RTS confirm they no longer have the episodes
New Zealand / NZBC	06/10/70	Wellington 04/09/70 – 09/10/70 Christchurch 18/09/70 – 23/10/70 Auckland 06/11/70 – 11/12/70 Dunedin 20/11/70 – 01/01/71	NZBC records show that the film prints arrived in the country on 21/10/69	NZBC records simply say 'Exp 31/08/73' – this is either the date the prints were sent on elsewhere, the date the rights to screen the story expired, or the date they were destroyed

APPENDIX I

Gibraltar / GBC	18/04/73	23/04/73 – 28/05/73		
Zambia / ZNBC	04/10/73	Kitwe ??/??/73 – ??/??/73 Lusaka 23/07/73 – 27/08/73		ZNBC confirm they no longer have the episodes
Nigeria / BPTV	24/10/74	11/03/75 – 15/04/75		

THE ICE WARRIORS (6 EPISODES)
EPISODES 2 & 3 MISSING

Country / TV Station	BBC Sales Date	Transmission Dates	Notes	What Happened to the 16mm Prints…?
Australia / ABC	20/08/68	Canberra 08/09/68 – 13/10/68 Sydney 08/09/68 – 13/10/68 Melbourne 15/09/68 – 20/10/68 Brisbane 22/09/68 – 27/10/68 Perth 29/09/68 – 03/11/68 Adelaide 06/10/68 – 10/11/68 Hobart 13/10/68 – 17/11/68 Brisbane 18/08/69 – 22/08/69 Adelaide 29/08/69 – 05/09/69 Perth 01/09/69 – 05/09/69 Canberra 12/12/69 – 22/12/70 Sydney 12/12/69 – 22/12/70 Hobart 22/12/69 – 06/01/70 Melbourne 21/01/70 – 30/01/70	ABC records show that the story was purchased on 13/03/68	ABC returned all six episodes to the BBC on 04/06/75 ABC confirm they no longer have the episodes
Germany / ZDF	Not purchased	Not shown	Prints of this story (possibly all six episodes) sent to ZDF as audition points in May 1968, but story (or series) not purchased	ZDF confirm they no longer hold the film prints

465

WIPED!

Country / TV Station	BBC Sales Date	Transmission Dates	Notes	What Happened to the 16mm Prints...?
Hong Kong / RTV	25/11/69	14/11/69 – 19/12/69		RTV confirm they no longer have the episodes
Singapore / RTS	04/05/70	16/04/70 – 21/05/70		RTS confirm they no longer have the episodes
New Zealand / NZBC	Sale not recorded by the BBC	Not shown	NZBC records show that the film prints arrived in the country on 28/10/70	Censors rejected – no further details NZBC confirm they no longer have the episodes
Gibraltar / GBC	18/04/73	04/06/73 – 09/07/73		
Zambia / ZNBC	04/10/73	Kitwe ??/??/73 - ??/??/73 Lusaka 03/09/73 – 08/10/73		ZNBC confirm they no longer have the episodes

THE ENEMY OF THE WORLD (6 EPISODES)
EPISODES 1, 2, 4, 5 & 6 MISSING

Country / TV Station	BBC Sales Date	Transmission Dates	Notes	What Happened to the 16mm Prints...?
Australia / ABC	08/11/68	Canberra 20/10/68 – 24/11/68 Sydney 20/10/68 – 24/11/68 Melbourne 27/10/68 – 01/12/68 Brisbane 03/11/68 – 08/12/68 Perth 10/11/68 – 15/12/68 Adelaide 17/11/68 – 22/12/68 Hobart 24/11/68 – 29/12/68 Adelaide 08/09/69 – 12/09/69 Perth 08/09/69 – 12/09/69 Canberra 02/01/70 – 09/01/70 Sydney 02/01/70 – 09/01/70 Hobart 12/01/70 – 20/01/70 Brisbane 18/08/70 – 21/08/70 Melbourne 24/08/70 – 28/08/70	ABC records show that the story was purchased on 18/06/68	ABC returned all six episodes to the BBC on 04/06/75 ABC confirm they no longer have the episodes

APPENDIX I

Country / TV Station	BBC Sales Date	Transmission Dates	Notes	What Happened to the 16mm Prints...?
Hong Kong / RTV	25/11/69	02/01/70 – 06/02/70		RTV confirm they no longer have the episodes
Singapore / RTS	04/05/70	28/05/70 – 02/07/70		RTS confirm they no longer have the episodes
New Zealand / NZBC	13/05/71	Wellington 03/05/71 – 07/06/71 Auckland 10/05/71 – 14/06/71 Christchurch 17/05/71 – 21/06/71 Dunedin 24/05/71 – 28/06/71	NZBC records show that the film prints arrived in the country on 04/11/70 NZBC records show that censors made edits to Episodes Four & Five	NZBC confirm they no longer have the episodes
Gibraltar / GBC	19/04/73	16/07/73 – 20/08/73		
Zambia / ZNBC	04/10/73	Kitwe ??/??/73 - ??/??/73 Lusaka 15/10/73 – 19/11/73		ZNBC confirm they no longer have the episodes
Nigeria / BPTV	24/10/74	22/04/75 – 27/05/75		

THE WEB OF FEAR (6 EPISODES)
EPISODES 2, 3, 4, 5 & 6 MISSING

Country / TV Station	BBC Sales Date	Transmission Dates	Notes	What Happened to the 16mm Prints...?
Australia / ABC	07/01/69	Canberra 01/12/68 – 05/01/69 Sydney 01/12/68 – 05/01/69 Melbourne 08/12/68 – 12/01/69 Brisbane 15/12/68 – 19/01/69 Perth 22/12/68 – 26/01/69 Adelaide 29/12/68 – 02/02/69 Hobart 05/01/69 – 09/02/69 Brisbane 02/01/70 – 09/01/70 Canberra 12/01/70 – 19/01/70	ABC records show that the story was purchased on 11/06/68	ABC returned all six episodes to the BBC on 04/06/75 ABC confirm they no longer have the episodes

467

WIPED!

Country / Broadcaster	Date	Transmission dates	Notes	Status
Australia / ABC	07/01/69	Sydney 12/01/70 – 19/01/70 Adelaide 15/01/70 – 23/01/70 Hobart 22/01/70 – 01/02/70 Perth ??/??/70 – ??/??/70 Melbourne 31/08/70 – 04/09/70	ABC records show that the story was purchased on 11/06/68	ABC returned all six episodes to the BBC on 04/06/75 ABC confirm they no longer have the episodes
Hong Kong / RTV	06/03/70	27/03/70 – 01/05/70		RTV confirm they no longer have the episodes
Singapore / RTS	04/05/70	09/07/70 – 13/08/70		RTS confirm they no longer have the episodes
New Zealand / NZBC	22/02/72	Wellington 14/06/71 – 19/07/71 Auckland 21/06/71 – 26/07/71 Christchurch 28/06/71 – 02/08/71 Dunedin 05/07/71 – 09/08/71	NZBC records show that the film prints arrived in the country on 09/11/70 NZBC records show that censors made edits to all six episodes	NZBC confirm they no longer have the episodes
Gibraltar / GBC	19/04/73	27/08/73 – 20/08/73		
Zambia / ZNBC	04/10/73	Kitwe ??/??/73 - ??/??/73 Lusaka 26/11/73 – 31/12/73		ZNBC confirm they no longer have the episodes
Nigeria / BPTV	24/10/74	03/06/75 – 08/07/75		

APPENDIX I

FURY FROM THE DEEP (6 EPISODES)
EPISODES 1, 2, 3, 4, 5 & 6 MISSING

Country / TV Station	BBC Sales Date	Transmission Dates	Notes	What Happened to the 16mm Prints...?
Australia / ABC	09/04/69	Canberra 02/03/69 – 06/04/69 Sydney 02/03/69 – 06/04/69 Melbourne 09/03/69 – 13/04/69 Brisbane 16/03/69 – 20/04/69 Perth 23/03/69 – 27/04/69 Adelaide 30/03/69 – 04/05/69 Hobart 06/04/69 – 11/05/69 Brisbane 13/01/70 – 21/01/70 Canberra 20/01/70 – 22/01/70 Sydney 20/01/70 – 22/01/70 Adelaide 27/01/70 – 02/02/70 Perth 24/08/70 – 31/08/70 Hobart 28/08/70 – 04/09/70 Darwin 15/08/71 – 19/09/71 Melbourne 23/08/71 – 30/08/71	ABC records show that the story was purchased on 22/01/69 ABC records show that censors made edits to Episodes Two, Four & Five	ABC have no records of them destroying/returning to the BBC any of the six episodes of this story However, ABC confirm they no longer have the episodes
Hong Kong / RTV	06/03/70	08/05/70 – 12/06/70		RTV confirm they no longer have the episodes
Singapore / RTS	04/05/70	20/08/70 – 24/09/70		RTS confirm they no longer have the episodes
New Zealand / NZBC	Sale not recorded by the BBC	Not shown	NZBC records show that the film prints arrived in the country on 01/12/70	Censors rejected – no further details. NZBC confirm they no longer have the episodes
Gibraltar / GBC	19/04/73	08/10/73 – 10/11/73		

WIPED!

THE WHEEL IN SPACE (6 EPISODES)
EPISODES 1, 2, 4 & 5 MISSING

Country / TV Station	BBC Sales Date	Transmission Dates	Notes	What Happened to the 16mm Prints...?
Australia / ABC	No BBC Sales Clearance History sheets are known to exist for this story	Canberra 13/04/69 – 18/05/69 Sydney 13/04/69 – 18/05/69 Melbourne 20/04/69 – 25/05/69 Brisbane 27/04/69 – 01/06/69 Perth 04/05/69 – 08/06/69 Adelaide 11/05/69 – 15/06/69 Hobart 18/05/69 – 22/06/69 Canberra 24/08/70 – 28/08/70 Sydney 31/08/70 – 07/09/70 Adelaide 04/09/70 – 11/09/70 Brisbane 14/12/70 – 21/12/70 Melbourne 18/12/70 – 28/12/70 Hobart 29/12/70 – 06/01/71 Perth 08/01/71 – 15/01/71	ABC records show that the story was purchased on 13/03/69 ABC records show that censors made edits to Episode Four	ABC have records of destroying all six episodes on 27/07/76 ABC confirm they no longer have the episodes
Hong Kong / RTV		13/02/70 – 20/03/70	Other BBC rights paperwork dates this sale as May 1970	RTV confirm they no longer have the episodes
Singapore / RTS		01/10/70 – 05/11/70	Other BBC rights paperwork dates this sale as May 1970	RTS confirm they no longer have the episodes
New Zealand / NZBC		Wellington 26/07/71 – 30/08/71 Auckland 02/08/71 – 06/09/71 Christchurch 09/08/71 – 13/09/71 Dunedin 16/08/71 – 20/09/71	NZBC records show that the film prints arrived in the country on 19/11/70 NZBC records show that censors made edits to Episodes Three, Five & Six	NZBC confirm they no longer have the episodes

APPENDIX I

Country / TV Station	BBC Sales Date	Transmission Dates	Notes	What Happened to the 16mm Prints…?
Gibraltar / GBC	No BBC Sales Clearance History sheets are known to exist for this story	17/11/73 – 22/12/73	GBC purchased the two stories either side of 'The Wheel in Space' on 19/04/73.	
Nigeria / BPTV		15/07/75 – 19/08/75		

THE INVASION (8 EPISODES)
EPISODES 1 & 4 MISSING

Country / TV Station	BBC Sales Date	Transmission Dates	Notes	What Happened to the 16mm Prints…?
Australia / ABC	No BBC Sales Clearance History sheets are known to exist for this story	Melbourne 03/07/70 – 21/08/70 Sydney 05/07/70 – 23/08/70 Brisbane 10/07/70 – 28/08/70 Perth 12/07/70 – 30/08/70 Adelaide 17/07/70 – 04/09/70 Canberra 19/07/70 – 06/09/70 Hobart 31/07/70 – 18/09/70 Canberra 20/01/70 – 28/01/70 Sydney 20/01/71 – 28/01/71 Adelaide 30/08/71 – 08/09/71 Darwin 05/12/71 – 23/01/72 Brisbane 16/12/71 – 24/12/71 Melbourne 17/01/72 – 26/01/72 Hobart 03/09/71 – 14/09/71 Perth ??/??/72 – ??/??/72	ABC records show that the story was purchased on 24/07/70	ABC returned all eight episodes to the BBC on 04/06/75 ABC confirm they no longer have the episodes
Hong Kong / RTV		25/09/70 – 13/11/70	Other BBC rights paperwork dates this sale as May 1970	RTV confirm they no longer have the episodes

WIPED!

Country / TV Station	BBC Sales Date	Transmission Dates	Notes	What Happened to the 16mm Prints…?
Singapore / RTS	No BBC Sales Clearance History sheets are known to exist for this story	21/01/71 – 11/03/71	RTS purchased the two stories either side of 'The Invasion' on 12/02/71	RTS confirm they no longer have the episodes
Gibraltar / GBC		25/04/72 – 12/06/72	Other BBC rights paperwork dates this sale as August 1972	

THE SPACE PIRATES (6 EPISODES)
EPISODES 1, 3, 4, 5 & 6 MISSING

Country / TV Station	BBC Sales Date	Transmission Dates	Notes	What Happened to the 16mm Prints…?
Australia / ABC	13/05/71	Melbourne 21/03/71 – 25/04/71 Adelaide 28/03/71 – 02/05/71 Canberra 11/04/71 – 16/05/71 Sydney 11/04/71 – 16/05/71 Brisbane 18/04/71 – 23/05/71 Perth 18/04/71 – 23/05/71 Hobart 09/05/71 – 13/06/71 Perth 14/01/72 – 21/01/72 Canberra 18/01/72 – 25/01/72 Sydney 19/01/72 – 26/01/72 Darwin 09/04/72 – 14/05/72 Hobart 09/05/72 – 17/05/72 Adelaide 12/05/72 – 18/05/72 Brisbane 07/05/73 – 14/05/73 Melbourne 14/05/73 – 21/05/73	ABC records show that the story was purchased on 25/08/70	ABC returned all six episodes to the BBC on 04/06/75 ABC confirm they no longer have the episodes
Hong Kong / RTV	13/05/71	05/02/71 – 12/03/71		RTV confirm they no longer have the episodes

APPENDIX I

Singapore / RTS	29/10/71	27/05/71 – 01/07/71		RTS confirm they no longer have the episodes
Gibraltar / GBC	09/08/72	28/08/72 – 02/10/72		
Zambia / ZNBC	01/04/76	Kitwe ??/??/76 - ??/??/76 Lusaka 18/03/76 – 22/04/76		ZNBC confirm they no longer have the episodes

WIPED!

APPENDIX II
THE ARCHIVES TODAY: 1963-1989

This Appendix looks at the current BBC archive holdings of classic-era *Doctor Who*, and details which is the best copy of each of the various episodes still existing. I've listed the format on which the best copy was originally held, but have also indicated where the BBC's archived copy is now on another format.

To summarise briefly, from 1963 through to 1983, *Doctor Who* was generally made and transmitted on two-inch videotape (the exceptions being the odd black and white episode shown from a 35mm telerecording, and 'Spearhead from Space' on 16mm colour film). From 'An Unearthly Child' to Episode Six of 'The Ice Warriors', this was 405-line black and white two-inch tape[92]. From Episode One of 'The Enemy of the World' through to the final episode of 'The War Games', this was 625-line black and white two-inch tape. From 'Doctor Who and the Silurians' through to 'The Five Doctors', the format was 625-line two-inch colour tape. After 1983, from 'Warriors of the Deep' through to 'Survival', the format switched to 625-line colour one-inch tape.

None of the black and white two-inch tapes survives at the BBC. About 50% of the two-inch tapes for the Jon Pertwee stories were also junked in the early 1970s, but the others, along with all of those for the Tom Baker and Peter Davison stories up to and including 'The Five Doctors', were kept by the BBC until 1993. That year saw the start of the Quad tape archiving project, which involved the BBC systematically copying all of its two-inch tapes (which numbered in excess of 69,000) onto D3 videocassette. Two copies of each tape were made – one was archived, one was kept as a viewing copy – before the original was sent to the National Film and Television Archive (NFTVA) in Hertfordshire for storage. From about 1997, this changed to making one Digital Betacam copy (the archived master) and one D3 copy.

While the two-inch tape archiving project was well under way, the BBC began archiving all of its one-inch tapes as well, this time onto Digital Betacam video cassette – the two projects overlapped. This included the broadcast masters of the remainder of the Davison stories, and all of the Colin Baker and Sylvester McCoy ones. Again, two copies of each tape were made for the Film and Videotape Library. Once the one-inch tapes had been copied, they were then junked, unlike the two-inch tapes.

---

92 For many years, the switch from 405-line to 625-line was thought to have occurred between Episodes Two and Three of 'The Enemy of the World', as this is when the difference was first noted on the BBC's P-as-C records. However, the BBC's videotape wipe forms consistently note that the first two episodes of 'The Enemy of the World' were 625-line recordings, so on the balance of probability, I have decided to go along with this information as correct.

In 2007, the BBC began transferring all of its D3 cassettes (including all the dubs of the two-inch material) onto Digital Betacam for long-term storage.

The Film and Videotape Library retains all its original film material, both 35mm and 16mm, colour and black and white. However, in *Doctor Who*'s case, a Digital Betacam copy has been made of nearly every black and white episode, as a by-product of them being re-mastered for DVD. The only black and white *Doctor Who* episodes the BBC don't hold as film prints are a few that have been returned from private collectors, where the BBC have taken only a videotape copy before returning the original print to the collector in question.

The BBC's policy on film prints in the 1970s and 1980s was that negatives were best. Therefore, if the BBC held material only as a positive print, a negative would be made from it, and this would become the archived copy, even though it was a generation down in quality. Prints loaned to the BBC from private collectors would usually have negatives made from them, which the BBC would archive before handing the print back. Because of this, it's sometimes difficult to pinpoint which is the best copy of an episode, as the archived negative might have been made from a non-archived positive. Whenever possible, I've tried to indicate in the sections below which is the best copy of an episode held on film.

A word about private collections. Over the years, collectors have played an important part in ensuring that material that was once junked by the BBC still survives in some shape or form. Nearly all of the items mentioned in this Appendix as being held in private collections have been made available to the BBC over the years, for use in documentaries or as bonus material on DVD releases. In some instances, the BBC has retained a copy of some, if not all, of the material. Sometimes it has not. So I have been occasionally vague when describing if some of the privately-owned material has had copies made by the BBC.

THE FIRST DOCTOR
WILLIAM HARTNELL (1963-1966)

AN UNEARTHLY CHILD (4 EPISODES)

Episodes One, Two, Three and Four all have black and white 16mm film negatives and positives (running to 877 feet, 922 feet, 886 feet and 1000 feet respectively), all with optical sound, plus separate magnetic soundtracks for all four episodes. These are all Stored Field recordings, made in 1967, as recovered from BBC Enterprises in 1978.

A 16mm film print of the untransmitted pilot episode is also held by the BBC, which runs to around 40 minutes, as it includes three takes of the final TARDIS scene. This is a Stored Field recording. A separate magnetic soundtrack exists for this

APPENDIX II

recording. This was always held at the BBC Film Library.

A 16mm positive print with a Spanish soundtrack of Episode One is also held, which came from BBC Enterprises in 1978.

A (mute) 16mm film negative labelled as 'stock shots' is held, running to 47 feet. This is held by the BBC Film and Videotape Library against Episode One's programme number and is stock colour film of stars and galaxies. It is not known precisely which – if any – episode of *Doctor Who* this stock film was used in, and so it is logged against the first episode as per the common practice for the BBC Film and Videotape Library.[93]

THE DALEKS (7 EPISODES)

All seven episodes have black and white 16mm film positives (running to 1000 feet, 900 feet, 900 feet, 900 feet, 900 feet, 900 feet and 900 feet respectively), plus 16mm film negatives of Episodes One to Six only. Nearly all the films have optical soundtracks, although the 16mm negative of Episode Four is mute. During remastering for the DVD release of this story in 2005, it was found that the prints of Episodes Five and Seven are Suppressed Field telerecordings (in Episode Seven's case, this is the *only* film copy), while the other five are all Stored Field recordings. Separate magnetic soundtracks exist for Episodes One, Two, Four and Seven.

When this story was recovered from BBC Enterprises in 1978, 16mm prints and negatives were found of all seven episodes. Only the negatives were archived as masters, while the positive prints were kept in the BBC Film and Videotape Library as viewing copies. During one viewing, the print of Episode Seven was damaged (mainly in the last five minutes), and so the negative was called up to have a new viewing print made. It was only then discovered that what was *thought* to be a 16mm film negative of the episode was actually just the separate magnetic soundtrack, which had been misfiled. Of the negative itself, which had been recovered in 1978, there was no trace. So for years, the only remaining copy of this episode had been used as a viewing print, and had been damaged in the process. Luckily a one-inch video copy made by BBC Enterprises in 1993 was located, and it was discovered that most of the damage had occurred after this copy was made.

A short section of Episode Five – a scene of the Daleks in their control room – also exists as a 35mm film telerecording. This was made sometime in 1964 from the original 405-line two-inch tape, for use in a feature in an edition of *Blue Peter*. This section is of a superior picture quality to the 16mm films of the episode, and was used

---

93 In the first edition of 'Wiped!', I mentioned that this film was 'thought to be the film sequence used when the TARDIS first dematerialises, mainly the shot of London fading away on the scanner'. The film has been viewed since the first edition was published, and found to be this colour 'stars and galaxies' material.

in the remastered version released on DVD.

A Spanish sound negative for Episode Seven is also held by the BBC Film and Videotape Library.

THE EDGE OF DESTRUCTION (2 EPISODES)

Episode One has both a 16mm film positive and negative (941 feet), while Episode Two has a 16mm film negative only (900 feet), although a poor quality viewing print is also held. Both episodes have optical soundtracks. Separate magnetic soundtracks also exist.

A 16mm positive film print of Episode Two with an Arabic soundtrack exists. This was found at BBC Enterprises in 1978.

During the remastering of this story for VHS release in 1999, the BBC's master negative of the second episode was found to have had the last five minutes of material spliced into it from another, inferior, negative of the same episode. The patched section was from a Suppressed Field telerecording. The rest of the episode, along with the prints of Episode One, were all Stored Field recordings.

MARCO POLO (7 EPISODES)

No episodes exist at the BBC.

Off-air audio recordings of all seven episodes remain. David Holman's are the best quality, although approximately 10 seconds is missing from his copy of Episode Seven. John de Rivaz also has audio recordings of all seven episodes.[94]

Director Waris Hussein retained Tele-snaps of six of the seven episodes (all bar Episode Four). A further eight off-air photos were taken by an Australian fan during the story's screening on the ABC in the 1960s.

THE KEYS OF MARINUS (6 EPISODES)

All six episodes have black and white 16mm film negatives (running to 872 feet, 944 feet, 892 feet, 930 feet, 937 feet and 900 feet respectively), plus 16mm film positives of Episodes Two, Three, Four and Six only (although viewing prints are available for all episodes). All six episodes have optical soundtracks. These were all found at BBC Enterprises in 1978.

A black and white 16mm fine grain duplicate negative exists at the BBC for Episode Five, although this isn't archived. It's probably the copy that was originally held by the BBC Film Library up to 1977.

A 16mm positive film print of Episode One with an Arabic soundtrack is also

---

[94] The quality of John de Rivaz's recordings for all the 1960s episodes has yet to be fully assessed, so it is possible than in due course some of these may supersede others as the copies judged to be the best surviving.

held, again hailing from BBC Enterprises in 1978.

When remastering this story for DVD release in 2008, it was discovered that a number of cuts had been made to Episodes Two and Four. Episode Two had five cuts, of 70 frames, 55 frames, 24 frames, 35 frames and 20 frames respectively, while Episode Four had three cuts, of 37 frames, 79 frames and 133 frames. The archive masters of this story were all Stored Field film recordings dating from 1967. An off-air DV recording of the story from early 2003-ish from ABC in Australia was also examined, and was found to be of Suppressed Field film telerecordings, which would have been made around the time the programme had aired in the UK. It was found that these Suppressed Field telerecordings were cut in an identical manner as well. The cuts were nearly all around scenes that had been physically edited on the original transmission tapes, and it is suspected that these physical edits may have caused picture off-locks when the tape was replayed, which were then edited out of the 16mm film prints.

David Holman retained off-air audio recordings of all six episodes, and these were used to restore the complete soundtracks to the two cut episodes for the DVD release, with the missing pictures covered with a mixture of cutaways, composite images and re-timed footage.

THE AZTECS (4 EPISODES)

All four episodes have black and white 16mm film negatives (running to 905 feet, 915 feet, 962 feet and 954 feet respectively), but there are no archived 16mm film positives of any episode. All four episodes have optical soundtracks on the negatives. Separate magnetic soundtracks also exist. These all originated at BBC Enterprises in 1978.

Viewing prints are available for all four episodes – these include the Suppressed Field film prints of Episodes One, Three and Four returned from Cyprus in 1985.

During remastering for DVD in 2002, the archived negatives of all four episodes were examined and found to be Stored Field telerecordings, made in 1967. The first few minutes of Episode One was found to be quite poor in terms of picture quality, although this soon improved and stayed consistently good thereafter. It was suspected that this was the result of some earlier damage to the negative, which was then repaired by having a section of duplicate negative spliced onto the start. The Cyprus-returned print of Episode One was also checked, and was found to be a Suppressed Field recording (as were the rest of the Cyprus-returned episodes), of markedly poorer quality than the duplicate negative section of the Stored Field negative. The film inserts in the archived second episode were found to be out of phase, although those in the third episode were fine.

A privately-owned print of Episode Four was loaned to the BBC for the DVD release. This had originated from Morocco, and contained an Arabic language version of the soundtrack. The film recording date for this episode was November 1967, according to the slate at the start of the film. This demonstrates that there were three different sets of telerecordings made by the BBC of this story between 1964 and 1967.

THE SENSORITES (6 EPISODES)

All six episodes have black and white 16mm film negatives (running to 1000 feet each), but there are no archived 16mm film positives of any episode (although viewing prints are available). All episodes have optical soundtracks on the negatives. All the negatives are Stored Field recordings, made in 1967, and hail from the find at BBC Enterprises in 1978.

THE REIGN OF TERROR (6 EPISODES)

A 16mm film print of Episode Six was located in a private collection in 1982, and loaned to the BBC, who made a duplicate negative of it as their archive master (running to 960 feet). This was a Stored Field telerecording. The collector's print was borrowed again by the BBC in 1994, and a D3 copy was made, avoiding the generation loss that a duplicate negative gave.

Episodes One, Two and Three (and another copy of Episode Six) were returned from Cyprus in 1985 as 16mm film positive prints with optical sound. These were all Suppressed Field film recordings. 16mm film negatives were made from these prints (Episode One runs to 914 feet, Episode Two to 911 feet, Episode Three to 960 feet, and Episode Six to 960 feet), which became the archived copies. Separate magnetic soundtracks were also made of the episodes.

A second 16mm film copy of Episode Three was located in a private collection in the mid-1980s, and the BBC were able to make a duplicate negative copy of it in 1985. Then, in 1994, they took a D3 copy of it, at which point it was found to be a Stored Field telerecording, and therefore better quality than the Cyprus print. However, it is more damaged than the Cyprus copy.

Off-air audio recordings of the story, including the missing fourth and fifth episodes, were made from the original UK broadcast. David Holman's are the best quality, although approximately one minute is missing from his copy of Episode Four. John de Rivaz also has audio recordings of all six episodes.

Small sections of material from both Episode Four and Episode Five were shot off-air on 8mm black and white film by an Australian fan in the 1960s. These mute clips are as follows:

APPENDIX II

Episode Four: The Doctor in Robespierre's office (two seconds)
Ian talking in Jules' house after his escape (three seconds)
Ian talking in Jules' house the following morning (one second)
Susan lying down in the surgery (one second)
Susan looks worried (two seconds)
Barbara tries to open the surgery door (one second)

Episode Five: Barbara in her cell, talking to the Doctor (four seconds)
Barbara remarking on the Doctor's disguise as an Officer (three seconds)
Ian talking to Leon in the crypt (two seconds)
The Doctor talking (one second)
The Doctor talking (one second)
Ian and Barbara in Jules' house (one second)

PLANET OF GIANTS (3 EPISODES)

All three episodes have black and white 16mm film negatives (running to 877 feet, 900 feet and 1007 feet respectively) held by the BBC, but there are no archived 16mm film positives of any of the episodes (although viewing prints are available). All episodes have optical soundtracks. A separate magnetic soundtrack for Episode Three also exists. In addition, 16mm positive film prints with Arabic soundtracks exist for all three episodes. All these elements were found at BBC Enterprises in 1978.

The National Film Archive also holds 16mm film copies of all three episodes of this story.

The third episode of this story was originally transmitted from a 35mm film telerecording, which would also have had a properly-mixed separate magnetic soundtrack. When the story was selected for VHS release in 2002, the surviving 16mm film prints were all that the BBC had. The original 35mm film print of Episode Three and accompanying magnetic soundtrack had been junked many years before. The surviving optical soundtrack for Episode Three *appeared* to be a duplicate of the optical soundtrack of the original 35mm transmission print, which was made from the cut-together sections of 35mm film, complete with a 20 frame 'overhang' on every sound edit. The original broadcast sound, i.e. the mixed separate magnetic soundtrack to this episode, exists only on the off-air audio recording that was made in 1964 by David Holman and on John de Rivaz's separate off-air recording.

The BBC also retains the stock film shots of the cat that were used to portray the 'giant cat' in this story.

WIPED!

THE DALEK INVASION OF EARTH (6 EPISODES)

Episodes One, Two, Three, Four and Six have black and white 16mm film negatives (running to 900 feet, 922 feet, 1017 feet, 888 feet and 966 feet respectively), but there are no archived 16mm film positives of any of these episodes (although viewing prints are available). These are all Stored Field telerecordings. All five of these episodes have optical soundtracks. Episode Six has an additional separate magnetic soundtrack. These were all found at BBC Enterprises in 1978.

Episode Five exists as a 35mm black and white film negative, with an optical soundtrack. This is held by the BBC over three separate reels of film, and runs to 2393 feet.[95] The optical soundtrack isn't the final transmitted sound, but the raw, unmixed sound as recorded in the studio. This is the film negative that was used to make the transmission print of the episode in 1964. A separate magnetic soundtrack – contained on two reels – is held for the episode, which contains the final mixed programme sound, and needs to be used in conjunction with the 35mm print. All this material was always held by the BBC Film Library.

No 35mm positive film print of Episode Five is archived. There are a number of 16mm viewing prints of it held by the BBC, including one that was recovered from the ABC in Australia, which is a Suppressed Field recording.

16mm positive film prints with Arabic soundtracks exist for Episodes One, Two, Four and Six of this story.

Two separate trailers for the story survive, both as 16mm film negatives, running to 30 feet and 50 feet respectively. These negatives are mute, but separate magnetic soundtracks for them survive, plus 16mm film positives with optical soundtracks.

Colour 8mm home movie footage of the cast rehearsing Episode Six is held by Carole Ann Ford, although the film has been 'double exposed' with footage of a gathering of her friends and family, and so the two images are irretrievably combined.

THE RESCUE (2 EPISODES)

Both episodes have black and white 16mm film negatives (running to 950 feet each) with optical soundtracks, plus 16mm film positives, again with optical soundtracks. These are all Stored Field recordings. Separate magnetic soundtracks exist for both episodes.

---

95 Andrew Martin of the BBC Film and Videotape Library explained to me why 35mm transmission prints are now cut into two or three spools at the BBC: 'These were probably all originally held as single 35mm reels, as the largest cans we had (see the reference to 'The Celestial Toymaker' 35mm telerecording footage) were 3000 feet. This was fine for transmission, but impractical for viewing on a Steenbeck, so all our large prints and mags were cut down (very carefully!) in the 1990s, and the mags were dubbed to polyester at the same time.'

APPENDIX II

Additionally, 16mm positive film prints with Arabic soundtracks exist for both episodes.

All these elements were found at BBC Enterprises in 1978.

THE ROMANS (4 EPISODES)

All four episodes have black and white 16mm film negatives (running to 917 feet, 879 feet, 997 feet and 877 feet respectively) with optical soundtracks. These are all Stored Field prints, and were found at BBC Enterprises in 1978. The BBC has also got archived 16mm film positive prints of all four episodes, but they have all been struck from the archived negatives, and were made comparatively recently.

Viewing prints are available for the first and third episodes only – these are the films originally held by the BBC Film Library in 1977. In the case of Episode Three, a good quality fine grain duplicate positive also exists.

THE WEB PLANET (6 EPISODES)

All six episodes have black and white 16mm film negatives (running to 900 feet, 983 feet, 900 feet, 976 feet, 988 feet and 1000 feet respectively) with optical soundtracks. These are all Stored Field prints, and were found at BBC Enterprises in 1978. There are also archived 16mm film positive prints of all but Episode Five, but these have all been struck from the archived negatives, and were made in recent years.

A number of viewing prints of Episode Five are held, some of which would have originated at the BBC Film Library in 1977. Additionally, a 16mm fine grain duplicate positive print of Episode Two exists, although this is damaged.

Further viewing prints of all six episodes were kept for a number of years, but were junked by the BBC in the early 1990s. Some of the prints of the first episode had the reprise from 'The Romans' edited out, while some of the last episode had a 'Next Episode' caption which read 'Next Episode: The Space Museum', rather than the correct 'Next Episode: The Lion'. However, the archived negatives of the episodes are complete and unedited.

Prints of all six episodes of this story were returned from Nigeria in 1985, and although some of these were retained as viewing copies, not all of them were kept by the BBC.

The BBC film and videotape library did once hold a Spanish-dubbed separate magnetic soundtrack to Episode Six, but this was junked many years ago.

THE CRUSADE (4 EPISODES)

Bruce Grenville's 16mm black and white film print of Episode One was borrowed by the BBC in 1998, and a Digital Betacam copy made via a wetgate telecine transfer. It was a Suppressed Field film positive, which was ex-TVNZ, having been sent to New Zealand in 1967.

Episode Three exists as a 16mm black and white film negative with an optical soundtrack, and runs to 1025 feet. A 16mm film positive with an optical soundtrack is also archived. A separate magnetic soundtrack for the episode also exists. During remastering for the DVD release on 'Lost in Time', it was discovered that the film inserts in this episode were out of phase.

Off-air audio recordings of all four episodes – including the missing second and fourth – were made at the time of UK broadcast. David Holman's are the best quality, although John de Rivaz also has recordings of all four episodes.

George Gallaccio (production assistant/production unit manager during Jon Pertwee's and Tom Baker's eras) retained Tele-snaps of all four episodes, after they were thrown out by the *Doctor Who* production office in the mid-1970s.

THE SPACE MUSEUM (4 EPISODES)

All four episodes have black and white 16mm film negatives (running to 897 feet, 834 feet, 890 feet, and 843 feet respectively) with optical soundtracks. These are all Stored Field telerecordings, and were found at BBC Enterprises in 1978. There are also archived 16mm film positive prints of all four episodes, but these have all been struck from the archived negatives in recent years.

No viewing prints exist apart from Episode Three, which has several. These are the 16mm films originally held by the BBC Film Library in 1977, and include a fine grain duplicate positive.

THE CHASE (6 EPISODES)

All six episodes have black and white 16mm film negatives and positives (running to 952 feet, 884 feet, 950 feet, 894 feet, 880 feet, and 1001 feet respectively) with optical soundtracks, plus separate magnetic soundtracks. These are all Stored Field recordings, made in 1967, and discovered at BBC Enterprises in 1978.

THE TIME MEDDLER (4 EPISODES)

The basis for the BBC's archive masters of this story are the four 16mm black and white positive film prints with optical soundtracks returned from Nigeria in early 1985 (which run to 800 feet, 954 feet, 900 feet and 900 feet respectively). From these prints (which are all Stored Field recordings), 16mm duplicate negatives were struck, plus a set of separate magnetic soundtracks.

The BBC already held a copy of Episode Two prior to the Nigerian discovery – as both negative and positive black and white 16mm films with optical soundtracks, plus a separate magnetic soundtrack.

Ian Levine loaned the BBC his unedited 16mm copies of Episodes One and Three in 1991, after it was found that the Nigerian prints had been edited. 16mm duplicate negatives of these were made, as well as telecine transfers onto D3 videotapes.

The Nigerian print of Episode Four is also edited, missing 12 seconds of footage of the two Vikings being stabbed by the Saxons, but this is the only extant copy of this episode.

D3 transmission masters were constructed for the story's 1992 BBC2 repeat, using the Nigerian prints of Episodes One, Three and Four – with the missing sections from the first and third patched from the Levine copies – and the print of Episode Two that was always held by the BBC.

New telecine transfers onto D3 videotape of Levine's 16mm film prints of Episodes One and Three were done in 1994.

Episode Two of the story contains a section of 35mm black and white news film, entitled *The Landing of the Vikings*, which dates from 28 June 1949. This film details the final part of the journey of a replica Viking ship from Denmark to Broadstairs in Kent. The 53 Danish men sailing the ship dressed as Vikings for the benefit of the news cameras. This film exists at the BBC and was used in the remastering of 'The Time Meddler' for DVD.

GALAXY 4 (4 EPISODES)

Terry Burnett's 16mm black and white film positive print of Episode Three was loaned to the BBC in late 2011. A telecine transfer of the episode was made onto Digital Betacam videotape, and the original film was returned to Burnett. The final 30 seconds or so of the episode plus the end credits were missing from the print. The missing material has been recreated for the 2013 DVD release of this episode, using the off-air audio recordings of this episode, cutaways of existing footage, and a newly recreated end credit roller caption.

A 30-second clip from Episode One was used in 'Whose Doctor Who'. This features a conversation between Maaga and the Doctor and Steven, about the uselessness of men. The footage was physically cut from a longer section of film that was duplicated for the documentary from a (now missing) 16mm print. This duplicated section originally ran to just under six minutes – beginning two-and-a-half minutes before the clip used in the documentary, and continuing for just under three minutes after it. These two discarded sections were retained by fan Jan Vincent-Rudzki after the programme was made. He later made them available to the BBC, and a D3 telecine transfer of the material was done.

A small section (10 seconds) of material from Episode One was recorded off-air

WIPED!

on 8mm black and white film by an Australian fan in the 1960s. This mute clip is as follows:

> Episode One: A pan across the TARDIS console as the Doctor operates the controls, while Vicki cuts Steven's hair in the background (10 seconds)

Off-air audio recordings of all four episodes were made at the time of UK broadcast. David Holman's are the best quality, although John de Rivaz and Allen Wilson also have recordings. No Tele-snaps exist for this story.

MISSION TO THE UNKNOWN (1 EPISODE)
Does not exist at the BBC.
   Off-air audio recordings of this episode were made at the time of the UK broadcast. David Butler's is the best quality, although David Holman and John de Rivaz also have recordings. No Tele-snaps exist for this story.

THE MYTH MAKERS (4 EPISODES)
No episodes exist at the BBC.
   Small sections of material from Episodes One, Two and Four were shot off-air on 8mm black and white film by an Australian fan in the 1960s. These mute clips are as follows:

> Episode One: Steven and Vicki watch the TARDIS scanner (nine seconds)
> Steven and Vicki discuss the possibility that they've landed in ancient Greece (ten seconds)
> Steven puts his cloak on (two seconds)
>
> Episode Two: Vicki looks worried as she watches the Trojans on the scanner (three seconds)
> More shots of Vicki looking at the scanner (three seconds)
> The Doctor and Steven talking on the plain (four seconds)
> More shots of the Doctor and Steven talking (four seconds)
> The Doctor talking (one second)
> Another shot of the Doctor talking (one second)
> Vicki leaving the TARDIS in Trojan dress (four seconds)
>
> Episode Four: The Doctor talking to Katarina (15 seconds)

APPENDIX II

Off-air audio recordings of all four episodes were made at the time of UK broadcast. David Holman's are the best quality, although John de Rivaz also has a recording, and Richard Landen has one of the final episode. No Tele-snaps exist for this story.

THE DALEKS MASTERPLAN (12 EPISODES)

The BBC hold Episodes Five and Ten as 16mm black and white positive film prints with optical soundtracks, as returned to them in 1983. (These run to 885 feet and 900 feet respectively.) From these prints (which are both Stored Field recordings), 16mm duplicate negatives were struck, plus separate magnetic soundtracks.

Francis Watson's 16mm black and white film positive print of Episode Two was returned to the BBC in 2004 (and runs to 914 feet). A telecine transfer was made onto Digital Betacam videotape.

A 35mm mute film (both positive and negative) of four insert sequences from Episode One of this story was found in a mislabelled film can in 1991 (running to 293 feet). These sequences are:

> Kert Gantry stumbling through the jungle on Kembel, and being exterminated by a Dalek (54 seconds)
> The TARDIS materialising on Kembel (12 seconds)
> The lights of the Dalek city (nine seconds)
> Mavic Chen's 'Spar' spaceship landing (28 seconds)

Another reel of 35mm mute positive film of four insert sequences from Episode Two of this story was kept by the BBC, prior to the episode itself being returned in 2004. (It runs to 293 feet.) This film mysteriously disappeared from the BBC's Film and Videotape Library in the late 1980s, but was returned in 1993. Unlike the insert reel from the first episode, this film also had a separate magnetic soundtrack reel to accompany the pictures. The sequences on the film are:

> The Daleks lighting their pyroflames and moving into the jungle (38 seconds)
> The Daleks burning the plants in Kembel's jungle (47 seconds)
> Mavic Chen's 'Spar' spaceship on the landing pad (12 seconds)
> A smoke overlay (30 seconds)

A clip from Episode Three also exists. Lasting 98 seconds, this starts with the Doctor, Steven, Katarina and Bret Vyon discussing landing on Desperus, and continues with the next scene of the Daleks in their ship reporting to the Dalek Supreme. This is held

WIPED!

on the two-inch colour videotape of the edition of *Blue Peter* from 25 October 1971, although the clip is a transfer from a 16mm black and white film print.

A clip from Episode Four exists as well, thanks again to *Blue Peter*. This time, the segment runs to 58 seconds, and shows the Doctor, Steven and Bret arguing about how best to help Katarina, who's being held hostage in the ship's airlock by the convict Kirksen. Katarina ends the dispute when she opens the airlock, killing both Kirksen and herself. This is held on the two-inch colour videotape of the edition of *Blue Peter* from 5 November 1973, although again the clip is a transfer from a 16mm black and white film print. The entire 16mm film print of this episode was loaned to *Blue Peter* in 1973 by the BBC Film Library, in order for a feature on *Doctor Who*'s tenth anniversary to be made, and was never returned.

A film stock shot of a faked sun that was used in this story also exists at the BBC.

Off-air audio recordings of all 12 episodes were made at the time of UK broadcast. Graham Strong's copies of Episodes Eight, Nine and Twelve are the best quality of those instalments, while David Holman's are the best quality of the others. John de Rivaz also has recordings of all 12 episodes.

No Tele-snaps exist for this story, although 20 off-screen photographs from Episode Seven do survive, taken by actor Robert Jewell, who played the clown in this episode.

THE MASSACRE (4 EPISODES)

No episodes exist at the BBC.

Off-air audio recordings of all four episodes were made at the time of UK broadcast. Graham Strong's are the best quality, although David Holman, Richard Landen and John de Rivaz also have recordings. No Tele-snaps exist for this story.

THE ARK (4 EPISODES)

All four episodes have black and white 16mm film negatives (running to 903 feet, 841 feet, 913 feet and 928 feet respectively) with optical soundtracks. These are all Stored Field telerecordings, and were located at BBC Enterprises in 1978.

The BBC has archived 16mm film positive prints of Episodes Two and Four, and separate magnetic soundtracks for these two episodes as well.

Viewing prints exist for Episode Three only. These are the 16mm films originally held by the BBC Film Library in 1977, although one of them is a 16mm fine grain duplicate positive.

THE CELESTIAL TOYMAKER (4 EPISODES)

Only Episode Four survives, as a black and white 16mm film print (running to 930

APPENDIX II

feet) with an optical soundtrack. This was returned to the BBC from the ABC in Australia (although it originated at RTS in Singapore), and is a Stored Field print. It is missing its 'Next Episode' caption. The BBC have used this print to make a 16mm duplicate negative for the archive, and also a separate magnetic soundtrack.

Off-air audio recordings of all four episodes were made at the time of the UK broadcast. David Holman's are the best quality, although Richard Landen and John de Rivaz also have recordings. No Tele-snaps exist for this story.

THE GUNFIGHTERS (4 EPISODES)

All four episodes have black and white 16mm film negatives (running to 895 feet, 894 feet, 926 feet and 897 feet respectively) with optical soundtracks. These are all Stored Field telerecordings, and were found at BBC Enterprises in 1978. No viewing prints exist for this story.

There is some confusion about how this story was originally broadcast by the BBC, as paperwork from BBC Enterprises suggests that only Episode One was retained as a two-inch 405-line videotape broadcast master for the purposes of making 16mm sales prints, with Episodes Two, Three and Four being held as 35mm film prints. When the BBC's negatives for this story were transferred in order to prepare the 2002 VHS release of this adventure, they were found to be comparatively poor quality. Certainly there was nothing about them that was inconsistent with the theory that the final three episodes were 16mm reductions from 35mm recordings. They had a number of printed-in artefacts, which suggested that they were actually duplicate negatives.

THE SAVAGES (4 EPISODES)

No episodes exist at the BBC.

Small sections of material from Episodes Three and Four were shot off-air on 8mm black and white film by an Australian fan in the 1960s. These mute clips are as follows:

Episode Three:	Steven hears a noise and takes cover (five seconds)	
	Steven and Dodo talking as they move along a corridor (three seconds)	
Episode Four	Dodo talking to the Doctor, with Nanina and Steven (three seconds)	
	Dodo smashes lab equipment (six seconds)	
	Jano talking (one second)	
	Jano talking again (three seconds)	
	Steven looks surprised (one second)	

WIPED!

> Steven decides to stay, Dodo runs over to him (six seconds)
> Steven says goodbye (three seconds)
> Steven shakes hands with the Doctor (five seconds)
> Steven looks back (one second)
> The Doctor comforts Dodo (six seconds)
> The Doctor and Dodo leave (one second)

Off-air audio recordings of all four episodes were made at the time of UK broadcast. Graham Strong's are the best quality, although David Holman, Richard Landen and John de Rivaz also have recordings.

A full set of Tele-snaps exists for all four episode of this story.

THE WAR MACHINES (4 EPISODES)

The basis for the BBC's archive masters for this story are the four 16mm black and white positive film prints with optical soundtracks returned from Nigeria in early 1985 (which run to 900 feet, 940 feet, 800 feet and 900 feet respectively). From these prints (which are all Stored Field recordings), 16mm duplicate negatives were struck, plus a set of separate magnetic soundtracks. Only Episode One is complete however. Censors edits have been made to the prints of Episodes Two, Three and Four.

The BBC already held a copy of Episode Two prior to the Nigerian discovery – this was a duplicate print made from a 16mm film owned by Ian Levine. Levine's print was itself a duplicate of a 16mm film owned by David Gee in Australia, which originated from the ABC. This copy of the episode is complete.

The material discovered by Damian Shanahan in 1996 at the Australian censors' archives includes material cut from Episode Three of this story. These 16mm black and white film print trims were copied onto D3 tape for the BBC. These scenes are:

> Episode Three: Major Green's speech: 'All human beings who break down
> will be eliminated' and the accompanying shot of man
> knocked down with blow to neck (17 seconds)
> The soldiers attack the warehouse – one is killed by spray
> from War Machine (37 seconds)

Additionally, a sequence that was edited out of the Nigerian print of Episode Four, of a War Machine attacking a man in a telephone box, was found to exist in the 1965 edition of *Blue Peter* that featured a War Machine visiting presenters Christopher Trace and Valerie Singleton in the studio.

35mm film sequences from Episodes Three and Four are known to exist in private collections. The sequences from Episode Three includes an 'outtake', as the 'burning' War Machine prop billows smoke, and the operator decides to make a quick exit from the back of the machine. This film is mute, although the separate magnetic soundtrack did exist at one point in time, and copies of the material with sound are available in fan circles. The material from Episode Four is also mute, and although the location of the physical film isn't known, domestic video copies were made of the footage.

Off-air audio recordings of all four episodes were made at the time of UK broadcast. Graham Strong's are the best quality, although David Holman, Richard Landen and John de Rivaz also have recordings.

When this story was released on VHS In 1998, and again on DVD in 2008, all these elements were combined to restore the story to an as-near-complete state as it was possible to achieve.

THE SMUGGLERS (4 EPISODES)

No episodes exist at the BBC.

Small sections of material from Episodes One, Three and Four were discovered by Damian Shanahan in 1996 at the Australian censors' archives. These 16mm black and white film print trims were copied onto D3 tape for the BBC. The scenes from this story are:

Episode One:	Cherub throws his knife into Longfoot's back. Longfoot then curses Cherub as he dies (23 seconds)
Episode Three:	Jamaica talking to Pike (three seconds)
	Pike lunging to kill Jamaica, and then a cut to Pike wiping blood off his hook with a piece of cloth, which he then drops on Jamaica's dead body (14 seconds)
	Kewper gets shot, Polly screams (four seconds)
Episode Four:	Pike pulls his sword out of Cherub's chest (three seconds)

Some of the location filming for this story centred around Trethewey Farm on 22 June 1966 was captured on mute 16mm colour film. This runs for just over two-and-a half minutes, and features scenes with Cherub, Pike and the Squire, plus William Hartnell's double, Gordon Craig. This material is held in a private collection, but has been made available to the BBC, and was included in the DVD release 'Lost in Time'.

Off-air audio recordings of all four episodes were made at the time of UK broadcast. Graham Strong's are the best quality, although David Holman, Richard Landen and John de Rivaz also have recordings.

A full set of Tele-snaps exists for all four episode of this story.

WIPED!

THE TENTH PLANET (4 EPISODES)

The BBC holds copies of Episodes One and Two as black and white fine grain 16mm film negatives (running to 869 feet and 871 feet respectively) with optical soundtracks. There are also archived black and white 16mm film positive prints with optical sound for these two episodes, plus separate magnetic soundtracks.

Episode Three is held as a black and white 16mm film positive print with optical soundtrack. A 16mm black and white duplicate film negative has been made from this, and also archived. The films of all three episodes have resided at the BBC Film Library since at least 1977. Viewing prints of all three episodes are also held. These are all Stored Field prints.

A 30-second clip from Episode Four also exists at the BBC – this is the key scene of William Hartnell's first Doctor regenerating into Patrick Troughton's second Doctor. This is held on the two-inch colour videotape of the edition of *Blue Peter* from 5 November 1973, although the clip itself is a transfer from a 16mm black and white film print.

Additionally, small sections of material from Episode Four were shot off-air on 8mm black and white film by an Australian fan in the 1960s. These mute clips are as follows:

Episode Four: The Doctor talking to Polly (four seconds)
More material of the Doctor talking to Polly (two seconds)
The Doctor addressing the Cyberleader (five seconds)
The Doctor talking again, same scene, slightly later (four seconds)
The Doctor talking again, same scene, slightly later (three seconds)
The Doctor talking again, same scene, slightly later (one second)
Polly being menaced by a Cyberman (two seconds)
Polly and the Doctor held prisoner on Cybership (three seconds)
Polly and the Doctor held prisoner on Cybership (one second)
Ben inside Cybership (one second)
Ben inside Cybership (one second)
The freed Doctor talking to Ben (two seconds)
The freed Doctor staggering towards the camera (three seconds)

APPENDIX II

> The start of the regeneration, the Doctor seen in silhouette, as the lights pulsate and the TARDIS controls operate themselves (19 seconds)

Off-air audio recordings of all four episodes were made at the time of UK broadcast. Graham Strong's are the best quality – in fact, they are better than the optical soundtracks on the surviving prints of Episodes One to Three – although David Holman, Richard Landen and John de Rivaz also have recordings. Strong's recording of Episode Four stops just at the point that the *Blue Peter* clip starts, so the full soundtrack to the episode has since been restored.

A full set of Tele-snaps exists for all four episodes.

THE SECOND DOCTOR
PATRICK TROUGHTON (1966-1969)

THE POWER OF THE DALEKS (6 EPISODES)

No episodes exist at the BBC. However, a large number of clips survive, from a variety of different sources.

A 40-second clip of the Daleks chanting 'Daleks conquer and destroy' from Episode Five is held by the BBC in the programme *Whicker's World*: 'I Don't Like My Monsters To Have Oedipus Complexes' (screened 27 January 1968), which was transferred directly from the original 35mm film inserts for this episode when they still existed. The same clip is also retained in an edition of *Blue Peter* from 27 November 1967, but is copied from a 16mm telerecording of the episode, and is therefore of poorer quality.

A shorter clip (11 seconds) from this same sequence exists as a film insert for the ABC programme *Perspectives*: 'C for Computer' (screened by the ABC 29 May 1974). This film insert was copied onto D3 videotape for the BBC in 1995, and contains two further clips from this episode. One is of a gunless Dalek gliding up to the camera while talking (ten seconds), the other is of the Daleks assembling in a room, waiting to attack (eight seconds).

Two clips from Episode Four of this story were also used in 'C for Computer' and were returned to the BBC at the same time as the others. The first is of two Daleks moving through a doorway into the capsule (ten seconds), the second is of a model shot of the Daleks on a conveyor belt (seven seconds). All of the 'C for Computer' clips were originally sourced from the 16mm telerecordings of the episodes sold to the ABC in the 1960s.

A second source for the two 'C for Computer' clips from Episode Four was

WIPED!

unearthed in the BBC archives in 2005, when a 16mm black and while film insert reel for the edition of *Tomorrow's World* originally screened on 28 December 1966 was used in an edition of the programme *Sunday Past Times* screened on 11 September 2005. However, the 1966 *Tomorrow's World* programme had sourced the clips from the original 35mm film inserts for this episode, which still existed at the time. Two further clips of the Dalek assembly line from Episode Four (running to eight seconds and six seconds respectively) were also found on the *Tomorrow's World* film inserts, again sourced from the original Episode Four film inserts, rather than from a 16mm telerecording.

An effects sequence of various Daleks exploding from Episode Six (duration six seconds) exists in the black and white 16mm film copy of the programme *Tom Tom* screened on 26 November 1968, and is still held by the BBC.

In 2003, a 16mm black and white programme-as-broadcast film copy of *Beyond the Freeze – What Next?*, shown on 5 November 1966, was found to contain an incomplete trailer for Episode One of this story, which includes a clip of the Doctor introducing Ben and Polly to the cobwebbed, immobile Daleks in the capsule (19 seconds). The trailer is incomplete as the film recorder was stopped and then re-started during the trailer's broadcast.

Small sections of material from Episodes One and Two were shot off-air on 8mm black and white film by an Australian fan in the 1960s. These mute clips are as follows:

Episode One:	Ben and Polly discuss the 'new' Doctor (five seconds)
	Ben and Polly discuss the 'new' Doctor (one second)
	Ben and Polly discuss the 'new' Doctor (one second)
	The Doctor awakens, muttering to himself (three seconds)
	The Doctor feels his new face (one second)
	The Doctor turns and slumps on the TARDIS console (three seconds)
	Ben and Polly watch the Doctor rummage in a trunk (six seconds)
	The Doctor sees his 'old' face in a mirror (two seconds)
	The Doctor bites his finger (two seconds)
	The Doctor pulls on his tall hat (one second)
	The Doctor quickly walks out of the lab (seven seconds)
	Ben and Polly with the cobwebbed Daleks (three seconds)
Episode Two:	The Doctor talks while Ben and Polly look on (four seconds)

APPENDIX II

> Polly in Lesterson's lab (three seconds)
> The Doctor looks towards the ceiling (one second)
> Lesterson wheels out a Dalek (four seconds)
> The Doctor with his 500 year diary (one second)
> Resno is exterminated (two seconds)
> The Doctor looks on as a Dalek enters (one second)
> The Doctor backs away from the Dalek (four seconds)
> The Doctor and the Dalek as it talks (four seconds)

Off-air audio recordings of all six episodes were made at the time of UK broadcast. Graham Strong's are the best quality, although David Holman, John de Rivaz and Richard Landen also have recordings.

A full set of Tele-snaps exists for all six episodes.

THE HIGHLANDERS (4 EPISODES)

No episodes exist at the BBC.

Small sections of material from Episode One were discovered by Damian Shanahan in 1996 at the Australian censors' archives. These 16mm black and white film print trims were copied onto D3 tape for the BBC. The scenes are:

> Episode One: Alexander McLaren stabs a redcoat (two seconds)
> Another shot of the redcoat being stabbed (one second)
> A Redcoat gives instructions for the hanging of the Doctor, Ben, Jamie and Colin McLaren (ten seconds)

A ten-second clip from the original 35mm film rushes of Episode One exists in private hands, although the BBC also has a copy of this material. It consists of a shot of the clapperboard used in filming, followed by the TARDIS door opening. This is an offcut from the finished insert film, and isn't technically a clip from the transmitted episode.

Off-air audio recordings of all four episodes were made at the time of UK broadcast. Graham Strong's are the best quality, although David Holman, Richard Landen and John de Rivaz also have recordings.

A full set of Tele-snaps exists for all four episodes.

THE UNDERWATER MENACE (4 EPISODES)

Episode Three exists as a 16mm film positive with an optical soundtrack (running to 908 feet). A fine grain 16mm black and white film negative with an optical soundtrack,

WIPED!

and a separate magnetic soundtrack, have been made from this print, and have been archived. A number of 16mm viewing prints also exist.

Small sections of material from Episodes One, Two and Four were discovered by Damian Shanahan in 1996 at the Australian censors' archives. These 16mm black and white film print trims were copied onto D3 tape for the BBC. The scenes are:

Episode One:	Polly being forced onto the operating table (14 seconds)
Episode Two:	The syringe being filled from a bottle (two seconds)
	Polly being menaced by a surgeon with the syringe (three seconds)
	Polly crying as she is held down (seven seconds)
	Damon prepares to inject Polly, is disturbed by the lights flickering (eight seconds)
Episode Four:	Zaroff drowns under the rising waters, trapped behind bars (three seconds)

Terry Burnett's 16mm black and white film positive print of Episode Two was loaned to the BBC in late 2011. A telecine transfer of the episode was made onto Digital Betacam videotape, and the original film was returned to Burnett. This film originated at ABC in Australia, and had the four cuts in it that had originally been made by the Australian censor. All four pieces of cut film were retained at the censor's archive and were re-transferred for the BBC in 2011, enabling the episode to be restored in full.

Off-air audio recordings of all four episodes were made at the time of UK broadcast. Graham Strong's are the best quality, although David Holman, Richard Landen and John de Rivaz also have recordings.

A full set of Tele-snaps exists for all four episodes.

THE MOONBASE (4 EPISODES)

Episodes Two and Four exist as 16mm black and white fine grain duplicate negatives with optical soundtracks (running to 927 feet and 881 feet respectively). From these, 16mm fine grain duplicate positive prints have been made, along with separate magnetic soundtracks for each episode. A number of 16mm viewing prints of both episodes also exist.

A duplicate 16mm film print of Episode Four was located in the early 1980s by Roger Stevens, and a wetgate transfer onto D3 videotape was made of this by the BBC in 1994. This print was of much better quality than the BBC's existing copy, but was missing the 'Next Episode' caption.

Off-air audio recordings of all four episodes were made at the time of UK

APPENDIX II

broadcast. Graham Strong's are the best quality, although David Holman, Richard Landen and John de Rivaz also have recordings.

A full set of Tele-snaps exists for all four episodes.

THE MACRA TERROR (4 EPISODES)
No episodes exist at the BBC.

Small sections of material from Episodes Two and Three were discovered by Damian Shanahan in 1996 at the Australian censors' archives. These 16mm black and white film print trims were copied onto D3 tape for the BBC. The scenes are:

Episode Two: Polly is held in a Macra's claws as Ben struggles to free her (15 seconds)
Polly and Ben hug each other as another Macra approaches (seven seconds)
Polly and Ben run into another Macra (three seconds)
On the screen, the controller is attacked by a Macra claw (one second)
Episode Three: The controller is attacked by a Macra claw (two seconds)

Small sections of material from Episode Three were shot off-air on 8mm black and white film by an Australian fan in the 1960s. These mute clips are as follows:

Episode Three: Opening titles (17 seconds)
The Doctor jokes about a bad rhyme in one of the colony's jingles (five seconds)
The Doctor looks around (five seconds)
The Doctor talking to the hypnotised Ben (six seconds)
Polly in the mine (four seconds)
Jamie in the mine (five seconds)
Jamie looks around the mineshaft (one second)
Polly and the Doctor talking (four seconds)
The Doctor realises that there's 'something' in the mine (five seconds)

Off-air audio recordings of all four episodes were made at the time of UK broadcast. Graham Strong's are the best quality, although David Holman, Richard Landen and John de Rivaz also have recordings.

A full set of Tele-snaps exists for all four episodes.

WIPED!

THE FACELESS ONES (6 EPISODES)

Episode One exists as a black and white 16mm film negative (running to 893 feet) with an optical soundtrack. This is a Stored Field telerecording. A separate magnetic soundtrack also exists. There is no archived 16mm positive print for this episode, although several viewing prints exist.

A 16mm film print of Episode One also exists in private hands, although this originated at the ABC in Australia and was edited to remove shots of DI Gascoigne's death and of the Chameleon seen at the episode's cliffhanger.

Episode Three exists as a black and white 16mm film negative (which runs to 900 feet) with an optical soundtrack, which was taken from Gordon Hendry's original 16mm film print. Hendry's print was damaged in several places, with approximately 19 seconds of footage missing in total throughout the episode. A further D3 videotape copy was made of this film print in 1994 by the BBC, which is a straight telecine transfer of the material.

A small section of material from Episode Two was shot off-air on 8mm black and white film by an Australian fan in the 1960s. This mute clip is as follows:

Episode Two: The imposter Polly brushes the Doctor aside as he questions her (three seconds)

Off-air audio recordings of all six episodes were made at the time of UK broadcast. Graham Strong's are the best quality, although David Holman, Richard Landen and John de Rivaz also have recordings.

A full set of Tele-snaps exists for all six episodes.

When Episodes One and Three were released on video and DVD, a great deal of clean-up work was undertaken on the third episode to repair the considerable damage sustained by the film print over the years. The soundtrack was fully repaired from the off-air audio recordings, and the missing picture elements were replaced by cutaways or composite images.

THE EVIL OF THE DALEKS (7 EPISODES)

Episode Two exists as a black and white 16mm film negative with an optical soundtrack, which was taken from Gordon Hendry's original 16mm film print (and runs to 1000 feet). A separate magnetic soundtrack was also made from Hendry's print, along with a number of viewing prints.

In 1994, the BBC borrowed the 16mm print again, and made a D3 videotape copy of it from a telecine transfer.

The clip of a Dalek killing Kennedy used in a scene at the end of 'The Wheel in

APPENDIX II

Space' Episode Six was taken from the cliff-hanger ending to Episode One of 'The Evil of the Daleks' rather than the reprise at the beginning of Episode Two. This was realised only when Episode Six of 'The Wheel in Space' was re-mastered for DVD release, and the scene was found to contain three extra frames not present in the reprise.

A small section of model film from Episode Seven exists, which shows two Daleks trundling through the wreckage of the Emperor's chamber. This runs to about ten seconds, although only three seconds of actual action is captured; the rest of the film is taken up by a pair of hands holding the models. As this is a film trim, it possibly wasn't seen as part of the transmitted episode.

The film designer, Tony Cornell, shot some silent 8mm black and white footage on 16 May 1967 during the filming of inserts for this story at the BBC's Ealing Film Studios. He compiled this footage into a short 'movie' called *The Last Dalek*, which still exists. It runs for about ten minutes and covers the filming of much of the action from the story's final episode.

Off-air audio recordings of all seven episodes were made at the time of UK broadcast. Graham Strong's are the best quality, although David Holman, Richard Landen and John de Rivaz also have recordings.

A full set of Tele-snaps exists for all seven episodes, plus a significant number of additional off-screen photographs from just the first episode.

THE TOMB OF THE CYBERMEN (4 EPISODES)

All four episodes exist as black and white 16mm positive film prints with optical soundtracks (with each episode running to 900 feet), as returned from Hong Kong in 1992. From these, a set of 16mm film negatives has been made by the BBC Film and Videotape Library, along with a set of separate magnetic soundtracks. A number of viewing prints have also been made.

THE ABOMINABLE SNOWMEN (6 EPISODES)

The BBC hold Episode Two as a 16mm black and white duplicate negative with optical soundtrack (which runs to 900 feet). This is taken from the 16mm positive print borrowed from Ian Levine (as found by Roger Stevens) in 1982.

This 16mm positive print was borrowed by the BBC again in 1994, and a D3 videotape copy made of a direct telecine transfer.

A 16mm black and white mute negative film of the location sequences for Episode Two exists as well at the BBC, alongside a separate magnetic soundtrack and a 16mm positive film print with an optical soundtrack. These are of a better picture quality than the sequences preserved in the telerecorded copy of the episode, and contain small amounts of material that was not used in the finished episode – including a blooper of Deborah Watling audibly slipping out of shot as she runs down the hillside towards the camera.

An edition of the BBC programme *Late Night Line Up* transmitted on 25 November 1967 contained two clips from Episode Four of this story. The first is a zoom shot of a Yeti stood next to the TARDIS (two seconds) and the second is of a group of Yeti walking up a hillside (six seconds). This edition of *Late Night Line Up* doesn't exist in full, but the film sequences that include these clips do survive as 16mm colour film (although the clips from this story are black and white).

Director Gerald Blake shot some behind-the-scenes footage covering the location filming of this story on 8mm colour mute film, which runs to about three-and-a-half minutes. Frazer Hines also took his 8mm camera to the location filming, and shot about a minute-and-a-half's worth of mute colour footage.

Off-air audio recordings of all six episodes were made at the time of UK broadcast. Graham Strong's are the best quality, although David Holman, Richard Landen and John de Rivaz also have recordings.

A full set of Tele-snaps exists for all six episodes.

THE ICE WARRIORS (6 EPISODES)

The BBC hold Episodes One, Four, Five and Six as black and white 16mm positive film prints with optical soundtracks (which all run to 900 feet). These were found at BBC Enterprises in 1988, when Villiers House was being cleared out. From these prints, the BBC has made 16mm duplicate negatives with optical soundtracks, plus additional magnetic soundtracks. Viewing prints have also been made.

Off-air audio recordings of all six episodes were made at the time of UK broadcast. Graham Strong's are the best quality, although David Holman, Richard Landen and John de Rivaz also have recordings.

A full set of Tele-snaps exists for all six episodes.

THE ENEMY OF THE WORLD (6 EPISODES)

Episode Three exists as a 16mm black and white film negative with an optical soundtrack (running to 867 feet). A 16mm film positive with an optical soundtrack is also archived. A separate magnetic soundtrack for the episode also exists.

Off-air audio recordings of all six episodes were made at the time of UK broadcast. Graham Strong's are the best quality, although David Holman, Richard Landen and John de Rivaz also have recordings.

Tele-snaps exist for five of the six episodes. Episode Four is not represented at all.

APPENDIX II

THE WEB OF FEAR (6 EPISODES)

The BBC hold Episode One as a black and white 16mm positive film print with an optical soundtrack (running to 950 feet). This was found at BBC Enterprises in the late 1970s. From this print, the BBC have made a 16mm duplicate negative with an optical soundtrack, plus an additional separate magnetic soundtrack. Viewing prints have also been made.

All six episodes of this adventure concluded with the end credits rolling over a pulsating moving image of the 'web'. A 16mm film print of the clean, specially-made end-credits sequence from this story also exists at the BBC.

Small sections of material from Episodes Two, Four and Five were discovered in 2005 in a private collection, as film trims made by the New Zealand censors. These 16mm black and white trims were copied onto Digital Betacam tape for the BBC. The scenes are:

Episode Two:	Two soldiers shoot at an advancing Yeti (14 seconds)
Episode Four:	Yeti strike down Professor Travis and Anne (11 seconds)
	The Doctor's group return to the fortress and Victoria discovers the dead soldiers (ten seconds)
	The web in the underground starts to pulsate, and Private Evans clutches his ears and screams (five seconds)
	Two soldiers shoot at the Yeti in a road (five seconds)
	A Yeti smothers two soldiers with a web gun (seven seconds)
	Colonel Lethbridge-Stewart hides from a Yeti in Covent Garden (three seconds)
Episode Five:	A Yeti comes to life to stop Victoria and Professor Travers escaping (three seconds)

Off-air audio recordings of all six episodes were made at the time of UK broadcast. Graham Strong's are the best quality, although David Holman, Richard Landen and John de Rivaz also have recordings.

A full set of Tele-snaps exists for all six episodes.

FURY FROM THE DEEP (6 EPISODES)

No episodes exist at the BBC.

A short clip from Episode One of the TARDIS landing on the sea (19 seconds) was reused in 'The War Games' Episode Ten, and survives in the 16mm film print of that episode.

WIPED!

Small sections of material from Episodes Two, Four and Five were discovered by Damian Shanahan in 1996 at the Australian censors' archives. These 16mm black and white film print trims were copied onto D3 tape for the BBC. The scenes are:

Episode Two:	Mr Oak and Mr Quill attack Mrs Harris (54 seconds)
Episode Four:	The Doctor and Jamie watch 'something' in the foam (three seconds)
	The Doctor and Jamie escape up the shaft away from the weed (14 seconds)
	Van Lutyens is attacked by the weed (14 seconds)
Episode Five	Robson overpowers a guard (17 seconds)
	Robson's hands are seen operating the helicopter (three seconds)
	Robson and the dazed Victoria in the helicopter (11 seconds)

16mm mute film trims from the recording of the climax of Episode Six were located in 2003 at the BBC Film and Videotape Library, where they were being used as spare filler and leader material. The footage runs to three minutes and 32 seconds, but consists of unused takes of scenes rather than the takes selected for inclusion in the episodes for transmission.

The Ealing film designer, Tony Cornell shot some silent 8mm colour footage behind the scenes during the filming of inserts for this story at the BBC's Ealing Film Studios. This still exists, and runs for about four minutes. It covers the filming of some of the action from the final episode of this story.

Off-air audio recordings of all six episodes were made at the time of UK broadcast. Graham Strong's are the best quality, although David Holman, Richard Landen and John de Rivaz also have recordings.

A full set of Tele-snaps exists for all six episodes.

THE WHEEL IN SPACE (6 EPISODES)

The BBC hold Episode Three as a 16mm black and white duplicate negative with optical soundtrack (running to 1000 feet). This is taken from the 16mm positive print borrowed from David Stead in 1984. A 16mm positive print was made from this negative, as was a separate magnetic soundtrack.

Stead's print was borrowed by the BBC again in 1994, and a D3 videotape copy made of a direct telecine transfer.

Episode Six exists as a 35mm black and white film negative, with an optical soundtrack. This is held by the BBC over two separate reels, and runs to 2,433 feet in total. The optical soundtrack on this film isn't the final transmitted sound, but the raw, unmixed sound as recorded in the studio. This is the negative that was used to make the print from which the episode was transmitted on BBC1 in 1968. A separate magnetic soundtrack – contained on two reels – is held, which contains the final mixed programme sound. A 35mm positive film print with (studio) optical sound is also archived. 35mm fine grain duplicate positive prints of both reels also exist. These were all held at the BBC Film Library in 1977.

A short model sequence of the Wheel hanging in space (four seconds) from the first episode was re-used in 'The War Games' Episode Ten, and so is preserved in the 16mm film print held by the BBC of that episode.

Two short clips of Duggan's death (one second and two seconds respectively) from Episode Four are amongst the censored material held by the Australian Archives and returned to the BBC on D3 videotape in 1996.

Further clips from Episode Five of a fight between Flannigan and two Cyber-controlled colleagues (totalling seven seconds) were discovered in a private collection in 2002, as film trims made by the New Zealand censors. These 16mm black and white trims were copied onto Digital Betacam tape for the BBC.

Off-air audio recordings of all six episodes were made at the time of UK broadcast. Graham Strong's are the best quality, although David Holman, Richard Landen and John de Rivaz also have recordings.

A full set of Tele-snaps exists for all six episodes.

THE DOMINATORS (5 EPISODES)

Episodes One and Two of this story exist as 16mm black and white positive film prints with optical soundtracks (running to 850 feet and 900 feet respectively). From these, 16mm black and white negatives with optical soundtracks have been made, alongside several viewing prints.

Episode Three exists as a 35mm black and white film negative, with an optical soundtrack. This is held on two separate spools, and runs to 2240 feet in total. The optical soundtrack on this film is of the raw, unmixed studio sound. A separate magnetic soundtrack is held for this episode, alongside a 35mm black and white positive film with optical soundtrack, which is possibly the transmission print from 1968. The origins of this 35mm material are uncertain, but it probably always existed at the BBC Film Library.

Another 16mm positive film print with optical soundtrack also exists for Episode Three, which was returned to the BBC from the ABC in Australia, together with a separate magnetic soundtrack. A 35mm fine grain duplicate positive print for the

WIPED!

episode also exists, split over two reels.

Episode Four exists as a 16mm black and white fine grain duplicate negative with optical soundtrack (running to 885 feet), plus an additional 16mm fine grain duplicate positive print with optical soundtrack, and a separate magnetic soundtrack. All these copies of this episode have censor edits made by a foreign broadcaster, possibly the ABC in Australia.

Episode Five exists as a 16mm black and white fine grain duplicate negative with optical soundtrack (running to 900 feet), although again this print has censor edits, again possibly from the ABC in Australia.

An uncut 16mm black and white positive film print of Episode Five exists in a private collection, and the BBC has been allowed to make a telecine transfer of this on DigiBeta videotape.

It has been known since the late 1970s that the British Film Institute (BFI) hold copies of all five episodes of this story. They were contacted again in 2008 about this, and were found to hold original 16mm film negatives for Episodes One, Two, Four and Five, which were all unedited and uncensored. The BBC had telecine transfers made of all the BFI's episodes, on DigiBeta videotape.

THE MIND ROBBER (5 EPISODES)

Episodes One, Two, Three and Four of this story exist as 16mm black and white film negatives with optical soundtracks (running to 806 feet, 814 feet, 722 feet and 722 feet respectively). Separate magnetic soundtracks for these four episodes also exist, as do 16mm positive viewing prints, all as found at BBC Enterprises in 1978.

Episode Five exists as a 35mm black and white film negative, with an optical soundtrack. This is held on two separate spools, which run to 1697 feet in total. The optical soundtrack on this film is of the raw, unmixed studio sound. A separate magnetic soundtrack is also held for this episode, alongside a 35mm black and white positive print with optical soundtrack. These would be the original BBC1 transmission components for this episode.

16mm black and white reduction prints of Episode Five exist as well.

D3 video copies of all five episodes also exist at the BBC, which were the transmission masters for the 1992 BBC2 repeat of this story.

THE INVASION (8 EPISODES)

Episodes Two and Six exist as 16mm black and white fine grain duplicate negatives with optical soundtracks (running to 950 feet and 1000 feet respectively), along with 16mm fine grain duplicate positive prints with optical soundtracks, and separate magnetic soundtracks.

APPENDIX II

Episodes Three, Five and Seven exist as 16mm black and white fine grain duplicate negatives with optical soundtracks (running to 891 feet, 1000 feet and 1000 feet respectively), along with 16mm positive prints with optical soundtracks, and separate magnetic soundtracks.

Episode Eight exists as a 16mm black and white film positive print with an optical soundtrack (running to 897 feet). From this, a 16mm fine grain duplicate negative has been made, again with an optical soundtrack, plus a separate magnetic soundtrack.

16mm positive viewing prints for all six surviving episodes are also held.

All of the film sequences in all six of the surviving episodes of this story are out of phase, with the single exception of a ten-second sequence in Episode Three.

Off-air audio recordings of all eight episodes were made at the time of UK broadcast, and are held by David Holman, Richard Landen and John de Rivaz. However, the best audio source for these episodes is an off-air recording made in Australia from an ABC broadcast.

No Tele-snaps exist for this story.

In 2005, the BBC's Interactive Drama and Entertainment department commissioned Cosgrove Hall (the award-winning Manchester-based animation studio) to animate from scratch new versions of Episodes One and Four of this story, matched up to slightly edited copies of the existing off-air audio recordings. These versions were released on DVD by 2|entertain in 2006.

THE KROTONS (4 EPISODES)

Episode One exists as a 35mm black and white film negative, with an optical soundtrack. This is held over two separate spools, and runs to 2100 feet in total. The optical soundtrack is of the raw, unmixed studio sound. A separate magnetic soundtrack is held, alongside a 35mm black and white positive film with optical soundtrack. These would be the original BBC1 transmission components for this episode. A 35mm black and white fine grain duplicate positive print plus 16mm black and white reduction prints of the episode exist as well.

Episodes Two and Three exist as 16mm black and white film fine grain duplicate negatives with optical soundtracks (running to 800 feet and 750 feet respectively). Separate magnetic soundtracks also exist for both these episodes, as well as 16mm fine grain duplicate positive prints and various 16mm viewing prints.

Episode Four exists as a 16mm black and white film negative with an optical soundtrack (running to 852 feet), and also has a separate magnetic soundtrack, plus several 16mm viewing prints. These were returned to the BBC by the BFI in 1977.

WIPED!

THE SEEDS OF DEATH (6 EPISODES)

Episodes One, Four and Six exist as 16mm black and white fine grain duplicate negatives with optical soundtracks (running to 850 feet, 937 feet and 915 feet respectively). They also have separate magnetic soundtracks and 16mm black and white fine grain duplicate positive prints.

Episodes Two and Three exist as 16mm black and white negatives with optical soundtracks (running to 915 feet and 932 feet respectively).

The best copies of all these episodes originated at BBC Enterprises in 1978.

Episode Five exists as a 35mm black and white film negative, with an optical soundtrack. This is held over three separate spools, and runs to 2300 feet in total. The optical soundtrack on this film is of the raw, unmixed studio sound. A separate magnetic soundtrack is held for this episode, alongside a 35mm black and white fine grain duplicate positive print with an optical soundtrack. These would be the original BBC1 transmission components for this episode.

16mm black and white reduction prints of Episode Five exist as well, one of which was returned from the ABC in Australia.

THE SPACE PIRATES (6 EPISODES)

Episode Two exists as a 35mm black and white film negative. This is held over two spools, and runs to 2500 feet in total. (Although listed as mute in the BBC's records, it's possible that this has an optical soundtrack of the raw, unedited studio stound, as per the other 35mm prints). A separate magnetic soundtrack is held for this episode, alongside a 35mm black and white positive print with an optical soundtrack. This is almost certainly the original transmission print from 1969. Various 35mm and 16mm viewing prints of the episode also exist.

A reel of mute 35mm film sequences for Episode Two also exists. This runs to 545 feet.

A reel of mute 35mm film sequences for Episode One was discovered at the BBC in 2004. The scenes are as follows:

> Episode One: Two pirates in space suits move along the hull of Alpha 1 (41 seconds)
> The black ship undocks and Alpha 1 explodes (24 seconds)

Off-air audio recordings of all six episodes were made at the time of UK broadcast, and are held by David Holman, Richard Landen and John de Rivaz. However, the best audio source of these episodes is an off-air recording made in Australia from an ABC broadcast.

No Tele-snaps exist for this story.

APPENDIX II

THE WAR GAMES (10 EPISODES)

Episodes One, Two, Three, Five and Six exist as 16mm black and white negatives with optical soundtracks (and run to 900 feet, 900 feet, 900 feet, 900 feet and 850 feet respectively). Episode Five has a separate magnetic soundtrack.

Episode Four exists as a 16mm black and white positive print with an optical soundtrack (and runs to 900 feet).

Episodes Seven, Eight and Nine exist as 16mm black and white fine grain duplicate positive prints with optical soundtracks (which run to 880 feet, 922 feet and 923 feet respectively), and have separate magnetic soundtracks.

Episode Ten exists as a 16mm black and white duplicate negative with optical soundtrack (duplicated from the BFI's negative of this episode) and runs to 900 feet.

16mm black and white viewing prints for all ten episodes also exist.

Episodes Two, Five, Eight and Nine were held by the BBC Film Library in 1977.

It has been known since the late 1970s that the BFI hold copies of all ten episodes of this story; and these were the source of the BBC's films of the first, third, fourth, sixth, seventh and tenth episodes. Duplicate 16mm film copies of these episodes were made and returned to the BBC to complete this story in 1977. The BFI were contacted again in 2008 about their film holdings for 'The War Games', and were found to actually hold the original 16mm film negatives for all ten episodes. The BBC had telecine transfers made of all of these, onto DigiBeta videotape.

A 16mm black and white film overlay of the forcefield effect from Episode Ten also exists at the BBC.

A copy of one spool of the soundtrack of the location rushes for this story, running to 20 minutes, exists in a private collection.

THE THIRD DOCTOR
JON PERTWEE (1970-1974)

SPEARHEAD FROM SPACE (4 EPISODES)

All four episodes exist as 16mm colour mute A and B roll negatives, and as 16mm mute colour positive prints, with separate magnetic soundtracks (and running to 1000 feet, 1000 feet, 1050 feet and 1000 feet respectively).

The original 16mm colour transmission prints from 1970 for all four episodes also exist at the BBC. When they were examined prior to the 1999 BBC2 repeat of the story, Episode One was found to be in good condition, but Episodes Three and Four were found to be suffering from film warp, and Episode Two was declared unsuitable for transmission due to film warp and print damage. A set of prints made in 1990 by BBC Enterprises had also been kept by the BBC, and Episodes Two, Three and Four

WIPED!

were found to be in very good condition. These three prints – along with the 1970 transmission print of Episode One – were thus transferred to DigiBeta to make the 1999 transmission tapes for the BBC2 screening.

A number of safety mags, viewing prints and black and white duplicate prints also exist for all four episodes.

DOCTOR WHO AND THE SILURIANS (7 EPISODES)

All seven episodes exist as 16mm black and white film negatives with optical soundtracks (running to 1000 feet, 1000 feet, 950 feet, 939 feet, 898 feet, 1000 feet and 1000 feet respectively). Most of the film inserts in all these episodes are out of phase.

Off-air NTSC colour copies of all seven episodes also exist, recorded from WTTW Channel 11 in Chicago in 1977. This transmission was of a compilation version of the story, and was therefore missing most of the original opening and closing credits, plus the reprises for most of the episodes. These domestic recordings were copied onto Betacam SP.

The story has been 'recolourised' three times, taking the colour information from the off-air NTSC recordings and adding it to the black and white signal from the better resolution film prints.

The first time was for BBC Video in 1993, when the story was released on VHS. Black and white film prints (although not the archived negatives) of all seven episodes were transferred to Betacam SP, and the black and white luminance signal combined with the colour from the NTSC domestic recordings. A portion of material on the NTSC colour recording – running to approximately 90 seconds and bridging Episodes Five and Six – had a fault and couldn't be used as a colour source. These 90 seconds were recolourised from scratch by a company called American Film Technologies Inc.

The story was repeated on BBC2 in 1999, and for this, a new broadcast master was made of all seven episodes. This took as its starting point the 1993 Betacam SP transfer of the 16mm black and white film prints. This time, though, more attention was given to removing dirt and noise problems in the picture, and the colour picture elements were colour-corrected and graded in a superior manner. Digital Betacam masters of all seven episodes were then made.

For the story's 2008 DVD release, a third restoration was done. First, new Digital Betacam transfers of the archived 16mm black and white film negatives were made of all seven episodes. These were combined with the 1992 Betacam SP recording of the NTSC domestic colour recording. VidFIRE was applied to the studio-recorded sections of the story, to restore the video look to the pictures. The sound was re-laid onto the episodes, using the off-air domestic recordings as the primary source for the first time. Extensive picture clean-up was also undertaken.

APPENDIX II

THE AMBASSADORS OF DEATH (7 EPISODES)

Episode One exists on its original two-inch 625-line colour transmission videotape (and is the oldest episode of *Doctor Who* to survive on its original transmission videotape). The BBC currently holds a D3 videotape copy of this, while the original has been donated to the National Film and Television Archive (NFTVA), where it is held in storage.

All seven episodes exist as 16mm black and white film negatives with optical soundtracks (running to 1000 feet, 924 feet, 926 feet, 924 feet, 1000 feet, 920 feet and 921 feet respectively). All of the film inserts in all seven episodes are out of phase.

Second generation off-air NTSC colour copies of all seven episodes also exist, recorded from WNED Channel 17 in Buffalo in 1977. These domestic recordings were copied onto Betacam SP. However, the recordings suffer from a large degree of interference, which manifests itself as rainbow patterns occurring frequently and randomly throughout the seven episodes (but particularly in Episodes Two, Three and Four).

In 1992, the *Doctor Who* Restoration Team attempted to restore this story to colour in the same manner as was done with 'Doctor Who and the Silurians'. Episode Five was fully recovered to colour, and nearly all of Episode Six too. However, the rainbow patterning in the off-air colour recordings saw the project abandoned partway through.

When the story was released on VHS in 2002, new Spirit telecine recordings of the 16mm black and white film negatives of Episodes Two to Seven were made, and new Betacam SP copies were made of the original Betamax NTSC colour off-air recordings. The black and white pictures were cleaned up, and VidFIRE was applied to the studio-recorded segments of Episodes Five and Six only. These two episodes were then completely recolourised using the NTSC colour.

Episodes Two, Three, Four and Seven were cleaned up, and where lengthy colour segments were available (unaffected by the rainbow patterning), these were intermittently added back to the pictures. The soundtracks to Episodes Two through to Seven were re-laid onto the episodes, using the off-air domestic recordings as the primary source.

The black and white film prints of Episodes Two to Seven were found to contain the chroma dots needed to apply the colour recovery process to this material, and these were used to finally restore the story to full colour for its 2012 release on DVD.

The trailer for Episode One of this story exists (retained at the end of the 16mm black and white film print of Episode Seven of 'Doctor Who and the Silurians', which is a programme-as-broadcast recording). This was recolourised partly by hand for its inclusion as an 'Easter Egg' on the DVD release of 'Doctor Who and the Silurians', and

WIPED!

by the chroma dot process for its inclusion on the DVD release of 'The Ambassadors of Death' itself.

The BBC also holds the clean opening title sequences for this story on 16mm colour film.

INFERNO (7 EPISODES)

All seven episodes exist as 525-line colour two-inch videotapes, as returned to the BBC from BBC Canada in 1983. These have all been transferred onto D1 videotape, still in the NTSC format, and the two-inch tapes have now been handed over to the NFTVA for storage. The version of Episode Five on the NTSC tape contains a scene removed from the transmission tape of the episode, which indicates it's an earlier edit.

All seven episodes have been reverse standards converted back to 625-line PAL colour, and are retained as Digital Betacam videotape copies.

All seven episodes also exist as 16mm black and white film negatives with optical soundtracks (running to 878 feet, 830 feet, 924 feet, 922 feet, 889 feet, 884 feet and 922 feet respectively), as found at BBC Enterprises in 1978.

The BBC also holds the clean opening title sequences for this story on 16mm colour film, which uniquely featured colour stock film of lava and volcanic eruptions, over which the story title and writer captions were overlaid.

TERROR OF THE AUTONS (4 EPISODES)

All four episodes exist as 16mm black and white film negatives with optical soundtracks (running to 926 feet, 932 feet, 881 feet and 831 feet respectively).

Off-air NTSC colour copies of all four episodes also exist, recorded from WTTW Channel 11 in Chicago in 1977. These domestic recordings were copied onto Betacam SP.

This story has been recolourised three times, taking the colour information from the off-air NTSC recordings and adding it to the black and white signal from the better resolution film prints.

The first time was for BBC video in 1993, when the story was released on VHS. Black and white film prints (not the archived negatives) of all four episodes were transferred to Betacam SP, and the black and white luminance signal then combined with the colour from the NTSC domestic recordings.

The story was scheduled to be repeated on BBC2 in 1999, and for this, a new broadcast master was made of all four episodes, before the decision was taken not to show the story after all. This took as its starting point the 1993 Betacam SP transfer of the 16mm black and white film prints. This time, though, more attention was given to removing dirt and noise problems in the picture, and the colour pictures were colour-corrected and better graded than before. Digital Betacam masters of all four episodes were then made.

Finally, when the story was prepared for release on DVD, new, high definition scans of the archive negatives were used as a basis for the restoration, which were VidFIREd where appropriate, and then combined with the colour from the NTSC recordings.

An insert tape for the magazine programme *Nationwide* from 1973, which was made for a feature about the departure of Katy Manning from the series, still survives at the BBC. This features a clip, running to just under a minute, of Jo's first meeting with the Doctor from Episode One in 625-line two-inch colour.

THE MIND OF EVIL (6 EPISODES)

All six episodes exist as 16mm black and white film negatives with optical soundtracks (running to 926 feet, 921 feet, 921 feet, 921 feet, 885 feet and 927 feet respectively).

Around six minutes of discontinuous footage from Episode Six exists as an off-air NTSC colour recording, recorded from WTTW Channel 11 in Chicago in 1977. This has been copied onto Betacam SP.

Episodes Two to Six have been recolourised using the chroma dot colour recovery process. However, no chroma dots were captured on the 16mm black and white film recording of Episode One, so it has not been possible to apply the same technique to this episode. For its 2013 release on DVD, the first episode will therefore have been coloured by hand. VidFIRE will be applied to the relevant sections of film.

THE CLAWS OF AXOS (4 EPISODES)

Episodes One and Four exist on their original 625-line two-inch colour transmission videotapes. These have each been copied onto D3 videotape, which is the format the BBC currently holds these episodes on, and the two-inch tapes have been donated to the NFTVA, where they are in storage.

Episodes Two and Three exist as 525-line two-inch colour videotapes, as returned from Canada in 1981. These have been transferred onto D1 videotape, still in the NTSC format, and the two-inch tapes have now been handed over to the NFTVA for storage. Both these episodes have been reverse standards converted back to 625-line PAL colour, and are retained as Digital Betacam videotape copies.

525-line two-inch tapes of Episodes One and Four were also kept by the BBC at one time, but these now reside at the NFTVA.

A 90-minute colour 625-line two-inch videotape of the studio recording session from 23 January 1971 for Episodes One and Two (which has the title 'The Vampire from Space' on the opening titles) was retained by the BBC. This was copied to D3 before being sent to the NFTVA.

The BBC also holds the clean opening title sequences for this story on 16mm colour film.

All four episodes also exist as 16mm black and white film negatives with optical soundtracks (each running to 1000 feet).

The story has been issued twice on DVD. The first time, NTSC Reverse Standards Conversions of Episodes Two and Three were used on the release. For the second issue, the 16mm black and white film prints of Episodes Two and Three were used as the basis for the restoration, with VidFIRE applied where appropriate, and then the colour from the NTSC RSC copies integrated over the black and white image.

COLONY IN SPACE (6 EPISODES)

All six episodes exist as 525-line two-inch colour videotapes, as returned from BBC Canada in 1983. These have been transferred onto D1 videotape, still in the NTSC format, and the two-inch tapes have now been handed over to the NFTVA. All these episodes have been reverse standards converted back to 625-line PAL colour, and are retained as Digital Betacam videotape copies.

All six episodes also exist as 16mm black and white film negatives with optical soundtracks (running to 914 feet, 856 feet, 892 feet, 914 feet, 952 feet and 953 feet respectively).

Three 16mm colour mute camera negative film trim rolls from the location filming of this story exist in a private collection, along with ten 16mm colour mute effects/modelwork film trim rolls and two 35mm colour mute effects/modelwork film trim rolls. The BBC have D3 videotape copies of this material.

THE DAEMONS (5 EPISODES)

Episode Four exists on its original two-inch 625-line colour transmission videotape. This has been copied onto D3 videotape, which is the format on which the BBC currently holds the episode, and the two-inch tape has been donated to the NFTVA, where it is kept in storage.

All five episodes also exist as 16mm black and white film negatives with optical soundtracks.

Off-air NTSC colour copies of all five episodes also exist, recorded from KCET Channel 28 in Los Angeles in 1978. This transmission was a compilation version of the story, and was missing opening and closing credits, plus reprises from most of the episodes. These domestic recordings were copied onto Betacam SP.

This story has been recolourised just the once to date, taking the colour information from the off-air NTSC recordings and adding it to the black and white signal from the better resolution film prints. This was done for a repeat screening on BBC2 in 1992, which was quickly followed by the release of the story on VHS. For this, black and white film prints (not the archived negatives) of Episodes One, Two, Three and Five were transferred to Betacam SP, and the black and white luminance signal was then combined with the colour from the NTSC domestic recordings to make D3 transmission masters.

Some of the location rushes of the burning milk van have been retained by the BBC for their 'stock shot' collection of films.

Mute colour 8mm film covering the location filming of this story in Aldbourne survives in a private collection.

DAY OF THE DALEKS (4 EPISODES)

All four episodes exist on their original 625-line two-inch colour transmission videotapes. These have each been copied onto D3 videotape for retention by the BBC, and the two-inch tapes have been donated to the NFTVA, where they are kept in storage.

THE CURSE OF PELADON (4 EPISODES)

Episodes One, Two and Four exist as 525-line two-inch colour videotapes, as returned from Canada in 1981. These have been transferred onto D1 videotape, still in the NTSC format, and the two-inch tapes have now been handed over to the NFTVA, where they are kept in storage. The colour 525-line two-inch tape of Episode Three, which was also returned from Canada in 1981, was junked by the BBC after it was first converted to 625-line videotape in 1982, although it was retained by Ian Levine. In 2008, it was borrowed back from Levine, and it too was transferred onto D1 videotape. All four episodes have been reverse standards converted back to 625-line PAL colour, and are retained as Digital Betacam videotape copies.

All four episodes also exist as 16mm black and white film negatives with optical soundtracks (running to 922 feet, 921 feet, 914 feet and 911 feet respectively).

16mm colour film sequences of the Doctor and Jo climbing the cliff from Episode One, and the fight between the Doctor and Grun from Episode Three, both exist in private collections. Both films have been loaned back to the BBC, and were used in the DVD restoration of this story.

The compilation version in two 50-minute episodes from the 1982 *Doctor Who and the Monsters* repeat season also exists on two-inch videotape (at the NFTVA) and D3 (at the BBC). These are normal standards conversions of this material.

WIPED!

THE SEA DEVILS (6 EPISODES)

Episodes Four, Five and Six exist on their original 625-line two-inch colour transmission videotapes. These have each been copied onto D3 videotape, and the two-inch tapes have been donated to the NFTVA, where they are kept in storage.

Episodes One, Two and Three exist as 525-line two-inch videotapes, as returned from Canada in 1983. These have been transferred onto D1 videotape, still in the NTSC format, and the two-inch tapes have now been handed over to the NFTVA. All three episodes have been reverse standards converted back to 625-line PAL colour, and are retained as Digital Betacam videotape copies. Episodes Four, Five and Six also exist in this format.

When this story was selected for repeat on BBC2 in 1992, it was found that the original 625-line two-inch videotape of Episode Five was badly scratched, and was deemed untransmittable. A conversion from the 525-line two-inch videotape was shown instead (and was also used for the VHS release of this story some time later). In 1997, Steve Roberts developed a scratch repair technique that was able to completely repair the damage to the tape. A new 625-line D3 master of this repaired episode was made for the BBC archives.

The BBC also has 16mm black and white telerecordings of all six episodes of this story.

A mute colour 8mm film covering the location filming of this story survives in a private collection. This runs to three minutes and 51 seconds, and was shot by one of the sailors at the naval base used as a location for this story. The BBC has a copy of this material, and it was included in the DVD release.

THE MUTANTS (6 EPISODES)

Episodes Three, Four, Five and Six exist on their original 625-line two-inch colour transmission videotapes. These have each been copied onto D3 videotape, and the two-inch tapes have been donated to the NFTVA, where they are kept in storage.

Episodes One and Two exist as 525-line two-inch colour videotapes, as returned from Canada in 1981. These have been transferred onto D1 videotape, still in the NTSC format, and the two-inch tapes have now been handed over to the NFTVA. Both these episodes have been reverse standards converted back to 625-line PAL colour, and are retained as Digital Betacam videotape copies.

All six episodes also exist as 16mm black and white film negatives with optical soundtracks (running to 917 feet, 916 feet, 1000 feet, 1000 feet, 1000 feet and 1000 feet respectively).

APPENDIX II

THE TIME MONSTER (6 EPISODES)
All six episodes exist as colour 525-line two-inch videotapes, as returned from Canada in 1981. These have been transferred onto D1 videotape, still in the NTSC format, and the two-inch tapes have now been handed over to the NFTVA, where they are kept in storage. All these episodes have been reverse standards converted back to 625-line PAL colour, and are retained as Digital Betacam videotape copies.

A 625-line two-inch low band (i.e. black and white, not colour) recording of Episode Six was made by the BBC on 1 December 1972 (according to the recording date noted on the spool). In 1992 Paul Vanezis combined the colour signal from the NTSC conversion of Episode Six with the black and white pictures from the 625-line recording, to produce a new copy of the episode that is almost as good as having the original 625-line two-inch colour transmission tape. This version is held by the BBC on Digital Betacam.

All six episodes also exist as 16mm black and white film negatives with optical soundtracks. A 16mm black and white viewing print of Episode Six also survives.

THE THREE DOCTORS (4 EPISODES)
All four episodes exist on their original 625-line two-inch colour transmission videotapes. These have each been copied onto D3 videotape, and the two-inch tapes have been donated to the NFTVA, where they are kept in storage.

CARNIVAL OF MONSTERS (4 EPISODES)
Episodes One, Two and Four exist on their original 625-line two-inch colour transmission videotapes. These have each been copied onto D3 videotape, and the two-inch tapes have been donated to the NFTVA, where they are kept in storage.

The original two-inch colour videotape of Episode Three was junked in 1981, when it was found to clog up on playback. A salvage dub was made, again on two-inch 625-line videotape, and used for the 1981 BBC2 repeat screening of the story. This has now been copied onto D3 videotape, and the two-inch tape has been donated to the NFTVA, where it is kept in storage.

A new version of Episode Four was also made for the BBC2 repeat in 1981, which at the request of the story's director, Barry Letts, removed some shots showing the bald cap worn by actor Peter Halliday as the character Pletrac starting to come loose. Again this was on two-inch videotape, and again, a D3 copy was made before the original was donated to the NFTVA.

The first edit of Episode Two also exists on its original two-inch colour videotape, which contains additional material and the unused 'Delaware' version of the theme tune on its opening and closing credits. This too has been copied onto D3 videotape, and the two-inch tape has been donated to the NFTVA, where it is in storage.

WIPED!

The 1972 BBC programme *Looking In* contains material shot on 16mm colour film from behind the scenes in the studio and gallery of this story during the recording of the final episode. This is kept in the BBC archive.

The BBC Visual Effects Department also kept a 16mm film of test footage shot for this story, showing the Drashig puppet tearing through various fake bulkheads, and footage of the spaceship landing. This is now in private hands, although the BBC has a copy.

FRONTIER IN SPACE (6 EPISODES)

Episodes Four and Five exist on their original 625-line two-inch colour transmission videotapes, which were always held by the BBC. Episodes One, Two, Three and Six exist as ex-ABC dubs on 625-line two-inch colour videotapes, returned to the BBC in 1983, which are probably third or fourth generation copies. All six episodes have all been copied onto D3 videotape, and the two-inch tapes have been donated to the NFTVA, where they are in storage.

The first edit of Episode Five also exists on its original 625-line two-inch colour videotape. This contains no extra material, just a longer reprise from the preceding episode, but has the 'Delaware' theme dubbed onto its opening and closing credits. This too has been copied onto D3 videotape, and the two-inch tape has been donated to the NFTVA, where it is in storage.

All six episodes also exist as 16mm black and white film negatives with optical soundtracks. These copies run to 876 feet, 907 feet, 902 feet, 886 feet, 900 feet and 950 feet respectively.

PLANET OF THE DALEKS (6 EPISODES)

Episodes One, Two, Four, Five and Six exist on their original 625-line two-inch colour transmission videotapes. These have each been copied onto D3 videotape, and the two-inch tapes have been donated to the NFTVA, where they are kept in storage.

Episode Three exists as a 16mm black and white negative with optical soundtrack (and runs to 847 feet).

In 2008, Episode Three was recolourised using the chroma dot colour recovery process. At about the same time, the US company Legend Films also recolourised Episode Three from scratch. By combining the colour elements from these two sources with a cleaned-up and VidFIREd copy of the black and white signal from the 16mm film negative, a full-colour version was created. This was used on the 2|entertain DVD release of this story.

D3 transmission tapes were made of all six episodes for this story's 1993 BBC1 repeat, which saw Episode Three screened in black and white. These tapes include the five-minute mini-documentaries that preceded each episode on that occasion (which were all made on Betacam SP, and then edited onto the D3 transmission masters).

THE GREEN DEATH (6 EPISODES)

All six episodes exist on their original 625-line two-inch colour transmission videotapes. These have each been copied onto D3 videotape, and the two-inch tapes have been donated to the NFTVA, where they are kept in storage.

The first edit of Episode Five, which has an unsyphered soundtrack, also exists on its original two-inch colour videotape. This too has been copied onto D3 videotape, and the two-inch tape has been donated to the NFTVA, where it is kept in storage.

THE TIME WARRIOR (4 EPISODES)

All four episodes exist on their original 625-line two-inch colour transmission videotapes. These have each been copied onto D3 videotape, and the two-inch tapes have been donated to the NFTVA, where they are kept in storage.

INVASION OF THE DINOSAURS (6 EPISODES)

Parts Two, Three, Four, Five and Six exist on their original 625-line two-inch colour transmission videotapes. These have each been copied onto D3 videotape, and the two-inch tapes have been donated to the NFTVA, where they are kept in storage.

Part One exists as a 16mm black and white duplicate negative with optical soundtrack (running to 1000 feet), copied from a 16mm positive print originally discovered by Roger Stevens in the early 1980s. A separate magnetic soundtrack and 16mm duplicate positive print were also made from this original print. The original was borrowed again by the BBC in 1994, and a telecine transfer made onto D3 videotape.

A 16mm mute positive black and white film cutting copy print for Part One also exists at the BBC (running to 700 feet). This contains all the location film sequences (only) for this episode, and includes a scene cut from the broadcast episode, of a looter being attacked by an off-screen dinosaur.

The first edit of Part Three also exists on its original two-inch colour videotape, which has an extra scene of Mike Yates rescuing the Doctor from a T-Rex. This too has been copied onto D3 videotape, and the two-inch tape has been donated to the NFTVA, where it is kept in storage.

An A and B roll 16mm colour mute negative of the location sequences for Part Five exists in a private collection, although a copy has been made by the BBC on D3 videotape. Other film sequences held in private collections include footage of the spaceship models and the vanishing pterodactyl.

The 16mm print of Part One contains the chroma dots needed to apply the colour

WIPED!

recovery process to this material. However, the result is not totally perfect, with a lot of blue detail missing from the picture. A recolourised version of the episode was included as an extra on the 2012 DVD release of this story by 2|entertain.

DEATH TO THE DALEKS (4 EPISODES)

Parts Two, Three and Four exist on their original 625-line two-inch colour transmission videotapes. These have each been copied onto D3 videotape, and the two-inch tapes have been donated to the NFTVA, where they are kept in storage.

A 625-line two-inch colour videotape of Part One exists in private hands. In 1992 a colour D3 videotape copy was made of this for the BBC.

Part One also exists as a 525-line two-inch colour videotape, as returned from Canada in 1981. This has been converted to 625-line two-inch videotape, although using a regular standards converter, and not by reverse standards conversion. A 625-line one-inch copy of this episode also exists, as returned from Australia in 1985, which has the opening scene edited out.

A 90-minute 625-line two-inch colour videotape of the studio recording session from 4 December 1973 for this story was retained by the BBC. This was copied to D3 before being sent to the NFTVA.

THE MONSTER OF PELADON (6 EPISODES)

All six episodes exist on their original 625-line two-inch colour transmission videotapes. These have each been copied onto D3 videotape, and the two-inch tapes have been donated to the NFTVA, where they are in storage.

A separate magnetic audio soundtrack recording of the film rushes for this story (around ten reels of tape) exists in private hands, although a copy has been made by the BBC.

PLANET OF THE SPIDERS (6 EPISODES)

All six episodes exist on their original 625-line two-inch colour transmission videotapes. These have each been copied onto D3 videotape, and the two-inch tapes have been donated to the NFTVA, where they are in storage.

The 625-line videotape of Part Two is quite badly scratched in places, and the D3 videotape copy of this episode retains these scratches.

The compilation repeat of this story, broadcast on BBC1 on 27 December 1974, also exists on its original two-inch colour transmission tapes. Due to its length (105 minutes), it is over two separate two-inch spools. These have been copied onto D3 videotape, and the two-inch tapes have been donated to the NFTVA, where they are kept in storage.

APPENDIX II

* * *

From this point onwards, every episode of *Doctor Who* was initially kept by the BBC on its original transmission videotape, with the sole exception of 'The Deadly Assassin' Part Three. These tapes were all two-inch 625-line colour tapes from 'Robot' in 1974 through to 'The Five Doctors' in 1983, and then one-inch 625-line colour tapes from 'Warriors of the Deep' in 1984 through to 'Survival' in 1989.

This section will cover any additional footage or programme notes for the stories from 'Robot' onwards, other than the transmitted episodes themselves. If a story isn't mentioned, it's because only the transmission tapes survive.

THE FOURTH DOCTOR
TOM BAKER (1974-1981)

ROBOT (4 EPISODES)

16mm mute colour film survives in a private collection of the script read-through for this story. This was shot for the documentary *Inside Television* in 1974, although the documentary was subsequently halted in early production and never finished. This film was junked by the BBC, along with the separate magnetic soundtrack, but the mute film survived. A copy has been made by the BBC.

A mute colour 8mm film covering the location filming of this story survives in a private collection. This runs to one minute and 45 seconds.

THE ARK IN SPACE (4 EPISODES)

16mm mute colour film (400 feet) of the various model sequences for this story exists in a private collection. The BBC has a copy.

The edited 70-minute repeat version also exists on 625-line two-inch colour videotape. The original two-inch tape is in storage at the NFTVA, while the BBC hold a D3 copy.

The BBC also has the original 1975 trailer for Part One of this story on 625-line two-inch colour videotape, transferred to D3.

THE SONTARAN EXPERIMENT (2 EPISODES)

The 50-minute repeat compilation of this story from 1976 also exists on two-inch tape. The BBC retains a D3 copy, while the two-inch tape has been sent to the NFTVA for storage.

GENESIS OF THE DALEKS (6 EPISODES)

The 85-minute repeat compilation version of this story from 1975, the two-x-50-minute compilation version from the 1982 *Doctor Who and the Monsters* repeat season

WIPED!

and the untransmitted longer 71 edits of the 1982 repeat version all exist on 625-line two-inch colour videotape (at the NFTVA) and D3 (at the BBC).

The 1975 repeat compilation was used by BBC Enterprises as the sound source for the 1979 LP release of this story, and the two-inch videotape was damaged in the process. The original two-inch videotape of Part One has also suffered a large degree of damage over the years through overuse.

The story was repeated again on BBC2 in 2000. Parts One to Three were transmitted from the D3 archive tapes with no restoration. Parts Four to Six were tidied up for transmission, with drop-outs, off-locks, and dirt and sparkle on the film sequences removed as best as possible.

REVENGE OF THE CYBERMEN (4 EPISODES)

This story was originally planned to be repeated in 2000 on BBC2, following 'Genesis of the Daleks'. In preparation, all four episodes were tidied up, with drop-outs, off-locks, and dirt and sparkle on the film sequences removed as best as possible. The repeat was subsequently cancelled.

TERROR OF THE ZYGONS (4 EPISODES)

This story was originally planned to be repeated in 2000 on BBC2, following 'Genesis of the Daleks' and (the ultimately abandoned) 'Revenge of the Cybermen'. In preparation, all four episodes were tidied up, with drop-outs, off-locks, and dirt and sparkle on the film sequences removed as best as possible. A private collector held the 16mm colour film sequences for half of Part Two, all of Part Three and all of Part Four. These were transferred to Digital Betacam on the BBC's Spirit telecine, and edited back into the new transmission masters for these episodes. The repeat was subsequently cancelled.

A separate magnetic audio soundtrack recording of the film rushes for this story (two reels of tape) exists in private hands.

A mute 16mm film print of the film rushes of Part One also exists in the private collection of original film editor Ian McKendrick. This includes the deleted scene of the invisible TARDIS arriving in Scotland. This was a cutting copy of the sequence, and had been assembled from both colour and black and white sources (there are nine shots in the sequence; five were in colour, four were in black and white). This film has been made available to the BBC, the black and white sections have been recolourised by hand, and the sound restored from the sound rushes. A 'Director's Cut' version of the episode, with this sequence restored into the narrative, has been prepared for the 2013 DVD release of this story.

APPENDIX II

PLANET OF EVIL (4 EPISODES)
48 seconds of material from the studio recording of the first episode of this story exists (purely by chance) at the end of the two-inch colour videotape of Part One. This has been retained on the D3 copies of this episode.

PYRAMIDS OF MARS (4 EPISODES)
The unused 16mm model film sequence of the TARDIS materialising on the alternative future Earth exists in a private collection, although the BBC has a copy.

Black and white timecoded Shibaden recordings of unsyphered early edits of Parts One, Two and Four also exist in a private collection. The BBC was able to take copies of this material when the story was being prepared for DVD release in 2003.

The 1976 edited 60-minute repeat version of this story also exists on two-inch colour videotape. The original two-inch tape is in storage at the NFTVA, while the BBC holds a D3 copy.

THE ANDROID INVASION (4 EPISODES)
A black and white timecoded Shibaden recording of an unsyphered copy of Part One exists in a private collection.

A separate magnetic audio soundtrack recording of the film rushes for this story (one reel of tape) exists in private hands.

THE BRAIN OF MORBIUS (4 EPISODES)
A small section of incidental music in Part One (in the scene where Sarah emerges from hiding near the end) was known to be missing from all screenings after the original transmission, and from the story's release on VHS. When the DVD was being prepared in 2007, it was discovered that the BBC's two-inch videotape master of the episode was a protection dub – the original was presumably damaged at some point in the past. It appears likely that the damage occurred during the scene with the missing music, and the damaged section was replaced with either the same section of action from the studio tape (assuming it still existed at that point), or a BBC Enterprises copy that was completely unsyphered. (The episode was accidentally sold to some US markets in the late 1970s with no music or sound effects at all.) An off-air audio recording of the episode was used to restore the missing music to the scene for the DVD.

The 1976 edited 60-minute repeat version of this story also exists on two-inch colour videotape. The original two-inch tape is in storage at the NFTVA, while the BBC hold a D3 copy.

A black and white timecoded Shibaden recording of an unsyphered copy of Part Two exists in a private collection

WIPED!

THE SEEDS OF DOOM (6 EPISODES)
A short outtake from this story exists on the BBC's *Thanks for the Memory* programme, shown as part of the *Festival 77* Silver Jubilee celebrations on 31 July 1977.

THE DEADLY ASSASSIN (4 EPISODES)
When this story was repeated on BBC1 in 1977, the master two-inch videotape of Part Three was physically edited to remove the freeze-frame cliffhanger as seen on the original broadcast, following a complaint by the National Viewers' and Listeners' Association. Around six seconds of footage was removed by editing the closing credits of the episode onto the master videotape just prior to the point the freeze-frame started – effectively wiping over the original ending. The footage was restored for DVD release by utilising off-air U-MATIC and Philips 1500 recordings of the original transmission.

THE FACE OF EVIL (4 EPISODES)
About 50 minutes of mute 16mm colour film trims of the Ealing film sequences of this story exists in private hands, although the BBC has been able to take a copy.

THE ROBOTS OF DEATH (4 EPISODES)
The two-x-50-minute repeat compilations of this story also exist on their original two-inch videotapes. The tapes are now at the NFTVA, while the BBC retains D3 copies.

A black and white timecoded Shibaden recording of an unsyphered early edit of Part One exists in a private collection, as does a further black and white timecoded Shibaden recording of all the model film sequences for the story. These were loaned to the BBC in 1999 for the DVD release.

THE TALONS OF WENG-CHIANG (6 EPISODES)
A black and white timecoded Shibaden recording of the final day's studio recording exists in a private collection. The BBC was able to take a copy of this material when the story was being prepared for DVD release in 2003.

A black and white timecoded Shibaden recording of an unsyphered copy of Part Six also exists in a private collection.

HORROR OF FANG ROCK (4 EPISODES)
A black and white timecoded Shibaden recording of an unsyphered copy of Part Four exists in a private collection.

THE INVISIBLE ENEMY (4 EPISODES)
A black and white timecoded Shibaden recording of an unsyphered early edit of Part

APPENDIX II

Three (which runs to a shorter length than the transmitted episode) exists in a private collection, as does a further black and white timecoded Shibaden recording of two of the studio recording sessions. These were loaned to the BBC in 2008 for the DVD release.

IMAGE OF THE FENDAHL (4 EPISODES)

A black and white timecoded Shibaden copy of all the film sequences from this story (including deleted scenes), plus a few studio scenes, exists in a private collection. This was made during the gallery-only studio session for this story. The BBC was able to take copies of this material when the story was being prepared for DVD release in 2007.

THE SUNMAKERS (4 EPISODES)

Black and white timecoded Shibaden recordings of unsyphered versions of Parts One, Three and Four exist in a private collection.

Several outtakes from this story exist on *White Powder Christmas*, a 1978 Christmas tape put together by BBC engineers for private viewing.

UNDERWORLD (4 EPISODES)

A VHS tape (approximately 40 minutes' duration) exists in a private collection showing part of a studio session in which Tom Baker and Louise Jameson record scenes against a CSO background.

Eleven black and white timecoded Shibaden tapes of the studio recording sessions (running to approximately seven hours of material) also exist in a private collection.

THE INVASION OF TIME (6 EPISODES)

A rehearsal copy[96] of the 16mm colour film sequences for all six episodes (including material not used in the finished programmes) were retained by the BBC. The film was transferred in 2007 in preparation for the DVD release of this story, and was found to be quite badly faded, with most scenes having a slightly red hue to them. This was due to the dyes used in the production of the film changing over time (and wasn't helped by being a rehearsal copy in the first place). The film was colour-corrected, and the appropriate sequences re-inserted into the DVD masters of all six episodes.[97]

An additional mute 16mm colour film exists in a private collection, which features

---

[96] A rehearsal copy or rehearsal print is a copy of the film sequences from a programme used as part of the studio rehearsal for the studio recorded portions of that programme. This was done so as to not risk any damage to the transmission (or 'master') print of the film sequences, which would be played in only during 'live' studio recordings.

[97] Due to an error made in the colour correction while grading the story for DVD, Borusa's and Rodan's robes appear a different colour in the re-inserted film sequences than in the scenes recorded in the TV studio.

WIPED!

a deleted scene between the Sontarans and Kelner.

THE PIRATE PLANET (4 EPISODES)
16mm colour film sequences for all four episodes (including material not used in the finished programmes) were retained by the BBC as both negatives and positive prints.

THE STONES OF BLOOD (4 EPISODES)
A 71 edit of Part Two also exists on its original 625-line two-inch tape, which contains material cut from the transmitted version. This two-inch tape is now in storage at the NFTVA, while the BBC holds a D3 copy.

THE ANDROIDS OF TARA (4 EPISODES)
A black and white timecoded Shibaden recording of an unsyphered early edit of Part Three exists in a private collection

Several outtakes from this story exist on *Good King Memorex*, a 1979 Christmas tape put together by BBC engineers for private viewing.

THE POWER OF KROLL (4 EPISODES)
A black and white timecoded Shibaden tape of some of the studio recording also exists in a private collection. The BBC was able to take a copy of this material when the story was being prepared for DVD release in 2007.

The BBC regional magazine programme *Variations* visited the location of this story during production, and made a six-minute feature about the filming. Although this programme no longer exists at the BBC, an off-air video copy does survive.

THE ARMAGEDDON FACTOR (6 EPISODES)
An incomplete black and white timecoded Shibaden recording of an unsyphered early edit of Part Four exists in a private collection, as does a black and white timecoded Shibaden recording of a studio session.

Several outtakes from this story exist on *Good King Memorex*, a 1979 Christmas tape put together by BBC engineers for private viewing.

CITY OF DEATH (4 EPISODES)
Three black and white Shibaden tapes with burnt-in timecode exist of the studio recording sessions on 22 May and 4/5 June 1979, running to just under four hours of material.

35mm mute film of the model effects and 'chicken sequence' exists in a private collection. Other 35mm and 16mm film material also exists in a private collection.

A sketch starring Tom Baker and John Cleese, recorded on the set of this story,

APPENDIX II

exists on *Good King Memorex*, a 1979 Christmas tape put together by BBC engineers for private viewing.

THE CREATURE FROM THE PIT (4 EPISODES)
A 71 edit of Part Three exists on its original 625-line two-inch tape (containing a cut scene of one of the guards being stabbed). This two-inch tape is now in storage at the NFTVA, while the BBC holds a D3 copy.

THE HORNS OF NIMON (4 EPISODES)
A black and white timecoded Shibaden recording of an unsyphered 71 edit of Part Two exists in a private collection

SHADA (6 EPISODES)
This was planned as a six-part story to conclude *Doctor Who*'s seventeenth season in early 1980. All the Cambridge location filming was completed on 16mm colour film, as was most of the model film work for the story. The studio material was then meant to be recorded at Television Centre in London in November and December 1979. The first three-day studio block in TC3 was successfully completed between Saturday 3 and Monday 5 November 1979, and the cast and crew returned to the BBC's Acton rehearsal rooms to prepare for the second block. However, that planned two-day studio, due to take place on Monday 19 and Tuesday 20 November 1979, had to be abandoned at the last minute due to industrial action at the BBC. All the sets were assembled in TC6, but the cast and crew just weren't allowed into the studio to record any material. The rehearsals for the last studio block were then cancelled, as was the last studio block itself, which had been due to take place between Saturday 1 and Monday 3 December 1979.

All the 16mm location and model film, plus the five two-inch tapes that contained all the studio material recorded in block one, were retained by the BBC Film and Videotape Library, under a special arrangement agreed between Sue Malden and incoming *Doctor Who* producer John Nathan-Turner. The two-inch tapes have since each been copied onto D3 videotape, and then donated to the NFTVA, where they are kept in storage.

When the 1983 story 'The Five Doctors' utilised two filmed sequences originally shot for 'Shada', the scenes were cut from the original 16mm film negatives and incorporated into the 16mm film sequences prepared for 'The Five Doctors'.

Some 35mm effects footage from 'Shada', filmed before the story was abandoned, exists in a private collection.

Mute colour 8mm footage covering the location filming of this story in Cambridge survives in a private collection.

WIPED!

THE LEISURE HIVE (4 EPISODES)
The 16mm colour film of the scenes on Brighton beach from Part One survive in a private collection, although the BBC does have a copy.

Black and white timecoded Shibaden recordings of unsyphered early edits of all four episodes also exist in a private collection. The BBC was able to take copies of this material when the story was being prepared for DVD release in 2004. Because these tapes contained the clean, unsyphered sound, a Dolby 5.1 soundtrack was able to be produced for the DVD.

Two colour U-MATIC tapes with burnt-in timecode exist in a private collection containing material from the studio recording sessions of this story. The BBC have copies of this material.

Mute colour 8mm film covering the location filming of this story in Brighton survives in a private collection.

MEGLOS (4 EPISODES)
Black and white timecoded Shibaden recordings of unsyphered early edits of all four episodes exist in a private collection.

FULL CIRCLE (4 EPISODES)
Mute colour 8mm film covering the location filming of this story survives in a private collection.

STATE OF DECAY (4 EPISODES)
35mm colour film of the model shots and visual effects used in this story exists in a private collection.

WARRIORS' GATE (4 EPISODES)
A 71 edit of Part Two exists on its original two-inch tape. This is now in storage at the NFTVA, while the BBC holds a D3 copy.

A colour U-MATIC tape of all the model film inserts exists in a private collection. The original colour 16mm film of the model filming exists in another private collection.

A black and white timecoded Shibaden recording of an unsyphered 71 edit of Part One exists in a private collection.

A colour timecoded U-MATIC unsyphered recording of the first eight minutes of Part Four exists in a private collection.

THE KEEPER OF TRAKEN (4 EPISODES)
A colour timecoded Philips 1500 recording of an unsyphered 71 edit of Part One

APPENDIX II

exists in a private collection, as does a black and white timecoded Shibaden recording of an unsyphered 71 edit of Part Four.

A colour U-MATIC recording with burnt-in timecode of the 71 edit of Part Four, minus the final scene, exists in a private collection.

LOGOPOLIS (4 EPISODES)

A mute 16mm colour rush print of some of the Barnett Bypass filming is held in a private collection. This was loaned to the BBC in 2006 when the story was being prepared for release on DVD.

A colour VHS tape with burnt-in timecode exists in a private collection, containing material from the final studio recording session of this story, including the regeneration sequence.

THE FIFTH DOCTOR
PETER DAVISON (1981-1984)

CASTROVALVA (4 EPISODES)

All the colour 16mm film sequences for this story, including the A/B roll camera negatives, exist at the BBC. These include scenes that were cut from the finished episodes.

Colour U-MATIC tapes with burnt-in timecode (duration approximately four and half hours, but 40 minutes of this material is mute) exists in a private collection, containing material from the studio recording sessions of this story.

FOUR TO DOOMSDAY (4 EPISODES)

A colour U-MATIC tape (duration approximately 60 minutes) exists in a private collection containing material from the first studio recording session of this story. This was the first hour of Peter Davison's first day as the Doctor in-studio.

KINDA (4 EPISODES)

71 edits of Parts One, Two and Three are held in a private collection on colour U-MATIC tapes with burnt-in timecode. These are dubs from VHS tapes (now wiped).

THE VISITATION (4 EPISODES)

All the colour 16mm film sequences for this story, including the A/B roll camera negatives, exist at the BBC.

A colour U-MATIC tape exists in a private collection containing material from one of the studio recording sessions of this story. However, it lasts approximately 20 seconds only, from a scene involving the Terileptils from Part Four.

WIPED!

BLACK ORCHID (2 EPISODES)
All the colour 16mm film sequences for this story, including the A/B roll camera negatives, also exist at the BBC. These include scenes that were cut from the finished episodes.

EARTHSHOCK (4 EPISODES)
All the colour 16mm film sequences for this story, including the A/B roll camera negatives, exist at the BBC.

The two-x-50-minute-episode compilation versions of this story from the 1982 *Doctor Who and the Monsters* repeat season also exist on two-inch videotape (at the NFTVA) and D3 (at the BBC).

A VHS recording of a studio session (recorded from a clean studio feed, not necessarily when the two-inch machine was also running) with burnt-in timecode, running to two hours and 30 minutes approximately, exists in a private collection, which the BBC has access to.

A VHS copy of the 71 edit of Part Four with burnt-in timecode also exists in a private collection, which the BBC has access to.

TIME-FLIGHT (4 EPISODES)
All the colour 16mm film sequences for this story, including the A/B roll camera negatives, exist at the BBC.

A 90-minute colour 625-line two-inch tape exists of one of the second studio block sessions for this story. This has been sent to the NFTVA for storage, but the BBC retains a D3 copy.

A number of VHS tapes with burnt-in timecode exist in a private collection, containing material from the studio recording sessions of this story. The BBC has copies of this material.

ARC OF INFINITY (4 EPISODES)
A 71 edit of Part Four is held on a colour VHS tape with burnt-in timecode in a private collection.

A number of U-MATIC tapes with burnt-in timecode exist in a private collection, containing material from the studio recording sessions of this story. The BBC has copies of this material.

SNAKEDANCE (4 EPISODES)
A 40-minute colour two-inch tape exists of iso-camera recorded material from one of the studio sessions for this story. This has been sent to the NFTVA for storage, but the

BBC retains a D3 copy.

A 71 edit of the last five minutes of Part Four is held on a VHS tape with burnt-in timecode in a private collection.

VHS timecoded recordings of unsyphered 72 edits of Parts One, Two, and Three also exist in a private collection.

MAWDRYN UNDEAD (4 EPISODES)

A mute 16mm colour film of location rushes from this story exists in a private collection, although the BBC has a copy.

A 16mm colour film – thought to be an audition print or trims – of location material from the first two episodes also exists in a private collection. This contains material that was cut from the finished episodes. Again, the BBC has a copy of this material.

TERMINUS (4 EPISODES)

A VHS tape with burnt-in timecode of some of the model shots filmed for this story exists in a private collection, to which the BBC has access.

ENLIGHTENMENT (4 EPISODES)

Colour 16mm film of the Ealing studio sequences from this story exists in a private collection.

In 2009, 2|entertain released a 're-imagined' version of this story, as an extra on the DVD release of the transmitted version. This was edited from a copy of the transmission tapes, with new CGI effects added, and presented as a single 75-minute feature, cropped to a 16:9 picture ratio.

THE FIVE DOCTORS (1 EPISODE)

A 71 edit of this story exists, contained on two 625-line two-inch tapes because of its duration (97 minutes 35 seconds). These tapes are now in storage at the NFTVA, while the BBC holds a D3 copy.

All the colour 16mm film sequences for this story, including the A/B roll camera negatives, also exist at the BBC.

All of the studio recordings for this story (carried out between Tuesday 29 and Thursday 31 March 1983) also exist on their original two-inch tapes. These six tapes have been sent to the NFTVA for storage, while the BBC retains D3 copies.

Other two-inch tapes also exist from the production of this story, which contain transfers of the 16mm film sequences, and copies of certain studio scenes that have been treated with additional effects, made during the gallery-only session for this

WIPED!

story. Again, these have been sent to the NFTVA, and D3 copies have been kept by the BBC.

A U-MATIC tape copy of all the film rushes (including outtakes) exists in a private collection. This was made by pointing a video camera at a television monitor replaying the film sequences, and so isn't a direct line copy. The BBC has a copy of this footage.

In 1995, BBC Video released a Special Edition of this story, produced by Paul Vanezis. He re-edited the story from scratch, utilising material from the two-inch studio, gallery and film transfer tapes only. New musical sequences were provided by Peter Howell, and the soundtrack was mixed in Dolby Surround. New graphics and effects were also added. This version, running to 102 minutes, is held by BBC Worldwide on D3 videotape.

In 1999, the Special Edition was released on DVD by BBC Worldwide. A new Dolby 5.1 soundtrack was produced for it, and some basic remastering was done on the original 1995 D3 material. This version is held by BBC Worldwide on Digital Betacam videotape.

In 2008, both the Special Edition and the transmitted version were released on DVD by 2|entertain. For this release, the colour 16mm A/B roll camera negatives of all the location film were transferred onto Digital Betacam via a Spirit telecine machine, and then re-edited into the new DVD masters of both the Special Edition and the transmitted version.

The story was edited into four 25-minute episodes for its repeat on BBC1 in 1984. This four-part version is held by the BBC as Digital Betacam dubs of the original one-inch tapes, which were subsequently junked.

A VHS recording of the unsyphered edit of this four-part version also exists in a private collection.

From 'Warriors of the Deep' onwards, the BBC occasionally kept a small number of one-inch studio and location tapes - plus the odd 71 edit – from the stories produced. However, just a few years later, from 'The Trial of a Time Lord' onwards, the amount of studio/location footage – plus 71 edits – retained by the BBC dramatically increased. This material was kept until all the Corporation's one-inch tapes were junked by the Film and Videotape Library in the early/mid 2000s. Unlike the one-inch transmission tapes, the BBC didn't retain copies of this unbroadcast material. These junked one-inch *Doctor Who* tapes were then all deposited with BBC Worldwide/2|entertain, so they could be accessed for potential DVD extras. Most of the tapes haven't been reviewed, so their exact content isn't known. Unfortunately, the long-term future of these tapes isn't guaranteed, and they may well be permanently junked at some point.

APPENDIX II

WARRIORS OF THE DEEP (4 EPISODES)
A colour U-MATIC timecoded recording of the unsyphered 72 edit of Part One exists in a private collection.

THE AWAKENING (2 EPISODES)
The 16mm colour location film for this story is still held by the BBC.

Mute 16mm colour film trims (material not used in the finished story) are held in a private collection. These include an outtake that was also featured on the edition of *The Late, Late Breakfast* Show transmitted on 10 September 1983 on BBC1, which also is retained by the BBC.

The 71 edit of Part One is held on colour VHS tape with burnt-in timecode in a private collection.

VHS timecoded recordings of the unsyphered 72 edit of both episodes also exist in a private collection.

The 50-minute repeat compilation of this story from 1984 is held by the BBC on Digital Betacam cassette, dubbed from the original one-inch tape, which was then junked.

FRONTIOS (4 EPISODES)
71 edits of Parts One (28 minutes 58 seconds), Two (25 minutes 10 seconds), Three (25 minutes 17 seconds) and Four (28 minutes and 13 seconds) are held on colour U-MATIC tapes with burnt-in timecode in a private collection.

RESURRECTION OF THE DALEKS (2 EPISODES)
This is a complicated one to explain! 'Resurrection of the Daleks' was originally written, produced and edited as a standard four-part *Doctor Who* story. All four episodes were initially made as overlong 71 edits, and then tightened up with a second edit to make 72 edits. These were syphered and prepared for transmission, and *would* have gone out in that form if the television schedules for the 1984 Winter Olympics hadn't got in the way.

With just weeks to go before transmission, it was decided that the story would have to be screened in two 50-minute slots instead. Parts One and Two were edited into a new Part One (which became a 73 edit), and Parts Three and Four were edited into a new Part Two (also a 73 edit). These two 50-minute transmission versions were made on 625-line one-inch colour videotape. They have since been copied onto Digital Betacam videocassette, and the one-inch tapes junked.

Similarly, all four 72-edit episodes were copied onto Digital Betacam, and the one-inch tapes junked.

WIPED!

The 71 edit of the original Part Two (duration 26 minutes 58 seconds) was junked by the BBC Film and Videotape Library, but retained by BBC Enterprises.

The 71 edit of the original Part One is held on colour VHS tape with burnt-in timecode in a private collection.

A one-inch tape of the 16mm colour film sequences from this story was kept by the BBC, which includes material not seen on screen. Also, a one-inch tape of the 'flashback' scenes from this story was kept. These have since been copied onto Digital Betacam, and the one-inch tapes junked.

A mute colour 16mm film of the model and effects work from this story exists in a private collection.

A U-MATIC copy of all the film rushes (including outtakes) for this story exists in a private collection. This was made by pointing a video camera at a monitor replaying the film sequences, and so isn't a direct line copy. The BBC has a copy of this material.

When this story was sold to America, the 50-minute version of Part Two was supplied completely unsyphered, with no music or effects. Many one-inch tapes of this time retained the unsyphered soundtrack on audio track two, with the mixed sound being laid back onto track one. It's possible that when the US's tape was copied, the wrong track was selected to be duplicated from the original one-inch tape.

PLANET OF FIRE (4 EPISODES)

All the colour 16mm film sequences for this story, including the A/B roll camera negatives, exist at the BBC.

VHS recordings with burnt-in timecode exist of some of the studio material from this story. These are held in a private collection.

The 71 edit of Part One is held on colour VHS tape with burnt-in timecode in a private collection.

VHS timecoded recordings of the unsyphered 72 edits of all four episodes also exist in a private collection.

In 2010, 2|entertain released a 're-imagined' version of this story, as an extra on the DVD release of the transmitted version of 'Planet of Fire' This was edited from a copy of the transmission tapes, with new CGI effects added, and presented as a single 65-minute feature, cropped to a 16:9 picture ratio.

THE CAVES OF ANDROZANI (4 EPISODES)

All the colour 16mm film sequences for this story (including material not used in the final episodes) exists in a private collection, although the BBC has a copy.

Colour mute 16mm film sequences of model and effects footage from this story exist in a private collection.

A high-band colour U-MATIC recording, running to 75 minutes, exists of iso-camera footage from the last day's studio recording. This includes material from the regeneration scene. This is held in a private collection, but the BBC also has a copy.

Colour U-MATIC timecoded recordings of the unsyphered 72 edits of Part One and Part Two (the latter incomplete) exist in a private collection.

A VHS timecoded recording of the unsyphered 72 edit of the last three minutes of Part Three also exists in a private collection.

THE SIXTH DOCTOR
COLIN BAKER (1984-1986)

THE TWIN DILEMMA (4 EPISODES)

Colour mute 16mm film sequences from this story are held in a private collection.

VHS timecoded recordings of the unsyphered 72 edits of Parts One and Two also exist in a private collection.

From 'Attack of the Cybermen', the series briefly moved away from the traditional 25-minute episode format, and was instead made in 45-minute episodes. This lasted only for the rest of the programme's twenty-second season, up to 'Revelation of the Daleks'. From 'The Trial of a Time Lord' onwards, the series returned to 25-minute instalments.

ATTACK OF THE CYBERMEN (2 EPISODES)

International versions were made of this story, re-edited into 4 x 25 minute episodes. These versions were made on one-inch tape. They have since been copied onto DigiBeta and the originals junked.

VENGEANCE ON VAROS (2 EPISODES)

A 90-minute colour one-inch tape of one of the studio sessions for this story was kept by the BBC. It has now been junked, but BBC Worldwide retain a Digital Betacam copy.

The 71 edits of Parts One and Two are held on colour U-MATIC tapes with burnt-in timecode in a private collection

International versions were made of this story, re-edited into 4 x 25 minute episodes. These versions were made on one-inch tape. They have since been copied onto DigiBeta and the originals junked.

WIPED!

THE MARK OF THE RANI (2 EPISODES)

The 71 edits of Parts One and Two are held on colour U-MATIC tapes with burnt-in timecode in a private collection.

International versions were made of this story, re-edited into 4 x 25 minute episodes. These versions were made on one-inch tape. They have since been copied onto DigiBeta and the originals junked.

THE TWO DOCTORS (3 EPISODES)

The 71 edit of Part One of this story (duration 47 minutes 38 seconds) was retained by the BBC on one-inch videotape. This tape was junked by the BBC Film and Videotape Library, but was retained by BBC Enterprises.

When preparing the DVD release of this story in 2003, it was found that one of the one-inch studio recording tapes was still held by the BBC Film and Videotape Library (containing mainly scenes of the Doctor and Peri exploring the deserted space station). This was copied to Digital Betacam, and the one-inch tape was subsequently junked.

A U-MATIC copy of all the film rushes (including outtakes) for this story exists in a private collection. This was made by pointing a video camera at a monitor replaying the film sequences, and so isn't a direct line copy of the material. The BBC has a copy of this material.

Colour mute 16mm film of location sequences and colour mute 16mm film of model sequences both exist in private collections.

Colour U-MATIC timecoded recordings of the unsyphered 72 edits of Parts One and Two, plus VHS timecoded recordings of the unsyphered 72 edit of Parts Two and Three, also exist in a private collection.

International versions were made of this story, re-edited into 6 x 25 minute episodes. These versions were made on one-inch tape. They have since been copied onto DigiBeta and the originals junked.

When I first began researching the *Doctor Who* holdings at the Film and Videotape Library in 1990, the BBC still retained 71 edits of all three episodes of 'The Two Doctors', plus all the 16mm location film *and* all the one-inch studio tapes. Basically, everything that was filmed or recorded for this story still existed. It was all junked – bar the 71 edit of Part One and a single studio tape – in early 1991. The loss of this material prompted Paul Vanezis to ask the Film and Videotape Library to retain *all* of its *Doctor Who* holdings from this point on, and to junk nothing without consulting with him first, which they agreed to. As a result, this was the last *Doctor Who* material to be junked by the BBC until the one-inch archiving project of the late 1990s.

APPENDIX II

TIMELASH (2 EPISODES)

International versions were made of this story, re-edited into 4 x 25 minute episodes. These versions were made on one-inch tape. They have since been copied onto DigiBeta and the originals junked.

A colour U-MATIC recording with burnt-in timecode of the unsyphered 72 edit of Part Two also exists in a private collection.

A colour U-MATIC recording with burnt-in timecode exists of the studio remount recorded on 30 January 1985. This was to record the extra TARDIS scene featuring the Doctor, Peri and Herbert that was required to prevent the second episode under-running. This studio session lasts for approximately 20 minutes.

REVELATION OF THE DALEKS (2 EPISODES)

The 71 edit of Part One of this story (duration unknown) was retained by the BBC on one-inch videotape. This was junked by the BBC Film and Videotape Library, but retained by BBC Enterprises.

The transmission one-inch tape of Part Two of this story had some material from an earlier edit of this episode retained at the end of the tape, after the closing credits. This included a brief scene of Peri being captured by the Daleks after the DJ's death, which was cut from the transmitted episode. As an editing exercise, Paul Vanezis created a new version of Part Two that incorporated this scene, edited on D3 videotape. This was then sent to the BBC's Film and Videotape Library.

When preparing the DVD release of this story in 2004, it was found that a one-inch tape containing some rough edits of various sequences from Part Two was still held by the BBC Film and Videotape Library. This was copied to Digital Betacam, and the one-inch tape was subsequently junked.

Colour mute 16mm film of location material and model effects exists for this story in a private collection, along with a mute 35mm colour film of the opening 'planet zoom' shot.

International versions were made of this story, re-edited into 4 x 25 minute episodes, which were also used for the BBC2 repeat in 1993. These versions were made on one-inch tape. They have since been copied onto DigiBeta and the originals junked.

From this point in the listings, the details of the one-inch material kept by BBC Worldwide/2|entertain are noted in a separate table for each story, but aren't referred to in the main text.

It's worth pointing out that studio spools were all originally logged against a specific episode on the BBC Film and Videotape Library database, but as the tapes

WIPED!

were from studio sessions or location recordings for the entire story, they probably contain material from more than just that single episode. Some of the durations given for the 71 edits listed on the BBC's system are probably wrong as well!

THE TRIAL OF A TIME LORD (14 EPISODES)

The opening model shot of the space station exists in full (and in a longer form than in the transmitted episode) on 35mm mute colour film at the BBC.

The French television station TF-1 purchased *Doctor Who* to screen in France for the first time in 1986. To promote the series, an edition of the science fiction magazine programme *Temps-X* ran a feature on it, which included material that they had specially shot behind the scenes during the making of Parts Five to Eight of this story. Although the BBC doesn't retain this footage, VHS copies are held in private collections.

BBC Worldwide	Part 1 – 1-inch 71 edit (duration n/k)
	Part 1 – 5 x 1-inch insert spools
	Part 2 – 1-inch 71 edit (duration n/k)
	Part 2 – 2 x 1-inch studio recording spools
	Part 3 – 1-inch 71 edit (duration n/k)
	Part 3 – 1 x 1-inch studio recording spool
	Part 4 – 1-inch 71 edit (duration n/k)
	Part 5 – 1-inch 71 edit (duration n/k)
	Part 5 – 5 x 1-inch insert spools
	Part 6 – 1-inch 71 edit (duration 25.50)
	Part 7 – 1-inch 71 edit (duration 25.22)
	Part 7 – 1-inch 72 edit (duration 28.00)
	Part 9 – 1-inch 71 edit (duration 29.30)
	Part 9 – 1-inch 72 edit (duration 24.45)
	Part 9 – 11 x 1-inch studio recording spools
	Part 10 – 1-inch 71 edit (duration 24.47)
	Part 10 – 3 x 1-inch studio recording spools
	Part 11 – 1-inch 71 edit (duration 23.55)
	Part 11 – 12 x 1-inch studio recording and insert spools
	Part 12 – 1-inch 71 edit (duration 25.47)
	Part 12 – 1 x 1-inch insert spool
	Part 13 – 1-inch 71 edit (duration 26.27)
	Part 13 – 1 x 1-inch studio recording spool
	Part 14 – 1-inch 71 edit (duration 30.33)
	Part 14 – 1-inch 72 edit (duration 30.21)
	Part 14 – 1-inch 74 edit (duration 27.06)
	Part 14 – 1 x 1-inch studio recording spool

APPENDIX II

THE SEVENTH DOCTOR
SYLVESTER McCOY (1987-1989)

TIME AND THE RANI (4 EPISODES)

An edition of the BBC's *Breakfast Time* programme ran a report on the location recording of 'Time and the Rani' in early 1987. This exists on one-inch tape at the BBC.

A one-inch tape of the computer-generated TARDIS flying through space, plus other computer graphics used in the story, exists in a private collection, although the BBC has access to it.

Mute colour 35mm film of the various model effect sequences exists in a private collection.

VHS recordings of the unsyphered 72 edits of Parts One and Two also exist in a private collection. These have the original 'ghostly' version of the Sylvester McCoy titles on them. (This version of the title sequence was also mistakenly used on transmitted version of Part Four.)

BBC Worldwide	Part 1 – 1-inch 71 edit (duration 27.00) Part 1 – 38 x 1-inch studio/location recording and insert spools Part 2 – 1-inch 71 edit (duration 27.00) Part 3 – 1-inch 71 edit (duration 28.00) Part 3 – 23 x 1-inch studio/location recording and insert spools Part 4 – 1-inch 71 edit (duration 20.00)

PARADISE TOWERS (4 EPISODES)

VHS recordings of syphered final-length versions of all four episodes, complete with the unused David Snell incidental music score, exist in a private collection.

BBC Worldwide	Part 1 – 1-inch 71 edit (duration 24.38) Part 1 – 14 x 1-inch studio recording and insert spools Part 2 – 1-inch 71 edit (duration 24.12) Part 3 – 1-inch 71 edit (duration n/k) Part 3 – 18 x 1-inch studio recording and insert spools Part 4 – 1-inch 71 edit (duration 26.30) Part 4 – 4 x 1-inch studio recording and insert spools

WIPED!

DELTA AND THE BANNERMEN (3 EPISODES)

Mute colour 16mm film of the various model effects sequences exists in a private collection.

An edition of the BBC children's programme *But First This...* filmed a report on the location recording in 1987. This exists on one-inch tape at the BBC. The colour 16mm film rushes for this segment also survive, featuring interviews with Sylvester McCoy, Bonnie Langford and Ken Dodd.

The local BBC news programme *Wales Today* also ran a feature on the location recording. This exists at the BBC on one-inch tape.

The 71 edits of Parts Two and Three are held on VHS tapes with burnt-in timecode in a private collection.

Quite a few outtakes from this story were used in the 'Clown Court' segment of one edition of the BBC programme *Noel Edmonds' Saturday Roadshow*. This also features an in-costume Sylvester McCoy defending himself. It exists at the BBC as a Digital Betacam dub of the original one-inch tape.

A spoof 'Making Of ...' documentary was put together by the *Doctor Who* production team for the amusement of cast and crew, featuring outtakes and behind-the-scenes material. The finished feature exists only on VHS tape in private collections, but the original material all probably survives on the one-inch location tapes.

BBC Worldwide	Part 1 – 1-inch 71 edit (duration 32.28)
	Part 1 – 47 x 1-inch studio/location recording and insert spools
	Part 2 – 1-inch 71 edit (duration 27.07)
	Part 2 – 1-inch 72 edit (duration 24.33)
	Part 3 – 1-inch 71 edit (duration 24.38)
	Part 3 – 16 x 1-inch studio/location recording and insert spools

DRAGONFIRE (3 EPISODES)

Mute colour 16mm film of the various model effects sequences exists in a private collection.

The 71 edits of Part One and the first 16 minutes of Part Two are held on VHS tapes with burnt-in timecode in a private collection.

20 minutes of studio-recorded material (mainly scenes of the young girl in the cafe) exists on VHS in a private collection.

BBC Worldwide	Part 1 – 1-inch 71 edit (duration 30.28)
	Part 2 – 1-inch 71 edit (duration 26.00)
	Part 3 – 1-inch 71 edit (duration 26.09)
	Part 3 – 11 x 1-inch studio recording and insert spools

APPENDIX II

REMEMBRANCE OF THE DALEKS (4 EPISODES)

Mute colour 35mm film of the various model effects sequences exists in a private collection.

A huge number of VHS tape copies (with burnt-in timecode) of the one-inch location and studio tapes – almost everything that was ever recorded for this story – exist in a private collection. Some of these duplicate the one-inch tapes held by BBC Worldwide, but others are unique copies of material that otherwise no longer exists.

BBC Worldwide	Part 1 – 1-inch 71 edit (duration 26.09)
	Part 1 – 4 x 1-inch studio/location recording and insert spools, plus 1 x 1-inch tape of the archive material from which the pre-credit sequence was edited from
	Part 2 – 1-inch 71 edit (duration 26.30)
	Part 2 – 4 x 1-inch studio/location recording and insert spools
	Part 3 – 1-inch 71 edit (duration 28.46)
	Part 3 – 14 x 1-inch studio/location recording and insert spools
	Part 4 – 1-inch 71 edit (duration 26.56)
	Part 4 – 3 x 1-inch studio/location recording and insert spools

THE HAPPINESS PATROL (3 EPISODES)

BBC Worldwide	Part 1 – 1-inch 71 edit (duration 34.00)
	Part 1 – 1-inch 72 edit (duration 24.49) – no end credits
	Part 1 – 13 x 1-inch studio recording and insert spools
	Part 2 – 1-inch 71 edit (duration 29.36)
	Part 3 – 1-inch 71 edit (duration 29.36)
	Part 3 – 1-inch 72 edit (duration n/k)

SILVER NEMESIS (3 EPISODES)

In 1993, BBC Video released this story on VHS as an extended Special Edition. Material was added back into the episodes from the 71 edits, and music cues were altered to accommodate these changes. This newly-created three-part version (which differs from the 71 edits) exists in BBC Worldwide's library.

The US New Jersey Network made a documentary entitled *The Making of Doctor Who* in 1988, which looked at the production of 'Silver Nemesis'. This was in the US's 525-line videotape format, and featured interviews with the cast and crew, plus behind-the-scenes material from many rehearsals and location recordings. BBC Worldwide have a copy of this programme, and a slightly edited 625-line conversion of it was

WIPED!

released on the VHS release of the 'Silver Nemesis' Special Edition.

Mute colour 35mm film of the various model effects sequences exists in a private collection.

Approximately seven hours of rushes exist on VHS tapes in a private collection.

BBC Worldwide	Part 1 – 1-inch 71 edit (duration 31.00)
	Part 2 – 1-inch 71 edit (duration 30.00)
	Part 3 – 1-inch 71 edit (duration n/k)
	Part 3 – 1-inch 72 edit (duration 27.00)

THE GREATEST SHOW IN THE GALAXY (4 EPISODES)

Mute colour 35mm film of the various model effects sequences exists in a private collection.

BBC Worldwide	Part 1 – 1-inch 71 edit (duration 27.00)
	Part 2 – 1-inch 71 edit (duration 23.05)
	Part 3 – 1-inch 71 edit (duration 28.50)

BATTLEFIELD (4 EPISODES)

In 1998, BBC Video released the story on VHS, with new edits of Part Two and Part Three that reinstated a number of scenes from the 71 edits. In 2008, the story was released on DVD, and included a new movie-format version, edited together from scratch. Both of these alternative versions of the story are held by BBC Worldwide.

The BBC's internal safety training course features footage of the water tank accident that occurred during the recording of this story, which is retained on videodisc.

BBC Worldwide	Part 1 – 1-inch 71 edit (duration n/k)
	Part 2 – 1-inch 71 edit (duration n/k)
	Part 3 – 1-inch 71 edit (duration 7.00)
	Part 4 – 1-inch 71 edit (duration 26.30)
	1 x 1-inch transfer tape from the gallery-only session, which consists of visual effects being overlaid onto studio and location material

APPENDIX II

GHOST LIGHT (3 EPISODES)

A VHS copy of parts of the final studio recording session, running to around three hours, exists in a private collection. A second VHS tape with approximately 150 minutes of studio-recorded material exists in a separate private collection.

VHS copies of the 71 edits of all three episodes exist in private collections, all with burnt-in timecode. A VHS copy of Part Two without timecode also exists in a private collection.

VHS recordings with burnt-in timecode of the unsyphered 72 edits of Parts Two and Three also exist in a private collection.

THE CURSE OF FENRIC (4 EPISODES)

In 1991, BBC Video released this story on VHS as an extended version. Material was added back into episodes from both the 71 edits and some (now-wiped) studio/location one-inch tapes, and new music cues were created to accommodate these changes. This newly created four-part version exists in BBC Worldwide's library. In 2008, the story was released on DVD, and included a new movie-format version, edited together from scratch. This version of the story is also held by 2|entertain/BBC Worldwide.

An edition of the BBC children's programme *Take Two* ran a report on the location recording of 'The Curse of Fenric' (then titled 'The Wolves of Fenric') in 1989. This exists on one-inch tape at the BBC.

A Beta SP tape of some of the Lulworth Cove rushes from this story, plus three further Beta SP tapes of original underwater camera material, exist in a private collection. Also, a VHS tape of the location recce, made before recording began, exists in a private collection.

VHS recordings with burnt-in timecode of the unsyphered 72 edits of Parts Two and Three also exist in a private collection.

BBC Worldwide	Part 1 – 1-inch 71 edit (duration 28.00)
	Part 2 – 1-inch 71 edit (duration 26.00)
	Part 3 – 1-inch 71 edit (duration 25.51)
	Part 4 – 1-inch 71 edit (duration n/k)
	1 x 1-inch location recording tape (of underwater footage)

SURVIVAL (3 EPISODES)

A Betacam SP tape of outtakes and fluffs from the making of this story was compiled and screened at the wrap-party held at the conclusion of recording. This runs to just over 16 minutes, and the tape still exists in a private collection.

WIPED!

Due to a wrong code being quoted on a requisition order in 1990, the BBC made a 16mm colour film copy of one of the (then extant) one-inch location recording spools of this story. This 16mm film was quickly junked, but still exists in a private collection.

VHS copies of the 71 edits of Parts One and Two exist in a private collection, both with burnt-in timecode.

BBC Worldwide	Part 1 – 1-inch 71 edit (duration 2.00 – almost certainly incorrect)
	Part 2 – 1-inch 71 edit (duration 25.15)
	Part 3 – 1-inch 71 edit (duration 5.00 – almost certainly incorrect)

APPENDIX III
GLOSSARY OF TERMS

One-inch Videotape: An open-reel videotape format. It replaced two-inch videotape as the BBC's main transmission format in the early 1980s, only to be replaced by the D3 cassette format in the 1990s.

Two-inch Videotape: Also known as Quad or Quadruplex. This was an open-reel videotape developed by Ampex in 1956, and adopted by the BBC as their original transmission format in 1958. It was replaced by one-inch tape in the early 1980s.

A and B roll: An editing technique when working with an original camera negative. Instead of preparing the finished film sequence on a single continuous roll, the negative is edited into two sections of identical length. Each section is prepared in a 'checkerboard' pattern, so that when a shot is edited into roll A, an identical length of opaque spacer is used on roll B. When the shot changes, the next shot is edited into roll B, with spacer now being used on roll A. This method allows dissolves and fades to be edited into the finished film. The A and B rolls are printed separately onto a single roll of raw stock, which is the finished cutting copy.

Betacam SP: An analogue component videotape cassette format developed by Sony, which separated the luminance and the chrominance on separate tracks. It was launched in 1986, and was a broadcast standard version of the Betacam format introduced in 1982.

Betamax: A domestic videotape format developed by Sony in 1975. Generally regarded as technically better than VHS, it had some initial success in the US in the late 1970s before VHS began to dominate the market. In the UK, it never achieved the market dominance that VHS managed, and was eclipsed in the mid 1980s.

Christmas Tapes: During the mid-to-late 1970s, every year the BBC VT engineers would put together a bawdy Christmas Tape, which would get shown at the end-of-year Christmas party. Copies would also be swapped with the various regional ITV companies, who produced their own equivalents. The Christmas Tapes would often include outtakes, as well as specially shot material featuring top television and musical personalities of the day. A copy of the 1978 edition, *White Powder Christmas*, was leaked to the *Sunday People* newspaper at the time, which ran a front page feature on the 'outrage'. Although the 1979 Christmas Tape, *Good King Memorex*, followed the same bawdy format, the practice of

WIPED!

making such tapes was eventually stopped by the BBC in the 1980s.

ComOpt Negative/ComOpt Positive: A film (can be a positive or a negative) that has an optical soundtrack.

Component Video: A video signal that keeps two or more elements as separate components. In broadcast equipment these elements are usually the luminance and chrominance. Domestic component equipment usually separates the red, green and blue (RGB) parts of a television picture.

Composite Video: An analogue video signal, which combines luminance and chrominance together.

Compression: A way of digitally storing picture information. Each frame of a picture is compared to the subsequent one, and any information that is found to be identical is kept only once. Thus only the picture areas that change between subsequent frames are encoded and stored.

D1: The first ever professional digital videotape format, introduced by Sony in 1986. This was an uncompressed digitised component format, and was characterised as being extremely expensive. It was never adopted by the BBC as a transmission format, although it was used for archival purposes and occasionally for special sequences such as graphics or effects.

D3: An uncompressed composite cassette videotape format, introduced by Panasonic in 1991. D3 replaced one-inch tape as the BBC's transmission format in the early 1990s, and remained the format for all material originated in 4:3 by the BBC.

Digital Betacam: A videocassette format launched by Sony in 1991 and commonly referred to as DigiBeta. Digital Betacam records a compressed component video signal, and became the BBC's transmission format for material made in 16:9 in the late 1990s. As 4:3 programme -making reduced, so Digital Betacam became the main tape format for the BBC.

Duplicate Negative: A duplicate negative, often referred to as a 'dupe neg', is a negative made from a print that has been made from another negative, and so is effectively two film generations down from its parent material.

APPENDIX III

Film Warp: This is a problem that film can suffer from when it shrinks due to age. As the film shrinks, the base doesn't shrink evenly, which creates a random, wavy pattern in the film. This can affect the spacing of the film perforations and prevent it from winding tightly on telecine equipment. Running warped film can cause it to be damaged.

Fine Grain Print: This is a very high quality positive film print, which is generally made so that equally high quality safety negatives can be made from it. In the motion picture industry, these films are also sometimes referred to as 'interpositives'.

Iso-camera: Almost all studio recordings of *Doctor Who* were made from the output of the vision mixer's desk, with the result that material from all the studio cameras was pre-mixed together. Some stories in the 1980s featured additional material recorded on a camera not linked to the vision mixer's console. This material would be edited into the episodes in post-production, during the creation of the initial 71 edit. Material from a single camera is referred to as 'iso-camera' (short for isolated camera) footage.

Mute: Generally refers to a silent film print.

Off-lock: These are usually caused by a bad physical splice in a videotape, which causes the machine replaying the tape to lose the sync-pulse needed to keep the picture stable. This often results in rolling television pictures, or some other form of picture instability, which usually stabilises within a few seconds.

Optical Soundtrack: An audio strip on film, located along one edge of the film itself. 16mm films with an optical soundtrack have sprocket holes running along only one edge of the film; the optical track is located where the second set of sprocket holes would normally be found.

Out of Phase: Where material originally shot on film has been transferred to videotape, and then telerecorded back to film with the field dominance incorrectly set up. This results in a burnt-in double image in the resultant telerecording.

'Philips': VCR was the official name of the domestic open reel videotape format launched by Philips in 1971, but most people refer to the machines as just 'Philips'. The square cassettes used half-inch wide videotape. The N1500 machine was launched in 1972 in the UK, and cost over £600 (which would be equivalent to £6000 in 2010). Later models such as the N1502 (launched in 1976) and the N1512 offered refinements to the system. The N1700 was launched in 1978 and was the first video recorder to be able to make 'long

WIPED!

play' recordings. The final model was the N1702, which further refined the system.

Separate Magnetic Soundtracks: When an episode is held on film, the film usually has an optical soundtrack printed onto it. Sometimes, an additional magnetic soundtrack (literally a spool of magnetic tape with the soundtrack recorded upon it) is held as well. In theory, this could have been recorded directly from the original two-inch videotape at the time that the 16mm telerecording was made. But more often than not in *Doctor Who*'s case, it is simply a safety back-up of the optical soundtrack, recorded from the 16mm film print.

Shibaden: An open-reel field video system, introduced in 1967. It could record pictures only in black and white, and playback was relatively unstable, especially on the later 1970s models. The BBC used the format for some years for making viewing copies of programmes during production. It was, at that time, the format on which episodes were supplied to incidental music composers and the Radiophonic Workshop when they were preparing their music and sound effects for an episode of *Doctor Who*. The first story for which Shibaden copies were used in such a manner was probably 'Terror of the Autons'. Shibadens were phased out of the BBC in the late 1970s when VHS became a cheaper and more practical format for this purpose.

Timecode: Most broadcast-quality tape formats record a timecode on a control track on the tape. When the tape is replayed on the appropriate machines, the timecode can either be displayed in-vision or be kept hidden. Copies made from such tapes during production – especially if they are intended for a purpose such as adding music and effects, or planning where to make cuts in order to edit the programme down to the required duration – sometimes have the timecode 'burnt in', i.e. permanently recorded on the picture. This applies to a lot of the 71 edits of the 1980s episodes that exist in private hands on either Shibaden or VHS. Timecodes for BBC programmes usually begin at 10.00.00.00 for the first frame. The numbers after the '10' are for minutes, seconds and then frames.

U-MATIC: One of the first-ever videocassette tape formats, released by Sony in 1971. The actual tape was ¾ of an inch wide, and recorded 330-lines of horizontal resolution. In the early 1980s, Sony released a broadcast-standard version of the system, which was referred to as 'high-band' U-MATIC. The original U-MATIC version then became known as 'low-band'.

VHS: The first domestic videotape format to win mass appeal with the public. Launched by JVC in Japan in the late 1970s, it initially competed with Sony's Betamax format. VHS

APPENDIX III

won out in the early 1980s due to its early dominance in the rental market; by the time Betamax machines became available to rent, VHS already had over 70% of the market.

Viewing Prints: Copies of episodes held by the BBC Film and Videotape Library for easy viewing. These are often damaged due to excessive use and handling, and are generally poorer than the archived master of the material.

Wetgate Telecine: A method of making a video copy of a film print. The film is run through a telecine machine that has the viewing gate submerged in a liquid with the same refractive index as the film stock. This reduces the effect of any dust, dirt or hairs, and helps cover up scratches and marks on the film's surface.

APPENDIX IV
DOCTOR WHO: THE MISSING EPISODES

For the first three seasons, *Doctor Who* stories had no overall on-screen story title. So when this book talks about Episode One of 'Marco Polo', for example, then that's really something of a misnomer (albeit a convenient one). A BBC film print of one of these earlier episodes would probably have the story's story code written on either the label or the film leader, along with the episode title. All of these episodes featured William Hartnell as the Doctor. The missing *Doctor Who* episodes from this era are:

Episode Title	Story Code	Also known as...
'The Roof of the World'	D	'Marco Polo': Episode One
'The Singing Sands'	D	'Marco Polo': Episode Two
'Five Hundred Eyes'	D	'Marco Polo': Episode Three
'The Wall of Lies'	D	'Marco Polo': Episode Four
'Rider from Shang-Tu'	D	'Marco Polo': Episode Five
'Mighty Kublai Khan'	D	'Marco Polo': Episode Six
'Assassin at Peking'	D	'Marco Polo': Episode Seven
'The Tyrant of France'	H	'The Reign of Terror': Episode Four
'A Bargain of Necessity'	H	'The Reign of Terror': Episode Five
'The Knight of Jaffa'	P	'The Crusade': Episode Two
'The Warlords'	P	'The Crusade': Episode Four
'Four Hundred Dawns'	T	'Galaxy 4': Episode One
'Trap of Steel'	T	'Galaxy 4': Episode Two
'The Exploding Planet'	T	'Galaxy 4': Episode Four
'Mission to the Unknown'	T/A	'Mission to the Unknown' Episode One
'Temple of Secrets'	U	'The Myth Makers' Episode One
'Small Prophet, Quick Return'	U	'The Myth Makers' Episode Two
'Death of a Spy'	U	'The Myth Makers' Episode Three
'Horse of Destruction'	U	'The Myth Makers' Episode Four

APPENDIX IV

'The Nightmare Begins'	V	'The Daleks Masterplan' Episode One
'Devil's Planet'	V	'The Daleks Masterplan' Episode Three
'The Traitors'	V	'The Daleks Masterplan' Episode Four
'Coronas of the Sun'	V	'The Daleks Masterplan' Episode Six
'The Feast of Steven'	V	'The Daleks Masterplan' Episode Seven
'Volcano'	V	'The Daleks Masterplan' Episode Eight
'Golden Death'	V	'The Daleks Masterplan' Episode Nine
'The Abandoned Planet'	V	'The Daleks Masterplan' Episode Eleven
'The Destruction of Time'	V	'The Daleks Masterplan' Episode Twelve
'War of God'	W	'The Massacre' Episode One
'The Sea Beggar'	W	'The Massacre' Episode Two
'Priest of Death'	W	'The Massacre' Episode Three
'Bell of Doom'	W	'The Massacre' Episode Four
'The Celestial Toyroom'	Y	'The Celestial Toymaker' Episode One
'The Hall of Doll'	Y	'The Celestial Toymaker' Episode Two
'The Dancing Floor'	Y	'The Celestial Toymaker' Episode Three

The remaining William Hartnell episodes from 'The Savages' onwards all had an on-screen story title, followed by an episode number. A BBC film print of one of these episodes would probably have the story title, episode number and story code written on the label or film leader. The missing latter William Hartnell episodes are as follows:

Story Title	Episode No	Story Code
'The Savages'	Episode One	AA
'The Savages'	Episode Two	AA
'The Savages'	Episode Three	AA
'The Savages'	Episode Four	AA
'The Smugglers'	Episode One	CC
'The Smugglers'	Episode Two	CC
'The Smugglers'	Episode Three	CC

WIPED!

'The Smugglers'	Episode Four	CC
'The Tenth Planet'	Episode Four	DD

The entirety of the Patrick Troughton era would also follow this format. The missing Patrick Troughton episodes are as follows:

Story Title	Episode No	Story Code
'The Power of the Daleks'	Episode One	EE
'The Power of the Daleks'	Episode Two	EE
'The Power of the Daleks'	Episode Three	EE
'The Power of the Daleks'	Episode Four	EE
'The Power of the Daleks'	Episode Five	EE
'The Power of the Daleks'	Episode Six	EE
'The Highlanders'	Episode One	FF
'The Highlanders'	Episode Two	FF
'The Highlanders'	Episode Three	FF
'The Highlanders'	Episode Four	FF
'The Underwater Menace'	Episode One	GG
'The Underwater Menace'	Episode Four	GG
'The Moonbase'	Episode One	HH
'The Moonbase'	Episode Three	HH
'The Macra Terror'	Episode One	JJ
'The Macra Terror'	Episode Two	JJ
'The Macra Terror'	Episode Three	JJ
'The Macra Terror'	Episode Four	JJ
'The Faceless Ones'	Episode Two	KK
'The Faceless Ones'	Episode Four	KK
'The Faceless Ones'	Episode Five	KK
'The Faceless Ones'	Episode Six	KK

APPENDIX IV

'The Evil of the Daleks'	Episode One	LL
'The Evil of the Daleks'	Episode Three	LL
'The Evil of the Daleks'	Episode Four	LL
'The Evil of the Daleks'	Episode Five	LL
'The Evil of the Daleks'	Episode Six	LL
'The Evil of the Daleks'	Episode Seven	LL
'The Abominable Snowmen'	Episode One	NN
'The Abominable Snowmen'	Episode Three	NN
'The Abominable Snowmen'	Episode Four	NN
'The Abominable Snowmen'	Episode Five	NN
'The Abominable Snowmen'	Episode Six	NN
'The Ice Warriors'	Episode Two	OO
'The Ice Warriors'	Episode Three	OO
'The Enemy of the World'	Episode One	PP
'The Enemy of the World'	Episode Two	PP
'The Enemy of the World'	Episode Four	PP
'The Enemy of the World'	Episode Five	PP
'The Enemy of the World'	Episode Six	PP
'The Web of Fear'	Episode Two	QQ
'The Web of Fear'	Episode Three	QQ
'The Web of Fear'	Episode Four	QQ
'The Web of Fear'	Episode Five	QQ
'The Web of Fear'	Episode Six	QQ
'Fury from the Deep'	Episode One	RR
'Fury from the Deep'	Episode Two	RR
'Fury from the Deep'	Episode Three	RR

WIPED!

'Fury from the Deep'	Episode Four	RR
'Fury from the Deep'	Episode Five	RR
'Fury from the Deep'	Episode Six	RR
'The Wheel in Space'	Episode One	SS
'The Wheel in Space'	Episode Two	SS
'The Wheel in Space'	Episode Four	SS
'The Wheel in Space'	Episode Five	SS
'The Invasion'	Episode One	VV
'The Invasion'	Episode Four	VV
'The Space Pirates'	Episode One	YY
'The Space Pirates'	Episode Three	YY
'The Space Pirates'	Episode Four	YY
'The Space Pirates'	Episode Five	YY
'The Space Pirates'	Episode Six	YY

INDEX

16mm	41, 44-46, 48-50, 52-53, 61-62, 65, 73, 77-79, 81-83, 85-86, 88-97, 99-100, 102-104, 106, 116-119, 123, 127-130, 138-140, 152, 160-162, 164, 166, 168-172, 174-176, 179, 185-186, 189-191, 193-195, 198-200, 203-211, 213-214, 216, 218-219, 225, 228-234, 236-248, 251-253, 256, 259, 261, 263-265, 267-278, 282-286, 288-291, 294, 296, 298, 301, 306-308, 310, 317, 325, 329-330, 333, 339, 351, 354, 358, 361, 367, 372-373, 375-376, 379, 385, 411-413, 416, 418, 424, 431-437, 439-440, 442-443, 445-449, 451-453, 455-467, 469-472, 475-485, 487-517, 519-535, 538, 542, 545-546
16x9 (16:9)	38, 529, 532 544
2|entertain	272, 277, 281, 429, 505, 516, 518, 529-530, 532, 535, 541
2nd House	201
35mm	15-16, 18, 20, 30, 40-42, 45, 48, 54, 58-60, 67-68, 70, 72, 77-91, 94-95, 103-105, 110, 160-161, 175, 179, 185-186, 190, 195, 198, 203, 227, 234, 241, 247-248, 268, 291-293, 309-310, 321, 434, 475-477, 481-482, 485, 487, 489-490, 493-495, 502-506, 512, 524-526, 536-537, 539, 540
405-line	15, 18-19, 30, 40-41, 45-46, 48, 52-53, 79, 86, 97, 100, 103, 138, 321, 475, 477, 489
4x3 (4:3)	38, 544
525-line	18, 97, 128, 205, 255-263, 265-267, 272, 276, 278-281, 411, 413-415, 417-418, 421, 510-515, 518, 539
625-line	19, 35, 40-42, 52, 61-62, 97, 102-103, 162, 180, 186, 208, 211, 251-253, 256, 258-261, 263, 265-270, 276-277, 279-281, 283, 290, 295-296, 412-414, 416, 418, 437, 475, 509-520, 524-525, 531, 539
71 edit	38-39, 520, 524-542, 545-546
72 edit	38-39, 225, 229, 531-541
73 edit	38-39, 290, 295, 531
74 edit	38-39, 536
8mm	301, 305, 308, 321, 329-331, 426, 429, 480, 482, 486, 489, 492, 494, 497-500, 502, 513-514, 519, 525-526
A and B roll (A/B)	269, 295, 412, 487, 507, 517, 527-530, 532, 543
A Day Out	24
A Quick Guide to Dr Who	114-115, 129-130, 136, 138, 193
A Tale of Two Cities	18
Abominable Snowmen, The	52, 56-57, 59-60, 71, 83, 95, 107-108, 113, 122, 125, 132, 161, 173, 181, 186, 192, 205-207, 219-220, 248, 276, 294, 319, 321, 327, 330, 345, 354, 360-361, 371, 375, 377, 381, 384, 400, 405-406, 409-410, 434, 463-464, 499
Abominable Snowmen, The: Episode 2	205-207, 219-220, 276, 434
Actor	13, 19, 22-24, 31-32, 118, 123, 128, 139, 147, 150, 231, 294, 321-323, 328, 330, 338, 370, 421, 427, 431, 488, 515, 524
Adam Adamant Lives!	40, 231-233, 423, 432
Adelaide	340-345, 412, 440, 443, 445-472
Aden (PDRY BS)	119, 334-335, 338, 361, 388, 390, 424, 437, 441-442, 444, 521-527, 546
Adventure World	209
Africa	215, 333-334, 339, 358-359, 363-364, 376, 378-379, 383-384, 432
Agnew, Mr (the mysterious)	206, 219
Air Lock (Galaxy 4: Episode 3)	47, 242-246, 436
Alaska	419-420
Aldbourne	513
Alexandra Palace	15, 17, 219
Algeria (TVA)	112, 120, 126, 128, 175, 192-193, 339, 409
Aliens: Special Edition	236
Amahl and the Night Visitors	288
Ambassadors of Death, The	65-66, 73, 133, 162, 169, 186, 196, 251-253, 256, 262-263, 267, 269, 272, 274-

WIPED!

	278, 282-285, 346, 413, 416-417, 419-420, 509-510
America / USA	13, 18, 34, 62, 97, 111, 128-129, 142, 254, 258, 261, 275-279, 281, 333, 335, 355-356, 412-413, 416, 418, 420-422, 508, 532
American Film Technologies Inc	276-277, 281, 508
Ampex	18-19, 31, 34-36, 543
Amsterdam	334
An Unearthly Child	9-10, 44, 46, 48, 51, 53, 55, 61-62, 67, 89, 94, 104-105, 111-112, 116, 118, 124, 126-129, 139, 160, 165, 167-168, 170-172, 185, 190, 193, 199, 201, 222, 226, 236, 247, 257, 287-288, 290, 315, 319, 325-326, 333, 335, 338-339, 342-343, 345-346, 352, 355-365, 367, 372-373, 376-384, 386-391, 393-394, 396-404, 407, 409, 434, 475-476
Anchorage	419-420
Android Invasion, The	93, 197-198, 521
Androids of Tara, The	524
Andy Pandy	97, 228
Animation / Animated	316, 321, 429, 505
Annan Committee, The	141
Anthony, Simon	272
Aperture Corrector	275
Arabia	120, 334, 338, 400, 418
Arabic	120, 126-127, 170, 175, 190, 192-193, 200, 290, 339-340, 362, 418, 478-479, 481-483
Arc of Infinity	528
Archive Selector	10, 65, 143, 152, 154-156, 159, 179, 205, 234, 251, 259, 273, 340, 434
Ariel	78
Arizona	419-420
Ark in Space, The	93, 129, 137, 197, 519
Ark, The	51, 69, 94-95, 105, 113, 120, 124, 131, 160, 167, 169, 173, 185, 191, 248, 306-307, 320, 327, 348-349, 353, 355, 366, 370, 372, 374, 379-380, 382, 384, 396-397, 399, 402, 406, 408, 488
Armageddon Factor, The	524
Armchair Theatre	227
Ascension Islands	225
Asia	234, 334, 360-361, 380, 382, 431
Asia Television	234, 360-361, 431
Associated Rediffusion (Malta)	333, 364
Attack of the Cybermen	533
Attenborough, David	24, 228
Auckland	238, 365, 372, 442, 444, 447-448, 450-451, 453-457, 459-461, 463-464, 467-468, 470
Audio	11, 17, 34, 36, 95-99, 123, 142, 146-147, 163, 167, 244, 270-272, 277, 287, 293, 308, 310-314, 316-320, 424, 427-429, 479-481, 484-491, 493, 495-503, 505-506, 518, 520-521, 532, 545
Audition Print	127-128, 341-342, 465, 429
Australia (ABC)	47, 50, 111, 113, 115, 118-123, 127-129, 132, 170, 179, 203-204, 208, 211-212, 237, 245-247, 259-260, 264-266, 271, 278, 291, 296-300, 305, 310, 318, 321, 328, 333, 337, 340-346, 248, 351-354, 366-367, 370, 373, 379, 386-388, 390, 393, 396-398, 400-407, 411-414, 416-417, 426, 432, 436, 439-440, 443-472, 478-480, 482, 486, 489-498, 502-506, 516, 518
Australian Film Censorship Board	298-299, 342, 346, 412, 447, 449
Avengers, The	423
Awakening, The	531
Ayres, Mark	271, 314-315, 318, 320
Aztecs, The	28, 45, 51, 67, 94, 105, 112, 124, 126-127, 130, 160, 168, 172, 185, 190, 193, 225-227, 247, 327-328, 335-336, 338-339, 352, 355-359, 361-365, 376, 378-380, 382-384, 387-390, 392-404, 407, 409, 479
Bahrain	418

INDEX

Baird, John Logie	14-15
Baker, Colin	9, 312, 415, 422, 475, 533
Baker, Tom	8, 10, 65-66, 129-130, 137, 162-163, 195, 203-204, 222, 270, 277, 312, 314, 377, 413, 415, 417, 421, 475, 484, 519, 523-524
Barbados (CBC)	112, 120-121, 334, 337, 354-355, 389, 395-397, 441, 444, 446-448, 451-452, 454
Barker, Ronnie	36
Barking	326
Barnett Bypass	527
Barnfather, Keith	138-139, 165
Barnham, Glen	22
Barrett, Ray	31-32
Barrett, Roger	424
Barrie	356, 441
Barry, Christopher	28, 32-33, 45, 323-324
Basil Brush Show, The	9, 128
Batman	363, 423
Battlefield	271, 540
BBC Audiobooks	312, 317, 428
BBC Birmingham	310
BBC Bristol	294
BBC Canada	205, 255, 258-259, 278, 510, 512
BBC Cardiff	180
BBC Choice	38, 182
BBC Cymru	180
BBC Drama Department	21, 44, 46, 49-52, 55-60, 62, 81, 83, 109, 218
BBC Ealing	218, 307, 435
BBC Engineering Department	20, 33, 42-44, 46, 49-50, 52-53, 55, 64, 104, 152, 172, 174
BBC Enterprises	7, 21, 23, 25, 43-44, 46-63, 65, 78-79, 81, 83-86, 88-90, 95-97, 100, 102-104, 106, 109-112, 114-119, 123-129, 136-140, 144-146, 150, 152, 161, 163-164, 166-168, 170-180, 182-183, 189-190, 192-195, 198-201, 205, 208, 210, 219, 224-225, 233-236, 241, 243, 245-246, 252-253, 265, 274, 289-290, 298, 333-335, 339-341, 346, 348, 354, 356-357, 361-362, 376, 381-384, 413-414, 416, 419, 421, 431, 434, 436, 440, 476-484, 488-501, 504, 506-507, 510, 520-521, 532, 534-535
BBC Exploitation	97
BBC Film and Videotape Library	24, 43, 53-54, 61, 64, 77, 83, 147-150, 155-157, 164, 166-167, 170, 175-176, 179, 181, 185, 189, 194-195, 198, 201, 203-205, 209-212, 214, 219, 225, 228, 230, 232-236, 251, 253, 255-256, 259, 261, 264-266, 268-269, 273-274, 280, 281-282, 290, 292-293, 301, 307, 309, 318, 358, 414-416, 431-432, 475-478, 482-483, 487, 499, 502, 525, 530, 532, 534-535, 547
BBC Film Library	7, 17, 19-21, 42-43, 64, 66, 77-90, 93-96, 104, 138, 142-144, 146, 152-153, 157, 161, 165-166, 174, 179, 183-184, 189-190, 193-195, 198, 200, 207, 209, 219-220, 253, 287, 289, 292, 434, 477-478, 482-484, 488, 492, 503, 507
BBC News Unit	77
BBC Pebble Mill	165, 180, 266, 275, 295
BBC Records	163
BBC Research Department	280, 282-283
BBC Script Department	13
BBC Sydney	118, 127, 212, 264, 341-342, 348, 366, 412-413, 452
BBC Television Centre	17-19, 24, 28, 43, 77, 82, 99, 178, 183-184, 233, 241, 244, 247, 266, 271, 387, 318, 435, 525
BBC Toronto	123, 255-256, 258, 260-261, 414-415
BBC Visual Effects Department	291, 294, 330, 516
BBC Wales	181-182
BBC Worldwide	281, 421, 530, 533, 535-542
BBC Written Archive Centre	118, 147, 154
BBC1	9, 13, 19, 21-22, 28, 33, 38, 41, 43, 47, 49-50, 52-56, 61-63, 76, 79, 83-83, 104-

555

WIPED!

	109, 111, 116-117, 163, 165, 170-171, 252, 257, 259, 269, 282, 285, 295, 308, 310, 336, 422, 424, 431, 437-438, 503-506, 516, 518, 522, 530-531
BBC2	10, 19, 21-22, 24, 36, 38, 40, 43, 47, 64-65, 89, 97, 114, 160, 166-167, 189, 221, 236, 257, 273-274, 293-294, 485, 504, 507-508, 510, 513-515, 520, 535
Beaulieu	242-243, 245-246
Benin	376-378
Bennett, Alan	24
Benny Hill Show, The	128
Bentham, Jeremy	10, 204, 207-208, 256, 323
Benue Plateau Broadcasting Corporation (BPBC)	376-377
Bermuda (ZFB1 & ZFBTV)	119, 334-335, 355, 388, 393, 441-442
Betamax	127, 261-262, 273, 278, 420, 509, 543, 546-547
Beyond the Freeze – What Next?	308, 494
Birmingham	15, 212, 221, 231, 244, 266, 310
Birt, John	155
Black & White Minstrel Show, The	435
Black Adder, The	37
Black Orchid	528
Blackpool	38, 163, 425
Blake, Gerald	330, 500
Blake's 7	9, 423
Bleak House	227
Blue Peter	9, 24, 61, 88, 127, 138, 166, 170, 193, 271, 289-291, 295, 317, 429, 435, 477, 488, 490, 492-493
Blu-Ray	127, 271
Bombay	338
Book of Lists, The	307
Boston	331, 419-420
BPTV (Nigeria)	465, 467-468, 471
Brain of Morbius, The	197, 521
Braybon, John	13
Breakfast Time	37, 537
Brentford	77, 144, 209, 414
Bridger, John	164-168, 175-176, 178
Briggs report, The	145, 151, 153
Briggs, Asa	147, 149, 151
Brighton	229-230, 232, 526
Brisbane	298, 340-345, 412, 440, 443, 445-453, 455-467, 469-472
Bristol	218, 294
British Film Institute (BFI)	139-141, 151, 172-173, 176-177, 179, 185, 195, 210, 214, 227, 245, 247, 424, 504-505, 507
British Rail	180, 182
Broadcasting House	14-15
Broadstairs	485
Browne, Andrew	282
Brunei	123, 412, 414, 416
Brunskill, Roger	224-226, 362
Bryant, Peter	56
Bryant, Steve	209-215, 226, 229-230, 232, 234, 259-261, 264
Buckingham Movie Museum	232
Buffalo	262, 419-420, 509
Build-up Material	269, 287-288
Burnett, Terry	242, 244-247, 485, 496
But First This…	538
Butler, David	320, 486
C for Computer	291, 296, 310, 493

INDEX

California	281, 419-420
Campbell, Bruce	207-208, 228-229, 234, 276
Canada (CBC, CKVU)	97, 111, 119, 123, 205, 254-260, 265, 278-279, 333, 335, 355-357, 365, 387-388, 412, 414-416, 439, 441, 510-515, 518
Canberra	340-344, 440, 443, 445-446, 448-449, 451-453, 455-467, 469-472
Cannes	163
Captain Pugwash	228
Caribbean	334, 354-355, 362, 382
Carnival of Monsters	10, 39, 66, 75, 134, 136, 162, 169, 187, 196, 206, 252, 254, 257, 264, 268-270, 286, 296, 413-418, 437, 515
Cash, Tony	138, 167, 176, 183, 195, 199, 201
Castrovalva	527
Caversham	118, 147, 154, 324-326
Caves of Androzani, The	156, 428, 532
CD	161, 272, 307, 318, 428-429
Celestial Toymaker, The	10-11, 41, 48, 56, 69, 79-81, 83-86, 94, 105, 113, 120, 124, 131, 160, 173, 185, 191, 211-212, 248, 317, 320, 322, 325, 327, 353, 355, 357, 366, 370, 374, 379-380, 382, 384, 396-397, 399, 402, 406, 408, 451, 482, 488
Celestial Toyroom	11, 209-210, 323
Censor	115, 127, 204, 237, 246-247, 265, 271, 297-300, 305-308, 342, 346, 348, 352, 365-367, 375, 412-413, 440, 442-443, 447-451, 453-463, 466-470, 490-491, 495-497, 501-504
CGI	529, 532
Channel 4	141
Chapman, Graham	62
Charet, Larry	261
Chase, The	51, 54-55, 68, 90, 94, 105, 112, 115, 124, 131, 160, 169, 172, 185, 191, 199-200, 203, 248, 305, 313, 327, 331, 338, 345, 347, 352, 355, 358-359, 362-363, 365, 376, 379, 381, 384, 391-394, 396-397, 399-404, 408, 484
Chicago	258, 261, 275, 419-420, 508, 510-511
Chile	120, 125, 193, 401, 404
Chislett, Julian	426
Christchurch (NZ)	365, 372, 442, 444, 447-448, 450-451, 453-457, 459-461, 463-464, 467-468, 470
Chroma Dot	117, 281, 283-286, 510-511, 516
Church of Jesus Christ of Latter-Day Saints	209-210
City of Death	524
Clapham	210
Claws of Axos, The	65-66, 74, 134, 162, 169, 186, 195-196, 199, 251-253, 255-256, 258-261, 263, 267-269, 281, 414-417, 511
Clearance History Sheets	125, 336, 338, 386, 411, 471-472
Cleese, John	62
Cliffhanger	80, 83, 87, 243, 260, 422, 498, 522
Clothes Show, The	274
Clown Court	538
Coburn, Anthony	13
Colditz	335
Colony in Space	65, 74, 129, 134, 162, 169, 186, 196, 252-253, 257-260, 270, 281, 284-285, 414, 416-417, 512
Colour Recovery Working Group	282
Commonwealth	111, 337-338, 340, 356-357, 363-365, 380
ComOpt Negative/ComOpt Positive	81, 544
Compilation	144, 197, 262, 269, 273, 275, 315, 508, 512-513, 518-520, 522, 528, 531
Component	37, 87, 94, 123, 272-273, 280, 307, 339, 504-506, 543-544
Composite	37, 273, 282, 479, 498, 544
Compression	544
Cook, James	340, 365

WIPED!

Cook, Terence	45
Cooper, George A	330
Cornell, Tony	308, 330, 499, 502
Cornwall	330
Coronation Street	424
Cosgrove Hall	429, 505
Counter Plot	
(The Daleks Masterplan: Episode 5)	209
Courtney, Nicholas	427
Craig, Gordon	330, 491
Creature from the Pit, The	525
Crockett, John	45
Crusade, The	54, 56, 68, 86, 89, 94, 105, 112, 124, 131, 160, 172-173, 185, 190, 195, 201, 216, 236-237, 248, 312-313, 319-320, 325, 327, 335, 343, 345, 352, 355-356, 358-359, 363, 365-366, 368, 373, 375-376, 379, 381, 384, 386, 390-394, 396-397, 401, 403, 408, 428, 431-432, 440, 445, 483
Cumming, Fiona	291-292
Cura, John	308, 321-326, 328, 329, 429
Current Ops	144, 183-184
Curse of Fenric, The	271, 541
Curse of Peladon, The	65, 74, 134, 162, 169, 187, 196, 199, 251-255, 257, 260, 263, 266-267, 269-270, 281, 284, 286, 312, 414-417, 513
Cybermen - The Early Years	214
Cyprus (CBC)	119, 216, 222-230, 266, 333, 336-358, 361, 383, 386, 389, 392-393, 441-442, 444, 479-480
D1	280, 510-515, 544
D3	37-38, 182, 214, 221, 229, 233, 266-267, 270, 274, 296, 300-301, 475-476, 480, 485, 490-491, 493, 495-499, 502-504, 509, 511-522, 524-526, 528-530, 535, 543-544
Da Silva, Howard	421
Dad's Army	9, 83, 128, 309
Daemons, The	8, 65-66, 74, 123, 134, 162, 169, 171, 187, 196, 199, 251-254, 257, 262-263, 267, 272-275, 277, 285, 315, 331, 412, 417-418, 420, 512
Dalek Invasion of Earth, The	27, 41, 48, 51, 54, 68, 79, 82-85, 89, 94, 105, 112, 115, 119, 124, 126, 131, 160, 164, 168, 172, 185, 190, 199-201, 237, 248, 261, 327, 330, 335-336, 338-339, 343, 345, 347, 352, 355-358, 360-366, 368, 373, 376, 379, 381-384, 387-390, 392-396, 398-404, 407, 409, 482
Daleks (spin-off), The	114-115
Daleks Masterplan, The	10, 51-52, 54-55, 69, 82, 88, 90, 94, 104-105, 113-116, 120, 124, 131, 136, 160, 166, 170-171, 173, 185, 191, 203, 209, 211, 241, 246, 248, 289-290, 292-295, 300, 311, 316, 318, 320-321, 327-328, 338, 346, 348, 353, 428, 432, 434, 449, 487
Daleks, The	40-41, 45, 48, 50-51, 55, 67, 79, 84, 94, 105, 112, 115, 118, 124, 126, 128, 160, 168-169, 172, 175, 185, 190, 193, 199-200, 226, 241, 247, 288, 313, 319, 323, 326, 335-336, 338-340, 345, 352, 355-359, 361-365, 367, 373, 376, 378-380, 382-384, 386-391, 393-394, 396-404, 407, 409, 434, 477
Darwin	340, 346, 469, 471-472
DAT Audio	318, 320
Dave Allen Show, The	307
David, Hugh	323-324
Davies, John	323-324
Davies, Kevin	294-295
Davis, Gerry	49, 427-428
Davison, Peter	259, 270, 290, 415, 421-422, 475, 527
Day of Armageddon	
(Daleks Masterplan: Episode 2)	90, 191, 241-242, 289, 292-294, 428, 434
Day of the Daleks	11, 63-64, 66, 74, 134, 162, 169, 187, 196, 252-253, 257-258, 261, 263, 267, 286,

INDEX

Day, Peter	295, 413-417, 513
	330
de Rivaz, John	244, 314, 318, 320, 478, 480-481, 484, 486-491, 493, 495-503, 505-506
Deadly Assassin, The	65, 162, 197, 519, 522
Death to the Daleks	65-66, 76, 93, 123, 135, 162, 169, 187, 196, 198, 203, 205, 251-252, 254-258, 264-266, 268, 271, 286, 412, 414-416, 418, 518
Delaware	39, 260, 413, 515-516
Delta and The Bannermen	538
Denmark	119, 128, 373, 386, 485
Derbyshire, Delia	39
Des Moines	419-420
Desperate People, The	227
Devil's Planet, The (The Daleks Masterplan: Episode 4)	289-290, 294
Diary of Samuel Pepys, The	308
Dicks, Terrance	8-9, 201, 225
Digital Betacam / DigiBeta	37-38, 239, 241-242, 245, 247, 270, 278, 282, 310, 475-476, 483, 485, 487, 496, 501, 503-504, 507-508, 510-515, 520, 530-535, 538, 544
Dikko, Umaru	216
Direct Line Copy (visual)	530, 532, 534
Direct Line Recording (audio)	311, 314, 316
Director	19, 28-29, 32-35, 44-45, 48, 81, 294, 313, 322-324, 326, 330, 478, 500, 515
Doctor Who and the Monsters	257, 269, 513, 519, 528
Doctor Who Appreciation Society (DWAS)	11, 138-139, 183, 200, 204, 209, 212, 221, 223, 229-230, 290, 301, 307, 312, 323, 329, 426
Doctor Who Bulletin (DWB)	11, 229, 236, 323-325, 328-329, 424, 427
Doctor Who Classic Comics	325
Doctor Who Club of Australia	298
Doctor Who Monthly/Magazine (DWM)	10-11, 194, 206-207, 209, 213-215, 221, 247, 256, 259-260, 311, 323-326, 423, 427
Doctor Who Production Office	27, 44, 201, 322, 324-325, 484
Doctor Who Programme Guide	224
Doctor Who: 25 Glorious Years	210
Doctor Who: The Beginning	166
Doctor Who: The Early Years	323
Dolby	530
Dominators, The	42, 57-59, 72, 82, 84-85, 91, 95, 113, 122, 125, 127, 133, 140, 161, 172-173, 177, 179, 186, 192, 195, 201, 214, 249, 261, 300, 316, 324, 328, 346, 351, 354, 359-361, 377, 381, 404, 406-407, 409-410, 503
Don, Monty	226
Doomwatch	128, 232, 423
Down, Richard	221
Dragonfire	538
Dubai	129, 265-266, 412, 414, 416, 418
Dubai Radio & Colour Television	265, 416
Duggan, Larry	238
Duke Of Edinburgh, The	16
Duke of York, The	229-230
Dunedin	365, 372, 442, 444, 447-448, 450-451, 453-457, 459-461, 463-464, 467-468, 470
Duplicate Negative/Dupe	161, 208, , 478-480, 489, 499, 501-502, 504-505, 507, 517, 544
Durbridge, Francis	227
DVD	8, 11, 103, 127, 166, 232, 242, 244, 258, 271-272, 277, 278, 281, 284-285, 305, 308-310, 316, 321, 330-331, 428-429, 476-479, 484-485, 491, 498-499, 505, 508-516, 518, 520-530, 532, 534-535, 540-541
Ealing	28, 31, 77, 82, 103-104, 163-164, 168, 178, 204, 218, 230, 233, 241, 266, 270,

559

WIPED!

	307-308, 330-331, 434-435, 499, 502, 522, 529
Ealing and Boston Manor Cine Club	331
Ealing Film Studios	28, 330, 435, 499, 502
Earthshock	257, 428, 528
East Tower	289, 435
Easterbrook, Jim	280-281
Eastern Nigerian Television (ENTV)	376
Eastman Kodak	329
Eccleston, Christopher	9, 428
Edge of Destruction, The	45, 50-51, 54, 67, 94, 105, 112, 118, 124, 126, 128, 136-137, 139, 160, 168, 172, 185, 190, 193, 226, 247, 326, 333, 335-336, 338-339, 342, 345, 352, 355-359, 361-365, 367, 372-373, 376, 378-380, 382-384, 386-391, 393-394, 396-404, 407, 409, 478
Elizabeth R	128
Enemy of the World, The	41, 52, 56, 58-61, 71, 90, 95, 108-109, 113, 122, 125, 132, 138, 161, 173, 186, 192, 194-195, 249, 317, 319, 321, 324-325, 328, 354, 360-361, 371, 375, 377, 381, 384, 401, 405, 409-410, 466, 475, 500
Enemy of the World, The: Episode 3	41, 90, 95, 192, 194-195
Enlightenment	529
Enright, Brian	144
Equity	22-23, 142-143, 147, 152, 159, 164
Escape Switch (The Daleks Masterplan: Episode 10)	209
Essex	433
Ethiopia (EBS/ETV/ETS)	112, 120, 334, 358, 407-408, 443, 445-446
Euston Road	241
Evil of the Daleks, The	10, 50, 53, 55-57, 60, 63, 70-71, 95, 107, 109, 113, 115, 121, 125, 132, 136-137, 147, 161, 173-174, 186, 191, 201, 220, 229, 231-232, 248, 261, 276, 288, 290, 312-313, 317, 319, 325, 327, 329-331, 345, 353, 357, 361, 366, 371, 375, 381, 403, 405-406, 437, 462-464, 498, 499
Evil of the Daleks, The: Episode 2	174, 229, 231-232, 276, 288, 290
Exchange and Mart	425
Ezeokoli, Victoria	215, 220
Fabric	157
Face of Evil, The	522
Faceless Ones, The	50, 55-57, 59-60, 70, 83, 90, 95, 107, 113, 121, 125, 132, 161, 173-174, 186, 191, 203-204, 229, 231-232, 248, 276, 305, 319, 325, 327, 331, 345, 350, 353, 361, 366, 371, 375, 381, 383-385, 398, 401-403, 405, 461, 463-464, 498
Faceless Ones, The: Episode 1	90, 95, 174, 191, 203, 204, 350
Faceless Ones, The: Episode 3	174, 229, 231-232, 276
Fawlty Towers	9
Feast of Steven, The (The Daleks Masterplan: Episode 7)	104, 136, 170-171, 328, 346
Federation of South Arabia, The (SABS & SATV)	334, 338
Festival 77	522
Film Buffs' Association	238
Film Clinic	235
Film Recording	15-16, 20, 40-42, 48, 50, 77, 80, 83, 86, 89, 98-99, 103-104, 116-118, 127, 161, 175, 181, 208, 252-253, 256, 272-275, 277-278, 282, 289, 479-480, 511
Film Trims	307-308, 501-503, 522, 531
Film Warp	507, 545
Filmsoc	241
Final Test, The (The Celestial Toymaker: Episode 4)	80, 211-212
Fine Grain Duplicate	478, 483-484, 488, 496, 503-507
Finklestone, Peter	272, 277

INDEX

Finland	335
Fitzroy Tavern, The	425
Five Doctors, The	37, 156, 270-272, 422, 475, 519, 525, 529
Five Faces of Doctor Who, The	22, 222, 257, 269, 434
Fletcher, Dean	238
FLOL (Flim Library On Line)	157
Florida	419-420
Ford, Carole Ann	329-330, 482
Forsyte Saga, The	307, 437
Four Hundred Dawns (Galaxy 4: Episode 1)	290, 301-302
Four To Doomsday	527
Frame, The	323
France	163, 536
Frenchs Forest Studio	211
Frick, Alice	13
Frontier in Space	65-66, 75, 92, 135, 162-164, 169, 187, 196, 198, 251-252, 254, 257, 259-260, 268-269, 286, 413-417, 437, 516
Frontios	531
Full Circle	331, 526
Fury From the Deep	10, 52, 59-63, 71, 95, 109, 113-114, 122, 125, 133, 161, 173-174, 186, 192, 233, 249, 288, 297-298, 307-308, 314, 317, 319, 321, 325, 328, 330, 345-346, 350-351, 354, 360-361, 366, 372, 375, 381, 403, 405, 409, 425, 428, 463, 469, 501
Galaxy 4	47, 51, 54, 69, 90, 94, 105, 113, 120, 124, 131, 136-139, 160, 163, 172, 176, 185, 191, 193-194, 199-200, 242-243, 245-246, 248, 290, 300-302, 312-313, 319-322, 327, 345, 347, 352, 355, 366, 369, 374, 379-380, 382, 384-385, 393, 397, 399, 401, 406, 408, 431, 436, 446, 485
Gallaccio, George	325, 484
Galton and Simpson	435
Gangster Show: The Resistible Rise of Arturo Ui, The	24
Gatiss, Mark	424
Gazelle	275
Gee, David	204, 461-462, 490
General Election Question Time	308
Genesis of the Daleks	93, 129, 137, 197, 257, 265, 277, 519-520
Geneva	334
Germany (ZDF)	128, 336, 465
Ghana (GRTC)	359, 391, 442
Ghost Light	271, 541
Gibraltar (GBC)	113-114, 119, 122-123, 128-129, 179, 334-335, 359-360, 388, 391, 408-409, 411-412, 416-417, 441-412, 416-417, 441-443, 445, 465-469, 471-473
Glasgow	14
Good King Memorex	524-525, 543
Goodies, The	9
Gordon Street	241
Goring, Marius	147
Gorrie, John	45
Grand Hotel, The (Birmingham)	212
Grand Hotel, The (Brighton)	229
Grandstand	9
Greatest Show In The Galaxy, The	271, 540
Green Death, The	66, 75, 123, 135, 162, 169-170, 187, 196, 198, 200, 252-254, 257-258, 264, 268-269, 286, 296, 412-415, 418, 517
Green, Benny	147
Grenville, Bruce	238-240, 483
Griffith University	298

WIPED!

Griffiths, Peter	325
Groves, Allan	319
Guam	419-420
Gunfighters, The	41, 46-48, 51, 56, 69, 79-81, 84-85, 90, 94-95, 105, 113, 116, 121, 124, 132, 160, 169, 173, 185, 191, 212, 248, 317, 322, 324, 327, 345, 349, 353, 355, 379-380, 382, 384, 396-397, 399, 406, 408, 489
Guyana (GBS)	334
Haining, Peter	210
Half-inch	437, 545
Halifax	220
Hamilton	355
Hammersmith	28
Hampshire	242
Hampshire, Susan	227
Hancock's Half Hour	435
Hand of Fear, The	197
Handley, Derek	326
Hanford, Anne	20, 64, 78, 89, 142-145, 152, 154-155, 179, 183
Happiness Patrol, The	539
Harriett Street	218, 237, 373-375, 442, 446, 459-460
Harris, Michealjohn	291, 330
Hartnell Years, The	166
Hartnell, William	27-28, 32, 41, 46-50, 52, 54-56, 61, 63-65, 79, 84, 94, 104, 112, 114, 118-119, 124, 126-130, 135-138, 160, 164, 166-172, 174, 175, 185, 187, 189, 194, 197-198, 201, 203, 211, 215, 224-225, 231, 236, 243, 247, 251-252, 278, 295, 306, 314, 317, 326, 330, 333, 338-339, 346, 351, 354-356, 358-360, 362-363, 367, 375, 378-385, 411-412, 414, 416, 418, 422, 439, 476, 491-492
Hearn, Marcus	324
Hendry, Gordon	230, 232, 276, 498
Henson, Jim	335
Hertfordshire	475
Highlanders, The	48-50, 52, 59, 70, 95, 106, 113-114, 121, 124, 132, 160, 171, 173, 186, 191, 248, 291, 297, 319, 323-325, 327, 349, 353, 361, 371, 374, 381, 383-385, 397, 401-405, 457, 495
Hill, Benny	322
Hill, Jacqueline	32
Hines, Frazer	308, 330, 500
HMV	236
Hobart	340-343, 345, 440, 443, 445-472
Hodgson, Brian	294
Hodgson, Paul	261
Hole, Tahu	17
Holland/Netherlands	129, 336
Holman, David	244, 312, 319-321, 478-481, 484, 486-491, 493, 495-503, 505, 506
Home Video	235, 265, 272, 274, 310, 435
Hong Kong (RTV)	112, 115, 119, 121-123, 128, 179, 226, 234-235, 312, 334, 338, 358, 360-361, 364, 390, 402, 405-407, 411-412, 417, 431, 439, 441-442, 444, 457-458, 460-464, 466-472, 499
Hope, Adrian	142
Horizon	128
Horns of Nimon, The	525
Horror of Fang Rock	522
Howard, Graham	306-307, 373
Howe, Antony	328
Howe, David J	324
Howell, Peter	530
Howlaround	288

INDEX

HSA-TV (Thailand)	382, 442, 444
Hulke, Malcolm	201, 225
Hunter, Keith	272, 274
Hussein, Waris	44-45, 326, 478
I Don't Like My Monsters To Have Oedipus Complexes	291, 493
I, Claudius	36, 184
Ice Warriors, The	55-56, 58-60, 71, 88, 95, 108, 113, 122, 125, 128, 132, 161, 173, 186, 192, 210, 233, 238, 248, 272, 301, 311, 319, 325, 327, 354, 360-361, 366, 371, 375, 381, 384, 400, 405, 409, 429, 436, 438, 465, 475, 500
Illinois	419-420
Image of the Fendahl	415, 523
Index record cards	138, 157, 166, 170, 172, 289
Infax	157, 182, 294
Inferno	65, 73, 92, 123, 133, 162, 169, 186, 196, 252-253, 256, 260-263, 267, 269, 281, 284-285, 412, 414-415, 417-418, 510
Insell, James	280, 282
Insert	29-31, 39, 79-80, 103, 290-291, 295-296, 310, 487, 493-495, 511, 536-539
Inside Television	519
Invasion of the Dinosaurs	63, 65, 76, 93, 117, 135, 162, 169, 180-181, 183-184, 187, 196, 203, 206-209, 219-220, 251-254, 256-257, 259, 264, 268-269, 276, 283-286, 411-412, 415, 421-422, 434, 517
Invasion of Time, The	66, 421, 523
Invasion, The	59, 61-62, 72, 95, 113-114, 122, 125, 127, 133, 161, 173-174, 180, 186, 192, 195, 199, 249, 256, 300, 321, 328, 331, 338, 351, 354, 359, 361, 381, 405-408, 427, 429, 471, 472, 504
Invisible Enemy, The	522
Ioannides, P	223
Iowa	419-420
Iran (NIR&T)	120, 127, 225, 362, 373, 386, 400, 431, 442-443
Irwin, Gerry	331
It Is Midnight, Dr Schweizer	16
Italy	335
ITC	16-17
ITV	16, 24, 141, 147, 278, 360, 364, 543
Ivanhoe	128
Jackson, David	235
Jacksonville	419-420
Jamaica (JBC)	334, 362-363, 391, 393, 403, 442, 444, 446
Japan	97, 335, 417, 546
JCA	235
Jearum, Arthur	163
Jewell, Robert	328-329, 488
Jim'll Fix It	9
Johnsonville	237
Jones, Dallas	298-299, 328
Jones, Terry	62-63
Jordan	120, 404, 416
Just William	159
Katy	227
Kearny/Hastings	419-420
Keeper of Traken, The	526
Keeping Television Alive	176
Kennedy, Robert	308
Kensington House	435
Kent	485
Kenya (VoK)	119, 334, 363-364, 393, 395, 442, 444

WIPED!

Keys of Marinus, The	45, 51, 54, 67, 94-95, 105, 112, 118, 124, 126, 130, 160, 167-168, 172, 185, 190, 193, 226, 247, 316, 327, 333, 335, 338-339, 345-346, 352, 354-359, 361-365, 376, 378-380, 382-384, 387-394, 396-404, 407, 409, 441, 478
Kinda	527
Kine, Jack	294
King George V	14
Kitwe	384-385, 442, 444, 446-448, 450-451, 543-454, 458-462, 465-468, 473
Korea	417
Krotons, The	10, 42, 57-59, 72, 82, 84-85, 91, 95, 113, 122, 125, 129, 133, 138, 140, 161, 172-173, 177, 179, 186, 192, 195, 199, 249, 257, 328, 354, 359, 361, 377, 381, 406-408, 410, 434, 505
Kuwait	416, 418
Lambert, Verity	13, 28, 34-35, 40, 322
Lambess, Neil	238-239, 376
Landen, Richard	311-313, 319-321, 323, 487-491, 493, 495-503, 505, 506
Lascelles, David	238
Last Dalek, The	330, 499
Late Night Line-Up	294, 500
Late Show, The	17, 273
Late, Late Breakfast Show, The	531
League of Gentleman, The	424
Lebanon	336
Lee, Adam	228, 234-235, 273, 292-293
Leeds	241
Legend Films	281-283, 516
Leigh, Gary	229, 328-329, 424
Leisure Hive, The	331, 526
Lengden, Gordon 'Drog'	329
Letts, Barry	8, 39, 56, 62, 269, 515
Levine, Ian	118, 163-172, 174-176, 178, 193, 204-209, 214-216, 218-221, 224, 229, 232, 254-255, 258-259, 261-262, 271-275, 277-278, 281, 289, 313, 319, 340, 376-377, 415, 420, 426, 485, 490, 499, 513
Libya	120, 403
Lime Grove	17-18, 28, 40, 77, 81, 165-166, 435
Lion (The Crusade: Episode 1)	86, 88, 161, 216, 236-238, 375-376, 428, 440, 483
Lionheart Television International	259-261, 421-422
Littlechild, Barry	435
Lively Arts, The	63-64, 85, 89, 138, 189, 194-195, 198, 201
Lloyd, Innes	49, 81, 322
Lodge, Bernard	287-288
Lofficier, Jean Marc	224
Logopolis	10, 257, 320, 527
London	14-15, 17, 19, 27-28, 33, 77, 140, 163, 181-182, 204, 207, 209-211, 216, 235, 239-241, 244, 255, 258-260, 262, 264-266, 300, 318, 334, 336, 341, 364, 375-376, 383, 413, 415, 425, 462, 477, 525
London Transport Assembly Rooms	28, 33
Longleat	213, 261-262
Looking In	269, 516
Loot	425
Lord, A V	99
Los Angeles (KCET)	254, 262, 273, 419-420, 512
Lost In Space	423
LP	97, 520
Lucarotti, John	13, 112
Lulworth Cove	541
Lundie, Tom	261-262, 420
Lusaka	384-385, 442, 444, 446-448, 450-451, 453-454, 458-462, 465-468, 473

INDEX

Lydiard, Simon M	224, 425-426
Lydiard-White, Peter	224
M&E (Music & Effects) Track	123-127, 339
Macra Terror, The	50, 55-57, 61, 63, 70, 95, 106-107, 113, 121, 125, 132, 161, 173-174, 186, 191, 248, 287-288, 297, 304-305, 312, 319, 323-325, 327-328, 350, 353, 361, 371-372, 374, 376, 381, 383-385, 398, 401-403, 405, 425-426, 432, 460, 464, 497
Madden, Paul	176-178
Magnetic Track/Soundtrack	87-88, 91-92, 161, 170, 193, 293, 476-485, 487-492, 496, 499-507, 517, 519, 546
Maidenhead	205
Making of Doctor Who, The (book)	201, 225
Making of Doctor Who, The (TV)	539
Malawi (MBC)	334, 378
Malden, Sue	10, 65, 143-145, 151-152, 154-156, 158-162, 172, 176-179, 194, 205, 207, 209, 219, 221, 251, 255-256, 258-259, 262, 340, 362, 415, 434, 525
Malta	112, 119, 333, 364, 387, 389, 412, 441, 443
Mammone, Robert	296
Man with a Flower in His Mouth, The	14
Manchester	505
Manning, Katy	295, 511
Marchwood	244
Marco Polo	45, 51, 67, 94, 105, 112, 118, 124, 127, 130, 160, 172-173, 185, 190, 226, 247, 300, 312-313, 319-320, 326, 328, 335-336, 338, 345-346, 352, 355-359, 361-367, 372-373, 376, 378-380, 382-384, 387-394, 396, 407, 425, 429-431, 440, 478
Marconi-EMI	15
Marham, Saied	229-232
Mark of the Rani, The	534
Marsh, Ronnie	62
Marter, Ian	427
Martin, Andrew	24, 54, 61, 77, 161, 179, 181, 307-309, 482
Martin, David	199
Martin, John Scott	295
Martin, Richard	323
Marvel	10, 256, 258
Masque of Mandragora, The	163, 197
Massachusetts	419-420
Massacre, The	51, 69, 94, 105, 113, 120, 124, 131, 160, 173, 185, 191, 248, 317-318, 327, 336-337, 345, 353, 355, 366, 369, 374, 379-380, 382, 384, 396-397, 399, 402, 406, 408, 449, 488
Mauritius (MBC)	334, 364-365, 394-395, 397, 442, 444, 446
Mawdryn Undead	529
Mawson, Enid	177-179
Mayfield	28
McCoy, Sylvester	422, 475, 537-538
McKendrick, Ian	520
Meglos	526
Melbourne	340-345, 412, 440, 443, 445-453, 455-460, 462-472
Mexico	120, 125-126, 193, 225, 333, 399
Miami	419-420
Michigan	416
Mickey Mouse	15
Midwest Television (MTS) Nigeria	376-378
Mind of Evil, The	65, 74, 123, 134, 162, 169, 186, 196, 252-253, 256, 261, 267, 277, 283-285, 412-414, 417-418, 425, 511
Mind Robber, The	42, 57-59, 72, 82, 84-85, 91, 95, 113-114, 122, 125, 133, 138, 161, 169, 173-174, 186, 192, 221, 236, 249, 312, 322-324, 328, 354, 359, 361, 381, 405-408, 504
Missing Believed Wiped	245, 247, 292-293
Missing in Action	424

WIPED!

Missing Years, The	238, 272, 301, 305
Mission to the Unknown	55-56, 61, 63, 69, 94, 105, 113-116, 120, 124, 131, 136-137, 160, 170, 172-174, 185, 191, 203, 211, 246, 248, 312-313, 320, 327, 338, 346-347, 352, 432, 447, 486
Molesworth, Richard	271
Monkhouse, Bob	210
Monster of Peladon, The	66, 76, 93, 136, 162, 197, 252, 254, 257-258, 268, 270, 286, 379, 412, 414-416, 418, 518
Montagu, Ralph	242-247, 271-274, 276-277, 280, 309, 314
Monty Python's Flying Circus	9, 62-63, 421
Moonbase, The	48-49, 55-57, 59, 70, 83, 95-96, 106, 113, 121, 125, 132, 161, 173, 186, 191, 194, 201, 206, 248, 276, 288, 319, 323-325, 327, 353, 361, 371, 374, 376, 381, 383-384, 398, 401-405, 428, 459, 496
Moonbase, The: Episode 2	95-96
Moonbase, The: Episode 4	95, 96, 191, 194, 206, 276
Moore, Dudley	436
Morgan, Wally	178
Mormon Unification Church	209-210
Morocco	120, 359, 398, 479
Morris, Gareth	154, 210
Muffin the Mule	97, 213
Mulkern, Patrick	323
Multi-Coloured Swap Shop	9
Mutants (B), The	130
Mutants (OOO), The	65-66, 75, 134, 162, 169, 187, 196, 251-253, 255, 257, 259-260, 263, 268, 284, 286, 331, 414-417, 514
Mute	86-88, 91-92, 192, 269-270, 292-293, 307-309, 318, 330, 370, 427, 477, 480, 482, 486-487, 489, 491-492, 494, 497-500, 502, 506-507, 512-514, 517, 519-520, 522-527, 529, 531-540, 545
MXF file	270
Myth Makers, The	51, 54, 69, 94, 105, 113, 120, 124, 131, 136, 160, 173, 185, 191, 248, 302, 311-313, 320-321, 327, 345, 353, 355, 366, 369, 374, 379-380, 382, 384, 396-397, 399, 401, 406, 408, 448, 486
Napier	238
Nash, Pamala	62, 104, 118, 168, 175-176, 178, 199
Nathan-Turner, John	39, 212, 224, 258, 261, 312, 525
Nation, Terry	13, 55, 114-115, 164, 291, 336, 365
National Film and Television Archive (NFTVA)	63, 179, 475, 509-522, 524-526, 528-530
National Film Archive (NFA)	141, 146-147, 151, 177, 227, 270, 481
National Film Theatre	262, 292
National Iranian Radio and Television (NIR&T)	362, 442-443
National Motor Museum	242
National Viewers' and Listeners' Association	522
Nationwide	295, 511
Neal, Giles	258
Nebraska	419-420
Negative/Neg	34, 47, 81, 85-88, 90-92, 116-119, 123, 125-126, 138, 140, 157, 161, 164, 167, 170-171, 174, 176, 178-179, 190-194, 196, 198-200, 204, 208, 214, 223, 253, 260, 264, 269, 275, 277-278, 282, 285, 293, 308, 324, 339-341, 431, 437, 440, 476-485, 487-490, 492, 495-496, 498-517, 524-525, 527-530, 532, 543-545
New Jersey Network	539
New South Wales	340-344
New York	334, 419-420
New Zealand (NZBC/TVNZ)	17, 47, 111, 113, 115, 119-123, 127, 129, 212, 218, 236-239, 264, 278, 305-307,

INDEX

	325, 333, 335, 337, 341, 352, 356, 362, 365-367, 370, 372-373, 375-377, 381-382, 386, 389, 398-399, 401-406, 408, 411-412, 414, 431-432, 439-440, 442-444, 446-457, 459-464, 466-470, 484, 501, 503
Newman, Sydney	13, 165-166
Nigeria (NTA/NTS/NBC/WNTV)	112-113, 118-119, 121-122, 128, 136, 215-218, 220, 224, 333-334, 368, 374, 376-378, 382, 389-389, 393, 409-410, 441, 443, 445, 465, 467-468, 471, 483-485, 490
No Trams to Lime Street	227
Noel Edmonds' Saturday Roadshow	538
Non-Theatrical Sales	163-164
Not Only But Also	436
Nothing At The End of the Lane	329
Novelisation	8, 201, 427-428
NTSC (National Television System Committee)	62-63, 123, 129, 254, 256, 258-262, 271, 274-281, 283-286, 296, 411-415, 417-419, 421, 508-515
O'Brien, Maureen	31-32
O'Hare, Gary	212
Off-air	143, 163, 204, 244, 254, 261-263, 271, 273-275, 277-278, 281, 287, 293, 301, 305, 308-312, 314, 317-318, 321, 323, 326, 328, 419-420, 426, 427-429, 437-438, 478-481, 484-503, 505-506, 508-512, 521-522, 524
Office of Film and Literature Classification (OFLC)	298-300
Off-lock	275, 479, 520, 545
Omnibus	10, 254, 269
Onedin Line, The	128
One-inch	34, 36-37, 123, 265, 437, 475, 477, 518-519, 530-544
Ontario	255, 258, 414-415
Optical Soundtrack	81, 86-91, 100, 123, 232, 239, 377, 317, 370, 477-484, 487-490, 492-493, 495-496, 498-517, 544-546
Orlando	419-420
Out of Phase	103, 479, 484, 505, 508-509, 545
Out of the Unknown	167
Outtake	291, 491, 522-524, 530-534, 538, 541, 543
Owen, Keith	178-179
Pagkalinawan, Evelyn	259
Pakistan (PTC)	334
PAL (Phase Alternating Line)	36, 123, 129, 256, 258-259, 262, 265-266, 271, 278-280, 285-286, 414, 416, 418, 510-515
Palfreyman, Dave	230
Palin, Michael	62
Palmer, Ben	288
PanoptiCon	229-230, 424
Paradise Towers	537
Paris	334
Parry, Ellen	298
PasB	8, 53, 79-70, 80, 181, 308, 367, 368
PasB (Programme As Broadcast)	8, 53, 79-80, 181, 308, 367-368
Paskewicz, Mary	260
PBS	254, 258, 418-419, 421-422
Pebble Mill at One	165
Pemberton, Victor	428
Pennsylvania	419-420
People's Republic of South Yemen (PROSYBS)	334, 338
Perry	167-168, 178
Personal Choice	308

WIPED!

Perspectives	291, 296, 493
Perth	340-345, 440, 443, 445-453, 455-472
Pertwee, Jon	7-10, 39, 56, 61-66, 82, 85, 117, 123, 128-130, 133, 135, 161-163, 169-170, 172, 179-180, 186-187, 194-195, 197-198, 200, 203-205, 208, 211, 225, 247, 251-254, 256, 258-262, 264, 266, 268, 270-273, 277-278, 280-284, 312, 360, 364, 367, 379, 381-382, 411-422, 475, 484, 507
Philadelphia	419-420
Philippines (RCO)	417
Phillips	315
Phoenix	419-420
Photo/Photograph	8, 213, 272, 287, 288, 321-326, 328-329, 427, 429, 478, 488, 499
Pilot (An Unearthy Child)	48, 51, 55, 61-62, 66, 105, 165-166, 185, 247, 476
Pinedene Films	213
Pirandello, Luigi	14
Pirate Planet, The	524
Pixley, Andrew	294-295, 324
Planet of Evil	93, 197, 521
Planet of Fire	532
Planet of Giants	40-41, 48, 54, 68, 79, 84, 94, 105, 112, 119, 124, 126, 127, 131, 160, 167-168, 172, 185, 190, 193, 214, 237, 248, 305, 327, 335, 338-339, 347, 352, 355, 358-366, 368, 373, 376, 378-379, 381-384, 387-390, 392-404, 407, 409, 481
Planet of the Daleks	65-66, 75, 92, 135, 162, 169, 187, 196, 198, 251-252, 254, 257, 260, 264-265, 268, 277, 281-283, 286, 382, 415-418, 421-422, 424, 516
Planet of the Spiders	66, 76, 93, 129, 136, 162, 187, 197, 252, 254, 257-258, 264-265, 268-269, 286, 412, 414-416, 418, 518
Polyester Track	161, 307
Porridge	36
Portland Place	15
Portsmouth	213
Portsmouth News, The	213
Positive/Pos	86-88, 91-92, 117-118, 170, 192, 195-196, 215, 223, 239, 264, 339, 476-485, 487-488, 490, 492, 495-496, 498-507, 517, 524, 544-545
Power of Kroll, The	524
Power of the Daleks, The	10, 42, 46, 59, 70, 81, 83-84, 87, 95, 104-105, 113-115, 121, 124, 132, 137, 160, 173, 186, 191, 220, 248, 291, 294, 296, 304, 308-310, 314, 319, 323, 325, 327, 353, 359, 366, 371, 374, 381, 397, 403, 408, 429, 432, 456, 493
Preddle, Jon	307, 419, 439
Prisoner, The	423
Private collection	83, 269, 292, 372, 433-434, 436, 440, 476, 480, 491, 501, 503-504, 507, 512-514, 517, 519-542
Producer	8, 13, 28, 36, 38-40, 49, 56, 62, 81, 138, 157, 199, 212, 224, 258, 261, 269, 273, 293, 312, 322, 325, 525
Pugsley, Steve	229
Purves, Peter	295
Pyramids of Mars	93, 197, 265, 521
Quad	18, 475, 543
Quarter-inch	34, 36
Quatermass Experiment, The	16, 423
Quatermass II	16
Queen Elizabeth II	16, 340, 356, 365
Queensland	340-344
Questech Charisma	274
Radio & Television of Singapore (RTS)	128, 333, 380-382, 417, 441, 444-445, 447-458, 460-464, 466-470, 472-473, 489
Radio Kaduna Television (RKTV)	376-377, 441, 443, 445
Radio Times	11, 14, 21, 46, 236, 244, 324, 426
Radiodiffusion Television Algerienne (RTA)	339

Randall & Hopkirk (Deceased)	231
Rank Cintel	243, 245-246, 271
Rank Organisation, the	17
RCA Company	19
Read, Hilary	255
Reason, Terry	329
Reconstruction	272, 316, 323, 429
Rediffusion Television	234, 360
Reel-to-reel	34, 310-311, 313, 316-317, 319-320, 438
Reign of Terror, The	51, 54, 67, 94, 105, 112, 119, 124, 130, 160, 172-173, 185, 190, 207-208, 216, 221, 224-229, 237, 247, 266, 276, 300-302, 312-313, 320, 327, 335, 338, 347, 352, 355-359, 361, 363-366, 368, 372-373, 376, 378-379, 381-384, 386-390, 392-396, 398, 407, 429, 431, 433, 443, 480
Reith, John	13-14
Remembrance of the Daleks	428, 539
Repeat	10-11, 16-17, 21-24, 35, 44-45, 50, 53, 62, 65, 73, 78, 98, 110, 115, 142, 153, 159, 162, 182, 197, 203-204, 221-222, 236, 240, 257, 269, 272-273, 276-77, 280, 282, 299, 305, 310, 316-317, 329, 339, 345, 351, 354, 357, 361, 367, 412-413, 415, 422, 424, 429, 434, 437, 485, 504, 507-508, 510, 513-516, 518-522, 528, 530-531, 535
Reprise	80, 83, 216-217, 260, 273, 288, 317, 319, 422, 483, 499, 508, 512, 516
Rescue, The	27-29, 33-34, 51, 54, 68, 94, 105, 112, 119, 124, 126, 131, 139, 160, 168, 172, 185, 190, 193, 199-200, 237, 248, 323, 327, 333, 335, 338-339, 343, 345, 352, 355-356, 358-359, 361-366, 368, 373, 376, 379, 381-384, 387-390, 392-393, 395-396, 398-404, 407, 409, 482
Resistance is Useless	273, 292-293
Restoration Team	242, 244, 271-273, 275-277, 280, 292, 305, 310, 425, 431, 437, 439, 509
Resurrection of the Daleks	37-38, 531
Retention Authorisation	21, 44, 46, 48-49, 52-53, 60-61, 79-81, 84, 104, 106, 109, 116, 166
Revelation of the Daleks	38, 533, 535
Revenge of the Cybermen	93, 129, 137, 197, 520
Rhodes, Cecil	378
Rhodesia (RBC/ZRBC/ZBC)	119, 378-379, 384, 389, 395, 441-442, 444
Riverside Studios	28, 33, 82
Roberts, Steve	221, 238-240, 242, 244-247, 271-273, 280, 293-294, 296, 300-301, 306, 514
Robin Hood – Prince of Thieves	236
Robin, Mr	347
Robinson, Bruce	
Robot	66, 129, 137, 162, 197, 413, 421, 519
Robots of Death, The	522
Rochester	419-420
Romans, The	28, 51, 68, 94-95, 105, 112, 124, 131, 160, 168, 172, 185, 190, 201, 216, 237, 248, 323, 327, 352, 355-356, 358-359, 363, 365-366, 368, 372-373, 376, 379, 381, 384, 390-394, 396-397, 399, 401, 403, 408, 433, 483
Rout, E R	99
Royal Charter	14, 20, 149, 378
RSC (Reverse Standards Conversion)	278-281, 284, 512
RTV (Hong Kong)	128, 334, 360-361, 417, 431, 441, 442, 444, 457-458, 460-464, 466-472
Russell	45
Russell, Gary	215, 324
Russell, James	271-273, 313-314, 319
Russell, Ken	313
Russell, Richard	283
Russell, William	32, 228, 325
Sallis, Peter	308
Salway, Kay	152, 155
Sampson, Terry	163

569

WIPED!

San Francisco	419-420
Sands, Basil	211-212, 259-260, 264-265, 348
Saskatchewan	415
Saudi Arabia (HZ-22/Dhahran TV)	120, 400, 418
Saunders, David	229-230
Savages, The	6, 47, 56, 69, 80, 95, 113, 116, 121, 124, 132, 136, 160, 173, 185, 191, 248, 302-303, 318, 323-325, 327, 345, 353, 355, 366, 370, 374, 379-381, 384, 396-397, 399, 402, 406, 408, 452, 489
Scoones, Paul	238-240
Scotsman, The	141
Scott	45
Scranton	419-420
Script Editor	8, 49, 201
Sea Devils, The	65-66, 74-75, 134, 162, 169, 187, 196, 199, 221, 225, 251-253, 257-261, 263, 267, 281, 284, 286, 312, 331, 414, 417, 514
Seeds of Death, The	42, 54, 57-61, 72, 82, 84-85, 91, 95, 110, 113, 122, 125, 129, 133, 161, 167, 169, 173-174, 186, 192, 195, 199, 201, 249, 328, 346, 354, 359, 361, 381, 384-385, 406-408, 410, 506
Seeds of Doom, The	197, 522
Sensorites, The	44-45, 51, 54, 67, 94, 105, 112, 124, 126, 130, 160, 167-168, 172, 185, 190, 193, 226, 247, 316, 327, 336, 338-339, 345, 347, 352, 355-359, 361-365, 376, 378-379, 381-384, 387-390, 392-404, 407, 409, 480
Seven of One	36
Shada	156, 331, 525
Shanahan, Damian	246, 298-300, 351, 490-491, 495-497, 502
Shawcraft Models	331
Shawcross, Alan	145, 152, 155
Shepherd, Ben	195
Shepherd's Bush	27
Sheridan, Tom	32
Sherwin, Derrick	56
Sheward, Ian	218-220, 276, 434
Shewring, Dean	
Shibaden	424, 437, 521-527, 546
Sierra Leone (SLBS)	120-121, 334, 337, 379-380, 396, 398, 401, 406, 442, 445-450, 452-454
Silence of the Lambs, The	236
Silurians, The	41, 61-62, 65, 73, 92, 128, 133-134, 162, 169, 186, 195-196, 199-200, 252-253, 256, 261, 263-264, 267, 272, 274-277, 285, 411, 416-420, 475, 508-509
Silver Nemesis	539-540
Singapore (RTS/TVS)	113, 115, 119-123, 128, 179, 211-212, 218, 333, 335, 337, 370, 374, 377, 380-382, 387, 390, 392, 403, 405, 407-408, 411-412, 417, 439, 441, 444-445, 447-458, 460-464, 466-470, 472-473, 489
Singleton, Valerie	490
Six Wives of Henry VIII, The	128
Skaro	425-426
Smallman, Michael	230-231
Smith, Justin	289
Smith, Matt	9, 428
Smith, Mr	213
Smugglers, The	56, 70, 95, 113, 121, 124, 132, 137, 160, 173, 185, 191, 248, 297, 318, 325, 327, 330, 349, 353, 355, 366, 371, 374, 379-381, 384-385, 396-397, 399, 402, 406, 408, 453, 491
Snakedance	528
Snell, David	537
Society of Motion Picture and Television Engineers (SMPTE)	245-246
Softly, Softly	234

INDEX

Soho Images	235
Sontaran Experiment, The	129, 137, 197, 519
Sony	36-37, 280, 437-438, 543-544, 546
South Arabian Television Service (SATS)	338, 441, 444
Southampton	213, 242, 244
Space Museum, The	51, 54, 68, 94, 105, 112, 124, 131, 136-137, 160, 169, 172, 185, 190, 193, 195, 199, 201, 203, 206, 216, 248, 316, 327, 331, 345, 352, 355, 358-359, 362-363, 365-366, 368, 372, 374, 376, 379, 381, 384, 391-397, 399-404, 408, 483-484
Space Pirates, The	42, 57, 59-60, 72, 82-85, 91, 95, 110, 113, 122, 125, 129, 133, 161, 173, 186, 192, 199, 249, 309, 320-321, 328, 346, 354, 359, 361, 381, 384, 385, 407-408, 410, 431, 437, 472, 506
Space Pirates, The: Episode 2	60, 82, 84, 91, 95, 110, 192, 199
Spanish	120, 124-127, 190, 193, 214, 336, 477-478, 483
Spearhead From Space	39, 61-62, 73, 82-85, 91, 133, 162, 169, 186, 195, 198, 203, 251-253, 256, 263-264, 267, 269, 277, 285, 379, 412-413, 416, 418, 475, 507
Special Edition	236, 271-272, 285, 530, 539-540
Spool	33, 35, 42, 54, 57, 61, 86, 100, 149, 168, 171, 180-182, 195, 198, 243, 265, 287, 292-293, 295, 309, 329, 375, 437, 482, 503-507, 515, 518, 535-539, 542, 546
Stammers, Mark	324
Stanstead	216
Star Trek	423
Star Wars	421
State of Decay	526
Stead, David	212-215, 228, 230, 234-236, 265-266, 276, 416, 502
Steenbeck	165, 482
Steer, Andrew	282
Steptoe and Son	9, 128, 436
Stevens, Roger	205-206, 209, 219, 276, 434-435, 496, 499, 517
Stirling, David	335
Stone, Cornelius	238
Stones of Blood, The	524
Stored Field	47, 50, 79, 102-103, 116, 118-120, 127, 166, 208, 228, 243, 246, 354, 357, 476-480, 482-484, 487-490, 492, 498
Strong, Graham	312, 316-321, 488, 490-491, 493, 495-503
Stuckey, Mrs	347
Studio Tape/Recording	27-28, 33, 36, 52, 83, 153, 156, 166, 268, 281, 511, 518, 521-524, 526-529, 533-534, 536-539, 541, 545
Sudan (SBS/STV)	334
Suez Canal	338, 416
Sunday Past Times	309-310, 494
Sunmakers, The	415, 523
Suppressed Field	47, 50, 101-102, 104, 106, 116, 118-120, 228, 237, 246, 354, 477-480, 482, 484
Surinam (SRS/STVS)	334
Surrey	312
Survival	37, 315, 475, 519, 541
Sussex	28
Sutton Coldfield	15
Sweden	336
Switzerland	335
Sydney	13, 118, 127, 165-166, 204, 211-212, 259, 264, 299, 340-345, 348, 366, 412-413, 440, 443, 445-446, 448-453, 455-472
Take Two	541
Talons of Weng-Chiang, The	415, 522
Target	8, 11, 111, 364, 427
Tasmania	340-345
Telecine	29-31, 98, 103, 214, 229, 233, 243-246, 276, 283, 293, 301, 306, 309, 483, 485, 487, 496, 498-499, 502, 504, 507, 509, 517, 520, 530, 545, 547

571

WIPED!

Telerecording	15-17, 19, 21, 40, 46-47, 77, 80-81, 83, 86, 97, 99, 101-104, 106-109, 116-117, 138, 166, 170, 189-190, 199, 208, 253, 282-283, 291, 310, 432, 435, 475, 477-478, 480-482, 493-494, 498, 545-546
Tele-snap	308, 321-326, 329, 429, 478, 484, 486-491, 493, 495-503, 505-506
Televisa SA (Mexico)	225
Television International Enterprises Ltd (TIE)	119, 334-335, 338, 355, 359, 383, 441-442
Television South (TVS) (Southampton)	242, 244
Telizya, Nick	258
TellyCon	231-232, 323, 424
Temps-X	536
Tennant, David	9, 428
Tenth Plane, The t: Episode 4	11, 56, 109, 138, 199, 231, 289, 303, 324, 424-426, 429, 435
Tenth Planet (shop)	326
Tenth Planet, The	11, 46, 53, 55-56, 60, 70, 95, 109, 113, 121, 124, 132, 137-138, 160, 173, 185, 191, 194, 199-200, 231, 248, 289, 303, 317-318, 324-325, 327, 330, 353, 366, 371, 374, 381, 397, 402, 408, 424-426, 429, 432, 435, 455, 492
Terminus	259, 529
Terror of the Autons	65, 74, 134, 162, 169, 186, 196, 252-253, 256, 260-264, 267, 272, 274-277, 285, 296, 360, 382, 416-417, 420, 510, 546
Terror of the Zygons	197, 261, 520
Texas	420
TF-1 (France)	536
Thailand (HSA-TV)	382, 394, 396, 442, 444
Thanks for the Memory	522
Thirty Years In The TARDIS	294-295
This Is The BBC	435
Thompson, Christopher	329
Three Doctors, The	10, 66, 75, 92, 135-136, 162, 169, 187, 196-198, 252-253, 257-258, 263, 265, 268, 286, 319, 379, 413-417, 515
Thunderbirds	423
Thunder-North Broadcast Services Ltd	258
Till Death Us Do Part	434-435
Time And The Rani	537
Time Meddler, The	51, 54, 68, 94-95, 105, 113, 124, 131, 136-137, 160, 163, 172, 174, 185, 191, 193, 201, 215-221, 236, 248, 276, 325, 327, 345, 352, 355, 359, 360, 363, 365-366, 368, 374, 376-377, 379-381, 384-385, 391-394, 396-397, 401, 403, 409, 434, 484-485
Time Monster, The	62, 65, 75, 128, 134, 162, 169, 187, 196, 200, 251-253, 256-257, 259-260, 263, 265, 268, 276, 281, 284, 286, 379, 411, 414-418, 515
Time Warrior, The	66, 76, 92, 117, 135, 162, 181, 187, 196, 208, 252-254, 257-258, 264, 268, 286, 412, 414-418, 517
Time Watcher	213
Timecoded	521-527, 529, 531-534
Time-Flight	528
Timelash	535
Time-Life	123, 254, 278, 412-413, 416, 418, 421
Title Sequence, Opening/Closing Titles	28-29, 31, 39, 91, 166, 198, 222, 229, 243, 260, 268-269, 287-288, 304, 308, 309, 319, 413, 422, 497, 510-512, 537
Tom Tom	294, 494
Tomb of the Cybermen, The	10, 52, 56-57, 60, 71, 95, 107, 113-114, 116, 122, 125, 132, 161, 171, 173, 186, 191, 213, 233-236, 248, 294, 312, 327, 345-346, 350, 354, 361, 366, 371, 375, 381, 400, 405, 427-428, 463-464, 499
Tomorrow People, The	231
Tomorrow's World	296, 310, 494
Top of the Pops	9, 274, 283, 308
Toronto	123, 255-256, 258, 260-261, 356, 414-415, 441

INDEX

Trace, Christopher	490
Trailer	18, 83, 86, 308-309, 321, 482, 494, 509, 519
Traitors, The (The Daleks Masterplan: Episode 4)	289
Trentacosta, Andrew	254-255
Trethewey Farm	330, 491
Trial of a Time Lord, The	38, 350, 533, 536
Trinidad and Tobago (TTT)	119, 334-335, 382-383, 392, 441-442, 444
Troughton, Patrick	7-8, 27, 42, 46-47, 53, 55-56, 59, 61, 64-65, 81-82, 94-95, 102, 110, 112, 114-116, 118, 124, 127-130, 132, 135-137, 140, 147, 160, 164, 167, 169-172, 174-175, 177-178, 180, 186-187, 189, 194, 197-198, 201, 203, 211, 213, 215, 230-232, 236-237, 248, 251-252, 261, 278, 287-288, 296, 306, 308, 314, 317, 333, 338, 345-346, 351, 359-361, 366-367, 372, 375, 377, 381, 383-385, 411-412, 416, 418, 422, 432, 438-439, 492, 493
Trumpton	128
Tucker, Rex	13, 81
Tunisia	120, 397
Tuscon	419-420
TV Ontario	255, 414-415
Twice a Fortnight	307
Twin Dilemma, The	533
Two Doctors, The	534
Two-inch	17-22, 28, 30-31, 33-37, 40, 42-44, 46, 48-66, 79, 81,-82, 85, 89, 97, 99, 103-105, 110, 128, 143, 152, 161-162, 166, 174, 180-183, 185-186 197-198, 203, 205, 208, 211, 251, 254-261, 265-270, 273, 276-278, 280-281, 283-286, 289-290, 295-296, 412-415, 417-418, 475-489, 492, 509-522, 524-526, 528-530, 543,546
UFO	231
Uganda (UTV)	119, 121, 226, 334, 357, 383, 390, 392, 401, 432, 441, 444, 457-459, 461-462
UK Gold	11, 276, 282
U-MATIC	164-165, 254, 262, 267, 275, 413, 417, 522, 526-528, 530-535, 546
Underwater Menace, The	48-49, 56-57, 59-60, 70, 95, 106, 110, 113, 121, 124, 132, 160, 173, 186, 191, 245-248, 297, 300-301, 319, 325, 349-350, 353, 361, 371, 374, 381, 383-384, 397, 401-405, 433, 436, 458, 495
Underwater Menace, The: Episode 2	245-246, 433, 436
Underwater Menace, The: Episode 3	95
Underworld	311, 415, 523
University College London Union	241
Unsyphered	87-88, 517. 521-527. 529-535, 537, 541
Uxbridge	331
Uxbridge Road	27
Vampire From Space, The	268, 511
Vampire Mutation, The	201
Vancouver	414
Vanezis, Paul	180, 221, 223-227, 230-232, 244, 247, 266, 271-272, 275-276, 295, 301, 308, 310, 317-320, 357-358, 362, 515, 530, 534-535
Vanity Fair	61
Variations	524
VCR (Video Cassette Recorder)	62, 274, 314, 545
Venezuela (RCT)	120, 125, 382, 394-395, 442, 444
Vengeance On Varos	533
VERA (Visual Electronic Recording Apparatus)	17, 34, 99
VHS	8, 11, 36-37, 127, 166, 180, 204, 214, 229, 231-232, 235-236, 238-240, 265, 271-272, 274, 276, 278, 282, 284, 294, 300-301, 325, 428-429, 433, 478, 481, 489, 491, 508-510, 513-514, 521, 523, 527-534, 536-543, 546-547
Victoria	340-344

WIPED!

Video & Audiovisual Review	142
VidFIRE (Video Field Interpolation Restoration Effect)	272, 277-278, 281, 283-286, 508-509, 511-512, 516
Viewing Print	150, 239, 342, 477-484, 488-489, 492, 496, 498-501, 503-508, 515, 547
Vigurs, R F	99
Villawood	299-300
Villiers House	7, 89, 97, 103-104, 137, 164, 167, 169-172, 174-179, 185,189, 192, 194, 200-201, 205, 219, 224, 233, 241, 289-290, 339, 434, 436, 500
Vincent-Rudzki, Jan	138-139, 167, 183, 200, 290, 301, 313, 426, 485
Virgin Islands, The (WBNB & WBNB-TV)	334
Virgin Publishing	324
Visitation, The	261, 527
Voice of Kenya (VoK)	363, 426, 442, 444
VT Cataloguing Unit	184
VTOL (Video Tape On Line)	157, 184
Wahine Gorge	238
Wales	180-182, 330
Wales Today	538
Walker, Graham	434
Walker, Stephen James	324
Wandsworth	209-210
Wapshott, Nicholas	141-142
War Games, The	55, 59, 61-62, 72-73, 95, 110, 113, 122, 125, 129, 133, 140, 161, 163, 172-173, 177, 179, 186, 192, 195, 199, 201, 249, 288-289, 315, 328, 345-346, 351, 354, 359-361, 381, 384-385, 407-408, 410, 475, 501, 503, 507
War Machines, The	47, 56, 61, 63, 69-70, 82, 95, 113, 118, 121, 124, 132, 136-137, 160, 173-174, 185, 191, 203-204, 215-218, 248, 271, 300, 318, 327, 349, 353, 355, 366, 370, 374, 377, 379-382, 384, 396-397, 399, 402, 406, 408-409, 432, 490
Warriors' Gate	526
Warriors of the Deep	37, 475, 519, 530-531
Warship	209
Washington DC	419-420
Waterman, Dennis	159
Watkins, Neville	221
Watling, Deborah	308, 500
Watson, Francis	241-242, 434, 487
Web of Fear, The	11, 52, 57-58, 60, 71, 95, 108-109, 113, 122, 125, 133, 161, 173, 186, 192, 194, 201, 205, 249, 288, 305-307, 319, 321, 325, 328-330, 345, 354, 360-361, 366, 372, 375, 377, 381, 384-385, 402, 405, 408-410, 427, 463, 467, 501
Web of Fear, The: Episode 1	60, 192, 194, 205
Web Planet, The	51, 54, 68, 94-95, 105, 112, 124, 131, 136-137, 160, 168, 172, 185, 190, 193, 195, 199, 201, 215-216, 218, 237, 248, 320, 327-328, 352, 355, 358-359, 362-363, 365-366, 368, 373, 376-377, 379, 381, 384, 390-397, 399-404, 408-409, 483
Webber, C E	13
Wellington	218, 237, 365, 372-376, 442, 444, 447-448, 450-451, 453-457, 459-461, 463-464, 467-468, 470
Western Nigeria Television (WNTV)	376
Wetgate Telecined	214, 229, 233, 483, 496, 547
WH Allen	210, 323
Wheel In Space, The	42, 53, 57-59, 71-72, 81, 84-85, 88, 90, 95, 109-110, 113, 122, 125, 127, 133, 161, 173, 186, 192, 201, 212-214, 249, 256, 276, 288-289, 298, 306-307, 319, 321, 325, 328, 338, 345, 351, 354, 357, 360-361, 366, 372, 375, 377, 381, 403, 405, 408-410, 470-471, 499, 502
Wheel In Space, The: Episode 3	84, 212-214, 276, 288
Wheel In Space, The: Episode 6	90, 95, 192, 256
Whicker's World	291, 493

INDEX

Whiston, John	273
Whitaker, David	13, 29, 31
White City	17, 434
White Powder Christmas	523, 543
Whitehouse, Mary	66
Whitsun-Jones, Paul	330
Whose Doctor Who	63-65, 81, 85, 89, 94-95, 125-126, 138-139, 163, 165, 167, 176, 180, 183-184, 189, 193, 198, 200, 205, 251, 253, 290, 301, 339, 485
Wiles, John	49, 322, 325
Williams, Graham	138
Williams, Roy	97
Wilson, Allen	244, 321, 486
Wilson, Donald	13, 40
Wiltshire	261
Windmill Road	77-78, 89, 94, 144, 156, 166-168, 174, 176, 178-179, 183-185, 189, 198, 201, 211, 229-230, 233-234, 255, 259-260, 264-265, 275-276, 292, 307, 435
Wipe/Junk Authorisation	20-21, 44, 48-52, 54-56, 60, 62-63, 83, 109
Withdrawn, De-Accessioned and Junked	140, 169, 171-172, 174-175, 200, 436
Wolf, Michael	323-324
Wolves of Fenric, The	541
Wood, C B B	99
Woodlands	233-234, 265
World at One	144
Writers' Guild	164
WTVA (Wider Television Access)	207
Wulf, Douglas	340
Xandir Malta	364, 441, 443
Yemen	334-335, 338
Yorkshire Television (YTY)	241
Young Ones, The	37
YTV (Canada)	415
Yugoslavia	335
Z Cars	24, 77, 227-228, 358
Zambesia/Zambezi	378
Zambia (ZNBC)	113, 119-122, 128, 337, 364, 378-379, 384-385, 391-392, 394, 399, 405, 409-410, 432, 441-442, 444, 446-448, 450-451, 453-454, 458-462, 465-468, 473
Zanzibar	338
ZDF (Germany)	128, 465
ZFB1 / ZFB-TV (Bermuda)	334, 355, 442
Zimbabwe (Rhodesia) (RBC/ZRBC/ZBC)	119, 378-379, 384, 389, 395, 441-442, 444
Zoo Quest	228

ABOUT THE AUTHOR

Richard Molesworth was born in 1968, and was hooked by *Doctor Who* when he first saw the Daleks menacing Jon Pertwee in 'Day of the Daleks' in 1972. He began writing for various *Doctor Who* fanzines in the mid 1980s, including *DWB*, where he first wrote articles about the BBC archive holdings. He has since contributed articles to publications such as *Doctor Who Magazine*, *Starburst* and *Sci-Fi Now*. In 1993, he acted as a researcher for *Thirty Years in the TARDIS*, the BBC documentary celebrating *Doctor Who*'s thirtieth anniversary, and became a member of the unofficial *Doctor Who* Restoration Team soon after. He worked with the team on various projects for BBC Worldwide/2|entertain in the following years, which included the first restoration of 'The War Machines' for its VHS release, and 'The Five Doctors: The Special Edition'. When *Doctor Who* started being released on DVD, he was responsible for a multitude of special features on many of the releases; producing audio commentaries with cast and crew, scripting on-screen production subtitles, and writing, directing and producing a number of documentary 'extra' features. He has also written *Surf 'n' Turf: The Unofficial Skins Companion* for Miwk Books, and has occasionally written for the *Mail on Sunday*.